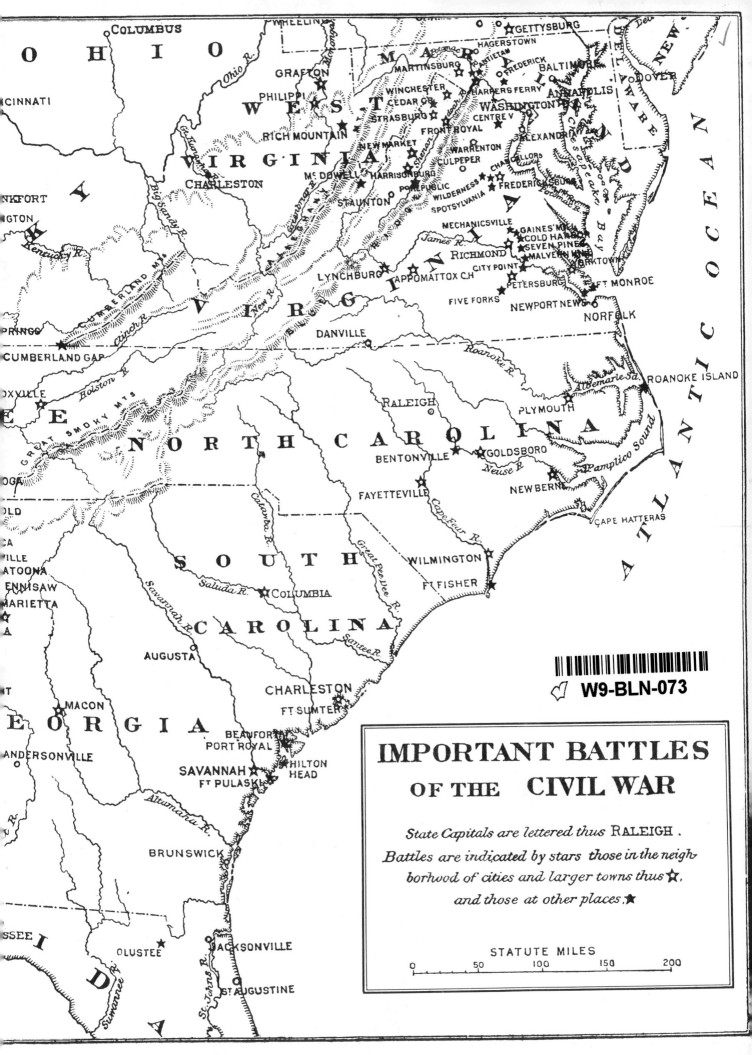

COLUMBUS
OHIO
CINCINNATI
WHEELING
GETTYSBURG
HAGERSTOWN
MARYLAND
GRAFTON
MARTINSBURG
ANTIETAM
FREDERICK
BALTIMORE
NEW
DOVER
PHILIPPI
WINCHESTER
HARPERS FERRY
ANNAPOLIS
WEST
CEDAR CR.
DELAWARE
RICH MOUNTAIN
STRASBURG
WASHINGTON
CENTRE V
CHARLESTON
NEW MARKET
FRONT ROYAL
ALEXANDRIA
VIRGINIA
WARRENTON
McDOWELL
HARRISONBURG
CULPEPER
CHANCELLORS
STAUNTON
PORT REPUBLIC
WILDERNESS
FREDERICKSBURG
SPOTSYLVANIA
Chesapeake Bay
FRANKFORT
KENTUCKY
MECHANICSVILLE
GAINES' MILL
COLD HARBOR
James R.
SEVEN PINES
RICHMOND
MALVERN HILL
LYNCHBURG
CITY POINT
YORKTOWN
APPOMATTOX C.H.
PETERSBURG
FT MONROE
FIVE FORKS
NEWPORT NEWS
VIRGINIA
NORFOLK
DANVILLE
Roanoke R.
CUMBERLAND GAP
Albemarle Sd.
ROANOKE ISLAND
KNOXVILLE
PLYMOUTH
GREAT SMOKY MTS
RALEIGH
TENNESSEE
NORTH CAROLINA
Pamlico Sound
Neuse R.
BENTONVILLE
GOLDSBORO
NEWBERN
FAYETTEVILLE
CAPE HATTERAS
SOUTH
Cape Fear R.
ATLANTIC OCEAN
WILMINGTON
FT FISHER
COLUMBIA
CAROLINA
Santee R.
AUGUSTA
GEORGIA
CHARLESTON
FT SUMTER
MACON
BEAUFORT
PORT ROYAL
ANDERSONVILLE
SAVANNAH
HILTON HEAD
FT PULASKI
Altamaha R.
BRUNSWICK
OLUSTEE
JACKSONVILLE
FLORIDA
ST AUGUSTINE

W9-BLN-073

IMPORTANT BATTLES
OF THE CIVIL WAR

State Capitals are lettered thus RALEIGH.

*Battles are indicated by stars those in the neigh-
borhood of cities and larger towns thus* ☆,

and those at other places ★

STATUTE MILES

0   50   100   150   200

BATTLE CHRONICLES
OF THE
CIVIL WAR
1862

JAMES M. McPHERSON, Editor

Princeton University

RICHARD GOTTLIEB, Managing Editor

Grey Castle Press

MACMILLAN PUBLISHING COMPANY
New York

COLLIER MACMILLAN PUBLISHERS
London

Text © 1989. *Civil War Times Illustrated*, a division of Cowles Magazines, Inc., Box 8200, Harrisburg, PA 17105.

Introduction, Transitions, Index and Format © 1989. Grey Castle Press, Inc., Lakeville, CT 06039.

Published by Macmillan Publishing Company
866 Third Avenue, New York, NY 10022

ILLUSTRATION CREDITS—Some sources are abbreviated as follows: Battles & Leaders, BL (*Battles and Leaders of the Civil War*); CWTI Collection (*Civil War Times Illustrated* Collection); Harpers, HW (*Harper's Weekly*); LC (Library of Congress); NA (National Archives); USAMHI (U.S. Army Military History Institute). Illustrations without credits are part of the *Civil War Times Illustrated* Collection.

Library of Congress Cataloging-in-Publication Data

Battle Chronicles of the Civil War.

   Includes bibliographies and indexes.
   Contents: 1. 1861—2. 1862—3. 1863— [etc.]
   1. United States—History—Civil War, 1861–1865—
Campaigns.   I. McPherson, James M.
E470.B29   1989   973.7′3   89-8316
ISBN 0-02-920661-8 (set)

Printed in the USA

Contents

1862—AN OVERVIEW

In the East . . .

It was all so grand and promising, General George B. McClellan thought. For seven months he had developed, drilled, and paraded an army that swelled to 130,000 men. Forced in February by Lincoln to commit the Army of the Potomac to action, McClellan devised an oblique drive on Richmond. He would transfer his huge creation by boat to the Virginia peninsula between the York and James Rivers. Then, as he moved westward up the peninsula toward Richmond, McDowell's Federal corps would come down from Fredericksburg to lend assistance. Naval forces meanwhile would sweep up the James to guard McClellan's other flank. Joseph E. Johnston's Confederate army, entrenched at Manassas and out-numbered more than two to one, would hardly present serious opposition.

The Peninsula Campaign began with the most famous naval duel of the war—if not of the century. Confederate naval officials had converted the captured Federal warship, *Merrimack*, into an ironclad vessel rechristened the *Virginia*. Packing ten guns and a battering ram, this revolutionary ship early in March gained momentary supremacy in Hampton Roads. Yet the Federals also had been perfecting an ironclad. The *Monitor* resembled "a tin can on a shingle"; and while it lacked the *Virginia*'s firepower, it surpassed the Confederate ship in maneuverability.

On March 9, the two vessels came face to face in Hampton Roads. For three hours

The battle that decided the fate of wooden warships: The fight between the Merrimack *(rechristened the* Virginia) *and the* Monitor *at Hampton Roads on March 9, 1862. (CWTI Collection)*

each ironclad tried futilely to sink the other. This seemingly inconclusive engagement had three major results: The duel marked the birth of steel navies; had the *Virginia* won, the North would have lost control of the Chesapeake Bay and its many waterways; and the *Monitor's* neutralization of the Confederate ironclad enabled McClellan to put his grand scheme into motion.

Transporting 121,500 soldiers, 14,592 animals, 1,200 wagons, and 44 artillery batteries required a flotilla of 389 vessels. By the end of March, McClellan was poised on the Peninsula's tip. So were Johnston and 60,000 Confederates who had hastened to the protection of Richmond. The Federals pushed their way through Yorktown and Williamsburg, then inched through the mud closer to Richmond. On May 31, with Richmond but nine miles away, a desperate Johnston turned and attacked at Seven Pines. Two days of fighting were indecisive, yet the battle had far-reaching consequences. When Johnston fell seriously wounded in the action, General Robert E. Lee succeeded to command of the Confederate forces. The ever-cautious McClellan ceased his advance to await dry roads and the reinforcements he deemed imperative. He extended his right flank northward for a hopeful link with McDowell's 40,000 men at Fredericksburg. Meanwhile, Confederate batteries at Drewry's Bluff on the James River repulsed a fleet of gunboats seeking to blast its way to Richmond. Federal pressures on the Capital were momentarily contained.

This respite gave Lee time to plan a daring counter-offensive. For the gamble he had in mind, additional troops were needed. He therefore summoned the army of "Stonewall" Jackson, who had just made history in the Shenandoah Valley.

Jackson's movements that spring were not in keeping with the nickname of "Stonewall," bestowed on him at First Manassas, for the stern Calvinist demonstrated that his real genius lay in mobility and surprise. When 1862 began, Jackson was defending the vital Shenandoah Valley. Not only was this area a rich producer of foodstuffs, but it also was a geographical avenue into the heart of the North. Control of the Valley was essential to either side. Hence, as McClellan's Army of the Potomac embarked for the Peninsula, 18,000 Federals under Nathaniel P. Banks moved into the Valley. Jackson's task was twofold and ominous: With but 8,500 soldiers, he had to hold the Valley and prevent Banks from sending aid to McClellan. On March 23, after a forced march, Jackson assailed part of Banks' army south of Winchester at Kernstown. Jackson lost 700 men and was forced to abandon the field, but the ferocity of his attack frightened Washington into holding Banks—and McDowell—as protective buffers for the Northern Capital.

To destroy Jackson and neutralize the Shenandoah, Lincoln then sent three Federal armies into the Valley. More than 63,000 Union soldiers advanced against Jackson from north, west, and east. Jackson obtained 8,000 reinforcements under General Richard S. Ewell—and then struck. Outnumbered as he was, Jackson realized that his only chance was to assail his adversaries separately before they could unite. He therefore left Ewell in Banks' front, marched swiftly up the Valley, turned west at Staunton, and on May 8 routed Robert Milroy's Federal forces at the Battle of McDowell.

The wily "Stonewall" then hastened back down the Valley, used the Massanutten Mountain as a screen, and attempted to get into Banks' rear by coming through the mountain pass at Front Royal. On May 23, Jackson's brigades struck the center of Banks' retreating columns at Front Royal. A running fight to and through Winchester followed before Banks retired across the Potomac. Jackson had little time to savor his successes. The lead elements of McDowell's corps were approaching from Fredericksburg; John C. Frémont's army was moving in from the west, and Banks' men recrossed the Potomac.

The Confederates barely escaped being caught in the convergence of those forces. Jackson retreated slowly through Harrisonburg—then turned suddenly. On June 8, Ewell's division inflicted a heavy defeat at Cross Keys on Frémont's forces. The

The bucolic Shenandoah Valley, where Thomas "Stonewall" Jackson's daring tactics gained him fame. (CWTI Collection)

following day, Jackson assaulted James Shields' division of McDowell's corps at Port Republic. By sundown that night, three battered Federal armies were retiring from the Valley.

In forty-eight marching days, Jackson's "foot cavalry" had trudged 676 miles, fought six formal actions and five pitched battles. Although outnumbered by more than three to one, Jackson had been victorious in nearly every engagement. His army inflicted 3,500 casualties, captured another 3,500 Federals, confiscated 10,000 muskets and 9 cannon, cleared the Shenandoah Valley of Federal threats, and so alarmed the Federal Government that the reinforcements McClellan urgently sought were never dispatched. All of this Jackson achieved at a loss of 2,500 men and three guns. Overnight his name became a byword; his fame buoyed the hopes of the South.

Jackson's successful Valley Campaign opened the way for Lee to seize the offensive at Richmond. Lee's cavalry, under the colorful "Jeb" Stuart, made an audacious reconnaissance in mid-June completely around McClellan's army and confirmed the fact that the Federal right flank was isolated by the rain-swollen Chickahominy River. Lee thereupon decided on his bold gamble: He would shift the bulk of his army from McClellan's front, unite with Jackson, and destroy the Federal army by shattering its exposed wing and taking the enemy in flank.

What ensued is known as the Seven Days' Campaign. On June 26, Lee's men

Sunday religious services at General George B. McClellan's headquarters prior to the start of the Seven Days' (Peninsula) Campaign. Sketch by Alfred R. Waud. (CWTI Collection)

Wagon trains of the Army of the Potomac ford Bear Creek one mile below Savage Station en route from Chickahominy to James River during the Peninsula Campaign. (Library of Congress)

launched heavy but futile assaults at Mechanicsville against the Federal corps of Fitz John Porter. That night, as McClellan's army began falling back, Jackson's troops arrived from the Valley. Lee attacked Porter again the next day at Gaines's Mill. He broke the Federal line after extremely costly fighting. The Army of the Potomac was now in full retreat to the James River. Lee pressed forward relentlessly in an effort to demolish McClellan's forces. Confederate attacks on the Federal rear, first at Savage Station (June 29) and then at Frayser's Farm (June 30), failed because of Southern commanders' lack of coordination and McClellan's skillful withdrawal tactics. At Malvern Hill on July 1, Lee hurled his army again at McClellan. Federal artillery broke the Confederate assaults. With Federal gunboats supplying both heavy fire-power and a secure line of logistics on the James, McClellan was now safe. The Peninsula Campaign was over. Fighting in the Seven Days cost McClellan 15,849 men. Confederate losses were 20,614—casualties the South could ill afford.

As McClellan extricated himself from the Peninsula, Lee turned to face a new menace to his beloved state. Union forces around Washington had been consolidated into an army under General John Pope, an untested commander who had won a few easy victories in the West. Pope started southward along the Orange & Alexandria Railroad. Lee detached Jackson to blunt this advance until the Army of Northern Virginia could get up into position. On August 9, Jackson's heavier force struck Banks' Federals at Cedar Mountain and won the field after indecisive fighting.

Lee now displayed daring strategy in his effort to destroy Pope before McClellan's army could arrive. He divided his forces by sending Jackson on a sweep northward through Thoroughfare Gap and around Pope's army. Jackson's men seized and destroyed the main Federal supply base at Manassas on August 26, then moved to a strong position on the old Bull Run battlefield to await Pope. The entire Federal army assailed Jackson unsuccessfully on August 29. The remainder of Lee's army came on the field the following day and delivered a counterstroke that sent a bewildered Pope and his beaten army back to Washington. Lee's September 1 attempt at Chantilly to sever Pope's line of retreat failed but cost the North the life of General Philip Kearny, New Jersey's most distinguished soldier. Pope's losses in this Second Manassas Campaign were 14,462 of 73,000 men engaged. Lee's 55,000 troops suffered 9,474 casualties.

A number of motives then prompted Lee to invade the North. Union forces in the East were badly demoralized from recent defeats in Virginia; Lee was anxious to relieve the Old Dominion from the telling pressures of war; the chances seemed good for the Confederacy to secure Maryland to its side; and a successful thrust into the Union might bring to the Confederacy the help and recognition from Europe so necessary for ultimate victory.

Early in September, Lee's columns tramped into Maryland and occupied Frederick. As consternation swept through the North, McClellan and the Army of the Potomac gave slow pursuit. Lee next resorted to a move as daring as it was dangerous. He sent Jackson and 25,000 men to capture Harpers Ferry—which would secure the gateway to the Valley—while the remainder of the Army of Northern Virginia proceeded toward Hagerstown. McClellan then became beneficiary of a stroke of good luck: He obtained a copy of Lee's orders outlining the disposition of the Confederate army. Yet the Federal commander still labored under delusions as to the enemy's strength. His pursuit continued at a wary pace.

Harpers Ferry, with 10,000 Federals and 30,000 small arms, fell to Jackson on September 15, the day McClellan's men fought their way through the passes of South Mountain. Lee suddenly found himself at Sharpsburg, with his back to the Potomac River and his numerically inferior army rendered even smaller by the absence of Jackson. McClellan's vacillation on the 16th enabled most of Jackson's force to rejoin Lee. Throughout the following day, McClellan launched powerful but disjointed assaults that made Antietam Creek "the bloodiest single day of the war." That Lee was able to repulse the onslaughts was due to skillful and heroic defense and the

Charge of the 23rd and 12th Ohio Volunteers against the 23rd and 12th North Carolina during fighting at South Mountain, Maryland, on September 14, 1862. (Library of Congress)

The Battle of Antietam or Sharpsburg, as the South called it: Dead soldiers lie before Dunker Church. (Library of Congress)

timely arrival of A. P. Hill's "Light Division," which double-timed seventeen miles from Harpers Ferry and delivered a surprise flank attack on the Federal left. Over 23,000 men fell dead or wounded that day.

Antietam Creek was in a sense a defeat for both armies. Lee's high hopes of Northern conquest ended at Sharpsburg. Yet McClellan permitted Lee on September 18 to retire unmolested to Virginia, thereby throwing away any fruits of victory. On the other hand, Lincoln exploited the battle by issuing five days afterward the preliminary draft of the Emancipation Proclamation. This bold decree granted freedom on January 1, 1863, to all slaves remaining in seceded territory. The Civil War was thus elevated to something more than the mere preservation of the Union, and the Proclamation rendered even more diplomatically perilous any pro-Confederate involvement by European nations.

"Jeb" Stuart gave a small boost to sagging Confederate morale in October, when he and his cavalry again rode around the Army of the Potomac. Stuart's second foray carried him as far north as Chambersburg, Pennsylvania, and provided Lee with much scouting information. This raid lasted twenty-seven hours, covered eighty miles, and cost Stuart but three men.

Lincoln's patience with McClellan's lack of initiative was exhausted. On November 5, he removed the general from command and appointed a Rhode Islander, Ambrose E. Burnside, as his successor. Burnside gained quick approval of a proposal that the Federal army move secretly and swiftly to Fredericksburg, cross the Rappahannock River on pontoon bridges, and advance on Richmond. If all went well, Lee would be outmaneuvered before he could ascertain Federal intentions.

All did not go well, however. The Federal vanguard reached Fredericksburg on November 17, only to find no pontoons available. By the time they arrived, Lee's army was solidly entrenched on the heights immediately to the south of the city. The Federal army crossed the Rappahannock on December 11. On the 13th, Burnside hurled his divisions in piecemeal frontal assaults against Lee's position. Wave after wave of bluecoated troops were ripped apart by Confederate artillery and infantry. Federal casualties soared to 12,653 men, while Southern losses were only 5,309. Burnside sobbed in his tent, while Lee remarked that "it is well war is so terrible;" otherwise, "we should grow too fond of it!"

In the spring of 1862, Federal forces were assailing Virginia from almost every

Union bombardment of Fredericksburg on December 11, 1862. Lee's army was entrenched on heights south of the city. Drawn by Rufus F. Zogbaum. (Battles and Leaders of the Civil War)

approach and were as close as nine miles to Richmond. By year's end, the only Federals within fifty miles of the Southern Capital were prisoners of war and soldiers suffering the frustrations of defeat.

In the West . . .

The supreme Confederate commander in the West was Albert Sidney Johnston, a veteran soldier and close friend to Jefferson Davis. Johnston was faced with an impossible task. The Confederate Government was resolved to hold onto every acre of seceded territory. Hence, Johnston's 48,000 men were scattered over a 600-mile front from Cumberland Gap to the Mississippi. Federal authorities soon discerned how thin the Southern line was. On January 19-20, 1862, George H. Thomas routed an undermanned Confederate army at Mill Springs, Kentucky.

A week later a second Federal army of 15,000 men, led by U.S. Grant, started through western Kentucky to attack the center of Johnston's defenses. Grant was about to initiate the "river war" by combining soldiers and gunboats to gain control of the inland waterways of the South. His goals were the Tennessee and Cumberland Rivers, the keys to Tennessee itself. The Confederates had constructed only a single fort for the defense of each stream.

On February 6, 1862, Federal gunboats blasted Fort Henry into submission while Grant was moving his troops into position. With the lower Tennessee River now under control, Grant turned his attention to Fort Donelson on the Cumberland. Federal tactics there had to be reversed. Confederate batteries repulsed the gunboats and forced Grant's men to operate on their own. Defective Confederate strategy and animosity between the Southern generals inside the fort were the decisive factors in the collapse of Donelson. When Grant replied to a Confederate overture by offering "no terms except unconditional and immediate surrender," more than 13,000 Southern soldiers on February 16 laid down their arms.

Union troops storm Fort Donelson, on the Cumberland in northern Tennessee. The capture of Forts Henry and Donelson were the first major Union successes of the war. (CWTI Collection)

The loss of these forts was a heavy setback to morale. A breach in the Confederate bastion had been made: The whole state of Tennessee, as well as Alabama and Mississippi, were now vulnerable to Federal attack. The New York *Times* commented: "The monster is already clutched and in his death struggle."

Grant pushed between the two wings of the Confederate army and forced Johnston to fall back to Corinth, Mississippi. By early April, the Federals were near the Mississippi border. However, the Confederates had been strengthening their forces for a counterattack. It came on April 6 at Shiloh, in southern Tennessee, and resulted in one of the severest battles fought in the West. Over 100,000 men took part in the two-day struggle

Johnston's initial assaults caught Grant's inexperienced troops by surprise. Regiments disintegrated as panic-stricken soldiers fled from the field. Determined Union resistance in an area known thereafter as the "Hornet's Nest" momentarily blunted

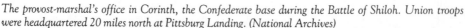

The provost-marshal's office in Corinth, the Confederate base during the Battle of Shiloh. Union troops were headquartered 20 miles north at Pittsburg Landing. (National Archives)

the Confederate drive. By nightfall, however, and despite Johnston's death from a bullet wound, Southern forces had driven Grant's army back a mile, to the bank of the Tennessee River. Don Carlos Buell's Federal reinforcements arrived after dark, and Grant counterattacked the following morning. Ten more hours of fighting ensued before weary Confederates began a sudden withdrawal to their base at Corinth. Halleck, superseding Grant, occupied the town near the end of May. At Shiloh, Grant lost 13,047 men; Confederate casualties were 10,694, about one fourth of their number engaged.

Many Northerners, appalled by Grant's high losses, implored Lincoln to remove him from command. The President replied to the criticisms with the statement: "I can't spare this man—he fights!"

Indians who fought at Pea Ridge. Note the war feathers that decorated their government-issued attire. (CWTI Collection).

Other Union armies in the West made advances during this same period. On March 7-8, at Pea Ridge (or Elkhorn Tavern), Arkansas, Iowan Samuel R. Curtis' 12,000 Federals withstood an assault by 16,000 Confederates that included 3,500 Indians. Curtis assumed the offensive on the second day and won the field, thereby giving the North permanent control of Missouri and northern Arkansas.

Coordinating with Grant's push through Tennessee, John Pope's Federal army embarked on an amphibious operation to clear the upper Mississippi of Confederate outposts. Gunboats and troopships bearing 12,000 men made up the armada that engaged in a March 3-April 8 campaign against New Madrid, Missouri, and Island Number Ten near the northwestern tip of Tennessee. Pope's forces captured both strongholds, as well as 5,000 prisoners, a number of artillery pieces, and large amounts of ammunition and supplies. Again the North had demonstrated the value of joint military and naval operations.

One of the Union's most brilliant successes came late in April. A naval squadron under Virginia-born David G. Farragut blasted its way into the Mississippi and seized New Orleans. Army forces under dour Benjamin F. Butler then clamped the city under such rigid military control that the Confederate Government ultimately branded Butler an outlaw. The capture of this all-important port closed the Mississippi to Southern commerce, deprived the Confederacy of a great deal of manufacturing and manpower capacity, and ranks with Vicksburg and Gettysburg as one of the decisive victories of the war.

Strangely enough, Federal advances in the West came to a close that spring. For a year thereafter, the Confederates generally would either be on the offensive or effectively holding their own against Northern onslaughts. Colonel John Hunt Morgan began this shift in military affairs when he led his "Kentucky Cavaliers" on a July

A Union fleet of ironclads and mortar boats under the command of Andrew H. Foote bombard Confederate defenses on Island Number Ten in the Mississippi River. (Library of Congress)

foray through his home state. Morgan won four battles, bagged 1,200 Federals, destroyed immense quantities of military stores, created havoc and confusion behind the Union lines, and returned safely to Tennessee—at a cost of fewer than 100 men. Morgan's cavalry compatriot, General Nathan Bedford Forrest, was also active. On July 13, his Tennessee troopers stormed into Murfreesboro and captured the entire Federal garrison of 1,040 Federals.

The major Confederate offensive in the West that year began in August. Braxton Bragg, now commanding the South's Army of Tennessee, invaded Kentucky with the hope of wrenching that state from the Union. On October 8, the armies of Bragg and Buell collided at Perryville. Leadership was lacking on both sides; neither general committed his whole force to action. Yet the fighting was sanguinary, producing 7,600 casualties. Bragg was forced to abandon Kentucky.

Meanwhile, General William S. Rosecrans in Mississippi gained for the Union such convincing victories at Iuka (September 19) and Corinth (October 3-4) that he was shortly named to succeed Buell as commander of the Army of the Ohio. But Rosecrans' confidence was short-lived. On December 31, he attacked Bragg's forces at Stone's River, near Murfreesboro, Tennessee. The two armies pounded each other unmercifully for three days. Bragg finally left the field, having suffered 11,739 losses. The "victory" cost Rosecrans 12,906 men and left his army so weakened that it did not take the offensive again for six months.

A concerted attempt to seize Vicksburg got underway in November when Grant and General William T. Sherman devised a two-pronged assault on the river fortress. But the destruction of a Federal supply base at Holly Springs, Mississippi, on December 20 by Southern cavalry under Earl Van Dorn forced Grant back to Memphis. Sherman then attacked alone (December 28-29) and was easily repulsed at Chickasaw Bayou.

In the meantime, John Hunt Morgan's cavalry had slashed again through Kentucky. This "Christmas Raid," which cost Morgan two killed and twenty-four wounded, netted 1,887 prisoners in addition to $2,000,000 worth of Federal property destroyed.

—*James I. Robertson, Jr.*

FORTS HENRY
AND DONELSON

Fort Henry by Edwin C. Bearss and Howard P. Nash
Fort Donelson by Stephen E. Ambrose

Fort Henry
by Edwin C. Bearss and Howard P. Nash

The Bombardment of Fort Henry as depicted in the March 1, 1862 issue of Harper's Weekly.

Three weeks after the Civil War began, Lieutenant General Winfield Scott suggested that the Union Army establish a chain of fortified positions along the Ohio and Mississippi Rivers from Louisville, Kentucky through Paducah, Memphis, Vicksburg, and New Orleans to the Gulf of Mexico. Such a river blockade, "in connection with the strict blockade of the seaboard" already begun by the Navy would, said Scott, "envelop the insurgent States and bring them to terms with less bloodshed than any other plan." Although Scott's *Anaconda Plan* was loudly derided by those who thought, as Horace Greeley did, that the Confederate states could be brought to terms by a quick thrust at Richmond, its merits were so obvious that it was immediately adopted by the government.

As one means of carrying out Scott's plan the War Department quickly took steps to organize a flotilla of gunboats for service on the western rivers. On May 16, 1861, the Navy Department sent Commander John Rodgers to Cincinnati in response to the War Department's request for advice and assistance in connection with this novel undertaking.

Mound City were 175 feet long, 51½ feet wide, and mounted six thirty-two-pounders, three VIII-inch Navies, and four forty-two-pounder Army rifles.

Eads was also given a contract by the quartermaster general to convert the giant salvage boat *Submarine No. 7* into a powerful ironclad to be known as *Benton.* The steamboat *New Era* was converted into the ironclad *Essex* by a St. Louis contractor. *Benton,* when commissioned, was the most powerful ironclad on the western waters.

While the North was building these gunboats the South occupied a defense line which extended from Columbus, Kentucky, on the Mississippi River, through Forts Henry and Donelson, Tennessee, to Bowling Green, Kentucky, then southeastward to Cumberland Gap. Long before the movement into Kentucky, the state of Tennessee had started work on Forts Henry and Donelson to guard the Tennessee and Cumberland rivers about seventy miles south of (upstream from) their confluences with the Ohio River. In mid-November 1861 these posts and the country between them were placed under the command of Brigadier General Lloyd Tilghman, a soldierly looking man with piercing black eyes and a resolute countenance. He had graduated from West Point in 1836, then resigned the same year to become a civil engineer with the Baltimore & Susquehanna Railroad. At the outbreak of the Mexican War he rejoined the army, serving on General Twiggs's staff and as a captain in a battalion of volunteers. After the war he was an engineer with several railroads until he entered the Confederate service.

On inspecting his new command Tilghman found Fort Henry to be a well-designed, five-bastioned earthwork situated just above a bend in the Tennessee where it could command a straight reach of river about three miles long. It was on low ground, however, liable to be flooded by spring freshets, and overlooked by hills on both sides of the river. As an artilleryman Tilghman immediately recognized that these hills could present the same sort of threat to Fort Henry that Dorchester Heights did to the British in Boston when General Washington occupied them. To offset this danger Tilghman ordered a work named Fort Heiman to be built on a bluff across the river almost opposite Fort Henry. The fact that Fort Heiman had not been completed by the beginning of February 1862 had an effect on future events.

When Tilghman took command of the area, Fort Henry mounted two twelve-pounders, one six-pounder, and six thirty-two-pounder smoothbore cannons. At his insistence its armament was increased to ten thirty-two-pounders, two forty-two-pounders, two twelve-pounders, one twenty-four-pounder, a ten-inch columbiad, and a rifled twenty-four-pounder (originally a smoothbore that had been rebored to take a sixty-two-pound conical projectile banded at the breech). Thus he had, all told, seventeen guns. As one of the

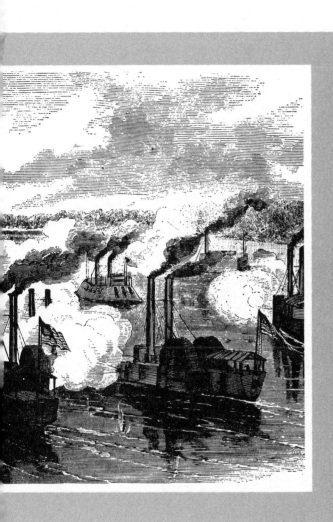

Rodgers found that steamers of the kind available in the West were poorly suited for use as fighting craft because, as he put it in an official report, they had "their high pressure boilers on deck with all their steam connections entirely exposed [to damage by gunfire], and with three-story houses of thin white-pine plank erected on their hulls." But, driven by the same necessity that caused the Navy to use ferryboats, excursion steamers, merchantmen, and the like to blockade the coast, he bought *Conestoga, Lexington,* and *A.O. Tyler.* A Cincinnati contractor converted these craft into gunboats of sorts by dropping their boilers below their main decks, lowering their steam pipes as much as possible, covering the thin walls of their deckhouses with oak planking five inches thick, and arming them with a number of thirty-two-pounder smoothbores, VIII-inch Navies, and VIII-inch Dahlgrens.

The War Department had contracted with James B. Eads to build seven ironclad gunboats big enough to carry heavy batteries and broad enough to provide steady gun platforms. *Cairo* and her sisters *Cincinnati, St. Louis* (later renamed *Baron deKalb*), *Carondelet, Pittsburg, Louisville,* and

Above: General Lloyd Tilghman, the Confederate commander of Fort Henry. Below: Commodore Andrew H. Foote, whose gunboats hammered Fort Henry into submission.

officers said, however, the twelve-pounders were so much like pot metal that they were test-fired, whereupon they burst.

Because the Confederates were kept well informed by Northern newspapers of the Union's gunboat building program, eleven of Fort Henry's heavy guns, including the columbiad and the twenty-four-pounder rifle, were placed on the river front where they could command the main channel east of Panther Island.

As was true of most Confederate installations throughout the war, Fort Henry had gunpowder of poor quality. Captain Jesse Taylor said that the fort's ammunition was so bad that "it was deemed necessary to add to each charge a proportion of quick-burning powder." Until this was done it was impossible to reach a target more than a mile distant.

During this fall of 1861 several Union Army and Navy officers told their superiors that they believed Fort Henry could be attacked without too much risk, and overcome without too much difficulty either by a couple of gunboats or by some troops assisted by gunboats. Flag Officer Andrew H. Foote, who had succeeded Rodgers as senior naval officer assigned to the Western Flotilla, and Brigadier General U.S. Grant were among the most ardent advocates of a joint movement.

At the beginning of the third week of January 1862, soon after the Eads gunboats were commissioned, Grant proposed such a movement to his department commander, Major General Henry W. Halleck. "Old Brains" curtly told Grant that the plan was preposterous. Halleck was then well known for his accomplishments in military and civilian life, whereas what little was known of Grant did not inspire confidence in him.

On January 28, 1862, perhaps at Foote's instigation, Grant again applied to Halleck for permission to move against Fort Henry. Foote helped by writing to Halleck: "General Grant and myself are of the opinion that Fort Henry . . . can be carried with four ironclad gunboats and troops, and be permanently occupied. Have we your authority to move for that purpose when ready?"

This concurrence of a navy man with Grant's opinion seems to have impressed Halleck, as well it might in view of Foote's record. In 1856, while Foote was commanding the USS *Plymouth* during a Sino-British war, a fort at Canton fired upon his vessel. He obtained permission from his superior to demand an apology. When this was refused he attacked the forts, four in number, employing the *Plymouth* and another sloop, the *Levant.* After breaching the walls of the largest fort he carried it by storm, with a loss of only forty men to four hundred for the Chinese.

Whatever his reasons may have been, Halleck telegraphed to Grant and Foote on Wednesday, January 29, that he would decide about their proposed movement as soon as he could receive a report on the condition of the road from Smithland, Kentucky to Fort Henry. Foote, who had become aware of Halleck's tendency to procrastinate, replied: "I have just received your telegram in relation to Fort Henry and will be ready with four ironclad boats early on Saturday. . . . As the Tennessee will soon fall, the movement up that river is desirable early next week (Monday), or, in fact, as soon as possible."

At or about the time these messages were being exchanged, Halleck heard, from what he supposed was a reliable source, that General Pierre G.T. Beauregard had been ordered from Virginia to the West with a large body of Confederate troops. Although this report was not entirely correct—Beauregard was being sent west, but without troops—it forced Halleck's hand. On January 30 he ordered Grant and Foote to move against Fort Henry.

Halleck's message reached Foote and Grant on the same day. By February 2 they had assembled a fleet of transports large enough to carry half of Grant's troops, and the gunboats *Conestoga, Tyler, Lexington, Carondelet, St. Louis, Cincinnati,* and *Essex.*

The *Essex* was commanded by William (Dirty Bill) D.

Porter. Since no one ever seems to have suggested that Porter was physically unclean, he probably earned his sobriquet by his methods of seeking professional advancement.

The plans for the movement against Fort Henry were kept a far better secret than was the case with most Civil War expeditions. Consequently the Confederates were taken completely by surprise when, to quote one of them, "countless transports" appeared below Fort Henry on February fourth.

Because it had been raining heavily for several days the Tennessee was at flood stage and its current was so rapid that the ironclads had to ride to double anchors and keep their engines running at full speed ahead while they were waiting for the transports to bring up the rest of the troops. A number of torpedoes (cylindrical mines about 5½ feet long, containing about seventy pounds of gunpowder), torn loose from their moorings by driftwood borne on the swift current, floated past the anchored boats. Foote had one of them fished out for examination. While he and Grant were watching the *Cincinnati*'s armorer dismantle it, a sudden hissing sound caused everybody to vacate the fantail. Foote, although the elder by sixteen years, beat Grant up the nearest ladder to the top of the casement. Reaching the top, and

The gundeck of a gunboat engaged in the attack on Fort Henry, as depicted in Harper's Weekly.

realizing that the danger, if any, had passed, Foote turned around to Grant, who was displaying more energy than grace, and said, "General, why the haste?"

"That the Navy may not get ahead of us," responded the general.

When the noise died down the armorer finished what he had been doing.

Late on the afternoon of February 5 the rest of the troops reached the rendezvous, some four miles below Fort Henry. Grant, on the fourth, had asked to have the *Essex* run him upstream close enough to the fort to permit him to have a good look at it. The *Essex,* accompanied by two other gunboats, stood cautiously up river. As the vessels chugged along, they shelled the woods on either side to see if they could flush any masked batteries. Passing up the main channel to the east of Panther Island, the gunboats took position near the mouth of Panther Creek. Having gained a point within one mile of Fort Henry, the vessels opened a deliberate fire on the Rebel works. Several of the gunboat's shells were seen to fall into the fort. The Confederates replied with their ten-inch columbiad and twenty-four-pounder rifle. Being inexperienced in handling the big guns, they had difficulty registering.

Grant having seen what he wanted, the gunboats started to turn around. A projectile from the rifled twenty-four-pounder screamed over the spar-deck of *Essex,* narrowly missing Grant and Porter, and struck the officers' quarters. After ripping through the cabin, captain's pantry, and steerage, the shell erupted from the stern, and dropped hissing into the river.

Foote and Grant met late on the fifth to draft final plans for a joint attack on Fort Henry. The soldiers were to advance up both sides of the river against Forts Heiman and Henry, while the gunboats were bombarding Fort Henry. (Fort Heiman did not seem important enough to warrant the gunboats' attention.) Originally Foote had supposed that the boats would have to use the main channel, which would permit the fort to bring them under fire at the extreme range of its guns—about three miles. His subordinates told him that high water would enable the boats to navigate a chute to the west of Panther Island, where they would be screened by dense woods until they were within a mile and a quarter of the fort. He gladly took advantage of this piece of good luck.

On February 6 Grant and Foote were ready to make their attack. The weather was ideal. A thunderstorm ended at daybreak, the temperature became comfortably mild, and there was enough wind to clear smoke away—an important consideration in the days of black powder. At 10:30 a.m., the flagship *Cincinnati* signalled "prepare for action." Thirty minutes later the gunboats got underway in line ahead. They cleared the upper end of Panther Island about 12:30 p.m., and formed in line abreast, with the *Essex* on the extreme right, the *Cincinnati, Carondolet,* and *St. Louis* to the left; the three wooden gunboats formed another line abreast about one-half mile astern of the ironclads and fired over them.

Opening fire at a range of seventeen hundred yards, the ironclads gradually closed to six hundred yards. As they neared the fort the fuses were cut from fifteen to ten to five seconds and the elevation of the guns was reduced from seven degrees to six, five, four and finally to three degrees.

Before the battle Foote had warned his gunners that every shot or shell they fired would cost the government eight dollars, so he wanted none of them wasted. To the grim amusement of the gunners of the other boats the *Cincinnati's* first salvo completely missed the fort. The boats seldom missed again and, as a Confederate officer remarked, their "shot and shell penetrated the earthworks as readily as a ball from a Navy Colt would pierce a pine board." This gunfire drove the Confederate gunners from their pieces and dismounted many of the cannon. Two thirty-two-pounders were hit, one of them squarely on the muzzle, almost at the same instant.

The Confederates' gunnery at first was as good as that of the gunboats. Seven hits were made on the *St. Louis* and nine or ten on the *Carondolet,* but neither of them was much damaged and neither suffered any casualties. The other ironclads were less fortunate. The *Cincinnati* was hit thirty-two times; two of her guns were disabled, her chimneys, main cabin, and small boats were badly damaged, one man was killed and eight were wounded. A shot that pierced the *Essex's* forward casement just above the port gunport killed one of Porter's officers, Acting Master's Mate Samuel B. Britton, Jr., in its flight; then it struck the middle boiler. Escaping steam and hot water killed ten and wounded twenty-three. Five men, who leaped overboard to escape being scalded, were never seen again. When it became possible to pass forward of the boiler room Pilot James McBride was found dead at his post, with one hand on the steering wheel, the other holding the engine room bell rope; James Coffey, a member of No. 2 gun crew, was found dead on his knees in the act of taking a shell from the box to be passed to the loader.

The Confederates suffered nearly as much from bad luck as they did from the Union bombardment. The fort's best gun, the rifled twenty-four-pounder, burst (perhaps because it was partly loaded with quick burning powder), killing one of its crew and wounding the rest. A few minutes later a priming wire jammed in the vent of the columbiad, putting it out of action. A premature discharge of a thirty-two-pounder (again possibly caused by quick burning powder) killed two men and disabled the piece.

As a consequence of these misfortunes and of the gunboats' accurate shooting, only four of Fort Henry's guns remained usable after seventy minutes. They were kept in action long enough to enable most of the garrison to escape to Fort Donelson. Fort Henry was then surrendered to Foote before Grant's troops, delayed by muddy roads, were in position to carry out their mission.

A s time passed and bigger battles were fought, the engagement at Fort Henry came to be regarded as of only minor importance. But by their capture of Fort Henry, the Federals had driven a wedge into the Confederate defense line guarding the heartland of the Confederacy. The left flank of this line had been anchored at Columbus, and the right on Cumberland Gap, and with the loss of Fort Donelson, this line was hopelessly shattered. To make matters worse, the Confederates had lost a powerful field army and an immense amount of war material.

The fruits of the victory at Fort Henry were quickly apparent. As early as February 8, two days after its fall, and in the face of the threat to Fort Donelson, General Albert Sidney Johnston had notified Secretary of War Judah P. Benjamin that he was giving up his position at Bowling Green and was retiring on Nashville. When Fort Donelson fell, Nashville was uncovered, and it was expected that Federal gunboats would ascend the Cumberland, compelling the Confederates to give up Nashville, a vital industrial and transportation complex. On February 17 and 18, Johnston evacuated the city and moved the main body of his Central Army of Kentucky to Murfreesboro. The Confederate rear guard left Nashville on the night of the twenty-third, and the vanguard of Brigadier General Don Carlos Buell's Army of the Ohio appeared the next morning on the right bank of the Cumberland, opposite the city.

At the same time, Columbus, the Confederate bastion on the Mississippi River, was rendered untenable. Major General Leonidas Polk was forced to order the evacuation of "The Gibraltar of the West." This was carried out on the night of March 2. The Union troops occupied Columbus the next day. Thus, by the capture of Forts Henry and Donelson and the destruction of the defending army, the Federals at one stroke had forced the Confederates to give up southern Kentucky, and virtually all of middle and west Tennessee. Falling back, the Confederates began to concentrate their troops for a new stand on Corinth in northeast Mississippi.

W ith the fall of Forts Henry and Donelson, the entire picture of the war in the West was changed almost overnight. Grant had seized the initiative and, despite temporary set-

backs, he was never to lose it. The deep wedge driven into the South by the fall of Forts Henry and Donelson would eventually split the Confederacy. Just over the horizon lay Shiloh, Corinth, Memphis and, seventeen months later, Vicksburg.

Abroad, the effects of the loss of these forts were quickly felt by the Confederate diplomatic agents who were seeking to persuade Great Britain and France to recognize their government and to denounce the Union blockade as ineffective. In March 1862 James Mason, writing from London, somewhat euphemistically said, "The late reverses at Fort Henry and Fort Donelson have had an unfortunate effect upon the minds of our friends here." And John Slidell, mincing no words, wrote from Paris that, if these defeats were not soon counterbalanced by some substantial victories, the Confederate government would not only have to give up hope for early recognition but must also expect that the declaration of the inefficiency of the blockade, which he had confidently expected at no distant date, would be indefinitely postponed. These defeats were not counterbalanced and the Confederate states never stemmed the tide that began to flow against them when Fort Henry fell.

Attack on Fort Henry. Operations from noon to midnight, February 6, 1862.

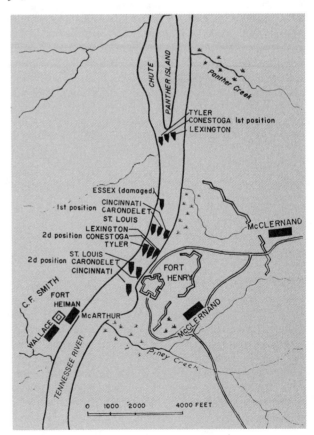

Fort Donelson

by Stephen E. Ambrose

"The blow was most disastrous and almost without remedy." So Albert Sidney Johnston described the loss of Fort Donelson and nearly fifteen thousand men. His powers as a prophet exceeded his abilities as a general. The Confederacy spent the three years in the West after February 1862 trying without success to recover from the blow.

It may be that the Confederacy was never strong enough to hold onto its vast western empire, that it just did not have the manpower to defend Tennessee, southern Missouri, Mississippi, Arkansas, Alabama, Texas, Louisiana, and southern Kentucky. Certainly the Confederate strategy of trying to protect everything was futile, and nearly all military historians today agree that Jefferson Davis should have concentrated his forces. Still, when the South did concentrate, as at Donelson and later at Vicksburg, the result was the capture of more men. In both cases, however, the Northern victory was primarily the result of timid Southern generalship.

The Donelson Campaign, like the Vicksburg Campaign a year and a half later, offered the Confederacy a glittering opportunity to surround and capture or destroy the most important Union army in the West. That the South let the opportunities pass was, in both cases, due to the lack of imagination and the cautious approach of two generals named Johnston. Neither seemed to realize that the Confederacy had to take chances to win. At Donelson, it was Albert Sidney Johnston who failed, and the failure was especially bitter because many, including President Davis, considered him the finest soldier in North America.

To be sure, Johnston's task was not easy. With a total force of less than seventy-five thousand men he was supposed to defend the entire area from the Appalachian Mountains to the Mississippi River. The Union had nearly two hundred thousand men in the vicinity, half under Don Carlos Buell in central Kentucky and half under Henry Halleck, with headquarters in St. Louis. Johnston had stationed his troops along a concave line that began at Columbus, Kentucky, on the Mississippi River, ran southeast to Forts Henry and Donelson, and then northeast to Bowling Green, Kentucky. He had a railroad for lateral communications, but the rivers were against him, as they ran perpendicular to his lines. The Cumberland and Tennessee Rivers offered natural highways to the Yankees, and the Union had river gunboats—Johnston did not. To seal off the rivers he had two forts, Henry on the Tennessee and Donelson on the Cumberland, ten miles apart at that point. Neither were good natural defenses nor did Johnston have them strongly garrisoned. He should have moved either forward or back to a better defensive line, but lack of troops forbade the one and states-rights politics the other.

Johnston's troops were raw recruits, untested in battle, led by untried junior officers, poorly armed and inadequately supplied. A Belgian who traveled across Kentucky that first winter of the war thought the Confederate men fantastic. What they wore for uniforms beggared description; he could not tell officers from privates nor soldiers from civilians, their weapons were often antiques, and he shuddered at the unshaven men who brandished "their frightful knives." They all looked dangerous, for "their determination is truly extraordinary, and their hatred against the North terrible to look upon, there is something savage in it." These Southerners would, someday, be among the world's finest fighting men, but it would take time.

The Yankees had problems, too. Their troops were better armed, supplied, and disciplined, but not necessarily better led. They had to take the offensive in an inhospitable territory plagued by bad weather and served by atrocious roads. They had no unity of command—Halleck and Buell were equals who reported to General-in-Chief McClellan, who in turn usually ignored them both. Worse, neither trusted the other nor the subordinate facing the Confederate forts, U.S. Grant.

But President Lincoln wanted action and Grant, at Cairo, Illinois, was anxious to move against Fort Henry, which he thought he could capture with two gunboats. Halleck still hesitated, but when on January 29, 1862, he heard that General P.G.T. Beauregard was coming west with fifteen regiments to reinforce the forts—a false rumor—Halleck gave Grant permission to seize Henry.

Grant began his movement early in February. By the sixth he had come up to the fort. The Confederate commander, Lloyd Tilghman, sent most of his men eastward to Fort Donelson before Grant's troops got close to his lines. Tilghman himself stayed in Henry to help a handful of men work the guns in an attempt to beat off the Yankee gunboats. They did a good job, disabling one of Flag Officer Andrew H. Foote's boats, but Foote's big guns soon broke down the Confederate parapets, dismantled some guns, and dismembered a few of the gunners. Early in the afternoon Tilghman hauled down his flag.

Johnston believed that the brief engagement had changed the entire situation in the West. His line was broken, the Tennessee River was open to the invaders (Foote sent a couple of gunboats tearing south on the river to spread panic throughout west Tennessee and northern Alabama), and his army was demoralized without ever having fought a battle. The bulk of Foote's gunboats had started back down the Tennessee—they were obviously going to swing east on the Ohio and then south on the Cumberland to attack Fort Donelson. Johnston thought the situation was approaching disaster; he met it with half-hearted measures. Instead of falling back to a new defensive line or, more appropriately, concentrating everything he had against Grant, Johnston

General Ulysses S. Grant on horseback at the battleline at Fort Donelson. Detail from a painting by Paul Philippoteaux. (LC)

sent half his men into Fort Donelson. He evidently hoped they could hold Grant. With the other half of his force he retreated, falling back from Bowling Green towards Nashville.

Johnston had put too few men into Fort Donelson to hold Grant, but more than he could afford to lose. He compounded the error by his selection of commanders at the fort. All the decisions Johnston made that winter can be, and have been, defended, save this one. Nothing a theater commander does is more important than his choice of subordinates, and here Johnston's failure was unmitigated. The man in charge at the fort was John B. Floyd, a one-time United States secretary of war who had no military experience, no leadership ability, no sense of responsibility, and whose sole concern was with his personal safety. Second to him was Gideon J. Pillow, formerly James K. Polk's law partner, a veteran of the Mexican War and the only Confederate toward whom Grant ever expressed outspoken contempt. His sense of responsibility about equalled Floyd's. The only real soldier in the fort was Simon Bolivar Buckner, and he was third in command. (Buckner was a year behind Grant at West Point and the two were close friends. In 1854, when Grant showed up broke in New York after resigning from the Army, Buckner had given him a life-sustaining loan.) Buckner was a professional who knew his business, but Floyd and Pillow saw to it that he never had a chance to show it. After the battle Buckner told Grant that if he had been in command the Yankees would not have invested the fort as easily as they did. Grant replied that if Buckner had been in command, "I should not have tried in the way I did."

Grant's great genius as a soldier, the characteristic in which he outdid every opponent he ever faced, was that he did not worry about what the enemy might do to him, but concentrated on what he might do to the enemy. Grant showed this trait at Donelson. Here he was, in midwinter in hostile territory with scarcely seventeen thousand men, dependent on a single river for supplies and reinforcements, surrounded by Confederates. From one point of view (Halleck saw it this way) he was a reckless subordinate in the heart of the enemy's territory with nothing to hold to in case of disaster. In effect, he was in a bag, with the enemy to the northeast, northwest, and directly in his front. If Johnston saw his opportunity and pulled the strings, Grant would be trapped. Most of Foote's gunboats and the transports that had carried his men up to Henry were gone. If Johnston had seen the situation as Halleck did, he might have changed the course of the war in the West. But he did not.

Neither did Grant. He figured that the Confederates were demoralized and panicky and that one more push would drive them out of middle and west Tennessee. He determined to cut loose from Fort Henry and march overland to Fort Donelson. Bad weather held him up for a few days; he started on February 11.

Fort Donelson was built in the early winter of '61 on a ridge just west of Dover, Tennessee. Its purpose was to deny the Yankees the use of the Cumberland River, and the batteries placed in the fort were well suited to the task. The fort itself consisted of little more than a series of shallow earthen entrenchments that extended in a semicircle around the batteries and just south of Dover. Hickman's Creek, to the north, and Indian Creek, to the south, gave additional protection to the flanks. The entire area was hilly and heavily forested, with only a few poor roads running through it. The most important of these was the Wynn's Ferry Road, running southwest from Dover.

Grant's forces were well up to the fort by February 13. He had a total of twenty-four infantry regiments, seven batteries of artillery, and several mounted units; Floyd had twenty-seven regiments of infantry and additional supporting troops. As Grant had expected, the enemy made no attempt to contest his advance. He later wrote that "I had known General Pillow in Mexico, and judged that with any force, no matter how small, I could march up to within gunshot of any intrenchments he was given to hold." Grant's forces were divided into two divisions: the 1st, under John A. McClernand on the right, or eastern end of the line, and the 2nd, under Charles F. Smith, on the left. McClernand was an Illinois politician whose military experience consisted of a few marches in the Black Hawk War. He was ambitious, untactful, hated West Pointers, and had little ability. By contrast,

Smith was Regular Army and an outstanding soldier. Lew Wallace described him: "He was a person of superb physique, very tall, perfectly proportioned, straight, square-shouldered, ruddy-faced, with eyes of perfect blue, and long snow-white mustaches." When reviewing troops, Smith had the bearing of a marshal of France. Rumor had it that he knew the Army regulations by heart. He was the only general officer in the Union Army who could ride along a line of volunteers in regulation uniform, plume chapeau, epaulets and all, without exciting laughter.

The infantry on both sides had a miserable day on the fourteenth. Grant had received some reinforcements, Lew Wallace's 3d Division, which had come up the Cumberland on transports behind Foote's gunboats. Wallace, a newspaper reporter, lawyer, politician, and veteran of the Mexican War, put his men into line between McClernand on the right and Smith on the left. There had been a blizzard the previous night, and as the troops could not have camp fires they had been cold, wet, and unhappy. A few wounded men froze to death.

Most regiments had a special company composed of their best marksmen, and during the investment of the fort they went out as individuals. The captain usually checked with them at first light. "Canteens full? Biscuits for all day? All right; hunt your holes, boys." They dispersed and like Indians sought cover behind rocks, stumps, or in hollows. Some dug holes, others climbed into trees. Once in a good spot they stayed there all day, shooting at anything in the enemy breastworks that moved. It was dangerous to show a head and impossible to start campfires. Both sides contented themselves with hardtack.

Grant's plan was to keep the Confederate infantrymen pinned within their lines while the gunboats attacked the batteries at close range. Both he and Foote thought that the boats would reduce the opposition at Donelson just as they had at Henry. When the batteries were destroyed and the fleet controlled the river, while Grant's men blocked the exits, the Confederates would have to surrender.

All of this depended on Foote, and was with his approbation. A Regular Navy man, he had had wide and varied experience. In the 'fifties, when the navy had been called upon to take certain Chinese forts, he had led a storming party across rice fields under heavy fire, holding an umbrella over his head for protection from the oppressive Oriental sun. On his ships sailors practiced total abstinence, refrained from profane swearing, and strictly observed the Sabbath; by the force of his personality Foote had maintained these rules without precipitating a mutiny.

Gunboats attack the water batteries at Fort Donelson.

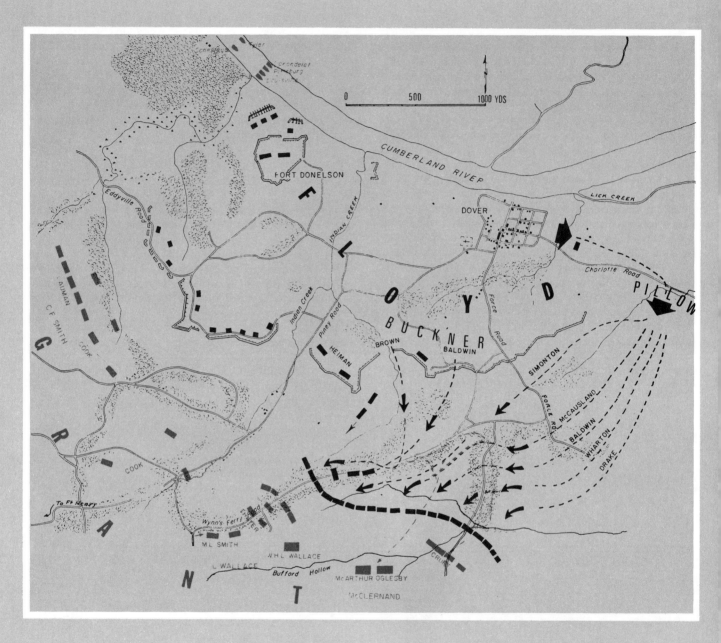

A simplified version of a map at Fort Donelson National Military Park by Edwin C. Bearss portrays the Confederate attempt to break out of Fort Donelson defenses from about 12:15 p.m. to 1 p.m. on February 15, 1862. In the sweep against the Union right flank, Pillow's command included Simonton's and Drake's brigades of Bushrod Johnson's division, Wharton's and McCausland's brigades of Floyd's division, and part of Baldwin's brigade of Buckner's division. Buckner, in the center, had Brown's and part of Baldwin's brigades of his own division. Confederate troops remaining in the trenches were Heiman's brigade of Johnson's division, the 30th Tennessee under Colonel J. W. Head, and in the fort itself two other Tennessee regiments under Colonel J. E. Bailey. Later in the afternoon the fort proper was commanded by Colonel C. A. Sugg. The gunboat attack of the 14th is shown at the top of the map. Small rectangles on the map represent regiments—Confederates in black, Federals in brown.

He was a little skeptical about this attack. He knew that the Donelson guns were stronger than those at Henry; but Grant urged speed, and so at mid-afternoon of the fourteenth he came up the river with his four ironclads, *Pittsburg, St. Louis, Carondelet,* and *Louisville.* Two unarmored gunboats, *Tyler* and *Conestoga,* followed. *St. Louis* was Foote's flagship.

Foote opened fire at about a mile's range. His shells fell short and he moved in closer—he had won at Henry by coming in close, and he was determined to do the same at Donelson. Slowly the distance lessened—three quarters of a mile, half a mile, a quarter of a mile. In the Crimean War the French and English fleets, composed of much larger ships than Foote's, had engaged the Russian shore batteries, which were little if any stronger than those of the Confederates at Donelson, from a maximum distance of eighteen hundred yards to a minimum of eight hundred yards. Still Foote moved in until he was only four hundred yards away. All the ironclads were taking hits, the decks were slippery with blood, the surgeons were absorbed in tending to the wounded, and the carpenters were busy making repairs. *St. Louis* alone took forty-nine hits. But the men cheered, for the fire from shore seemed to slacken and lookouts reported that the enemy was running.

Foote moved in, too closely this time. At 380 yards a solid shot tore through the pilot-house of *St. Louis.* It carried away the wheel, mortally wounding the pilot and injuring Foote. At the same instant the tiller ropes of *Louisville* were disabled. Both vessels were unmanageable and began to float down the current, whirling round in the eddies like logs. *Pittsburg* and *Carondelet* closed in to cover them. Foote was compelled to retreat, and the fleet backed up with the best grace and most speed it could manage. Any victory won at Fort Donelson would have to be won by the army.

Grant was disappointed at Foote's failure, but he did not panic. He knew that the Confederates could not get significant reinforcements into the fort nor bring supplies to the besieged men. He was fairly certain Johnston was not going to mount an attack on his rear. He was willing to wait for starvation to bring him victory.

The Confederates decided not to wait. That night Floyd held a council of war and all present agreed with his plan to attack the Union right wing and force a breakout. The Southerners spent the night of February 14 preparing for the

This engraving of a gun explosion on the Carondelet *during the attack on Fort Donelson was based on a sketch by Rear Admiral Walke. (BL)*

attack. Most of the troops left their rifle pits and massed over on the left. They made every effort to keep silent, but heavy gun carriages just could not be moved without making some noise. Yet, because of high winds from the tail of the blizzard, the Yankees did not hear them.

At dawn, when the woods were ringing with reveille and the numbed Union soldiers were rising from their icy beds and shaking off the snow, the Confederates struck. Pillow led the attack on the left, Buckner in the center. The general direction was along Wynn's Ferry Road. After the first confused moments, with shots and shouts ringing out in the cold air, McClernand's brigade commanders got their units formed into line and began to return the Confederates' fire. Both sides slugged away for the better part of the morning, spreading a lurid red over the snow, toppling limbs from trees, and sending up a continuous roar. The Yankees held.

About noon officers from various regiments rode up to the Union brigade commander on the right, Richard J. Oglesby, with news that their men were running out of ammunition. They asked where they could get more, but he could only weakly reply, "Take it from the dead and wounded." Actually, there was plenty of ammunition all around him, but at that early stage of the war junior officers were not very good at their distribution functions. Before the officers could even get back to their men, Oglesby's right-hand companies began to give way, the men holding up their empty cartridge boxes as they retreated to prove that they were not cowards.

Seeing them, the Southerners gave a whoop and swept around Oglesby's flank, quickly appearing in his rear. Sick at heart, he gave the order to retire.

The commander of the next brigade to the left, W.H.L. Wallace, looked to his right and saw the crumbling line. Coming towards his own unprotected flank was Bedford Forrest and the Confederate cavalry. Wallace's men were also out of ammunition, and he quietly told them to join the by now general retreat. The Confederates had control of the Forge Road; the road to the southeast and Nashville was open to them.

The time had come to begin the retreat to the south. There can be no doubt that had the Confederates started out at noon they would have made it safely to Nashville. The Union force probably would not have even mounted an effective pursuit, since Grant was not on the scene to direct it. He had left before daybreak to consult with Foote, and was in the middle of the Cumberland River on the *St. Louis*. But Pillow, the hero of the morning, now proceeded to make himself ludicrous. He convinced himself that Grant's whole army was fleeing in rout for Fort Henry. Ignoring Floyd, he rode over to Buckner and accused him of cowardice. Napoleon, he exclaimed, followed up his victories, and the Confederates would do no less. Pointing to a road that ran up a gorge in front of Buckner, he ordered an attack. Then he sent an

aide to the nearest telegraph station with a dispatch for John-ston, asserting on his honor as a soldier that the day was his. His head swimming with his own glories, Pillow abandoned all thought of a Confederate retreat to Nashville.

McClernand's division had retreated to Bufford's Hollow south of Wynn's Ferry Road, and Wallace had sent two bri-gades of his division over to the right to help out. Buckner's men were coming along the road, anxious to pour more minie [rifle] balls into McClernand's ammunition-less men. Wal-lace, riding over, saw a Union officer gallop by, shouting, "All's lost! Save yourselves." Behind him, riding at a walk, with one leg thrown over his saddle horn, and looking for all the world like a farmer coming home from a hard day's plowing, came W.H.L. Wallace and what was left of his brigade.

"Good morning," Lew Wallace said.

"Good morning," W.H.L. Wallace replied.

"Are they pursuing you?" "Yes." "How far are they be-hind?" W.H.L. Wallace calculated, then said, "You will have about time to form line of battle right here." "Thank you. Good-day." "Good-day."

Lew Wallace looked behind him and saw Battery A, 1st Illinois Light Artillery, and Colonel John M. Thayer's six-regiment brigade coming up. He placed the artillery across the road, with the infantry on either side and in reserve. The

The interior of Fort Donelson as depicted in Harper's Weekly.

Confederates hit the roadblock at full speed and rebounded like a rubber ball. For the next ten minutes they tried to break through, finally decided it was impossible, and stopped to catch their breath. A lull settled over the field.

Just then Grant rode up. He had ridden the entire length of his line, and was satisfied with what he saw on the left and in the center. On the right, however, "I saw the men stand-ing in knots talking in the most excited manner. No officer seemed to be giving any directions. The soldiers had their muskets, but no ammunition, while there were tons of it close at hand."

It probably never occurred to Grant that he should have panicked, that he should have begun riding this way and that, shouting orders, making threats, beating enlisted men with the flat of his sword. Most officers would have reacted in this way. Not Grant. His solidity and basic common sense were never in better evidence than here at this, one of the most decisive moments of his career.

Noticing the full knapsacks on the Confederate dead, Grant immediately realized that Floyd and Pillow were trying to cut their way out. He began walking his horse along the line, calling out to the men, "Fill your cartridge boxes, quick, and get into line; the enemy is trying to escape and he must not be permitted to do so." It worked. The men cheered, set to work, and quickly re-established the line on the right.

Grant then decided to launch an attack of his own. He was sure that Floyd must have stripped his entrenchments to make the attack, so he rode over to Smith's headquarters and told that general to attack.

The position was a mean one, uphill and criss-crossed with felled trees. Smith, in what Grant called "an incredibly short time," got his men into line and began the movement. Smith himself went to the front and center of the line to keep his men from firing while they worked their way through the abatis. From time to time he turned in his saddle to make sure the alignment was kept. He looked as if he were on review; one private remarked, "I was nearly scared to death, but I saw the old man's white mustache over his shoulder, and went on." Confederate fire began to increase, men began to fall. Smith's line hesitated. The general put his cap on the point of his sword, held it aloft, and called out, "No flinching now, my lads! Here—this is the way! Come on!" Most of his men followed him, broke through the abatis, and scattered the Confederates.

Grant now held an important section of the Southern en-trenchments. Lew Wallace and McClernand meanwhile had reorganized their men and launched their own attacks, driv-ing Pillow's and Buckner's men back into their entrench-ments. The Confederate attempt to break out had failed.

30

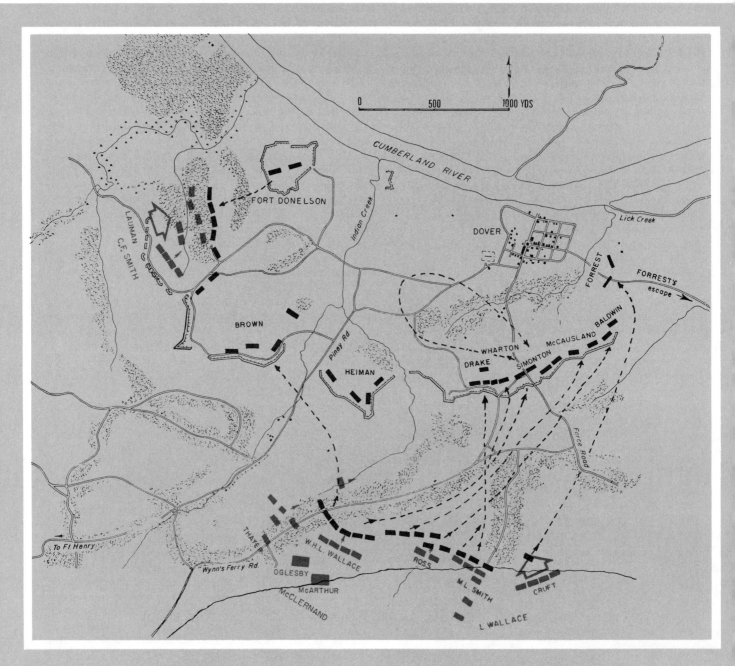

This map shows Grant's counterattack on February 15 from about
2:15 p.m. to 3 p.m., when he drove the Confederates back into
their entrenchments. The broken lines and arrows show the general
directions rather than exact routes taken by the withdrawing and
advancing troops.

Right: *Confederate infantry escaping from Fort Donelson. Drawing
by W. A. Rogers. (HW)*

That night, as both sides gathered their wounded, Floyd and Pillow argued about ways of extricating the army from its embarrassing position. Unable to reach an agreement, at one a.m. they called a meeting of all general officers and regimental and brigade commanders. When most of the leaders had assembled, Floyd began to speak. His scouts had just discovered that Grant had five regiments of reinforcements coming to join his army. Floyd wanted to get out before Grant's reinforcements arrived, and he ordered his officers to have their men ready to march by four a.m. The brigade and regimental commanders left to make their preparations; Floyd, Pillow, and Buckner remained in Dover at Pillow's headquarters. Buckner argued that Floyd's orders were as unrealistic as Pillow's actions had been the preceding morning. The troops had fought all day and were exhausted. There had been no regular issue of rations for days, the ammunition was nearly expended, Grant had four times as many men and half of his were fresh. It would be madness to try to fight their way through. If he persisted, Floyd would lose three-quarters of his men, and Buckner said he "did not think any general had the right to make such a sacrifice of human life." Pillow argued that they ought to hold on and wait for transports to carry them across the river; then they could make their escape by way of Clarksville, and "thus save the army." Buckner pointed out that Smith had already

gained their entrenchments—the Yankees would overrun them the next day.

Pillow stood up and declared, "Gentlemen, if we cannot cut our way out nor fight on there is no alternative left us but capitulation, and I am determined that I will never surrender the command nor will I ever surrender myself a prisoner." Floyd chimed in, "Nor will I; I cannot and will not surrender." Pillow added that he thought "there were no two persons in the Confederacy whom the Yankees would prefer to capture than himself and General Floyd." He then asked Floyd if he could scurry off with him. Floyd replied, "It was a question for every man to decide for himself."

At this point Forrest entered the room, looked at the gloomy faces, and demanded to know if they intended to surrender. Someone nodded. Forrest stomped out of the room, assembled his officers, and announced, "Boys, these people are talking about surrendering, and I am going out of this place before they do or bust hell wide open." He got his troops together and marched them through the icy streams and creeks to safety—most of the eastern end of the line was unguarded.

After Forrest left, the comic opera at headquarters reached its climax. Floyd started the last act. "General Buckner," he said, "I place you in command; will you permit me to draw

out my brigade?"

"Yes, provided you do so before the enemy act upon my communications," Buckner replied.

Turning to Pillow, Floyd said, "General Pillow, I turn over my command."

Pillow exclaimed, "I pass it."

Buckner grimly declared, "I assume it; bring on a bugler, pen, ink, and paper." While Buckner began his bitter duty, Floyd and Pillow dashed out and got down to the river, where they were expecting a steamboat. Just before dawn the boats arrived. Floyd and his Virginia troops got on and sailed away. Pillow and his staff crossed the river on a flatboat and later rejoined Floyd.

Dover Tavern, General Buckner's headquarters and the scene of the surrender, as it appeared in 1884. (BL)

Johnston, now in Nashville, knew nothing of these proceedings, and did nothing to change the situation at Donelson.

Buckner, who held to his old-fashioned belief that a general's responsibility extended to going into captivity with his men, composed his note to Grant, asking for terms of capitulation. Grant received it just before daylight. His reply was terse: "No terms except unconditional and immediate surrender can be accepted. I propose to move immediately upon your works."

Buckner was shocked. He had not slept in over thirty hours, had spent most of the previous day engaged in hard fighting, and was disgusted with his superiors. He did not quite know what Grant meant by "unconditional surrender," as the term was a new one, and he did not like to think about the implication of it. Perhaps he allowed himself a fleeting thought of further resistance. But he had a role to play, and he was determined to play it out to the end, with dignity. So he wearily wrote his reply to Grant. "The distribution of the forces under my command incident to an unexpected change of commanders and the overwhelming force under your command compel me, notwithstanding the brilliant success of the Confederate arms yesterday, to accept the ungenerous and unchivalrous terms which you propose." So Donelson was gone, and with it all of western Kentucky and Tennessee.

The Confederates had run the gamut from glittering opportunity through brilliant victory to buffoonery and finally bitter defeat. All three senior officers had blundered, or worse. Only Buckner emerged untarnished, and he at least managed to restore some dignity to the last act.

Later that morning Grant rode into Buckner's headquarters. The two commanders made final practical arrangements—the prisoners went north on Yankee transports, Buckner went with them—and gave each other cigars. At the conclusion of the meeting, when Buckner was walking off, Grant stopped him and said, "Buckner, you are, I know, separated from your people, and perhaps you need funds; my purse is at your disposal." Buckner declined, then thanked him for the offer. It was a strange war.

THE BATTLE
OF SHILOH

by Wiley Sword

Occupation of
Pittsburg Landing

"**In numbers engaged, no** such contest ever took place on this continent; in importance of results, but few such have taken place in the history of the world." The author of this terse assessment was a general destined to become one of the most famous of American soldiers—later Lieutenant General Ulysses S. Grant. The battle he referred to was the one he came to regard as "more persistently misunderstood than any other engagement between National and Confederate troops during the entire rebellion"—the terrible bloodbath of Shiloh.

Grant had good reason to regard Shiloh with unfeigned respect. It was a conflict that nearly cost him his reputation, his military career, and even his life. Feeling he had been "shockingly abused" by the press, he wrote to his wife shortly after the battle: "I am thinking seriously of going home. . . ." Following

Ulysses S. Grant, victor in the Henry-Donelson Campaign, was ordered to conduct the "decisive movement" that would probably end the war. (U.S. Army Military History Institute)

The Battle of Shiloh on April 6-7, 1862, was one of the bloodiest fought in the western theater, producing enormous numbers of casualties on both sides and ending forever Confederate hopes of recovering west and middle Tennessee. (CWTI Collection)

the war General Grant continued to reflect upon the battle's bloody significance. "Shiloh was the severest battle fought at the West during the war, and but few in the East equalled it for hard, determined fighting," he asserted in his memoirs.

Yet Shiloh has suffered from a want of general understanding. Long accorded a controversial and complex status, the Battle of Pittsburg Landing, as the South referred to it, represents a paradox in American military history. Fought essentially to restore a disastrously lost war balance, the battle only compounded an already dire military situation in the South. But the conflict represented perhaps the Confederacy's greatest opportunity for a devastating victory in the West, one that might have altered the course of the war. By the narrowest of margins a disaster of the greatest magnitude was averted by the Federal army at Shiloh. Although, as Bruce Catton has written, the fact that this effort came close to being a dazzling victory did not offset the failure, the story of that miscarriage at Shiloh is as remarkable as it is fascinating, befitting one of the pivotal events in our nation's history.

The mastermind of the Federal Tennessee expedition was Henry Wager Halleck, the 47-year-old major general whose bulging eyes and receding hairline had earned him the nickname "Old Brains." As commander of the Department of the Missouri, Halleck had been constantly harassed by President Abraham Lincoln during the winter of 1861–1862 concerning the inactivity in the Western Theater. Confronted by a virtual stalemate in the military situation, with the Confederates occupying a vast defensive network stretching from Columbus to Bowling Green, Kentucky, Halleck sought an early opportunity to penetrate the Middle South.

In January 1862, a conference at his St. Louis headquarters with Brigadier Generals George W. Cullum, Halleck's chief of staff, and William T. Sherman, his friend and subordinate, produced a tentative plan that envisioned the Tennessee River as "the true line of operations."

To the rather obscure, middle-aged Illinois brigadier general who had led the combined Army and Navy expedition up the Tennessee against Fort Henry during the first week in February 1862, the operation afforded an outstanding opportunity at a minimum risk. Utilizing the Navy's gunboats almost exclusively, Ulysses S. Grant quickly reduced the two uncompleted works, Fort Heiman, on the west bank, and Fort Henry, on the eastern shore. Both Confederate forts had been erected on low ground near the river's edge for political rather than strategic considerations, and a climactic artillery duel on February 6 proved the vulnerability of Fort Henry. The fort surrendered

after a bombardment of two hours and ten minutes, and Grant was thus provided with easy access to another major Confederate defensive bastion.

Fort Donelson, only twelve miles distant across a narrow neck of land, and guarding the Cumberland River approach to Nashville, was invested on February 12 by Grant's army. Following some horrendous generalship on the part of Confederate Generals John Floyd and Gideon J. Pillow it was decided to surrender the fort and garrison. On February 16 about 9,000 prisoners, thirteen heavy cannon, and nearly 15,000 small arms were turned over to Grant's troops. Famous almost overnight, Grant was promoted to major general, and Halleck was granted his ardent wish—command of several consolidated departments, which made him virtual commander west of Knoxville, Tennessee.

Recognizing the enormous importance of having breached the Confederates' outer line of defense, Halleck immediately prepared to capitalize on the opportunity. Using the Tennessee and Cumberland rivers as broad avenues of access, Halleck sent Federal gunboats deep into the Middle South's interior.

On the Tennessee, Union vessels cruised as far south as Florence, Alabama, wrecking bridges, breaking up numerous militia camps, and destroying Rebel shipping. Then, in late February, following the fall of Nashville, a major invasion column was organized, again under Grant's command. His orders were to conduct the "decisive movement" that would probably end the war.

Henry W. Halleck tried to remove Grant from field command, but he was quickly forced to back down. (CWTI Collection)

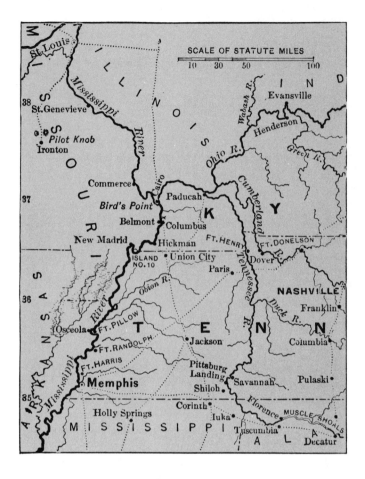

At this point several untoward incidents involving army high command occurred to retard the campaign. Perhaps sensing an emerging rival in the arena of popular esteem, Halleck in early March callously removed Grant from field command on the pretext of neglect and inefficiency. Alleging that Grant had returned to his former whiskey drinking habits, which had reportedly caused him to resign from the Regular Army in 1854, Halleck attempted to justify his actions with the administration in Washington.

Within a week, however, Halleck learned that President Lincoln had become involved and that he would be required to provide specific information on his allegations against Grant. Halleck quickly backed down. Restoring Grant to active command of the Tennessee expedition on March 13, he attempted to cover his culpability in the affair by forwarding a copy of an exonerating letter to Fort Henry for Grant's perusal.

Meanwhile, Brigadier General C. F. Smith,

Grant's replacement, had led a column of sixty-three transports forward for the purpose of destroying the vital enemy railroad bridge over Bear Creek, near Eastport, Mississippi. This would sever the major east-west artery, the Memphis & Charleston Railroad, that provided interior mobility and crucial supplies to the Mississippi Valley region.

Numbering about 25,000 men, with twelve batteries of artillery, Smith's column approached Savannah, Tennessee, on March 11. "The weather was soft and fine," an officer recorded, and from the long, winding column of transports flags fluttered and bands played. To one observer the grand and awesome column of boats made it seem "we had men enough . . . to clean out the Confederacy and half of Europe."

Savannah had been chosen as a base of operations, it seems, largely because of a planned rendezvous with Major General Don Carlos Buell's Army of the Ohio, then at Nashville.

Wasting little time to achieve his immediate objective of cutting the enemy's railroad communications, Smith ordered two successive raids by elements of his column on March 12. The first foray, led by the dapper Indiana Brigadier General Lew Wallace (later the author of *Ben Hur*), failed in its objective of seriously damaging a bridge on the north–south route of the Mobile & Ohio Railroad. Thereafter Wallace's troops remained concentrated on the southern bank of the Tennessee at Crump's Landing.

The second raid ordered by C.F. Smith was led by the irascible and controversial William Tecumseh Sherman, who had been relieved from command less than six months earlier as being temporarily "unfit for duty"; physically and mentally broken. Like Wallace's attempt, Sherman's venture resulted in little net gain, but became important in the rapidly unfolding scheme of events. Forced by inclement weather to return from Yellow Creek in northern Mississippi, Sherman had been unable to reach the Memphis & Charleston Railroad, about nineteen miles inland.

Since the Tennessee had been rapidly and heavily swollen by a sustained torrential rain—the river had risen fifteen feet in less than twenty-four hours—Sherman returned upriver to the first landing site above water—Pittsburg Landing, Tennessee.

Here on March 16, 1862, in conjunction with Brigadier General Stephen A. Hurlbut's division, which had also moved up to the landing site as support, Sherman disembarked his men to make another attempt on the Memphis & Charleston Railroad east of Corinth. Following a minor skirmish Sherman concluded that he would not be able to strike the railroad from this site without a severe conflict since the enemy was watching all approaches too closely.

Sherman had been favorably impressed by the location as a major base of operations though. Pittsburg Landing not only provided a strategic position from which to strike the railroads. It also afforded an "admirable camping ground for a hundred thousand men," and the terrain "admits of easy defense by a small command," said Sherman.

Ironically, the man who was to act upon Sherman's observations had only belatedly arrived upon the scene. "Sam" Grant, as his friends knew him, had at last been restored to field command by Halleck, and had hastened upriver from Fort Henry, arriving on the 17th. C.F. Smith, who had recently scraped his leg on boarding a small yawl and had been stricken with a tetanus infection, and Sherman were the only West Point officers commanding divisions in the expedition. Grant placed full confidence in both, and remembering Sherman's gallant gesture in offering to waive seniority during the Donelson Campaign, readily accepted Sherman's strong endorsement of Pittsburg Landing as a base. All troops remaining at Savannah, except later Major General John A. McClernand's division, were accordingly ordered forward nine miles to Pittsburg Landing.

By the last week in March most of Grant's command, later officially designated the Army of the Tennessee, had encamped within a three-mile perimeter of the nearly 100-foot-high bluffs at the landing. Only Lew Wallace's division remained detached at Crump's Landing, four miles north along the river. As the men observed, Pittsburg Landing and vicinity "excited nothing but disgust and ridicule." One officer described the area as "an uninteresting tract of country, cut up by rough ravines and ridges." Within a few weeks of its occupation by Grant's troops, however, the vast wilderness site had been transformed into a teeming quasi-city, cluttered with army tents, parked wagons, boxes of munitions, and dozens of steamboats vying for the limited landing access. "Men were everywhere," wrote an awed young private, and another volunteer noted that a person might "march for miles and . . . see nothing but the white tents of infantry, cavalry, and artillery. . . . The sound of drums and the blowing of trumpets," he observed, "fill my ears from morning to night."

The original purpose of the concentration at Pittsburg Landing, as a base from which to readily strike the enemy's railroads, had been substantially changed in light of recent strategic developments. Henry Halleck, at last endowed with the authority he had long

Pittsburg Landing, on the west bank of the Tennessee River. (Harper's Weekly)

courted—over-all command in the Western Theater—had ordered the concentration of Buell's 36,000-man army with Grant's troops along the Tennessee River. Buell, who acknowledged orders for a joint offensive on March 10, was allowed to march overland from Nashville rather than move by river transport. Accordingly, on March 16 Buell's leading division broke camp and began its direct march toward Savannah, the point of rendezvous. Although Buell had reckoned that he could "move in less time, in better condition, and with more security . . ." by marching overland than by river, he failed to consider the route. Ahead lay a 122-mile backwoods road, rutted and muddied by early spring rains, and inundated by several badly swollen rivers.

As Buell's troops laboriously trudged south in late March, Grant's men languished at Pittsburg Landing. Among more than 51,000 Union soldiers reported there and at Crump's Landing, the inevitable sickness an internal bickering over food and seniority undermined the troops' morale. Constant drill and inspections were tedious, and the monotony of camp life was boring in the extreme. "It will be two weeks tomorrow since I done anything but eat and lay around the encampment," wrote a disgruntled Illinois soldier.

With the advent of April the skies cleared and a warm sun dried the ground and brought forth a profusion of leaves and blossoms. It became so hot that it was uncomfortable in the daytime, thought one soldier, but the health and spirits of the troops improved rapidly with the weather. Regarding their encampment as a sort of martial picnic ground, the men roamed through the surrounding woods filled with "johnny-jump-ups" and other wild flowers. Delicate pink peach blossoms fluttered by the thousands in the breeze throughout the numerous orchards adjacent to their encampments, and one private observed that "the nights are delicious, just cool enough to sleep well."

The Counter Offensive

A measure of the enormity of crisis in the Mississippi Valley region during March 1862 was suggested by the furor that arose within the Confederacy over the retention of General Albert Sidney Johnston as commander in the Western Theater. Following the loss of Forts Henry and Donelson, forcing the abandonment of much of Kentucky and Tennessee to the enemy, the Southern press, many congressmen, and even several of his high ranking subordinate generals openly criticized Johnston and demanded his removal.

Confederate General Albert Sidney Johnston (left) and his second-in-command, General Pierre G.T. Beauregard (right). By the end of March they had gathered nearly 50,000 troops at Corinth. (Both photos: CWTI Collection)

The son of a former New England doctor and his second wife, Sidney Johnston had grown up in Kentucky and become a dedicated soldier. After graduating from West Point in 1826, he took up an active military career that included service in the Texas Revolution of 1836 and the Mexican War. Despite several lackluster assignments, including duty as a paymaster on the Texas frontier during the 1850's, Johnston had been appointed colonel of the newly formed 2d U.S. Cavalry in 1855. Partly responsible for this good fortune had been Jefferson Davis, Secretary of War in the Franklin Pierce administration and Johnston's close friend and admirer since their college days at Transylvania University. A brigadier general commanding the Department of the Pacific in 1861 when war broke out, Johnston immediately resigned to cast his lot with the South. Jefferson Davis had amply rewarded Johnston by appointing him a full general with rank second only to Adjutant General Samuel Cooper, an administrative official. As commander of Confederate Department No. 2, Johnston was responsible for a huge area of the South, including all or portions of seven states stretching from the Appalachian Mountains to Indian Territory.

Johnston's tenure in this assignment had been anything but successful, however. In January 1862 a subordinate, Brigadier General Felix K. Zollicoffer, had been soundly defeated at Logan's Cross Roads, Kentucky, opening east Tennessee and the Cumberland Gap to enemy incursions. Following the loss of Forts Henry and Donelson, important sites such as Columbus, Kentucky, and Nashville had been abandoned.

Though Johnston's subordinates had been generally responsible for these disasters, the department commander was bitterly criticized. One congressman, traveling with the army, wrote to Jefferson Davis that Johnston had committed inexcusable "errors of omission, commission, and delay." Coupled with other vociferous protests, the pressure to remove Johnston was extensive; all but one of Tennessee's congressmen called on Davis to demand his removal. Davis' reply revealed his unshakable confidence in his close friend. If Sidney Johnston was "no general," he said, they had best give up the war, for they had no general.

Johnston, aided by another of the South's premier generals, P.G.T. Beauregard, rapidly determined on a bold plan to recoup lost Southern fortunes. Sent west in February 1862 following political difficulties with the Davis administration, the victor of Bull Run had tentatively suggested to Johnston in late February that he might wish to co-operate with or join the independent command then being gathered by Beauregard to defend the vital railroads about Corinth, Mississippi.

Sidney Johnston reached a decision almost immediately. Stating that defense of the Mississippi Valley was "of paramount importance," he would risk interception by Buell's Federal army to join with Beauregard. This "hazardous experiment," as Johnston termed it, was initiated in late February, and following a three-week combined march and journey by

Above: Members of the Ninth Infantry, Indiana, which saw fierce action at Shiloh. (National Archives)

Below: A group of Confederate artillerymen, typical of those who fought at Shiloh. (Library of Congress)

railroad, the vanguard of Johnston's army reached Corinth without mishap.

Including the troops from Columbus, Kentucky, and contingents from the Gulf states, Beauregard had managed to gather about 21,000 troops for defense of the railroads. To these were added about 10,000 men in mid-March from Major General Braxton Bragg's Department of Alabama and West Florida. Sidney Johnston's command further swelled the Confederate forces in and about Corinth to nearly 50,000 by the end of the month.

Reorganized as the Army of the Mississippi, this formidable gathering was to be further augmented by Major General Earl Van Dorn's Trans-Mississippi Army, ordered on March 22 to join at Corinth as soon as possible. Yet events along the Tennessee River had occurred so rapidly that Confederate plans soon became largely reactive in nature.

Following the initial occupation of Pittsburg Landing by Sherman's troops on March 16, a growing apprehension had developed for the safety of the Memphis & Charleston and Mobile & Ohio railroads, deemed "the vertebrae of the Confederacy" by one general. Various detachments had been posted at outlying locations along the railroads, and a series of false alarms soon began to wear upon the nerves of the Confederate generals. At Bethel Station, twenty-three miles northwest of Corinth on the Mobile & Ohio road, a strong force of infantry and cavalry under Brigadier General Benjamin F. Cheatham had been posted. Sent to this site to defend the region from an advance by Lew Wallace's Federal division, part of which was reported at nearby Adamsville, Cheatham was instructed to establish a strong outpost at Purdy, four miles distant in the direction of the enemy. While carrying out his instructions on April 2, Cheatham's movement was discovered by Federal scouts lurking in the vicinity.

Fearing that an attack was pending on his lone brigade stationed at Adamsville, Federal Colonel Charles R. Woods immediately sent word of a Confederate "advance" to Lew Wallace at Crump's Landing. The alarmed Wallace promptly started two brigades to Woods's relief, and before midnight stood with his entire division in line of battle, waiting for an attack that never came.

Cheatham's cavalry scouts, meanwhile, had observed Wallace's forced march to Adamsville. Compounding the error, they alarmed Cheatham, who sent an urgent telegram to Corinth about 10 p.m., warning of a Federal movement in force. Placed in Beauregard's hands, Cheatham's telegram precipitated a major crisis. Concluding that Wallace's ag-

gressiveness suggested that a junction of Buell's and Grant's armies was near at hand, and that the enemy was preparing to advance in strength, Beauregard endorsed Cheatham's telegram: "Now is the moment to advance and strike the enemy at Pittsburg Landing." This message was entrusted to Adjutant General Thomas Jordan, who immediately carried it to General Johnston for final disposition.

Johnston was still awake and, being uncertain of the tactical implications, walked across the street to Bragg's quarters to confer with his chief of staff. Bragg, after being roused from bed, soon became involved in a critical discussion. Both Bragg and Jordan, speaking on Beauregard's behalf, allegedly urged an immediate advance against the enemy. Johnston was said to be reluctant, but was influenced by several related developments. On the previous day, one of Johnston's staff officers, Lieutenant Thomas M. Jack, had returned from Richmond bringing important dispatches from Jefferson Davis and Robert E. Lee, the President's military adviser. Both letters urged Johnston to strike the enemy before the arrival of Buell's army, enroute from Nashville. Further, it is believed that during the evening of April 2 a report on the rapid approach of Buell's 36,000 troops was received from two detached companies of Louisiana cavalry, watching Buell's movement along the Duck River in middle Tennessee.

This coincidence of information served to support the theory that the junction of the two Federal armies was near at hand. Accordingly Johnston ordered preparations for an advance at 6 a.m. the following morning, drafting the orders in Bragg's bedchamber after midnight. Final plans and arrangements were written by Beauregard early in the morning of April 3, and somewhat belatedly, about midafternoon, the advance elements of the army cleared Corinth.

However, due to widespread confusion over the proper roads to take, the poor condition of the narrow backwoods wagon trails, and improper communications, the march was so protracted as to require three days to traverse the approximately twenty-three miles to Pittsburg Landing. A light rain began to fall during the afternoon of the 4th, miring the already soft roads. Thereafter the widely dispersed troops often found their way blocked by bogged wagons and artillery.

Though it had been intended to attack during the early morning of April 5, Johnston found this plan thwarted by a heavy rainstorm that lasted nearly three hours during the night. By dawn the roads were vast quagmires of mud and standing water, and the scattered corps were unable to move faster than a slow crawl. Although the front line, Hardee's Corps, was in position by 10 a.m. the second and third assault waves lagged far behind, creating huge gaps in the Confederate array.

By late afternoon, when most of the troops were finally deployed, the nerves of the Confederate commanders were so frayed that several wanted to call off the entire operation. Braxton Bragg, in a surly mood and commenting unfavorably on the troops' lack of secrecy and their insufficient provisions, urged a withdrawal. Even Beauregard, who had initiated the movement and planned much of the attack, also proposed a retreat. The noise of the inexperienced troops and the delay, said Beauregard, had alerted the enemy, and they would be found "entrenched to the eyes."

Sidney Johnston was astounded. Supported by Leonidas Polk, commander of the I Corps, Johnston declared, "Gentlemen, we shall attack at daylight tomorrow." The enemy, he reasoned, could present no greater front than the Confederates, and thus he would "fight them if they were a million."

That night the Confederate army slept within two miles of Shiloh Church, which marked the outer perimeter of Grant's army. Although it had been originally intended to attack corps abreast, Beauregard had earlier decreed a battle formation modeled after "Napoleon's order for the Battle of Waterloo." Thus, succeeding waves of infantry, with corps in tandem aligned across the entire front, were ordered deployed. The basic premise, advised a staff officer, was that "no force the enemy could [amass] could cut through three double lines of Confederates." In the heavily wooded terrain, with scattered enemy encampments throughout affording natural pockets of resistance, Beauregard's plan presented a fatal flaw.

Johnston, who had determined to trust in the "iron dice of battle," by now was more intent on the tactical objectives of the attack. By turning the enemy's left flank, the Federal army's line of retreat to the Tennessee River might be cut off, and the opposing troops forced back against deep Owl Creek, "where [they] will be obliged to surrender," said Johnston.

Mindful of his recent assertion: "The test of merit in my profession with the people is success. It is a hard rule, but I think it right," Sidney Johnston's terse battle orders urged resolution, discipline, and valor. "The eyes and hopes of eight millions of people" were resting upon them, Johnston told his soldiers. They were to fire at the feet of the enemy to avoid overshooting, and soldiers would not be permitted to break ranks "to strip or rob the dead." Anyone running away on any pretext would be "shot on the spot."

Oblivious of the dire implication of these words, Johnston's soldiers prepared for the morrow's fight with considerable, if ill-judged, enthusiasm. Campfires, although forbidden by orders, were ablaze in a wide perimeter throughout the Confederate lines. Shouts, bugle calls, and drum rolls echoed through the forests. "I have a great anxiety to see and be in a great battle," wrote one Confederate before the fight, and another talked of his "breathless anxiety" as Beauregard had ridden past on the 5th, saying, "Fire low, boys, fire low." In all, the campaign was largely looked upon as a grand adventure by the many soldiers who would soon be involved in their first combat. Unfortunately for many, it would also be their very last experience.

The Surprise

To William Tecumseh Sherman, the events of the first week in April reflected the dire inexperience of his untried division. Since most of his men were recruits unfamiliar with army life, he had ordered daily drill and instruction. On April 3 Colonel Ralph Buckland's brigade had marched three miles out the Corinth road to perform this routine duty. Actually, the men of the 70th Ohio remembered the jaunt as "a kind of picnic excursion." After marching a few miles the men stacked arms for dinner, sending out a small picket detachment. These pickets were advancing to their posts when they were suddenly fired on by Confederates.

According to one private, a hasty retreat by the pickets was followed by a short council among the officers, and they decided to withdraw promptly to their Shiloh Church encampment. When later informed of the affair, Sherman regarded it as so minor that he made no report to army headquarters.

On the following day, April 4, another of Buckland's regiments, the 72d Ohio Infantry, was drilling in the open fields near their outpost pickets. About 2:30 p.m. sharp firing in the nearby woods resulted in a further advance by a few companies of the regiment. They soon learned that an entire outpost consisting of a lieutenant and six men had been captured by Confederate cavalry. When two of the 72d's companies sent into the woods as flankers failed to return, a strong 150-man detachment of the 5th Ohio Cavalry was sent by Sherman to investigate.

Guided by the sporadic sound of firing, the cavalrymen soon came up with Buckland's missing companies, then engaged with a larger force of enemy cavalry. The Ohio cavalrymen burst on the scene with a shout and chased the scattering Confederates

On April 3, after they were unexpectedly fired on by Confederates, Colonel Buckland's brigade quickly returned to the Union encampment at Shiloh Church. (Harper's Weekly)

for nearly a quarter-mile, capturing about thirty prisoners.

Atop a nearby knoll the pursuers suddenly came face to face with a Confederate battle line of infantry supported by artillery. Surprised by the blast of musketry and three cannon shots, the Ohioans fled the scene, losing most of their prisoners in the confusion. Unknowingly, Sherman's cavalrymen had uncovered the advance elements of Hardee's Corps, marching to their assigned position as spearhead of the planned assault on the Federal camps.

When the retreating Federals returned to the line of outposts, they found Sherman present, and in a surly mood. Angrily upbraiding Buckland for nearly drawing the whole army into battle, Sherman further chided his officers for their "irregular proceedings." Even the commander of the Ohio cavalry, Major Elbridge Ricker, was scoffed at by Sherman for his alarmist report of having encountered a strong enemy force. "Oh!—tut, tut. You militia officers get scared too easily," remarked Sherman.

After returning with his men to their Shiloh camps, Sherman sent a routine report to Grant estimating that the Confederates occupied the village of Monterey in considerable force, and inferred that

Buckland had perhaps encountered a brigade making a reconnaissance in force.

Since he was informally the camp commander, despite the presence at Pittsburg Landing of Major General John A. McClernand, who ranked him, Sherman was responsible only to Grant, who was then quartered at Savannah awaiting Buell's arrival. Alerted by several preliminary reports of an attack on the army's outposts, Grant hastened to Pittsburg Landing late that night. He arrived in the midst of a driving rainstorm and was unable to reach Sherman's camps at Shiloh Church. In the darkness and slippery footing Grant's mount fell heavily, pinning the major general's leg. Although the soft ground prevented a fracture, Grant's ankle became so swollen that his boot had to be cut off. During the next several days Grant was unable to walk without crutches.

Several of Grant's staff officers had reported all quiet along Sherman's front, however, and thereafter the skirmish of the 4th was largely disregarded. The following day, Saturday, April 5, Sherman sent word to Grant: "I have no doubt that nothing will occur today more than some picket firing. The enemy is saucy, but got the worst of it yesterday, and will not press our pickets far. I will not be drawn out far unless with certainty of advantage, and I do not apprehend anything like an attack on our position."

Sherman, as suggested by the evidence, was deeply embarrassed by the affair of the 4th. Disdainful of his officers and men, he wrote that they had "as much idea of war as children." The officers, in particular, he thought were "afraid of the men," and extremely careless. "I will do all I can with my division, but regret I have not better discipline and more reliable men," he confided.

Orders that served as a demeaning critique were soon issued to his division. In case of alarm, regiments were to await orders before going to the front. Brigade commanders were to go no farther than the advanced pickets without Sherman's order. Detachments adjacent to the flank of a marching column were absolutely prohibited—on and on read the lengthy orders.

Thereafter, Sherman was particularly harsh in dealing with his alarmist officers. On April 5, when the colonel of the 53d Ohio Infantry formed his men following an exchange of shots between pickets, Sherman sent over a staff officer with a caustic comment: "General Sherman says: 'Take your damned regiment [back] to Ohio,'" announced the staff officer, "'There is no enemy nearer than Corinth.'"

Yet if Sherman remained indifferent in his attitude, his resulting lack of vigilance was shared by others, including the man who later came to be regarded as one of the heroes of the battle.

Brigadier General Benjamin M. Prentiss was a curious addition to Grant's command. A quarrelsome Illinois politician who had feuded with Grant over seniority during service in Missouri in 1861, Prentiss was also on unfriendly terms with several of his subordinates. As commander of the newly created 6th Division, Prentiss was allocated ten recently arrived regiments, only one of which had been in battle. The commander of this unit, the 25th Missouri Infantry, was Colonel Everett Peabody, a highly competent if headstrong former railroad engineer known for his outspoken manner. Peabody had been wounded and captured during the siege of Lexington, Missouri, by Price's Confederates in September 1861. Upon his exchange his old unit had been quickly reorganized and sent east into Tennessee. As an experienced senior colonel, Peabody, upon assuming a brigade commander's responsibility, objected to the "kind of loose" camp life permitted in the division. During the evening of April 5 Peabody had gone to Prentiss with a suggestion that the division be put in a condition to resist an attack, and that at least one battery of artillery be deployed to protect the outer line.

Prentiss, undoubtedly regarding Sherman's adjacent camp at Shiloh Church as the outer portion of the army most exposed to any enemy buildup, is said to have "hooted" at Peabody's suggestions.

Although forming a portion of the army's outer periphery, since it was on the immediate left of Sherman's camps, Prentiss' pickets were stationed only about 300 yards in front. Several officers who reported about a dozen "butternuts" observing a review of the 6th Division from the underbrush on the afternoon of the 5th had felt uneasy enough to urge Prentiss to make a reconnaissance patrol late that afternoon. Routinely obliging these officers, Prentiss had allowed five companies under Colonel David Moore of the 21st Missouri to march into the brush to search out the offending Confederates. Moore had returned after dark and reported no contact of any sort. Apparently, Moore marched only about a mile diagonally across Sherman's front to an "old cottonfield," where several Negroes said they had seen a few Rebel cavalry that afternoon.

Consequently, Prentiss was convinced, like Sherman, that his men were unduly alarmed, and that few enemy were nearby.

After listening to taunts from the handful of Confederates captured during the skirmish of the 4th—"If you ain't mighty careful, they'll [Confederates] run you into hell or the [Tennessee] river before tomorrow night," said one prisoner—an undercurrent of apprehension had, indeed, run through the Federal ranks. One rather dismayed lieutenant colonel of an Illinois regiment had gone bathing at a nearby creek along the front and found no Federal pickets guarding the approaches. The army must have some "queer generals" he surmised in his diary.

Yet, almost at the very last possible moment, events occurring on the evening of April 5 were to result in a crucial detection of the Confederates, in time to provide a narrow margin of survival for perhaps the entire army.

About 8:30 that evening an officer of the outer picket guard, Captain Gilbert D. Johnson of the 12th Michigan Infantry, returned to camp and reported to the officer of the day that "he could see long lines of camp fires" and "hear bugle sounds and drums." Fully concerned, the officer of the day, Lieutenant Colonel W.H. Graves, promptly went to see Prentiss with this information.

Prentiss, however, had recently received Moore's negative report, and merely told Graves to withdraw Johnson's company, saying the cause of concern was only an enemy patrol. When Johnson dutifully returned to camp with his men about 10 p.m., however, he had been further alarmed by the continuous noise in the woods. Again Graves went to see Prentiss, this time taking Johnson with him. But the Illinois brigadier rather abruptly told them not to be alarmed, that everything was "all right."

Frustrated by Prentiss' lack of concern, they went to the tent of their brigade commander, Everett Peabody, and told him of the recent events. Although it was then about midnight, Peabody pondered the alternatives. At last, saying he would not be taken by surprise, he ordered out upon his sole responsibility a reconnaissance patrol consisting of three companies of the 25th Missouri and two companies of the 12th Michigan regiments. Under the command of a veteran Regular Army officer, Major James E. Powell, the patrol was hastily organized and marched from camp about 3 a.m.

Working their way forward about a mile to an obscure cotton field known as Fraley's Field, Powell's men approached the open spot cautiously, just as the first streaks of light gathered on the horizon. Three warning shots rang out in the semi-darkness, but Powell pressed forward into the clearing, his men deployed in a long skirmish line.

Ahead, the advanced pickets of Brigadier General S.A.M. Wood's Confederate brigade were surprised to see the approaching Federals. Following an exchange of shots between Powell's men and a few forward vedettes, Wood's outpost pickets, 280 men under Major A.B. Hardcastle, opened fire with a volley. A second lieutenant of the 25th Missouri was here struck down, becoming the first of what was soon to be a dreadful butcher's bill of casualties.

The first fire had occurred at about 4:55 a.m., and doggedly Powell's and Hardcastle's units continued firing, both sides losing an increasing number of men. A half-hour passed before word came from Wood's headquarters for Hardcastle to hold his ground until the general advance could begin. Yet another half-hour went by, and still the Federals stubbornly refused to yield in front.

Acting under Peabody's orders to "drive in the guard, and . . . develop the force," holding the ground as long as possible, Powell also had anxiously awaited his own reinforcements. About 6:30 a.m., however, a long battleline of men in butternut uniforms emerged from the woods and swept into Fraley's Field, their muskets glimmering in the soft morning sunlight. A portion of Hardee's corps, which comprised the first of three successive Confederate battlelines, this frontal assault column numbered more than twenty-two regiments, in all about 9,000 effective troops. The awesome sight was enough to convince Powell of his danger, and a hasty withdrawal was initiated by a bugler sounding retreat. Chased by the skirmishers of two Arkansas infantry

The landing at Savannah, nine miles north of Pittsburg Landing. (Battles and Leaders of the Civil War)

units, Powell's men disappeared into the woods at a run, heading for camp along the same route by which they had earlier advanced.

At Savannah, Ulysses Grant was asleep in his headquarters at the Cherry house, having been up "to a very late hour" the previous evening while socializing with his officers aboard the steamboat *Tigress.* The advance elements of Buell's army, William Nelson's division, had arrived only yesterday following a forced march. Grant had no boats to transport these troops upriver, however, and he had assured one of Buell's officers, "I will send boats for you Monday or Tuesday, or sometime early in the week. There will be no fight at Pittsburg Landing; we will have to go to Corinth, where the Rebels are fortified."

At Pittsburg Landing the normal camp routine was already underway. With the usual Sunday morning inspection in the offing, many of the men in Hurlbut's and Sherman's divisions were cleaning their equipment. Breakfast was being prepared in many of Prentiss' camps, and one 20-year-old Wisconsin private, having just returned from all-night picket duty, was so exhausted that he told his sergeant he was "going to sleep today, even if Abe Lincoln comes." Another soldier, a newly appointed brigadier general, was at breakfast, unaware that his wife had just arrived at the landing for a surprise visit and even now, dressed in her Sunday finery, was preparing to go to him.

Even the crusty, bedridden brigadier, C.F. Smith, was in fine spirits that morning, laughing and joking with several visiting officers. Only yesterday Smith had offhandedly commented on the army's current welcome respite. The enemy, he said, are "all back in Corinth, and, when our transportation arrives, we have got to go there and draw them out, as you would draw a badger out of his hole."

The Onslaught

Albert Sidney Johnston had risen early, and was discussing the general plan of attack with General Beauregard that morning when they heard the sound of gunfire. Mounting his thoroughbred bay, Fireeater, Johnston appeared to be in fine spirits, and told his staff, "Tonight we will water our horses in the Tennessee River."

As the advancing lines hurried forward, it seemed to Beauregard, who remained in the rear forwarding reserves, that the dense columns were as irresistible as "an Alpine avalanche." The weather had cleared and a bright sun was now rising in a cloudless sky, prompting an officer to remark that it must be another "sun of Austerlitz."

But in the rough terrain south of Shiloh Church, brigades and regiments were already experiencing difficulty in maintaining an intact battleline. Gaps appeared and widened as much of Hardee's line veered northeast toward Prentiss' camps. Consequently, frequent delays occurred as troops were realigned or moved forward into the void.

At a small clearing near Fraley's Field, Shaver's Arkansas brigade belatedly encountered a regiment of Federals, sent by Peabody to reinforce Powell's patrol, which was known to be in difficulty by the trickle of wounded returning to their camp. Expecting to meet only a skirmishing party, the reinforcements had joined Powell's retreating men, but their commander insisted on pressing forward into the open field. Colonel Moore, who had returned to the scene of his earlier reconnaissance, was almost immediately shot down by a heavy volley from behind a fence row. Although his men promptly fell back, taking position along a timbered knoll fronting a small ravine south of their camp, they were soon assaulted by overwhelming numbers of Confederate infantry, and scattered in confusion.

In Prentiss' camp about 7 a.m. the sharp volleys issuing from the nearby woods had caused Colonel Peabody to order a drummer to sound the "long roll," calling the division to arms. As the men were forming, down the line galloped their irate general. Prentiss reined in his horse in front of Peabody, and angrily demanded to know if the colonel had provoked an attack by sending out a force without orders. Peabody attempted to explain, but the general cut him short by shouting, "Colonel Peabody, I will hold you personally responsible for bringing on this engagement."

The two men glared at one another. With obvious contempt, Peabody remarked that he was personally responsible for all of his actions, then mounted his horse and rode away. In Prentiss' official report, his lingering anger was manifested by omitting all men-

The Confederate charge on Prentiss' Sixth Division early on Sunday morning. (Battles and Leaders of the Civil War)

tion of his senior colonel, except listing him as a brigade commander.

Advancing toward the sound of the nearby firing, Peabody soon encountered the fugitives from Shaver's attack. The sun was already two hours high, and Peabody rapidly deployed his brigade along a prominent oak ridge south of camp. Seventy-five yards away the onrushing Confederates swept over the crest of an opposite ridge. To one Federal private it was the "grandest scene" he had ever witnessed. A seemingly endless line of men covered the ground in front.

Yet miraculously, Peabody's deadly volleys of musketry soon brought the Rebel line to a halt, and even caused a few units to break and run away on the enemy's left flank. Soon the Confederates returned to the fray, however, and about 8:15 a.m. a peculiar, high-pitched cry rang from the woods in front, followed by the appearance of a massive column of brown-clad infantry with fixed bayonets.

To Private Henry Morton Stanley, one of Shaver's men, it was the first time he had heard the bloodcurdling Rebel yell. According to Stanley it "drove all sanity and order" from them, and inspired the men with the wildest enthusiasm.

Attacked by nearly two full brigades of Confederate infantry, Peabody's line was overlapped and enveloped in what seemed like an instant. As rapidly as they could go, the remnants of Peabody's line began streaming back through their camp, losing in the process much of their organization and discipline.

Everett Peabody, bleeding from four wounds—in the hand, thigh, neck, and body—vainly attempted to reform his men. Unable to find Prentiss, he galloped among the tents urging his frightened soldiers to "stand to it yet!" Perhaps cursing Prentiss for refusing to allow artillery to be parked in front of his brigade camps the night before, Peabody was still mounted on his big horse, gesturing and shouting amid the swirling smoke. Having earlier believed he would be killed, he had shaken hands that morning with his officers and bid them good-bye. Now he was struck by a fifth missile, which entered his upper lip and passed out the back of his head, killing him instantly. His terrified mount bolted away, and the colonel's body was tossed limply against a log. Not yet 32, Everett Peabody's premonition of death had been fulfilled.

For Peabody's men, the next few minutes became utter chaos. Unable to reform in sufficient strength to stabilize a defensive line, they rapidly melted away in the face of the approaching enemy. One youthful Wisconsin lieutenant, realizing that their camp would soon be lost, ran to his tent to retrieve a tintype of his fiancée. Emerging just in time to avoid capture, he

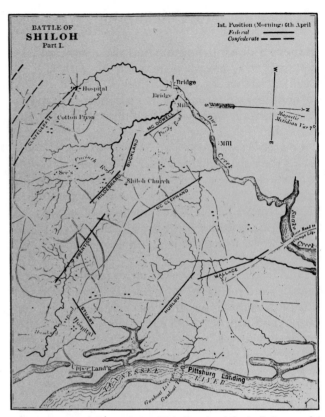

Troop positions on the morning of Sunday, April 6. At that time, the Hornet's Nest was between the lines of Prentiss and Hurlbut. (Battles and Leaders of the Civil War)

raced away down the company street, a hail of musket balls whizzing close about his ears.

By 8:45 a.m. all of Peabody's camps were in Confederate hands, and the mass exodus toward the river landing had begun, most of the Federal units being so scattered that they ceased to exist as regiments during the remainder of the battle. While many men joined with other regiments and continued to fight, others simply clogged the roads and wandered about aimlessly. Said one private with unabashed candor, ". . . [by now] everybody was running, . . . so I ran too." Inevitably these fugitives were joined by the remainder of Prentiss' division, including their sorely pressed commander.

Prentiss' remaining brigade, led by Colonel Madison Miller of Missouri, had earlier formed in a small parade ground clearing known as Spain Field. Attacked by Brigadier General Adley H. Gladden's brigade, Miller's men, assisted by two batteries of 6-pounder guns, had handily beaten off the first assault. Indeed, Gladden had been mortally wounded by a Federal shell, and nearly an hour was lost in attempting to re-form and reinforce the Confederate line at this point. Then, with Peabody's camps lost, the Confederates had renewed their assault on Miller. The brigades of Chalmers and Gladden, the latter now commanded by Colonel Daniel W. Adams,

pressed forward so rapidly that several of Prentiss' cannon were overrun before they could be withdrawn.

One of Miller's regiments just off the boat, the 15th Michigan, had marched from the landing that morning to join their new command. En route, they had passed several idle camps where some of the 15th's men had inquired about the firing heard ahead. The unconcerned soldiers told these greenhorns that some of the pickets were likely "shooting squirrels." Farther on, the regiment encountered several wounded men. When asked about the pickets shooting squirrels, one soldier held up a bloody hand and said they were the "funniest squirrels" he ever saw.

Once on the firing line, the 15th was rushed into position in time to confront Gladden's Confederates. Yet, somehow, the regiment had marched to the front without ammunition, and they now stood with empty Austrian rifles, unable to return the enemy's fire. The regiment was soon withdrawn and marched to the rear; they were unable to draw ammunition and fight until much later in the day.

As the order to fall back spread through Prentiss' remaining regiments, so many men had already abandoned the fight that only an estimated 150 men of an original 862 were present in one Wisconsin regiment.

In the chaos and confusion of Miller's retreat, the scene became "perfectly awful," according to one officer. Sick and wounded soldiers were running in all directions, some dressed only in underclothes. A young lieutenant of artillery who had witnessed the loss of his section and the virtual annihilation of the battery, was found crying like a child.

Prentiss' shattered division was by now nearly a total wreck. Of the approximately 5,000 fighting men, only two or three regiments retained enough effective strength to continue functioning as units. Much of their artillery, many small arms, and all of their camps and equipment with seven stands of colors were already in Confederate hands. To add to the misery, a portion of the abandoned camps caught fire, utterly destroying their former occupants' possessions. One of Prentiss' privates, having run in full flight for a half-mile, was convinced that they were forever disgraced. "What will they say about this at home?" he pondered in utter frustration.

Reacting with obvious alarm to the sound of nearby firing, the most advanced of Sherman's regiments, the 53d Ohio Volunteers, had formed on their color line about 6 a.m. When word of this was sent to

Routed Federals flee to the river bank at Pittsburg Landing, as reinforcements land. (Frank Leslie's Illustrated Newspaper)

Henry Lovie's drawing of Brigadier General William Sherman's troops hurrying to meet the Confederate attack. Shiloh Church is shown on the left. (National Archives)

Sherman's headquarters, an officer rode over and told the colonel, "General Sherman says you must be badly scared over there."

Yet before 7 a.m. the advancing columns of the enemy could be detected in the timber by the bright flash of their gun barrels glinting through the green leaves.

Riding a magnificent "sorrel race mare" captured from the enemy several weeks earlier, William Tecumseh Sherman rode into Rhea Field in front of the 53d Ohio's camp shortly after 7 a.m. His attention was caught by a body of troops marching across the distant end of the field, and he uncased his telescope to study their movements.

Screened by brush bordering a small stream about fifty yards to the right, the skirmishers of Cleburne's brigade now emerged into the field and discovered a mounted party of Federals diagonally in their front. Raising their muskets, they prepared to fire at what was obviously an important officer. At the last instant, one of the 53d Ohio's officers gasped a warning. "General, look to your right!"

Sherman dropped his telescope and whirled about, just as the skirmishers fired. "My God, we are attacked!" he blurted out, and threw up his hand as if to ward off the bullets. Close by his side Private Thomas D. Holliday, his orderly, was struck and

immediately killed. Too, Sherman at this point was probably struck in the hand by a single buckshot (part of a "buck and ball" cartridge containing a ball and three buckshot, commonly used in .69 caliber smoothbore muskets). Immediately dashing to safety, Sherman merely shouted to the astonished Ohioans to hold their position, he would bring them support.

Advancing at the time onto Rhea Field was one of the most aggressive fighters in all the Confederacy, Brigadier General Patrick Ronayne Cleburne. A 34-year-old Irishman with daredevil courage, Cleburne had experienced bad luck that morning. His brigade had been split apart by "an almost impassable morass," and now he faced the 53d Ohio's position with only two small regiments present. Immediately attacking, his men were surprised and cut down by cannon fire from a strategically placed Federal battery atop a nearby hill. Waterhouse's Illinois battery had been prepared for inspection when the alarm sounded that morning, hence these guns were harnessed and ready for action almost immediately. Waterhouse's rifled cannon continued to fire downhill with shell and canister, even as another attempt was made by Cleburne to get past the 53d Ohio's camp.

Charging unsupported by artillery or their companion regiment, which was too broken to re-form in time, the 6th Mississippi moved alone through Rhea Field. A small regiment, 425 men strong before the fighting began, the Mississippians again endured a terrific storm of fire. Although their attack caused the 53d Ohio to flee the field when their colonel, his nerves at the breaking point, called out, "Retreat and save yourselves," the Confederates were driven back in disorder. In less than a half hour these Mississippians had sustained a loss of 300 men, representing the fourth highest loss during the entire war by any Southern regiment in a single battle.

Unable to press the Federals further in this sector until reinforcements arrived about 8 a.m., Cleburne galloped around the intervening swamp to see to his remaining regiments. Here on the left he found four of them, in all about 1,500 men, attacking a strong Federal brigade posted in their front. Here Buckland's brigade of Sherman's division had not only more men, but also a favorable field of fire from behind heavy timber. Again Cleburne's units met a bloody repulse.

At last, the advance elements of Braxton Bragg's second Confederate battleline made their appearance about 8:30 a.m. But due to the colossal mistake of arranging each corps in tandem across a wide front, Bragg's units had already become so intermixed and retarded by the rough terrain that effective deployment was almost impossible. Bragg's leading brigade, James Patton Anderson's, had advanced only a mile in two and one-half hours, and being unsupported, had had to wait until one of Polk's brigades, Russell's, appeared. Part of the third Confederate battleline, by marching along the main Corinth road this brigade had made faster progress than most of Bragg's units.

Together, Russell and Anderson attempted to assail Waterhouse's deadly guns, posted on the knoll beyond the 53d Ohio's camp. They quickly became entangled in the same morass that Cleburne had found impenetrable, however. Regiments and companies were separated in the heavy going, and when these units emerged in piecemeal fashion, they were taken in flank by Barrett's Federal battery, posted opposite Shiloh Church. The result was a bloody repulse that further mixed and confused the survivors. When another trailing brigade, Bushrod Johnson's, came up, this unit was jumbled and intermixed with Russell's and Anderson's men, creating an unwieldy mass. So many Confederates were soon found advancing, however, prodded on by an angry Braxton Bragg, that the 57th Ohio, one of two remaining regiments supporting Waterhouse's guns, broke and ran away.

Waterhouse's cannoneers next limbered up and started for the rear, only to have one of Sherman's staff officers halt and redeploy the battery, thinking their retreat was too hasty. Here one of Russell's regiments, the 13th Tennessee, swung around to the east and approached from the flank, taking the battery unawares. The hard-charging Confederates were within fifty yards before any attempt was made to bring off the guns. In the smoke and confusion three cannon were wheeled away but the remainder of the equipment was lost. Disgustedly, a nearby Federal officer watched the enemy claim the cannon that had cost the Confederates so many lives. "They swarmed around them like bees," he said. "They jumped upon the guns, and on the hay bales in the battery camp, and yelled like crazy men."

Alone on the extreme left flank of Sherman's line stood the 77th Ohio, doggedly fighting near Shiloh Church. Although this unit promptly changed front, attempting to compensate for the loss of Waterhouse's battery and the other two Ohio regiments, the Rebels began working around their flank, causing the regiment to gradually break up. Then three of Bushrod Johnson's regiments, separated by the swamp, pushed directly toward Shiloh Church from the south. The pressure was too great for the 77th Ohio, and "they ran like sheep," said an officer of Barrett's battery.

Left alone to confront the attacking Confederates, Barrett's unsupported guns put out such a devastating fire that the enemy regiments in front ultimately broke and withdrew in disorder. In front of the smoking cannon, the Confederates lay in windrows. Devastated by effective Federal artillery fire, and wasted in piecemeal attacks lacking counter-battery support and proper brigade co-ordination, the Confederates had suffered a severe reverse at the hands of a Federal brigade half their strength.

First position of Captain Waterhouse's battery, near the left of Sherman's division. (Battles and Leaders of the Civil War)

Yet, ironically, the vicious fighting and stout defense of the Federal artillery went for naught. Although the fighting momentarily abated in Barrett's front, it was quickly understood that Sherman's left flank had been turned. The enemy could be seen in the rear, advancing at almost right angles to Barrett's guns, and Sherman sent word for the plucky cannoneers to fall back.

Sherman, despite the close call that morning in Rhea Field, had refused to believe the attack was anything more than a foray against his own camp until the appearance of Bragg's men—"a beautiful and dreadful sight," he observed. Embroiled in the fighting near Shiloh Church, a grimly determined Sherman had endured such a withering fire that staff officers when approaching were seen to bend low in their saddles, as if in the midst of a driving rainstorm. At least three horses had been killed under Sherman that morning, including his "sorrel race mare." All about him were astounded by his imperturbable demeanor, and an aide said his cool conduct "instilled . . . a feeling that it was grand to be there with him." Calmly smoking a cigar, his short, scraggly red beard masking a stern expression, Sherman gave the impression that ice water ran through his veins.

Once again Sherman was called upon to handle a burgeoning crisis, which had its beginning in the chaos that developed upon his initial withdrawal from the Shiloh Church area. At ten minutes past ten, following nearly three hours of fighting, the order to fall back to the Purdy-Hamburg road, about 500 yards in the rear, was passed along Sherman's line.

All of Buckland's nearby regiments, and Colonel John A. McDowell's right flank brigade, were ordered to fall back to join with the remnant of the Shiloh Church defenders at this location. After both brigades withdrew and re-formed in the middle of the Purdy road, they created an opportunity for disaster. Captain Frederick Behr's 6th Indiana battery, ordered from McDowell's right flank to replace Barrett's guns, now low on ammunition, soon came dashing down the Purdy road at a full gallop. Because of the heavy brush on each side of the road, Buckland's men still jammed the right of way, and were abruptly shoved out of the road by the wildly careening guns and caissons. In the resulting confusion a mass of fugitives running up the road from the opposite direction added to the disorder. Then the onrushing Confederates, following in the tracks of the retreating Federals, burst upon the scene. Behr's battery, attempting to unlimber near the crossroads, here took a point-blank volley that felled their captain. Sherman later recalled that the men then became panic-stricken and abandoned their guns without so much as firing a shot.

Sherman's Purdy road line now shuddered in total disorder. When the Confederates again charged, the line gave way almost completely. Only McDowell's brigade, farther up the road, remained intact. Still, Sherman's desperate stand had counted for much. The division's lengthy ordeal had bought sufficient time for the more distant divisions to form a strong defensive line. With the rapidly growing confusion of intermixed units in the belatedly victorious enemy impeding their rapid pursuit, additional time, soon to be a key element, was afforded.

To Sherman, his shirt collar twisted askew, his hand bloodied, and his uniform torn and besmudged by the grime of battle, the events of that morning involved the essence of effective battlefield leadership. His personal example continued to fire his men's souls. It inspired bravery and steadied their nerves. Sherman's genius was never more evident than in the fiery crisis of battle. On an occasion when he, more than others, had reason to fear the result, Sherman appeared to one admiring officer to be "the coolest man I saw that day."

A Rude Awakening

Ulysses Grant had been eating breakfast that morning at his Cherry House headquarters in Savannah when an orderly came in to report the sound of firing coming from the direction of Pittsburg Landing. Leaving his breakfast unfinished, Grant walked outside, heard the distant gunfire, and immediately boarded the *Tigress*. While steam was being generated Grant dictated several messages to the advanced elements of Buell's army that had only yesterday arrived at Savannah, asking them to proceed to Pittsburg.

Then, about 8:00 a.m., Grant hastened upriver to Crump's Landing, not knowing if that point was under attack. Finding Lew Wallace there aboard a transport, Grant merely told him to hold his troops in readiness to march, then sped ahead to Pittsburg Landing.

Grant arrived on the field of battle at about 9:30 a.m. Convinced for the first time that his Pittsburg Landing camps were the true object of the enemy's attack, he sent word by a staff officer to Lew Wallace to "come up" to Pittsburg Landing. By the time Captain A.S. Baxter had proceeded with the *Tigress* to Crump's Landing and met Wallace some distance inland it was about 11:30 a.m.

Wallace had his troops concentrated at Stoney

Transports at Pittsburg Landing a few days after the battle. The second steamer from the right is Grant's headquarter's boat, the Tigress. *(U.S. Army Military History Institute)*

Lonesome, a point midway on the road to Purdy, since he was uncertain if the enemy might approach from that direction. Deciding to utilize an interior road that led to Sherman's camps at Shiloh Church, rather than the so-called river road direct to the landing area, Wallace was confident that this was the shorter of the two routes.

Actually, Wallace was courting disaster. The road he had chosen was not only about three miles longer, but it also led to what was now the rear of the Confederate army, where his entire division might be cut off or even captured. Following a half-hour delay for "dinner," Wallace's troops marched briskly toward the sound of the raging conflict, heedless of their danger.

At Savannah, Buell's commanders had desperately sought a means to get to Pittsburg Landing, but without success. The roads along the river were swampy at best and were now inundated by water. No transports were then at Savannah to provide river transportation. With difficulty, about noon a local doctor was found who knew a backwoods route estimated at eight miles, five of which were through a "black mud swamp." Thus, about 1:30 p.m., Colonel Jacob Ammen's brigade began their arduous journey, not knowing if they could get through at all.

At Pittsburg Landing, Grant, dressed in his full major general's uniform complete with sword and sash, was soon in the midst of the heaviest fighting. Concerned by the rapidly deteriorating military situation, Grant dispatched another note to Lew Wallace to "hurry forward" with all speed.

Then, following a brief chat with Sherman, he attempted to return to the small log cabin on the hilltop at Pittsburg Landing designated as his headquarters. With his staff officers at his side, Grant galloped across the northern fringe of Duncan Field in order to reach the Pittsburg-Corinth road.

In the opposite fringe of timber a Mississippi battery had just unlimbered and rapidly trained its guns on what appeared to be an important group of Federal officers. At the discharge of these guns Grant said, "the shells and balls whistled about our ears very fast. . . ." A staff officer's horse was killed, and following a rapid dash for cover, Grant discovered that his sword had been struck just below the hilt, the missile striking with such force it had broken his scabbard and blade nearly in two.

Soon returning to Pittsburg Landing, Grant was later found on board the *Tigress* by General Buell, who had commandeered a passing steamboat at Savannah. Buell said of Grant at the time that he looked much worried and certainly lacked "that masterly confidence" that was a highly publicized character trait.

Grant had obvious cause to be greatly concerned.

Already a milling crowd of fugitive soldiers, estimated in the thousands, had gathered at the riverbank by the landing. As was discovered by nearly all who attempted to rally these men, they for the most part were so frightened and panic-stricken as to be insensible to entreaty or threats.

A Crucial Mistake

Albert Sidney Johnston had confidently advanced with the front line that had swept through Prentiss' camps about midmorning. In the camp of the 18th Wisconsin Johnston had picked up a little tin cup, saying that such would be his share of the spoils today. Here he detached his personal physician, Dr. D.W. Yandell, to look after the many wounded Federals until other medical officers could be found.

It was at this point that a critical turn in the battle occurred, without so much as involving an exchange of shots.

On the extreme Federal left was an isolated brigade attached to Sherman's division, originally assigned to watch the bridge crossing Lick Creek from the direction of Hamburg. This minimal command of 2,811 men was led by a Chicago lawyer turned soldier, Colonel David Stuart, who by midmorning was thoroughly alarmed by his isolated position. Stuart had formed his three regiments about 8 a.m., and as the morning hours continued he shifted his men from location to location, not knowing from what direction an enemy attack might come.

This constant shuffling and defensive activity resulted in one of the battle's major mistakes. Captain S.H. Lockett of Braxton Bragg's staff, and the assistant chief engineer of the army, had been sent by Bragg to scout the critical sector nearest the Tennessee River early that morning. Taking with him Lieutenant S.M. Steel, an engineer who had surveyed the region before the war, Lockett proceeded to the Lick Creek area and observed Stuart's camp. Following the opening of the battle on the distant left, Lockett and Steel saw "alarming" activity among these Federal troops. Mistakenly interpreting this force to be a "division," Lockett sent a report to headquarters expressing fear that these troops would "swing around and take ours in flank, as it was manifest that the Federal line extended farther in that direction than ours."

Johnston ultimately received Lockett's report, following the collapse of Prentiss' line. Since the Confederate right flank was the most critical sector, requiring the overwhelming of all Federal resistance at this point so as to roll the enemy army back against

Recent studies suggest that Johnny Clem, the unofficial drummer of the 22d Michigan and the so-called "Drummer Boy of Shiloh," may not actually have participated in this battle. In later years Clem became a major general; he died in 1937 and was buried in Arlington Cemetery. (Library of Congress)

Owl Creek, Johnston acted promptly in accordance with the master plan. Staff officers were sent to bring then Brigadier General John C. Breckinridge's Reserve Corps forward to the extreme right. Further, two frontline brigades that had helped in overrunning Prentiss' camps, Chalmers' and Jackson's, were pulled out of line and sent on a roundabout circuit over two miles to reach a point not even a half mile distant by direct line. The ultimate consequence was a delay of several hours in engaging these withdrawn brigades, and the depletion of the Confederate front line at a most inopportune time.

Benjamin Prentiss, following the loss of his camps and the virtual breakup of his division, had been surprised to see two brigades of Stephen A. Hurlbut's division hastening to his support about 9 a.m. Approaching from the rear, Hurlbut soon deployed his nearly 5,400 men about a half mile behind Prentiss' camps, since it was apparent that the Federal troops along the outer perimeter had been routed.

Although without Colonel James C. Veatch's brigade, which had been sent to Sherman's support, Hurlbut occupied a strong position, fronting moderately open ground. Many of his troops were behind an old split rail fence, with a peach orchard, fragrant with delicate pink blossoms, in their front. A minimum of 300 yards of mostly cleared ground lay between Hurlbut's line and any approaching Confederates, providing a favorable field of fire. To support this line Hurlbut had three well-equipped batteries of artillery deployed at the critical angles.

Although Chalmers', Jackson's, and Adams' (Gladden's) Confederate brigades had observed Hurlbut's deployment, and were preparing to attack, two of these units had been pulled out of line and sent to the right by Johnston's order just as their skirmishers were becoming engaged. Since Wood's and Shaver's brigades had gone to the left to help in the struggle against Sherman, Gladden's brigade, commanded by Colonel Daniel Adams, remained alone in front of Hurlbut. But Adams reported his regiment nearly out of ammunition, and soon withdrew a short distance pending reinforcement.

While a rather desultory artillery duel occurred between opposing batteries in this sector, Sidney Johnston sat patiently astride his horse, awaiting the appearance of Breckinridge's troops. He had nearly two hours to wait. The protracted delay on Hurlbut's front was to become one of the decisive factors in the battle.

When the Confederates failed to pursue their advantage, Hurlbut allowed the remnant of Prentiss' division to form as an extension of his right flank. Among these men were what remained of two of Peabody's regiments, including Major James E. Powell with a fragment of the 25th Missouri. When another Missouri unit came up—the 23d Infantry, fresh off a

transport at Pittsburg Landing—Prentiss' command was more than doubled in size and now numbered perhaps 1,000 men. The position they took, in a sunken road worn by many years' use as a wagon trail, was further strengthened by eight field guns that remained from Prentiss' artillery.

Ironically, Prentiss' improvised command was to occupy one of the critical sections of the field, being the means of linking another large segment of the makeshift Federal perimeter then forming.

Brigadier General W.H.L. Wallace, still ignorant of his wife's presence at the river landing, had gone forward on the main Corinth road with his two remaining brigades shortly after Hurlbut's advance along the Hamburg-Savannah road. Taking position about 10 a.m. along the northern fringe of Duncan Field, Wallace's men were appalled by the stream of fugitives going to the rear. Among these stragglers was a wagon containing a few Confederate prisoners. When one of the captured enemy taunted an Iowa regiment, calling them "damned Yankees," and cursing them heartily, one soldier said he "never felt more like shooting a Rebel."

With about 5,800 men in line, W.H.L. Wallace anchored the right flank of what had become a great convex battle formation, stretching more than a half-mile along the wagon road ridge. Although loosely tied together the two main segments, Hurlbut's and W.H.L. Wallace's, were linked by Prentiss' command at the apex of the arc. In all, more than 11,000 men supported by seven batteries of artillery totaling thirty-eight field guns now confronted the advancing Confederates. Instead of attacking highly vulnerable and fragmented enemy defenses, the protracted delay in pursuit now compelled the Confederates to dislodge a formidable Union battleline.

Oddly, the first troops to advance against this Federal stronghold were from the third Confederate line, Polk's Corps. Braxton Bragg, who, like his fellow corps commanders, was exasperated at the confusion and delays occasioned by the tandem battle formation being utilized, already had been compelled to improvise a makeshift arrangement. The three primary Confederate lines had become so intermixed by midmorning that Bragg had agreed to control all troops in the center if Polk and Hardee would go to the left and direct operations there.

Unfortunately for the South, Braxton Bragg was one of the worst combat tacticians in the army. A supremely adept organizer and disciplinarian, Bragg was more suited for the role of chief of staff than active battle command. The sector in which he had chosen to exercise control was the middle of the battlefield, directly in front of the Hurlbut-Prentiss-W.H.L. Wallace line.

Brigadier General Benjamin F. Cheatham, leading the mostly Tennessee brigade of Colonel William H. Stephens, had been ordered into the fight by Colonel Thomas Jordan, Beauregard's roving adjutant general. Appearing in front of the left of W.H.L. Wallace's line defending Duncan Field about 11 a.m., Cheatham attacked unsupported, his three regiments going up against portions of three Federal divisions.

Caught in a terrible crossfire, Cheatham's men were slaughtered in the open field, only their right flank regiment closing to within ten yards of the Federal line in heavy brush. A half-hour after the attack was launched the Confederate dead "literally covered" the ground in front of one of Colonel Jacob Lauman's Indiana regiments, and Cheatham's soldiers were so bloodied that they withdrew from the fighting.

Next, a lone brigade under Colonel Randall Lee Gibson was found standing idle nearby, and Bragg personally ordered an attack on the Federal stronghold. Leading his four regiments forward at noon, the dapper Yale graduate Gibson marched straight for the sunken road perimeter. Like Cheatham's men they were murdered at short range, being unable to see far ahead in the thick undergrowth there. Terming this ground a "valley of death" the Confederates broke and ran back after suffering grievous losses.

Bragg, who had remained nearby, was incensed at what he regarded as Gibson's premature withdrawal, and sent a staff officer to rally these men and order another attack. Directed to attack this same position without the aid of other infantry or even artillery support, Gibson protested, yet complied with Bragg's orders. Again this sadly depleted Louisiana and Arkansas brigade rushed forward, screaming the high-pitched, eerie Rebel yell.

Prentiss' soldiers, supported by a fresh regiment detached from W.H.L. Wallace's line, braced for the attack by lying prone in the sunken road. With their covering artillery firing charges of double canister into the Confederates the din was terrific. Despite obviously severe losses Gibson's men pressed grimly on. Then, when the onrushing gray line was about twenty yards distant the Federal infantry jumped to their feet and delivered a point-blank volley. So many Confederates were shot down that a private later described the scene as a "slaughter pen." Yet the remaining enemy rushed up to the very muzzles of the Federal cannon. In hand-to-hand fighting the Confederates were finally overwhelmed and driven off.

As the thick cloud of gunsmoke gradually cleared, the Federal defenders looked out on a scene of com-

Gibson's brigade charges Hurlbut's troops in the Hornet's Nest. Throughout April 6, seven Rebel assaults were made on Hurlbut's line. (Battles and Leaders of the Civil War).

plete devastation. The enemy bodies lay in piles observed an Indiana colonel. The brush had been so cut to pieces that, said another eyewitness, it had "the appearance of a Southern corn field that had been topped." To the survivors among Gibson's brigade the storm of enemy missiles had seemed like facing a swarm of hornets, and they appropriately named the Federal stronghold "the Hornets' Nest." Incredibly, Gibson's men were again required to attack this formidable line unsupported. Bragg, further enraged by what he regarded as a repulse due to enemy "sharpshooters occupying the thick cover," sent orders for still another frontal attack.

Colonel Henry W. Allen of the 4th Louisiana, a bullet hole through each cheek, seized his colors from Bragg's staff officer, and bitterly led the remnant of the brigade forward. In a few minutes they stumbled back repulsed in another, the fourth, forlorn attack on this front. By now it was nearly 3 p.m., and important action was occurring on the opposite, or left flank of the Federal perimeter.

Following a wait of nearly two hours, the extreme left of Grant's army had at last been engaged by Brigadier General James R. Chalmers' and Brigadier General John K. Jackson's brigades. The Federals in their front by this time numbered two brigades; a three-regiment unit commanded by the colorful Scotsman Brigadier General John A. McArthur had been detached earlier by W.H.L. Wallace and sent to help Stuart.

Commencing at about eleven o'clock, the action on the Stuart-McArthur front had been desultory until about noon. Fighting "like Indians," behind trees and logs in heavily timbered terrain cut by huge ravines, the blue-coated soldiers had been able to hold their ground. Yet with a dwindling supply of ammunition and the prospect of added pressure being applied by approaching Confederate reinforcements, Stuart began to consider a retreat. Unknowingly, these two Federal brigades, seemingly fighting an isolated battle on the outer periphery, were anchoring the entire left flank of Grant's army. Should they retreat, an entire corridor direct to Pittsburg Landing would be open.

Although Chalmers and Jackson had been bolstered by the arrival of Breckinridge's Reserve Corps about noon, the more than 8,000 infantry with

Also on April 6 in the Hornet's Nest: Prentiss' troops, supported by Hickenlooper's battery, repulse an assault by Hardee's troops. (Battles and Leaders of the Civil War)

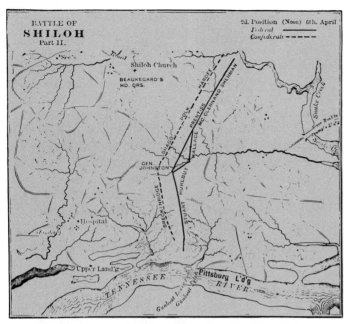

The position at noon. (Battles and Leaders of the Civil War)

four batteries of artillery had been unable to break the Federal line. Beyond cautiously maneuvering in McArthur's front, the Confederates had wasted considerable time in attempting to mount a coordinated attack in the rugged terrain.

Sidney Johnston, riding Fire-eater, had gone with Brigadier General John S. Bowen's brigade of Breckinridge's Corps. Meanwhile, Statham's brigade, farther to the west, had encountered the extreme left flank of Hurlbut's peach orchard line. Hearing of confusion among Tennessee troops here, Johnston had sent his volunteer aide Governor Isham G. Harris to rally this line, and also ordered a bayonet attack by Statham's men.

Breckinridge presently confronted Johnston, saying he could not get the brigade to charge. Johnston then personally came up and addressed the men. Apparently on the spur of the moment, he determined to lead the attack. Passing along the line and touching their bayonets with the little tin cup taken earlier that morning, Johnston cried, "I will lead you."

Word was passed to Bowen's brigade on the right and to Stephens' bloodied brigade on the left, recovered from their initial assault on the Hornets' Nest. This entire line was to go forward in a coordinated effort to break the Federal left flank.

An officer pulled off his cap, placed it on the point of his sword, and raised it high in the air. It was approximately 2 p.m. as the long line swept forward with a loud shout.

First to break under this tremendous pressure was McArthur's thin line of fewer than 2,000 men. Bowen, joined by several of Jackson's regiments, enveloped the Federal flank, bypassed Stuart, and chased McArthur's crumbling line nearly a quarter of a mile.

On Bowen's immediate left, Johnston's bayonet attack was aimed directly at the Peach Orchard line defended by Hurlbut. Although an entire Federal brigade quickly fell back, their artillery continued firing until the last moment. After clearing the orchard, Johnston's men, however, encountered severe resistance along the wooded ridge that led to the sunken road.

Having sustained heavy casualties crossing the generally open ground, the Confederates here took cover and returned the fire. Stephens' brigade, in fact had been repulsed. Caught in an old open cottonfield, they had lost so many men that their dead "looked like a line of troops laying down to receive our fire," thought a Federal infantryman.

In the rear of Statham's line, Sidney Johnston sat for nearly a half-hour, issuing orders and preparing to renew the attack. Amazingly, no one noticed that he was then desperately wounded. During the attack on the Peach Orchard Johnston had been struck perhaps four times. Only one projectile had broken the skin, however. A minie ball, nearly spent, had entered his right leg behind the knee joint and cut the large artery. Judging from the location of the wound, it is possible that one of his own men had accidently launched the fatal missile. The blood flowed into Johnston's high boot, and no one noticed the wound, even when he collapsed in the saddle.

Moved to a ravine nearby, his staff desperately tore off his shirt looking for the wound, and poured brandy down his throat. No physician was nearby, Johnston having ordered Dr. Yandell to remain with the Federal wounded at Prentiss' camps. In Johnston's pocket was a field tourniquet that might have staunched the flow. Johnston never regained consciousness. About 2:30 p.m. the awful truth dawned on those present. The highest ranking field general in the Confederacy was dead from an acute loss of blood, the fatal wound not being discovered until it was too late. Hastily, a note advising Beauregard that he was now in command was sent to the rear, yet little was done to alter the lull that now occurred in the battle.

Although, as noted above, Stuart had been bypassed by Chalmers, this last remaining segment of the Federal left was ordered to retreat about 2:15 p.m. Fired into by the pursuing Confederates and confused by the rugged terrain, Stuart's men ultimately fled all the way to Pittsburg Landing.

The death of Johnston, the highest-ranking officer of either South or North to be killed in the war. (CWTI Collection)

A huge gap of nearly three-quarters of a mile now existed all the way to the vital core of the Federal army, Pittsburg Landing, only a mile and a half distant. Yet Sidney Johnston was dead and no one seemed to be in control in this vital sector. Moreover, instead of advancing due north to envelop the entire Federal army, most Confederate commanders, following Beauregard's earlier instructions to march toward the sound of the heaviest fighting, soon turned in a wide arc toward the Hornets' Nest line. To complicate matters, Bragg ultimately arrived upon the scene, still intent on reducing the deadly Federal stronghold by frontal assault.

A Mass Surrender

Stephen A. Hurlbut, observing the debacle on his left flank involving Stuart's and McArthur's troops, acted promptly to protect his exposed left flank. Pulling Lauman's entire brigade out of line, he rushed these troops to a ten-acre clearing known as Wicker Field. Lauman was just in time to meet the mass of Confederates pursuing McArthur. In a stubborn firefight Lauman's men temporarily held Chalmers' brigade at bay. About 3:30 p.m., however, Hurlbut saw that the enemy was working around his left flank and he ordered a general retreat. Although he hoped to make another stand near his line of encampments, in the confusion of the movement Hurlbut's division was virtually fragmented and only one regiment stood to cover their withdrawal.

Moreover, Hurlbut's withdrawal exposed the rem-

Above: Brigadier General Stephen A. Hurlbut, who commanded the Union's 4th Division. (U.S. Army Military History Institute)

Below: Brigadier General John A. McArthur, who commanded a three-regiment unit of Union soldiers. (Library of Congress)

nant of the original Hornets' Nest line under Prentiss and W.H.L. Wallace. His line now bent back in the shape of an elongated U, Prentiss sought to cover the void, convinced he could still hold his ground. Although Bragg hurled the remnant of Gladden's brigade against the center of this line—only to be beaten off—and had directed another forlorn attack by Shaver's brigade against W.H.L. Wallace's troops, the buildup on all sides of Prentiss convinced him that he was surrounded. Still he refused to retreat, believing, so he said, that Lew Wallace's division might yet come up.

To add to the Federal woes at this point, Confederate Brigadier General Daniel Ruggles had brought up and organized the largest concentration of artillery yet seen on the North American continent—eleven batteries and one section, a total of sixty-two field guns. In all, two separate concentrations had developed, fronting the sunken road and Duncan Field perimeters. About 4 p.m. these cannon unleashed a devastating fire that sounded to one Federal lieutenant "like a mighty hurricane." The brush and trees around the position were so blasted by this fire that it seemed a relief to a Federal captain when he observed the Confederate infantry advancing upon them.

Major General Leonidas Polk, an Episcopal bishop, was later killed in action at Pine Mountain, Georgia. (CWTI Collection)

Soon one of W.H.L. Wallace's brigades, depleted by detachments to more hotly contested parts of the Hornets' Nest, began to break up. Colonel Thomas W. Sweeny, the one-armed Irishman who led this brigade, had taken another wound—in his good arm. Here his two Illinois regiments observed massed Confederate troops maneuvering beyond their extreme right flank.

These Confederates, Polk's troops, were pursuing the remnant of McClernand's division, which had shored up Sherman's battered line, and were already north of the Hornets' Nest defenders. The commanders of Sweeny's two regiments ran their men out to the northeast, precipitating the breakup of W.H.L. Wallace's entire command.

Following a sustained fight of nearly six hours, W.H.L. Wallace at last realized that his position was untenable. After hastily issuing orders for a retreat, Wallace and his staff tried to gallop past the encircling Confederates. Several advancing Rebel skirmishers drew a bead on the fleeing party, and Wallace went down with a mortal head wound.

In the confusion of the precipitate retreat all discipline was lost, and the withdrawal quickly became a "mad race" to escape to the landing. When it was found that the Confederates were on all sides, having "marched to the sound of the heaviest fighting," white handkerchiefs began fluttering throughout the thicket in token of surrender. Only one of W.H.L. Wallace's regiments, the 7th Illinois, escaped without serious loss.

The only remaining defenders of the Hornets' Nest line, Prentiss' improvised command, by now had realized that they were caught in a deadly trap. Pushed back by a spirited cavalry charge led by Colonel (later Lieutenant General) Nathan Bedford Forrest, Prentiss' line numbered eight regiments, nearly 2,000

Confederate Brigadier General Daniel Ruggles, who commanded a total of 62 field guns. (U.S. Army Military History Institute)

The tree under which Prentiss surrendered to Polk shortly after 5 p.m. on April 6. (Chicago Historical Society)

men, although only about 300 men remained of his original division.

Attacked on three sides about 5 p.m., Prentiss finally gave the order to retire. But it was too late. A small ravine behind the Hornets' Nest was found to be a valley of death as bullets crisscrossed from several directions.

Those few who escaped the ravine ran straight into Polk's infantry blocking escape to the north. In one of Hurlbut's abandoned encampments several Tennessee soldiers charged to find Prentiss "holding aloft the white flag." In the space of a half-hour about 2,000 Federals surrendered; it was the largest capture yet made by the Confederacy. Although the jubilant Southerners demonstrated their joy by tearing up the 8th Iowa's cotton flag for souvenirs, and numerous Confederate officers were observed laden with bundles of the surrendered swords of their Federal counterparts, the Hornets' Nest defenders could well be proud of their accomplishments. Their stubborn defense had taken a tremendous toll among the enemy. Many of the Federals had been armed with Enfield rifles, and the fire of these deadly accurate weapons had been so effective that nearly a dozen separate charges were repulsed. Indeed, never in the history of warfare had the efficacy of rifled arms been so apparent.

On The Brink of Disaster

The scene of a great army verging on collapse was "humiliating in the extreme," wrote a Federal eyewitness. Thousands of men, routed and weaponless, were milling about the landing area, some so panic-stricken that they rushed aboard and nearly swamped several transports laden with wounded in their effort to escape the mounting danger.

Adding to the chaos at the landing were many of Sherman's and McClernand's troops, present at this spot since midday. McClernand's division had originally supported Sherman's line along the main Corinth road, a quarter-mile in the rear. Here McClernand had been attacked by many of Hardee's, Polk's, and Bragg's troops, fresh from their victory over Sherman.

Despite such mistakes as allowing a Confederate unit to approach unopposed, thinking their state flag was a Federal banner, McClernand's units fought hard, but were quickly overwhelmed. The division had been all but broken up by 11 a.m., and only the presence of a lone brigade sent by Hurlbut, Colonel James C. Veatch's, had prevented a rout.

Yet the Confederates were so weakened by the losses sustained against Sherman and McClernand

The "Last Line" of the Union defense, one mile from Pittsburg Landing, repulsing the Confederates on Sunday evening. (Frank Leslie's Illustrated Newspaper, May 17, 1862)

that they stalled in effective pursuit. By the time ammunition was replenished and the Southerners had rested, Sherman and McClernand were able to piece together a defensive line amid McClernand's camps.

The effort to break this patchwork Federal right flank had involved nearly five additional hours of fighting by often isolated Confederate units. Finally gaining some cohesion with the appearance of Trabue's brigade of Breckinridge's Reserve Corps, the Confederates about 5 p.m. forced Sherman's and McClernand's remnants back to within a quarter-mile of the landing.

So many Southern brigades had already either retired for want of ammunition or had gone toward the center to participate in the assault on the Hornets' Nest line, however, that it was readily perceived that the danger was greatest on the Federal flank nearest the river.

Precisely at 2:50 p.m., the wooden gunboat USS *Tyler*, responding to an urgent plea from Hurlbut for

help, had begun firing her 8-inch naval shells in the direction of the Confederates. Although these shells overshot the mark, generally falling in the extreme enemy rear, the deafening noise from the bursts added to the dismal battle scene. A massive pall of smoke rose from the fought-over ground, making the day seem like night, a Federal officer thought.

With the routed blue soldiers streaming in broken clusters back to the high ground about the landing, "all appeared lost," wrote an exhausted private, who considered that "it was Bull Run over again."

As the afternoon wore on, U.S. Grant anticipated that the enemy would make a "desperate effort" to capture the landing. Accordingly, plans were made to defend the high bluffs in a final stand. Grant's chief of staff, Colonel Joseph D. Webster, had been busy moving a battery of heavy siege cannon into position a quarter-mile from the river. Intended for use in besieging Corinth, the chance presence of these five monster 24-pounder guns enabled Grant to form a stout defensive line. As other artillery units came back they formed an elongation of this original line. By 6 p.m. this Federal artillery concentration consisting of at least ten batteries extended nearly a half-mile. Yet infantry supports were seriously lacking. The remnants of Hurlbut's and W.H.L. Wallace's divisions were in line fronting south, with McClernand and Sherman bent back along the "river road" to the north. In all, Grant's last line covered a perimeter barely more than a mile in length, all that remained of a fighting force that had numbered more than 40,000 men that morning.

To make the dismal situation even worse, it was learned that Lew Wallace's division would not arrive in time to be of help. Several of Grant's staff officers, sent to hurry this division forward, had found Wallace about 2 p.m. on the "wrong road." Belatedly convinced of his error, Wallace was persuaded to countermarch, but he was so cautious and dilatory as to double his leading brigade back through the entire line, rather than to face about and reverse his line of march. Too, Wallace first refused to leave behind his

artillery, which marched behind his advance brigade, and insisted on ordering halts to keep his column "closed up." In all, said an irate staff officer, Wallace's march seemed more like a cautious reconnaissance than a forced march to relieve a hard-pressed army. Near sundown Lew Wallace's men had still not crossed Snake Creek, although they could hear the terrific crashes from the heavy artillery in the distance, warning that the last line of the army was engaged.

Braxton Bragg, in company with Generals Breckinridge and Polk, had been active in organizing a final assault in the last hour of daylight remaining. Gathering all available troops they pushed forward toward a deep chasm known as Dill Branch. On the opposite ridge they could see Grant's line of heavy artillery, largely unprotected by infantry. It was about 6 p.m. as Chalmers' and Jackson's brigades pushed forward, their massed lines resembling some "huge monster clothed in folds of flashing steel," said an eyewitness.

The sight of these attacking Confederates was spec-

Battery of 24-pounder siege guns that formed a part of the Union's "Last Line" above Pittsburg Landing. The photograph was taken a few days after the Battle of Shiloh, before the guns had been moved from their battle position. (Library of Congress)

tacular in the extreme, a Michigan private later remembered. The sun hung as a huge fireball, slowly falling out of sight, and the gleaming bayonets of the enemy sparkled in its waning rays.

Across the river from Pittsburg Landing the vanguard of Buell's army had appeared about 4:30 p.m. Belatedly, several steamboats had been appropriated to ferry the men of Jacob Ammen's brigade across. Touching shore about 5:20 p.m., Buell's advance contingent hastened up the bluff, shouting "Buell" to encourage the mob of disheartened troops milling about—now estimated at between 7,000 and 10,000 men "frantic with fright and utterly demoralized."

With only the 36th Indiana and a portion of the 6th Ohio in line, Grant's army braced for the oncoming attack, directed at the extreme flank nearest the river. The roar from the great guns and the supporting infantry created a noise "not exceeded by anything I . . . heard afterward," said a staff officer. Chalmers' brigade advanced into Dill Branch ravine but was beaten back by the storm of fire, and Jackson's men, on their left, lay down behind the crest of a ridge to escape the deadly missiles. Bragg and others, however, were bringing up reinforcements when Jackson's brigade suddenly pulled back.

Unknown to many of the Confederate generals present, one of Beauregard's staff officers, Major Numa Augustin, had ordered a halt to the fighting and a withdrawal by the front line to the captured enemy camps. Beauregard, in the rear near Shiloh Church, had been persuaded to put an end to the fighting because of the widespread disorder in the Confederate rear, and a belief that the victory was sufficiently complete for the day. Years later he confided that he believed his men "demoralized by the flush of victory," and that he had Grant "just where I wanted him, and could finish him up in the morning." This opinion of disarray was undoubtedly enhanced by the bursts of the gunboat shells in the rear, spreading confusion, plus the widespread looting and pillaging observed in the captured camps.

Being thus distant from the scene of the fighting, Beauregard had made what Bragg later termed one of the great mistakes of the war on the basis of other than first-hand information. "One more charge, my men," Bragg had previously told his troops, "and we shall capture them all."

When darkness finally put an end to the sporadic fighting, there was an immense sense of relief within the Federal army. Although driven to the brink of disaster, Grant's men could now anticipate more favorable prospects for the morrow. Indeed,

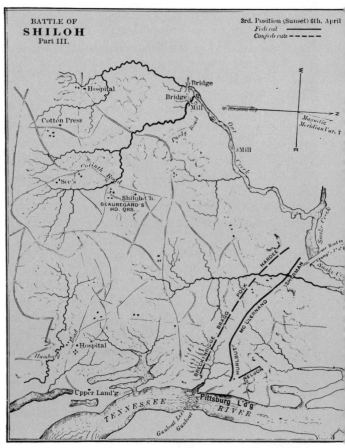

Positions at sunset. (Battles and Leaders of the Civil War)

throughout the night Buell's advanced troops were ferried across the river, while others were brought up from Savannah by transports. By daylight about 7,500 men of Buell's army were present, including most of two divisions, Brigadier Generals William Nelson's and Thomas Crittenden's. A third division, McCook's, was ashore by early morning on the 7th, expanding Buell's force to nearly 15,000 men. Buell, in fact, had already contemplated a counteroffensive, and issued orders for an attack by his men at daylight. Almost contemptuous of Grant for what he regarded as the disgraceful rout of his army, Buell considered his army independent, and merely "presumed" Grant would be in accord with his plans.

Grant, preoccupied with getting Lew Wallace's division up, did not meet with Buell that night. With Wallace finally present along the river road beginning about 7:15 p.m., Grant also anticipated an advance on the 7th, though he issued no specific orders that night. Lew Wallace's more than 7,000 troops represented the means to achieve "a great moral advantage" by becoming the attacking party, said Grant, and he planned accordingly.

Hungry, beaten Federal troops bivouac on the battlefield, kept awake by a cold, driving rain and the noise of fire from Federal gunboats. (Battles and Leaders of the Civil War)

Unable to sleep under a towering oak because of a raging thunderstorm that began about midnight, Grant went to the little log cabin near the landing, now being used as a hospital. Again he was unable to sleep in the presence of the grisly amputations being carried on continuously during the night. His injured ankle paining him severely, he then hobbled back to his "tree in the rain," thoroughly exhausted.

The night of April 6, later wrote one of Buell's soldiers, "was the worst night of our entire three years service." The cold driving rain continued until after 3

a.m., and the hungry, beaten Federal soldiers huddled in dire misery. "It seemed like the Lord was rubbing it in," wrote an Ohio youth. One private, unable to find a dry spot, put his blanket over his shoulders, stuck his bayoneted musket into the ground, placed his chin on the butt, and slept standing up. To add to the misery, about 9 p.m. the Federal gunboat *Tyler*, acting under instructions from General Nelson, began firing 8-inch naval shells in the enemy's direction at ten minute intervals. Taken up by the USS *Lexington* about 1 a.m., the fire continued

The Tyler *and* Lexington *shelling Confederate positions on the night of April 6. (Battles and Leaders of the Civil War)*

throughout the night, the deafening concussions doing little damage, but keeping men on both sides awake.

For the Confederates the night of April 6 represented a further crucial breakdown in communications. Sent by Nathan Bedford Forrest to spy on the enemy's activities that night, a detachment of scouts discovered Buell's troops debarking and returned to Forrest with this vital information. Forrest quickly informed Hardee and Breckinridge, but was directed to find Beauregard. Unable to locate the commanding general's headquarters after a lengthy search, Forrest returned to see Hardee, who told him merely to return to his regiment and report all hostile movements. Beauregard, ensconced in Sherman's captured tent near Shiloh Church, apparently had not left word where he could be found. On the afternoon of the 6th, Beauregard had received a telegram from a colonel near Florence, Alabama, reporting elements of Buell's army marching toward Decatur, Alabama. Thus within the span of twenty-four hours the circumstances had been substantially reversed. It would be the Confederates who were to be surprised on April 7.

Reversed Fortunes

The fighting on April 7 began with a few lingering Confederates being driven from Lew Wallace's front by artillery fire at daylight. Although Wallace began his attack about 6:30 a.m., his advance was so cautious in the face of minimal opposition that he had advanced only to the main Corinth road by midday.

Most of the initial action during the morning oc-

curred on the Federal left flank, where Buell's troops confronted the large concentration of Southern infantry remaining from the Hornets' Nest fight of Sunday. However, since many of these units had withdrawn to the captured camps of Sherman's and Prentiss' divisions, the Confederates allowed more than a mile of hard-won ground to be occupied by Buell's troops before they offered serious resistance.

About 10 o'clock Hardee, who seemed to be the "master spirit" on this front, ordered a counterattack in the vicinity of the much fought over Peach Orchard. Shouting taunts of "Bull Run! Bull Run!" at Buell's advancing men, several Confederate regiments swept into the underbrush, and were soon fighting hand-to-hand with their blue enemies. Soon discovering that they were outnumbered, the Confederates broke and ran back. One overly ambitious Federal brigade, Colonel William B. Hazen's, which pursued too closely was in turn routed by some reserve Louisiana troops, and became scattered.

Yet Hardee, his magnificent black horse having been shot from under him and his coat torn by several rifle balls, was unable to prevent the Confederate line from falling back under a heavy artillery fire. Several brief counterattacks stabilized the line, however, and by noon a general stalemate existed. Amid a burgeoning artillery duel, the men on both sides lay down to rest as best they could. One Federal private, exhausted by the events of the past two days, was found fast asleep under a tree despite the storm of shot and shell that raged about him.

In the center of the battlefield Crittenden's division and some of Bragg's troops had struggled for possession of thickets in the vicinity of the Hornets' Nest. Again Bragg had insisted on hurling fragmented and often isolated units against the Federal line in piecemeal assaults. One Kentucky regiment, marching into action singing the "Kentucky Battle Song," had been fearfully decimated in halting a Federal advance. Here the Confederate provisional governor of Kentucky, serving in the ranks, was mortally wounded.

Slowly driven back to the vicinity of Sherman's former headquarters in heavy fighting, by 1 p.m. the middle of the Confederate line verged on collapse. Several batteries had been lost, and many of the men were so demoralized that an officer, found cowering under a tree with some of his men, refused to re-form his command. He didn't give a damn what any general might call him, said the officer, he was not going back into the fighting. By now stragglers in a steady stream were making their way to the rear, while a critical shortage of ammunition compounded the growing difficulties.

Beauregard, at last aware of Buell's reinforcements,

Monday at 2 p.m.: Beauregard, at Shiloh Church, sends orders to begin the retreat. (Battles and Leaders of the Civil War)

refused to panic, however. To a Louisiana regiment he seemed cool and collected, and told the men, "The day is ours—you are fighting a whipped army, fire low and be deliberate."

Yet, as his staff surmised about midday, many of the troops were beyond further effort. While several officers were sent to gather all the arms and ammunition about the camps and load them into wagons to be taken to the rear, Beauregard organized his remaining troops for one last attempt to achieve an overwhelming victory.

Since noon a raging conflict had been underway in the vicinity of Water Oaks Pond, near the main Corinth road. Here Lew Wallace's troops, aided by the remnant of Grant's army, had advanced and then retreated in what one Federal general termed "one of the severest conflicts" of the two days of fighting. Pat Cleburne had attacked here, ordered by Bragg to make an assault without support. Though Cleburne protested what were obviously foolish tactics, he had led the remnant of his brigade, reduced from 2,700 men to about 800, in a forlorn charge.

About 2 p.m., Beauregard in person brought Colonel Preston Pond's relatively fresh brigade forward in a final effort to break the Federal line. Supported by several other random regiments the tattered grey line

sprang forward and fell on some of Buell's troops, McCook's division, only recently arrived on the field. "The fires from the contending ranks were two continuous sheets of flame," observed Alexander McCook, and his men were pushed back to a point near McClernand's camps. Still, the Federal artillery punished the attackers severely, and a reserve unit, Lauman's brigade, was brought into action with decisive results.

About 3:30 p.m. the Confederate infantry began streaming to the rear and Beauregard ordered a general retreat.

Slowly and ponderously, the jaded Confederate army trudged away from the smoldering battlefield. Several of the Federal camps were on fire, and the windrows of dead bodies, already swollen by the heat, presented a gruesome sight. Some of the retreating men were so fatigued that they could not move rapidly. "I never was exhausted so completely in my life," said one Southern soldier.

Grant's men made little effort to pursue the retreating enemy, however. "I was without cavalry," lamented Grant, who also noted that his men were scattered and had no knowledge of the various country roads. Buell likewise was content to let the Confederates go, even believing that defensive preparations should be made "for tomorrow's fight." Shocked by the carnage they found in the recaptured camps, the men bedded down for an uneasy sleep. Thousands of wounded had to be attended to; the confusion and disorder were extreme following what was then the bloodiest battle in the nation's history.

A steady, cold rain fell throughout most of the night, adding further misery to the terrible ordeal. One Confederate private, unable to walk farther, stood under a tree for shelter but fell asleep standing up. When he awoke he lay down and slept in a pool of water, content to lie there all night.

Despite an abortive pursuit by Sherman's division on April 8, which involved a fight with Nathan Bedford Forrest's cavalry at Fallen Timbers, the Battle of Shiloh had ended by mutual consent.

Although both sides claimed a victory, the newspapers were subsequently filled with controversial and indignant accounts citing the many mistakes and lost opportunities. What was largely overlooked in the tremendous publicity that ensued, however, was what was most evident to those who had fought at

Overleaf: Recapture of artillery at Pittsburg Landing by the 1st Ohio under Brigadier General Lovell H. Rousseau, on Monday, April 7. (Frank Leslie's Illustrated Newspaper)

Vicinity of the Hornet's Nest. The stump in the field to the right marks the spot where Albert Sidney Johnston was killed. By the end of the fighting in this area, there were so many dead soldiers that, said Grant, it would have been possible to walk across "stepping on dead bodies without a foot touching the ground." Drawing by W. Lathrop. (Grey Castle Press)

Shiloh. "It is time our people were getting rid of the idea that the courage is all on our side," wrote an enlightened Federal captain, "It is a mistake. The enemy seemed to fight determinedly and I know they fell back steadily when forced to, contesting every step of the way." It was a sentiment equally appropriate for both sides.

Shiloh witnessed the metamorphosis of the American soldier. Beyond the aspects of territory won or lost, of initiative gained or squandered, of new technology implemented, or unspeakable horror viewed, it produced a radical change in the attitude of fighting men both North and South. The hardening of perspective and the heightening of dedication that ultimately resulted in such bloody trials as Stone's River, Vicksburg, Chickamauga, and on through the Atlanta and Carolinas campaigns, was first manifested and nurtured at Shiloh.

William Tecumseh Sherman saw this vital aspect clearly when he stated after the war: "That victory [Shiloh] was one of the most important which has ever occurred on this continent. I have always estimated the victories . . . at Fort Donelson and Shiloh the most valuable of all, because of their moral effect. They gave our men confidence in themselves. . . ."

The true significance of the battle lay in its vital personal influence. From the cauldron of Shiloh sprang the tenacity of a Grant, the icy, calculating nerve of a Sherman, and the furious combative ardor of a Forrest and a Cleburne. If an enigma, the indelible impression Shiloh produced on the soldiers who fought there would never be effaced in the subsequent course of the war. That, perhaps, may serve as an explanation for the battle's fascination, even to this day.

The Eastern Theater at the Beginning of 1862

Union victories in Tennessee did much to reverse the moods of gloom in Washington and confidence in Richmond that had prevailed during the early winter of 1861–62. In December, a diplomatic showdown between Britain and the United States had threatened to add a second war to Abraham Lincoln's problems. A Union naval ship had stopped the British steamer *Trent* on the high seas and taken from it the Confederate diplomats James Mason and John Slidell, who were on their way to England to seek British diplomatic recognition of the Confederacy. Uproar ensued in London, where the British government branded this action an outrageous violation of British neutrality and freedom of the seas. War between Britain and the United States loomed until the Union government backed down and released Mason and Slidell. "One war at a time," was Lincoln's wise philosophy. But the letdown following this affair added to the discouragement that gripped Washington in the weeks surrounding Christmas.

The *Trent* affair had provoked a brief panic in northern financial circles. Banks suspended specie payments (the backing of their notes circulating as money with gold or silver), and Secretary of the Treasury Salmon P. Chase found it difficult to sell bonds to finance the war. General McClellan fell ill with typhoid fever. Lincoln had prodded McClellan in vain to take some action on the Virginia front with his splendid army. Now it was clear that, though he would recover, McClellan would remain out of action for a month or two. From General Henry W. Halleck in the West in January came negative reports on the prospects of an advance in that quarter. "It is exceedingly discouraging," Lincoln told a friend. "The people are impatient; Chase has no money; the General of the Army has typhoid fever. The bottom is out of the tub. What shall I do?"

But in February came news of the captures of Forts Henry and Donelson and the occupation of Nashville by Union troops. Burnside's victories in the Albemarle and Pamlico sounds of North Carolina were followed by reports of the Union victory at Pea Ridge in Arkansas. Now it was Richmond's turn for despair at "this disgraceful . . . shameful . . . catalogue of disasters." Jefferson Davis was formally inaugurated as president of the Confederacy on February 22, 1862 (he had previously been provisional president). When someone asked Davis' coachman why the president and his footmen were dressed in black for the occasion, the coachman replied wryly: "This, ma'am, is the way we always does in Richmond at funerals and sichlike."

While Davis conceded in his inaugural address that the Confederacy had "recently met with serious disasters," northern newspapers gloated that "the cause of the Union now marches on. . . . Every blow tells fearfully against the rebellion. The rebels themselves are panic-stricken, or despondent." The news of the bloody repulse of the Confederate counterstroke at Shiloh further depressed southern morale. The Union Congress solved northern financial problems by enacting new taxes, authorizing new bond issues, and passing the Legal Tender Act that authorized the issuance of treasury notes as money—the famous "greenbacks" that, in modified form, still serve as the main form of money today.

The USS San Jacinto stops the Trent on the high seas, precipitating an international crisis. (CWTI Collection)

Optimistic northerners viewed Union victories in the West as the first half of a one-two punch that would knock out the Confederacy. The second half would be the Army of the Potomac's advance in Virginia. Recovered from his illness, McClellan persuaded a reluctant Lincoln to authorize a flanking movement around Joseph Johnston's Confederate army at Manassas. Instead of attacking Johnston directly, McClellan proposed to transport his force down Chesapeake Bay to the mouth of the Rappahannock River, forcing Johnston to retreat in order to cover Richmond. Before McClellan could act, however, Johnston in early March anticipated him by withdrawing his army to a new defensive position behind the Rappahannock.

This only caused McClellan to alter his planned flanking movement another fifty miles southward, to Hampton Roads at the tip of the peninsula formed by the James and York Rivers seventy-five miles southeast of Richmond. Although this would give McClellan's army a secure supply line by water, Lincoln did not like it. Unless enough troops were left behind to defend Washington, the capital would be vulnerable to a sudden raid by rebel forces in northern Virginia or the Shenandoah Valley. Besides, Lincoln told McClellan, "by going down the Bay in search of a field, instead of fighting near Manassas, [you are] only shifting, and not surmounting, a difficulty. . . . [You] will find the same enemy, and the same, or equal, intrenchments, at either place."

Lincoln was beginning to suspect that McClellan lacked the will to fight. He was right. But in March 1861 the general, brandishing his professional military training before the civilian president, obtained Lincoln's consent for the Peninsula campaign against Richmond on the condition that he leave behind enough troops to protect Washington. The South, though, was counting on a secret weapon to overcome northern naval superiority and prevent any such operations in the Hampton Roads area. The secret weapon was the ironclad warship *C.S.S. Virginia.* But in one of history's most famous naval duels, the North's *U.S.S. Monitor* neutralized the *Virginia*, allowing McClellan's Peninsula campaign to go forward.

—James M. McPherson

BOUND FOR HAMPTON ROADS

Bound for Hampton Roads by Edward Miller

Notes on the Navies by James I. Robertson, Jr.

Bound for Hampton Roads
by Edward Miller

The duel between the *Monitor* and the *Virginia*, painted by J.O. Davidson. (*CWTI* Collection)

It was a cold, bleak day in February 1862 when Samuel Lewis, alias Peter Truskit, first saw Ericsson's *Monitor*. A U.S. Navy quartermaster, he was considered an experienced sailor and had spent most of his life at sea, including service on men-of-war. He was familiar with timbers of oak, long spars, and sailing canvas, and had watched with curiosity the gradual introduction of steam machinery onto ships during the 1850's. But ships were still rated in his mind by the number of guns in their broadside and the thickness of their oak. So as he stepped on the iron deck of the *Monitor*, penetrating cold may have shivered up his back at the sights about him on the strange and mysterious vessel.

Lewis could not comprehend the tremendous change that was taking place, or the effect it would have on history. Too busy adjusting to this new style of warship, he had no time to speculate on such questions. He would let chance and destiny decide these issues for history. A much more practical man, he would fulfill his part, keeping one hand for himself and one for the ship.

We sailors generally shipped under some other name on account of danger of running foul of bad captains or bad ships, when we might have to decamp at the first port, and were not particular about leaving any clues behind. That is why I called myself Truskit . . .

I and my partner, Joe Crown, were in Bombay when the war broke out. We had both served in the Navy before, and were anxious to get into it again. I had medals for service on both British and Russian men-of-war, and the news that there was fighting over the water sort of fired men up. Well, the upshot of it was that Joe and I shipped for New York and when we got there, enlisted. We went on-board the receiving ship *North Carolina* and had followed the dull daily routine for a week or so when Ericsson's *Monitor*, about which something had been whispered among the men, was completed, and a call was made for volunteers to go and man her. We understood that she was bound for Hampton Roads. . . .

The next day we went on-board. She was little bit the strangest craft I had ever seen; nothing but a few inches of deck above the water line, her big round tower in the center, and the pilot house at the end . . . We had confidence in her though, from the start, for the little ship looked somehow like she meant business.

History records that great events and technological breakthroughs were many times spawned during periods

her under way if necessary. Commodore Charles S. McCauley, commanding the navy yard, had been cautioned earlier not to take any steps that would provoke the citizens of Norfolk towards secession, and as a result few preparations were made at the yard for war.

The yard commander, fearing the storming of the facility by local secessionist militia, was mistakenly not informed that relief was on the way; confronted by seemingly overwhelming odds, he abruptly panicked in mid-April 1861. Even though the sizeable garrison at Fort Monroe was only a short distance away, McCauley ordered preparations made to destroy the yard and to scuttle the ships on the 20th of the month. But at 8:00 P.M. on the same day the order was given, Commodore Hiram Paulding arrived with a relief force of 450 marines and infantrymen to find all the ships, including the *Merrimack*, already settling to the muddy bottom and men scattering combustibles preparing to set the yard afire. The commodore, considering the situation too far gone to salvage, decided to complete the job already begun. He ordered the remaining ships and facilities burned.

The next day, after the Federals had been evacuated by Paulding, the Confederates occupied the yard, only to find it just partially destroyed. They were able to put out many of the fires, saving the machine shops, vast amounts of supplies and munitions, and some 1,200 heavy cannon, including 300 modern Dahlgren guns. And most important to the young Confederate navy, the stone graving dock was saved by a Union petty officer who had interrupted a deadly black powder train to protect the nearby homes of friends.

It was a humiliating loss for the Federal navy. The Confederacy had obtained a $10 million establishment, substantially intact, without a fight. And newly-appointed Confederate Secretary of the Navy Stephen R. Mallory, one of those willing to gamble with technology, was well prepared to exploit the South's good fortune.

of crisis when men were forced to take great risks. In 1862, many Northerners felt that the risks were too great, and the chances of another Ericsson failure too high, to share Truskit's intuitive confidence in the *Monitor*. But in the South there were others — people to whom a gamble with technology appealed.

After the firing on Fort Sumter, the Union dissolved quickly and the attention of U.S. Secretary of the Navy Gideon Welles focused on the Gosport Navy Yard at Norfolk, Virginia. It was the largest in the country and contained vast stores of war material, including cannon, ammunition, and stockpiles of powder. The yard was equipped with complete repair facilities, machine shops, and a stone graving dock deep enough to accommodate the largest ships in the fleet. Most important, however, were the warships at berth, particularly the new screw-driven steam-frigate *Merrimack*, in the yard for overhaul of her machinery.

Welles immediately dispatched Engineer in Chief Benjamin Isherwood and Captain James Alden to Norfolk to reassemble the *Merrimack*'s engines and to get

As a U.S. Senator from Florida in the 1850's and as chairman of the U.S. Senate Committee on Naval Affairs, Mallory had kept abreast of the development of ironclad ships in Europe. Now serving a new nation, he was convinced that a well-armored fighting vessel would make up for the Confederacy's deficiency in warships. Only days after the fall of Gosport, Mallory wrote:

> I regard the possession of an iron-armored ship as a matter of first necessity. Such a vessel at this time could traverse the entire coast of the United States, prevent all blockades, and encounter, with a fair prospect of success, their entire Navy.
>
> If to cope with them upon the sea we follow their example and build wooden ships, we shall have to construct several at one time; for one or two ships would fall an easy prey to their comparatively numerous steam frigates. But inequality of numbers may be compensated by invulnerability; and thus not only does economy

but naval success dictate the wisdom and expediency of fighting with iron against wood, without regard to first cost.

His arguments were convincing and on May 10, 1861, the Confederate Congress appropriated $2 million for the construction of ironclads. But money alone would not give the South an armored ship. Since February, Mallory had been investigating the availability of needed resources and industrial skills. It appeared that none of the rolling mills in the non-industrialized South could provide armor plating of sufficient thickness. Subsequently, he decided to first seek the acquisition of ironclads abroad. But Mallory also directed naval ordnance expert Lieutenant John M. Brooke to submit an idea for an armored vessel.

Confederate naval engineer John M. Brooke.

In June, Brooke submitted his preliminary design which, without any major modifications, would become the prototype of most ironclads built in the South. Then after consulting with Engineer in Chief William P. Williamson and Naval Constructor John L. Porter to refine the concept, Brooke finalized the design. What resulted was nothing revolutionary for current naval technology, but the vessel embraced a simplicity and practicality appropriate to the South's industrial capacity.

The ironclad was to be a shallow-draft vessel, sharply pointed at the bow and rounded at the stern, whose deck in battle trim would be barely awash. Amidships, running almost the entire length of the vessel was

an iron covered casemate sloping to the sheer at an angle of 40° and thoroughly backed with wood.

Guns mounted broadside were to be run out through gunports protected by iron covers, while two pivot guns at the ends would swivel to fire, fore and aft. For protection the boilers and all machinery were placed below the waterline. All those features, combined with an iron prow for ramming, would create a formidable warship capable of taking on the largest ship of the Union fleet. Having a good plan, Mallory instructed Brooke and Porter to find the means of getting it from the drafting table to the launching ways.

The search started at Norfolk for the necessary engines and other machinery. At the Tredegar Iron Works in Richmond, they were told they could obtain the 1-inch plate which, when laid in several courses, was thought to be sufficient. However, the necessary engines were not to be found anywhere in the South. When hearing this Williamson remarked on June 25th, "It will take at least twelve months to build her engines unless we can utilize some of the machinery in the *Merimac* [sic]." So additional discussion ended in agreement on the idea of adapting their design to the already existent, and salvaged hull of the Federals' *Merrimack*.

In May, the hulk had already been raised from the mud of the Gosport yard and placed in the surviving graving dock. Brooke and Porter rushed to inspect the charred wreck and determined that it was suitable for the conversion. On July 10, the scheme was presented to Mallory and immediately adopted. Regardless of the many compromises that would be required, the economy and speed of converting an existing steam warship, rather than constructing a new one, would give the Confederacy a formidable and perhaps, decisive edge against the Union blockade. Mallory envisioned the new ironclad would free-up commerce and entice Great Britain, hungry for Southern raw materials, to enter the conflict.

Work, already started before receiving Congressional approval, almost immediately ran into snags because of shortages of materials. The charred timbers were cut down to the berth deck and a new gun deck was installed. Over this the wooden casemate was constructed and backed with timber, the whole awaiting iron. The engines were not much improved by their submersion and Acting Chief Engineer H. Ashton Ramsay, one of the engineers on the old *Merrimack*, loudly complained that more cantankerous engines could not have been found. Indeed, they had been condemned and awaited replacement when Gosport was abandoned. Disliking them even more than before, Ramsay would have to coax the old machinery as best he could. He was secretly assured that the new ironclad would never be sent where her unreliable engines would endanger her. Another inherent defect was the converted vessel's deep draft. In any future engagement, the new ironclad

Converting the *Merrimack* into the ironclad *Virginia* at the stone graving dock at Gosport.

would be restricted to only those navigable channels that would severely handicap a shallow-draft vessel.

The work went at a feverish pace. There were as many as 1,500 men working, often at night and on Sundays. To Porter's chagrin, rush orders came almost daily from Richmond, cautioning against sabotage and requesting progress reports. Soon the word was out. "The government is constructing a monster at Norfolk," declared a War Department clerk. This started one of the most interesting attempted deceptions of the war. Initially, rumors were planted in Norfolk papers saying the salvaged hulk was worthless. Then the new warship started to take on enormous proportions in the Northern press as additional reports were received of the conversion. Soon a cry went out from Union port-city mayors pleading for protection because it was believed all Northern ports, commerce, and even the Capitol in Washington were to be within range of the ironclad's batteries.

John-Ericsson, a Swedish import, was already known in Washington as a "mechanic of some skill" when the *Merrimack* scare began ripping through the town. But there was no love lost between the U.S. Navy and the fifty-three-year-old engineer due to the regrettable 1844 *Princeton* incident where Ericsson was blamed for a gun explosion that killed the secretary of state and others (not an endearing method of obtaining future government contracts). However, it seemed as though fate had determined that the engineer's long nurtured concept of an armored battery would have its day of trial as Ericsson, having finally gotten approval, skillfully orchestrated the construction of an ironclad ship in New York while continually dispersing bureaucratic hesitancy and fear of another failure in Washington.

Progress, meanwhile, on the ironclad taking shape in Norfolk was slow and frustrating. To obtain the needed iron for the ship's armor, the Confederates had to scour the countryside of northern Virginia tearing up railroad iron. And the simplest tasks became major chores as procurement problems plagued the project.

In September, Tredegar Iron Works was midway through the production run of 1-inch plate, when

Brooke decided as a result of firing tests, that 2-inch plate would be needed instead. Aside from lost time and wasted money in making new plate, frequent design changes made by Porter and Brooke necessitated the relocation of drilled holes in the iron, in some instances as often as four times. Adding to this aggravation, by mid-October, with nearly 100 tons of the iron ready for shipment, a shortage of railroad rolling stock occurred. Some of the plate sat at the ironworks for more than four weeks, waiting for delivery. To expedite matters, flatcars were specifically assigned for the shipment of the plate and an officer was dispatched from Norfolk to insure delivery. However, fate decreed that speedy delivery was just not to be. The officer and his train were routed from Richmond to Norfolk by way of Weldon, North Carolina. As a result, it was not until February 12, 1862, that the last of the armor arrived in Norfolk.

From Washington on January 11, Commodore Smith of the navy's ironclad board wrote to a Lieutenant John Worden to discuss the new Ericsson battery. He said, "this vessel is an experiment, I believe you are the right sort of officer to put in command of her." Worden replied by asking to inspect the vessel first before making a decision. After a hasty examination, he told Smith he believed she might prove to be a success and he was "quite willing to be an agent in testing her capabilities."

The seeds of conflict, sown long before Abraham Lincoln took *his* oath, presented the president with one of his first tasks in office—keep the lumbering Federal Government functioning while many in the bureaucracy abandoned their oaths and began scheming to dismantle the Union. Seven states had already seceded and almost daily reports reached Washington of federal buildings, forts, and arsenals being turned over to state authorities. Confidential messages and letters immediately became known to secessionists because of spies and unfaithful couriers. One exception was a forty-four-year-old naval officer who was to have the distinction of being the first Federal officer to be taken prisoner. Lieutenant John Lorimer Worden was sent to Fort Pickens, Pensacola, Florida, with a secret message committed to memory instructing the commander there to hold the fort despite demands for its surrender. A navy veteran of twenty-seven years, the lieutenant was a native of New York and his loyalty was certain. On his return by the same route, just after Fort Sumter, he was captured by Confederates. For his loyalty he spent seven months in Southern prisons before being released in an exchange of prisoners. When he reported to New York to take command of Ericsson's battery on January 16, 1862, it was his first opportunity to take an active part in the war.

Having a ship, Worden needed a crew. After carefully considering the requirements for manning the vessel, he selected a total of fifty-seven men—ten officers and the rest crew. He decided that nineteen would be the maximum allowed in the turret to work the guns and to handle the heavy port-stoppers. "Peter Truskit" was made a loader and his partner Joe Crown was made a gunner's mate. Worden selected Lieutenant Samuel Dana Greene, a Marylander who had just turned twenty-one and recently graduated from the Naval Academy, to be his executive officer. Others included Paymaster William F. Keeler, a man whose letters to his wife would vividly detail life aboard the *Monitor*. On February 25, Ericsson's battery was put into commission. With rumors that the *Merrimack* would be coming out any day, no time was lost putting stores aboard and making ready for sea.

On Thursday, March 6, following weeks of accidents and difficult engineering trials, the *Monitor* finally departed the Brooklyn Navy Yard. The new ironclad was taken under tow by the tug *Seth Low* to speed the voyage and as a precaution against heavy weather. Two other vessels accompanied them, giving added assurance to the crew taking an ironclad to sea for the first time. A last minute directive from the Navy Department ordering *Monitor* to proceed directly to Washington to defend the capital went undelivered because the small

Battles and Leaders of the Civil War

The *Monitor*'s executive officer, Samuel Dana Greene. At the time he served on her he was just twenty-one years old.

flotilla had already cleared New Jersey's Sandy Hook Lighthouse. The battery, her crew closely quartered beneath her iron deck, was bound for Hampton Roads.

In Norfolk, work on the Southern ironclad was nearing completion. On February 17th she was floated in the graving dock, her crew was ordered aboard and the converted vessel was commissioned the C.S.S. *Virginia*, although many of her crew from the "old" navy and the Northern press would persist in calling her the *Merrimack*. On the 24th, Flag Officer Franklin Buchanan was given command of the Confederate navy's James River Squadron which consisted of several small, unarmored gunboats and the *Virginia*. Buchanan, a well-seasoned naval officer with forty-six years of naval experience, had helped establish the U.S. Naval Academy in 1845 and had served as its first superintendent. A native of Maryland, he had resigned his commission after riots in Baltimore, being unwilling to bear arms against his state. When Maryland did not secede, he asked to be reinstated, but was coarsely told his name had been dropped from the rolls. However, his brother retained his commission in the Federal navy and was known by Buchanan to be aboard the *Congress* blockading Hampton Roads.

Buchanan recognized the *Virginia*'s shortcomings as an ironclad, but was anxious to test her qualities under fire. Sharing Secretary Mallory's vision of the great effect "dashing cruises" up the Potomac and even to New York would have for the Southern cause, Buchanan wanted first to test the new vessel against the Union fleet at Hampton Roads. But it was not until March 7, that sufficient powder and ammunition was placed aboard; the department claimed, "Every pound of powder that could be procured has been sent to Norfolk for the *Virginia*." Even then Buchanan had to beg for additional powder from the army and other vessels in Norfolk.

Having gotten all the powder he was going to get, and all aboard nearly ready, Buchanan waited for clear weather. On the morning of March 8, 1862, he made his move. At eleven o'clock, the *Virginia* steamed down the Elizabeth River. The shoreline was crowded with cheering spectators and soldiers. The *Virginia* was just as novel and untried to the Confederates as the *Monitor* was to her crew.

> The officers and crew were strangers to the ship and to each other. Up to the hour of sailing she was crowded with workmen. Not a gun had been fired, hardly a revolution of the engines had been made, when we cast off from the dock and started on what many thought was an ordinary trip.

But Buchanan had decided to strike. At anchor off Fort Monroe were the U.S. frigates *Minnesota* and *Roanoke*, sister ships of the old *Merrimack*, and the 50-gun sailing frigate *St. Lawrence*. A large fleet of foreign warships was also at anchor there, where they had waited for several months in anticipation of the ensuing

Franklin Buchanan, *Virginia*'s first commander and, one day, a Confederate admiral. In his long U.S. Navy career he traveled with Perry to Japan.

engagement. Off Newport News, seven miles above the Union's Fort Monroe, were the 50-gun *Congress* and the 30-gun *Cumberland*. Buchanan steered for Newport News. He had decided to ram the *Cumberland* first, apprehensive of the new 70-pounder rifled pivot gun she had aboard. There seemed little notice of the approaching ironclad among the anchored warships. And it took the *Virginia* nearly one and a half hours to reach the Roads. This seemed like an eternity to the waiting gun crews.

> From the start we saw that she was slow, not over five knots. She steered so badly that with her great length it took from thirty to forty minutes to turn . . .

The Union fleet was seemingly unprepared for the encounter everyone else had expected for months. Commodore Goldsborough, commanding the blockading squadron, had continually received warnings from Washington about the progress on the *Virginia* and had, the day before, received word that her flags were flying, that she had taken on crew, and was ready for action. However, when the *Virginia* steamed out into the Roads, Goldsborough was many miles away in the Carolina Sound overseeing another opera-

tion, and Captain William Radford, commanding *Cumberland* was attending a court-martial board ashore. Although he returned at the gallop, he arrived just as his ship was sinking.

The initial response to the sighting of the *Virginia* was catastrophic for the Union fleet. The *Roanoke*, *St. Lawrence*, and *Minnesota* ran aground as they tried to get underway without the assistance of the steam tugs. The *Virginia* approached to within three-quarters of a mile of the *Cumberland* before she had cleared her decks and "beat to quarters." The gunners on the *Virginia* incredulously peered out their gunports.

> The day was calm and the two ships were swinging lazily by their anchors . . . Boats were hanging to the lower booms, washed clothes in the rigging. Nothing indicated that they were expecting us.

The first shots were fired by a small picket boat and the shore batteries at Newport News. The *Virginia* seemed to ignore them, steadily advancing towards the warships. Buchanan waited until he was within easy range of the *Cumberland* before he opened up with the 7-inch Brooke rifle bow gun. It was a direct hit on the starboard quarter showering the decks with lethal wooden splinters that wounded several marines. Soon the firing became brisk with returning Union shells having no effect upon the ironclad. As the *Virginia* passed the *Congress*, the vessels exchanged broadsides. This had a devastating effect on the *Congress*, put several guns out of action, and killed entire gun crews. The Union gunners stared in terror as their combined broadside made little difference to the ironclad, steaming straight-ahead for the *Cumberland*.

> She looked like a huge half-submerged crocodile . . . At her prow I could see the iron ram projecting, straight forward somewhat above the waters edge, and apparently, a mass of iron . . . it was impossible for our vessel to get out of her way.

Buchanan ordered the *Virginia*'s engines reversed before ramming the *Cumberland* under the fore rigging on the starboard side. Above the din of battle there was no audible smashing of timbers and just a slight jar as the *Virginia* buried its prow into the side of the war-

When *Virginia* passed Craney Island on her way to attack the Federals at Hampton Roads, Rebel troops stationed there cheered her.

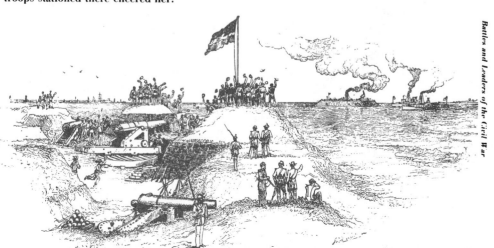

Buchanan expertly knifed *Virginia*'s ram into the U.S.S. *Cumberland* on the first try.

around. Due to her deep draft and large turning radius, he was forced to go quite some distance up the James River. At first thought to be retiring, it soon became evident that the ironclad was turning around. And at that point the *Virginia* was joined by three other vessels of the James River Squadron, and together they started raking the *Congress* with deadly fire.

The *Congress* had attempted to get underway by slipping her anchor and had run aground in such a manner that she could not bring her broadside to bear on the enemy. Her two deck-mounted pivot guns returned the fire as best they could. As one gun crew was cut down, others would jump in their place until the guns were dismounted. It became evident that the *Congress* would soon meet the same fate as the *Cumberland*. A Lieutenant Pendergrast took command after Lieutenant Joseph Smith, son of Commodore Smith in Washington, was beheaded by a shell that also dismounted the last gun that could be brought to bear. With the ship on fire in several places and wishing to prevent further needless slaughter of his crew, Pendergrast ordered the colors hauled down in surrender.

While the C.S.S. *Beaufort* and C.S.S. *Raleigh* were alongside the *Congress*, removing wounded and prisoners, a heavy fire from Federal infantry on shore drove them off, wounding several of their crew. Angered by this breach of military etiquette, Buchanan exposed himself needlessly on top of the *Virginia* while shouting at the enemy and was himself hit in the thigh. Infuriated, he ordered the *Congress* destroyed by hot shot and incendiary shells. She would burn long into the night.

It was now five o'clock with only an hour of daylight remaining. Lieutenant Catesby Rogers Jones relieved Buchanan after his injury, and had every confidence that the *Virginia* would return the next day on high tide to complete her destruction of the Union fleet.

As dusk fell on the bloodied water and the smoke of the retiring Confederate ironclad still hung in the distance, the *Monitor* was entering Hampton Roads, her crew grateful to be still afloat after experiencing mechanical problems on their trip. They had heard the sound of guns and seen the peculiar puffs of white

ship, seemingly marrying the two vessels together. Still the opposing batteries exchanged shots, causing the ironclad to seem like she was "frying from one end to the other." The grease spread on the armor to help deflect shells sizzled and combined with the burning powder smoke of the guns. The two ships were engulfed in smoke, with the *Virginia* noticeably down by the bow from the weight of the sinking warship above her. Many of her crew were afraid they would join the *Cumberland* in her fate. Gradually, the *Virginia* pivoted almost parallel to its sinking adversary before sluggishly withdrawing and leaving the poorly attached ram in the side of her prey. Soon the *Cumberland* listed to starboard and settled rapidly with gun crews still firing their guns until submerged. Many were trapped there for lingering too long trying to help their wounded shipmates. When she came to rest her masts protruded from the surface of the water and her battle colors were still flying. The surface of the water was littered with the debris from the fight and men struggling to save themselves. In less than an hour, one of the most powerful ships in the Federal navy had been sent to the bottom with 121 men lost. The *Virginia* suffered two men killed and eight wounded. The muzzles of two of her guns had been shot away, along with her boats, railing, and anchors. Her smoke stack was riddled, but her armor had proved impenetrable, having undergone a severe test.

Buchanan's attention now turned to the *Congress*, but in order to get at her, he would have to turn the *Virginia*

Buchanan's lieutenant, Catesby ap Rogers Jones. After long years of U.S. Navy service and Confederate naval combat, he died in 1877 in a personal quarrel.

Finally, Acting Master Samuel Howard volunteered and the battery proceeded to take her station alongside the stranded *Minnesota*, arriving there at 1:00 A.M.

Shortly after daybreak the *Virginia* was sent steaming from her anchorage towards the warships off Fort Monroe, obviously bent on continuing the destruction of the previous day. As the *Virginia* approached the *Minnesota*, Lieutenant Jones caught a first glimpse of his new adversary. Some thought it to be a water tank or perhaps a ship's boiler being sent ashore for repairs, but Jones knew it must be Ericsson's battery.

At 7:00 A.M. *Monitor* had her steam up and raised her anchor. All the hatches were battened and the vents and stacks were stowed below. At 8:00 A.M. Worden told the *Minnesota* he would stand by her to the last and do his best to protect her. A little later, the first shot from the *Virginia*'s bow gun was heard overhead, directed not at the *Monitor*, but at the *Minnesota*.

Going below, Worden paused in the turret as the crews were loading the guns. As a word of encouragement he said, "Send them that with our compliments, my lads." The gun crews stood in dimly lit silence, waiting for the sound of enemy shells against their untried armor, and wondering if it would protect them

smoke which for them was the first indication that the Union fleet had come under attack.

At 9:00 P.M. the *Monitor* anchored near the *Roanoke*. Worden went aboard to confer with Captain Marston and learned of the events of March 8. Worden and Marston decided to disregard any order to send the *Monitor* to Washington. Instead she would remain at Hampton Roads to defend the *Minnesota*, still hard aground. In the opinion of both officers, the *Monitor* was the only vessel in the Union fleet that had any chance of averting further disaster.

The *Monitor* needed a pilot to negotiate the Roads and nearly two hours were spent trying to locate one.

The *Monitor* apprehensively steams into Hampton Roads. Her presence there was a mistake; she should have been in Washington, D.C.

Working the guns in the *Monitor*'s turret. Young Samuel Greene, at the right, pulled the lanyard for every shot.

any effect on the other it seemed. Inside the revolving turret, Greene was having difficulty knowing where his target was. The speaking tube from the pilot house was broken early in the engagement and instructions had to be passed to the gunners by messenger. Worden would tell Greene the *Virginia* was on the starboard beam or the port quarter, but Greene had no idea where these were; his white marks on the deck noting the ship's true designations had been rubbed out early in the action.

Greene fired every gun himself. The pilot house could be directly in the line of fire and would be easily damaged by the *Monitor*'s own guns if they were fired carelessly. Then additional problems developed with the turret mechanism; "it was difficult to start revolving, or when, once started, to stop it." Further difficulty with the heavy port-stoppers that required a whole gun crew to move, caused Greene to experiment with firing the ready gun while the turret was still moving. This decreased their accuracy, but increased their firing rate to once every eight minutes. Several times Greene thought he had penetrated the enemy's armor and would later

against the guns of the Rebel behemoth.

Worden instructed the gunners, "Tell Mr. Greene not to fire till I give the word, to be cool and deliberate, to take sure aim and not to waste a shot."

Worden steered directly for the *Virginia*, which at first ignored its opponent. The *Monitor* then drew up alongside the *Virginia*, stopped her engines and Worden gave the command, "Commence firing!" Rotating the iron turret, Greene ordered a port-stopper up, a gun run out, and then he pulled the lanyard. Truskit peered out the gun port and later wrote, "You can see surprise on a ship just the same as you can see it in a human being, and there was surprise all over the *Merrimac* [*sic*]."

Not being able to get any closer to the *Minnesota* in the shallow water, Jones decided to devote his full attention to the Federal ironclad. At first the two vessels circled at long range, but frequently Worden would bring the *Monitor* in close, until the ships almost touched. Worden took good advantage of his ship's superior speed and maneuverability, making the gunners on the *Virginia* complain, "We never got a sight of her guns except when they were about to fire on us."

Neither ironclad had

lament that he was not allowed to use full powder charges. He had been limited to 15 pounds per charge on instructions from Washington. Both vessels attempted to ram the other. Then *Virginia* struck a glancing blow, but did little damage without her iron ram. The *Monitor* parried by trying to carry away *Virginia*'s rudder and propeller, but missed the mark.

As the engagement wore on, the Confederate ironclad started to show signs of weakness. In several places her armor had been cracked and the wood backing started to come away. Another solid shot hitting in an already dented spot might have penetrated her iron. The *Virginia* was leaking badly in the bow and had her pumps constantly in motion.

For a short while the *Monitor* pulled off into shallow water to replace ammunition and powder in the turret, but soon renewed

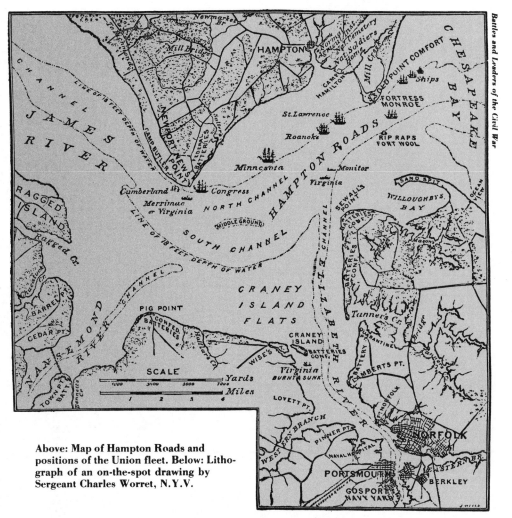

Above: Map of Hampton Roads and positions of the Union fleet. Below: Lithograph of an on-the-spot drawing by Sergeant Charles Worret, N.Y.V.

the fight. Shortly after noon, however, the gunners of the *Virginia* directed their attention at the *Monitor*'s pilot house. Previously they had had no effect when firing on the turret. At a distance of about ten yards, the after pivot gun of the *Virginia* scored a direct hit on the new target. Worden was peering out the slit at the time and was badly wounded in the face. In the confusion this created, the *Monitor* ran off some distance while assistance was given to Worden, and Greene was summoned from the turret.

The result was that the *Monitor* broke off the fight. After inspecting the damage, Greene returned to the pilot house to resume the fracas but the Rebel ironclad had already turned towards the Elizabeth River thinking it had delivered a deadening blow, winning the battle. Similarly, the crew of the *Monitor* felt they had sent the *Virginia* back to Norfolk in a sinking condition.

Stalemate, victory, or defeat was a real issue to the men who served on those first ironclads. But to history the common element between the two ships was the heroism of those who fought on them. Neither was decisively defeated, and each vessel attained some success, and all, it seems, to fulfill a solitary purpose—their one chance engagement on March 9, 1862.

Notes on the Navies

by James I. Robertson, Jr.

Rumors that the Confederates were constructing an ironclad ship led the Union to construct the Galena and, above, the New Ironsides. These were ships of conventional design overlaid by iron plating. They were to play important roles in the Union's victory. (CWTI Collection)

During the American Revolution, George Washington stated a basic tenet of military strategy: "In any operation, and under all circumstances, a decisive naval superiority is to be considered as a fundamental principle, and the basis upon which every hope of success must ultimately depend." This axiom applied pointedly to the Civil War, for Union naval power in the 1860's proved so important that its effects on the defeat of the Confederacy can hardly be exaggerated.

The U.S. Navy faced an awesome dilemma at war's outset, when Lincoln proclaimed a blockade of the South. The Navy had but a handful of ships available to isolate the 3,500 miles of Confederate seacoast. Both sides realized how absolutely dependent the Southern nation was on European sources of supplies. For the North to win the war, an effective blockade was imperative. The Navy was also needed for military operations along the coast and in the rivers, as well as for the protection of American commercial vessels at sea.

The very presence of the Navy in the war's first weeks had a substantial effect on the outcome. Federal cruisers in the Potomac River and Chesapeake Bay in 1861 probably saved Washington, D.C., and Maryland from falling into the hands of the Confederacy, and there can be little doubt that Federal naval control of the upper Mississippi and Ohio Rivers helped to keep Kentucky and Missouri in the Union.

It is a testimonial to Lincoln's hardworking Secretary of the Navy, Gideon Welles, that Northern strength afloat became as highly potent and effective as it did. While the few ships at hand began blockading the major Southern ports in 1861 (and captured 150 blockade-runners that first year), Welles and his equally brilliant assistant, Gustavus V. Fox, worked indefatigably to build a mighty sea force. Construction and purchase of craft continued at a rapid pace as Welles secured every type of ship "from Captain Noah to Captain Cook." From only forty-two serviceable vessels in 1861, the Navy reached 671 ships by 1864. Many of these were so radically new in design and performance that the Civil War truly ushered in the modern era of naval power.

The *Monitor* is an excellent case in point. Invented by John Ericsson and constructed during the winter of 1861–1862, this revolutionary vessel possessed a number of startling innovations. It was a small, all-iron ship, with its hull only inches above the water line. On its deck were but two superstructures: a revolving gun turret that could withstand a ten-inch shell at close range, and a small pilothouse. High maneuverability was one of its chief tactical advantages.

The famous 1862 *Monitor-Virginia* duel has already been summarized. Neither ship emerged victorious from the Hampton Roads confrontation. Yet the fact that the *Monitor* held its own against the larger, more ominous looking, *Virginia* did much to dash Confederate hopes of a naval super-weapon. A few weeks later, the *Virginia* was run aground and burned to prevent its capture by the fleet that accompanied McClellan's army to the Peninsula. The original *Monitor* was also ill-fated. On the night of December 30–31, 1862, it sank in a storm off Cape Hatteras, North Carolina.

Increasingly effective as the blockade was, Lincoln and Secretary Welles did not regard it as sufficient alone to cut the South's commercial strings with foreign markets. Occupation of key points along the seacoast would strengthen the blockade, jeopardize those ports still open, give the Navy fueling stations closer to the areas of operation, and enable fleets to move in greater concentration against the remaining prime targets.

Such "hop-scotch" tactics began in August 1861, when an amphibious expedition secured Forts Clark and Hatteras on the North Carolina coast. These captures put a stop to Confederate privateering in the area. Two months later, Flag Officer Samuel F. Du-Pont commanded Federal forces in the capture of Port Royal, South Carolina, giving the Union control of the town of Beaufort and the vital sea islands nearby, plus a needed naval base deep in the South. During February-March 1862, General Ambrose E. Burnside led a heavy armada that overpowered the Confederate defenses at Roanoke Island. The fall of this strategic bastion led to the Union occupation of the North

A joint army-navy expedition overpowers Confederate defenses at crucial Roanoke Island, which controlled the passage between Pamilco and Albemarle sounds. This amphibious exercise won a promotion to major general for Ambrose E. Burnside. (Library of Congress)

A *"powder monkey" poses on the deck of the U.S.S. New Hampshire. (Library of Congress)*

Carolina coastal towns of New Berne, Edenton, and Elizabeth City—and, in addition, left the Carolina interior vulnerable to attack. The capture of Fort Pulaski in April all but closed the Savannah River and Georgia's leading seaport. The recapture of Norfolk, also that spring, sealed the Virginia coast.

By 1864, the Confederacy held but four of its major ports: Charleston, South Carolina; Mobile, Alabama; Wilmington, North Carolina; and Galveston, Texas. They became the focal points for Federal naval attacks in the war's last year.

Charleston, "the seedbed of the Confederacy," proved especially thorny. For 587 consecutive days in 1863–1864, the city was besieged by fleets under DuPont and Admiral John A. Dahlgren. Southern batteries played havoc with monitors, gunboats, and frigates that ventured into range. Union amphibious assaults against outlying works were likewise unsuccessful. The proud fortress-city stood battered but defiant until February 1865, when the approach of Sherman's army led to its fall. Charleston's long stand in the face of seemingly overpowering Federal might is one of the heroic sagas of the Confederacy.

Mobile became the South's chief gulf port after the April 1862 fall of New Orleans, and Confederates strengthened it accordingly with shore forts, underwater mines (known then as "torpedoes"), and a fleet spearheaded by the deadly ram *Tennessee*. The Federal navy prepared carefully until August 5, 1864, when "the Victor of New Orleans" struck again. Crusty David G. Farragut led his fleet of ironclads and frigates up the dangerous channel. Confederate artillery raked the Union warships and inflicted heavy damage. Yet Farragut, lashed to the rigging of the flagship *Hartford*, refused to turn back. Whether Farragut actually shouted "Damn the torpedoes! Full speed ahead!" is debatable. Nevertheless, he steamed into Mobile Bay and achieved one of the paramount naval victories of the war. (See Volume 4.)

The Confederacy's last Atlantic opening was Wilmington, situated several miles up the Cape Fear River. Powerful Fort Fisher, guarding the river's junction with the sea, was the key to Wilmington itself. Confederates inside the fort repulsed a December 1864 land-and-sea assault by forces under General Benjamin F. Butler and Admiral David D. Porter. The following month, Porter's fleet and 8,000 Federal infantrymen under General Alfred H. Terry silenced the guns of Fort Fisher and overran the works. The fall of the fort and of Wilmington ended Confederate blockade-running.

Galveston, Texas, held out until after the end. Located on the frontier of the Confederacy, it never

Union sailors aboard a warship relaxing with games and music. (National Archives)

became a principal object for attack as did New Orleans, Charleston, and Mobile. On June 2, 1865, almost two months after Appomattox, the city officially capitulated to Union authorities.

Of equal or possibly greater importance than Federal naval efforts at sea was the work done by the various river squadrons and fleets working in conjunction with Union armies. In many of the war's major campaigns, Federal armies followed waterways and depended upon them for support, logistics, and a safe retreat if necessary. Much of the story of the war in the West can be told in terms of joint army and navy operations. Ulysses S. Grant, more than any other general in the Civil War, realized the full potential of sea power—and made the most use of it. His first campaign, at Belmont, Missouri, was largely amphibious. Grant's drives against Forts Henry and Donelson were successful only because he utilized ships for rapid transportation of soldiers and because the Union gunboats gave him "inland control of the sea" by proving more than a match for Southern shore batteries. Federal warships protected Grant's flank on the drive through Tennessee, and salvos from those gunboats were a large factor in Grant's victorious counterattack at Shiloh. The North's final investment of Vicksburg, and ultimate control of the Mississippi River, could not have resulted but for the floating firepower of the U.S. Navy.

Similarly, McClellan's entire 1862 Peninsula Campaign depended upon naval support. His huge Army of the Potomac could not have disembarked at Fortress Monroe if the menace of the *Virginia* had not been checked by the *Monitor*. Federal squadrons on the James River paralleled McClellan's advance on Richmond and gave constant protection to his left flank. When Lee's counter-offensive crumbled the Federal right, McClellan was saved from disaster by retreating to the James, where he had both the protective batteries of naval gunboats and a secure line of logistics by water. McClellan's dilemma and eventual salvation by the Navy was the "Dunkirk" of the war.

Two years later, when Grant was hammering futilely in front of Richmond, he was able to shift across the James and move on Petersburg because Federal ships controlled all waterways to the east. The U.S. Navy made possible the climactic, nine-month siege that followed. It alone ensured during those months the food and equipment for Grant's enormous army. How vital Grant considered the Navy is best revealed by his fears when Confederate ironclads late in 1864 attempted to break the James River supply line.

The Southern Confederacy had no real navy and never acquired the facilities for building one. Stephen R. Mallory, the Confederate naval secretary, was unable to surmount the additional obstacles of obtaining enough funds for sufficient foreign purchases and of overcoming the North's superior overseas diplomacy. Confederate naval efforts were thus restricted to privateering, blockade-running, menacing Union commercial ships on the high seas, and to a series of revolutionary counter-weapons such as mines, torpedoes, and tactical submarines.

What glory the Confederacy achieved at sea came from a score of cruisers that, under adventuresome crews, preyed singly on Federal naval and maritime vessels. This had the dual effect of drawing Federal warships from blockade duty (thereby increasing the odds for blockade-runners) and of denting Northern commercial interests. The first of such sleek raiders was the 500-ton steamer *Sumter*. Her commander was Raphael Semmes, the Confederacy's most brilliant sailor. A native of Alabama, Semmes had a quarter-century's naval experience behind him when civil war began. He captained the *Sumter* for only six months, yet during that period the cruiser captured eighteen Federal ships in the Atlantic and Caribbean.

On August 24, 1862, Semmes took command of the South's premier cruiser, the *Alabama*. This 1,000-ton steamer was equipped with eight guns and two 300-horsepower engines. Its crew of 144 men included more English sympathizers than Confederate seamen. During its two-year reign of terror on the high seas, the *Alabama* came to be regarded as a ghost ship. It ranged from Newfoundland to Singapore, always appearing as if from nowhere to assail its victims. The *Alabama*'s sixty-nine prizes included the USS *Hatteras*, which she sank after capture.

The Confederate cruiser destroyed more than $10,000,000 worth of Federal shipping and literally drove the American merchant marine to cover. But on June 19, 1864, the *Alabama* was cornered off the coast of France by the USS *Kearsarge*. For an hour, the two vessels exchanged broadsides at a range of 900 yards. The *Alabama* sank with twenty-six hands; the remainder were picked from the sea by the *Kearsarge* and nearby European vessels that had witnessed the classic battle.

The CSS *Florida*, under Captain John Newland Maffitt, was a privateer that seized thirty-seven prizes during eighteen months of cruising in the Caribbean and South Atlantic. Her capture in a Brazilian seaport by the USS *Wachusetts* was a violation of neutral rights that the United States later disavowed. The *Tallahassee*, a former blockade-runner operating out of Wilmington, took thirty-nine prizes during her 1864 saga. Last of the Confederate cruisers was the fabled *Shenandoah*, a sailing steamer under Captain James I. Waddell. The raider sailed from England in October 1864 to disrupt the Northern whaling fleet in the Bering Sea. Among the *Shenandoah*'s forty-

Confederate naval efforts included menacing Union commercial ships on the high seas. Above: The Confederate's premier cruiser, the Alabama, leaving the merchant ship Brilliant on October 3, 1862, after placing her under bond. (CWTI Collection)

Below: The fabled C.S.S. Shenandoah, which captured 48 Union ships, shown entering Hobson's Bay, Australia, on January 25, 1865. (Illustrated Australian News, February 23, 1865)

The Confederates capture the U.S.S. Harriet Lane at Galveston, Texas, using a fleet of merchant steamers fortified with bales of cotton on the decks. (Harper's New Monthly Magazine)

eight captures were eight whalers burned collectively two months after Appomattox. When Captain Waddell learned of the war's termination, he returned to Liverpool. There, on November 6, 1865, the last Confederate naval ensign was furled.

Confederate blockade-runners provided some of the highest drama in the Civil War. A typical blockade-runner was a lean, low, paddle-wheel steamer, painted a dull gray and burning almost smokeless anthracite coal. Having telescoping smokestacks and other streamlined features, these sleek vessels were capable of speeds up to fifteen knots. Their usual tactic, when approaching the Southern coast with a full cargo, was to keep out of sight until nightfall. Then the vessel would make a dash for port in the darkness. Confederate coastal guns would lay down a heavy bombardment on Federal blockaders while the vessel was making its run for safety. If the ship were severely damaged by Federal gunfire, it was deliberately run ashore so that at least part of its cargo could be salvaged.

The Confederacy devised several novel weapons for use in coastal defense. Various types of water mines were developed but never proved highly effective. In January 1863, Texas soldiers fortified some merchant steamers with bales of cotton on the decks and launched attacks on blockading squadrons. At Galveston the "cotton-clad" fleet captured the USS *Harriet Lane* and routed half a dozen other blockaders. The strange-looking flotilla moved on to Sabine Pass and seized two other Union warships before Federal naval reinforcements arrived.

Experimentation by the South with "torpedo boats" centered around the *David*, constructed at Charleston in the autumn of 1863. The *David* was a small, cigar-shaped vessel, propelled by steam. It cruised almost submerged and attacked by means of a torpedo attached to a long spar projecting from the bow. Thus armed, the *David* did extensive damage to the blockader *New Ironsides* before running aground at Charleston.

Unique among Confederate naval innovations was history's first tactical submarine, the *H. L. Hunley*. Its short career is a story of perseverance in the face of repeated failure.

Designed and financed by Horace L. Hunley, the submarine was built in the spring of 1863 at Mobile. The vessel sank on its initial trial run, but all hands escaped. The Confederate Government showed no interest in the enterprise. Hunley thereupon enlisted private financial support for the construction of a second submarine, which was completed that summer and shipped by rail to Charleston. On its first trial run there, a passing ship flooded the open hatches and sent the *Hunley* to the bottom of the harbor with a loss of eight of nine crewmen. The ship was raised and repaired—only to go down again three weeks later from a similar accident. Six seamen perished in that disaster.

Again the vessel was brought to the surface. Hunley then assumed personal command for an experimental attack run. The designer intended to dive beneath the CSS *Indian Chief* and have a dummy torpedo being pulled by a line strike the *Indian Chief*'s hull. Midway through the run, the *Hunley*'s ballast tanks burst. Hunley and eight crewmen drowned. The vessel was brought to the surface several days later and its occupants interred with military honors in Charleston.

A volunteer crew under Lieutenant George E. Dixon then took the *Hunley* into action. On the night of February 17, 1864, with a torpedo attached to a bow spar, the *Hunley* moved among the Federal blockading fleet and sank the USS *Housatonic*, the world's first victim of submarine attack. However, the *Hunley* also sank in the explosion, with a loss of all hands. No trace of the vessel has ever been found.

The South's many land forts and shore batteries were no match for the heavy and mobile firepower that the U.S. Navy brought to bear against the Confederacy. While the C. S. Navy had daring officers and courageous seamen, it never had the materiel necessary to mount a force sufficiently strong to challenge its Northern counterpart. On the basis of what was accomplished in the face of almost no resources, Confederate naval undertaking must be judged as little short of miraculous.

In the end, however, the effect of the U. S. Navy was overwhelming. President Lincoln spoke for posterity when he observed during the war: "Nor must Uncle Sam's web feet be forgotten. At all of the watery margins they have been present. Not only on the deep sea, the broad bay, the rapid river, but also up the narrow, muddy bayou, and wherever the ground was a little damp, they have been and made their mark."

Two Fronts in Virginia

The standoff between the *Monitor* and *Virginia* on March 9 translated into a strategic victory for the Union. Though the two ships never fought each other again, the *Monitor's* presence prevented further attacks by the *Virginia* on the Union fleet at Hampton Roads. It also prevented Confederate interference with McClellan's Peninsula campaign. During the latter half of March a huge assemblage of 400 freighters, transports, and barges began ferrying McClellan's army of 100,000 men and their supplies, 300 cannon, and 25,000 horses, mules, and cattle from Washington to the tip of the Peninsula at Fortress Monroe. It was an impressive feat of logistics, and it forced Joseph Johnston to transfer his army of 50,000 from northern Virginia to join the 17,000 Confederate defenders on the Peninsula to resist McClellan's advance.

Lacking the power to interdict McClellan's move by water, Confederate strategists planned a diversion on land to prevent reinforcements joining McClellan from Union divisions that had advanced to Fredericksburg and up the Shenandoah Valley. Guarding the Valley for the Confederates was a small army commanded by General Thomas J. Jackson, who had earned his sobriquet of "Stonewall" at First Manassas. Jackson's real genius as a military leader, however, consisted less in standing like a stone wall on the defensive than in utilizing secrecy and mobility to make slashing surprise attacks on the offensive. He was just the man to make diversionary attacks in the Shenandoah Valley.

This enterprise turned out even better than the Confederates had hoped. For Jackson launched his campaign at a time when Lincoln discovered that McClellan had left behind fewer troops to defend Washington than he had promised. Jackson's

Fort Monroe, originally called Fortress Monroe, was some 11 miles north of Norfolk. It was built between 1819 and 1834 to command the entrance to Chesapeake Bay. (CWTI Collection)

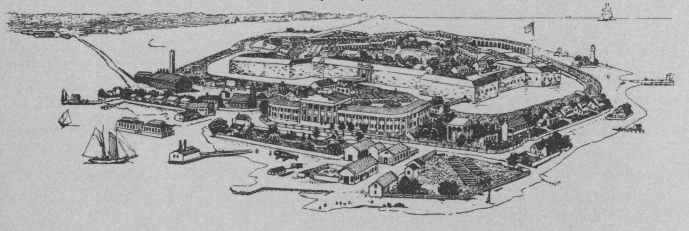

Fort Monroe.

The town of Harrisonburg, in the bucolic Shenandoah Valley—one of the two fronts in Virginia on which action now took place. Sketch by Edwin Forbes. (CWTI Collection)

bold operations with a small force in the Valley misled Union intelligence to believe that he had a large army there that could pose a danger to Washington. So Lincoln withheld reinforcements that McClellan had expected. Even though he still had a large numerical superiority over southern forces on the Peninsula, McClellan's habitual caution and his chronic tendency to overestimate enemy numbers caused him to proceed at a snail's pace. This gave the Confederates time to build up their defenses and to take the initiative. In this way Jackson's famous campaign in the Shenandoah Valley from March to June 1862 decisively affected events on the Peninsula 140 miles away.

—James M. McPherson

STONEWALL
IN THE
SHENANDOAH

by James I. Robertson, Jr.

The fertile Shenandoah Valley was an important breadbasket for the Confederacy as well as a key to military movements in the Eastern Theater. (Harper's Weekly, November 9, 1861)

One of the most famous campaigns in the annals of military history, it lasted barely three months. It began with the withdrawal of a small Confederate army of 4,600 ill-equipped soldiers; it ended with three Federal armies totaling 64,000 men in full retreat. For embattled Virginia at that time (to alter a phrase by Winston Churchill): "Never have so few done so much for so many."

A few words are necessary about the stage and the leading actor in this drama.

The Shenandoah Valley is one of the most beautifully contoured and deeply fertile regions in the world. It lies between the two easternmost ranges of the Allegheny Mountains. Its eastern boundary is the famed Blue Ridge, with the Alleghenies proper to the west. An average of 30 miles wide, the Shenandoah stretches 165 miles from Lexington northward to Harpers Ferry, where the Baltimore & Ohio Railroad—the main line of transportation between Washington and the West—crossed the Potomac, and where the Shenandoah flows into the great river. The Valley loses altitude as it stretches northward. Hence, and in contrast to general terminology, one journeys northward *down* the Valley and southward *up* the Valley.

The Shenandoah region was a veritable breadbasket, first for Virginia and then for the Confederacy. Grain of all kinds, orchards, large herds of livestock, all were in great abundance. The Upper South's very existence depended in great part on the harvests of the Shenandoah. Moreover, the Valley was of primary military importance. It was a natural avenue into both North and South. Any army in the Eastern Theater that launched an invasion had of necessity to have control of the Valley. Otherwise, it left itself dangerously vulnerable to flank attack and/or counter-invasion. In short, the Valley was the key to military movements, if not military supremacy, in the East.

By early 1862, this important area was under the command of an eccentric, ingenuous man now regarded nationally as almost a legend.

His name was Thomas Jonathan Jackson. History remembers him as "Stonewall." His men called him "Old Jack" or "Old Blue Light"; and cadets at the Virginia Military Institute (where Jackson had been a professor of military science before the war) dubbed him "Tom Fool" because of his consistently odd behavior.

Jackson was a large man, strong of build and close to six feet in height. Deep-set blue eyes stared directly ahead. His hair and beard were brown and slightly curly. A partial deafness in one ear sometimes made it difficult for him to detect distant artillery fire or to determine the direction from which it came. His uniform customarily was a single-breasted, threadbare coat that he had worn in the Mexican War, a battered kepi, which he wore with the broken visor pulled far down over his eyes, and an outsize pair of flop-top boots that covered feet estimated at size fourteen.

Correspondent George Bagby of the New Orleans *Crescent* interviewed Jackson in February 1862, and wrote that he was "a spare man, above the medium stature with dark hair and eyes, a sallow complexion, and a habit of holding his head back so that he never looks at the ground. He is as brave and cool as a human being can be; a Presbyterian who carries the doctrine of predestination to the borders of positive fatalism. . . . Silent and uncommunicative, exceedingly polite, yet short and prompt in his speech, he has but little to do with the commanders under him, but is devoted in his attention to the men. . . ."

He was a plain man who put on no airs. He was also a man of few words; and on those rare occasions when he laughed, he threw back his head, opened his mouth widely—and emitted no sound whatsoever. He lived simply, required little sleep, arose early, worked hard, and considered *duty* as the primary responsibility of a soldier.

Jackson could aptly be termed a religious fanatic. A staunch, unyielding Calvinist, he prayed regularly, attributed everything to God's will, and sometimes interrupted his soldiers at their poker by strolling through camp and passing out Sunday School pamphlets. His men came in time to believe that he was in direct communication with the Almighty. Many of his men hoped so, for Jackson took them places, and ordered them to perform deeds, that seemed beyond human accomplishment.

Even his marching pace was a test of endurance: fifty minutes of each hour at a jog, then ten minutes for rest. A one-hour lunch period was the only respite from a marching day that usually lasted seventeen hours. Most Civil War units were lucky to make eighteen miles a day. Jackson expected his men to do twenty-five or thirty miles—and then fight a battle, if

Thomas "Stonewall" Jackson, whose brilliant strategy gained him fame in the Shenandoah, where his outnumbered, fast-moving troops repeatedly defeated the Federals. (CWTI Collection)

necessary. He tolerated no excuse for soldiers breaking ranks. To him, a sick soldier and a straggler were but two of a kind. One of his officers observed that Jackson "classed all who were weak and weary, who fainted by the wayside, as men wanting in patriotism. If a man's face was as white as cotton and his pulse so low you could scarcely feel it, he looked upon him merely as an inefficient soldier and rode off impatiently."

Jackson's diet was as odd as his behavior. To ease the pain of dyspepsia, he subsisted on cornbread, milk, and butter—supplemented by lemons, dozens of lemons which he sucked feverishly. He refused to use seasoning on his food. Pepper, he claimed, made his left leg ache.

On the march, "Old Jack" was easily recognizable. A begrimed man who slumped awkwardly in the saddle, he rode a small tanglefoot named Little Sorrel. The horse's gait bore a resemblance to the rhythm of St. Vitus' Dance; and as the little beast loped down the road, Jackson's big feet were always dangerously close to the ground. The rider and his mount had little likeness to a champion on his charger, but together they would alter the course of modern warfare.

Jackson had been given command of the Valley in November 1861. In the three months that followed—quiet months broken only by Jackson's trying winter campaign against Romney, the Confederate general concentrated on the fundamentals of drill and discipline. His headquarters was Winchester, twenty-six miles southwest of Harpers Ferry. Winchester guarded all of the mountain passes in the lower Shenandoah and, hence, was the key to that entire area. Jackson's force consisted of 3,600 infantry, 600 cavalry, and 6 batteries of 27 guns. All of the men were Virginians save for a small battalion of Irish "navvies." Most of the troops were from the Valley. As such, they were familiar with the mountainous countryside and accustomed to outdoor life.

Late in February 1862 a Federal force began inching into the Valley. It numbered 38,000 men (including 2,000 cavalry and 80 guns). Like their Confederate opponents, these troops were mostly farm boys; products of the hardy life in Ohio, Indiana, Wisconsin, and western Virginia. The commander of this army, and of the newly created Department of the Shenandoah, was 56-year-old Major General Nathaniel P. Banks.

Tall, thin, and heavily mustached, Banks had risen from a laborer in a cotton mill to a political power in Massachusetts. He had served ten terms in Congress, gained national prestige as Speaker of the House of Representatives, was governor of Massachusetts, and a principal organizer of the Republican party. He owed his general's stars to the unrealistic custom in the Civil War of granting field command to men of political prominence. Banks had an air "of one used

Jackson's camp near Harrisonburg, sketched by Frank Vizetelly. Intended for the Illustrated London News, *the sketch was intercepted by a Federal blockade off Charleston. (Harper's Weekly)*

Jackson's opponent: Major General Nathaniel P. Banks, Governor of Massachusetts prior to the war and commander of the newly created Department of the Shenandoah. (National Archives)

to command"; even captured Confederates remarked that they "never saw a more faultless-looking soldier." Yet in the words of his chief biographer, Banks "had courage but was short on talent and experience." He proved to be a devoted servant who gave the military everything he had. The weakness was that, by both training and intuition, Banks had very little to give.

In the face of Banks's army, Jackson's tasks remained the same as they had been since he took command of the Valley. He had to protect the left flank of the Confederate army at Manassas, guard Virginia's breadbasket against all intrusions, and carry out these two duties with no expectation of reinforcements. (The closest body of Confederate troops was at Culpeper, sixty miles away on the other side of the formidable Blue Ridge Mountains.) If Jackson was upset over this seemingly superhuman assignment, he made no display of it. However, his determination was strongly evident in a letter he wrote at this time to a congressional friend: "If this Valley is lost," Jackson stated, "Virginia is lost."

Jackson's little army was no match for the hordes that Banks was concentrating. A Federal move on Winchester late in February left Jackson no choice but to abandon the city. On the night of March 11,

the Confederates slowly withdrew from the area and marched southward up the Shenandoah. The citizens of Winchester hardly greeted Banks's men with open arms. A New York cavalryman characterized the town as being "as rebellious and aristocratic as it was beautiful. Thoroughly loyal Union families were there, but they were like angels' visits, 'few and far between.'"

A few miles south of Winchester, Jackson halted his columns. He had no intention of relinquishing Winchester without some sort of demonstration. On the night of March 12, the Confederate general summoned a council of war composed chiefly of regimental commanders from the Stonewall Brigade. Jackson came quickly to the point: He wanted to launch a night attack on the Federal army. Banks's men were inexperienced, Jackson stated; Confederate morale was high; and the confusion of a night attack might possibly send the Federals scurrying back across the Potomac. On these premises, orders were issued. Jackson directed the wagon trains to be parked immediately south of Winchester. He then made a social call while his lieutenants attended to final details for the surprise assault.

When Jackson returned to the army a few hours later, he learned that, through some misunderstanding, the wagons had gone to Kernstown and Newtown, from three to eight miles distant, and that the Stonewall Brigade was already en route to those points to obtain rations. The men would have to march hard in the darkness for ten miles in order to strike Banks. Jackson's face blazed with anger. In calling off the proposed attack, he snarled: "That is the last council of war I will ever hold!" It was.

The Confederates then fell back to Strasburg, eighteen miles south of Winchester. When Banks dispatched another political appointee, Brigadier General James Shields and his division of 11,000 men and 27 guns toward that village, Jackson withdrew 25 miles southward to Mount Jackson. The Confederate general hoped that the Federals would continue in pursuit so that he could pull them farther from their Winchester base. Yet by then Banks had learned Jackson's true strength, and for the time being he regarded Jackson more as a nuisance than as a threat.

Several Federal officers did not share Banks's feelings. Colonel George H. Gordon, a Massachusetts soldier of proven ability, later wrote: "Much dissatisfaction was expressed by the troops that Jackson was permitted to get away from Winchester without a fight, and but little heed was paid to my assurances that this chieftain would be apt, before the war closed, to give us an entertainment up to the outmost of our aspirations."

Meanwhile, Major General George B. Mc-Clellan began moving a massive Federal army toward the Virginia peninsula for a campaign against Richmond. McClellan, who had a penchant for drawing reinforcements from all sectors, wanted another Federal army to swoop down on Richmond from the north in a simultaneous assault. He thus ordered two of Banks's three divisions to leave the Valley and proceed to Fredericksburg. Banks complied routinely with the order, at the same time directing Shields to fall back to the more secure ground around Winchester.

Brigadier General James Shields, like his commander, Banks, a political appointee. He led a division of 11,000 men and 27 guns toward Strasburg. (Battles and Leaders of the Civil War)

Shields's division contained some devoted elements, but his command had early acquired a reputation for rowdiness and mismanagement. A New York *Times* reporter described a regiment of Germans in the division as being "as lawless [a] set as ever pillaged hen roosts or robbed dairy-maids of milk and butter." An Ohio captain summarized the general inefficiency prevailing with the comment: "When a supply of nails finally arrived, they came consigned to the medical director. The difficulty with which they were rescued from his clutches would lead one to suppose that the surgeon thought them a newly invented tonic intended to promote the digestion of our country's defenders."

On a dark, sleety March 21, Shields's men abandoned Strasburg and started slowly down the Valley toward Winchester. Jackson learned of the withdrawal that evening. The news came to him from his ever-alert cavalry chief, Brigadier General Turner Ashby. One of the South's most romantic idols, Ashby was a dark-skinned, dark-haired, militarily untutored officer who hated Yankees passionately because of the murder of his younger brother in the war's first months. Ashby was a born leader: a gentle and soft-spoken man off the field, but daring and impetuous in battle. That Jackson trusted him implicitly was a high testimonial in itself. Jackson immediately realized the implications of Shields's withdrawal and resolved to stop Banks's army from uniting with McClellan. The fate of Richmond could depend on what now happened in the Valley.

Jackson had his men on the road early the next morning, March 22. Ashby's 280 troopers rode hard and struck Shields's picket line a mile south of Winchester. In the skirmish that followed, fragments from a shell fractured Shields's arm and removed him from the battle that followed. Jackson's infantry covered twenty-five miles that day and tramped an additional sixteen miles the next day—a cold, raw Sunday—before arriving at Kernstown, two miles south of Winchester, at 2 p.m.

The Confederate army defending the Valley now numbered no more than 3,000 men, for Jackson's fast pace had left 1,500 stragglers scattered along the road from Mount Jackson. Nevertheless, when Ashby reported that only four regiments of Shields's division were blocking the way, Jackson decided to attack and, by winning, to contain Shields in the Valley.

Two factors gave Jackson pause for consideration. He himself had made no reconnaissance of the Kernstown situation; and—more disquieting to Jackson—that day was the Sabbath. Jackson normally refused even to write a letter on the Lord's Day. To do battle on Sunday might be tempting the power of Satan. Yet

Left: Brigadier General Turner Ashby, Jackson's ever-alert cavalry chief and a born leader. Right: Brevet Major General Nathan Kimball, who assumed command of the Federal forces at Kernstown. (Both: Battles and Leaders of the Civil War)

every military exigency demanded prompt action. If Jackson were to continue to do the Lord's work, no time could be wasted. His brigades were quickly deployed in attack formation.

At 3 p.m. (only an hour before Jackson struck), Banks confidently went to Harpers Ferry. He was totally unaware that an attack was pending. Thus, with Banks gone and Shields hospitalized, command of the Federal forces at Kernstown fell to Colonel Nathan Kimball. Born in southern Indiana in 1822, Kimball was a physician by profession. However, he had served as a captain in the Mexican War and, prior to Kernstown, had proven his worth in the Cheat Mountain campaign. His troops referred to him affectionately as "that stout old fighter."

The late afternoon sun glistened off a countryside made spongy from constant rain. Jackson's troops could clearly see Federals in the distance, but everyone was of the opinion that only a thin rearguard of Shields's division blocked the way. The Union line extended on both sides of the Valley pike, with the heaviest concentration appearing to be east of the road. To the west of the pike was a sparsely wooded knoll called Pritchard's Hill. A Federal picket line was visible at the base, and two Union batteries stood posted on the summit.

Jackson made hasty plans to turn the apparently weak Federal right, which would then give him control of the commanding ridge overlooking the entire area. Ashby's cavalry would cover the turnpike while two Confederate infantry brigades and Carpenter's battery swung westward from the pike to assail what every Southerner was convinced was only a weak screen of troops.

At 4 p.m. the battle opened explosively. Federal

cannon began a bombardment from a mile away and received an answer from Carpenter's guns, posted along the turnpike. Some 2,000 Confederate infantrymen moved quickly under the artillery duel and, in twenty minutes, seized Pritchard's Hill. The 5th Virginia then took a supporting position in the rear. The remainder of the Stonewall Brigade, reinforced by the 21st Virginia and three battalions, drove forward along the ridge. Jackson's battle plan was working perfectly.

Suddenly and unexpectedly, from the woods to the north, came a loud, long roar of musketry. Too late Confederates realized that Shields's entire division was in battle position! The 27th Virginia was the lead element of Jackson's advance, and it reeled from a point-blank volley of Federal rifle fire. The Confederates faltered momentarily, then drove ahead and overran two Federal skirmish lines. On the far left, the 37th Virginia in Colonel Samuel Fulkerson's brigade was advancing into an open field when it saw Federal troops entering the field from woods at the opposite end. A stone fence bisected the clearing. Blue and gray troops made a simultaneous dash for this cover. The Virginians arrived first and delivered a heavy volley of musketry that shattered a Pennsylvania regiment only a few yards away. The remaining Federals retired to the cover of the trees.

The whole battle line now became a flaming stalemate. For two hours soldiers fired muskets that often became red-hot. A Massachusetts infantryman was convinced that "there was not an interval of a second between the firing of the musketry." A lieutenant in the 5th Ohio observed that "a perfect whirlwind of

The battlefield at Kernstown. Jackson, who fought against heavy odds, formed his line of battle on the near side of the stone wall. (Battles and Leaders of the Civil War)

The Union charge on the stone wall at Kernstown, based on a sketch by Alfred R. Waud. Though tactically a stunning defeat for Jackson and his Confederate forces, the question persists whether Kernstown was a strategic setback for them. (Harper's Weekly, April 12, 1862)

balls was flying, as if the air was filled with hissing snakes." Five times his regimental flag fell to the ground as one colorbearer after another was hit. A reserve unit, the 14th Indiana, rushed into action; and in the smoke, confusion, and excitement of battle, the Hoosiers fired precipitately into the rear of the 5th Ohio, inflicting several casualties. George L. Wood of the 7th Ohio commented: "The roar of musketry was now deafening. The dying and the dead were lying thick upon the hillside, but neither army seemed to waver. The confusion attending the getting of troops into action ceased. The great 'dance of death' seemed to be going forward without a motion. The only evidence of life on that gory field was the vomiting forth of flame and smoke from thousands of well-aimed muskets."

Kimball now had his entire Union division in action. Union fire maintained a destructive volume, and the Confederates began running low on ammunition. Slowly the Federal line surged forward on the Southern flanks. In the center of Jackson's line, Brigadier General Richard B. Garnett saw his Stonewall

Below: A marks the first position of Kimball's and Sullivan's brigades. Sullivan remained; Kimball moved to B and finally to the main battlefield, F, where he joined Tyler, who had been at C and then at D. Jackson had marched to F from his initial position at E. (Battles and Leaders of the Civil War)

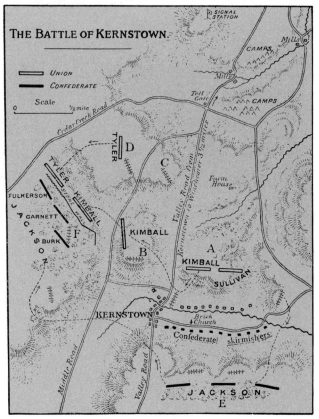

Brigade in real danger of being totally overwhelmed. No time existed to await orders. Garnett instructed his regiments to withdraw. On his left, Fulkerson's men had no choice but to follow suit in order to protect their flank. The whole Confederate line fell back, Southerners fighting and firing as they gave ground. An astonished Jackson rode up and attempted to rally the broken line. But it was no use. His army was in disorganized retreat.

The 5th and 42d Virginia made a gallant stand against hordes of oncoming Federals. The 84th Pennsylvania charged three times and withdrew only after its colonel fell dead. As night descended, the final elements of Jackson's army abandoned the field. The Confederates fell back to the wagon trains at Newtown, four miles south.

Jackson's men were exhausted after three hours of intense battle against heavy odds. One of Jackson's staff officers wrote: "In the fence corners, under the trees, and around the wagons [at Newtown] they threw themselves down, many too weary to eat, and forgot, in profound slumber, the trials, the dangers, and the disappointments of the day." A member of the 21st Virginia verified this statement by stating: "I never felt so tired and broke down in my life."

Shields's division bivouacked that night on the field it had successfully held. "All night long," one Federal soldier reported, the wounded "were brought in by the wagon load, every empty house and room in town was filled with them." Early the following day, a member of the 2d Massachusetts walked over the battlefield. "The hardest fighting," he noted, "was along a ridge which the enemy attempted to hold. Along it for nearly a mile, the bodies of our soldiers and those of the enemy were scattered thick. . . . In one little piece of thick woods, there were at least thirty of the enemy lying just as they fell; they were sheltered by a ledge of rocks, and most of them were shot through the head and had fallen directly backwards, lying flat on their backs with their arms stretched out in an easy, natural manner over their heads."

Federal losses at Kernstown were 568 men; Jackson's casualties numbered 455 men, in addition to 263 soldiers missing and presumed captured.

Jackson retired unmolested up the Valley. Banks termed the Confederate withdrawal a "flight" and commented that Jackson was now "not in condition to attack, neither to make strong resistance."

Kernstown was tactically a stunning defeat for Jackson. Yet the question persists whether Kernstown was a strategic setback. To be sure, Jackson was driven from the field and suffered the higher losses. General James Shields never let the world forget that. An Irish soldier in his fifties, Shields had served in the U.S. Senate from both Illinois and Minnesota. He was a lean, combative man who had once challenged Abraham Lincoln to a duel. He now tried hard to take all the credit for the Kernstown victory, even though he was miles from the field throughout the engagement. Nevertheless, he boasted thereafter that Jackson was afraid of him—a statement Jackson was to refute abruptly and painfully.

Many Federal soldiers openly and derisively referred to Shields as "Dirty Dick." Major George Wood of the 7th Ohio spoke for his compatriots when he wrote of Kernstown: "Colonel Kimball was mainly instrumental in achieving the victory. The skillful manner in which the troops were managed was entirely due to him; and the authorities regarded it in that light, for he was immediately made a brigadier general. . . ."

In a number of respects, however, Kernstown can be regarded as a Confederate victory in disguise. Jackson's small army had given Shields's division a rough treatment. Jackson was not boasting when he stated that "night and an indisposition of the enemy to press further terminated the battle." Moreover, Lincoln promptly stopped the transfer of Shields's division from the Valley. Banks was detached from McClellan's command and, with Williams' division, ordered back into the Valley. It was hoped that his 16,000 men, plus an additional 9,000 troops transferred from Major General John C. Frémont's forces would enable Banks to drive Jackson up the Valley.

The Union army now outnumbered Jackson by no less than 6 to 1. Although McClellan ordered Banks to "push Jackson hard," the Federal general made a casual and cautious pursuit. He established outposts at Tom's Creek, seventeen miles south of Kernstown, and was content thereafter to leave the Confederates alone. In reality, Banks fell victim to a host of imagined dangers and minor obstacles. He considered his men weary and short on supplies. The weather was not to his liking. Part of his army needed shoes. He was always in fear of an exposed flank. "Jackson and Ashby are clever men," one of Banks's officers moaned. "We are slow-w-w!"

In the meantime, Jackson was sternly reorganizing his army. Here he demonstrated how iron-willed he could be. He cashiered one of his best generals, Richard B. Garnett, for withdrawing the Stonewall Brigade prematurely from battle. Granted, the brigade was out of ammunition, badly outnumbered,

Stonewall Jackson's admirable "foot cavalry," from a drawing by Allen C. Redwood. (Battles and Leaders of the Civil War)

and in danger of being flanked on both sides. A withdrawal was but common sense. Yet in this instance common sense ran counter to duty. Anyhow, Jackson snorted, the men could have held their position by using the bayonet—an instrument that no one but Jackson admired.

This stigma on Garnett's reputation proved fatal: the following year, the young brigadier in quest of vindication threw himself into the jaws of death at Gettysburg. Yet the episode of Garnett's removal had a memorable effect on the soldiers, as well as on all other generals who served under Jackson.

In those post-Kernstown weeks, Jackson's foot soldiers slowly acquired a new faith in their commander. Perhaps grudgingly, they came to understand his careful attention to details, his devotion to Virginia, and his sense of urgency about the war. He searched the countryside for food and clothing for the soldiers, and he personally molded his tattered, beaten force into a new army with an indomitable will of its own. On April 17, Jackson optimistically wrote his wife: "Our gallant little army is increasing in numbers, and my prayer is that it may be an army of the living God as well as of its country."

It was also during this inactive period that Jackson and General Robert E. Lee worked out a plan so daring as, by its sheer audacity, to have a chance for success. What Jackson wanted to do was to pin down all Federal forces west of the Blue Ridge firmly to the Valley theater, thereby preventing any of them from concentrating with McClellan against Richmond. Then, if Jackson could keep them separated one from the other, he could assault and defeat each one individually. This would take a degree of luck; but since Jackson defined luck as "the assistance of an ever kind Providence," he was confident of the outcome.

Both Lee and Jackson were painfully aware of the odds they faced. By April, the lower end of the Shenandoah was literally swarming with Union forces. Banks's large army was solidifying near Winchester. To the west, beyond the Alleghenies, was another Federal army under Frémont. Handsome and magnetic, a general who "gave at the same time an impression of wise maturity and buoyant youth," Frémont was a champion of the abolitionists and a hero to every Republican. "The Pathfinder" had a reputation both exalted and overblown; in reality, his military activities—like himself—proved to be "showy and futile."

Jackson's trick, simple but at the same time dangerously complicated, was to keep the forces of Frémont and Banks from uniting. Jackson concluded that he could accomplish this through a combination of speed, deception and, most of all, desperate marching. Any other factors involved, Jackson was content to entrust to God's keeping.

Jackson and his chief engineer, Jedediah Hotchkiss, now made a careful study of the lower Valley. Winchester was the northern key to the Shenandoah. Moving southward up the Valley, one passed Strasburg (with Front Royal a few miles due east), then New Market, Harrisonburg, and Staunton. From Harrisonburg to the Front Royal-Strasburg area, however, there are actually *two* valleys. The reason for this is an imposing eminence, known as Massanutten Mountain, that is situated in the middle of the Valley floor. A tree-covered, uninhabited range that runs some fifty miles down the Valley, the Massanutten contains a lone pass at New Market. Otherwise, it splits the lower Valley into separate halves. Movements in one sector cannot be perceived in the other. Jackson carefully memorized these details.

In mid-April, Jackson received the only reinforcements he was to get: 8,500 infantry and 500 cavalry under Major General Richard S. Ewell. This eccentric, spry bachelor was a short man in his mid-forties—a tough old soldier who spoke awesome profanity with a sort of twittering lisp and who subsisted on a diet of cracked wheat in order to calm the pain of dyspepsia. Ewell had a sharp nose and bald head, which he frequently let droop toward one shoulder. Bulging eyes and prominent mouth added to an appearance that some people regarded as similar to that of an eagle. Others thought the likeness more akin to a buzzard. Ewell was a West Pointer who had spent too many years on the frontier. He always regarded his command—whether brigade, division, or corps—as of regimental size. Once, when his 8,000 men complained of a shortage of beef, Ewell left camp and

Major General Richard S. Ewell, who headed the only reinforcements Stonewall Jackson was to receive. (Library of Congress)

returned triumphantly with a solitary, aged bull in tow.

Jackson effected a union with Ewell's division by moving to secure Swift Run Gap, a strategic pass that would give him a link with Ewell's troops on the upper Rappahannock. On April 18, after a leisurely march of fifty miles, Jackson reached the gap. With Ewell's division and 2,800 men under Brigadier General Edward Johnson in western Virginia, Jackson's force had now swelled to 16,000 troops and forty-eight guns.

Meanwhile, morale in the Federal armies was deteriorating badly. From "Camp Misery," two miles south of New Market, a Massachusetts soldier wrote on April 21: "The regiment has been here for three days without tents, on a bare field, with no other shelter than what the men could rig up out of rails and straw. The rain has been pouring down, in torrents most of the time, making the whole surface of the ground a perfect mire. We are lying around, like pigs, in straw, with wet blankets, wet feet, wet everything, and a fair prospect of nothing for dinner. We

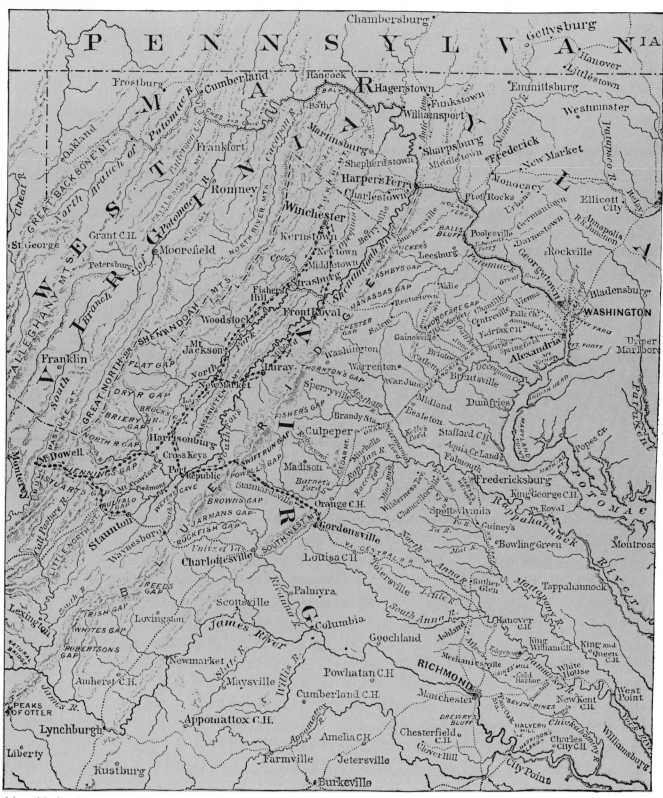

Map of Jackson's campaign in the Shenandoah Valley. The crosses and arrows indicate Jackson's troop movements from Staunton on May 6 westward to McDowell two days later; northward to Front Royal, Newton, and Winchester on May 23, 24, and 25; south to Cross Keys on June 8; and finally to nearby Port Republic on June 9. (Battles and Leaders of the Civil War)

have had some pretty tough times lately, but this knocks everything else higher than a kite!"

Major Wilder Dwight of the 2d Massachusetts stated the Union case more succinctly: "Here we are, eighty miles from our supplies, all our wagons on the road, our tents and baggage behind, our rations precarious, and following a mirage into the desert."

Jackson now went into action with a zeal that had become customary, and with tactics that always seemed incredible. Leaving Ewell's men at Conrad's Store to check Banks, Jackson on April 30 began withdrawing his own brigades southward up the Valley. The march was a nightmare: rain poured incessantly, and the mud became ankle-deep. Soon Jackson turned left, and the column headed eastward. Confederate soldiers muttered dejectedly as Banks happily reported that Jackson was abandoning the Valley and marching toward Richmond.

A few miles down the road, however, Jackson halted his men at a rail junction. Trains soon appeared; the soldiers boarded cars; and, to the surprise of the Southerners, the trains left the station moving westward. The cars rumbled through Staunton without stopping and proceeded several miles beyond. Jackson's men detrained and found themselves uniting with Johnson's command of just under 3,000 men. On May 7, this combined Confederate force marched sixteen miles westward, overran a Federal picket, and continued up the Staunton-Monterey turnpike to within two miles of the hamlet of McDowell. That village had been occupied two days earlier by 3,700 Federals under Brigadier General Robert H. Milroy. "The War Eagle," as this Indiana-born officer was known, was a proven soldier of great energy and courage. His McDowell command consisted of the 3d West Virginia, 32d and 75th Ohio, Hyman's battery and detachment of cavalry. At Jackson's approach, Milroy rapidly concentrated his forces and sent an urgent call for reinforcements to his superior, Frémont. Recent snowstorms and heavy rains would delay the arrival of Federal troops in strength.

Early on Thursday morning, May 8, Jackson put his army in motion. Johnson's brigade of six regiments took the advance; Brigadier General William Taliaferro's small brigade of three regiments followed; Colonel John A. Campbell's three regiments came next; and Brigadier General Charles S. Winder's Stonewall Brigade brought up the rear. The numerical superiority of the Southern army forced Milroy back into McDowell. Jackson's forces immediately occupied Bull Pasture Mountain, which lay to the north of the turnpike and overlooked the McDowell valley.

The Confederates wasted no time in fortifying the broken, hilly summit of Bull Pasture Mountain. From an eminence one and a half miles away, Hyman's Federal battery unleashed several salvos in a vain attempt to dislodge the Confederates from their commanding position.

Near 10 a.m., the Federal brigade of Brigadier General Robert C. Schenck arrived from Franklin after a tortuous march of thirty-four miles in twenty-three hours. Milroy then dispatched a strong skirmishing party to clear a section of Bull Pasture Mountain known as Sitlington's Hill. Yet the 52d Virginia, comprising Jackson's left, easily repulsed this Federal stab. The situation for Milroy was becoming increasingly critical. As Captain E.R. Monfort of the 75th Ohio stated, Milroy's little army "was in a position of great peril, for, should the Confederates succeed in planting a battery on Sitlington's Hill, they could, with a plunging fire, clear the valley very soon."

Hence, Milroy took the offensive. "His restless nature and love of conflict prevailing," he sent the 25th and 75th Ohio across Bull Pasture Mountain and up Sitlington's Hill in a heavy assault on Jackson's left. The attacking column was under the command of Colonel Nathaniel C. McLean of the 75th Ohio. Captain Monfort later stated: "McLean formed his men quickly for the charge, which was made up the precipitous mountain-side. Suddenly the whole mountain seemed ablaze with the flashes of rebel guns that thundered and vomited forth showers of leaden hail. The rocks, and crags, and trees seemed clothed in the wild sublimity of the glory of a natural storm, as when mountain-tops salute each other with heaven's artillery."

The 12th Georgia was in the center of the Confederate line that caught McLean's attack. When the Union ranks swept up the hillside, the Georgians displayed more valor than judgment by standing up to shoot down at their enemy rather than withdrawing behind the hill. Silhouetted against the sky, they were ideal targets for Federal soldiers. All too soon, the Georgia regiment sustained losses of 19 officers and 156 men.

The Ohioans gained the mountaintop. Completely unsupported, they nevertheless withstood Confederate assaults for four and one half hours. Meanwhile, Milroy had rushed the 32d and 82d Ohio, plus the 3d West Virginia, to turn Jackson's unengaged right flank. This assault was initially successful; but Jackson swiftly ordered in the 25th and 31st Virginia regiments to support the 44th Virginia, which had borne the brunt of the Union onslaught.

A curious battle developed in one small sector. Members of the 3d West Virginia suddenly discovered that they were fighting neighbors serving in

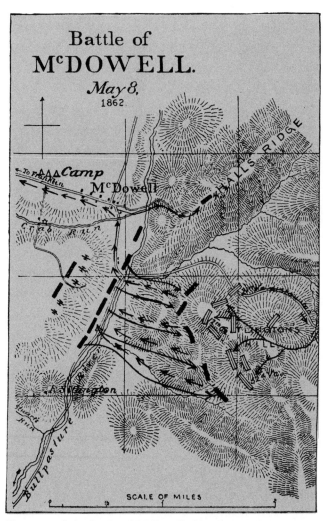

This map of the Battle of McDowell, like that of the Battle of Kernstown, was drawn by Major Jed. Hotchkiss, Jackson's topographical engineer. (Battles and Leaders of the Civil War)

the 25th Virginia. Both regiments had been formed in the same western Virginia counties. The fighting here was particularly vicious. Yet at times, when men on opposite sides recognized one another, they exchanged greetings.

With the Confederate left now stabilized, Jackson dispatched the 21st Virginia to turn the attacking column on his right. Neither side would give ground, and for several hours the battle raged without interruption. Many of the soldiers later remembered a large Newfoundland dog that was a mascot in Milroy's brigade. The animal ran back and forth along the battle line, "barking and snapping at the flying missiles, but before the fight was over he fell, pierced by a score of balls."

At 8:30 p.m., with darkness settling over the field, the Battle of McDowell ended. The Federal regiments had been repulsed at every point, and nothing was left for them to do but to retire in order from the

field. Jackson could organize no counterattack because of approaching nightfall, the confusion on the field, and the rugged terrain where the conflict had been waged. Jackson had suffered 498 casualties, while Milroy had lost but 256 men. Yet the Federal position at McDowell was now untenable. That night Milroy withdrew his forces toward the west and the mountains. Whereupon Jackson contemptuously turned his back on Frémont's menacing army, closed off the mountain passes, sent a cryptic battle report to Richmond ("God blessed our arms with victory at McDowell"), and returned to more serious business in the Valley.

The South by then was desperately in need of a victory, for those spring days of 1862 had been beset with disaster. Early in April, General Albert Sidney Johnston had lost a battle and his life at Shiloh; the vital port of New Orleans had surrendered three weeks later; McClellan had a toehold on the Virginia peninsula and was pushing westward toward Richmond with an army three times in size what General Joseph E. Johnston could bring to bear in defense. The capital city of Richmond was already preparing for evacuation.

Jackson was cognizant of these setbacks, but now, with his left flank protected after the success at McDowell, he was ready to concentrate against Banks. This Federal general had a measure of bravery born of ignorance. He was firmly convinced that the size of his army would more than compensate for any thrust that Jackson might be so foolish as to make. Indeed, Banks considered his position in the lower Valley so secure that he again made preparations for transferring Shields's division to McClellan. Such an action substantiated the belief of many of Banks's officers that he had never learned to reconnoiter well or to utilize all components of his army.

In mid-May, Shields's 11,000 men began departing the Valley. Banks was left with only 8,000 soldiers to guard the main passage northward. To protect himself, Banks fell back from New Market to Strasburg.

His men by then were unhappy and dispirited. One Federal soldier commented that every dooryard on the retreat was full of "jeering men and sneering women"; others added that secessionist-minded roosters perched on fenceposts and crowed derisively as the Union columns passed. A Federal brigadier was apprehensive that "if the amount of swearing that has been done" in the ranks of the Union army "is recorded against us in Heaven, I fear we have an account that can never be settled." Despondent Federals then plodded into Strasburg, which a Massachusetts chaplain characterized as the "dirtiest, nastiest, meanest, poorest, most shiftless town I have yet

Federal cavalry conducts reconnaissance of the Confederate position at Strasburg, prior to the town's occupation by Frémont. (Frank Leslie's Illustrated Newspaper, June 28, 1862)

seen in all the shiftless, poor, mean, nasty, dirty towns of this beautiful valley." Obviously, morale in Banks's army was sagging.

While this slow retreat was taking place, Jackson was on the move. He drove his men rapidly down the Valley. On May 20, Ewell's division joined Jackson at New Market. Jackson now found himself in a blissful situation: For the first time in his career, he had an army that could do full battle. Small wonder that the first glimpse many of Ewell's soldiers had of Jackson was a man contentedly sitting on a rail fence and sucking a lemon as he watched the gray lines pass. In the gray light of dawn, May 22, Jackson's army marched northward from New Market. Soon the column turned right and advanced toward the pass through the Massanutten. None of the soldiers knew their destination, and Jackson made no effort to erase their bewilderment. Only he knew that the army was headed into the Luray Valley—that portion of the Shenandoah east of the mountain, and an area completely screened from Federal view.

Right: "The peaked mountain from New Market," by "Porte Crayon." (Harper's New Monthly Magazine, 1867)

In Washington, Northern optimism was at its height. The national Capital was regarded as so secure that recruiting offices had been closed. President Lincoln and Secretary of War Edwin Stanton were preparing to leave for Fredericksburg in anticipation of the imminent fall of Richmond.

Had Banks been more sharply alert to topography and reconnaissance, he might have avoided disaster. He was correct in regarding his position at Strasburg

as "dangerously exposed." Yet he took no action to have a clear road for possible retreat; he retained his supplies, and his sick and wounded, with him rather than release these burdens to the safety of Winchester; and he gave little or no heed to possible dangers from the Luray Valley.

Thus, when Jackson's 16,000 troops entered the Luray, they stood squarely between Banks and eastern Virginia. The Massanutten Mountain would effectively hide any movements they made. More dangerously, Jackson now had an almost unobstructed route to Front Royal, the flank of the Federal army. Once Front Royal was seized, the Confederates would then have a straight shot at Winchester, Banks's major supply base. When Jackson's men realized the opportunities that lay ahead, not even persistent rain and occasional hail could deter their march northward.

Jackson, unlike Banks, knew that the Luray Valley's key city of Front Royal was completely indefensible. High ground looked down on it from almost every side. In addition, the small Federal garrison stationed there consisted principally of Colonel John R. Kenly's 1st Maryland (U.S.) Infantry. Jackson's plan was to seize Front Royal with such speed as to gobble up Kenly's men and prevent any warning from reaching Banks.

Friday, May 23, was clear and intensely hot. Late in the morning, Kenly's Marylanders were seeking cool relief from the sun's rays when suddenly from the forests emerged long gray lines of men and a deadly explosion of musketry. George W. Clarke, an army correspondent of the New York *Herald*, was staying in the Front Royal home of the aunt of the famous Confederate spy, Belle Boyd. When gunfire erupted, Clarke bounded down the stairs and shouted: "Great Heavens! What is the matter?"

"Nothing to speak of," Miss Boyd replied coolly. "Only the rebels are coming, and you had best prepare yourself for a visit to Libby Prison."

Clarke was en route to prison that night.

Kenly tried desperately to put up a fight against the hordes of Confederate soldiers swarming against his lines. Soon word reached him that Southern cavalry were galloping around his right flank. Kenly ordered his men—many of whom were grappling fiercely with their Southern counterpart, the 1st Maryland (C.S.) Infantry—to fall back. The Federals made a short stand at Guard Hill, an eminence north of Front Royal; but again Confederate numbers drove them from their positions. Kenly's troops then retired to the hamlet of Cedarville, three miles farther. They had barely formed a line when Jackson's "foot cavalry" seemingly struck from every direction.

A view of Strasburg during its occupation by Federal troops under Banks. Fort Mountain is on the left.
Sketch by Edwin Forbes. (Frank Leslie's Illustrated Newspaper, April 26, 1862)

The small Federal force disintegrated. When Kenly fell, desperately wounded, most of his men laid down their arms. Barely an hour after Jackson had struck, the fight for Front Royal was done. Jackson had inflicted 904 casualties (including 600 prisoners), and had captured a wagon train—all at a cost of fewer than 50 men. Moreover, he was now in a clear position to isolate Banks from the Federal supply base at Winchester.

A courier carried news of the Front Royal disaster to Banks at Strasburg. "By God, sir," Banks shouted, "I will not retreat!" He was initially inclined to dismiss the Front Royal incident as a Confederate raid. At the same time, the adverse effect on his political standing in the North if he did retreat created in Banks an obstinate expediency. "We have more to fear from the opinion of our friends," he remarked to a fellow officer, "than from the bayonets of our enemies."

Through the night of May 23–24, Banks refused to consider withdrawal. Not until 3 a.m. did the despondent general finally agree to dispatch his sick and wounded to Winchester. Only at midmorning of the 24th did the division begin the march to Winchester. By then, Jackson's troops were closing fast from the east. An air of panic filled the Federal ranks. One writer observed: "A few soldiers had lost all sense of discipline. Steadier troops were hampered by the tangle of bewildered fugitives and by the crush of military wagons. Ambulances packed with the disabled were blocked by the smashed remains of vehicles that had collided in the mad excitement. Frightened horses were stampeding, army teamsters had deserted their stations. The baggage train stood still, and it looked as though Banks's army would crack up before it met the enemy."

A wild race for Winchester now ensued, with Banks hurrying down the macadamized Valley Turnpike from the south and Jackson lunging through the mud from the southeast. Despite his inward despair, Banks presented an outward appearance of calm and confidence. One Federal trooper stated: "General Banks (God bless him!) was here, there, everywhere, urging the men on, and determined to fight the cruel foe until the last."

The Federal army enters Front Royal. The Manassas Gap Railroad and Blue Ridge Mountains are in the distance. Sketch by Edwin Forbes. (Frank Leslie's Illustrated Newspaper, *July 5, 1862)*

Midway through the afternoon of May 24, Jackson's foot cavalry struck the Valley pike and collided with the rear third of Banks's retreating columns. A Confederate soldier observed: "The rout of Banks surpassed in many respects anything of the kind I saw during the war. It beggared description. Pell-mell, helter-skelter, without check, without any effort to rally or form, the retreating mass of men, horses, artillery and wagons rushed down the Valley Turnpike, everything going at breakneck speed. . . ." Discarded Federal wagons and equipment littered the road for a full six miles, as Banks literally raced for his life.

Banks momentarily escaped from the panic gripping his army and began to display a real talent for retreat. He bought precious time by discarding wagons and supplies that he knew would prove a tempting distraction to Jackson's hungry soldiers. The ploy worked. To Jackson's chagrin, Ashby's cavalry stopped their forceful pursuit of Banks's columns in order to plunder. Moreover, Colonel George H. Gordon, in charge of Banks's rearguard, used ambuscades and other devices to blunt Jackson's advance. Such tactics

enabled most of the Federal army to reach Winchester ahead of Jackson's forces.

Banks considered Winchester "the key to the valley, and for us the position of safety." He was confident that Jackson would not dare attack him there. Comforted by this rationale, Banks sent a reassuring telegram to Washington and then went to his rooms for a leisurely bath. Yet the bluecoats desperately strengthening the earthworks south of town did not share their general's optimism. The sound of small arms fire continued to come closer as the nighttime hours passed. By midnight, even Banks realized that Jackson was not stopping the pursuit. Banks thereupon ordered his military train to start toward the Potomac. The wagons were still moving slowly through the city streets when dawn came—and with it Jackson's onslaught.

The indefatigable Confederate general subjected his men to a test of endurance that night of May 24–25. Most of the Southern troops had marched at least eighteen miles on the 24th; many of them were actively engaged in heavy skirmishes with Federals; and none of the Confederates had eaten since dawn. They were, in short, jaded by nightfall. But Jackson sensed a smashing victory; and at such a time, personal feelings were of little importance. On through the night he pushed his men. The few rest periods were of the briefest duration. In the end, Jackson achieved his objective: Sunlight of the 25th found the Confederate army massed in battle array on the southern outskirts of Winchester.

Losses at Front Royal and on the retreat had reduced Banks's force to no more than 6,500 men. Jackson was bringing to bear against him more than twice that number. Jackson's battle plan was simple: Ewell would assail the Federal left; and, while a portion of Jackson's command held the Federal center in check, the remaining Confederate regiments would turn the Federal right and dash for Winchester.

A mist hung over the rolling hills when, at 5 a.m., the Confederates struck. Jackson's skirmishers brushed aside the Federal pickets and made contact with Banks's weak lines. Skirmishing gave way to an artillery duel, and soon intense musketry drowned out the noise of cannon. Federals manning the left met Ewell's initial advance with "murderous" volleys that ripped one Confederate regiment to shreds and left Ewell's forces (according to one Union soldier) "fumbling in the fog." On the Federal right, however, Jackson's men pushed forward in such heavy numbers that Banks's men were hard-pressed to maintain their position.

For three hours the Federals managed to hold fast. Then Jackson dispatched eleven regiments to turn the enemy's flank. This turning movement broke Banks's right into fragments, and it came just at the moment when Ewell's determined soldiers curled around the Federal left. Banks, on the field, now saw that he had been flanked for half a mile on either side. His order to retreat was not heard, for the remaining elements of his army had already broken from the lines. Across the way, Jackson was riding among his own soldiers and shouting: "Order forward the whole line! The battle is won!"

When the entire Confederate line surged forward in triumph, Banks watched horrified as his army disintegrated. Outflanked, beaten, and bewildered, the Federals lost all semblance of order. Blueclad soldiers streamed into Winchester "like a muddy torrent with the sunlight glittering on its turbid waves." Once in town, all remaining discipline vanished, for dozens of local residents began taking shots at soldiers in the crowded streets. A member of the 10th Maine, which was guarding the downtown, observed: "Nothing that day was more trying than standing there in the streets of Winchester, with that panic-stricken mob rushing past our front, from left to right, every one telling a different tale, but all saying, 'They're coming!'—'Right on you!'—'Hurry up or you'll be lost!' . . ."

Banks himself tried desperately to halt the tide. He encountered the 3d Wisconsin in headlong flight. "Stop, men!" he shouted. "Don't you love your country?"

One soldier looked back over his shoulder and replied: "Yes, by God, and I'm trying to get back to it just as fast as I can!"

Hundreds of Federal soldiers discarded their weapons in the frantic dash northward. Fear-crazed troops commandeered horses, wagons, carriages—even cattle—to speed the trip to safety. Every effort by Banks to reorganize and restore order failed. Sheer exhaustion brought a brief halt at Martinsburg; at sundown the retreat resumed and did not stop again until the army reached Williamsport, Maryland. Federal soldiers had raced thirty-five miles in fourteen hours. "All of us," a New England soldier confessed, "had our feet blistered, some having more blisters than natural skin, but to describe the thousand aches and cramps we felt cannot be done." Yet even Banks admitted that "there were never more grateful hearts . . . than when at midday on the 26th we stood on the opposite shore [of the Potomac]."

Jackson was disappointed that the bulk of the Federal army escaped his clutches. Only the tardiness of the Confederate cavalry in going into action north of Winchester, he felt, saved Banks from total disaster. Yet the harvests of victory were enormous. In three days of fighting, Banks lost 3,030 of 8,500 men. Jackson's casualties were fewer than 400. The Confederates had bagged 9,300 new muskets, two cannon, and veritable storehouses of medical supplies and military equipment. The Southern soldiers had handled Banks with such ease, and were consuming his supplies with such regularity, that he became known as "Old Jack's Commissary General." Of greater import, Jackson's thrust had cancelled Federal Major General Irvin McDowell's intended advance from Fredericksburg to Richmond. And, for the moment, the Valley was clear of Federal forces.

Authorities in Washington were abruptly awakened to the awesome realization that the Shenandoah Valley was like a loaded musket aimed at the heart of the North—with Stonewall Jackson fingering the trigger. The Washington *Star* snorted editorially that Jackson was "popping around" in the Valley "like a quill of quicksilver in a hot shovel." Such popping had created terror in the national Capital and waves of panic throughout the North.

Lincoln thereupon interceded and made hasty but concrete plans to destroy Jackson once and for all. This would have the added dividend of giving the North control of the Shenandoah. Lincoln's strategy called for a giant pincer movement. A reinforced Banks would push southward straight up the Valley; Frémont would close in from the west; Shields would retrace his steps and come in from the east. Together, these three Federal armies (totalling 64,000 men) would trap Jackson somewhere between Winchester and Strasburg. Then, with Banks, they would strike Jackson from three directions—with each Federal army at least as large as Jackson's force of 16,000 men.

It was a daring and desperate counterattack, and it came within a hair of succeeding. Jackson, comfortably quartered at Winchester, and with the Stonewall Brigade in the van thirty-six miles farther north at Harpers Ferry, did not realize what was taking place until almost the last moment. Then, on the night of May 30, Jackson ordered his scattered command to fall back toward Strasburg. The retreat began on the morning of the 31st. Federal prisoners, escorted by the 21st Virginia, led the way. Jackson's infantry and wagon trains followed. The Confederate column, a full seven miles long, moved slowly southward.

Meanwhile, Frémont was closing fast on Strasburg; and Shields, by occupying Front Royal, locked the door to the Luray Valley. A few more hours, and the single remaining escape route for Jackson would be blocked.

Thereafter, for the North, occurred a series of er-

Frémont's vanguard arrives above Strasburg on June 1 to intercept Jackson, who was moving south in the Valley. Here, Frémont's advance party sights the tail end of Jackson's train which, escorted by troops in the background, is about to clear Strasburg. The incident illustrates how closely Jackson calculated his time-and-place factors. Sketch by Edwin Forbes. (Battles and Leaders of the Civil War)

rors. Banks was still so battle-scarred that his "forceful advance" up the Valley did not begin in earnest until June 10—the day after the campaign ended. No communication existed between Frémont and Shields, for Jackson held the country between those two Federal armies. Yet this point was probably academic. With the destruction of Jackson within their grasp, Shields and Frémont both failed to exercise the speed and determination necessary for success.

Shields tardily left Front Royal and led his men westward to the cutoff point at Strasburg. An Ohio officer summarized caustically what then happened: "It was late in the afternoon before Shields got ready to move, and then owing to some blunder never clearly explained, he took the road to Winchester." By the time the mistake was discovered, it was nightfall. Shields lost fully half a day as his men angrily retraced their steps.

Frémont's conduct is even more inexplicable, if not inexcusable. To Frémont, Lincoln sent a number of telegrams emphasizing the need for prompt movement. "Put the utmost speed into it," the President wired. "Do not lose a minute." Yet Frémont mysteriously chose to take a different route into the Valley from the one that Lincoln had ordered. As a result, it took Frémont's army eight days to cover seventy miles—at a time when Jackson's "foot cavalry" were marching fifty miles in two days. Nevertheless, Frémont's men reached the top of the Allegheny Mountains in ample time to deliver a smashing blow. Clearly visible below to Frémont was Jackson's army, strung out along the Valley floor, with flanks unprotected and burdened by seemingly endless wagon trains.

The Federal opportunity to wreak destruction, however, came to naught. Instead of attacking, Frémont began constructing defenses on the mountains six miles west of Strasburg. After a painful delay, he dispatched a timid probe into the Valley. Jackson countered by sending Ewell's division westward in full battle array. Ewell's advance so paralyzed Frémont that a Confederate officer stated contemptuously: "Sheep would have made as much resistance as we met."

Jackson then spent several hours waiting for the Stonewall Brigade and his cavalry to rejoin the army. The men in Jackson's brigade never forgot the living hell of that dash for survival. They had been at Harpers Ferry when the orders came to fall back rapidly. In thirty-six hours, through driving rain and bottomless mud, and with neither food nor rest, those men trudged forty-five miles. On reaching the safety of Jackson's army, many of the infantrymen collapsed in the road where they stood and fell asleep

Major General John C. Frémont, whose troops displayed unexpected alacrity in early June. (Library of Congress)

half-buried in the mire. Fatigue was so all-engulfing that few of the men knew where they were.

Their general was never content merely to be safe. Jackson's army was intact, but his beloved Valley was still in the grip of heavy Federal pressure—and his primary responsibility remained the security of that region. Early in June, the hunted became the hunter.

By then, rains had turned the countryside into mud. A series of cavalry engagements marked those first days of June as Ashby's troopers contested first Shields and then Frémont. The Confederate cavalrymen also burned all bridges between the two Federal hosts so as to keep them from uniting. Jackson's plan was to allow Frémont and Shields to converge upon him, and then to strike each before the two could merge into a superior force.

Frémont's army in those first days of June displayed an alacrity that its commander had never before shown. His cavalry galloped rapidly up the Valley and began closing on the Confederates. On the afternoon of June 6, Ashby's horsemen repulsed a force of 800 Federal cavalry some three miles from Harrisonburg. Frémont quickly dispatched heavy reinforcements. In the fierce fighting that ensued, the Confederates began to give ground. Ashby then rode up and called on his men to charge. Suddenly his horse collapsed from a fatal bullet wound. Ashby leaped to his feet and shouted: "Charge, men! For God's sake, charge!" The gray ranks swept out into the open and sent the Federals into general retreat. Yet on the field lay Ashby, "the idol of his troopers," dead from a musket ball through the head.

Several weeks earlier, a New England officer had written of Ashby: "He is light, active, skillful, and we

Frémont's division marching through the woods, en route to battle. (Frank Leslie's Illustrated Newspaper, July 5, 1862)

Depiction by W. L. Sheppard of the charge of the 1st Maryland Regiment at the death of Turner Ashby near Harrisonburg on June 6. Ashby, "the idol of his troopers," was also highly esteemed by Jackson, who viewed his loss as a personal tragedy. (Library of Congress)

are tormented by him like a bull with a gad-fly." A New York cavalryman echoed these sentiments by observing: "His exploits had been so daring, quick, and so generally successful, that he had made himself a great name, and become a terror to our forces."

For Jackson, Ashby's loss was a personal tragedy. Jackson viewed the remains in a room at Port Republic and stated: "Poor Ashby is dead. He fell gloriously—one of the noblest men and soldiers in the Confederate army."

By now, Shields was bursting with confidence. Referring to Jackson's army as "a broken, retreating enemy," he urged Frémont on June 7 to push hard against "the demoralised rebels." Shields was convinced that if Frémont would launch an attack, Shields's own forces could then come "thundering down on Jackson's rear."

What Shields incredibly overlooked was that muddy roads, swollen streams, and the strangeness of the terrain had converted his army into a disconnected series of brigades scattered almost the length of the Luray Valley.

Jackson was well aware of that fact. His army waited quietly at the point where the two main roads of the Federal advances converged. His main body was at Port Republic, with Ewell's division four miles northwest at Cross Keys. Jackson was not immediately concerned about Shields, since his division was strung out twenty-five miles down the Luray Valley. Frémont's army was closer and more concentrated. Jackson's main attention, therefore, was given to it.

On Sunday, June 8, Frémont's army moved out of Harrisonburg. Federal skirmishers and Ewell's pickets became engaged at 8:30 a.m. Ewell had at hand about

Above: Mount Jackson, where Frémont made his headquarters on his advance to Harrisonburg, a "handsomely built" village with "several common schools, several taverns, and...blest with one weekly newspaper." (Frank Leslie's Illustrated Newspaper, July 5, 1862)

6,000 infantry and 500 cavalry; Frémont's army numbered 10,000 infantry, 2,000 cavalry, and twelve batteries of artillery. The Federal superiority in numbers could have been used to decisive advantage. Yet, as one historian has stated, "Frémont was more afraid of losing the battle than anxious to win it." He therefore "sought refuge in half-measures, the most damaging course of all."

Of twenty-four regiments at his disposal, Frémont gingerly dispatched five into action. This was the German brigade of Brigadier General Louis Blenker, which attacked the Confederate right. The Federals got to within sixty yards of Ewell's position when a concentrated volley of musketry rolled down the Southern lines. The German regiments broke and fell back in disorder. For a short while the field was quiet. Brigadier General Isaac Trimble, commanding the right of Ewell's line, then received permission to make a counterattack against Frémont's left. This onslaught caught the Federals by surprise. Frémont's left crumpled back a mile from its original position.

Trimble's attack came just as Frémont was probing

Right: Some of the officers of Brigadier General Louis Blenker's division. Blenker is right center, his hand resting on his belt. At Blenker's left is Prince Felix Salm-Salm, a Prussian military officer. At Blenker's right is then-Brigadier General Julius Stahel. (National Archives)

Above: The Battle of Cross Keys on June 8, viewed from the Union position, looking east. Sketch by Edwin Forbes. (Battles and Leaders of the Civil War)

other sectors of the Confederate works. A line of bluecoated skirmishers tested the Confederate center and found it too strong to break. On the Federal right, Milroy and Schenck advanced on their own, drove in the Confederate skirmishers, and were making satisfactory progress when Frémont ordered them

Below: A map of the Battle of Cross Keys, drawn by Major Jed. Hotchkiss. (Battles and Leaders of the Civil War)

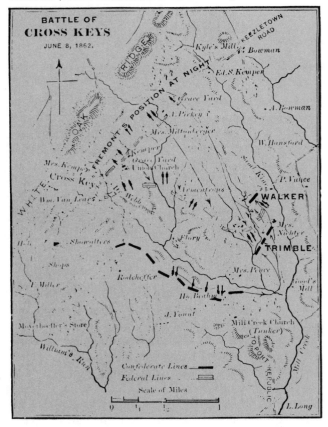

back to protect his shattered left. Under Frémont's prodding, his troops frantically constructed earthworks; and from their strong positions, they warily watched the Confederates for the remainder of the day.

The battle of Cross Keys was a relatively minor affair. Frémont's casualties were 684 men, as compared to 288 Confederate losses. The 8th New York in Blenker's brigade was "almost annihilated."

An Ohio officer aptly described Jackson's subsequent strategy: "Jackson's plan for the next day [June 9] was to leave a brigade to amuse Frémont, for whose enterprise and military talents he seems to have entertained a profound and not ill-founded contempt; to throw the remainder of his troops across the river and polish us [Shields's division] off in short order; then to return and put a quietus on Frémont."

At 5 a.m. on Monday, the Stonewall Brigade opened the battle of Port Republic by advancing across an open expanse against a strong Federal position. Shields again was absent from the field. He remained at Conrad's Store throughout the day. Command of the Federal forces fell to Brigadier General Erastus B. Tyler, who had at his disposal two brigades of 4,000 men plus sixteen guns. The remainder of Shields's division was strung out far to the rear. However, most of the regiments under Tyler's command had been at Kernstown and had witnessed the rare spectacle of Jackson being defeated. Small wonder that the Federals had a measure of confidence as they prepared to meet Jackson's attacks.

Winder's Stonewall Brigade struck hard at the Federal right but soon was forced back by intense fire from Tyler's lines. As the Valley brigade launched another assault, Brigadier General Richard Taylor's Louisianians swept around the Federal left and, after severe fighting, seized a key Federal battery near an abandoned coaling station. The Federals were now hard pressed, but they maintained their position with grim determination and continued to inflict casualties on Jackson's army. Near 10 a.m., the lead elements of Ewell's forces reached the field. The 44th and 58th Virginia reinforced the Stonewall and Louisiana brigades in a third assault that shattered Tyler's lines. Defeated Federals streamed down the Luray Valley in unbroken columns. Jackson's men gave pursuit for nine miles before falling back to Port Republic.

This battle was the most costly engagement of the Valley Campaign. Jackson lost over 800 of 5,900 engaged, while Tyler's casualties constituted one fourth of his command. The fighting at Port Republic was

Hospital.   Cavalry in Position.

*The Battle of Port Republic, sketched by Edwin Forbes. Frémont and his staff appear at bottom right. The
battle opened at 5 a.m. on June 9, when the Stonewall Brigade advanced against a strong Federal position.*
(Frank Leslie's Illustrated Newspaper, *July 5, 1862*)

second to none in the Shenandoah. The outcome
might have been different had Frémont advanced on
Jackson's left flank. Yet Frémont steered clear of making further contact with the Southern army, and his
apathy proved costly. By nightfall of June 9, both
Frémont and Shields were in retreat. Banks was warily approaching Winchester, with no intention of ven-
turing farther. The great Valley Campaign was over.

On June 12, a New York cavalryman wrote home
from the Valley: "It cannot be denied that this Jackson is a man of decided genius, and that very few in
our army are fit to compete with him."

Indeed, in the Valley Campaign lies a model example of how to get the most from the least. A quiet
gentleman from Lexington—an unpretentious officer
who persistently sucked lemons and spoke little—had
saved Richmond and preserved his beloved Valley
through a series of some of the most extraordinary
movements in military annals. Jackson's feats
changed the thinking of many people, just as they
altered the course of the Civil War.

General Richard Ewell spoke for many Confederates when he made a confession to one of his officers.
At the beginning of the campaign, he stated, he
thought Jackson insane. "I never saw one of Jackson's
couriers approach without expecting an order to assault the North Pole." Now, Ewell admitted, "I take it
all back and will never pre-judge another man. Old
Jackson is no fool. He knows how to keep his own
counsel, and does curious things, but he has a
method in his madness."

Ewell also remembered being censured by Jackson
for ordering his men at Cross Keys not to kill a
Federal officer who valiantly rode a white horse in
the front of his attacking column. Jackson was not
impressed by such heroism. "This is no ordinary
war," he told Ewell. "The brave and gallant Federal
officers are the very kind that must be killed. Shoot
the brave officers and the cowards will run away and
take the men with them."

On the day after Port Republic, Jackson wrote his
wife Anna and summarized the campaign of recent
weeks with a succinct statement: "God has been our

Gen. Fremont and Staff

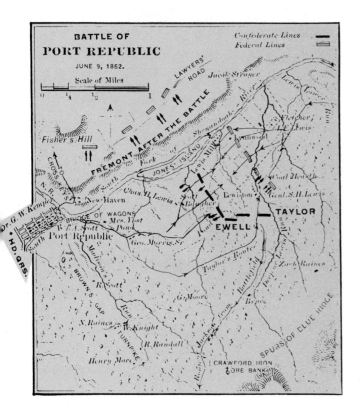

shield, and to His name be all the glory." Yet, when pressed for an explanation of the Valley Campaign—in other words, Jackson's means toward God's ends—"Old Jack" stated that only two rules needed to be followed for victory in the field.

First, he stated, "always mystify, mislead, and surprise the enemy, if possible. And when you strike and overcome him, never let up in the pursuit so long as your men have strength to follow; for an army routed, if hotly pursued, becomes panic-stricken, and can then be destroyed by half their number. The other rule is, never fight against heavy odds if by any possible maneuvering you can hurl your own force at only a part, and that the weakest part, of your enemy and crush it. Such tactics will win every time, and a small army may thus destroy a large one in detail, and repeated victory will make it invincible."

Jackson transformed such strategy into the tactics of the 1862 Valley Campaign, and the results were astounding. With never more than 16,000 men, he

Left: Map of the Battle of Port Republic by Major Jed. Hotchkiss. By nightfall, the Federals were in retreat; the Valley Campaign was over. (Battles and Leaders of the Civil War)

completely frustrated the designs of 64,000 Federals whose generals were assigned the simple, solitary task of accomplishing his destruction. Jackson fought four pitched battles, six large skirmishes, and countless minor actions. With the exception of Kernstown, where even his defeat had highly important offsetting results, Jackson accomplished his main tactical purpose in every movement he made. Moreover, when one considers that what Banks, Frémont, McDowell, and McClellan did was directly related for a time to Jackson's movements, British historian G.F.R. Henderson was not exaggerating when he observed that Jackson's 16,000 "absolutely paralyzed" 175,000 Federals.

In all but two of the Valley engagements (Kernstown and Cross Keys), Jackson confronted his opponents with superior strength ranging from 2 to 1 to 17 to 1 odds—despite the fact that in total numbers his army was outnumbered by 4 to 1. That Jackson continually concentrated in battle more manpower than his adversaries, when superior numbers of Federals were always just beyond the horizon, is sheer genius to be envied.

Much of this genius, if not most of it, was based on hard marching. In forty-eight marching days, Jackson's foot cavalry tramped 676 miles. In the end, the rewards were enormous: 3,500 Federal casualties, another 3,500 captured, 10,000 muskets seized, 9 cannon acquired, plus valuable railroad rolling stock, medical supplies, and quartermaster stores too voluminous to inventory. All of this Jackson achieved at a cost of no more than 2,500 casualties.

In addition, Jackson so alarmed Washington as to prevent 38,000 Federal soldiers from joining McClellan and effecting the capture of Richmond. Instead, three Union armies had been isolated in the Valley, where they gained nothing and lost much. The "Rebel Napoleon," wrote a New York *Tribune* reporter, had succeeded in monopolizing, "for the amusement of the world, the attention of six distinguished [Federal] generals."

But even beyond this were deeper, more intangible achievements. The Valley Campaign gave the South its first lasting hero, and "Stonewall" Jackson became a legend in his own time. Moreover, the effect of the Valley Campaign on morale, North and South, was tremendous. Federals and Confederates were about equally exhausted when the fighting ended; yet from this campaign came traditions of victory and defeat. Banks, Frémont, and Shields had their commands so shattered as to lose the last vestige of esteem any of the three enjoyed. Conversely, "repeated victory" (a

term Jackson used) began to instill in the Confederate soldiers a feeling of invincibility. Because this campaign came after a long interlude of retreat and discouragement, its success gave a fierceness to the Confederate soldiers' pride both in their general and in themselves.

To be sure, Jackson drove them mercilessly; and he had nothing but contempt for the man who fell ill or straggled. When his "foot cavalry" reached the field of battle with mouths dry and bones aching from fatigue, Jackson flung them into combat and disregarded losses until the battle ended. Jackson then gave all credit for victory to God. The only thing that the men received was the knowledge of victory. Yet that was enough. Jackson's success sustained a losing cause, inspired a people, and created a heritage.

The Valley Campaign gave the Confederacy its first lasting hero: Thomas "Stonewall" Jackson became a legend in his own time. (Battles and Leaders of the Civil War)

From the Valley to the Peninsula

By the time Jackson's Valley campaign came to an end after the battle of Port Republic, Robert E. Lee was commander of the forces defending Richmond. Jefferson Davis had transferred Lee from his desk job to field command after Joseph Johnston was wounded May 31 at the inconclusive battle of Seven Pines, a half-dozen miles from the Confederate capital. Lee's reputation had been tarnished by the failure of his western Virginia campaign the previous autumn. But Davis believed in Lee; the sequel proved him right.

Lee planned a counterattack on the Union forces closing in for a siege of Richmond. He ordered Jackson to bring his troops from the Valley in utmost secrecy to fall on McClellan's right flank. This launched the Seven Days battles—the climax and defeat of McClellan's three-months' campaign against Richmond. Together, Jackson and Lee led a remarkable revival of Confederate military fortunes, which had looked so dark in May after the uninterrupted string of Union victories that had started with the capture of Fort Henry. By midsummer 1862, the Northern forces were reeling back in defeat and discouragement.

—James M. McPherson

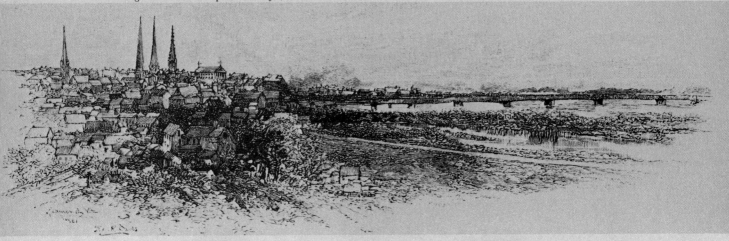

Richmond, Virginia, which Lee would defend in the bloody battles at Seven Pines and Seven Days. Richmond, chartered as a city in 1782, became the Confederate capital in July 1861. During the war, five Union generals tried to capture the city. (CWTI Collection)

Bayonet charge of the New York Excelsior Brigade, Colonel Hall commanding, at the battle of Seven Pines (or Fair Oaks, as the North called it) on June 1, 1862. The two-day battle, only a half-dozen miles from Richmond, ended indecisively, with both sides claiming victory. Drawing by Alfred R. Waud for the August 16, 1862 issue of Harper's Weekly. (Library of Congress)

THE PENINSULA CAMPAIGN

The Invasion of the Peninsula by Emory Thomas
Desperate Defense of Richmond by Emory Thomas
A New Confederate Commander by Emory Thomas
The Defenders Take the Offensive by Emory Thomas
Victory and Defeat at Malvern Hill by Emory Thomas

The Invasion of the Peninsula
by Emory Thomas

In 1624 Captain John Smith wrote of the Virginia Tidewater, "The mildnesse of the ayre, the fertilite of the soyle, and the situation of the rivers are so propitious to the nature and use of man, as no place is more convenient for pleasure, profit, and man's sustenance. . . ."

In May 1862 Confederate Major General D.H. Hill recorded rather different sentiments about the region that would come to be known as the Peninsula. "Our Revolutionary sires," he wrote, "did not suffer more at Valley Forge than did our army at Yorktown, and in the retreat from it. . . . the rain, mud, cold, hunger, watching, and fatigue."

Confederate troops during the months of March and April occupied a thin line of field fortifications which stretched across the Virginia Peninsula from Yorktown on the York River to the Warwick River, a short tributary of the James. On the other side of this line, at the tip end of the Peninsula, the Army of the Potomac gathered itself for what it hoped would be a

McClellan (on the rearing horse) arrives on the bank of the James at start of the Peninsula Campaign. Drawing by Larkin Goldsmith Mead.

decisive assault upon the Rebel line. The Federals planned to overrun the Confederates, press on to Richmond, and win the Civil War within a few weeks. Then during the evening of May 3, almost on the eve of the Union attack, the Confederates withdrew up the Peninsula under cover of darkness. At this point the Peninsula ceased to be scenery en route to Richmond and became instead a battleground, the site of a campaign.

It rained on the evening of May 3, just as it had rained for the better part of twenty of the thirty days preceding. Soldiers on both sides who had crouched in trenches knee-deep in water, slept in mud, and eaten in ooze, now had to try to move themselves and their equipment over the sodden countryside.

"The whole soil of that section," recalled a Southern artillerist, "seemed to have no bottom and no supporting power. The roads were but long strings of guns, wagons, and ambulances, mixed in with infantry, artillery, and cavalry, splashing and bogging through the darkness in a river of mud." The Confederates averaged

Harper's Weekly, August 2, 1862

McClellan, "the Young Napoleon," strikes a Napoleonic pose in his major-general's uniform.

less than a mile per hour. And even at such a snail's pace, they outdistanced their pursuers. The Union quartermaster stated flatly that he had "never seen worse roads in any part of the country."

Responsible for choosing this bottomless sponge as a theater of war was Union Major General George Brinton McClellan. His decision to assault Richmond from the east up the Peninsula had plunged these two armies, perhaps 170,000 men altogether, into that morass. In the beginning, when the campaign existed only on paper in Washington, the Peninsula route to Richmond and victory appeared quite promising.

McClellan arrived in Washington in July 1861 following the Union debacle at Bull Run. He had won

battles in the Kanawha Valley in western Virginia, and his small victories so contrasted with the gloom of the North's larger failure, that the press and politicians hailed McClellan as savior of the Union. At age 35 the "Young Napoleon" had had no experience as a national hero; yet rather quickly he began to enjoy the role and more important, he began to believe his flatterers and to feel messianic.

He collected, organized, and trained a wonderful army, displayed himself on horseback to those who admired, and dared even to snub Abraham Lincoln when he was weary from these duties. Once Lincoln came to call upon the general to try to find out what he intended to do with his army and when he intended to do it. McClellan was out, and the President chose to await his return. But when McClellan arrived, he went straight to bed and left his commander in chief sitting in the parlor.

Lincoln was only one of many who wanted to know McClellan's plans and wanted to get the war over soon. The general knew it was not that simple, and he wanted those who did not understand war's complexity to let him alone. By the late fall of 1861 he realized that he would have to wait until spring to move, and so he had to stall and avoid aggressive action all winter. The obvious, simple way to crush the rebellion seemed to be what Irvin McDowell had tried to do the previous July —attack the Confederate position on Bull Run near Manassas Junction. McDowell had failed, and General Joseph E. Johnston, who now commanded the Southern army at Manassas, had enjoyed many peaceful months improving a line which had already proven impenetrable. Thus McClellan determined to bypass Johnston's army, make use of his superior naval power, and land his own army closer to Richmond. For a time he favored striking at the small port of Urbanna on the Rappahannock River. A landing at Urbanna would place McClellan's army nearer Richmond than Johnston's and would force the Confederates to retreat in haste. When this happened McClellan planned to fall upon his foes, destroy the retreating Southern fragments, and claim victory at Richmond.

Unfortunately, in early March Johnston evacuated Manassas and took up a new position at Culpepper Court House. From there the Confederates would be able to move with equal ease against McClellan's army whether it approached Richmond from the north or the east. Hence McClellan settled upon the Peninsula as his primary axis of advance. He planned to transport his army, more than 100,000 strong, to Fort Monroe, which remained in Union hands throughout the war. Then while the navy protected his flanks with gunboats and supplied him along secure water routes, he would march up the Peninsula to Richmond.

Lincoln was not completely happy with McClellan's concept of operations. But he wanted and needed action, and to that end he had trusted McClellan and tolerated

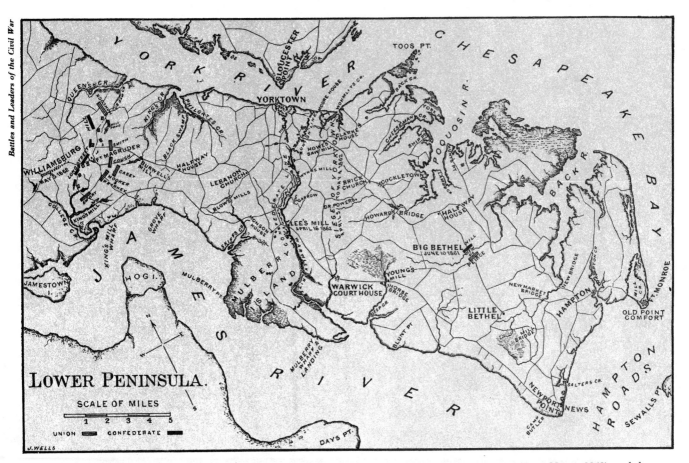

Map of early Peninsula operations, showing engagement at Big Bethel (June 10, 1861), Siege of Yorktown (April 5 to May 4, 1862), and the Battle of Williamsburg (May 5, 1862).

his behavior. And because he had invested so much in the general already, he was unwilling to withdraw his support now. Consequently the President bowed to the general's professional judgment—with two conditions. First, McClellan must leave a covering force near Manassas to hold northern Virginia, and second, Washington must have enough defenders at hand to keep the Capital secure. Lincoln never forgot his sleepless anxiety during the night after the Battle of Bull Run; never again would Washington be so vulnerable.

Thus, with the President's guarded approval, McClellan's campaign began. By the end of March, the Army of the Potomac was on the Peninsula and McClellan with more than 100,000 men set out on April 1 to confront the Yorktown line, manned by about 10,000 Confederates. At this juncture, however, Lincoln and Secretary of War Edwin M. Stanton counted noses and realized that McClellan had not fulfilled the two conditions upon which the campaign rested. Not enough Federal troops guarded northern Virginia and the Capital. Moreover, an unknown number of Confederates commanded by Major General Thomas J. "Stonewall" Jackson were menacing Union forces in the lower— northern—Shenandoah. Jackson's activities, limited thus far to a repulse at Kernstown on March 23, did not in themselves frighten Lincoln. Jackson's presence did, however, remind the President that McClellan had not

kept his bargain. Accordingly, on April 3 Lincoln decided to enforce his agreement unilaterally. He ordered Stanton to retain a corps under McDowell for the defense of Washington and rebuked McClellan for what he considered duplicity.

The general did not understand—in fact he never would. Convinced that the Confederates had "probably not less than 100,000 men, and possibly more" in his front, he wrote his wife that the President's action in withholding McDowell's troops was "the most infamous thing that history has recorded." And because he believed badly overestimated reports of the Confederate strength, McClellan answered Lincoln's plea for action with a decision to invest the Yorktown line and conduct siege operations. He continued siege operations for a full month until the Southerners withdrew on May 3. Then on the morning of May 4, he sent his army plunging into the mud after the retreating Confederates.

Leading the Confederate retreat up the Peninsula toward Richmond was Rebel General Joseph Eggleston Johnston. The man was certainly no coward; he had served with dash and courage in the "old army," and at 55 he still displayed "gamecock jauntiness." No, Johnston led the withdrawal because he never intended to fight on the lower Peninsula in the first place. He marched his army from Culpeper Court House, through

126

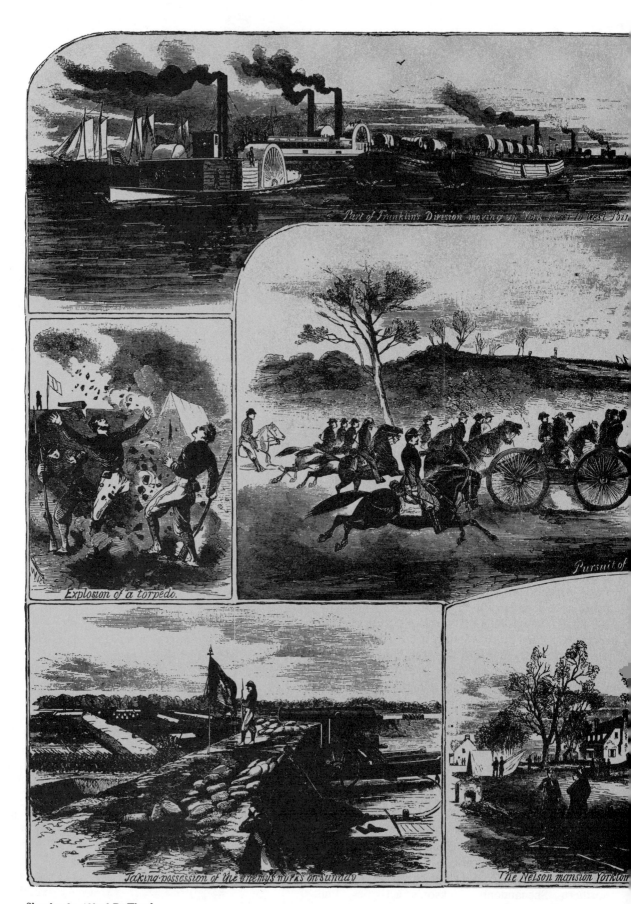

Part of Franklins Division moving up York River to West Point

Explosion of a torpedo.

Pursuit of

Taking possession of the enemys works on Sunday

The Nelson mansion Yorktown

Sketches by Alfred R. Waud.

ad to the land face of the Yorktown fortifications Union forces & balloon

rebels

Magazine at the head of the ravine Yorktown

Rebels as a hospital.

Fortifications at Yorktown looking toward the river.

128

Richmond, and into the works at Yorktown only because Jefferson Davis ordered him to do so. Although Johnston was a bit more "professional" in his dealings with Davis than was McClellan with Lincoln, the two opposing commanders shared similar opinions of their respective commanders in chief.

When Johnston resigned from the United States Army and offered his services to the Confederacy, he held one of the highest ranks—brigadier general—among officers who "went South." So when Davis ranked him fourth on his first list of full generals (behind Samuel Cooper, A.S. Johnston, and R.E. Lee), Johnston protested, and a feud began which lasted long after the Lost Cause was lost. Johnston's military talents were many, and to his credit Davis entrusted the general with crucial commands throughout the war. But Johnston never quite trusted his President; he resented Davis' pretensions to military wisdom, accused him of interference, and complained that the Richmond government neither supported him nor his armies with sufficient will or enthusiasm.

When McClellan's intentions for the Peninsula Campaign became clear, Johnston journeyed to Richmond to confer with his government about some response. On April 14 the general with two of his subordinates, Major Generals James Longstreet and G.W. Smith, met with the President, the President's military adviser Robert E. Lee, and Confederate Secretary of War George Wythe Randolph. At this council of war Johnston argued that he meet McClellan near Richmond; Lee and Randolph urged a confrontation on the Peninsula; Davis assumed the role of judge and only stated that he would not submit the army to a siege at Richmond. After 14 hours of discussion and debate, the President announced his "verdict": Johnston would fight on the Peninsula.

Battery #4, with its thirteen-inch Union mortars emplaced for the siege of Yorktown.

Principal street in Yorktown. The court house is behind the trees to the left.

Naturally the general was less than enthusiastic about his assignment. Still, he followed the letter, if not the spirit, of his orders. He marched down the Peninsula, determined that McClellan's force was too strong to confront at Yorktown, and marched right back up the Peninsula again. As he explained later in his memoirs, "The belief that events on the Peninsula would soon compel the Confederate government to adopt my method of opposing the Federal army, reconciled me somewhat to the necessity of obeying the President's order." Now that he was withdrawing to the vicinity of Richmond, Johnston's prophecy reached self-fulfillment.

McClellan, however, did not intend to allow the Southerners to withdraw at leisure. He sent his cavalry, commanded by George Stoneman, after J.E.B. Stuart's horsemen, the last Confederate troops to leave the Yorktown line, and committed five divisions of infantry to the chase. In addition McClellan planned to dispatch four more infantry divisions by water to West Point where the Pamunkey and Mattapony Rivers flow together to make the York. From West Point the general hoped he could cut Johnston's retreat and capture his supply trains, if not his army. But while McClellan supervised the embarkation of the first of the divisions bound for West Point, the rest of his army overtook the Confederate rearguard near Williamsburg. After almost two months, the Peninsula Campaign finally generated a battle.

It was a semi-spontaneous affair. Some months previously Confederate Major General John Bankhead Magruder, the original architect of the Yorktown line, had established another line of field works about 2 miles east of Williamsburg. In the center of this line was Fort Magruder; smaller earthen redoubts flanked the fort and composed the "line" which extended altogether for about 4 miles. The position was crude and tentative, and on the afternoon of May 4 members of the Confederate rearguard, were inclined to trudge on past it. But Federal cavalry became menacing; consequently one brigade and then a second took shelter in Fort Magruder and some of the nearby redoubts and fought the Federals until dark.

It rained throughout the night of May 4. Anticipating McClellan's move to West Point and anxious about the security of his supply trains, Johnston at 2 o'clock on the morning of May 5, hurried the bulk of his army eastward from Williamsburg. Longstreet's division, designated as rearguard, inherited the position around Fort Magruder. Longstreet had six brigades, two of which were occupying the fort and redoubts. But as another soggy day broke on May 5, two full Union divisions, Brigadier General Joseph Hooker's and Brigadier W.F. Smith's, appeared before the Confederates. Both sides opened artillery fire and sent skirmishers forward. Longstreet brought his entire division up. The Southerners repulsed an attack by men from Hooker's divi-

Tent with McClellan's headquarters at Camp Winfield Scott, before Yorktown. Photograph by James F. Gibson, May 1862.

sion, then counterattacked. Hooker's troops gave ground grudgingly, and the fighting remained inconclusive.

Around noon Johnston himself arrived at the front, which was really his rear. He had been trying with limited success to expedite his withdrawal through Williamsburg and now realized that his rearguard would have to hold until dark. Since Rebel Major General D.H. Hill's division had not yet left Williamsburg, Johnston recalled this unit to support Longstreet.

Meanwhile the Union brigade commanded by Winfield Scott Hancock (part of Smith's division) was making a long flank march in an attempt to turn the Confederate's left flank. As Hill's Confederates reached the scene, Hancock's troops appeared behind the Southern left. Moreover, the Federals had the good fortune to find two of Magruder's old redoubts unoccupied; amid the rain, dark, and combat of the preceding 24 hours, the Confederates simply never realized that the vacant positions existed. Hancock's Federals were quick to exploit their find and soon were pouring artillery fire into Longstreet's flank and rear.

Leading Hill's division into the fray was the brigade commanded by Brigadier General Jubal A. Early, a tobacco-chewing veteran with an aggressive disposition. Early could not see his enemy, but advanced toward the

low ridge from which Hancock's men were firing. As he drew near the Federals, Early realized that they could not see him either, and thus he suggested to Hill that he attack Hancock's right and outflank Hancock's flanking position. Hill relayed the request to Longstreet who refused at first, then agreed to the attack. Hill and Early acted in haste. As a result the units involved reached the Union position at different times and from a variety of directions.

From the standpoint of military science the Confederate attack was a ragged, mismanaged failure. As Hancock later reported, "no man had left the ground unhurt who had advanced within 500 yards of our line." In terms less scientific, however, the assault was, as Early later recalled it, "one of the most brilliant of the war." Early referred to the gallantry of troops who stormed forward, without orders, into the hail of minie balls, exploding shells, and canister. Such gallantry was costly. Participating regiments lost as many as half their numbers, and no accurate count exists because most of those responsible for casualty reports, the officers, were casualties themselves. Throughout the confused, dripping day the Federals lost about 2,200 men; the Confederates lost around 1,700, probably more.

McClellan's army on the road between Yorktown and Williamsburg.

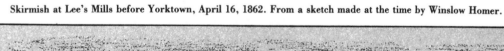

Skirmish at Lee's Mills before Yorktown, April 16, 1862. From a sketch made at the time by Winslow Homer.

132

Major General John B. Magruder (left), Major General James Longstreet, and General Joseph E. Johnston (right).

Mercifully darkness ended the action. By that time Johnston had left the field, gone to hasten his retreat up the Peninsula. McClellan was never really near the field at Williamsburg; he arrived late from Yorktown as the makeshift battle wound down.

The Union general elected not to press the Confederate rear further. Instead he concentrated upon cutting Johnston's retreat by way of West Point. Unfortunately for McClellan the transport of four divisions from Yorktown to West Point took some time, more time as it happened than it took Johnston's army to slog along the muddy ground. Consequently on May 7 Mc-

Clellan had but one division near West Point, and the ever-wiley Johnston had a division of his own there to oppose the Federals. On May 7 near West Point, actually nearer places on the south bank of the Pamunkey, Barhamsville and Eltham's Landing, Major General Gustavus W. Smith's Confederates attacked Brigadier General William B. Franklin's Federals. Franklin's troops repulsed the attack, and there the affair ended because McClellan had ordered Franklin only to hold his ground until reinforced. As a result Johnston made good his escape, and the two armies battled mud instead of each other for a while. Both army commanders seemed

"General Hancock's brigade charging the Rebels at the Battle of Williamsburg" by Alfred R. Waud.

satisfied with the way things were going up to that point. McClellan rejoiced over the taking of Yorktown and his pursuit of the Confederates. "The success is brilliant . . ." he wrote, and then promised, "to push the enemy to the wall." Johnston relished his escape. He termed the actions at Williamsburg and Eltham's Landing (Barhamsville) successes, and he seemed to believe that "living to fight another day" was the best for which he could hope.

Neither president was happy. Lincoln, with Secretary of War Stanton, arrived on May 6 at Fort Monroe to survey the scene. The President wanted to speak with McClellan, ascertain his plans, and as always urge him forward. But the general was too busy; he was in Williamsburg much involved with his army, and so it was "really impossible" for him "to go to the rear." Hence Lincoln wandered about and conferred with the army and navy officers on hand. He even acted out his impatience by setting in motion the capture of Norfolk. The port city was doomed by Johnston's withdrawal, but no one had yet pressed the issue. So Lincoln did. He ordered the navy to shell Confederate batteries in the vicinity and personally accompanied a reconnaissance of landing sites near the city for Union troops. The Confederates evacuated Norfolk on May 9, and when they did, they left their famous ironclad *Virginia* without a port. The *Virginia* had wreaked havoc with the Union's wooden fleet on March 8 and then the next day fought her inconclusive duel with the *Monitor*. Since then the Southern ironclad had seen no action, yet her presence alone was enough to bar the James River to Federal ships. Shortly after Norfolk fell, the *Virginia's* crew had to scuttle her and thus opened the James all the way to Rich-

mond. Lincoln heard the news as he returned to Washington and was well aware that he had had a hand in the event. From McClellan, though, he only heard more complaints. The general was piqued that Lincoln was not more impressed with the victory at Yorktown, and he lamented the rain and mud which hampered his advance toward Richmond. "McClellan," Lincoln told his secretary, "seemed to think, in defiance of Scripture, that heaven sent its rain only on the just and not on the unjust."

Lincoln was anxious and irritated; Davis was thoroughly alarmed. In none of his correspondence did Johnston even mention making a stand. Would the Confederate Army retreat forever? And more important, if the James River remained undefended, it would matter little what Johnston or McClellan did with their armies. Richmond would fall to the Federal Navy. Davis all but begged Johnston for some assurance, some plan, and Johnston responded by asking how his army would be supplied if Richmond were lost.

Nor was Davis alone in his fears. Anyone in Richmond could discern the crisis at hand. When Johnston's army marched through the city on its way to Yorktown, the citizens lined the streets and offered food and cheers. In the aftermath of Williamsburg, as one observer noted, "They straggled into Richmond muddy—dispirited—exhausted; and, throwing themselves on cellar doors and sidewalks, slept heavily; regardless of curious starers that collected around every group. Never had a Southern army appeared half so demoralized; half so unfit to cope with the triumphant and well-appointed brigades pressing close upon it."

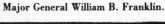
Major General William B. Franklin.

McClellan's Own Story, 1886

General McClellan reconnoitering at Yorktown. The artist, Alfred R. Waud, pictures himself (third from right) with the general's staff.

Desperate Defense of Richmond

by Emory Thomas

Charge of Casey's division to save the guns at Fair Oaks. Engraving from a painting by Alonzo Chappel.

On the evening of May 9, 1862, Varina and Jefferson Davis held a reception at the Executive Mansion in Richmond. The handsome house was alive with light and wit, while hosts and guests tried to act out society-as-usual and forget for a time the massive Federal Army closing upon the Capital. A uniformed courier interrupted the gaiety, spoke privately with President Davis for a few minutes, and left. Davis then returned to his guests, and the evening went on as before. When all but a very few of the revelers had gone, however, the President told his wife that she must leave Richmond the following day. The courier bore news that a Union fleet had started up the James River toward Richmond. No

one quite knew if Confederate forces could stop the ships; if they could not, the Federals would be able to shell the city from the river and land troops at its wharves.

For two months the Confederates at Richmond had lived with the threat of George B. McClellan's massive Union Army which approached slowly but steadily up the Peninsula between the York and James Rivers. Southern General Joseph E. Johnston with about 60,000 men retreated before McClellan's force of over 100,000 and offered no assurances that he could do more than slow down the Federals. McClellan was slow enough, even without Johnston's resistance. And the rainiest spring in memory further retarded the Union advance. By the second week of May the rival armies were on opposite sides of the Chickahominy River, a sluggish, meandering stream which flowed around Richmond on the north and east at a radius of from 5 to 8 miles before it eventually joined the James.

However, while most Richmonders watched the marching and maneuvering of the land forces, a more immediate threat developed on water. When the Confederates abandoned Yorktown and the lower Peninsula, they exposed the port city of Norfolk to capture. And when the Federals seized Norfolk, they rendered the ironclad *Virginia* homeless, without a port. When her crew blew up the *Virginia*, they in turn destroyed the only obstacle to the ascent of the James by the Union Navy. Now that ascent was under way. Federal ironclads, the *Monitor* and the *Galena*, were leading a parade of wooden warships up the James.

Varina Davis and her children left Richmond for Raleigh, North Carolina, on May 10, ostensibly to relieve her husband of concern for his family that he might devote his attention more thoroughly to the deepening crisis. The same day Secretary of War George Wythe Randolph ordered his bureau chiefs to pack up all but the most current files and have them ready for a hasty departure. This was only a "prudent step," Randolph assured his subordinates, "There is no need . . . for panic in the city." But panic there was. The Davis family was not the only one to seek a safer locale during the emergency, and Mrs. Davis at Raleigh greeted friends arriving from Richmond with nothing but the clothes they wore. The Confederate Congress had already responded to the situation. On April 22 the solons voted themselves a raise in pay and adjourned.

Most of those who remained in Richmond to defend the city and the Confederacy agreed that their best chance to stop the Union ships on the James lay at a place called Drewry's Bluff. There, about 7 miles below Richmond, the river was fairly narrow and the south bank was a sheer cliff perhaps 80 to 100 feet high. The Yankees called the site Fort Darling, but since a man named Drewry owned the land and since the military all but ignored the fort until Johnston left Yorktown, the place was known as Drewry's Bluff. Local farmers dug gun emplacements and finally the President and his adviser Robert E. Lee took action to shore up the position. Lee's oldest son, Custis, supervised the installation of

Richmond as seen from the Manchester side of the James River.

Battles and Leaders of the Civil War

Captain John Taylor Wood, CSN.

heavy guns and the sinking of weighted hulks in the river channel as obstructions. The elder Lee, exceeding his advisory authority, detached a brigade of infantry to support the position, and the crew of the *Virginia* took charge of the guns on the bluff. These preparations were frantic and makeshift, and there was no way to predict what would happen when the Federal flotilla challenged Drewry's Bluff.

At 5 o'clock on the afternoon of May 15 large numbers of Richmond residents answered the call of Virginia Governor John Letcher to attend a mass meeting for the purpose of organizing companies of citizen-soldiers for the city's final defense. They had heard guns booming to the southeast, and most people realized that the Federal ships were at hand. Letcher promised to see the city destroyed before he surrendered it, and Mayor Joseph Mayo promised some other mayor would have to give up the city. A short while later, as if Letcher's and Mayo's pugnacity had been merely theater, news arrived that Drewry's Bluff had held.

The channel obstructions blocked the heavy-draft ironclads; nor could the *Monitor* and *Galena* elevate their guns high enough to fire at the batteries on the bluff. Moreover, the *Galena* proved much less than impervious to Southern shot and shell. She sustained considerable damage and many casualties, and by the time the Federals broke off the engagement, the *Galena* was severely crippled. The three wooden ships which accompanied the ironclads remained out of range throughout the conflict.

John Taylor Wood, a naval officer who had served on board the *Virginia*, rejoiced with his shipless comrades at their victory over the *Monitor*. But Wood wisely observed that had the Federal ships been supported by ground forces in any strength, the outcome at Drewry's Bluff might well have been different. However moot, Wood's point was well taken. Yet both army commanders seemed oblivious to the potential of naval forces in the Peninsula Campaign. Johnston failed to foresee that his evacuation of Yorktown would cost the Confederacy Norfolk, the *Virginia*, and a secure James River. Accordingly he had had nothing to do with the hurried preparations at Drewry's Bluff. McClellan, although he talked about cooperating closely with the navy and relied upon Federal ships for supply and troop transport, did nothing to support the Federal assault up the James on May 15, or afterward.

In Richmond the repulse at Drewry's Bluff produced profound relief. As Davis informed his wife, "The panic here has subsided, and with increasing confidence there has arisen a desire to see the city destroyed rather than surrendered." Yet the Confederacy was still imperiled; McClellan was still across the Chickahominy with an army which outnumbered Johnston's by more than three to two. Wisely, Davis realized that the army, not the capital, was vital to his would-be nation's survival. Thus he refused to consider siege tactics, and as he explained to Varina, was prepared to abandon Richmond in order to salvage Johnston's army. "I have told them that the enemy might be beaten before Richmond, or on either flank, and we would try it, but that I could not allow the army to be penned up in a city."

Regularly the President rode out to his army (which by then was within several miles of Richmond) and conferred with Johnston. The two men shared the conviction that McClellan must be beaten outside of Richmond if he were to be beaten at all. Davis was naturally anxious to strike the blow, but Johnston was naturally concerned that when the blow was struck it would not miss the mark and lead to disaster. Johnston also nursed old wounds from his dealings with Davis and resented the President's constant questions and his presence at headquarters. In the middle of the situation was Lee. Like everyone else he desired a victory, and he was well aware of the latent conflict between Davis and Johnston. Lee consequently offered his advice to Johnston and Davis in such a way as to make them feel that they had had the idea first. And because general and President most often communicated with each other through Lee, he was able to soften language and pour oil over potentially troubled waters.

Lincoln and McClellan had no Lee to mediate their communication, and their relationship made that of Davis and Johnston appear almost blissful. Convinced that he was outnumbered, McClellan demanded reinforcements, and when he received none or fewer than he

Harper's Weekly, May 31, 1862

A balloon view of the Federal attack on Fort Darling on Drewry's Bluff (above).
A closer view of the fort and bluff shows river obstructions (below).

Harper's Weekly, June 28, 1862

requested, he became all the more convinced that his government was betraying him. He especially distrusted Secretary of War Edwin M. Stanton who occupied the same sort of diplomatic middle ground held by Lee. "Those hounds in Washington are after me again," he lamented to his wife, "Stanton is without exception the vilest man I ever knew or heard of."

As it happened, McClellan's force vastly outnumbered its foe. But McClellan, relying upon the intelligence offered by Alan Pinkerton and his agents, remained convinced that he faced odds of two to one. Perhaps the general thought it curious that a superior force should retreat so consistently before an inferior one. Still, he persisted in his conviction, moved with extreme caution, and renewed his pleas for reinforcements. On May 21 an exasperated Lincoln relented and informed McClellan that the corps-sized unit commanded by Irvin McDowell would march overland from the vicinity of Fredericksburg to join the effort on the Peninsula.

Within 3 days, however, the direction of McDowell's marching orders changed 90 degrees. McDowell would remain near Fredericksburg and detach 20,000 men for service in the Shenandoah Valley. The reason for the sudden shift in plans was the presence of an indeterminate number of Southern troops in the Shenandoah Valley commanded by Thomas J. "Stonewall" Jackson.

As fanatically aggressive as he was intensely religious, Jackson drove his Valley army hard. The troops earned the sobriquet "foot cavalry," and whether on the march or in close combat their impact far exceeded their numbers (at this point about 16,000 men). When Jackson's Valley Campaign threatened the lower (northern) end of the Valley, Lincoln and his government once again became alarmed over the security of Washington. Hence the President diverted McDowell's force to the Shenandoah Valley and left McClellan with his fears about a superior enemy in front of him and his fantasies about treason in his rear. To his wife the general petitioned, "Heaven save a country governed by such counsels."

Despite McClellan's trepidation his army continued to advance and because of his trepidation the army advanced with such caution that Johnston could find no opportunity to strike back successfully. Throughout the campaign McClellan had had his base of supply of the York-Pamunkey river system. For a short time he used West Point, then shifted to White House Landing on the Pamunkey. This base, site of Lee's son "Rooney's" home, offered the advantage of a navigable river and access to the Richmond & York River Railroad which crossed the Pamunkey at this point to connect Richmond with West Point. In order to use the base at White House most efficiently, McClellan's army remained mostly on the north side of the Chickahominy. But to

White House Landing in Virginia, McClellan's second supply base. The White House was "Rooney" Lee's home.

take Richmond the Federals would have to cross this swampy stream and approach from the east as well. Hence, even as Lincoln sent a telegram advising, "the time is near when you must either attack Richmond or give up the job and come to the defense of Washington," McClellan was shifting troops south of the Chickahominy and pondering logistical problems.

By the end of May the Federals occupied a broad front. Three corps were north of the Chickahominy; two more were south of the river. The line extended from Beaver Dam Creek on the north all the way around to White Oak Swamp to the east. Moreover, the Union troops of Brigadier General Erasmus Keyes's IV Corps were at the village of Seven Pines astride the Williamsburg Road and Fair Oaks Station on the Richmond & York River Railroad.

Brigadier General Erasmus Keyes.

Seven Days commanders. Major Generals Gustavus W. Smith, CSA (left); Silas Casey, USA; and Daniel H. Hill, CSA (right).

While the Federals were expanding this front, moving laterally toward the James, the Confederates plotted an attack. When he learned that McDowell had been ordered south, Johnston realized that he must act before the fresh troops joined McClellan. Accordingly, he made plans to strike across Beaver Dam Creek on May 29. Then, learning that McDowell was not en route to join McClellan, Johnston cancelled his attack.

Finally on May 30 nature presented Johnston with an opportunity he could not refuse. As if to underscore the unusually sodden spring, the skies opened again and in the afternoon and evening poured rain upon eastern Virginia. The storm transformed the Chickahominy into a torrent and washed away the bridges which linked one portion of the Federal Army to the other. In haste Johnston prepared to attack Keyes' isolated corps at Seven Pines and rout it before Major General S. P. Heintzelman's III Corps could reinforce.

On paper, at least, the battle plan appeared simple enough. Three roads from Richmond converged eventually at Seven Pines; Johnston sent Major General D. H. Hill's division down the Williamsburg Road, Major General James Longstreet's division down the Nine Mile Road, and Brigadier General Benjamin Huger's division down the Charles City Road. Brigadier General W. H. Chase Whiting's division (behind Longstreet's), and Huger's division were to support the principal thrusts by Hill and Longstreet. The only complexity involved Huger's assignment to relieve a portion of Hill's command stationed south of Seven Pines before the assault began. Orders to all commanders except Longstreet were in writing; Johnston gave Longstreet verbal instructions during a lengthy conversation on May 30. The movement was to commence at dawn on May 31.

Hill's troops first went down the Williamsburg Road. Longstreet, however, marched his men out the Nine Mile Road, then over to the Williamsburg Road where

he had to wait for Hill's troops to pass. In this process Longstreet obstructed the columns first of Whiting, then of Huger. Longstreet's route delayed Whiting and detained Huger, who could not then release Hill's missing brigade. Furthermore, while Longstreet and Huger argued about the right-of-way, Hill was alone nearing a position of attack at Seven Pines.

Johnston soon learned of the mix-up, but refused to believe it. He sent couriers down the empty Nine Mile Road in search of Longstreet. His second courier even went so far as to blunder into Federal lines and alert Keyes to the fact that the Southerners were coming. Finally Johnston rode off to correct the confusion and

Major General Benjamin Huger, CSA.

Kirby's Federal battery meeting Confederate attack in the Battle of Fair Oaks, fought May 31 to June 1, 1862.

try to salvage his battle. When Johnston discovered where Longstreet really was, he confided to an aide that he wished all his troops were back in camp. But by this time it was too late to turn back.

At about 1 o'clock in the afternoon Hill alone launched the attack which was supposed to commence in the early morning with Longstreet's support. Hill's

troops collided with those of Brigadier General Silas Casey's Federal division and drove them back about one and a half miles beyond Seven Pines. But then Brigadier General Philip Kearny's Federal troops appeared in support and the Confederate drive faltered and fell back.

Late in the afternoon Whiting's division, sent by Johnston to take up Longstreet's original assignment

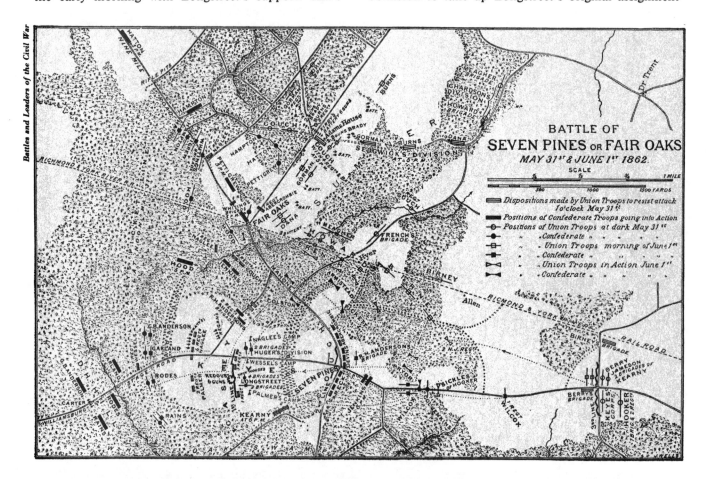

pressed his concern for Johnston, then realized that he had a leaderless army in desperate contact with the enemy. Major General Gustavus Smith succeeded Johnston for the moment. Next day, however, Davis appointed Lee to the command.

Meanwhile, Smith tried to salvage the situation. Thus far Hill had fought a gallant but unsupported battle at Seven Pines; then Johnston had directed Whiting's troops in a bloody standoff around Fair Oaks. Smith in the early morning of June 1 directed Longstreet to renew the attack near Seven Pines. In fighting so intense that Longstreet believed he faced the entire Union Army, the Federals repulsed the Confederate attack, counterattacked, and recovered the ground lost the previous day. Shortly after noon, Lee appeared at Smith's headquarters, assumed field command, and ordered a withdrawal.

The fighting at Seven Pines and Fair Oaks served notice that the Confederates were capable of offensive action and so fed McClellan's caution. Yet the offensive was badly bungled, and the battle was a Federal victory. The mix-up in roads and routes, the untimely appearance of Sumner from north of the Chicahominy, and the lack of coordination of the Southern assaults turned the promise of victory to failure. Johnston planned to engage twenty-three of his twenty-seven available brigades at Seven Pines; yet at no time were more than four in action. The Confederates sustained 6,134 casualties, the Federals, 5,031. But even these figures do not reveal the depth of Johnston's failure. Because so few brigades were actually involved, several Southern units were almost destroyed, sustaining losses near 50 percent.

McClellan allowed his enemy to withdraw and planned more and better bridges across the Chickahominy. "I only wait for the river to fall," he wrote, "to cross with the rest of the force and make a general attack . . . ." McClellan, overcautious though he was regarding his foes and near paranoia as he was regarding his government, was on the verge of victory.

along Nine Mile Road, encountered Union resistance near Fair Oaks. The Union troops were part of Brigadier General John Sedgwick's division from the other side of the Chickahominy. Sedgwick's corps commander, Major General Edwin V. Sumner, had, against the council of his engineers, led the advance across Grapevine Bridge to come to the aid of his comrades. The action at Fair Oaks between Sedgwick's and Whiting's divisions was fierce but inconclusive.

Johnston himself directed some of the movement in this quarter and paid dearly for it. In the fading light of dusk, as he rode among his forward units, Johnston suffered a flesh wound in the shoulder from a rifle ball. Seconds later a shell fragment tore into his chest. Carried from the field on a stretcher, Johnston was in severe pain; some thought his wound mortal. President Davis was on hand, trying to find out what was happening. He ex-

The "First Minnesota Squad" after the Battle of Fair Oaks.

A New Confederate Commander

by Emory Thomas

On June 1, 1862, Robert E. Lee was not yet a hero, not yet the great, gray knight, and not yet a mythical Southern god. He was a professional soldier, known by other professional soldiers to be a good one.

Son of a hero in that "other" revolution, "Light Horse Harry" Lee, he had served in the United States Army for 32 years. Commissioned an engineer officer, he had been conspicuously brilliant during General Winfield Scott's campaign for Mexico City in 1847, and he had been superintendent of West Point from 1852 to 1855. On April 18, 1861, Scott offered Lee command of Federal troops in the new war, and Lee made the difficult decision to reject the command, resign his commission and remain a Southerner.

Lee first commanded Virginia State Troops, then accepted charge of the Confederate expedition to the Kanawha Valley in western Virginia. The campaign was a failure; it made a hero of Lee's rival commander, George B. McClellan. Then Lee journeyed South to command Southern troops along the South Carolina-Georgia coast. He arrived just in time to hear news that the Federals had occupied Port Royal between Charleston and Savannah. Thus Lee was left with the prudent but unpopular task of burning cotton bales on the coast and withdrawing his forces to defensible lines in the interior. Next Lee returned to Richmond to act as President Jefferson Davis' military advisor, an informal chief of staff for the Commander in Chief. Thus far during the Peninsula Campaign Lee had displayed a talent for diplomacy in mediating matters between the President and his field commander Joseph E. Johnston. Otherwise he was an unknown quantity.

After Johnston sustained a serious wound at the Battle of Seven Pines, or Fair Oaks, Davis gave Lee command of the Army of Northern Virginia. The new commander had little reputation with the public and press of his nascent nation. And he hardly made an auspicious beginning with the army. His first order was to retreat—back from the futile field of Seven Pines into lines before Richmond. Then he ordered his troops, men who considered themselves seasoned warriors, to dig holes in the ground, field fortifications. The Southern troops resented the task Lee set for them, and the man who would become "Marse Robert" was first the "King of Spades." Nor did many people believe Lee's defensive works would be effective against McClellan's blue host which was approaching the Confederate Capital.

At least one man knew better. Joe Johnston would envy Lee later, but at this juncture he sustained his successor. When a visitor remarked that Johnston's wounds were calamitous to the "Cause," the general responded, "No Sir! The shot that struck me down is the very best that has been fired for the Southern cause yet. For I possess in no degree the confidence of our government, and now they have in my place one who does possess it, and who can accomplish what I never could have done—the concentration of our armies for the defense of the capital of the Confederacy."

There were others, of course, whom Lee had impressed. Obviously Davis trusted him. And so, no doubt, did Mrs. Mary Amanda Stewart. Mrs. Stewart lived just outside Richmond, and back in March when the campaign was developing far down the Peninsula, some engineers surveyed the Stewart property in preparation for the construction of breastworks near the house. Anxious that the war might come into her backyard, Mrs. Stewart wrote to Lee. And the then military advisor responded personally. "I regret to hear," Lee wrote, "that your residence is said to occupy the best position for defending the approach by the road . . . I hope some other position may be taken. At all events I beg you will not give yourself any uneasiness yet on the subject as every effort will be made to satisfy the question without disturbing your house."

Lee was a gentle man whose instincts were such that he took time in the midst of a war to allay a lady's fears. But he was first a professional soldier, and Southerners other than Johnston, Davis, and Mrs. Stewart would learn about that aspect of the man before anything else. Yet if the "King of Spades" set the Army of Northern Virginia to digging field works (in Mrs. Stewart's yard and elsewhere) in order to conduct a static defense, he was playing directly into the hands of his foes.

George B. McClellan still believed he was outnumbered before Richmond, and he still seemed more concerned about not losing his Peninsula Campaign than about winning. Unlike Lee he remained in command not because he enjoyed the confidence of his government, but because Abraham Lincoln had boundless patience. Nevertheless Lincoln's patience and McClellan's caution appeared destined to produce victory for the Union. For the Federal general envisioned a victory resulting from a series of "regular advances." McClellan might believe himself outnumbered, but he knew he was not outgunned. And he proposed to use his superior firepower to compensate for his assumed numerical inferiority and to economize his casualties. When defined battle lines developed in front of Richmond, McClellan intended to deploy his big guns, batter the Confederate line into submission, and move forward. This process he would repeat, until he was blasting the city itself. Then finally his infantry would take possession of the rubble, and McClellan would have destroyed the Rebel Army, Capital, and Cause.

Thus in the aftermath of Seven Pines, the Federals advanced on a broad front east of Richmond. McClellan massed four army corps south of the Chickahominy River and left one corps north of the stream. No less than eleven bridges insured that elements of the Army of the Potomac would never again be isolated from each other as they had on the eve of Seven Pines. And McClellan began bringing up his guns. He had 101 pieces of siege artillery including twenty-five 10-inch mortars, ten 13-inch mortars, two 200-pounder Parrotts and eleven 100-pounder Parrotts. These were huge weapons, capable of altering an entire landscape. To bring them to bear upon Confederate works and eventually Richmond itself, McClellan depended upon barges towed up to White House Landing on the Pamunkey River and then upon the Richmond & York River Railroad for overland transport. Given time, the security of his supply line, and customary prudence, McClellan would succeed and he knew it. He wrote his wife that he would "make the first battle mainly an artillery combat." Then he would "push them in upon Richmond and

Library of Congress

General Robert E. Lee. A photograph taken in the late war years, after he had become the idol of his army.

behind their works . . . bring up my heavy guns, shell the city, and carry it by assault."

By committing his army to the preparation of field fortifications, Lee seemed to be in partnership with McClellan's venture. But such was not the case. On June 5 the new commander wrote an almost *stream of consciousness* letter to the President and revealed his perception of the situation. "McClellan," Lee wrote, "will make this a battle of posts. He will take position from position, under cover of his heavy guns, and we cannot get at him without storming his works, which . . . is extremely hazardous. You witnessed the experiment Saturday [at Seven Pines]." Siege operations at Richmond, Lee observed, would take 100,000 troops, which he did not have, and "would only prolong" the inevitable. Then in mid-paragraph Lee stated his plan, "I am preparing a line that I can hold with part of our forces in front, while with the rest I will endeavour to make a diversion to bring McClellan out."

Lee devoted his first ten days of command to securing his front with field works and concentrating what heavy guns he had upon the rail line McClellan would have to use to advance his siege weapons. Then he began working on that "diversion to bring McClellan out."

First he did an odd thing. He detached nearly four brigades from his outnumbered army and sent them to "Stonewall" Jackson's "Valley Army." Did he wish to deceive "those people," as Lee termed the Federals, into thinking that Jackson would make a desperate attack upon Washington? If so, he failed. Abraham Lincoln realized that Richmond was the critical point. "Jackson's game," Lincoln wrote, "—his assigned work—now is to magnify the accounts of his numbers and reports of his movements, and thus by constant alarms keep three or four times as many of our troops away from Richmond as his own force amounts to. . . . Our game is not to allow this." Actually Lee sent reinforcements to Jackson, not as part of any bluff, but to allow Jackson the means to conclude his campaign in the Shenandoah. Then, as Lee proposed to Davis, ". . . Jackson can then be directed to Ashland, where I will

Stuart in camp. Drawing by Frank Vizetelly.

re-enforce him with fresh troops, with directions to sweep down north of the Chickahominy, cut up McClellan's communications and rear, while I attack in front." While Jackson prepared to leave the Valley and join the army before Richmond for a showdown with McClellan, Lee was gathering information about the Union right flank.

Brigadier General James Ewell Brown "Jeb" Stuart was the quintessential cavalryman. His spurs jingled and his staff accompanied their movements with banjo music. Stuart was young—29—and wore a huge beard to conceal his youth and, some said, a weak chin. A queer amalgam of vanity and piety, of tireless competence and ostrich plume exhibitionism, Stuart had risen rapidly in rank and responsibility during this young war. Now on June 11 Lee, whose aide Stuart had been during John Brown's raid on Harpers Ferry, entrusted the dashing general with a crucial mission. Stuart was to move in the Federal right rear north of the Chickahominy, determine the enemy's strength and disposi-

tion, and disrupt his communication and supply lines as much as possible.

Stuart preserved the secrecy of the expedition until two o'clock on the morning of June 12, when he awakened his staff and announced cheerfully, "Gentlemen, in ten minutes every man must be in the saddle." No doubt it took longer than ten minutes for 1200 troopers to stir themselves and their horses. Yet very soon the Confederate column moved off, heading due north out the Brook Turnpike from Richmond. Still Stuart concealed his mission, and many of the men guessed they were going to join Jackson in the Valley. After 22 miles Stuart ordered a halt and camped on the night of June 12 near the North Anna River.

Before dawn the next day rockets went up to recall the men to their saddles. The column soon turned eastward, and the Confederates then realized that they were going to challenge the Federal flank. They first made contact at Hanover Court House, where the Southerners chased off a small picket force of Federals. Then Stuart turned south and continued the march through another brush with Federal cavalry at Haw's Shop towards Old Church which lay on the supply line used by McClellan's right wing. The Southerners could anticipate sterner resistance at Old Church; indeed Stuart had reason to believe that his father-in-law, Brigadier General Philip St. George Cooke, would command the opposition. Cooke was not at Old Church, but other Union horse soldiers were, and there was a brief, spirited clash. The Confederates prevailed and drove the Federals from the field and their camps. Captain William Latané who led the charge was killed, but the Confederates suffered no other casualties in the fray.

While his men burned the Federal camp and destroyed supplies (except for a keg of whiskey) Stuart pondered his next move. Already he knew what Lee needed to know—that the enemy was not present in strength in the Pamunkey Valley. Now his duty was to return to his lines and make his report. Should he retrace his hoof prints and return the way he had come? Or might he with less risk continue in the Federal rear and ride completely around the Army of the Potomac? Perhaps exaggerating in his mind the prospect of am-

bush if he returned over the same ground, Stuart convinced himself to do what he wanted to do—press on around McClellan's army. After hearing and brushing aside some discouraging words from his subordinates, Stuart led the column off at a trot.

The route was parallel to the Pamunkey and led first to Tunstall's Station on the Richmond & York River Railroad. Near that place the two artillery pieces bogged down in a mud hole and refused to budge. Concerned that he not have to abandon the guns, the lieutenant in charge, on the advice of his sergeant, placed the captured keg of whiskey on one of the gun carriages and told the men they could have the keg if they extricated the guns. Within minutes the pieces were on dry ground. Unfortunately the lieutenant was unable to get the artillery to Tunstall's in time to damage a Federal train which passed while the Confederates held the station.

At Tunstall's Station Stuart resisted as too risky the temptation to swoop down upon White House Landing, only 4 miles away. The next challenge was thus the

White House, home of Brigadier General William H.F. Lee, General Robert E. Lee's second son. This was McClellan's supply base on the Pamunkey River. Inset: Ruins of White House after the Federal occupancy. From drawing by Alfred R. Waud.

Battles and Leaders of the Civil War

Harper's Weekly, June 5, 1862

Stuart's raiders attack a Federal supply train at Tunstall's Station, near White House Landing. Sketch by Larkin Goldsmith Mead.

Chickahominy. Tired men and worn horses reached the river about dawn on June 14 and found a flooded ford and a destroyed Forge Bridge. Strained hours passed as exhausted troopers rebuilt the bridge while they listened for sounds of pursuers. Finally the column crossed, and the rearguard fired the bridge. Within 10 minutes a small party of Federal horsemen appeared on the opposite bank.

Once across the Chickahominy Stuart placed Fitzhugh Lee, the commanding general's nephew, in charge of the ride home and hastened ahead himself to report. On the morning of June 15 Stuart clattered into Richmond. The rest of the column arrived the next day. They had ridden 150 miles around an army of more than 100,000 men and lost only one of their number. Some days later Stuart answered an invitation to visit Virginia Governor John Letcher. He found a crowd on hand in front of the Governor's Mansion and answered their call for a "few words." A listener reported that Stuart said, "he had been to the Chickahominy to visit some of his old friends of the United States Army, but they, very uncivilly, turned their backs upon him."

The "ride around McClellan" brought Lee the information he required about the Federal right flank. But of even greater value to a people who desperately needed to hear some good news was the morale value of the ride.

McClellan responded to Stuart's ride and the prospect of Jackson's arrival with indecision. The Confederates had made him painfully aware that his lifeline

from White House Landing to the Chickahominy was vulnerable. Accordingly, he alerted the Union Navy to a possible change of base from the Pamunkey to the James. McClellan resisted the move, however, because the most likely base on the James, Harrison's Landing, lacked a rail line over which to move supplies and heavy guns. As for the right flank, he wondered whether to reinforce Fitz John Porter's corps north of the Chickahominy or to make a general assault on the Confederate lines east of Richmond. He satisfied himself with ordering a limited attack from the east on June 25. After that McClellan's options narrowed severely.

On the afternoon of June 23, Lee convened a meeting at his field headquarters at the Dobb's house on Nine Mile Road. In attendance were Major Generals James Longstreet, D. H. Hill, A. P. Hill, and a weary Stonewall Jackson. Jackson's troops were on the march, and their commander had ridden ahead to discuss their mission. Lee began the meeting by explaining in outline his plan of attack. He proposed to leave 25,000 men commanded by Major Generals Benjamin Huger and John B. Magruder between the Army of the Potomac and Richmond. The divisions of the two Hills and Longstreet, roughly 47,000 troops, he would order to form near Mechanicsville to attack and drive Porter's 30,000 Federals. Jackson's force of 18,500 would envelope the Union right and force the Federals out of their works. If all proceeded as planned the Confederates

would sieze McClellan's supply line at the same time they forced the Army of the Potomac to fight in the open, away from their works and their big guns. Lee's ultimate goal was not relief from a potential siege, but no less than the destruction of McClellan's army.

However rich the prize, the risk was greater. If McClellan realized how thin were the ranks between the bulk of his army and Richmond, he could assault them and capture the city. Then what was left of Lee's army would be cut off from its base of supply. Lee did not believe McClellan would act so perceptively and decisively. And on the faith of this belief he determined to go ahead with his plan. He left to his four subordinate generals the date of the assault. Jackson volunteered to be in position for battle on June 25. Longstreet suggested that he give himself one more day. Thus Lee fixed the morning of June 26 as the time of truth.

Stuart's route in his ride around McClellan. His cavalry rode 150 miles around an army of more than 100,000 and lost only one man.

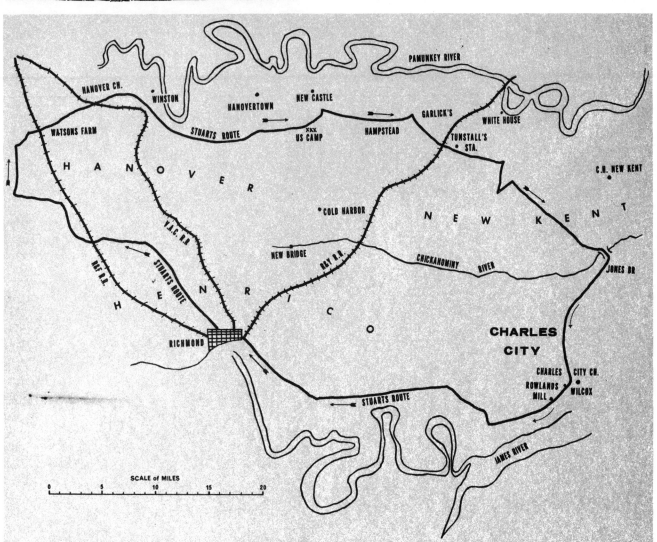

The Defenders Take the Offensive

by Emory Thomas

It began with General Orders No. 75. Six paragraphs and the phrase "By command of General Lee," written on June 24, 1862, launched the week of nearly constant combat known as the Seven Days Battles.

General Robert E. Lee was committing his entire Army of Northern Virginia, 88,000 men, to a desperate fight; in so doing he was gambling the safety of the Confederate Capital and perhaps the very existence of the Confederacy upon the result. Lee's rival commander Major General George B. McClellan and 115,000 men of the Army of the Potomac were closing upon Richmond from the east. Since March the Federals had been working their way up the Peninsula from Fort Monroe, and now they lay within striking distance of the city. Lee believed that the Federals were too strong to attack frontally. Therefore he was posting a token force, 25,000 troops commanded by Major Generals Benjamin Huger and John B. Magruder in front of Richmond, bringing Major General T.J. "Stonewall" Jackson's army secretly from the Shenandoah Valley, and hurling Jackson's force and three other divisions at the Federal right flank, the 30,000-man corps of Brigadier General Fitz John Porter. With this assault Lee intended to drive his enemies away from their fortifications, their supply lines, and their big guns. Then, in open combat, Lee hoped to annihilate McClellan's army.

There were crucial contingencies, however, in General Orders No. 75. Paragraph I described a rapid approach of 18,800 troops under the command of Jackson; these men were to fall upon the Union rear and force Porter's corps to flee. As soon as Jackson went into action, Major General A.P. Hill's division was to clear the town of Mechanicsville and the bridge across the Chickahominy River. Divisions of Major Generals James Longstreet and D.H. Hill were then to move forward in support of A.P. Hill and Jackson respectively. These four commands would "sweep down the Chickahominy," presumably in pursuit of a confused and frightened Federal Army. Paragraph II ordered Huger and Magruder to "hold their positions in front of the enemy" during the early action and join the chase if and when it developed.

Two potential problems fairly leapt from the page containing these instructions. First, if McClellan realized Huger's and Magruder's thinly spread ranks were

all that stood between him and Richmond, surely he would attack in strength and win a relatively easy victory. Second, if the four generals leading the attacking troops on the Confederate left failed to coordinate their movements and press the advantage offered by Lee's strategy, the crushing blow might be blunted and come to naught.

Lee and his Commander in Chief, Jefferson Davis, worried considerably about the first of these possibilities. And to Huger the commanding general wrote that he was to hold his lines "at the point of the bayonet if necessary." The second potential problem caused much less anxiety. The two Hills, Longstreet, and Jackson

An engraving depicting elaborate Federal defenses at Ellerson's Mill during the Seven Days.

were veteran soldiers who would instinctively exploit their advantages. Especially this was true of Jackson. Apostle of Calvin and Mars, Jackson had recently concluded a brilliant campaign in the Shenandoah Valley. His "foot cavalry" had moved fast and fought hard in the course of defeating a combined enemy force more than twice its size.

On the day he signed General Orders No. 75, Lee expressed his primary concern by riding off to the Williamsburg Road and observing some skirmishing on his vulnerable right. The errand caused him to miss a visit by President Davis who, no doubt, came to Lee's headquarters seeking reassurance about the same sector.

Next day, June 25, McClellan gave Lee and Davis moments even more anxious. Although he had not yet

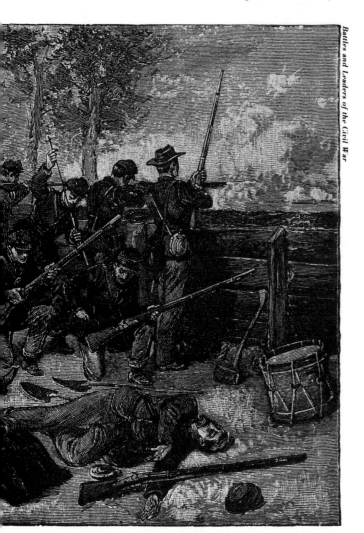

Battles and Leaders of the Civil War

prepared an attack order, McClellan was on the verge of delivering a blow. In preparation for a general attack upon Confederate lines east of Richmond, he ordered the divisions of Brigadier Generals Philip Kearny and Joseph Hooker to advance through the mile or so of empty woods between them and the Confederates and conduct a limited assault. The Federals moved in the morning through swamp and brush and emerged in the afternoon on a broad field. Through the drizzling rain the men saw on the other side of the open space the Southern breastworks. Sharp fighting flared as the blue infantry drove back pickets and skirmishers and tested the Confederate line. McClellan himself appeared on the scene to view the action. Then in the late afternoon came the order to halt, throw up breastworks, and wait. McClellan was adhering to his plan for "regular advances."

He was also responding to some very bad tidings. While on the Williamsburg Road overseeing Hooker's and Kearny's advance, a courier brought word to McClellan that a Confederate deserter had appeared at his headquarters with news that Jackson, who was supposed to be in the Shenandoah Valley, was actually behind the Federal right flank. McClellan hurried back to his headquarters and, as far as possible, confirmed his fears.

Aware of the worst and able to guess what Lee intended for the next day, McClellan did not immediately respond to the peril of Porter and his men. First he took time to compose a message to Washington. He informed his superiors that Jackson was nearby, predicted the attack on his right flank, and projected the enemy strength at 200,000. "I am in no way responsible . . .," he protested, "I have not failed to represent repeatedly the necessity for reenforcements . . . if the result of the action . . . is a disaster, the responsibility cannot be thrown on my shoulders; it must rest where it belongs." Of course McClellan in fact outnumbered his foe, and he had been reinforced, although never to the extent he desired. But McClellan was convinced that his superiors, President Abraham Lincoln and Secretary of War Edwin Stanton, had not supported his campaign, and he alternately suspected their wisdom and their patriotism. Thus in anticipation of Lee's attack he committed his absolution to writing and entered it upon the record. Then only did he ride to Porter's headquarters and prepare to meet the attack.

Rebels ripping across the field at Beaver Dam Creek to turn the Federal flank.

No one knew it at the time, but the action of June 25 on the Williamsburg Road was the first of the Seven Days Battles. Variously named the Battle of Oak Grove, King's School-House, French's Field, or French's Orchard, the action cost the Union 516 casualties. The Confederates lost 316 men. McClellan unwittingly had probed the most glaring weakness in Lee's scheme and not discovered his opportunity. Instead he was acting as though he were following, not countering, General Orders No. 75.

At 3 o'clock on the morning of June 26 Jackson's troops were supposed to be forming around Ashland for the advance to Porter's rear. They were late. By 10 o'clock that morning, they were on the march but already six hours behind schedule. At 3 o'clock in the afternoon, Jackson was still nowhere near the scene.

A.P. Hill could restrain himself no longer. The 36-year-old general with his red beard and red shirt watched as skirmishers cleared the Federal pickets in front of his division. He waited anxiously in the steaming heat, listening for sounds indicating Jackson's approach. Like McClellan, Hill's roommate at West Point, who also waited for Jackson, he did not like the strange silence. Finally Hill decided to move in anticipation of Jackson's arrival. He assumed that Jackson must be nearby and on that belief ordered the attack to begin.

Five infantry brigades with attendant artillery swung into action and swept through the small hamlet of Mechanicsville. Then as they advanced on line they

encountered Porter's well-prepared position behind Beaver Dam Creek, just about a mile from Mechanicsville. Federal artillery raked the Southern ranks and rifle fire followed. Commanders on the field attempted to turn the Federal flank to no avail. As darkness descended, the day seemed a failure for Lee and the Confederates.

But Lee determined to make one final charge and attempt to flank Porter's left. Brigadier General Roswell S. Ripley's brigade from D.H. Hill's division had finally struggled across the Chickahominy, the first of Hill's command to do so. Lee ordered Ripley to attack the Federal left immediately. Soon after receiving Lee's order, Ripley received almost the same command from Jefferson Davis. The President had ridden to the scene and without Lee's

Right: Southerners pouring through Mechanicsville in hasty retreat. A June 22, 1862, sketch by Alfred R. Waud.

knowledge, repeated his order. Ripley's two regiments charged forward into the open twilight toward the darkening undergrowth which fringed Beaver Dam Creek. As they came on, the Federals opened fire with artillery and small arms. A few Confederates reached the opposite bank of the creek—too few to breach the Union works. And in the end, they all fell back—all but 477 casualties left behind in the growing darkness.

Lee's masterful plan miscarried. Instead of maneuvering Porter's troops out of their entrenchments, the Confederates assaulted them frontally. The day's action cost the Union 361 casualties and the Confederacy 1,484. Perhaps Hill should not have assumed so much when he ordered the advance without hearing from Jackson. Certainly Lee and his staff should have been better able to coordinate actions once the battle began. But the main blame seemed to be Jackson's for his uncharacteristic tardiness. While Ripley's doomed brigade was forming for its futile charge, Jackson's troops were making camp a few miles away, within earshot of the battle. What had happened to the Valley army and its vaunted commander?

Several factors contribute to an explanation of Jackson's actions or lack of them on June 26. He was

Confederate Brigadier General Roswell S. Ripley.

slow in forming his troops and pushing them onto the road, and once on the march the columns met harassment from Federal cavalry. He was in unfamiliar territory without adequate maps or guides, and when he neared the scene of action, he was blind to what was taking place at Beaver Dam Creek. These circumstances were important, but they do not fully explain Jackson's lassitude. Nor do they explain Jackson's subsequent failings during the Seven Days.

The most plausible solution to the riddle of Jackson's behavior during this period has been described variously as "fog of war" or "stress fatigue." The man was simply worn out from marching, fighting, responsibility, and sleeplessness. On the morning after the Battle of Mechanicsville (June 27), Jackson resumed his cautious approach until he found the war. There was symbolism, though, in the fact the first artillery shells Jackson's men fired after discovering Lee's and McClellan's armies fell among some troops of A.P. Hill's division.

During the night McClellan had ordered Porter to fall back from his exposed position on Beaver Dam

154

Brigadier General John Bell Hood, whose troops broke the Union line.

Grapevine Bridge across the bloody Chickahominy.

The red-shirted general, A.P. Hill.

Creek and form a new line to the southeast behind Gaines's Mill on Boatswain's Swamp. Lee was committed to continue pressing the issue against Porter and so followed the Federals, again with the intent of flanking them out of position with Jackson and D.H. Hill. In the early afternoon of June 27, A.P. Hill again led the assault on the Federal line, while Jackson again blundered. This time he got lost as he attempted to gain Porter's right flank and chose to backtrack. A.P. Hill's troops fought all but alone against the Federals for five hours and by early evening the tide of battle seemed to be turning in favor of Porter's outnumbered men.

Finally at about 7 o'clock in the evening Lee was able to mount a general assault. Jackson roused himself to send a vigorous message to his subordinates: "this affair must hang in suspense no longer; sweep the field with the bayonet."

The break came first where it was least expected, in the center of Porter's line. There the men had engaged A.P.

Mass.—MOLLUS Collection

Above: One-armed Major General Philip Kearny

Below: Kearny leading troops at Williamsburg. A wash drawing by A.R. Waud.

Library of Congress

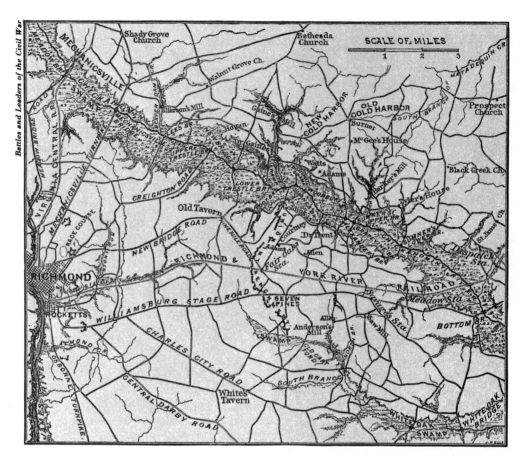

Map of the Richmond-Chickahominy area showing neighboring country and battlefields.

Hill's Confederates since 2 o'clock and now fresh attackers came at them. Credit for the breakthrough is given usually to Brigadier General John Bell Hood's brigade. They held their fire as they approached and suffered their losses without responding. But they continued to advance. The Southern troops were on the verge of using bayonets when the first rank of Federals fled. Then Hood's men commenced firing, moving forward, and firing again. At last they crashed through and saw before them a steady retreat by bluecoated soldiers from many sections of the front.

In an attempt to stop the oncoming Confederates and permit an orderly withdrawal, Brigadier J. E. B. Stuart's father-in-law, Federal Brigadier General Philip St. George Cooke, ordered a cavalry charge. The gallant gesture turned into a fiasco, however. Having breached lines held by entrenched infantry, the Confederates had little fear of men who had to shoot at them from galloping horses. Consequently, the charge became a stampede to the rear, and Porter later claimed that he lost fourteen guns because of the confusion Cooke created.

Once again darkness halted the battle action on this the third of the Seven Days, known as the Battle of Gaines's Mill or First Cold Harbor or the Chickahominy. The casualty figures were frightening: 6,837 Union and 8,750 Confederates. In the dark, Porter managed to get his shattered corps across the Chickahominy to join the rest of the Army of the Potomac. Lee, grateful for his

first bona fide victory, set to work reorganizing his forces to press the advantage.

Thus far Lee's counteroffensive had been only a limited success. McClellan's army was still very much intact; indeed only one of his five corps had even been engaged. And Lee was still gambling that his attacks on McClellan's right would threaten his supply line to the Pamunkey and distract the Union commander from the thin Southern ranks directly in front of Richmond. On the night of June 27, Lee's audacity paid dividends. Even though the Federal line had bent instead of broken, McClellan was frantic for the safety of his army. He determined to "change his base" of supplies from the Pamunkey River to the James and accordingly ordered a general withdrawal in the direction of Harrison's Landing. Of course, it took no genius to pronounce McClellan's "change of base" a retreat. Lincoln termed it a "fall back;" one Federal soldier was more graphic in calling the move a "great skeedadle."

McClellan reached this conclusion when near the field at Gaines's Mill. Even before Hood's troops broke the center of Porter's line, the Union commander hurried to his headquarters to organize the movement. He did not act without opposition from his subordinates. Joseph Hooker and Phil Kearny, especially, were loud in their demands to storm Richmond with their divisions. Both men had realized that Magruder's and Huger's bluff was precisely that and wanted to prove it. But McClellan believed he knew better. Convinced his army was outnumbered and his supply line imperiled, McClellan persisted in his decision to retreat.

Somewhat earlier in the day the Federal headquarters had received a message from Washington. In an effort to serve the defense of the Capital, Lincoln and Stanton had formed the Army of Virginia and brought John Pope east to command the new force. Pope, under the proper circumstances, was available to support McClellan from the north. For now, though, Pope offered only advice. Lincoln informed McClellan, "General Pope thinks if you fall back it would be much better toward the York River than toward the James." Such counsel McClellan did not want to hear and so did not even bother to reply.

Late in the evening of June 27, however, McClellan determined to set his government straight about his circumstances. So he sent a long telegram which revealed the state of his mind at this critical juncture:

> If we have lost the day we have yet preserved our honor, and no one need blush for the Army of the Potomac. I

have lost this battle because my force was too small. I again repeat that I am not responsible for this, and I say it with the earnestness of a general who feels in his heart the loss of every brave man who has been needlessly sacrificed today. I still hope to retrieve our fortunes, but to do this the government must view the matter in the same earnest light I do. . . . As it is we have lost nothing but men, and those the best we have. . . . I know that a few thousand men would have changed this battle from a defeat into a victory. As it is, the government can not and must not hold me responsible. . . .

McClellan concluded the message, "If I save the army now, I tell you plainly that I owe no thanks to you or to any other persons in Washington. You have done your best to sacrifice this army." Mercifully Lincoln was spared his general's closing insubordination; the telegraph supervisor deleted the final two sentences before sending the message to the President.

Having cleared away his bitterness, McClellan resumed his concern for saving his army. Across the Chickahominy, Lee, though he did not know it yet, had the opportunity to transform a costly victory into the annihilation of his foe.

Yankee artillery playing on the Rebels at the Battle of Gaines's Mill.

Victory and Defeat at Malvern Hill

by Emory Thomas

McClellan blows up his supply dumps and begins his retreat toward the James River in this sketch by Alfred R. Waud.

On the morning of June 28, 1862, General Robert E. Lee rode out upon the ground his army had secured the evening before. He wanted to survey the field as any victorious general might and, like any other father, he also wanted to find his youngest son, a private in the Rockbridge Artillery. Fruits of the victory in the Battle of Gaines's Mill, however, seemed overripe; on the field were dead, dying, and wounded soldiers and the horrible debris of battle. Lee found young Robert safe and asleep, while details of soldiers began the grisly task of burying those whose sleep was permanent. There were so many corpses and so little time. As a result, graves were often shallow, and when local hogs reclaimed the land, they would root up skulls and bones for some time to come.

The Peninsula Campaign still required conclusion, even though Lee's Army of Northern Virginia had broken a portion of the lines held by General in Chief George B. McClellan's Army of the Potomac the night before. Since March, when McClellan's minions had landed on the Peninsula, the Confederates had feared for Richmond and their fragile nationhood. The Federals had marched to Richmond's suburbs before a bungled counterattack by the Southerners resulted in wounds to Joseph E. Johnston. Lee then assumed command and immediately began planning what became the Seven Days Battles. Leaving an uncertain screen before Richmond, Lee loaded his left, brought Major General T.J. "Stonewall" Jackson down from the Shenandoah Valley and struck McClellan's right flank. Three days of close contact and heavy fighting brought the armies to a decisive point on June 28; McClellan had determined to retreat to the James, but Lee did not know it.

The Confederates could see Union wagons moving down the bank of the Chickahominy River and none coming the other way. They saw smoke and sensed that the Federals were lightening their load for movement. Yet no one could be sure that McClellan was withdrawing or if he were, in which direction. Lee sent Brigadier J.E.B. Stuart's cavalry to try to discern the Federal intent and likewise dispatched Major General Richard S. Ewell's infantry division down the east bank of the Chickahominy. Back on the scene of the bloody battle of June 27 and throughout the Southern line, Lee ordered the work of reorganization to hasten and all units to

stand ready for the pursuit of McClellan's veterans.

On the Union side McClellan was proceeding prudently. Convinced he was outnumbered and in a desperate way, McClellan ordered Brigadier General Fitz John Porter's corps, which had born the brunt of the fighting for the last two days, to march south and secure Malvern Hill covering the escape route. In reality, the bluecoats were numerically superior and options still remained to seize Richmond from the lines they held; but McClellan persisted in believing that his army was about to be destroyed. Consequently, he dispatched his 5,000 wagons toward Harrison's Landing on the James and ordered his infantry to follow. His former supply base at White House on the Pamunkey River was to be ordered de-

The sick and wounded in this Union field hospital Station were left behind by McClellan's retreating army. Photograph by James F. Gibson.

stroyed. When Stuart's cavalry troops reached the scene somewhat later, they found two square miles of smoldering devastation.

As the June sun was nearing the western horizon on the 28th, Lee resolved to act. He acted more from calculated guess and instinct than from any firm intelligence about McClellan's movements. Yet he realized that if the Federal Army were enroute to the James, he would have an opportunity to destroy it only if he moved rapidly and decisively. Lee took a characteristic risk and ordered an all-out pursuit. He ordered the divisions of Major Generals John B. Magruder and Benjamin Huger, men who had been screening Richmond from the bulk of the Federal Army for several nervous days, to move forward (to the east) and attempt to strike the retreating columns on the flank. To Jackson, who had been a disappointment thus far in the Seven Days, Lee

Louisiana State University

Major General John B. Magruder, rebuked by Lee for his delay at the Battle of Savage's Station.

gave Major General D.H. Hill's division and orders "to press directly upon McClellan's rear with his whole force." The divisions of Major Generals A.P. Hill and James Longstreet were to march southeast and strike the Federals below White Oak Swamp, at least wounding their flank and perhaps cutting off the retreat entirely. Lee even ordered Major General Theophilus H. Holmes and his division from picket duty south of the James (near Drewry's Bluff) and pressed them into the chase.

Even though June 29 was a day devoted for the most part to reorganization and readiness in both armies, there was fighting at Garnett's and Golding's Farms near the Gaines's Mill battlefield and at Dispatch Station, where Ewell's division attempted to discern McClellan's intentions. Lee's orders prescribed the grand pursuit to begin early on June 29.

"**P**rince John" Magruder remained awake and active throughout the night of the 28th, preparing his subordinates for the next days' actions. His stomach was boiling, perhaps from nervousness and certainly from the

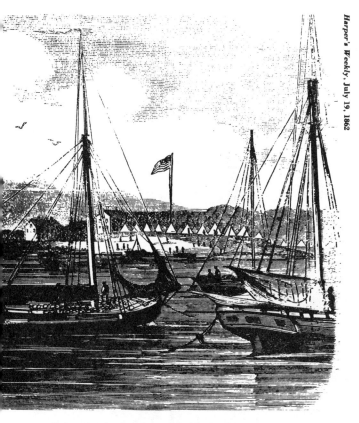

Harper's Weekly, July 19, 1862

Finally, prodded by Lee, Magruder ordered a "general" assault. Yet of six brigades on hand, he employed only two and one half. The advance thus sputtered near Savage's Station. The Confederates sustained 354 casualties before darkness and a thunderstorm combined to close the action. Lee's comment on the day and the Battle of Savage's Station was as close as the courtly commander could come to a stinging rebuke. To Magruder, Lee wrote:

> I regret very much that you have made so little progress today in pursuit of the enemy. In order to reap the fruits of our victory the pursuit should be most vigorous. I must urge you, then, again to press on his rear rapidly and steadily. We must lose no more time or he will escape us entirely.

Lee, of course, might have directed similar words of censure at others among his subordinates. Jackson, for example, consumed the entire day of June 29 rebuilding Grapevine Bridge and did not cross the Chickahominy until the early morning of June 30. Stuart spent the 29th allowing his troops to help themselves to the

medicine he had taken for his indigestion. At 3:30 on the morning of the 29th he began his march along the axis of the Richmond & York River Railroad down the Nine Mile and Williamsburg Roads. He realized that his would be the first troops to strike the enemy, but he depended upon Jackson to cross Grapevine Bridge over the Chickahominy and support his left. And he depended upon Huger whose men were proceeding down the Charles City Road to support his right.

Magruder moved cautiously. As he neared the old battlefields at Seven Pines and Fair Oaks he slowed his advance, then stopped. Anxiously he inquired of Jackson's movements and of Huger's. Then he became convinced that the Federals to his front were about to attack with force superior to his own. Consequently he requested and received two brigades of Huger's division and set about preparing a defensive position from which to receive the attack. By this time many precious hours had slipped away.

Artist A.R. Waud's on-the-spot drawing of artillery of Smith's division engaging the Rebels at White Oak Swamp.

Library of Congress

Mass.—MOLLUS Collection

Major General Fitz John Porter. His forces were sent to Malvern Hill to cover the Union retreat.

162

The Battle of Savage's Station from a sketch at the time by Alfred R. Waud (above). Union supply wagons and railroad box cars on the siding at Savage's Station, June 27, 1862 (below).

McClellan's army destroyed this railroad bridge at White Oak Swamp during its retreat (above). Photograph by Mathew Brady. Franklin's corps of General W. F. Smith's division comprised part of the Union rearguard at White Oak Swamp (below). Painting by Julian Scott.

Federal leavings at White House and gathered little useful intelligence during the pursuit. But might-have-been victories could not concern Lee on the morning of June 30; he still hoped his forces would be able to converge upon the withdrawing Federals and drive together for the jugular.

McClellan was in no position to blame or praise anyone regarding his thus far successful escape. After Gaines's Mill he was never on the scene of battle. Accordingly his corps and division commanders had to work out their separate salvations with little active guidance from the commanding general.

On June 30 Lee's planned convergence again miscarried. Again Jackson was slow and indecisive in his advance. Again Magruder vacillated, and Huger allowed felled trees across the Charles City Road to block his advance. As a result Longstreet's and A. P. Hill's divisions were all but alone in the assault which began about four o'clock in the afternoon against the Federal division commanded by Major General George A. McCall.

The Confederates were successful at first. They broke McCall's line and even captured McCall who was reconnoitering a position for reinforcements and searching for some of the wounded. But Hill and Longstreet struck very near the geographical center of the Army of the Potomac

and reinforcements were near at hand. Brigadier Generals Philip Kearny's and Joseph Hooker's divisions along with Brigadier John Sedgwick's closed the gap. In brutal, often hand-to-hand fighting amid tangled undergrowth which resulted in the wounding of Sedgwick, the battle, later named Frayser's Farm or White Oak Swamp or Glendale, raged into the night. When it was over the Union line had held, and McClellan's escape was all but secure.

During the night of June 30 four Union corps took up positions on Malvern Hill. McClellan's remaining corps (Brigadier Erasmus D. Keyes's) occupied Harrison's Landing about seven miles away. The huge wagon train of the Army of the Potomac was at Harrison's Landing too, safely under the guns of Federal warships on the James. Malvern Hill was the last place on which the blue army needed to make a stand before reaching the relative sanctuary of Harrison's Landing. Fitz John Porter's corps had been on the ground since June 29, and these veterans of Mechanicsville and Gaines's Mill appreciated the natural strength of the position. Flanked by Turkey Run and Western Run, the plateau was a mile wide. It overlooked open fields of fire to the north, and beyond the open ground was dense, swampy forest. Only one practicable road led through the forest; thus any army approaching Malvern Hill would have to deploy for attack on the open ground at the base of the plateau.

Men of Kearny's division repulse Confederate attack in the Battle of White Oak Swamp (also called Glendale or Frayser's Farm). Drawing by A.R. Waud.

Straw-hatted troops of the 16th New York wait to go into action in the Battle of White Oak Swamp. On the hilltop Slocum's artillery engages Huger's on the Charles City Road. Drawing by A.R. Waud.

On July 1 such a position held in strength by four-fifths of McClellan's army naturally gave Lee pause. He considered flanking the Federal right and attempting to impose his army between Malvern Hill and Harrison's Landing. Such a plan, however, was much easier to order than to execute, and the Army of Northern Virginia had not distinguished itself by coordinated movements and aggressive marching during recent days. Consequently Lee dispatched Longstreet to reconnoiter the situation and determine "the feasibility of aggressive battle."

Longstreet returned to report around noon of July 1. He had climbed a hill beyond the Federal left and surveyed the Union position. It was formidable, Longstreet confirmed; but, as he recalled later, "the tremendous game at issue called for adventure." Massed artillery where he was (near the Crew house) on the right and more massed artillery on the left (at the Poindexter Farm) might catch the enemy's guns in a deadly crossfire. Then with the Federal artillery in disarray and the lines of infantry raked with shot and shell, Confederate foot soldiers might carry the position with a vicious charge. Such was Longstreet's vision. And Lee saw it too.

He had exercised field command for exactly one month. He had forged a splendid army, but that army's organization was still very much makeshift. If Lee could not entirely depend upon his subordinate commanders to execute his orders with speed and vigor, he had faith in his soldiers. The situation at Malvern Hill was scarcely as sanguine as had been the circumstances on the other

six of the Seven Days. But had he and his army come this far only to shrink from the moment of truth? He must not allow McClellan to slip away into sanctuary, and here was the last chance. Perhaps the same thoughts and emotions took charge of Lee before Malvern Hill as dominated him later—before Cemetery Ridge at Gettysburg. Aware of the odds, he gambled upon total victory.

Lee's order seemed simple: "Batteries have been established to rake the enemy's line. If it is broken, as is probable, Armistead, who can witness the effect of the fire, has been ordered to charge with a yell. Do the same." Brigadier General Lewis A. Armistead led the Confederate brigade at the foot of Malvern Hill directly before the Federal position. It was Armistead who was to initiate the charge when he determined the artillery barrage had done its work. Little more than a year later

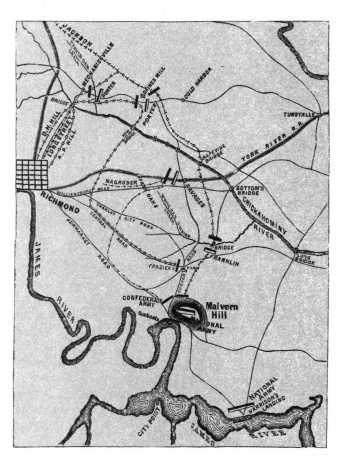

Map of the Union retreat to Harrison's Landing.

Brigadier General Lewis A. Armistead led the first Confederate charge at Malvern Hill.

Armistead would lead another charge—Pickett's at Gettysburg—and die in the attempt.

As it happened, the Southern artillery never really fought its duel with the Federal guns at Malvern Hill. Faulty organization, faulty staff work, and outranged guns prevented the Confederates from massing their pieces where Longstreet had indicated with the speed Lee required. Consequently the reserve artillery never got into action and "massed guns" never materialized. As D.H. Hill described it, the artillery fire was "almost farcical."

All this was evident by three o'clock in the afternoon. Lee saw no need to cancel his order, as the charge had been contingent upon the artillery's success. With Longstreet the commanding general rode toward the left of his lines to investigate the possibility of a flanking maneuver. He asked Longstreet to move to the left, and then he rode back toward the center. There he found that some of the Federals before him were withdrawing.

Armistead's men drove back Union skirmishers and moved forward apace. Lee believed—perhaps he wanted to believe—that McClellan was resuming his retreat. This was absolutely the last chance. Thus Lee ordered an immediate, general advance.

Fitz John Porter described the result:

> An ominous silence, similar to that which had preceded the attack in force at Gaines' Mill, now intervened, until, at about 5:30 o'clock, the enemy opened upon both [George W.] Morell and [D.N.] Couch with artillery from nearly the whole of his front, and soon after pressed forward in columns of infantry, first on one, then on the other, or on both.
>
> As if moved by a reckless disregard of life equal to that displayed at Gaines' Mill, with a determination to capture our army or destroy it by driving us into the river, brigade after brigade rushed at our batteries; but the artillery of both Morell and Couch mowed them down with shrapnel, grape, and canister, while our infantry, withholding their fire until the enemy were in short range, scattered the remnants of their columns, sometimes following them up and capturing prisoners and colors.

The charge, or rather the ragged succession of charges, was a disaster. At dark the men on both sides remained more or less where they were and in the night

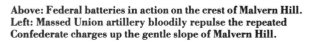

Above: Federal batteries in action on the crest of Malvern Hill. Left: Massed Union artillery bloodily repulse the repeated Confederate charges up the gentle slope of Malvern Hill.

Northern and Southern soldiers mingled in their efforts to minister to the wounded and dying. On Malvern Hill were 8,000 casualties; the Confederates lost over 5,000 men and the Federals fewer than 3,000.

Next morning, July 2, the field lay in a thick mist. As the sun burned away this veil a Federal officer observed: "A third of them [bodies on the field] were dead, but enough were alive and moving to give the field a singular crawling effect. The different stages of the ebbing tide are often marked by the lines of flotsam and jetsam left along the seashore. So here could be seen three distinct lines . . . marking the last front of three Confederate charges of the night before."

The Seven Days Battles and the Peninsula Campaign to which the battles belonged were over, although no one could be sure of this then. The last week of daily conflict had cost the Union 16,000 casualties of 115,000 men involved. The Confederate loss was about 20,000 of their 88,000 total. The Army of the Potomac was safe; Richmond was safe. Neither commander was satisfied.

Lee had established himself and his Army of Northern Virginia, and in Richmond he was a savior. But he knew he had lost opportunities to destroy his adver-

Union gunboats covering the retreat to Harrison's Landing.

saries. To President Davis, he reported on McClellan at Harrison's Landing: "I fear he is too secure under cover of his boats to be driven from his position. I discover no intention of [his] either ascending or crossing the river at present." To his army Lee announced, "Today the remains of that confident and threatening host lie upon the banks of James River, thirty miles from Richmond, seeking to recover, under the protection of . . . gunboats, from the effects of a series of disastrous defeats." But to his wife, he confided, "Our success has not been as great or as complete as I could have desired," and later reported, "Under ordinary circumstances the Federal Army should have been destroyed."

McClellan, the would-be conqueror, surveying the blood and mud in which his army lay at Harrison's Landing, began thinking about renewing the offensive, and then lapsed into anxiety about the security of his force. He asked for 100,000 reinforcements, and Lincoln informed him there were not 75,000 more soldiers anywhere in the Eastern Theater. Then on July 8 Lincoln came to see for himself the state of the army at Harrison's Landing. McClellan took advantage of the Presi-

dent's presence to give him in writing his views about how this war should be conducted. The general favored a limited war which disturbed neither slavery nor property; the President read the letter and put it in his pocket.

After Lincoln returned to Washington, McClellan was left to watch his army lick its wounds and to reflect. About the President, McClellan wrote his wife, "I can never regard him with other feelings than those of thorough contempt." At the urging of some Northern politicians, he even flirted with the notion of marching on Washington and staging a coup. In the end he did nothing. In August the army began evacuating the Peninsula to join Pope before Washington.

The Army of the Potomac, like its adversary, had proven itself in adversity on the Peninsula. But at Harrison's Landing its major achievement belonged to Brigadier General Daniel Butterfield, who had led one of Porter's brigades until wounded at Gaines's Mill. While the army lay inert under the hot Virginia sun remembering the Peninsula Campaign, Butterfield altered an old army bugle call—and produced *Taps*.

SECOND
MANASSAS

by Dennis Kelly

August 1862: The rout of the Federal Army of Virginia at Second Manassas (Second Bull Run), was a severe setback for the Union. Sketch by Alfred R. Waud. (Library of Congress)

An Impudent General

The year 1862 was half over. It had begun as a year of promise for the Union, a year promising extermination for the Confederacy. Kentucky, Missouri, and western Virginia were in Union hands. Tennessee had been pierced by Union armies, New Orleans captured, and the Atlantic coastline overrun. With the Federals' Army of the Potomac advancing up the Virginia Peninsula on Richmond, President Abraham Lincoln's sometimes impulsive Secretary of War, Edwin M. Stanton, became so confident no more soldiers would be needed, that the end of war was so close at hand, in April he closed down army recruiting stations. Confederates, by contrast, resorted to conscription to keep manpower in the ranks.

Then, just as the Union war wagon seemed to be rolling smoothly, its wheels came off. That elusive Confederate, Major General Thomas J. "Stonewall" Jackson, appeared and disappeared in the Virginia countryside with his troops, defeating Major General John C. Frémont in the mountains west of the Shenandoah Valley. Stanton, from piles of contradictory reports, concluded Jackson was withdrawing from the valley. Major General Irvin McDowell believed he might surface on his front at Fredericksburg. With

speed unimagined by the Federals, Jackson doubled back from the mountains and struck at Front Royal, then again two days later at Winchester, defeating Major General Nathaniel P. Banks and sending his soldiers fleeing across the upper Potomac River.

Jackson's whereabouts and intentions now seemed assured—he was advancing on Washington! From Baltimore, Maryland, and Washington, D.C., every available fighting man rushed to where he was figured to surface next: Harpers Ferry, Virginia. Appeals for help were telegraphed to the Northern states; militia and home guard regiments were hurried to rescue the capital.

It was all for nothing. Jackson had already accomplished his objective; any threat to the capital was a ruse. He was withdrawing back up the valley. McDowell's corps, which had been ordered to advance on Richmond and reinforce Major General George B. McClellan, simply dispersed, defeated without having fought. The president and his war secretary had hoped to intercept and destroy the impudent Jackson by squeezing him between Frémont, marching from the west, and McDowell, moving from the east. But Jackson's fast-marching infantry had slipped between the two, defeated Frémont at Cross Keys, then beat McDowell's leading division at

Port Republic before entraining to join the main Confederate army in front of Richmond.

Far away in St. Louis, a 40-year-old major general named John Pope, temporarily on leave of absence from his command in Mississippi, received an urgent telegram from the War Department ordering him to Washington immediately. The president, with whom Pope was on friendly terms, was absent at West Point, New York. So on arrival in the capital Pope reported to the War Department asking after his orders. There he met Secretary Stanton, a man who seemed to have "lost much sleep and was tired in both body and mind." The armies of Frémont, Banks, and McDowell needed to be united, declared the war secretary in his usual curt, dictatorial manner. Together they should threaten Rebel railroad communications at Gordonsville and Charlottesville. That would draw off some enemy forces confronting McClellan, making it easier for him to storm Richmond.

Stanton was not merely musing. He held the general's new assignment. A new army, christened the Army of Virginia, was officially brought into being and Pope placed in command on June 26, 1862. Ironically, this was the very day that Confederate General Robert E. Lee—not McClellan—initiated the battles for Richmond: Mechanicsville, Gaines' Mill, Savage's Station, Frayser's Farm, Malvern Hill. And each blood-spattered place was a little farther away from the Confederate capital than the one preceding.

To Richmond and the South, these fights, the Seven Days' Battles, signified redemption. An enemy on the verge of victory was turned away. Not since the Battle of Manassas, nearly a year past, had there been a cause for Southern celebration. Confederate President Jefferson Davis looked and felt relieved. In seven days, Robert E. Lee had made himself the South's foremost soldier.

To McClellan, the sacrificial week was not a retreat, but a change in the base of operations. He believed his move from the Pamunkey to the James River was accomplished through masterful strategy. To him the Seven Days was a salvation of a different sort. Incompetent spies had deluded McClellan into believing the Confederates had twice the men he had. McClellan felt he and the Army of the Potomac had been deliberately placed in jeopardy, nearly sacrificed by scheming Washington politicians. He was irrationally bitter at the civil administration for not supplying reinforcements he demanded in impossible numbers. His army shared this belief. Now camped twenty-five miles from Richmond at Harrison's Landing, he felt he too had turned back an enemy intent on destroying him.

For the Lincoln Administration and the Union

Robert E. Lee. His Army of Northern Virginia had pushed the enemy from Richmond to the outskirts of Washington in three months. (Harper's Pictorial History of the Great Rebellion)

cause, the week of retreat amounted to a disaster. Jackson's raid in the valley had created local alarm, but the failure on the Virginia Peninsula bred deep gloom, national gloom, a feeling that crept over the Northern states like a sickness. Recruiting offices reopened, and the president issued a call for 300,000 more soldiers. The response was feeble.

The Confederacy was rejuvenated, ascending its pyramid of military power in the summer of 1862. The Union was despondent, its enthusiasm sapped, its strategic initiative stolen, its leadership quarreling among itself, the very purpose of its cause in question. Thus the campaign that culminated in the Second Battle of Manassas (Bull Run) began not at a geographic location, with generals pointing at their maps deciding this or that northern Virginia railroad intersection was strategically important. It began at a point in time.

New Leaders and New Plans

The president had grown dissatisfied with the management of the war. He returned to Washington from the crowded, unhealthy camps at Harrison's Landing, hardly reassured by McClellan. The general had repeated what he had so often written: if an advance on Richmond were to be resumed, he would need heavy reinforcements. He still firmly believed the Confederates greatly outnumbered him.

Despite his misconceived situation, McClellan found time to write his president a long letter, purely political in substance, advising military force not be used as an instrument to upset "the relations of servitude." He believed Americans would rally to the cause of reuniting the nation, but not to freedom for the Negro. If slavery were tampered with, he warned, "our cause will be lost." Lincoln, pondering the necessity of emancipation for some time, replied he was much obliged, and put the document in his pocket.

Soon Lincoln would have two Union armies in Virginia, McClellan's and Pope's, widely separated with the Confederates between them. What should be done with them? Should McClellan be withdrawn to reinforce Pope, or could the two perhaps cooperate and attack Richmond from two directions at once?

The president and Stanton took to reading military manuals. But Lincoln at last concluded strategy was something more than a pair of industrious lawyers could easily master by borrowing primers from the Library of Congress. Expert military judgment was needed. On July 11, Major General Henry Wager Halleck was called from the western theater to Washington to direct all Union forces. John Pope tarried in the capital at the president's request, acting as an unofficial adviser before Halleck arrived.

Lincoln was well acquainted with the Pope family; the general was connected to Mary Todd Lincoln's family by marriage. His father was a Federal judge, and his uncle was a United States senator from Kentucky. He was a West Point graduate, class of 1842, and a Mexican War veteran. And Pope was the polished type of officer, one who preferred staff duty with the topographical engineers to frontier posts and chasing marauding Indians.

At White House dinners he told stories to Lincoln, and Lincoln liked stories. Pope always tried to say the right thing to the right Republican. To an abolitionist like Treasury Secretary Salmon P. Chase, he appropriately mentioned that slavery must perish. To others he spoke forcefully of vigorously prosecuting the war. Among McClellan's many political enemies, when the subject was brought up, he criticized his generalship and endorsed McClellan's removal from army command. He liked telling of his own relatively bloodless victories at New Madrid, Missouri, and Island No. 10 on the Mississippi River earlier in the year. And it was duly noted that what John Pope especially liked to talk about was John Pope.

Pope made a good first impression in his uniform, maintained good eye contact, and had a stiff, rectangular beard. Nevertheless, he did not always impress everyone the way he intended. He was known as the "bag of wind" to his fellow officers in the Regular army. Presidential adviser Postmaster General Montgomery Blair told Lincoln the general's father, Judge Pope, was "a flatterer, a deceiver, a liar, and a trickster; and all the Popes are so." Lincoln admitted Pope's many faults, but credited him with "great cunning."

The general of "great cunning" remained in Washington for several weeks. There he conferred with dignitaries, devised plans, defined procedures and policies, and took stock of his scattered command. He drafted a series of general orders designed to deter any hostile activities behind his troops' Virginia lines, orders that would go harshly on the noncombatant populace of the state. Guerrilla warfare would not be tolerated; guerrillas and anyone who aided them would be shot. Virginians would either take an oath of allegiance to the United States or relocate beyond Union lines. If they violated their oath or returned, they would be treated as spies and shot. No commander was to furnish guards for private property; he was to confiscate whatever horses, forage, or other supplies he needed.

The most severe parts of these orders were not

Union leaders. Left: John Pope, commander of the Army of Virginia at Second Manassas. (Library of Congress) Center: Nathaniel P. Banks, nicknamed "Old Jack's Commissary" for the beating he took from Stonewall Jackson in the Shenandoah, commanded the Army's II Corps. (U.S. Army Military History Institute) Right: Franz Sigel, commander of the I Corps. (USAMHI)

enforced—probably no one was shot. But civilians were outraged, and for good reasons. Many a plantation, farm house, or log cabin in the path of Pope's far flung Army of Virginia suffered pillage at the hands of renegade bands of Union soldiers. "General Pope's orders," they cracked to defenseless families being robbed.* Even Pope was appalled when he learned how his orders were being misapplied, and he threatened severe punishment to miscreants.

The Army of Virginia consisted of three corps, all formerly the forces of three military departments headed by Major Generals Frémont, Banks, and McDowell. Frémont, insulted because he was Pope's senior in rank, resigned his command the day after he learned the general was to be his new commander. About 11,500 men, the Army of Virginia's I Corps, was the new command of Frémont's successor, Major General Franz Sigel. Sigel was enthusiastically received by the corp's predominantely German-American regiments. He was a German-born exile, a veteran of Europe's 1848 insurrections, and he had fought with some distinction in the Civil War's early western battles in Missouri and Arkansas. His personal popularity was such that abolitionist German immigrants swarmed to fill his ranks. This gave his corps a decidedly ethnic tang. Within his three divisions were leaders with names like Schenck, Steinwehr, Shurz, Bohlen, Schimmelfennig, and Kryzanowski. But enthusiasm had its limits. Not long after taking command the corps, encamped in the lower Shenandoah Valley at Middletown, was "in very bad condition in regard to discipline, organization, equipment, and to a great extent, demoralized," Sigel reported to Pope.

Not far from Sigel was the II Corps, commanded by Major General Nathaniel Prentiss Banks, sometimes called "the Bobbin Boy of Massachusetts" because his start came from his father's Bay State cotton mill. Banks was a "political" soldier, which was close to saying he was no soldier at all. He had been Speaker of the House of Representatives in 1856, and was governor of Massachusetts at the outbreak of the war when Lincoln appointed him general because he strongly advocated the Union cause. He was brave and energetic, but Stonewall Jackson's Rebels had captured so much of his foodstuffs that they derisively called him "Old Jack's Commissary General." His two divisions numbered only 8,800 men, hailing mainly from New England, Ohio, New York, and Pennsylvania.

*Later in the war such policies would be considered routine, but at the time Pope became notorious as a moral monster.

Commanding the III Corps was Major General Irvin McDowell, a luckless general who magnified his own misfortunes. He could be rude, ill-tempered, pompous; he was obese and renowned for his indulgence. "While he drank neither wine nor spirits, he fairly gobbled the larger portion of every dish within reach," wrote an officer who once dined with McDowell. That evening he had finished his meal "with an entire watermelon, which he said was 'monstrous fine!'"

His soldiers hated him, and for some irrational reason they believed McDowell was a traitor in league with the enemy. It was McDowell who had commanded in the Union disaster at Manassas the previous summer, and the stigma of failure still lingered. His two divisions were huge, totalling 18,500. One was located at the old battleground, Manassas, the other at Fredericksburg. The corps was predominantly made up of New Yorkers and Pennsylvanians. In this corps was also a conspicuous brigade of westerners from Wisconsin and Indiana.

Completing the complement of troops was a small reserve corps under Brigadier General Samuel D. Sturgis that had been assigned to Pope but was undergoing organization at Alexandria and not yet available. Together with some 5,000 run-down cavalry divided into two brigades, the Army of Virginia totalled 43,800 men.

Pope's mission had undergone only slight modification since he first reported to Stanton. He was to protect Washington; secondly, secure and guard the Shenandoah Valley (now free of Confederates since Jackson departed for Richmond) and, last, help McClellan by operating against enemy communication lines at Gordonsville and Charlottesville.

Even as McClellan was "changing his base" on the Peninsula, Pope issued orders to concentrate his forces along the upper Rappahannock River. Sigel was to move up the Shenandoah Valley to Luray, cross the Blue Ridge at Thornton's Gap, and post himself at Sperryville. Banks was to march across the mountains at Chester Gap and proceed to Little Washington. Brigadier General James B. Ricketts' division of McDowell's corps was to move from Manassas to Waterloo Bridge on the Rappahannock.

The march was slow and disjointed, quickly using up Pope's scant supply of patience. Instead of prompt compliance with his orders, Pope encountered procrastination, excuses, and questions. Instead of pressing forward, subordinates inquired about designated routes of retreat, or what should be done if the enemy were encountered.

"Do?!" roared Pope, "Fight 'em, damn 'em, fight 'em!"

Pope felt his command needed inspiration; it needed to be infused with fresh enthusiasm. "Let us understand each other. I have come to you from the West, where we have always seen the backs of our enemies. . . ." He said he assumed he was called to Virginia "to pursue the same system." He was tired of hearing from subordinates who worried about lines of retreat and their bases of supplies. "Let us study the probable lines of retreat of our opponents, and let our own take care of themselves. Success and glory are in the advance," he closed, "disaster and shame lurk in the rear."

An egoist's attempt to get tough and "create a cheerful spirit," Pope's address was a flat failure. Worse, it backfired. His men, many of them good soldiers, were humiliated by their recent defeats, sensitive to criticism, resentful of any of his comparisons to Westerners. Pope's tactlessness made him the object of scorn and ridicule in three armies—his own, McClellan's Army of the Potomac, and Robert E. Lee's Army of Northern Virginia.

As if this *faux pas* was not bad enough, Pope was said to have told a newspaper reporter that his headquarters would be located "in the saddle." Everybody everywhere howled, saying this general did not know his headquarters from his hindquarters.

Halleck, the eagerly awaited Western expert, reported to Washington in mid-July and immediately departed for Harrison's Landing to confer with McClellan. He, like Pope, had come out of the West with an aura of prestige, based on victories won by his subordinates. Halleck was a West Pointer, author of a book on military science, and a successful San Francisco businessman and lawyer. No one could have foreseen it, but Halleck was not a man on the rise; he had already passed his zenith. Called "Old Brains," he was little more than a scholarly bureaucrat, an officer whose hand was better fitted to the pen than the sword.

When the two generals sat down, McClellan, who recently held the post of general-in-chief and regarded Halleck's appointment "as a slap in the face," told Halleck his 101,000 troops were outnumbered by Lee two to one. Halleck pointed out that Pope was making threatening gestures southward and it was necessary for McClellan's army to do likewise. McClellan said he could attack only if he had 30,000 more men. Halleck responded that the government would be strained to come up with 20,000. McClellan promised he would try if given those reinforcements.

The two men also briefly touched on the idea of removing the Army of the Potomac to northern Virginia and uniting it with Pope's; Halleck created the impression that McClellan would command the force. McClellan maintained this would be a bad idea; the true shield to Washington, he argued, was with his continued presence on the Peninsula.

No sooner had Halleck returned to Washington than McClellan telegraphed, crying he would require no less than 35,000 more men to advance to Richmond. This time, his routine reinforcement demands and overassessments of enemy strength finally caught up with him. Rubbing his elbows while pondering the matter (an irritating and distracting mannerism displayed whenever he was engrossed in thought), Halleck reflected on the estimated size of the Confederate army and reasoned it would be unsound strategy to approach the enemy capital with divided forces. McClellan's and Pope's armies must be united as quickly as possible. On August 3, the Army of the Potomac got its orders: Board transport vessels in the James River and proceed by convoy for the Chesapeake Bay and up the Potomac River to Aquia Creek near Fredericksburg. This would be the army's new base of operations. There, it would be situated to defend Washington, support Pope, and begin a fresh overland campaign against Richmond. Also, Major General Ambrose E. Burnside's IX Corps, returning from a successful expedition to North Carolina, and now aboard transports at anchor off Fort Monroe, was to sail for the same base.

Burnside moved promptly. McClellan, seething with resentment, did not. If his army were recalled then the long, painful trek to Richmond and back would have led to nothing and McClellan would be a failure. He protested as strenuously as he could. The order was a week old when he requested permission to advance on Richmond, but the administration was adamant. Despite repeated messages from Halleck to speed things up, eleven days passed before McClellan got the hated movement underway. Even then he moved with deliberate slowness.

While the Federals made changes, Robert E. Lee rested, refitted, reorganized, and reinforced his Army of Northern Virginia. Its successful defense of the Confederate capital established Richmond as *the* symbol of the Confederacy, much as Washington was the symbol of the Union. So between drills, Confederate soldiers spent a great deal of time digging earthworks around it, a precaution that would make it easier for Lee to make detachments for field operations elsewhere. Meanwhile, the hero of the Shenandoah Valley, Stonewall Jackson, was chafing to take an offensive, one that would extend to an outright invasion of the enemy's country. Jackson would get his chance soon enough.

On July 12 the Confederates received information that part of Pope's forces had entered Culpeper, Virginia. That meant they were just twenty-seven miles above Gordonsville, a community on a northerly bend of the Virginia Central Railroad. This was ominous. Any threat to that railroad, the lone vital rail supply link between Richmond and the Shenandoah Valley, had to be countered whatever the risk, whatever the cost. The Shenandoah produced food the army and much of the northern Confederacy needed. The very next day Lee ordered Jackson with his own division and Major General Richard S. Ewell's division, to board trains for central Virginia.

For two weeks nothing happened. At Gordonsville, Jackson was unable to learn much about Pope's strength or movements. Pope, commanding from Washington, was still concentrating his army along the upper Rappahannock. Only an advance brigade was at Culpeper. McClellan remained idle on the Peninsula, whining for more men.

Lee next dispatched Major General Ambrose Powell Hill's Light Division to reinforce Jackson, bringing Stonewall's strength to 24,000. He retained only 56,000 in the Richmond earthworks to resist a possible advance by McClellan.

Lee had been moved to the depths of his knightly soul by Pope's threats and live-off-the-country measures against his fellow Virginians. For no other opponent did he ever possess the personal dislike he developed for John Pope. "I want Pope suppressed," he told the departing Hill. And Pope "ought to be suppressed, if possible," he wrote his Confederate president. Now with Hill, Jackson might have enough men to suppress Pope and, if necessary, still return to deal with McClellan.

While Jackson waited for an opening, he set up camps in the lovely Virginia Piedmont country, with its lush crops, good water, grassy fields, and groves of timber, far away from the old camps and unhealthy swamps of the Peninsula and the fights for Richmond. For Stonewall it was a new beginning. His performance in the Seven Days had been disappointing, at best. But Lee never expressed one word of dissatisfaction over it. He believed in this general. Formerly a mediocre professor at the Virginia Military Institute, Jackson was a reclusive eccentric with a somewhat unkempt appearance who was profoundly, if not fanatically, religious. His field library consisted of just three books: the *Holy Bible*, *Webster's Dictionary*, and Napoleon's *Maxims of War*. With a fresh start, in the days ahead he would need all three.

Temporarily in command of Jackson's old division was Brigadier General Charles S. Winder, who had a reputation as a tyrant. He had about thirty of Jackson's old troops, the Stonewall Brigade, "bucked"—a humiliating and painful form of punish-

176

Confederate officers. Left: Richard S. Ewell, Jackson's popular subordinate in the Stonewall Brigade, nicknamed "Old Bald Head." (USAMHI) Right: Charles S. Winder, Jackson's tyrannical subordinate. (Battles and Leaders of the Civil War)

ment*—for straggling during the march to Gordonsville. Half of the punished deserted that night; the others swore revenge, threatening the next battle "would be the last for Winder." Beside the Stonewall Brigade was a Louisiana brigade, and another unit, three Virginia regiments brigaded with an untried pair from Alabama. Relatively weak, the division numbered only 4,000 soldiers.

Second in popularity to Stonewall or "Old Jack," was "Old Bald Head," Major General Richard S. Ewell, Jackson's premier subordinate in the Shenandoah. In peculiarities he was not unlike Jackson; both suffered from stomach ulcers and had unnatural sleeping habits. But Ewell was an exdragoon and Indian fighter who habitually cursed in a high-pitched lisp. The two of them got along famously. Ewell's division consisted of Virginians, Louisianans, and a heterogeneous brigade of one regiment each from Alabama, Georgia, and North Carolina. Together, they totalled 7,200 men.

Half of Jackson's infantry, 12,000 men, were in the six-brigade Light Division of A.P. Hill. Two brigades were from North Carolina, one each from South Carolina, Georgia, Virginia, and one predominated by Tennesseans. Hill was a hothead, a proud, sensitive sort with an explosive temper. In part, Lee sent this division away from Richmond to head off an impending duel between Hill and Major General James Longstreet. But after two weeks with Jackson, Hill was bickering again.

Under Brigadier General Beverly Robertson's command, with whom Jackson was displeased, were the

*Each soldier was seated with his hands and feet tied. His knees were drawn up, and a rod inserted, horizontal to the ground, between the arms and the backs of the knees.

1,200 cavalry. "Where's the enemy?" Jackson had asked with a rare smile. "I don't know," replied Robertson. Jackson's face fell and without a further word to Robertson he wrote to Richmond calling for cavalry commander Major General J.E.B. Stuart.

Then came the news Jackson was awaiting. Scouts and spies returned reporting the Yankee army was converging on Culpeper, but only a portion of their force was there now. This was Bank's corps. Ricketts' division of McDowell's corps was also nearby, but a Union division led by Brigadier General Rufus King was far away at Fredericksburg protecting that place until Burnside arrived. Sigel's corps was strung out along the road between Culpeper and Sperryville, one of its divisions still loitering in camp at the base of the Blue Ridge. For some time Jackson had believed Pope would advance to Culpeper. With a swift march he might be able to crush the Federal vanguard before Pope could concentrate his troops or reinforce Banks.

This required a twenty-mile march to the hamlet of Orange. The hike went well on August 7, but the men did not march as tightly knit columns of disciplined troops. The temperature was in the sweltering 90s, and everybody was miserably hot. The army straggled badly. Several men keeled over and died from sun stroke. Only eight miles were covered the next day. Without informing Hill, the secretive Jackson changed the route of march, producing an exasperating mix up. Hill blamed Jackson, Jackson blamed Hill, and a bitter feud between the two began. When one of the staff asked Hill about their next destination, Hill glumly replied he supposed they would go to the top of the next hill, but that was all he knew. Jackson was irritated and gloomy; by now Federal cavalry had obviously reported his location. He decided to press on to Culpeper on August 9, anyway.

A Fight At Cedar Mountain

Major General Pope, who had at last joined his army on July 29, was developing a plan to threaten the Virginia Central Railroad at Charlottesville. He had heard Rebels were coming. But despite urgings from Halleck to be cautious until reinforced, Pope prepared for a fight. Bank's corps was to stop the Confederates, who, Pope decided, were making a reconnaissance in force, until the entire army could be brought up.

Banks' two divisions, under Brigadier Generals C.C. Auger and A.S. Williams, marched forward to support the advance brigade of Brigadier General Samuel Crawford. Crawford, in turn, was supporting a cavalry screen eight miles south of Culpeper along

Cedar Run. Concealing Williams' division on the right flank was a thick woods northwest of the Culpeper Road. Three-quarters of it surrounded a large, rectangular wheat field. Southeast of the road were Auger's troops, hidden in rolling corn fields, his left reaching toward immense Cedar Mountain. It was also known ominously as Slaughter Mountain, after Dr. Slaughter the landholder who farmed its shoulder.

Banks, with 8,000 troops and several cannon, would be on his own. Ricketts' division of McDowell's corps was just three miles to his rear, but Ricketts would spend the day idle. He had no orders to participate. Nor would Sigel take part in the fight. Sigel halted his troops on the only road between Sperryville and Culpeper and stupidly inquired which route to take.

Again the temperature was climbing toward 100° in the late morning when Banks' cannon muzzles blazed fire and roared thunder over Cedar Run, bringing the Confederate vanguard to a halt. Jackson galloped past his columns of puffing men to where he found General Ewell, amusing himself, playing with some little children on a porch. Jackson spread a map and the two studied it. The obvious key terrain feature was Cedar Mountain. Jackson instructed Ewell to take two brigades and some artillery over its shoulder and turn the enemy's left flank. Ewell's remaining brigade, commanded by Brigadier General Jubal A. Early, was to sheer off and proceed straight ahead. Winder's small division was to support Early in echelon along the Culpeper Road. Hill's division would be the reserve. With 20,000 men within reach, Jackson held all the advantages.

A little past 2 p.m., Early's brigade easily drove away Federal cavalry. Then, as they hiked over a ridge, they were hit by Federal artillery fire. Confederates galloped three field pieces to the front. Early had them unlimber in a grove of cedars, and a spirited duel began.

He detached one regiment on his right to partially cover the mile distance between him and Ewell, whose men were approaching the summit of Cedar Mountain. Then Winder's men neared the danger area along the road to Early's left. Four mangled corpses lay victims of one cannon shot. "What is the matter?" a tuckered-out Confederate by the roadside was asked. "I don't want to fight" he replied. "I ain't mad with anybody."

Winder had been ill. Pale and sick, he pulled himself from an ambulance and hurried to the front on horseback, where he deployed Brigadier Generals Richard Garnett's and William Taliaferro's brigades along the road at right angles to Early, and withheld the Stonewall Brigade as reserves. Adjacent to their

position were five cannon answering the Union artillery. Winder dismounted, removed his tunic and began to direct their aim. Far away on the mountain, Ewell was booming away with six guns placed in Dr. Slaughter's yard. Books from Slaughter's library were strewn around the cannon. Yankees had paid an earlier visit.

For two long hours under the smothering August sun the opposing artillerists rammed, primed, and fired at each other. Infantry, for the most part, kept out of sight.

Peculiar things were noticed. In Winder's artillery, every man hit was an officer; not a private was scratched. One officer was given a short ride by a low-flying projectile, but was otherwise unhurt. Some of the infantrymen pinned slips of paper to their jackets with their names and units on them for identification in case they were killed. And some darted from their marching columns to hide things under leaves by the roadside—decks of playing cards. It would be embarrassing to many to be found dead with the Devil's playthings in their pockets.

Gradually, Federal batteries gained the upper hand. Winder was considering a charge across Early's front to take them when the Union guns began shifting their positions. Shouting some inaudible orders to a nearby cannoneer, Winder put his hand to his mouth to repeat himself. A shell tore through him, causing a ghastly, mortal wound. He fell straight backwards. Brigadier Taliaferro, who knew virtually nothing of Jackson's or Winder's plans, was notified the division command had devolved upon him.

After five o'clock the artillery's exchange of iron slackened. Suddenly, Union infantry came swarming out of the woods, charged across the wheat field on the left, over a rise and through the corn in the center. All of Banks' two divisions, less one brigade, were in the assault.

Why Banks attacked later provoked heated controversy. That morning a staff officer from Pope delivered Banks' verbal orders; Banks had him commit them to paper. They read: "General Banks to move to the front immediately, assume command of all forces in the front, deploy his skirmishers if the enemy advances, and attack him immediately as he approaches, and be reinforced from here." Pope contended Banks knew full well he was only supposed to take a strong defensive position and hold it until help arrived. Banks flaunted the message, retorting the language gave him discretion to attack. Banks, "Old Jack's Commissary," was probably looking for a chance to even the score with Jackson, and as soon as he thought he saw an opportunity, he seized it. Like Pope, he had no inkling Jackson's force outnumbered his by more than two to one.

Banks' attack dealt the Confederate army an unex-

pected and staggering blow. "I tell you they slaughtered our men," one Virginia officer wrote home. Crawford's Union brigade crossed the wheat stubble and struck Garnett's brigade in the flank, shattering it. The 1st Virginia Battalion was nearly destroyed. Union Brigadier General George H. Gordon's brigade followed on the heels of Crawford's. Here, where it counted, there were more Federal troops than Confederates.

Taliaferro's men, aligned in the roadway shooting to their front, suddenly found Yankees coming from their left and rear. Their artillery limbered up quickly and cleared out. Brutal hand to hand fighting followed. "We were literally butchered," wept a Virginian. The 47th and 48th Alabama, new regiments, fled in panic—"ran like turkeys," commented another Virginian. "Raw men can't stand that kind of music."

The terrible tune spread to Early's brigade across the road. Brigadier General Edward L. Thomas' brigade had come up on Early's right, and together the two were holding back Auger's Union division. Now out of the woods came Crawford's Federals and Early's left began to melt away. It looked as though Jackson's whole army was on the verge of a rout.

Stonewall Jackson spurred his horse into the smoking melee along the Culpeper Road. There armed men and their deadly missiles seemingly came from all directions at once. Witnesses said he was a transformed man, the "light of battle" was in his grim eyes. He was in danger; his army was teetering on the brink of disaster. He went for his sword, but it was stuck in its scabbard. Unfastening its clasps, he waved the cased sword. "Rally, brave men, and press forward! Your general will lead you," he cried. "Jackson will lead you. Follow me."

His presence was electric. The Southerners began to resist. "What officer is that, Captain?" a captured Federal lieutenant asked. When told, dazzled at being in the presence of a celebrity, he shouted, "Hurrah for General Jackson! Follow your general, boys." (His captors released him then and there.)

The Stonewall Brigade advanced from its reserve position. It was partly broken and driven back. Jackson galloped to the rear for A.P. Hill's division. He found the leading brigade in ranks and Brigadier General Lawrence O'Brian Branch exorting his North Carolinians with a speech. In few words Jackson ordered Branch to lead the counterattack. Brigadier Generals William D. Pender's and James Archer's brigades followed closely behind to his left.

Now the Federals were outnumbered and overwhelmed. Fresh masses of Rebels were coming up through the trees, and the exhausted Northerners broke ranks and tumbled out into the wheat field, the North Carolinians in hot pursuit. A Wisconsin field officer, conspicuously turning to rally his regiment, was felled by a volley that riddled him. Ewell had descended from the mountain and was turning the Federals' left. Early and Thomas had stopped Auger's attack and now began to push it back. "General," called one of Early's colonels, "my ammunition is nearly out; don't you think we had better charge them?"

Williams' and Auger's divisions were steadily forced back across Cedar Run, where they had started their attack an hour and a half before. The Yankees made

August 9, 1862: The charge of Union troops on the left flank of Jackson's army at Cedar Mountain. Both Pope and Jackson claimed victory but, indeed, the battle changed nothing strategically. Drawing by Edwin Forbes. (Library of Congress)

regarded Cedar Mountain the most successful of his exploits." He wrote to Lee: "God has blessed our army with victory."

Even so, he was six miles short of Culpeper and had failed to prevent Pope from concentrating his army. There was no fighting on August 10 or 11; the dead were buried and the wounded removed. The night of the Cedar Mountain fight, the Confederate army left its camp fires burning and by morning had fallen back behind the Rapidan River.

A Lost Hat, Lost Orders, Lost Chances

Pope's first impulse was to pursue (exactly what Jackson hoped for), but he was held in check by General Halleck. The Battle of Cedar Mountain changed nothing strategically. Pope was to hold his position and prevent any Confederate advance while McClellan moved to join him. Pope believed when that happened, Halleck would come from Washington and assume field command; with Pope and McClellan as wing commanders, the combined armies would take care of Lee and Jackson.

Lee's desire to quickly dispose of Pope was increasing. Of course he was delighted with the victory, but he recognized Jackson did not have enough strength

one last thrust. A 164-horse battalion of the 1st Pennsylvania Cavalry came thundering down to blunt the Confederate attack and cover the artillery's withdrawal. Every able Southerner drew a bead and fired, sending riders and horses crashing to the ground. Only seventy-one men returned from the charge.

The fighting was all but over by 7:00 p.m.; Hill's division was pursuing Banks with fresh units. Jackson got a report that a second enemy corps, Sigel's, was not far away. He ordered the men to camp where they were.

Pope rode to the scene, inspected the damage and, after nearly getting himself captured, rode away again. He later pronounced the battle a Union victory. One of his surprised officers, more honest than Pope, wrote to his parents: "I'm sorry I can't twist the facts into a glorious victory. It was a glorious defeat if such an adjective can be used with a noun. A hotter fire than that endured by our men. I do not believe was ever poured upon soldiers, certainly not in this war."

Banks' losses totalled 2,377, of whom 400 men and a brigadier general were prisoners. Some of the Southerners noted, however, the prisoners did not behave like beaten men. The Federals knew they had fought well and their jaunty, cocky attitudes reflected this.

Confederate casualties numbered 1,276. General Winder's death was mourned everywhere save the Stonewall Brigade. Because of his personal participation, certainly not because of his tactics, Jackson

Pope headquartered at Culpeper, near the depot of the Orange & Alexandria Railroad. This posed a threat to the Confederate's vital supply link, the Virginia Central Railroad. (USAMHI)

While the Confederates depended on the Virginia Central Railroad, Pope's only supply line from Washington was the Orange & Alexandria Railroad bridge over Bull Run. (USAMHI)

to exterminate Pope or eliminate the threat to the Virginia Central Railroad. On August 13 he started three divisions under Major General James Longstreet for Gordonsville, leaving scarcely 25,000 men to protect the capital. That same day rumors that McClellan's army was departing the Peninsula were confirmed; it was leaving, Lee concluded, to join Pope. Two days later Lee himself departed.

The race was on. If Lee could move quickly enough, using railroads and taking advantage of the shorter route, he might be able to put an end to Pope's army before McClellan's arrived. Whoever won this race might win a great victory. On the other hand, whoever lost stood a chance of losing the war.

By August 15 Pope had about 52,000 soldiers under his command. Burnsides' IX Corps, 8,000 veterans under Major General Jesse Reno, had joined him from Fredericksburg, and Rufus King's division of McDowell's corps had arrived, too. Lee had about the same number, but he quickly divined Pope had his army in a potentially dangerous place.

They were camped in a horizontal "V" between the Rapidan and Rappahannock rivers, along the Rapidan's banks. The Orange & Alexandria Railroad, Pope's supply and communications line with Washington, ran back at a diagonal to the northeast. Studying his maps, Lee saw Clark's Mountain. If he could move his army undetected behind the mountain, throw it across the Rappahannock around Pope's left while cavalry demolished the Rappahan-

nock railroad bridge, Pope would be helpless and might be destroyed. The opportunity was there. Speed was essential. Lee planned to strike on August 18.

But the Confederates did not assemble quickly enough, and the cavalry blundered. J.E.B. Stuart, in charge of all Southern horsemen, ordered cavalry to rendezvous in back of Raccoon Ford prior to crossing the Rappahannock, but his orders did not stress the urgency involved. Riding up to the hamlet of Verdiersville, he found no one knew anything about the Confederate cavalry camp that was supposed to be nearby. An aide was dispatched to locate the missing brigade of Brigadier General Fitzhugh Lee, the commanding general's nephew, while a puzzled Stuart and the rest of his staff bedded down on a porch. About daybreak a cavalry column clattered up the road toward them. Stuart sent two men to investigate. Instead of a hearty welcome from Fitz Lee there came pistol shots. "Yankee cavalry!" was the warning. The staff scattered. Stuart was on his horse in an instant and jumped it over the garden fence.

Everyone escaped except the officer designated to locate Fitz Lee. Stuart, in his haste, left behind his cloak, plumed hat, and more serious, his haversack containing maps and orders. "Where's your hat?" greeted him for several days. Stuart was humiliated. "I intend to make the Yankees pay dearly for that hat," he wrote to his wife.

What happened was that Fitz Lee, utterly ignorant of the timetable, took a roundabout route and was a day late. At the same time a brigadier who had gone visiting pulled away two Georgia infantry regiments, supposedly guarding the ford road, and had them prepare rations. The unhindered Federal patrol came and departed with all the information they needed. Combined with the overall unpreparedness of the army, the incident caused Lee to postpone the attack until the 20th. By then it was too late.

Halleck in Washington worried that Lee might overwhelm the Army of Virginia before the sullen McClellan joined, and on the 16th he telegraphed Pope to seek a more convenient position behind the Rappahannock. Pope, warned fully by both friends and foes, withdrew from the trap.

For the time being, all the advantages seemed to be with the defending Federals. Deployed along the higher Rappahannock north bank for seven or eight miles above Kelly's Ford, Pope had simply to guard the crossings, protect the railroad, and fend off Lee until the army of the Potomac arrived. With each passing day, Lee's chances grew smaller. He could not afford to lose time or men fording the Rappahannock. His strategy was to maneuver upstream and at the first opportunity swing the Army of Northern Virginia across the first undisputed ford and attack the Union right. For his part Stuart rode ahead of Jackson and Longstreet to probe the fords. But wherever the Confederates moved, there was Pope, alert and blocking their jabs.

Stuart for his part was still smarting over the loss of his hat and haversack. He proposed a cavalry raid to break the Orange & Alexandria Railroad. Lee approved.

On August 22 Stuart crossed the Rappahannock at Waterloo Bridge with about 1,500 troopers and two cannon. Quickly covering the seven miles around Pope's right he rode into Warrenton. So far so good. The excited residents said no Yankees had been around for days. But as the jangling column rode for Catlett's Station and the railroad bridge over Cub Run, massive dark clouds gathered. Late that afternoon they erupted into a violent Virginia summer thunderstorm.

Approaching Catlett's in the evening, Union sentinels were silently eliminated by Stuart's men and replaced by Confederates. A reconnaissance by Captain W.W. Blackford, Stuart's engineer officer, revealed "a vast assemblage of wagons and a city of tents, laid out in regular order and accompanied by the luxuriously equipped quartermasters and commissaries . . . but no appearance of any large

Union soldiers beside damaged rolling stock of the Orange & Alexandria Railroad. Often during the war, both sides tried to use railroads to best their opponent. (Library of Congress)

organized body of troops." Captured Federal guards disclosed even more exciting news—this was Pope's headquarters!

A contraband Negro, one freed from slavery by virtue of residing in Union-occupied territory, was also captured and agreed to guide the raiders to the headquarters tent. Fitz Lee and Stuart selected one of Robert Lee's sons, Colonel W.H.F. "Rooney" Lee, and his 9th Virginia for that task. Two regiments were to hit the camps on the far side of the depot. Another led by Blackford the engineer would set fire to the railroad trestle. When the bugle sounded, everyone was to give a "Rebel Yell."

Union officers that day did not even bother to verify a report that Confederate cavalry was on the move. Some were sitting on the verandah of a house, feet up on the railing, watching the rain. One was having some friends over for a drink. "Now this is something like comfort," said a guest, lifting his glass. "I hope Jeb Stuart won't disturb us tonight." Just then a bugle was heard—close, but the call was drowned out by 1,500 screaming Rebels and their running horses. "There he is, by God!"

Tables and tents were knocked over in the scramble. "I went in with the leading regiment," recalled Blackford later, "and the consternation as we charged down the main street, scattering our pistol balls promiscuously right and left, made men laugh until they could scarcely keep their saddles." Some Pennsylvania infantrymen grabbed rifles and returned the fire from the depot, but the Virginians vaulted their horses onto the platform and crashed into the freight room, ending resistance. A couple of raiders shinnied up telegraph poles, and with a few quick saber swipes the Union army was out of touch with its capital.

General Pope was out for the evening, but to Stuart's delight, his hat, cloak, and one of his dress uniforms were left behind. Most important, the Army of Virginia's headquarters dispatch book and a number of recent messages fell into Confederate hands. This in itself more than compensated for the raid's lack of total success.

The thunderstorm let up a while then broke out anew. Only lightning lit what Stuart called "the darkest night I ever knew." Gusting winds driving a deluge foiled attempts to burn the captured property or the trestle, and by now the recovering Federals were beginning to resist from across the stream. Stuart gave it up as hopeless.

With dawn approaching and rising streams a cause for worry, Stuart recalled his soaking, happy troopers. Hundreds of horses and mules, 300 prisoners and valuable military property, plus the Army of Virginia's money chests, were netted. Pope was broke. Unmolested, the Confederate caravan returned to the Rappahannock the way it came.

Stuart, as a prank, offered to trade Pope's coat back to him in exchange for his plumed hat. Receiving no reply, he sent the coat to Richmond, where it was put on public display. Pope's anger was surely aroused (in Culpeper he gave his lagging troops "a salutation of profanity . . . that would have graced a Mississippi stevedore much better than a major general of the United States Army"), but of that there is no official record. When the telegraph was repaired he told Halleck the damage was "trifling; only some officers' baggage destroyed."

The information gleaned from the raid proved a turning point in the campaign; Lee now knew the plans and strength of his opponents. The situation was grave. To fight now, with Pope and McClellan about to merge forces, would be too dangerous. If Lee could not attack, he could maneuver and force Pope to keep pace with him, all the while moving Pope away from McClellan's reinforcements. This, too, would remove the ravaging Yankees from the agricultural districts of central Virginia.

On Sunday, August 24, Lee rode to Jackson's headquarters at Jeffersonton and conducted a conference outlining his strategy. Jackson was to take his 24,000 men up the Rappahannock and get around the Federal rear and seize the Orange & Alexandria Railroad. The Bull Run Mountains would screen a great part of his movement. Longstreet's 28,000 rifles would take over Jackson's river position, deceive the Federals temporarily, and give him a good start. Speed and surprise were vital; risks were immense. If Pope discovered Confederates were dividing their forces, he could keep them separated, overwhelm one, then the other with superior numbers.

Jackson was excited and drew a rough diagram on the ground with his boot. Napoleon Bonaparte had used similar maneuvers many times in his campaigns, and no doubt Jackson was familiar with them. He made preparations immediately and began the great march before dawn the next morning, Monday, August 25.

Ewell's division took the lead, then A.P. Hill's Light Division, followed by Jackson's under Taliaferro. Only ordnance wagons and ambulances were taken, no extra baggage, and knapsacks were left behind. The regiments and batteries departed their bivouac areas even before rations could be cooked. Many a soldier ate nothing but green apples and raw corn for several days. Covering twenty-six miles the first day, they went past Amissville, across a tributary of the Rappahannock called Hedgemen's River, to Orlean, then another dozen northward miles to Salem on the Manassas Gap Railroad. Villagers and rural folk along the way handed out biscuits, cold chicken, ham, and dippers of water, which were gratefully snatched up by the trudging columns. Homes were besieged by hungry soldiers looking for something to eat. "Please, ma'am," called one South Carolina joker to a lady, "give me a drink of water. I'm so hungry, I ain't got no place to sleep."

The march was continued on August 26, through White Plains toward the looming wall of the Bull Run Mountains. Having turned in an easterly direction now, the men knew their destination was the Union rear. Had Thoroughfare Gap been disputed, there might have been trouble, but not so much as an enemy outpost was encountered. True to his address, Pope was letting his rear take care of itself.

At Gainesville Stuart's cavalry screened the flank toward Warrenton. The last long leg of the journey was to Bristoe Station on the railroad, twenty miles behind Pope's army. Stuart's troopers jumped a small Union guard post there, and Pope's supply line belonged to the Confederates.

They just missed a northbound train, which rumbled through a hasty barricade before it was quite ready. The next two were not so fortunate. The first was derailed and riddled by small arms fire as it turned on its side and crashed down an embankment.* A second train rammed the rear cars of the first. It, too, plunged down the bank in a twisted wreck. The engineer of another train sensed danger, applied the brakes and chugged backward into the gathering darkness, eventually to warn Pope.

Jackson had moved an extraordinary fifty-four miles in forty hours. Not only was he on the enemy's supply line, but he learned their supply base was at Manassas Junction, only three more miles away. Brigadier General Isaac Trimble was asked to take his brigade and seize the junction. "I don't need my brigade," he said. "Just give me my two twenty-ones"—the 21st Georgia and 21st North Carolina.

Stuart's horsemen moved along a parallel road while Trimble's boys hiked the railroad tracks. At midnight they swept over a pair of earthen forts guarding the depot. A battery of artillery was captured, but not before it got off a few token shots.

"Give 'em another round, boys, it's only some damned guerillas." Having hollered that, the battery's officer felt a tap on his shoulder and a Georgia voice drawled from the darkness, "I reckon, colonel, you have got in the wrong crowd."

Maneuvering For Advantage

Pope, **after a poor** start, had handled his army well along the Rappahannock line. Halleck instructed him to hold on for two days and help would be with him.

*This train was pulled by the locomotive "President." To the Rebels' glee, Mr. Lincoln's portrait on the steam dome had a bullet hole through it.

Pope put off Lee for the greater part of a week, throwing him back from the fords, dueling furiously with artillery, keeping cavalrymen always in their saddles.

At last, nineteen days after the order to evacuate the Peninsula, installments from the Army of the Potomac began arriving. First came the Pennsylvania Reserve Division, about 4,700 men under a first-rate Pennsylvanian, Brigadier General John F. Reynolds. These were assigned to McDowell on the northern flank near Warrenton. Pope had become so dissatisfied with Sigel's mishandling of his corps that Sigel, too, was placed under McDowell's guidance. The two corps—McDowell's and Sigel's—and Reynold's division would constitute an informal wing. Pope himself directed the rest of the army from Warrenton Junction on the railroad.

Following Reynolds by several days, on the last leg of a leisurely march upstream from Aquia Creek, was the V Army Corps of Major General Fitz John Porter; two divisions of 10,000 men, one composed mainly of U.S. Regulars, the other of volunteer state troops. These were McClellan men; Porter and his troops had fought and won two of the Richmond battles almost on their own. Once Pope and Porter finally met, Pope noticed Porter's attitude seemed one of "listlessness and indifference not quite natural under the circumstances." If the two were not already enemies they quickly developed an intense mutual dislike for one another. Both orally and in writing, Porter freely expressed his discontent at being under Pope's orders. This would later have bitter and tragic consequences for him.

By rail, another pair of divisions came down, one by one, from the Potomac River wharves at Alexandria. This was the 15,000-man III Army Corps of Major General Samuel P. Heintzelman, a gruff, old Regular, suspected by Pope of being another McClellan supporter. His two divisions' commanders were outspokenly anti-McClellan, so Pope chose to deal directly with them. The first was Brigadier General Joseph Hooker, never one to get along with any of his superiors. Through a journalistic slip he had recently become known as "Fighting Joe Hooker," a nickname he never quite lived down nor up to. The other was one-armed Brigadier General Philip Kearny, a Mexican War veteran. A leader with dynamic qualities, he had also fought for the French in the Italian War of 1859, leading cavalry charges with the bridle reins clenched in his teeth. Kearny hated McClellan. He wrote to a friend up North, "McClellan is a dirty, sneaking traitor."

As fighting material, the reinforcements were excellent. Including a brigade from the mountains of western Virginia awaiting transportation, Pope now commanded more than 75,000 soldiers. Two additional corps of Peninsula veterans were due to disembark at Alexandria within a few days.

But if the movement to reinforce the Army of Virginia was slow, it was also nearly chaotic. Neither Heintzelman nor Porter had wagons or ambulances. Heintzelman's artillery was still en route; Porter had no reserve supply of artillery ammunition. One of Reynolds' brigades was on the verge of riot because it was being fed irregularly.

Their problems could never be solved as long as a communication chasm existed between the generals. Pope and McClellan had not been on speaking terms for six weeks and each dealt directly with Halleck, the general-in-chief. Halleck in his War Department office was evading responsibilities and becoming irritable. Despite what Pope believed, he had no intention whatever of taking the field. When Pope complained he was in the dark about McClellan's forces, Halleck wired: "Just think of the immense amount of telegraphing I have to do and then say whether I can be expected to give you any details as to the movements of others, even when I know them."

To McClellan, now at Falmouth near Fredericksburg desiring information on the whereabouts of Pope, Halleck replied: "You ask for information I cannot give. I do not know either where General Pope is or where the enemy in force is. These are matters which I have all day been most anxious to ascertain." His orders were indefinite, he ignored pressing dispatches. In those last August days Halleck devoted three-quarters of his time to recruiting new troops and to matters far away in the West.

When the telegraph line to Washington went dead on the evening of August 26, Pope first believed Rebel cavalry had done him a favor. He chafed at being tied down to the Rappahannock line; there had been a great deal of marching and counter-marching without accomplishing much. Jackson's flanking maneuver had been detected, and to Pope it seemed likely the Rebel army was heading back to the Shenandoah Valley. He wanted to conduct a reconnaissance in force and, if his guesses were correct, he planned to pitch into their rear. But within twenty-four hours he recognized the situation had taken a turn for the worse; something wrong was going on in *his* rear.

On the morning of Wednesday, August 27, Pope sent word to Halleck through the Falmouth telegraph office; he believed the Confederate army was now at White Plains, northwest of the Bull Run Mountains. They had thrust "a strong column" to Manassas and destroyed the railroad bridges, he reported. "I think it possible they may attempt to keep us in check and throw considerable force across the Potomac in the direction of Leesburg."

This was Pope's appraisal: The enemy was making a large-scale raid and they would have to attempt an escape. For the next four days he would obstinately cling to his false belief. No amount of persuasion, no compilation of contradictory evidence, would shake his convictions.

To counter the Confederates, Pope about-faced his forces and had them march northeastward, creating a moving wall of Federal soldiers to penetrate the twenty-mile gap between the supposed raiders and the main army. McDowell, with Sigel's corps leading, and Reynolds' division, followed by his own corps, took the Warrenton Turnpike toward Gainesville. This would seal off the obvious Confederate retreat route to Thoroughfare Gap. Kearny's division and a corps commanded by one of Burnside's recent arrivals from the Carolinas, Major General Jesse L. Reno, moved toward Greenwich. (This put them about in the center, where they would be within supporting distance of McDowell.) Pope himself took command of the southern flank. Hooker's division was to go back up the tracks to Bristoe Station, followed by Porter's corps, just now arriving from Aquia Creek. Banks' beaten-up corps guarded the trains and brought up the rear.

Meanwhile, Jackson ordered Hill's and Taliaferro's divisions to join Trimble at Manassas Junction. Ewell remained behind at Bristoe to watch for approaching Federals; the cavalry patrolled the roads in all directions. Trimble's men guarded a small military city of tents and warehouses alongside two half-mile-long railroad trains, all filled with great quantities of quartermaster and commissary stores bound for their enemies. Trimble considered them Confederate property; Hill's hungry men saw them as rewards and began helping themselves. Artillery booms signaled Yankees were coming. Officers hustled grumbling, hungry men to defensive positions on the east edge of the storage area.

Cautious, a Washington garrison outfit serving as infantry, the 2d New York Heavy Artillery, called "heavies," advanced from the Centreville area toward a large brick house called Liberia. It had been General P.G.T. Beauregard's headquarters the previous year during the Manassas battle. Near it long ranks of Hill's Confederate Light Division forming into battle array and bursting Rebel artillery shells confirmed the New Yorkers' suspicions. These were not guerrilla raiders. The heavies beat a hasty retreat.

Next, farther south, came Brigadier General George W. Taylor's four New Jersey regiments. This brigade, sent by train from Alexandria, jumped out east of Bull Run to disperse what Taylor had been told was Confederate cavalry. They blundered straight into a hornet's nest. Waving a handkerchief and calling them to surrender, Jackson actually tried to save the Jerseymen. One of them took a shot at him; it was their only response. They were beaten bloody. Taylor was mortally wounded, and his troops fled back across Bull Run. Fitz Lee, returning from a reconnaissance to Fairfax, finished off what was left of them. It was all over before noon.

The remainder of Wednesday afternoon was spent plundering Manassas storehouses, a feast and frolic such as few of these Sons of the South ever attended. There were new shoes for the barefooted, new Union-blue clothes for the ragged, saddles for cavalrymen, medicines for surgeons, blankets, candles, tooth-brushes, and soap for all. Best, of course, was the food. Hardtack and coffee were plentiful. There were sutler stores, luxury items even the average Union enlisted man rarely saw: lobster salad, fresh fruit, sardines, pickled oysters, cigars, canned meats, French mustard, white wine, and for the German Yankees, beer. Some men could not decide what to take, there was so much, while those who fought during the day griped that all the delicacies were consumed before they arrived, especially by Ewell's men.

Ewell got into a sharp fight at Bristoe with Hooker, each side losing nearly 300 men. Stonewall's instructions were to not risk a general engagement, so late in the afternoon, Ewell fell back across Broad Run to Manassas. There, his men sat down to eat. Since only a minute fraction of the captured goods could be hauled away, the rest were put to the torch. To the relief of a Louisiana chaplain who feared temptation had overcome his rowdy Confederate flock, near dusk the men formed ranks and began to march away. They had to get away from Manassas quickly before Pope arrived with his whole army.

The first part of Jackson's mission was successfully completed. Federal supplies were interrupted, and Pope was rapidly moving away from the Rappahannock. Now Jackson had to safeguard his command until the two separated Confederate wings could be reunited. A disguised cavalryman brought word that Lee and Longstreet had departed the Rappahannock on August 26, the previous evening. Good news, for sure, but they still had a long distance to travel. What Jackson felt he needed was a position near Thoroughfare Gap, a concealed place to hide, one strong enough defensively to hold a day or two. From there he could strike at Pope and prevent the Federal army from retreating any farther toward Washington.

He selected a long, partly wooded ridge about a mile northwest of the year-old Manassas battleground. This ridge roughly paralleled a stretch of the Warrenton to Alexandria turnpike, near a hamlet called Groveton. Taliaferro's division took the direct route, Sudley Springs Road, while Hill went to Cen-

treville, and turned west. Ewell crossed Bull Run and sidled upstream toward Stone Bridge. (Actually, the march by three routes was a lucky blunder on Jackson's part, for it added to the confusion of an already confused John Pope.)

Just as Hooker's fight with Ewell was concluding, Pope rode to Bristoe and learned for the first time it was Stonewall Jackson confronting him. The thought of destroying the arch Rebel was intoxicating to Pope. He lost his head and forgot strategy. His scouting cavalry was worn worthless, so he relied on his intuition as a substitute for facts. He imagined he had surprised Jackson, who probably would fight.

Pope ordered his army to concentrate at Manassas on August 28. Porter was to march at 1:00 a.m. to Hooker's support; Hooker's men were low on ammunition and Jackson might attack. (Pope's foot soldiers carried 100 rounds of ammunition, the Army of the Potomac men had only 40.) Reno's, Kearny's, and McDowell's wings were to "move at the very earliest blush of dawn." If everyone moved promptly and acted expeditiously, said Pope, "we shall bag the whole crowd."

But Porter did not move promptly. His corps started two hours late and reached Bristoe at 10:00 a.m. instead of daylight. While the Confederates marched through the night, Porter claimed it was too dark to see the road and a wagon train blocked his way.

McDowell did not move fast. Sigel was five hours late getting started. Then his wagons stalled one of McDowell's divisions led by Major General Rufus King. Next, instead of keeping to the left of the Manassas Gap Railroad, he inclined to the right, explaining he thought the unnamed railroad in the order meant the Orange & Alexandria, seven miles farther south. Finally, McDowell entrusted a copy of Pope's marching order to a courier. Dispatched in the very direction the order stated the enemy was located, the courier was, of course, captured.

Still, McDowell had a much clearer idea of Lee's intent than Pope. The man Lincoln had called a general of "great cunning" had completely lost sight of the fact that most of the Confederate army was somewhere beyond the Bull Run Mountains. When he rode into the smoldering ruins of his supply base and questioned witnesses, Pope jumped to the conclusion Jackson was fleeing by way of Centreville. This was his reason for changing his orders and directing the army to concentrate there.

McDowell had an efficient cavalry-man on his left flank named Brigadier General John Buford, and Buford reported to McDowell that Longstreet was at White Plains. Far from believing Jackson was escaping to rejoin Lee, McDowell correctly suspected Lee was coming to join Jackson. To hold Longstreet west of the mountain, McDowell detached Ricketts' division to Thoroughfare Gap.

Sigel and Reynolds were to countermarch, King to continue ahead, and the three to converge on Centreville.

Meanwhile, Lee was accomplishing what McDowell feared. Two days earlier he had set out with Longstreet's wing to follow Jackson's tracks. One division, Major General Richard Heron Anderson's, was left behind to watch the Rappahannock line for an additional day.

Including Anderson, Longstreet's command amounted to about 30,000 men, organized loosely into five divisions, usually of three brigades each. Divisions were commanded by senior brigadiers: D.R. Jones, Cadmus Wilcox, James L. Kemper, and John B. Hood. None of them was particularly outstanding except for Hood.

By late afternoon Lee was approaching Thoroughfare Gap. Couriers had arrived with the welcome news of Jackson's success at Manassas and his march to Groveton. The two could unite the next day. Then came the rolling, reverberating sound of artillery fire in the mountain pass. It boded ill. The Yankees might make a stubborn stand. Longstreet might be held off long enough for Pope to demolish Jackson.

James B. Ricketts, usually a capable soldier, hardly put up a fight at all. Lee got D.R. Jones' division to push straight up the mountain on either side of the pass, while some of Hood's men found a trail leading through a cleft in the rocks on the left. Wilcox, three miles farther on, tried Hopewell Gap. Ricketts sensed he was being flanked, decided his position was untenable, and withdrew toward Gainesville, the way he came. The distant rumble of gunfire coming from over his right shoulder might also have influenced him.

Groveton Combat

It was nearly 5 o'clock that August 28 afternoon, when Rufus King's division of McDowell's corps came plodding eastward along the Warrenton Turnpike. For a while, a lone horseman appeared on a rise bordering the road. He trotted back and forth, and stopped several times to study the Yankee column intently. Then he turned toward the distant woods and was gone.

"Here he comes, by God," exclaimed one of the gathered Confederate officers in the trees. Stonewall Jackson, the line rider, reigned up, touched his cap in salute and, without any trace of excitement said, "Bring up your men, gentlemen."

The men, when they saw the group of conferring officers break up, knew what was about to happen. From the woods one of them remembered there arose "a hoarse roar, like that from cages of wild animals at the scent of blood." General Taliaferro, on the right, started his division forward. Ewell had two brigades on his left. Three batteries jangled to the front. General Trimble took his place at the head of his troops and in a voice so loud it echoed, bellowed, "Forward, guide center, *march!*"

Federal Brigadier General John Gibbon was trotting ahead of his brigade, the second in the passing Yankee column. He passed through a belt of timber to a knoll for a look around. Gibbon was a North Carolina Yankee who had three brothers fighting against him. He was a West Pointer and had been an artillerist before his promotion to lead a brigade of Westerners, men who stood out not only because of where they came from, but also because in the field they wore the U.S. Army's dress uniforms—knee length frock coats topped by black, high-crowned hats. They were nicknamed the "Black Hat Brigade." Except for the 2d Wisconsin, which ironically had fought nearby at Bull Run the year before, the outfit had never burnt powder.

Scanning the horizons, Gibbon noted that Union Brigadier John P. Hatch's brigade had already passed the cluster of houses and haystacks at a crossroad called Groveton and was out of sight. In the other direction, through a vista, he made out several parallel lines of horsemen approaching, about a half-mile distant. As he began to speculate which army these cavalry belonged to, the horse columns veered simultaneously, and Gibbon's artillery experience told him that this was not cavalry at all, but field artillery going into battery.

Behind their general, the 6th Wisconsin regiment had just cleared the timber and one soldier was loudly complaining how they had been in the service for a year and not seen combat yet: "I tell you, this damned war will be over and we will never get into a battle." Then came six, rapid, distant booms, followed a second or two later by screaming shells exploding in the treetops. The neat column scattered for the road bank. The second round, closer, sent a horse tumbling over and over, smashing it against a rail fence.

At this point, Gibbon believed since Hatch's brigade had passed this way a half-hour before, no enemy infantry was around; the guns probably belonged to J.E.B. Stuart's roving cavalry. They needed to be chased off or, better yet, captured, so that the march could continue. Gibbon called for his old battery, and soon up the roadway, kicking up a cloud of dust, came Battery B of the 4th U.S. Artillery, commanded by Captain J.B. Campbell. A rail fence was kicked over and six Napoleon guns unlimbered by Gibbon's side. While the general rode off to locate

Rough-and-tumble Midwesterners who fought for the Union. Men much like the ones in this unidentified group made up Brigadier General John Gibbon's hard-fighting "Black Hat Brigade." (Milwaukee Public Museum of Milwaukee County)

an infantry regiment to take the Rebels in flank, Battery B opened a well-aimed, destructive counter-battery fire. West of the woods, the 2d Wisconsin left-faced into a two rank fighting formation and started across a large broomsedge field. The field sloped upward toward an orchard. There, silhouetted peacefully against the evening skyline, trees surrounded the log house rented by a farmer named John Brawner.

Rebel skirmishers suddenly rose from the grass and began firing. Then the Wisconsin men saw them: Confederate infantry, six brigades strong, advancing swiftly over the crest, crimson battle flags dancing over their heads.

At seventy-five yards the two lines halted, and the long tearing sound of musketry started. Seeing he needed more force, Gibbon ordered up the rest of his brigade and called on the division for support. The 19th Indiana and 7th Wisconsin rushed to their comrades in the 2d; the 6th Wisconsin, recovering from their initial shock, moved up on their right.

Advancing astride the woods created a massive gap in the Federal front. But with rapid blasts of cannister, Battery B kept the Rebels from penetrating it until two regiments from Brigadier General Abner Doubleday's brigade, untried like those of Gibbon, came over and sealed the dangerous hole.

For over an hour and a half the two battle lines stood locked in a deadly shooting contest. Part of the Stonewall Brigade got some protection from

Brawner's house and orchard, and Doubleday's two Union regiments were deployed in the edge of the woods, but for the most part, soldiers stood upright loading and firing without cover of any sort. The Civil War rifle-musket, at 100 yards, could place its bullets within a 12-inch circle. Here the only hindering conditions were fading light and the hovering gray haze of gunsmoke. The effect of the gunfire in the open belies imagination.

Casualties accumulated at a frightful rate. General Taliaferro went down with three wounds. Colonel John E. Neff of the 33d Virginia was killed. Lawson Botts, once defense council for abolitionist raider John Brown, now a Confederate soldier, fell mortally wounded. Among the 200 dead from the Stonewall Brigade's ranks was Jackson's young hometown friend, Lexington, Virginia's 16-year-old Willie Preston. (It was said Jackson broke down and cried that evening when he learned of the boy's death.) General Ewell ventured too near the firing line and caught a bullet in his knee.*

On the Union side, 900 Black Hats were killed or wounded, and Doubleday's two regiments counted 350 more. Every field grade officer of the 7th Wisconsin was shot, including the distinguished Lieutenant Colonel Charles A. Hamilton, former Secretary of

---

*Not all wounds were fatal or so serious. Oddly, Private Ned Moore, a cannoneer, noticed that three-quarters of those Confederates passing to the rear with slight wounds had been hit in the left hand.

the Treasury Alexander Hamilton's grandson. Still they fought. "Don't mind us," called stricken Federal men to their friends leaving the ranks to aid them. "Whip 'em, whip 'em!"

The sky darkened, but this was a fight nightfall did not stop. When the 6th Wisconsin moved a little to its left, Brigadier General Alexander Lawton's brigade charged to get around the Yankee flank; but Battery B stopped them cold by using Rebel muzzle flashes for targets. Jackson, to get a decision from the standoff, ordered twenty artillery pieces to the front. Only a few guns, however, successfully navigated the terrain. Captain John Pelham, cavalry commander Stuart's young artillery chief, managed to get two cannon within sixty yards of the 19th Indiana's flank, but the fire only caused the Federals to step over bodies and refuse their left.

At last, about 9 p.m., the firing subsided as the lines slowly drew apart. Returning to the pike, the 6th Wisconsin shouted three defiant cheers into the night. No reply came from the Rebels.

More than one-third of the Federals had been shot. The Confederates suffered about the same. Confederate engineer W.W. Blackford, when he inspected the human debris the next morning, found "a painfully interesting sight." The rival lines were marked by long ranks of prostrate bodies. "On each front the edge was sharply defined, while towards the rear it was less so, showing how men had staggered backward after receiving their death blow." A cow and a half-grown colt lay dead in Brawner's farmyard. And Confederate Private Ned Moore noticed a dead rabbit and a dead field lark.

While the Black Hats took their wounded to a cabin on the pike for treatment, their generals huddled around a camp fire across the road. McDowell was absent. Having left his command that afternoon to seek General Pope at Manassas Junction, he had become lost in the woods somewhere. Next in command was Rufus King. He was an epileptic and had remained in Gainesville, missing the battle, "sick in body and mind." Their last orders were to proceed to Centreville, now a dubious proposition. Gibbon said if they did anything other than retire to Manassas, where the bulk of the army was thought to be, they would be annihilated at daylight.

After some discussion, that was what was decided. Sometime after midnight, the weary Federals stole off silently toward Manassas, relinquishing the battlefield to the Confederates. King notified Pope of his men's fight with Jackson, wildly overestimating the enemy force. And Ricketts, after his fight with Longstreet at Thoroughfare Gap, began withdrawing to Bristoe.

Here was another serious Federal mistake. The route for Lee to unite with Jackson was entirely undefended. Of lesser importance, King's and Ricketts' movements were not what General Pope had wanted.

But at 10:00 p.m. Pope was elated and still poorly informed. He had learned of Gibbon's fight and believed McDowell's wing had run head-on into Jackson's retreat and stopped it. Presuming McDowell with 25,000 men blocked the turnpike west of the Rebels, and knowing he himself had an equal number around Centreville, Pope believed Jackson would be crushed between the two wings the next morning. Orders were dispatched for McDowell to hold his position at all cost; his men would serve as an anvil, Pope's would be a hammer, Jackson's would be smashed between them. At Centreville, Kearny was to take the Warrenton Pike at 1:00 a.m., make contact as quickly as possible and attack at dawn. Hooker and Reno would be close behind. Fitz John Porter, the McClellan man at Manassas, was to move to Centreville and be the reserve.

Toward morning, however, Pope was not so cheerful: "God damn McDowell," he swore when he discovered his left wing was scattered over half of Prince William County. "He's never where I want him." Sigel's corps and Reynolds' division, which attempted to march toward Gibbon's battle before dark halted them, were bivouacked on the hills above the Stone House intersection, about midway between Groveton and Bull Run. Pope ordered these units "to attack the enemy vigorously as soon as it was light enough to see, and bring him to [a] stand if possible." Jackson must not be allowed to escape. Old General Sam Heintzelman was instructed to join the attack with Kearny and Hooker as soon as he reached the battlefield.

Far from fleeing, Jackson was ready to fight and waiting on Lee. After the bloody fight with Gibbon, he drew his men back to an interesting position, an abandoned railroad right-of-way. The independent line of the Manassas Gap Railroad was to have connected at Gainesville, and run to Alexandria. For five years after 1853, picks and shovels and barrels of black powder hacked out a roadbed, but no bridges or trestles were ever built, no track was ever laid. Financial difficulties in 1858 halted the project. What remained was a series of cuts and embankments which rendered ready-made trenches and breastworks along two miles of Confederate front. From Catharpin Run near Sudley Church on the left, the Confederate line ran along the base of Stoney Ridge southeastward to a point on the unfinished railroad north of Brawner's farm.

If the position had any weakness, it was on the left, where A.P. Hill oversaw the Sudley Springs Road, the Confederate escape route to Aldie Gap. There a thick forest blanketed the front for several hundred yards, offering good concealment but shrinking the field of fire. Hill therefore arranged his brigades in two lines: Brigadiers Maxcy Gregg, Charles Field, and Colonel Edward Lloyd Thomas in the front line supported in depth by Lawrence Branch, William D. Pender, and James J. Archer close behind.

The center, where a lane between Sudley Church and Groveton crossed the railroad grade, was held by two brigades of Ewell's division. Ewell's knee wound required his leg's amputation during the night, so now his men were led by Brigadier Alexander Lawton. The other two brigades, detached under Jubal Early, guarded Jackson's right along the Warrenton Turnpike and watched for Longstreet's approach from Thoroughfare Gap.

On the right, where the fields of fire were unobstructed and the land more elevated, Jackson placed his own battered division, commanded by Brigadier General William E. Stark. Some regiments were virtually without officers and had been reduced to the size of companies. Totaled, Jackson had about 20,000 men to face Pope's Yankee hordes, more than double his number.

Forty Confederate cannon massed into 24-gun and 16-gun concentrations on Stoney Ridge overlooked the left and right flanks, positioned to converge their fire on almost any avenue of approach. Stuart's cavalry secured the flanks. The positions and dispositions proved ideal. Not only defensively strong, they were strategically located where Lee, only a few hour's march away, could unite quickly with Stonewall's outreaching right. Jackson's immediate task now was to hold on and beat back Pope's attacks until Longstreet arrived and Lee took over.

The Battle Begins

At 5:30 a.m. on Friday, August 29, following Pope's attack-at-dawn order, Sigel began to move his 9,000 soldiers forward across a wide front. Brigadier General Carl Schurz with one division moved north toward the Rebel left. Brigadier General Robert Schenck with the other division headed west along the Warrenton Pike. Brigadier General Robert Milroy, with his Independent Brigade, advanced into the intervening vacuum. McDowell, who had at last surfaced from parts unknown, directed Reynolds' division to cooperate with Schenck and advance on his left.

Once across a stream called Young's Branch, Schurz, a scholarly-looking general, could see an expanse of open, rolling land ahead. There were a few scattered farms, and farther on in the long stretch of green forest, the enemy was supposed to be waiting. Schurz formed his division into regimental marching columns, Colonel Alexander Schimmelfennig on the right, Colonel Wladimir Krzyzanowski on the left, and skirmishers well ahead. All was quiet and still for an hour, until they entered the woods. Two shots, a silent pause, then a round of musketry, and the battle was on.

The Rebels seemed to give ground, but Schurz was unsure exactly what was happening because he could see so little in the smoky woods. Despite all the shouting and waving of swords by company officers trying to hold their units together, the tangled underbrush broke the men into irregular squads. After advancing for what seemed to Schurz about a half-mile, the sound of fire suddenly increased.

A.P. Hill's Light Division barred progress. The 1st and 12th South Carolina of Maxcy Gregg's brigade struck back in a bruising counterattack, knocking Schimmelfennig's brigade back on its heels. His and Krzyzanowski's brigades had drifted apart, struggling through the woods; another sortie first threw their center into confusion, then threw it out of the woods.

By late morning, though his center and left had barely fought, Sigel decided his corps was outnumbered and had made its contribution. Milroy, with his brigade, advanced about a mile under a brisk shelling. But once near the enemy, Milroy got nervous, sent two regiments to help Schurz, feebly attacked with the remaining two and was easily repulsed. General Schenck, a reputed expert on the game of draw poker, did little more with his division. Not up for gambling, cautiously, slowly, he moved west along the turnpike past Groveton to about where Gibbon's fight took place the evening before. Confederate artillerists saw him coming and moved twelve guns down the ridge to meet him with fire, and Schenck stood pat. He dueled them with his artillery until it ran out of ammunition, called for more guns, then sent a brigade to help Milroy. By this time the Union's John Reynolds, using a circuitous southern route, came up beside Schenck's left and advanced a brigade north of the turnpike. Instead of attacking, the two generals took alarm when they discovered a great body of Confederates on their flank and beat a hasty retreat.

"It is Longstreet!" cried a courier. The general called "Old Pete" had arrived. After an eight-mile march, his long columns began filing off the pike into battle position behind a screen of woods. Hinged on Jackson's three divisions, extending northeast along the unfinished railroad, Longstreet's line formed nearly southward, so that the Confederate front formed a great V of about 160°, facing a bit southeast.

The angled front was strongest at its apex, where Confederate John B. Hood's division and Major J.B.

Walton's battalion of New Orleans' Washington Artillery connected with Jackson's right. Perpendicular to the pike, and behind Hood's left, was Brigadier General Cadmus Marcellus Wilcox's division, with Brigadier General James Lawson Kemper's division alongside his right. To the south, fresh from their service at Thoroughfare Gap, was D.R. Jones' division; its right sat on the Manassas Gap Railroad. The front was now nearly four miles long. When Richard Anderson's division arrived, expected late in the afternoon from its Rappahannock River guard duty, it would bring Lee's strength to 55,000 men, all he could expect to put into action.

His instinct was to launch an immediate attack, employing Longstreet's fresh troops, against the Union left.

Longstreet, however, was not satisfied. Never one to jump into anything too quickly, Old Pete wanted to examine the ground first and see if any Yankees were around his flank.

Lee consented, and Longstreet rode to a hill for a long, careful look. When he returned he was most apprehensive. The Yankees were extended far south of the turnpike, he said, and he was not at all pleased with the terrain. To attack might expose his flank to any Federal force approaching from the direction of Manassas.

Lee was disappointed but still favored an attack. While the two generals debated, a message from Stuart arrived saying a strong Yankee force was indeed approaching from Manassas; he was having his cavalrymen drag bundles of brush behind their horses to raise dust clouds and create an impression of thousands of marching Confederates moving to meet them. If the high command wanted to hold the ground, they needed reinforcements immediately.

Wilcox's division started off to move to D.R. Jones' right, and Longstreet went with them to investigate.

As Lee studied the land in front of him, Stonewall Jackson rode up and briefed him on what had occurred since their meeting four days earlier. As they talked, Longstreet returned, still cautious. He reported that the force he saw was not dangerous, but there was dust behind them.

"Hadn't we better move our line forward?" Lee asked. "I think not," replied Longstreet; "we had better wait till we hear more from Stuart about the force he has reported moving against us from Manassas."

Jackson said nothing. The volume of gunfire from his sector was rapidly increasing and he quickly departed. Stuart arrived and confirmed what Longstreet observed, and he added the Yankees belonged to the corps of Fitz John Porter from McClellan's army. Lee, growing impatient, mounted his horse

"Traveler" and rode to the right to look the situation over for himself.

Pope, meanwhile, had arrived on the battlefield from Centreville at about the same time as Lee (approximately noon) and established headquarters on Buck Hill behind the Stone House tavern there.

Believing Jackson's the only Confederate force before him, Pope's plan was for Sigel, Reno, and Heintzelman to attack in front, while McDowell and Porter came up from Manassas to deliver the crushing blow on Jackson's right flank and rear. It was a good plan in concept, but Pope possessed only sketchy knowledge about the lay of the land, where his own troops were, or for that matter, even where the enemy was.

He had about 33,000 men on the field by then. The Union front paralleled the unfinished railroad and overlapped Jackson's line slightly at either end. As Reno came up, Sigel dispersed the small corps to reinforce his own line; nevertheless, Sigel reported to Pope that his line was weak, his divisions cut up, and he wanted permission to retire. Pope sternly replied that no replacements were available and Sigel must hold his ground. McDowell and Porter would strike soon, he added.

From about 1:30 to 4:00 p.m., Federal brigades launched a series of disjointed, unsupported attacks against Stonewall Jackson's position. Hardly was

The Stone House tavern, sited on the Gainesville & Centerville Turnpike, was built in 1828. When Pope arrived on the battlefield about midday on August 29, he established his headquarters on Buck Hill, behind the house. (CWTI Collection)

there a time when an assault was not in progress. Most of the action fell on Confederate A.P. Hill.

Between the right of Maxcy Gregg and the left of Colonel Edward Thomas' Georgians, a dangerous 150-yard interval had been left undefended. Schurz got a second attack going after his boys crept silently into a railroad cut opposite the opening; they came out threatening to snap off Gregg's brigade from the rest of the Confederate army. The 14th South Carolina and 49th Georgia countercharged, exchanged blazing musket fire at a 10-yard range, forcing the Federals back and putting an end to the threat. Another Southern counterstroke broke three regiments holding the Federals' center and again sent them flying out of the woods. But Schurz had a battery and a regiment in reserve; pursuing Rebels entering the open fields were cut down in their tracks.

The Federals went back once more, reached the railroad grade and held it, but Schurz was fought to a

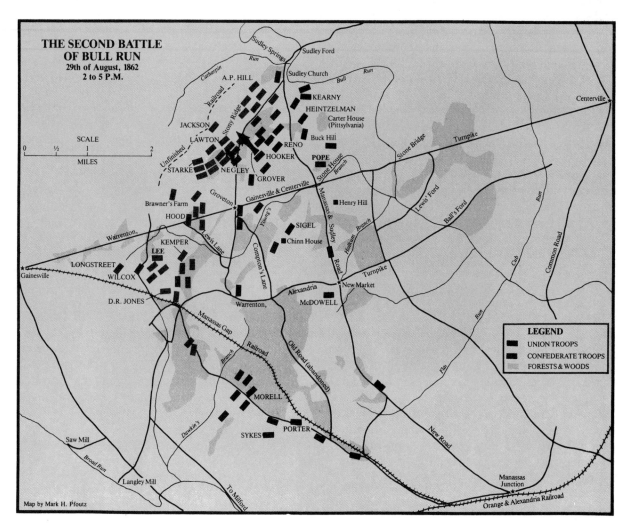

THE SECOND BATTLE OF BULL RUN
29th of August, 1862
2 to 5 P.M.

SCALE
0   ½   1   2
MILES

LEGEND
■ UNION TROOPS
■ CONFEDERATE TROOPS
░ FORESTS & WOODS

Map by Mark H. Pfoutz

standstill. Hooker's and Reno's troops came forward and relieved Schurz.

Colonel Joseph B. Carr's brigade took over from Krzyzanowski and engaged in a hot skirmish fire, keeping the Rebels pinned in place. At 3:00 p.m. Union Brigadier General Cuvier Grover received orders to carry the embankment in front and hold the woods beyond.

"Where are my supporters?" asked Grover.

"They are coming," assured a staff officer. Grover's brigade got no help from anybody.

They were New England regiments, mostly: 1st, 11th, 16th Massachusetts, 2d New Hampshire, and 26th Pennsylvania. Grover rode the length of his line saying they would rely on the bayonet. Moving through the woods to the attack, they stepped over dead and wounded from Milroy's earlier effort.

A sudden explosion of Rebel musket fire was answered by a 1,500-man Yankee cheer; they went up to the top of a 10-foot embankment. Here a short, brutal hand-to-hand struggle occurred. The Virginians of Charles Field's brigade had already fired, and most of them got caught hugging the shelter of the bank, expecting a return volley that never came. Those who tried to fight were shot, bayoneted, or had their skulls crushed by musket butts; many threw up their hands and surrendered; some "played possum," feigned death. Others made a run for it and Grover's men were right behind.

The fragments of the first line stampeded into a supporting line, which the 2d New Hampshire also overpowered. A third Confederate line held. On the 2d's left, the 11th Massachusetts carried the embankment and got into a savage fight with the second Rebel line while artillery fire tore at its flank. Grover tried getting the 16th Massachusetts through the 2d's penetration, but the Rebels had recovered. It was the Yankees' turn to run. As they recrossed the embankment, they were exposed to a murderous crossfire. "To say nothing of the very bad language used by the Rebels in calling us to stop," a survivor added. In twenty minutes the brigade lost 487 men. One thinned regiment had its flag torn away; its scattered men answered to the command "Rally 'Round The Pole."

Next came a brigade of Reno's corps, the men of Colonel James Negley. They had come up through the backwash of battle, heard all the discouraging remarks, watched men in bloodied blue uniforms being carried rearward to surgeons at the operating stations. Remembering it later, one of them wrote sagely: "Such sights were enough to make the stoutest and bravest man look pale." Their officers dismounted and the resting brigade got to its feet; it was time to go in.

Some of Pope's staff officers urged them on, bawling, "Porter is in their rear; you'll hear his guns in a minute. Fight sharp, boys, and you've got 'em sure!" Once they entered the woods, unseen Rebels peppered the air with bullets and Negley's soldiers fired and reloaded on the move. They hit Jackson's center about where a back country lane crossed the railroad grade. Across the deeply rutted lane they charged, leaping into a cut with bayonets level, up the other side and beyond. Then from underbrush on their left came a roar of gunfire. It cut into the flank of the 6th New Hampshire. Back to the cut, hollered the officers. Swearing it was their comrades of the 48th Pennsylvania shooting at them by mistake, the 6th's colorbearer angrily waved the Stars and Stripes.

The response was more bullets. Colonel Peter Starke's and Johnson's Confederate brigades wheeled around, and Negley's men abandoned their dead and wounded—nearly 50 percent their original number—and scrambled out of the woods into a field. The Confederates swept out into the open after them and hit General Nelson Taylor's unsuspecting Excelsior Brigade square in the flank, turning its men into a disordered mob. The 14th Louisiana captured a cannon and merrily had it hauled back to their lines using downcast Yankee prisoners hitched up like draft horses.

Porter's Ruin
Longstreet's Position

In his official report of the battle, Pope dismissed the afternoon fighting in a single sentence, calling it "very severe skirmishes . . . at various points." What most concerned him was the silence from the southwest. What had happened to McDowell and Porter?

Porter, an able general, but dedicated to McClellan, earlier received Pope's orders to countermarch and head northwest for Gainesville instead of Centreville. Rufus King was ill. His division, now commanded by Brigadier John P. Hatch, was also temporarily attached. About noon Porter received the so-called "Joint Order." It read: "HEADQUARTERS ARMY OF VIRGINIA, Centreville, August 29, 1862. Generals McDowell and Porter: You will please move forward with your joint commands toward Gainesville. I sent General Porter written orders to that effect an hour and a half ago. Heintzelman, Sigel, and Reno are moving on the Warrenton turnpike, and must now be not far from Gainesville. I desire that as soon as communication is established between this force and your own the whole command shall halt. It may be necessary to fall back behind Bull Run at Centreville tonight. I presume it will be so, on account of our supplies. . . .

"If any considerable advantages are to be gained by departing from this order it will not be strictly carried out. One thing must be had in view, that the troops must occupy a position from which they can reach Bull Run tonight or by morning. The indications are that the whole force of the enemy is moving in this direction at a pace that will bring them here by tomorrow night or the next day. My own headquarters will be for the present with Heintzelman's corps or at this place. Jno. Pope, Major-General, Commanding."

General George Morell's division, in the lead, halted short of a stream called Dawkin's Branch on the road out of Manassas heading for Gainesville to verify a report that hostile troops blocked the way. When General McDowell arrived on the scene about noon, the two discussed Pope's instructions. (By any standard, the Joint Order was a dreadful piece of writing.) They rode northward for a distance and decided it was impractical to cut cross country to the battlefield, especially since dust columns raised by the ruse of Stuart's cavalry seemed to indicate Confederate troops were moving east toward Jackson. McDowell had a dispatch written at 9:30 a.m. by

cavalry General John Buford stating he had observed seventeen enemy infantry regiments with artillery and cavalry pass through Gainesville. He showed it to Porter, but did not make an effort to forward it to General Pope. Obviously, the moving enemy troops belonged to Confederate General James Longstreet.

Neither McDowell, who was senior in grade, nor Porter seemed sure of what to do. McDowell then decided he should take Hatch's division and backtrack up the Sudley Springs Road and go to Pope.

Left with the Joint Order in his hands, Porter had several options. He could fight his way toward Gainesville, but McDowell had advised against that, saying his present position was "too far out." He could remain where he was. Or, since Pope said the whole army might fall back to Bull Run that night, he could probably retreat without disgrace. Pope's sentence about "considerable advantages . . . gained by departing from this order" gave him a great deal of leeway.

Porter concluded to stay where he was. His couriers were apparently captured by Rebels so he had no contact with the main force. He listened to his skirmishers fire at the enemy, and debated whether the

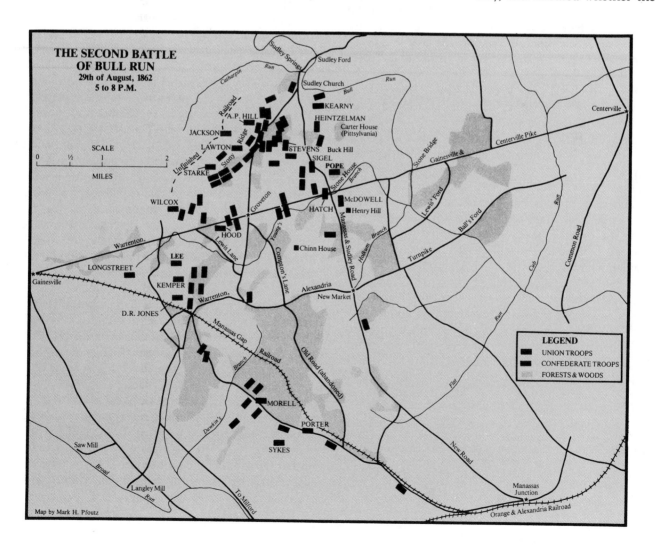

intermittent artillery fire he heard three miles beyond the trees indicated Pope was fighting a battle. Late in the afternoon the noise seemed to recede to the east. Porter wrote a dispatch to McDowell saying he was going to fall back to Manassas. Then he did not do it. Instead, he ordered a reconnaissance across Dawkin's Branch by Morell with four regiments.

At 6:00 p.m. Captain Douglas Pope, the general's aide and nephew, delivered another order: "HEAD-QUARTERS IN THE FIELD, August 29-4:30 p.m. Major General Porter: Your line of march brings you in on the enemy's right flank. I desire you to push forward into action at once on the enemy's flank, and, if possible, on his rear, keeping your right in communication with General Reynolds. The enemy is massed in the woods in front of us, but can be shelled out as soon as you engage their flank. Keep heavy reserves and use your batteries, keeping well closed to your right all the time. In case you are obliged to fall back, do so to your right and rear, so as to keep you in close communication with the right wing. John Pope, Major-General, Commanding."

Porter urged Morell to hurry, but Morell was sick. He was worried about his flanks, the heavy odds he believed he faced, and the lateness of the day. Porter finally agreed it was too late and halted the moving lines before they became engaged. In the end, Porter had done nothing all day.

After the battle was lost and Pope removed from command, Porter was courtmartialed for disobedience of orders and misbehavior in the face of the enemy. Charges were preferred by Pope's inspector general, but it was no secret the actual accuser was Pope.

The court convened in November, in an atmosphere of gloom brought about by a season of Union defeats. The deck was stacked against Porter from the onset. The majority of court officers were Porter's juniors in rank, his defense council was a civilian who handled the case badly, and much of the prosecution's case was based on a distorted map showing incorrect troop positions for both Porter and the enemy. Pope testified Longstreet had not arrived; Jackson's flank was vulnerable all afternoon and Porter failed to attack it. In January 1863, the court found Porter guilty and sentenced him to be dismissed from the service.*

*For the next fifteen years Porter attempted to get a new hearing. This finally occurred in 1878. A more objective board convened at West Point, heard new evidence, listened to ex-Confederates, including General James Longstreet, and decided in Porter's favor. He was restored to the army rolls (for purposes of pension and honor) twenty years after his alleged transgression.

But all of that was in the future. On August 29, Porter's corps sat inert.

Back on the battlefield, Pope, believing Porter would attack any minute, ordered a fresh attack at five o'clock by Kearny and Reno against Jackson's depleted, but undefeated left. Kearny, filled with enthusiasm, his kepi tilted jauntily, took two brigades across the Sudley Springs Road and wheeled to the left so they would come down behind and along the length of the railroad grade. They wore a red patch on their caps, and when they were not called the "Red Diamond Division" they were called "Phil Kearny's thieves." Stevens' division of Reno's Corps added their weight to that of the "thieves" by attacking more frontally, to the Red Diamond Division's left.

Facing them, A.P. Hill's men were desperately short of cartridges. "Good for you, boys! Give them the rocks and the bayonet," Hill encouraged. "Hold your position and I will soon have ammunition and reinforcements for you." Hill's staff filled their pockets and haversacks with cartridges for distribution while he rode to consult Jackson, reporting his men might not be able to stave off another onslaught. Jackson replied they must.

A loud crash of gunfire swept the field. "Here it comes," said Hill.

"I'll expect you to beat them," Jackson called after him.

Maxcy Gregg's South Carolinans began stepping backward under the pressure. General Gregg strode along the line waving his old Revolutionary War sword, saying, "Let us die here, my men, let us die here!" Officers popped with their pistols. The Federals pressed so close some found they could save themselves by anticipating a shot from the other side. One soldier reflected on his experiences afterwards: "One may fight at long range as a patriot and a Christian, but I believe that no man can engage in one of those close struggles, where he can look into the eyes of his adversary and see his blood, but he becomes for the time, at least, a mere beast of prey."

Hill's line was forced to a position almost at a right angle with the railroad, his men fighting with all the strength left to them. Colonel Henry Forno's brigade of Ewell's division was thrown in on the left. Then, typical this day, the Federals lost some of their impetus and cohesion. Confederate reinforcements rushed to tip the balance. Jubal Early's brigade, returning from outpost duty after Longstreet arrived, charged toward the bending flank. With the 8th Louisiana and 13th Georgia picked up and added to either flank along the route, Early's Virginians surged over Gregg's prone troops and slammed into the fragmented Yankees. Once more thrown out of the woods, all the lost Confederate ground recovered, the Federals were forced back to where they launched their first attack that morning.

A courier rode to Stonewall Jackson announcing the good news. Jackson, with one of his rare smiles, answered: "I knew he would do it."

Kearny, furious at the setback, rode to Pope's headquarters for reinforcements. Pope replied none were to be had. For a moment Kearny showed his dismay, but only for a moment. "Look at that! Did you ever see the like of that? Isn't it beautiful?"

To the distant west a blood-red sun was setting behind enormous billowing clouds, brilliant hues above a landscape of dark forest green. Below the horizon, tiny blinking lights were visible, twinkling like fireflies. There was a battle going on along the Warrenton Turnpike, but it was all color. Not a sound could be heard. All the gathered Union officers and their staffs paused to admire the spectacle.

War could be admired by commanders at a distance, but up close for participants it was another outbreak of confusing, deadly violence.

McDowell had reported to Pope with Hatch's division at the height of Kearny's assault. Since the resounding noise indicated Kearny was winning, and a fresh report said the enemy was moving troops to their right, presumably to confront Porter, McDowell was told to make an attack down the turnpike. He rode to the double-quicking 76th New York and yelled they were on the heels of a retreating foe. "Push 'em like hell!"

Lee, that afternoon, had encountered nearly the same difficulty as Pope: getting a subordinate to make an attack. He returned from a personal reconnaissance satisfied Longstreet's line was longer than the Federals', and it outnumbered theirs. For the third time he urged Longstreet to make an attack. Longstreet remained immobile. In his opinion it was too late; a full-scale advance might result in disaster. He preferred making a forced reconnaissance with General Hood. Lee, sometimes unwilling to force his will on a subordinate, finally acceded; Longstreet got his way. Cadmus Wilcox's division was ordered back to support Hood, if necessary.

And so two divisions collided along the highway in the twilight—Hood's coming from the west and Union General Hatch's from the east—in a battle Pope, Kearny, and the other commanders watched in awe from a distance. From the Federal vantage point on Buck Hill, the twinkling lights advancing from the west increased, those from the east grew weaker, receded, and finally sputtered out. Hood's line, longer, had come out of a dark wood on Hatch's left, crumpled it, and driven the Federals splashing across

Young's Branch. A major in the 76th New York nearly made himself a prisoner of war when in the confusion he began to rally the 2d Mississippi. For the Federals, confusion had also been typical this day.

Night Of Pain, Morning Of Indecision

Evening turned to dark night and ended the terrible fighting of August 29. The atmosphere at Pope's headquarters mixed elation with frustration. The major general commanding optimistically appraised the day's bloody events and believed his army had fought successfully. Although he figured his army had lost between 6,000 and 8,000 killed and wounded, he was sure he had inflicted greater damage on Jackson. Hooker estimated the enemy loss at two to one. Kearny thought it closer to three to one. First thing in the morning Pope would wire General-in-Chief Henry W. Halleck that "the enemy was driven from the field, which we now occupy." Pope's frustration stemmed from Fitz John Porter's failure to deliver the death blow to the enemy.

"I'll arrest him!" snapped Pope when he learned of Porter's inaction at Dawkin's Branch. His belief Porter would at some point deliberately let him down seemed substantiated. But McDowell interceded. Porter was an overrated general who made a mistake through incompetency, not deliberate motive, he said. Why take such severe action when they were winning a great battle? Pope listened, and yielded. Nonetheless, he wrote Major General Porter a menacing dispatch: "Immediately upon the receipt of this order, the precise hour of receiving you will acknowledge, you will march your command to the field of battle of today and report to me in person for orders."

Porter's corps turned out of its blankets at 3:00 a.m. and began a sleepy trudge to the battlefield.

Pope made no plans or changes in position during the night. He had decided to wait for August 30. He was deeply troubled about the condition of his army. The troops were exhausted, famished, lacking commissary supplies. At dawn, a courier arrived from the Manassas telegraph station with a message from Major General William Buel Franklin, written at McClellan's direction. Pope read the words, crumpled the paper in his fist, and without a word to anyone, walked away from his officers for a short distance before turning around to return.

"What is it, General?" asked one of the staff. Pope handed him the note. Washington was well aware of his acute supply problem. Several times Pope had requested rations and forage. McClellan's reply,

As night sets in and fighting cools, the wounded are gathered from the battlefield. Neither army disturbed such parties in their mission of mercy. (Battles and Leaders of the Civil War)

through Franklin, was that his requested supplies would be loaded when Pope sent cavalry to Alexandria as an escort to the railroad trains. In the middle of battle, it was a petty, impossible condition. One of his friends on the staff later recalled he only knew Pope to feel downtrodden once: "That was when he got that damned dispatch from McClellan at Alexandria telling him that he and his army could go starve."

In the morning hours of Saturday, August 30, Pope called his commanders together at his Buck Hill headquarters. The night before, McDowell gave him Buford's message about the seventeen regiments passing through Gainesville, but Pope placed no credence in it. He was still under the delusion that Jackson, and Jackson alone faced him. His impulse was to follow upon Kearny's previous afternoon's success and resume attacking. He felt this would be a safer course than retreat. McDowell and Heintzelman were to assail the Rebel left, aided by Porter, whose corps was due to arrive shortly.

But by noon, the August 30 plan of operations had undergone considerable revision. Pope and several of his chief subordinates had come to the fantastic belief the enemy was retreating. Information came from

Hatch's front along the Warrenton pike that John B. Hood's division was gone. (This was true. Hood had withdrawn to the main Confederate line at 2:00 a.m.) Paroled Union prisoners said the Confederates had been retreating all night long. For a man of action, oddly enough, Pope seemed confused. "General Pope seemed wholly at a loss what to do or what to think," a witness observed.

While Pope was plagued with indecision, McDowell and Heintzelman rode up the Sudley Springs Road to inspect their attack zone. Jackson's line was concealed deep in the woods, and the two generals, seeing no evidence of it, or of Confederate wagon trains (wagons had been parked behind Sudley Church the day before), hastily deduced Jackson had gone. Franz Sigel, whom they met on the way back to headquarters, had come to the same conclusion.

Pope cut them off before they could speak: "I know what you are about to say, the enemy is retreating." Pope was himself again. Based entirely on reports from Hatch's front, Pope had come to the same erroneous conclusion they had: Jackson had had enough and was pulling out. McDowell and Heintzelman confirmed this belief. The attack plan was dropped. Pope now thought in terms of pursuit.

By the oddest, ironic contrast, Lee had the feeling Pope might retreat. Except for a desultory exchange of cannon shots, the Federal side of the battlefield was perfectly calm. Occasional grass fires lifted white smoke toward gathering clouds. Lee's thoughts, as he sat down to write a report to Confederate President Jefferson Davis, were not on the probability of a battle, but on more marches to maneuver the Yankees out of Virginia. His moves so far, he said, had "drawn the enemy from the Rappahannock frontier and caused him to concentrate his troops between Manassas and Centreville. My desire has been to avoid a general engagement, being the weaker force, and by maneuvering to relieve the portion of the country referred to."

If the Federals did not attack that day, Lee decided Longstreet should create a diversion in the afternoon while Jackson slipped across the Bull Run at Sudley Springs after dark, and once again thrusted at the enemy's rear. If they did attack, Lee was confident the Yankees would be repulsed in two hours.

Jackson also began to doubt there would be a battle. He rode to the right of his line to watch for Federal movements, but could detect little. "Well," he said to Colonel William Smith Hanger Baylor of his old brigade, "it looks as if there will be no fight today, but keep your men in line and ready for action."

Pope, after a full morning of hesitation, determined to begin his pursuit and strike Jackson's rear guard. Porter's corps reached the Stone House about

9:00 a.m. and relaxed in the fields near the John Dogan place. There hungry men husked and boiled corn until Southern artillery burst shrapnel around them and officers ordered the fires extinguished. Since Porter's corps had done next to nothing on August 29, Pope reasoned these soldiers would be freshest. About 11:30 a.m. he dispatched a verbal order to Porter: "Attack, King [Hatch] will support."

At noon, realizing more coordination would be needed, he dictated a written general order placing McDowell in charge of the pursuit of the supposedly retreating Confederates. Porter's corps, followed by Reynolds' division, and King's old division, now commanded by John Hatch, were to push west along the Warrenton pike. Ricketts' division, which had at last reached the field after a circuitous retreat from Thoroughfare Gap via Bristoe and Manassas, was to cross the Bull Run at Sudley Springs and turn west on the Haymarket Road. (This route roughly paralleled the pike several miles north.) Heintzelman's corps would follow Ricketts. The remainder of the army—Sigel's, Reno's, and Banks' men and the Federal wagon train at Bristoe—would wait in reserve.

No sooner was this order written, than the Union command became aware they had guessed wrong about the Rebels.

Ricketts, before he could lead the northern procession, had to put his division back together. When it arrived that morning, McDowell detached two of its brigades to relieve Philip Kearny's men. "Apparently no opportunity for dividing and scattering commands was to be lost," one of Reno's officers disgustedly observed. Rebel artillery commenced beating on one of Ricketts' brigades as it began to assemble. Another brigade was skirmishing with the enemy. Ricketts came to McDowell firmly convinced the Rebels "had no intention of retiring." When it attempted to move, Heintzelman's corps met Confederate fire, too.

McDowell ordered Ricketts to abandon pursuit and resume his position. Reynolds' Pennsylvania Reserves, meanwhile, broke camp and fell into marching formation. Some men, too weak to participate, were permitted to go to the rear. The hungry 3d Regiment was told sadly by its colonel there were no rations for issue, only cartridges. Moving out with these men (the Pennsylvania Bucktails) covering the front, Reynolds kept just south of the pike. He had his troops wade across Young's Branch, step over corpses from Hatch's evening fight, and enter the woodlands near Groveton.

They bumped into Longstreet's Confederates again. Sporadic skirmish fire began. The Bucktails requested a supporting regiment, then another. Some Rebel sharpshooters had climbed trees and were sniping from the foliage. Their locations were revealed by

The battle on August 30. Special artist Edwin Forbes sat on the Bald Hill while he sketched this scene for Frank Leslie's Illustrated Newspaper. The numbers on the sketch refer to the following: (1) Thoroughfare Gap, through which Lee's army marched. (2) Confederate line of battle. (3) The old railroad embankment behind which the Confederates were posted. (4) The Stone House. (5) Warrenton Turnpike. (6) Bald Hill. (7) Henry Hill. (8) Union line of battle. (9) McDowell's Corps moving to the left flank to repel Longstreet's attack, which had just commenced. (10) Hadley Springs road. (Library of Congress)

smoke puffs. The Pennsylvanians huddled into small squads and blew them from their nests with short bursts of fire.

Reynolds became suspicious, especially when one of his regiments fled across a clearing and flopped down to take cover. Rebel infantry was preparing to attack, their colonel reported; they were masked by a line of cavalry pickets. "Impossible!" snorted Reynolds, riding into the clearing to see for himself. One glance was enough. The enemy seemed to be waiting at right angles to his flank. The report was correct. Reynolds whirled his horse around just as the opposite woodline erupted with shots. The general escaped, but his orderly was killed.

McDowell, underestimating the magnitude of the uncovered peril, ordered Reynolds to pull back slightly to a defensive position. Porter was notified of the change; if he needed support, Pope would send him Sigel's troops. But Sigel, too, was suspicious of a Confederate presence south of the pike and conveyed the information to Pope. Pope digested the report, then, with a wave of his arm, instructed the aide to return to General Sigel and have him send a brigade and a battery to "the bald hill."

"What bald hill?" asked Sigel. "He said, the bald hill," responded the officer, mimicking Pope's arm gesture. Sigel ordered Brigadier General Nathaniel McLean's Ohio brigade to Chinn Ridge, a treeless plain topped by a whitewashed frame farm house, a mile in Reynolds' rear. There they could be of no immediate help, whatever, to Reynolds.

By early afternoon Pope and most of his senior generals were conscious that the Confederates had not retreated as they had at first supposed; and some of them were also vaguely aware of an enemy menace brewing behind the woods south of Groveton. The only result Pope's noontime pursuit order produced was confusion, especially in Porter's corps. These men still believed they were to sweep over Jackson's rear guard.

Against light skirmish fire, two great divisional columns of Porter's Peninsula veterans closed in on the strip of woods bordering the Groveton-Sudley lane. This day the volunteer division was commanded by Brigadier General Daniel Butterfield. (During the night General Morell with two brigades, because of a misunderstanding, had marched to Centreville instead of the battlefield. Butterfield would miss them.) Butterfield's division lay down in the woods. Brigadier General George Sykes' division of Regulars halted in the fields on their left. From behind the railroad grade across a meadow came brisk musket fire.

"Now, men," cautioned a Federal sharpshooter officer, "if there are any here who think they are going to have an easy time on this skirmish, change your tune now." These were the marksmen of the 1st United States Sharpshooter Regiment, a group of men who each could shoot ten consecutive shots into an 8-inch bull's eye at 200 yards. They rushed over the field, making for the cover of a dry stream bed about half way across. "There was very little chance for a man to escape being hit at this place," one of them said, "even if he lay very low." Minié bullets smacked into the dirt bank or whizzed close overhead. Bullets riddled their knapsacks. Three infantry regiments were rushed out to help their pinned-down comrades.

Porter and Butterfield observed how the Rebel-held railroad grade ran off diagonally to the left of their corps' front. The outlook was bleak. An enfilade

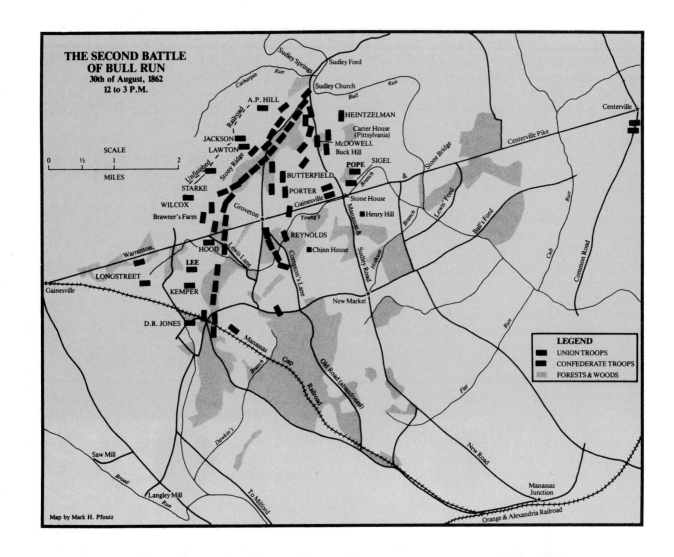

**THE SECOND BATTLE
OF BULL RUN**
30th of August, 1862
12 to 3 P.M.

SCALE

0   ½   1   2

MILES

Sudley Springs

Sudley Ford

Catharpin   Run

Sudley Church

Bull   Run

A.P. HILL

HEINTZELMAN

Carter House
(Pittsylvania)

JACKSON

McDOWELL

LAWTON

Buck Hill

Railroad

POPE   SIGEL

Unfinished

Stony Ridge

BUTTERFIELD

STARKE

PORTER

Centerville

WILCOX

Groveton

Gainesville

Stone House

Henry Hill

Centerville Pike

Stone Bridge

Brawner's Farm

Young's

Lewis Ford

Ball's Ford

Warrenton,

REYNOLDS

HOOD

Lewis Lane

Chinn House

Compton's Lane

Sudley Road

Manassas &

Branch

Cub   Run

LEE

LONGSTREET

KEMPER

New Market

Common Road

Gainesville

D.R. JONES

Flat   Run

Manassas

Branch

Gap

Old Road (abandoned)

Railroad

Saw Mill

Dawkin's

New Road

Broad

Langley Mill

Run

To Milford

Manassas
Junction

LEGEND

■ UNION TROOPS

■ CONFEDERATE TROOPS

▨ FORESTS & WOODS

Orange & Alexandria Railroad

Map by Mark H. Pfoutz

fire from the right was checking progress. To the southeast, Confederate batteries posed trouble. Belatedly, Porter called for Hatch's division to come up on his right. It was done "slowly and in a confused manner." Hatch would lead. After Butterfield's division took the railroad grade, it was to wheel left and go for the enemy's artillery. It was three o'clock in the afternoon when the Union attack finally got rolling.

Finished On Familiar Ground

"Here they come" the Confederates warned one another. They shifted their cartridge boxes to the front of their uniforms for quicker access. The Yankees came pouring out of the woods giving "three deafening cheers." For a moment they wavered in the lane as Confederate bullets peppered their ranks. They scaled a rail fence, then formed into regimental fighting lines. Colonel Bradley Tyler Johnson rushed his Virginia regiments out of seclusion to join his skirmish line at the "Deep Cut," where the railroad excavation was lowest. The Stonewall Brigade, all that remained of it, hurried forward from thickets on Johnson's left.

W.W. Blackford, the cavalry engineer, rode forward to watch the Federal attack sweeping across the front of Colonel Stephen D. Lee's artillery battalion. Later he wrote: "The advance began in magnificent style, lines straight as an arrow, all fringed with glittering bayonets and fluttering with flags. But the march had scarcely begun when little puffs of smoke appeared dotting the fields in rapid succession just over the heads of the men, and as the lines moved on, where each little puff had been lay a pile of bodies, and half a dozen or more staggering figures standing around leaning on their muskets and then slowly limping back to the rear."

Colonel Leroy Stafford, on Johnson's left, had his Louisiana brigade protected by a high embankment. They poured a deafening volley over it. The noise was followed by the frantic rattling of steel ramrods. "We all knew," said a 24th New York private, "that our only hope lay in getting there before they could reload their guns. Over half our men had now fallen, but the rest swept on in an unbroken wave." The 24th scrambled up to the top of the bank, delivering their own volley, and causing a convulsive shudder in the Louisiana ranks. A mounted Union officer, sword raised high, got clear to the top. From the astonished Southerners came the spontaneous cry, "Don't kill him!" But bullets plunged into both horse and rider and they both went down in a heap.

The 50-yard gap in the embankment to Stafford's left was where peacetime railroad architects had envisioned a trestle. The place was called "the dump."

Jackson protected this weak area with a motley collection of stragglers and other petty ne'er-do'-wells; "I suppose as much for punishment as for the real benefit they might be," speculated Captain William C. Oates, an Alabaman. The right of Oate's 15th Alabama obliqued their fire to lend a hand.

The attacking Union forces, hugging the embankment slope, poked their rifles over their heads and pulled the triggers without exposing themselves. The defenders, short of cartridges, hurled cannonball-size rocks down on them. "The flags of the opposing regiments were almost flapping together," said Oates.

"The shouts and yells from both sides were indescribably savage," a 24th New York lieutenant wrote. "It seemed like the popular idea of pandemonium made real, and indeed it is scarcely too much to say that we were really transformed for the time, from a lot of good-natured boys to the most blood-thirsty of demoniacs."

Back on Johnson's front, the Yankees in Butterfield's division lost a great number of men to a crossfire: from Southern artillery on their left, and from small arms fire from in front and on their right. Some regiments changed direction under fire in order to approach the Rebel line more squarely. Up a slope they clambered to a short plateau where, as a Michigan sergeant said, "the slaughter commenced." The 17th New York sprawled on the ground and fired. Most of the other regiments stood erect, exchanging bullets with Confederates sheltered in the Deep Cut. Colonel Johnson reported he "saw a Federal flag hold its position for half an hour within ten yards of one of the regiments in the cut and go down six or eight times."

Though the Yanks melted fast, the Virginians began to run out of ammunition. They took it from the cartridge boxes of their dead and wounded comrades. They picked up stones and threw them, the range was that close. (Lieutenant Lewis Randolph, a grandson of President Thomas Jefferson, was reported to have killed a Federal with a rock.) The Union regiments would stand the punishment for as long as they could, then break and flee for protection at the base of the slope. While officers reformed them for another attempt, the Confederates ran forward to retrieve their supply of stones.

All the while, S.D. Lee's battalion of eighteen cannon pounded on the exposed Union flank. They burst shells and case shot among Union reserves trying to advance and support the attacking forces. Then they drove them back into the woods. Federal counter-battery fire was ineffective; only two batteries fired and did nothing to neutralize the Confederate cannon. A feeble lunge toward the Rebel guns was blasted with discharges of canister at 200 yards.

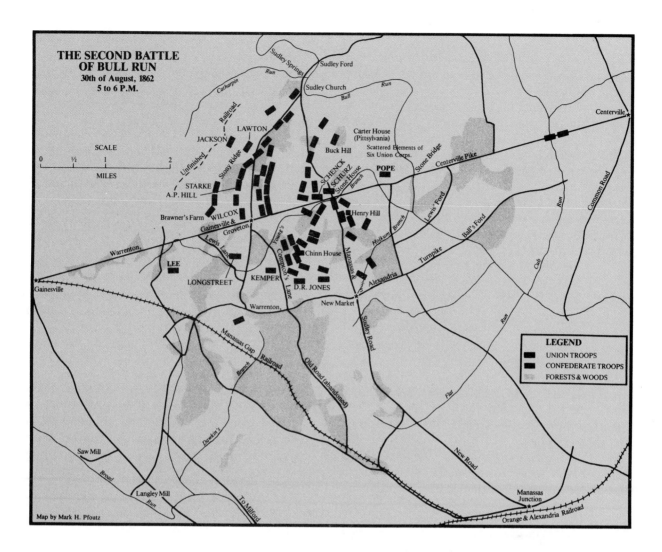

THE SECOND BATTLE
OF BULL RUN
30th of August, 1862
5 to 6 P.M.

LEGEND
UNION TROOPS
CONFEDERATE TROOPS
FORESTS & WOODS

Map by Mark H. Pfoutz

There was no hope of Federal assistance from the rear. A wounded lieutenant under the embankment watched the reinforcements advance, "many of them holding their arms before their faces, as though to keep off a storm." They broke under the metallic hail, tried to reform, then fled for their lives.

A Confederate staff man rushed to Jackson's side reporting Colonel Baylor was shot. His successor requested reinforcements.

"What brigade, sir?" asked Jackson, missing the connection.

"The Stonewall Brigade," he answered.

"Go back," commanded Jackson, "give my compliments to them, and tell the Stonewall Brigade to maintain her reputation." Jackson began wondering whether his soldiers could hold out much longer. He signaled a message to Lee requesting reinforcements.

General Longstreet, galloping to the front, learned of Jackson's plight. With one look out across the smoky plain at what S.D. Lee's guns were doing to Porter's flank, Longstreet called for a pair of his own batteries and placed them near where the Union's John Gibbon had positioned his on August 28. As the first battery began to boom, Longstreet received a request from Robert E. Lee to send a division to Jackson. "Certainly," he replied cheerfully, "but before the division can reach him, that attack will be broken by artillery fire."

The Union assault forces began retiring, losing as many men retreating across the open meadow as when they advanced. They could not break into the railroad bed, they could not be reinforced, they could not remain in an untenable position any longer. Unaccountably, Porter had made the attack with only half the troops he had available; Sykes' entire division and two brigades of Hatch's were never sent into action.

At this point, General McDowell committed a colossal blunder. Sigel's corps was near the J. Dogan house directly in Porter's rear. Reynolds' division was south of the turnpike protecting the Union left. With ample evidence that Longstreet's Confederates were facing Reynolds, McDowell sent a hurried, thoughtless call to run the division across the pike to bolster Porter. Lieutenant Charles Hazlett's battery of U.S. Regulars was all that was left to cover the Union flank.

Hazlett was horrified by what he saw happening. Not even pickets were being left behind. An orderly was sent galloping for help. From Sykes' division came about 1,000 men, his volunteer brigade: the 5th New York and 10th New York Infantry, Colonel G.K. Warren commanding. No sooner had they hustled into the woodlands and deployed on Hazlett's left than Longstreet began the great Confederate counterattack.

Anticipating the order from General Lee, Longstreet seized the initiative at precisely the right time and place. Porter was repulsed; the Federal left was in a state of confusion. Longstreet struck with 28,000 fresh Confederates where Pope and McDowell had only 1,000 New Yorkers to oppose them. Five divisions swept forward along a two-mile crescent. General John B. Hood's Texans led the great charge.

The six companies of the 10th New York on the skirmish line barely had time to shoot before they were overrun. They rallied on their 5th New York comrades, standing erect in a clearing, rifles at the ready. The 5th's men were dressed like French Zouaves: tasseled fezzes, flashy blue jackets, bright red pantaloons, and white gaiters. They were about to set a ghastly record.

Hood's 5th Texas and Carolinian Major General Wade Hampton's "Legion" staggered a moment under a point-blank zouave volley, then surged ahead, firing as they came, swarming around the zouaves' flanks. "It looked like a slaughter pen" around the colors, said a survivor. The New Yorkers' colonel fell from his saddle; he was wounded seven times that day. An officer's stampeded horse dragged its rider across the ground. Hazlett's guns were positioned in such a way that they could not possibly help. The battery was hastily limbered up and withdrawn.

The zouaves were right behind. As they fled for the rear, some men darted in a zig-zag fashion to avert a shot in the back. Those who turned to fire a last time were usually shot themselves. In fifteen terrible minutes, the 5th New York suffered the highest percentage of men killed outright in a single Civil War battle—124 slain, 223 wounded, out of 490 men present. An irreverent Texan described them as "gaudy corpses."

After dispatching the zouaves, Hood's division next slammed into the rear of Reynolds' men, catching Union Brigadier General C.F. Jackson's brigade, in column, headed for the north side of the pike. Caught surprised, the Pennsylvanians tried to make a stand, but the Texans destroyed the brigade and captured four cannon.

The great Southern V-shaped vise began to close relentlessly. As Longstreet's left swept ahead, his right ponderously wheeled to the northeast. The ground there was uneven, cut by gullies, ravines, and long hollows, with the upper slopes covered with trees and undergrowth. Longstreet's divisions would hit not as one solid mass but as a series of brigade-sized punches and flanking attacks. Although parts of Stonewall Jackson's Confederate force emerged from their railroad cut stronghold, their depleted condition prevented them from keeping up with Longstreet's pace.

Sykes' U.S. Regulars gave ground grudgingly. Gibbon's now-veteran Black Hats covered Hatch's backward move, always facing to the front. They backed up to a defensive line the erstwhile Federals Sigel and Schenck had drawn up near the J. Dogan place. There they lay down, the Confederates coming from the woods cautiously. When the Rebels came within easy range, Gibbon barked the fire command. Canister knocked them down like tenpins.

Pope and McDowell worked frantically to get enough forces in front of Longstreet to stop him. McDowell sent Brigadier General Zealous B. Tower with his own and Brigadier General George Hartsuff's brigades of Ricketts' division to Chinn Ridge. Sigel sent Brigadier Robert Milroy's brigade, followed soon after by Krzyzanowski's and a Colonel John Koltes' men. As soon as Reynolds reached the north side of the pike, his two remaining brigades were rushed toward an old Battle of Manassas site, the Henry Hill. Sykes' Regulars and the one service-

able brigade of Jesse Reno's division followed them. Pope moved his headquarters there, too. For the moment, however, the only Yankees in front of Longstreet were Colonel Nathaniel McLean's four Ohio regiments and a battery of New York artillery.

The 75th Ohio boys were occupying themselves by taking pot shots at some Texans reforming in the thickets off their right flank. Apparently they were not conscious of the whooping sound coming from the woods in front. Out of the trees burst Brigadier General Nathan G. "Shanks" Evans' brigade of South Carolinians, two ranks deep and 75 yards away. Their objective was Pope's "bald hill," the Chinn Ridge. The Ohio regiments fired by file: Two men at a time discharged their rifles from one end of the line to the other. The batterymen switched from shell to canister, then, double-shotted canister. Evans' soldiers recoiled under the furious blasting, but quickly returned for a second try, reinforced now by Brigadier General Micah Jenkins' South Carolina brigade.

Then two Virginia brigades—Colonel Eppa Hunton's and Colonel Montgomery Corse's of Brigadier General James L. Kemper's division—moved up from the south, threatening the Federal flank resting by a cornfield fence in front of the Chinn house atop the ridge. Hunton's brigade halted momentarily to

dress its ranks. Union Colonel McLean was ordering a section of the New York battery to turn and blast them when someone yelled those were reinforcements. McLean peered hard through the thick gray smoke, but all he could detect was that they wore dark uniforms, like Federal blue. He probably guessed they belonged to Milroy's Union brigade, last seen moving laterally across the valley of nearby Chinn's Branch behind McLean's rear. He was unfortunate in his belief; Milroy had actually halted and reversed his march.

Hunton and Corse charged toward the side of the house and sent a deluge of bullets into the Yankees' flank. The 73d and 25th Ohio fell back over the ridge crest for shelter but Confederate artillery, in their rear, jarred them with banging shells. General Schenck, who for the longest time did not know Sigel had detached McLean from his division, rode into the action rallying his men and was hit by three bullets in rapid succession. The last one caused him to be carried off the field delirious.

As McLean gave the order to retreat, reinforcements took over. Tower's four regiments fought bravely, but ineffectively, unable to deploy under demoralizing pressure. Among these troops, in Hartsuff's brigade, was the 12th Massachusetts of Colonel Fletcher Webster, son of the great statesman, Daniel Webster. These men got back on top of the ridge, but could not hold it; Webster was killed and they were forced back with the others.

Charging the Union battery, Lieutenant Colonel F.G. Skinner, a giant of a man riding ahead of his 1st Virginia, nearly decapitated a Yankee cannoneer with one powerful slash of his sword. He killed another with a thrust, before an infantryman plunged a bayonet into him, driving him backward out of the saddle. Wounded so seriously that later, parts of three ribs had to be removed, Skinner shrugged off attempts to aid him, exclaiming, "Bah! Witness gentlemen, I took this battery."

Swarming down the slope, the Virginians were attracted by a test of their marksmanship, a moving target. To save his piece from capture, a Federal artillery driver dashed between the dry creek bed of Chinn's Branch and advancing Confederate troops. A stream of bullets was directed his way as he whipped his lead horses, the gun bounding behind. He steered along the brink of the creek bed, Rebels yelling, shooting, and closing the range with every step. "Let the man alone and shoot the horses," hollered a captain. "You are shooting too high," he screamed. "Shoot the horses!" The captain estimated

Stubborn Union troops make a stand at Henry Hill and prevent a Confederate rout. (Battles and Leaders of the Civil War)

500 shots were fired at that Yank, and yet somehow he escaped. He pulled up on a knoll out of range, turned around and waved his cap. The Confederates, appreciating his daring, responded with a cheer.

Koltes' and Krzyzanowskis' men then charged into the fight with abandon; coupled with Federal artillery fire from around Dogan's house, they made Longstreet's attack sag momentarily.

The Confederates had plenty of guns of their own, leap-frogging from one ridge to another, delivering a few rounds until the Federals were out of range, then repeating the process. General Robert Lee reigned up next to one of these, the Rockbridge Battery, and was told one of the cannoneers wanted to speak with him—not an unusual request in the Confederate army. "Well, my man, what can I do for you?" he said pulling down his binoculars. "Why General, don't you know me?" Under the grime covering him Lee did not see at first it was his youngest son, Private Robert E. Lee, Jr.

South and east of the main battle area, near New Market Crossroads, in back of a building called the Conrad house, Confederate Brigadier General Beverly H. Robertson, with a brigade of troopers, hoped to swing around Pope's rear and intercept the Yankees' retreat. The 2d Virginia Cavalry galloped in the van. Rebel Colonel Thomas T. Munford spied a lone squadron of Yankee horsemen strung out along the base of a ridge. When he took the bait, ordering a charge, two of Brigadier John Buford's Federal regiments trotted over the crest, and Munford found himself in a wild saber-swinging melee. "Go for the Colonel," cried a Union sergeant. But as he delivered a saber slash his horse went down and Munford caught only a glancing cut. Stuart, with the 7th and 12th Virginia, thundered to the rescue, overwhelmed Buford's disorganized troopers, and sent them fleeing for Lewis' Ford over Bull Run, leaving 300 prisoners in Confederate hands.

It was getting late in the afternoon. Gathering dark clouds threatened an evening rain. Pope, his generals, and men were beaten. Their only salvation was to keep open the route of retreat across Bull Run and its Stone Bridge. If the Confederates seized control of the bridge approaches, all was lost.

North of the turnpike, to conform with the retirement of the Union left, Sam Heintzelman began pulling his corps east of the Sudley Road to the vicinity of the brown Carter mansion, called Pittsylvania. Sigel, in the Federal center, abandoned the Dogan house plateau area. Along the length of the Warrenton Turnpike for miles, from the Stone House across Bull Run toward Centreville, there was a tangled throng of Union army wagons, broken batteries, ambulances, fragmented infantry units, and confused, defeated men.

All that stood between them and destruction at the hands of James Longstreet was one last Yankee line, drawn up in ranks near a pile of rubble. A year before it had been the dwelling of old Mrs. Judith Carter Henry, a civilian victim of the First Battle of Manassas. The defenders were the two serviceable brigades of the Pennsylvania Reserve Division (it had done a great deal of fruitless marching so far but not much fighting), Robert Milroy's brigade, a brigade of Jesse Reno's corps, and a patchwork of companies, squads, and individuals who refused to quit. Beyond the Sudley roadway they watched Longstreet's exultant Rebels crush or push aside whoever tried to stop them.

Infected with victory, the Rebels began ascending Henry Hill, nearer and nearer, their officers urging them on. Against the setting western sun they "came on like demons emerging from the earth."

General John Reynolds drew his breath and hollered, "Forward, Reserves!"

Two charging lines collided head-on at the Sudley Road, the Pennsylvanians jumping into the eroded depression for shelter. In the evening there was bitter fighting again. It equaled any that had gone before it. Reynolds seized the flag of the 2d Pennsylvania and, as if charmed, galloped the length of the front untouched. The Rebels brought up their reserve division, Richard H. Anderson's, and extended their right east of the road. In the nick of time, Federal George Sykes arrived with his Regulars and took over from Reynolds, skillfully pulling the flank back to keep it out of the enemy's reach. A volunteer regiment fired by mistake into the Regulars' backs, and at the height of the crisis an artillery battery panicked and bolted for safety. But, this time the Yankees could not be moved.

At long last the sun went down and the Rebels fell back to Chinn Ridge and went into bivouac. Lee and his generals gathered around a camp fire. There, Hood exclaimed Confederate battle flags moving forward that afternoon had been a thrilling sight. Lee answered gravely, "God forbid it should ever see our colors moving in the opposite direction."

At eight o'clock Pope ordered a general withdrawal to Centreville. Banks was instructed to destroy everything at Bristoe that could not be transported and march for Centreville, also. An odor of black powder smoke polluted the air, and as the darkness deepened, a steady rain began to fall, soaking the tired soldiers to the skin and turning the road to a thick paste. Reflecting on their adventures and misadventures long afterward, many old Union veterans remembered the retreat to Centreville as the gloomiest, most miserable single night of the whole war.

The rank and file seethed with anger. They knew they had fought as well as the Confederates; they had been out-generaled and mis-generaled. Of all the lies Pope ever told, perhaps his greatest was the dispatch telegraphed to General-in-Chief Henry Halleck from Centreville that evening. After outlining the facts, Pope had the gall to write: "The troops are in good heart, and marched off the field without the least hurry of confusion." True, there was no panic as there had been after the first defeat, but there was a great amount of confusion. And there was ugly talk.

"Scoundrel!" a soldier called to McDowell. "Traitor!" yelled another. One infantryman said loudly he would rather put a bullet through McDowell than Stonewall Jackson. And Pope got his share. A Horace Greeley reader hailed him with "Go west, young man. Go West!"

Preparing For The Future

Next morning, Sunday, August 31, Pope had his army in the old Confederate fortifications along Centreville heights. Major General William Buel Franklin's corps had arrived the night before. Major General Edwin V. Sumner's was coming in from Alexandria, too, giving Pope 20,000 fresh troops to make a new fight if he wanted.

First he believed he did: "I shall attack again tomorrow if I can; the next day certainly." Then his mood changed to despair. He inquired if Halleck felt "secure about Washington should this army be destroyed." He hinted darkly about "unsoldierly and dangerous conduct" by some of McClellan's old Army of the Potomac officers.

Pope's talk of this conduct filtered down to the ranks. Franklin's reinforcements treated Pope's dispirited men with contempt and scorn; they lined the route of retreat and "greeted us with mocking laughter, taunts and jeers," said one of McDowell's officers. "They held us back," a Wisconsin soldier told the Black Hats. When General Franklin was questioned why it took three entire days to march from Alexandria to Centreville, he replied he had McClellan's orders in his pocket.

Three miles to the west, Longstreet's Confederates drew the grisly task of undertakers. The casualties were nearly equal: the Union lost about 20 percent of their strength, the Confederates about 17 percent. Pope's 70,000 lost about 1,750 killed, 8,450 wounded, and 4,250 captured or missing. Lee's 55,000 lost 1,550 killed, 7,750 wounded, and about 100 unaccounted for. The battlefield was horrible. Clods of mud were heaped in the shallow trenches and graves, for there was much work and very little time. Hundreds received no burial at all. The Confederate army had to move.

Stonewall Jackson already had his tired men slogging north on another circling maneuver. Lee had beaten the Federal army badly, but he had not destroyed it as he had hoped. He wanted to try again before they retreated to the safety of the defenses of Washington. Jackson crossed Bull Run at Sudley Springs and headed for the Little River Turnpike, where he turned sharply to the right on the route to Fairfax, eight miles in Pope's rear. Roads were muddy, rations again short, troops fatigued, and by day's end Jackson had covered only ten miles. The next day, September 1, the weather was dismal and the going even slower. Late in the day, near a Virginia country estate named Chantilly, the Federals came from the south looking for a fight.

Pope, aware something was afoot north of him, began withdrawing toward Fairfax, at the same time dispatching troops to block the Little River Turnpike. Brigadier General Issac Stevens' division marched cross-country and attacked immediately. Jackson faced his three divisions south to meet him. When Stevens' line crossed a fenced cornfield advancing toward a Confederate held woodline, the gathering dark clouds rolled with thunder, lightning split the sky, and rain came down in torrents. Stevens pushed his line forward in the downpour until he fell dead, shot through the temple. The attack came to a soggy halt.

The driving rainstorm made it impossible for soldiers to load without soaking their cartridges. But when one of A.P. Hill's colonels requested his outfit be relieved because his rifles were useless, the army's commander, Jackson, sternly replied the enemy's ammunition was just as wet as his.

One-armed Phil Kearny splashed to the front at dusk and tried to get the Union attack going again, but the conditions were so bad, the men so miserable, even he could get no response. Galloping through the storm he rode into a Confederate skirmish line and was shot to death before he could escape. "Poor Kearny," said A.P. Hill, viewing the body. "He deserved a better death than that."

After Kearny fell, the inconclusive fighting sputtered to an end in the darkness. The Federals lost two of their best generals and about 1,000 men, the Confederates about half as many. Jackson's maneuver was thwarted, and the Federals slipped off to Fairfax.

On September 2, Old Pete Longstreet's corps joined the troops and the whole army rested. Stuart reported the Federal army heading for Washington. Fortifications there were much too strong for a successful assault, and the suffering Confederate supply situation compelled Lee to look toward Maryland, beyond the Potomac. He could not remain where he was, idle. Western Marylanders were pro-Southern. They might provide recruits and provisions. With the defeated Federal army recovering in Washington, Lee believed he would have time for his own army to refresh itself in the enemy's territory before they marched out for a fight.

In scarcely three months since taking command, Lee had moved the war from the suburbs of Richmond to the environs of his opponent's capital. Washington lived on rumors while Pope's army was out of communication. Then muffled gunfire shook the breezes coming out of the southwest from Virginia. A bulletin from the Treasury Department first announced a great victory. At Secretary of War Edwin Stanton's call, surgeons and male nurses were urged to journey to the battlefield and minister to the Federal wounded, said to number 10,000. Then came shocking news of a military disaster.

Frightened and bewildered crowds gathered. Some said the Army of the Potomac had refused to fight; some of its officers, supposedly, deliberately caused the defeat. One wild rumor said McDowell had committed a treasonous act and Franz Sigel had shot him. General Schenck's arriving ambulance was surrounded by an agitated crowd. "Why, General, is that you?" "Yes," replied Schenck uncovering his wound, "and they have shattered me." All across Washington it was repeated; Schenck had said "our army is scattered."

President Abraham Lincoln called his personal secretary John Hay from his bedroom—"Well, John, we are whipped again, I'm afraid."

All the while the great engagement took place in Virginia, a different sort of battle was being waged across the Potomac. While Jackson's Confederates feasted on Federal supplies at Manassas Junction, General George McClellan had arrived at Alexandria, and reported for duty to Halleck. Part of his assignment was to forward reinforcements from his own Army of the Potomac to Pope, his despised rival. Halleck agreed to his suggestion to have Edwin Sumner's corps protect Washington, but he wanted William Franklin's sent to Pope as soon as possible. McClellan ordered Franklin to move, then countermanded the order. There was no cavalry escort, and the corps' artillery had no horses; the corps was not in fighting condition.

While Pope's soldiers were storming the blazing railroad embankment, McClellan reported he heard Lee with 120,000 Rebels was about to descend on the capital. He wanted to know if Halleck was certain Franklin should leave the capital. Halleck sent peremptory orders for Franklin to move at once. Franklin's force "crawled" ten miles to Annandale and halted. Halleck angrily telegraphed, "this is contrary to my orders." McClellan cooly wired back he had obeyed orders; henceforth Halleck should be more specific with his instructions, "for I have simply exercised the discretion you committed to me."

While Pope's beaten troops retreated across Bull Run, Halleck collapsed in bed "utterly tired out."

Lincoln was among those who believed McClellan had wanted Pope to fail. In proposing alternatives for Washington's safety, McClellan had used the phrase "leave Pope to get out of his scrape."

Secretary of War Stanton, who had been passive since Halleck came east, sent a demand to Halleck's office for a full record regarding McClellan's movement from the Peninsula to northern Virginia and he asked if any slackness had endangered national security. Halleck's reply was, all things considered, McClellan could have moved faster. Stanton and Treasury Secretary Salmon Chase prepared a protest for other cabinet members' signatures. Addressed to Lincoln, it demanded McClellan's dismissal. Chase's real opinion was that McClellan should be taken out and shot.

Lincoln, however, had his ear to the political ground. McClellan and his vision of the Union cause was espoused by the Democratic party, and McClellan was beginning to be regarded as the leader of the opposition. Lincoln needed support from the Democrats for recruits and war legislation. Furthermore, the army, upon whose strained shoulders the nation depended, was devoted to this general. The army wanted McClellan, and if any part of the current rumors were true, it might not fight for anyone else. Indeed, there was no one else. Pope was finished. Halleck had collapsed under pressure. "There is no man in the Army," concluded Lincoln, "who can man these fortifications and lick these troops of our's into shape half as well as he."

On September 2, after a stormy night, General McClellan was at an early breakfast at his house on H Street when the president and General Halleck came and asked him to take command of Washington and the troops falling back from Manassas. For the time being, the future was his.

Politics, Slavery, and Diplomacy in the Antietam Campaign

By all odds, Lee's victorious but exhausted army should have gone into camp for rest and refitting after Second Manassas. Supplies were short, and thousands of men were without shoes and with mere rags for uniforms. But southern leaders believed the war had reached a crucial turning point. Confederate armies in the western theater had marched north in a thus-far successful invasion of Kentucky. A parallel invasion of Maryland might win the war. At the very least, it might win Maryland for the Confederacy. It also would take the armies out of war-ravaged Virginia during the fall harvest. So on September 4, 1862, Lee's ragged veterans began wading across a ford forty miles up the Potomac from Washington.

A great deal was riding on the backs of these soldiers. One issue at stake was British and French diplomatic recognition of the Confederacy. This had been an important goal of southern diplomacy from the war's outset. Official recognition of the Confederacy's independence by the world's most powerful nations would give a tremendous boost to the South's cause. It might lead to foreign aid for that cause, as it had in the American Revolution. In 1861, Confederate leaders had counted on "King Cotton" to win British support. The English economy was dominated by the textile industry, which obtained 80 percent of its cotton from the American slave states. Southerners reasoned that the British navy would have to break the Union blockade in order to get cotton. Unfortunately for the South, the bumper cotton crops of the late 1850's had piled up almost a year's surplus supply in British warehouses by 1861. And in any case, British foreign policy was governed by *Realpolitik*. Before Prime Minister Viscount Palmerston and Foreign Minister Lord John Russell would risk estrangement of the United States by recognizing the Confederacy, the South would have to prove beyond all doubt its capability of winning and sustaining its independence.

Confederate victories in the Seven Days battles and Second Manassas went a long way toward fulfilling that condition. Moreover, the cotton famine had finally hit the textile industry, throwing tens of thousands of employees out of work. The British and French governments contemplated a joint offer of mediation to end the carnage across the Atlantic and reopen the cotton trade. The Union army "got a very complete smashing" at Bull Run, wrote Palmerston to Russell on September 14, "and it seems not altogether unlikely that still greater disasters await them, and that even Washington or Baltimore may fall into the hands of the Confederates. If this should happen, would it not be time for us to address the contending parties and recommend an arrangement upon the basis of separation?" Russell replied enthusiastically, adding that if the Lincoln administration refused such an offer of mediation—as it most certainly would have—"we ought ourselves to recognise the Southern States as an independent State." Palmerston agreed, on condition that Lee won another "smashing" victory in Maryland. If not, "we may wait awhile and see what may follow."

Both the Union and Confederate governments were well aware of the potential foreign-policy consequences of Lee's invasion. To sway British diplomacy was one of the South's goals in the campaign. Another was to influence the 1862 congressional elections in the North. In a bipartisan effort, most northern Democrats had supported Lincoln's war policies in 1861. But as those policies evolved from a limited war to restore the old Union toward a total war to destroy the Old South and build a new Union on its ashes, Democrats went into opposition. In 1862, Lincoln and the Republican majority in Congress took a number of steps against slavery. In July Congress passed a confiscation act providing for the seizure of the property, including slaves, of persons in rebellion against the government. Lincoln contemplated an emancipation proclamation applying to all slaves in Confederate states. Tens of thousands of slaves fled their rebel masters to find sanctuary in Union lines. Yankee soldiers also seized or destroyed other southern property. Northern Democrats opposed all these measures as harsh and revolutionary. They had looked forward to restoration of a Union in which southern slave–owning Democrats would retain their wealth and power, and combine with northern Democrats to form a national majority as before the war.

But Republicans were no longer fighting that kind of war. They regarded southern Democrats as traitors. They demanded unconditional surrender and called for measures to mobilize all northern resources to "crush" the rebellion. These measures included confiscation of slaves, to take their labor power from the Confederacy and add it to the northern war effort. It also included conscription of state militias, sanctioned in the militia act passed by Congress in July 1862. Denouncing these measures, many northern Democrats increasingly denounced the war itself. Some of them, branded "Copperheads," expressed sympathy with the Confederacy. Union officials arrested many anti-war activists. Democrats added these"arbitrary arrests" to the catalogue of Republican sins. They intended to make the congressional elections of 1862 a referendum on Republican war policies.

In September, it appeared that the Democrats had a good chance to win a majority in the next House of Representatives. Northern voters were discouraged by Union defeats in the Seven Days and Second Manassas battles, as well as by Confederate advances in Tennessee and Kentucky. Perhaps the Democrats were right, many voters reasoned; perhaps Lincoln's hard-war policies could never restore the Union; perhaps the Democrats should be given a chance to negotiate a compromise with the South. A successful Confederate invasion of Maryland and another victory over the Army of the Potomac might provide the final blow to discredit Lincoln and prod northern voters to repudiate his policies. That was what Robert E. Lee hoped to accomplish as his weary warriors splashed across the Potomac on September 4.

For Lincoln, more than the fate of his party in the elections was at stake in the military campaign shaping up in Maryland. Back in July he had decided that because "slavery is the root of the rebellion," emancipation was "a military necessity, absolutely essential to the preservation of the Union," because it would "weaken the rebels by drawing off their laborers." The North could no longer fight this war "with elder-stalk squirts, charged with rose water," said Lincoln. "We want the army to strike more vigorous blows. The Administration must set an example, and strike at the heart of the rebellion."

On July 22, Lincoln informed the cabinet of his decision to issue an emancipation proclamation. Most cabinet members approved, but Secretary of State Seward advised withholding the edict until Union arms won a military victory. Otherwise, coming in the wake of defeats in Virginia and setbacks in the West, the proclamation might be viewed "as the last measure of an exhausted government, a cry for help . . . our last *shriek*, on the retreat." Lincoln accepted this advice. But the wait for a victory was a long one. In August and September came more bad news from Tennessee, Second Manassas in Virginia, and Lee's invasion of Maryland. Nerves were stretched to the breaking point in Washington during those bleak days of September 1862 as Lincoln anxiously awaited news from the front.

—*James M. McPherson*

THE BATTLE
OF ANTIETAM

by Stephen Sears

The "Lost Order"

Major General George B. McClellan had never taken more pleasure from his military accomplishments. It was 9:30 on the morning of September 15, 1862, and he was writing a hurried note to his wife. The Army of the Potomac had "gained a glorious & complete victory: every moment adds to its importance," he told her. ". . . How glad I am for my country that it is delivered from immediate peril. I am about starting with the pursuit & must close this. . . . If I can believe one tenth of what is reported, God has seldom given an army greater victory than this. . . ."

He telegraphed the good tidings to Washington. His information was "perfectly reliable," he announced, that the enemy was fleeing "in a perfect panic, & that Genl Lee last night stated publicly that he must admit they had been shockingly whipped." A report just in, he wrote in a second telegram, "completely confirms the rout & demoralization of the rebel Army. . . . It is stated that Lee gives his loss as fifteen thousand." After reading these dispatches,

President Abraham Lincoln replied, "God bless you, and all with you; destroy the rebel army if possible."

The subject of General McClellan's euphoria was the Battle of South Mountain, Maryland, fought the day before. His pursuit was undertaken to drive the Confederates out of the state and across the Potomac River back into Virginia. For over a week he had tried to track the invaders across some 600 square miles of western Maryland on a military chessboard that extended from Harpers Ferry, Virginia, on the Potomac River, northward to Hagerstown, near the Pennsylvania line, and from Frederick westward across South Mountain to the Maryland village of Sharpsburg. With this one victory, he thought, he had won the campaign.

As was his habit, however, he was indulging in a good deal of wishful thinking. He furnished the Lincoln Administration with more overheated rumor than fact. Confederate General Robert E. Lee had not lost anything close to 15,000 men at South Mountain, nor did he say publicly (or privately) that he had been "shockingly whipped." Nor was his

Harpers Ferry as seen from Loudon Heights, while still occupied by Federal troops. Early in their Maryland Campaign, the Confederates seized the town to prevent the Union garrison there from threatening their flanks at Sharpsburg. (The Soldier in Our Civil War)

General Lee marched for Sharpsburg that day because it was the most convenient spot on the Maryland side of the Potomac to concentrate his widely scattered army. It offered good defensive ground and was a position not easily turned. As he directed his men to their postings behind Antietam Creek, one of them heard him say, "We will make our stand on those hills."

Lee was puzzled by General McClellan's unexpected aggressiveness that had brought on the fighting at South Mountain, but unwilling to give up his campaign because of it. A primary rationale behind his entire plan of operations in Maryland was the fact that George McClellan commanded the Federal army, and he was not yet persuaded by the events of the past thirty-six hours to change his opinion that his opponent put caution ahead of all other military considerations.

As Lee suspected, whatever had suddenly impelled McClellan to go on the offensive, it was not due to a change of character. It was pure chance. Two days

Army of Northern Virginia fleeing "in a perfect panic."

Indeed, news that began reaching McClellan's headquarters at midday no doubt tempered his enthusiasm. From the summit of South Mountain a lookout reported the enemy had stopped retreating and was taking up a line of battle "on the other side of Antietam creek and this side of Sharpsburg." The sighting was confirmed by Captain George Armstrong Custer of McClellan's staff, riding with the advance: "They are in full view. Their line is a perfect one about a mile and a half long. . . . We can employ all the troops you can send us."

Confederate General Robert E. Lee, who resolved to carry the war into Northern territory. (CWTI Collection)

earlier, on the morning of September 13, McClellan was handed what became famous as the "Lost Order." It was lost, apparently, through the carelessness of a Southern courier or staff officer, and found by Corporal Barton W. Mitchell of the 27th Indiana in a meadow near Frederick, Maryland, where Mitchell's regiment was making camp. Headed "Special Order No. 191, Headquarters Army of Northern Virginia" and dated September 9, it was a copy of Lee's field order for his complex operation against the Federal garrison at Harpers Ferry. Here, in full detail, was listed every major command in the Confederate army, the objectives and routes of march for each, and a timetable. When McClellan telegraphed the president at noon that day, "I have all the plans of the rebels," he was not exaggerating. It was the intelligence coup of the Civil War.

The situation was one of considerable irony, for if McClellan had had his way there would have been no Federal garrison occupying Harpers Ferry and no need for Lee to issue "Order 191" for its capture. When the Confederates began crossing the Potomac into Maryland at White's Ford on September 4, every Federal outpost to the west in Virginia's lower Shenandoah Valley was in immediate danger of being cut off and captured. McClellan pointed this out to Union General-in-Chief Major General Henry W. Halleck, and suggested that the troops at Harpers Ferry, the most important of these outposts, be withdrawn and added to his field army. Halleck refused. He believed Lee was crossing into Maryland merely as a feint to draw the Federal army away from Washington, the Confederates' real objective. By McClellan's account, Halleck insisted that the Harpers Ferry garrison "was perfectly safe where it was. . . ."

Fresh from his victory at the Second Battle of Bull Run (Second Manassas) on August 29 and 30, 1862, General Lee had every intention of retaining the strategic initiative but no intention of attacking Washington's strong fortifications. He invaded Maryland for a number of reasons—to forestall another Federal offensive into Virginia, to provision his army, to put pressure on the Lincoln Administration's shaky political coalition, among them. But above all Lee was looking to pull McClellan far from his Washington base for a showdown fight on a field of his own choosing. He wanted him out of his lines so he "could get at him," he said in an interview after the war. "I went into Maryland to give battle, and could I have kept Gen. McClellan in ignorance of my position and plans a day or two longer, I would have fought and crushed him." He told the interviewer that he had regarded McClellan as an able general but a timid one.

Lee had intended the battlefield of his choice to be somewhere in the Cumberland Valley of Maryland and Pennsylvania, an extension of the Shenandoah Valley of Virginia. Moving that far west meant running his supply line through the Shenandoah, and to protect that line something would have to be done about the Federals at Harpers Ferry. Instead of simply masking the garrison there, obstructing the view of his operations, he devised a plan to divide his army so as to surround and capture it—men, supplies, ordnance, and all. In drawing up "Order 191" he assigned six of his nine divisions to the task, under the overall command of Major General Thomas J. Jackson—the famous "Stonewall," renowned for his mastery of independent operations.

In carrying out the Harpers Ferry movement the Confederates maneuvered for several days behind the northern barrier of South Mountain in ways that McClellan could not fathom. "From all I can gather secesh is skedadelling & I don't think I can catch him unless he is really moving into Penna," he wrote his wife on September 12. ". . .I begin to think that he is making off to get out of the scrape by recrossing the river at Williamsport. . . . He evidently don't want to fight me. . . ." He told Washington authorities the same thing, telegraphing that night that he feared the Rebels would make their escape to Virginia "before I can catch them."

But by noon on September 13 he had the "Lost Order" and understood all these movements, and he promised Lincoln "no time will be lost" in catching Lee in his own trap and punishing him severely. A swift advance across South Mountain would put his forces squarely between the widely scattered elements of the Rebel army. "My general idea is to cut the enemy in two & beat him in detail," he told one of his generals. For George McClellan, however, losing no time meant starting first thing next day. It was eighteen hours before any Federals marched in response to the finding of the "Lost Order."

The Battle of South Mountain on September 14 would be fought for the two main passes through the mountain—Turner's Gap to the north, where the National Road from Frederick crossed the range, and Crampton's Gap to the south, where a road crossed into Pleasant Valley and went on to Harpers Ferry. Had McClellan in reality lost no time and ordered strong forces to advance to within striking distance of the passes during the afternoon of September 13— seven hours of daylight were available in which to march the ten or twelve miles to the foot of the mountain—the next morning he would have met only slight opposition at Turner's Gap and nothing but a

The 23d and 12th Ohio charge the 23d and 12th North Carolina in the Battle of South Mountain, Maryland. Fought on Sunday, September 14, the battle caused the Confederate troops to retire to Sharpsburg. Painting by A.A. Fasel. (Library of Congress)

cavalry screen at Crampton's Gap. A vigorous offensive begun at first light on September 14 would have put the Federals across South Mountain by midday and in position to divide and conquer Lee's army—and to rescue the Harpers Ferry garrison.

To be sure, General McClellan could not forecast all these favorable circumstances. Yet the question remains: Why did the tactics of speed and surprise not occur to him as the most logical responses to the "Lost Order"? Issuing directions for an immediate advance toward South Mountain the moment he read "Order 191" on September 13, even before working out the final details of his plan, could do no possible harm and might bring great rewards. The answer may be that whenever McClellan had to improvise rapid responses to situations he had not anticipated—learning all the plans of the enemy could hardly be anticipated—he always found (or imagined) risks that outweighed opportunities. Lee's sense of the man was astute: he was indeed acting as the most timid of generals.

As it happened, it was late afternoon on the 14th before a full-fledged attack was mounted at either pass. By then the Confederates had enough troops on the scene to make a fight of it, and when darkness ended the firing the Federals had reached no farther than the crest of the mountain. In the meantime, Stonewall Jackson drew his noose tightly about Harpers Ferry. He notified Lee that he expected to capture it in the morning.

At daylight on September 15 the ranks of Jackson's guns surrounding Harpers Ferry resumed their bombardment, and at 8:00 a.m. the garrison raised the white flag of surrender. The closest rescue force from the Army of the Potomac, Major General William B. Franklin's VI Corps at Crampton's Gap, was half a dozen miles away and a day late. Jackson's spoils included 11,500 men, 13,000 small arms, 73 pieces of artillery, and a huge stock of supplies. Franklin reported to McClellan that the artillery firing had stopped, which he thought could only mean that Harpers Ferry had surrendered. That unhappy news,

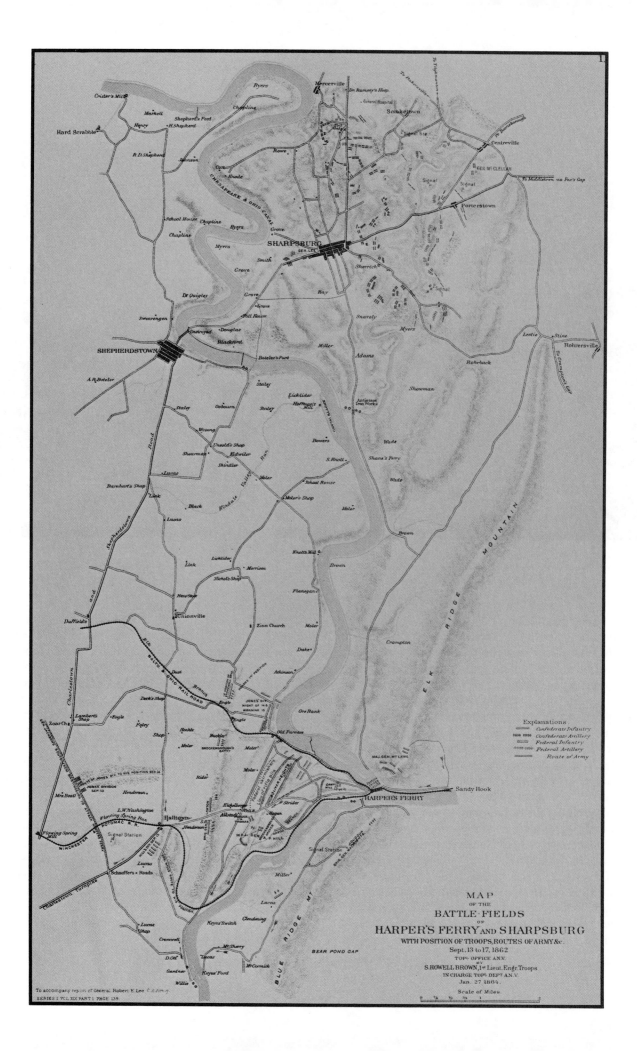

MAP
OF THE
BATTLE-FIELDS
OF
HARPER'S FERRY AND SHARPSBURG
WITH POSITION OF TROOPS, ROUTES OF ARMY &c.
Sept. 13 to 17, 1862
TOP'L OFFICE A.N.V.
BY
S. HOWELL BROWN, 1st Lieut. Engr. Troops
IN CHARGE TOP'L DEPT A.N.V.
Jan. 27 1864.
Scale of Miles.

Explanations
Confederate Infantry
Confederate Artillery
Federal Infantry
Federal Artillery
Route of Army

To accompany report of General Robert E. Lee C.S. Army
SERIES 1 VOL XIX PART 1 PAGE 139.

along with the report that the enemy in front of him was making a stand at Sharpsburg, gave McClellan further cause to rethink his entire course of action.

His inflated view of the results of the fighting at Turner's and Crampton's Gaps had at first led him to think the Maryland campaign was all but over; his notion of pursuit was little more than a gesture to see the Rebels off as they fled back to Virginia. He remained miles to the rear at his headquarters east of South Mountain, savoring his army's first offensive victory since he took command more than a year before. The march of the Federals that morning was badly directed, with units delayed and getting in one another's way and no one from headquarters to straighten out the tangles. It was only a six- or seven-mile march to Antietam Creek, but the first Yankee infantry did not reach the scene until two o'clock in the afternoon. McClellan did not appear until an hour later. He made what he described as a "rapid examination" of Lee's position and decided (as he reported to Washington) that "it was too late in the day to attack."

McClellan was a prudent man by nature, but what activated his almost unnatural caution in military matters was the picture of the enemy he carried in his head. It dominated his every action. In contemplating the situation on September 15, he based his calculations on the belief that Lee had invaded Maryland with 120,000 men, an army 25 per cent larger than his own. Even after he knew from the "Lost Order" that the Army of Northern Virginia was widely scattered, he remained preoccupied with the odds he might face. ". . .I have the mass of their troops to contend with," he told General Halleck in announcing his find, "& they outnumber me when united."

He had almost 60,000 troops under his immediate command that day—the army's right wing led by Major General Ambrose E. Burnside, consisting of the I and IX Corps and supported by a division of Major General Fitz John Porter's V Corps (another of Porter's divisions would arrive the next day); and the army's center under Major General Edwin V. Sumner, containing the II and XII Corps. Franklin's 19,000 men—his VI Corps and an attached division under Major General Darius N. Couch—were in Pleasant Valley beyond Crampton's Gap. "Shall I make the necessary dispositions to attack?" Sumner asked when he reached Antietam Creek. "And shall I attack without further orders?" McClellan replied that nothing was to be done until he reached the scene.

As McClellan reckoned it from the "Lost Order," Lee had opposed him at Turner's Gap with 30,000 men. Consequently, there ought to be only that number at Sharpsburg, less whatever losses (substantial losses, by his count) were suffered in the Turner's Gap fight. Yet here was his opponent standing defiantly in line of battle, apparently perfectly willing to resume the fight.

Perhaps his calculations were flawed; perhaps the plan in the "Lost Order" had been changed and those hills and woodlots and orchards around Sharpsburg concealed uncounted Rebel reinforcements. In his dispatch Sumner warned, "The enemy is drawn up in large force in front. . . . As we don't know the number of their lines it is impossible to estimate their *entire* force." The I Corps' Major General Joseph Hooker was heard to say that their force was at least 40,000. McClellan concluded there was not time enough left that day to launch a coordinated, fully manned, carefully planned attack. To attempt anything less would be a dangerous improvisation. Tomorrow would be soon enough to act.

In addition, McClellan had Stonewall Jackson to worry about. Franklin's report about the Harpers Ferry surrender was a troubling development. Jackson might already be marching for Sharpsburg. If he moved up the Virginia side of the Potomac and crossed the river at Harpers Ferry and followed the direct Sharpsburg road west of Elk Mountain (a range parallel to and west of South Mountain), he would come in on Lee's right. However, if he marched to the east of Elk Mountain, through Pleasant Valley, it would put him on the flank and rear of the Federal forces facing Antietam Creek.

Subsequently, McClellan watched his left flank with great care on September 15. It was seventeen miles from Harpers Ferry to Sharpsburg by the shortest route, but Jackson's men were known to be prodigious marchers. Franklin's wing was ordered to remain on guard in Pleasant Valley, and for the better part of the day four divisions under Burnside and Porter took position to reinforce Franklin. So September 15 passed without event, and General McClellan wasted a second major opportunity to divide and conquer the Army of Northern Virginia.

Unaware that his opponent knew all the workings of his Harpers Ferry operation, Lee was running a substantial bluff that day. He had scarcely 15,000 men in the line of battle, McClellan observed in his hurried inspection. Lee had his gunners put every piece of artillery they had in the line, with orders to fire on any Federals they saw.* Then, about noon, a courier brought Lee confirmation of the capture of

---

*One target that attracted their attention was McClellan's reconnoitering party. The general sent his staff to seek cover while he went on with his inspection.

Harpers Ferry, along with the welcome news that Jackson would have his troops on the road by evening and be at Sharpsburg the next day. But, even when the army was reunited, Lee would have less than 40,000 fighting men of all arms.

Robert E. Lee did not stand and fight at Sharpsburg because he was cornered and forced to it. He might have continued his retreat from South Mountain on September 15 and very likely crossed the Potomac into Virginia before the Federal pursuit caught up. He could certainly have made the crossing safely under the cover of darkness. Instead, he stood his ground north of the river and challenged McClellan to attack him.

Gambling on a Timid General

To fight there was the boldest and most hazardous decision of any Lee made during the Civil War. Some would term it foolhardy: not until the final doomed hours at Appomattox Court House in April 1865 did he again stand so great a chance of losing his entire army. And only in those last days of the war would the Army of Northern Virginia be as small as it was at Sharpsburg.

Lee and his generals had good enough intelligence sources, and they had seen enough of the Federals at Turner's Gap and as they arrived before Antietam Creek to estimate the size of McClellan's force. They figured rightly that they were outnumbered by as much as 2 to 1. And they knew it was not even certain that all Confederate commands could be reunited in time to meet a Federal attack. But on this last point, General Lee felt secure in his judgment of his opponent's caution and how much that timidity would benefit him. "If he had had a well-equipped army of a hundred thousand veterans at his back," a Confederate officer recalled, Lee "could not have appeared more composed and confident."

The troops that Lee did have were in wretched physical condition. Most of them had lived primarily on green corn and apples for two weeks and more, and thousands were suffering debilitating chronic diarrhea. Thousands were shoeless and footsore. "They nearly worried us to death asking for something to eat. They were half famished and they looked like tramps . . .," a Sharpsburg woman recalled. And nearly every man in the ranks was tired and worn beyond mere exhaustion. During the Second Bull Run Campaign in August they had marched all across northern Virginia and in September they marched through a sizable part of western Maryland, and during the past two weeks straggling had reached

epidemic proportions. From September 1 onward, the Army of Northern Virginia lost more than one-fifth of its numbers through straggling. One of Jackson's officers wrote home: ". . . I am completely tired out with our constant marching. . . . It is too much as the state of our ranks show, and if Jackson keeps on at it, there will be no army for him to command." Another officer remarked simply, "none but heroes are left."

The battlefield Lee chose at Sharpsburg, wrote Confederate artillerist E. Porter Alexander, "was a fairly good one for defence as positions go in a well-settled agricultural country, but it was by no means as strong as it is often said to be." Its greatest weakness was that there were too few men to defend it; the Army of Northern Virginia promised to be stretched very thin trying to hold its lines from flank to flank. Another serious drawback was the fact that the Potomac River was only three miles to the rear. The bridge at Shepherdstown had long since been burned, and the only crossing was Boteler's Ford, deep and rocky and not easily negotiated. Should the 2 to 1 odds be too much for the Rebels and force them to retreat under fire, chances were poor that many would escape across the river in the face of vigorous pursuit. It was for just this reason that the military textbooks warned against an army fighting with a river at its back, yet here was Lee risking seeing his army utterly destroyed on the banks of the Potomac if McClellan's offensive succeeded.

Why did he take such a gamble? Certainly pride was a factor in his decision. He had launched an ambitious campaign to gain a decisive victory on Northern soil, with all that would mean for the goal of Confederate independence, and to have it end in a humiliating withdrawal, with only the capture of the Harpers Ferry garrison to show for it, was not something he could easily accept. He had come north to give battle, and he had confidence in himself and in his troops. Furthermore, he believed the Federals to be disorganized and demoralized after their recent defeats. If Sharpsburg had to be the battlefield rather than the Cumberland Valley, if he had to fight defensively rather than maneuver against his opponent offensively, he would make that choice. Considering the unexpected weakness of his army he could hardly count on the decisive victory he had originally hoped for, but a victory of whatever sort might buy time and set back Federal plans for the rest of the year.

And there was more to it than that. After cataloging all the disadvantages of making a fight at Sharpsburg, E. Porter Alexander listed the advantages: "There is a single item, but it is an important one." General McClellan brought an army superior in numbers and equipment to the field, he wrote, "but he brought *himself* also. Perhaps the anticipation of that fact encouraged Lee to risk the odds. . . ." To Lee's way of thinking, that was the equalizer. He was sure beyond doubt that he could defeat George McClellan on any field of battle.

At dawn on Tuesday, September 16, a thick ground fog blanketed the hollows and woods around Sharpsburg and hid the Confederate positions from the Federals east of Antietam Creek. McClellan began the day with seeming confidence. He was in "excellent spirits," he telegraphed his wife at 7:00 a.m. "Have reached thus far & have no doubt delivered Penna & Maryland." At the same hour he telegraphed General Halleck in Washington that the fog "had thus far prevented our doing more than to ascertain that some of the enemy are still there. Do not yet know in what force. Will attack as soon as situation of the enemy is developed." To General Franklin in Pleasant Valley he wrote: "I think the enemy has abandoned the position in front of us, but the fog is so dense that I have not yet been able to determine. If the enemy is in force here, I shall attack him this morning."

These promises to bring Lee to battle promptly were straightforward enough, but there was no substance to them. McClellan had not yet completed a plan for an offensive nor moved troops into attacking position. When at mid-morning the fog burned off and revealed the Confederate army still in place, the pretense ended. "It became evident from the force of the enemy and the strength of their position that desperate fighting alone could drive them from the field, and all felt that a great and terrible battle was at hand," he explained. The day would be devoted to preparation—"obtaining information as to the ground, rectifying the position of the troops, and perfecting arrangements for the attack." A Union staff man recalled that no one seemed to be in a hurry that day. "Corps and divisions moved as languidly to the places assigned them as if they were getting ready for a grand review instead of a decisive battle."

McClellan's unhurried actions on September 16 may best be explained in the telegram sent that day to Pennsylvania's Governor Andrew G. Curtin by Captain William J. Palmer, chief scout for the governor's intelligence service. Captain Palmer had spent the previous night at General McClellan's headquarters, and he gave Curtin the general's view of affairs. The general believed, he wrote, that Harpers Ferry had surrendered on the morning of the 15th, "and that Jackson re-enforced Lee at Sharpsburg last night. . . . Rebels appear encouraged at arrival of their re-enforcements."

There is nothing in the Army of the Potomac records or in McClellan's papers to document the belief that Jackson had marched his entire force from Harpers Ferry to Sharpsburg on September 15—no reports by Federal cavalry or scouts, no sightings by civilians, no information from deserters or prisoners. It was pure deduction on McClellan's part, and from it he made the further deduction that with Lee's army now reunited there was no need for hasty action. He could act with his usual deliberation. That he thought Stonewall Jackson could complete all the Harpers Ferry surrender arrangements, reassemble his men and their artillery from the various besieging positions, organize and provision them in their (imagined) scores of thousands and then march them seventeen miles, all in the space of twelve or fourteen hours, suggests McClellan not only multiplied the Confederates' numbers in his mind, but that he gave them superhuman qualities as well.

Up to that time, McClellan had gained remarkably little profit from his possession of "Lee's Order 191." The engagements at South Mountain cost him 2,300 men, including one of his ablest corps commanders, Major General Jesse Reno, killed by a Rebel sharpshooter. And fighting there failed to put him in position to crush Lee's scattered commands one by one.

The badly managed pursuit on September 15 gave further life to the Army of Northern Virginia. On the morning of September 16 McClellan could put four times as many men on the firing line as his opponent, but once again the opportunity for an overwhelming victory slipped away. "If he had used the priceless hours of the 15th September, and the still precious, though less precious hours of the 16th as he might have," wrote Francis W. Palfrey, an Antietam veteran turned historian, "his name would have stood high in the roll of great commanders; but he let those hours go by. . . ." Now only a single advantage remained to be gained from the "Lost Order": on September 17, 1862, Robert E. Lee would have to fight a different sort of battle than he had planned, and fight it sooner and with fewer men than he had intended.

It was not until midday on September 16 that Jackson and the vanguard of his force reached Sharpsburg. They had made what Jackson admitted was "a severe night's march" and the exhausted men continued to straggle in throughout the afternoon. And two trailing divisions, under Major Generals Lafayette McLaws and Richard H. Anderson, did not get even as far as the Potomac ford on the 16th. Lee greeted Jackson, then, together with his other chief lieutenant, Major General James Longstreet, they arranged the posting of the troops. One of Jackson's staff, Colonel Henry Kyd Douglas, overheard a group of Longstreet's soldiers arguing about whether Jackson had really arrived. One of them insisted he was still "over in Virginny, somewhere, up to something lively, I'll be bound." His friend approached Douglas and asked him to settle the argument.

Yes, Douglas told him, Stonewall was back with the army. "That's he, talking with your General, 'Old Pete'—the man with the big boots on."

"It is? Well, bless my eyes! Thankee, Captain." He turned back to his comrades, waved his hat, and shouted, "Boys, it's all right!"

Lee could count six of his nine divisions with him now, and the lack of activity across the valley of the Antietam made it obvious that he would not have to face a serious attack that day. He put Jackson in command of the left of the line and Longstreet in command of the right. Jackson spent the afternoon reconnoitering the terrain on his front and positioning his forces. Longstreet, too, was carefully examining the ground he would be defending and the dispositions of the Federals facing him. He rode slowly along the high ground in front of Sharpsburg, binoculars to his eyes, indifferent to the sporadic shelling of the Federal batteries.

Lee sent orders to McLaws and Anderson south of the Potomac to resume their march in time to be at Sharpsburg early on the 17th. Another courier galloped off to Harpers Ferry with orders for Major General A. P. Hill, whose division Jackson had left to manage the details of the surrender, to set off first thing in the morning to rejoin the army. Lee had concluded that McClellan would grant him no more gifts of time. Gunners were told to hold their fire and save their ammunition for a battle the next day.

Despite the potential risk in fighting with a river at his back, Lee chose his ground well, carefully calculating its defensive possibilities. Sharpsburg was a farming community of 1,300 people at the center of a network of roads—turnpikes leading north to Hagerstown, northeast to Boonsboro, and southwest to Shepherdstown, and local roads running to Pleasant Valley and to Harpers Ferry. To the west the Potomac River made serpentine bends as it followed its southward course; to the east, copper-colored Antietam Creek flowed within a mile or so of the town on its way to a junction with the Potomac three miles to the south. It was good farming country, and in many of the fenced fields corn stood thick and head-high. The woodlots, free of undergrowth and dotted with stacks of farmers' cordwood, provided additional cover. Autumn had not yet touched western Maryland, and the trees were in full foliage.

From a military perspective, a low north-south ridgeline, along which ran the Hagerstown turnpike, dominated the landscape. South of Sharpsburg, toward the mouth of the Antietam, the ground was broken and steeply sloped, marked by wooded hills and ravines. To Federal observers the ground appeared more open and level north of the town, although this impression proved to be (as a Northern war correspondent wrote) "completely deceitful." The terrain there was full of little hollows and creases and jutting outcroppings of limestone, offering many sites for concealment and defense. A network of town and farm roads behind the ridgeline, and the Hagerstown pike itself, simplified troop movements for the Confederates.

Lee erected no fieldworks on the 15th or 16th, in part because his men had few entrenching tools but mainly because he felt, at this stage of the war at least, that such works hampered his opportunities for maneuver; clearly he was thinking of an offensive defense. This lack of fortifications was not as significant as it might seem, however. During the battle Rebel soldiers would take full advantage of the many terrain features suited to defense, and they improvised rough fieldworks of their own from logs and fence rails. A Federal officer, in recalling the battle, wrote that Jackson "had sheltered his reserves behind rocky ledges waist-high, and wonderfully adapted for defense, had deepened natural depressions into rifle-pits, had laid up long lines of fence-rail breastworks, and so was all ready for a formidable resistance."

Antietam Creek was another important battlefield feature, for it was just wide enough and deep enough to complicate Federal movements in any offensive,* particularly for the artillery and the ammunition trains. Three arched stone bridges crossed the Antietam in the vicinity of Sharpsburg. The Rohrbach Bridge, the most southerly of the three, on the Sharpsburg-Pleasant Valley road, would soon be made famous by the name "Burnside Bridge." The Middle Bridge was almost due east of Sharpsburg, on the Boonsboro turnpike. The Upper Bridge was some two and a half miles to the north, on the road to Williamsport on the upper Potomac.

As Lee posted it that day, his line of infantry and artillery extended some four miles. From north to south it ran along the face of the ridgeline and generally parallel to and in front of the Hagerstown turnpike, covered Sharpsburg, and ended on high ground

---

*McClellan regarded it as a line of defense as well, and did not resort to fieldworks of his own as he had done so often in a campaign he had waged against the Confederate capital in Spring 1862. Fought on Virginia's Peninsula, south of the capital, Richmond, it, too, was a campaign characterized by slowness.

overlooking Antietam Creek below the Rohrbach Bridge. One brigade of Major General J.E.B. Stuart's cavalry guarded the army's southern flank along the lower Antietam, and another the northern flank on the Potomac. Stuart positioned fourteen guns on Nicodemus Hill, the highest ground on the northern flank.

From his first look at the field on September 15, General McClellan decided to throw the main weight of his offensive against that northern flank. Not only did the ground on the Confederate left seem best suited for maneuver, but the approach to it by the Upper Bridge was beyond the reach of the enemy's artillery. Another inspection of the field on the 16th made him comfortable with this decision, and by noon that day he was ready to order the movement. It would be the first time in his Civil War career that he planned and directed an offensive battle, and the first battle of any kind that he directed, or even witnessed, from start to finish. Before Antietam, wrote Francis Palfrey, "there was almost always something for McClellan to do more important than to fight his own battles." He issued no written order outlining his plan and called no meeting of his generals to explain it.

While McClellan's tactical plan at Antietam was dictated by terrain and his mental picture of the enemy, the method he used to carry it out was very much shaped by his confidence (or lack of it) in his subordinates and troops. His first decision was to alter his triad command structure. He had devised this system—left wing under Franklin, center under Sumner, right wing under Burnside—to manage his advance into Maryland, and he retained it for the fighting at South Mountain. Now the way he had disposed of his forces made it impractical, but an equally basic reason for changing it on the eve of battle was his doubts about two of his senior major generals. During his Peninsula Campaign, waged in Virginia in Spring 1862, McClellan complained to his wife that Sumner had nearly brought the army to defeat and was "even a greater fool than I had supposed." His disillusionment with his old friend Burnside was more recent. He had decided Burnside acted sluggishly in pursuing the enemy after South Mountain and was slow to put his troops into position on September 16. He issued Burnside a sharply worded rebuke that brought a chill to their relationship.

Other men seemed to please him more. McClellan arranged it so that the two major generals he rated most highly—"Fighting Joe" Hooker and Fitz John Porter—would play crucial roles in his battle plan. Hooker and his I Corps were to lead off the attack on the Confederate left. Porter and his V Corps formed the main reserve, to exploit victory or to serve as the last line of defense in case of defeat. On the afternoon

Left: Major General Ambrose E. Burnside. (National Archives) Right: Brigadier General Jacob D. Cox. (U.S. Army Military History Institute) McClellan's command shifts prior to the Battle of Antietam disgruntled Burnside and confused Cox.

of September 16 Hooker crossed the Antietam at the Upper Bridge and took position astride the Hagerstown turnpike opposite Lee's left flank. When he called for support lest he be left out on a limb, McClellan that night sent him Major General Joseph K.F. Mansfield's XII Corps. By Hooker's account, McClellan promised him that the XII Corps was his to call on if he needed reinforcement for the morning's attack.

Removing Mansfield from Sumner's command and putting him at Hooker's call was part of McClellan's deliberate effort to keep Edwin Sumner in check. Old Sumner (he was age sixty-five and had fought Indians on the far frontier before George McClellan was born) was all determination and courage. But the job of leading a third of the army, of even a corps, was beyond his abilities. He was ordered to hold his II Corps behind the Antietam and to be ready to march in the morning. When Sumner went into action it was McClellan's intention that he be in support of Joe Hooker and therefore come under Hooker's direction as the general commanding on the field.

In this scheme Hooker was taken from Burnside's control and Burnside himself was posted with the IX Corps on the far left of the army, as far from the I Corps as it was possible to be. Burnside took this as a demotion and it soured his normally genial disposition. Brigadier General Jacob D. Cox, who had succeeded to command of the IX Corps after Jesse Reno's death at South Mountain, offered to give up the post and return to his division, but Burnside would not accept that course; it would only be an acknowledgment of his humiliation. The result was an awkward and ill-defined situation. Burnside had command responsibility for the IX Corps but Cox commanded the troops; whatever initiative either might exercise in the coming battle would be smothered in confusion.

To further complicate affairs, it was not really clear to these two generals what the IX Corps was expected to do in the Sharpsburg battle. With the possible exception of his confidant and unofficial second-in-command Fitz John Porter, McClellan seems to have discussed his plans for the fight with no one but Joe Hooker. As Burnside and Cox understood it, upon orders from headquarters in the morning they were simply to mount a diversion at the Rohrbach Bridge to prevent the Confederates from withdrawing troops from their right to meet the main attack on their left. For such a diversion to succeed it would have to be made when Hooker opened his attack or soon afterward, but there was no certainty about McClellan's actual intentions on this point. (Through the post-

war years McClellan wrote several accounts of his Antietam battle plan. The accounts vary and perhaps reflect his own uncertainty on the matter.)

For equally vague reasons, McClellan held Franklin's corps in Pleasant Valley throughout the day on September 16, and only that evening sent orders for it to march the next morning to rejoin the main army. Then he directed General Couch's division to Harpers Ferry, an errand he never explained, and perhaps could not explain. As a result, of Franklin's 19,000 men, only 12,000 (two of his three divisions) arrived on the battlefield on September 17, and only when the battle was half over. Couch's troops were removed to a distance from where they could be of little help—and when that help did come, it was too late. (In telling contrast, that day General Lee ordered two late-arriving divisions commanded by Major Generals Lafayette McLaws and Richard H. Anderson to march at midnight so as to be at Sharpsburg by sunrise on the 17th; for General McClellan, sunrise was early enough for Franklin to start his march.)

During the fighting the Federal command displayed a noticeable lack of knowledge about the battlefield. McClellan gained what he could by direct observation, riding his lines from flank to flank on the 16th, but for whatever reason few of his generals showed any initiative in the matter. A newspaper correspondent found Sumner and Hooker waiting idly for their orders at headquarters, well to the rear. A third corps commander, Mansfield, had only arrived to take over the XII Corps on September 15 and was too occupied learning his new command to look over the ground where it might fight. To the south,

Major General James E.B. ("Jeb") Stuart, Lee's commander of cavalry. (Life and Campaigns of General J.E.B. Stuart)

Major General Joseph Hooker. His nickname, "Fighting Joe," came from a press wire that read, "Fighting—Joe Hooker." (Harper's Magazine, June 1865)

General Burnside literally sulked in his tent. McClellan sent his staff engineers to inspect the ground there and place troops, and they apparently did so officiously, further offending Burnside. As a result, on September 17 the top officers of the IX Corps would demonstrate ignorance even of the ground on their own side of the creek.

Normally cavalry scouted the terrain and developed the enemy's positions and observed their movement. On the evening of September 16, Confederate Major General "Jeb" Stuart was doing precisely that, locating the new posting of Hooker's I Corps. Lee would be informed and fully prepared to meet the morning's opening assault. The Federal cavalry, however, performed no such role at Antietam. McClellan placed Brigadier General Alfred Pleasonton's 4,300-man cavalry division alongside Porter's corps at the center of his line, intending it to deliver the finishing blow if there was to be one. This was a tactic of an earlier day, and quite out of touch with the reality of the 1860's. During the Napoleonic Wars mass cavalry charges had their place against infantry armed with short-ranged, inaccurate smoothbore muskets. Against Civil War infantry with rifled muskets it was a hopeless, murderous tactic. Yet McClellan proposed just such a charge to Pleasonton on September 17. (Pleasonton ignored the suggestion.)

Of more significance, in this posting the cavalry ceased to act as the eyes of the army.

At the headquarters of McClellan's Army of the Potomac, staff officers pictured the size of the enemy force just as their commanding general did. Lieutenant Colonel David Strother of McClellan's personal staff wrote in his diary that the Confederates faced them with 100,000 men "in round numbers." General Porter's chief of staff, Colonel Alexander S. Webb, wrote home a few days later, "We knew they outnumbered us," and put Lee's strength at from 100,000 to 130,000. A newspaper correspondent, taking his count from headquarters, gave the total of the two armies at 200,000. McClellan later testified to a Congressional committee that at Antietam he was opposed by "pretty close upon 100,000 men." Presumably, he meant this as Lee's effective strength; he had within his reach on September 16 some 94,000 men present for duty, of which perhaps 75,000 could be put on the firing line. That night he announced to his staff what was at stake: "To-morrow we fight the battle that will decide the fate of the republic."

In view of that, and of the odds he supposed he faced, he intended to fight the battle in such a way as to prevent being defeated. His would be a defensive offense. In his "design," as he termed it, he would open the fighting with the troops he had the least confidence in, and follow up with those in whom he had the most trust. The initial attack on Lee's left was to be made by men who had recently come to the Potomac army from the ill-starred Army of Virginia.* They had been soundly beaten at the Second Battle of Bull Run and McClellan was dubious about them. He put Joe Hooker in command, he said, to "make them fight if anyone can." Behind Hooker was the XII Corps, another transplant from the Army of Virginia. Their support would come from Sumner's powerful II Corps, veterans of the Spring 1862 Peninsula Campaign. The Burnside-Cox IX Corps, which had seen its first action with the Army of the Potomac at South Mountain, would carry the battle against Lee's right. The cavalry and the Peninsula veterans of Porter's V Corps and (when they arrived) Franklin's VI Corps formed the general reserve, to exploit victory or salvage defeat.

At sunset there was a brief, sharp clash between Hooker's advance and Lee's outposts north of Sharpsburg. "The fight flashed, and glimmered, and faded, and finally went out in the dark," a newspaperman wrote. Men in the ranks of both armies took this as the forecast of a far greater fight the next day. It was

---

*A short-lived organization put together specifically for a summer campaign in northern Virginia led by Union Major General John Pope. Following Pope's defeat at the Second Battle of Bull Run in August 1862, it was disbanded.

an uneasy night, with a steady drizzle of rain, broken by alarms and bursts of picketline firing. Some men slept the sleep of exhaustion. Many others remembered lying awake with the torment of what they might face at daylight.

Brigadier General Alpheus S. Williams, a XII Corps divisional commander who had brought his men across the Antietam in support of Hooker, expressed a common recollection of those nighttime hours in a letter to his family. It was, he wrote, "so dark, so obscure, so mysterious, so uncertain; with the occasional rapid volleys of pickets and outposts, the low, solemn sound of the command as troops came into position, and withal so sleepy that there was a half-dreamy sensation about it all; but with a certain impression that the morrow was to be great with the future fate of our country. . . ." Another soldier recalled that "time flew with slow wings" that night; "conjuring up the hosts who are to blaze at you . . . is not pleasant."

The Bloodiest Day

At first light on Wednesday, September 17, Joe Hooker rode forward to his picket line on the Joseph Poffenberger farm to examine the ground he would be fighting for. Looking due south along the Hagerstown turnpike, he could see about a mile from where he was standing a small whitewashed brick building in a fringe of woods alongside the pike. Many soldiers that day thought it was a schoolhouse, but it was actually a church of the German Baptist Brethren, a pacifist sect that believed church steeples to be an expression of vanity and whose practice of baptism by total immersion caused them to be known as Dunkers. Just across the turnpike from the church was an open plateau-like area crowded with Confederate guns. Hooker concluded that if he could seize that area he would be in a fair way toward rolling up the enemy flank.

Apparently his instructions from McClellan were no more specific than to assault the Confederate left; how and in what strength was left to him. He understood, he later testified to Congress, that attacks on the enemy right and center would be made "simultaneous with my attack." Joe Hooker would prove that day to be a hard fighter but a cautious planner. He determined to open the attack with only his own three divisions—8,600 fighting men in all—and leave Mansfield's XII Corps well to the rear, to be called up should he need help.

In narrowly focusing on his intent to take the Dunker church and the area around it Hooker did

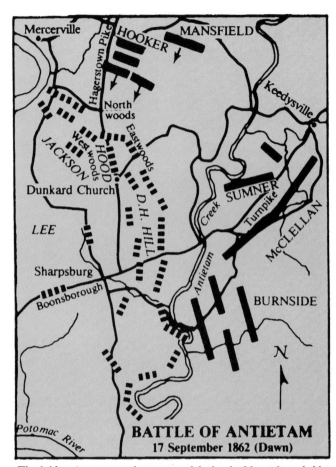

The field at Antietam at the opening of the battle. Union forces led by Major General Joseph Hooker are advancing to engage Major General Thomas "Stonewall" Jackson on the Confederate left. (CWTI Collection)

himself a disservice. He gave no thought to seizing the Nicodemus Hill, the high ground off to his right that dominated both the Federal and Confederate positions. Jeb Stuart's guns on that hill played a major part in the first few hours of fighting, but neither Hooker, nor the other Federal generals on the scene, nor McClellan back at headquarters, took any action against this key site beyond ordering Union artillery to fire back. Had the Federals captured Nicodemus Hill and posted batteries on it, an observer wrote, Jackson's position "could not have been held fifteen minutes."

Brigadier General Abner Doubleday's division made up the right wing of Hooker's assault force and Brigadier General James B. Ricketts' division the left. Doubleday's brigade-wide front ran from the woodlot behind the church—the West Woods, it would be labeled on the military maps—across the turnpike and into farmer David Miller's 30-acre cornfield— soon to win a grim fame as *the* Cornfield. Ricketts' front extended eastward from the Miller farm into a patch of woods that would come to be known as the East Woods. Two brigades of Union Brigadier General George G. Meade's division were held back as a reserve; Meade's third brigade was well advanced on the extreme left, at the edge of the East Woods, where it had skirmished with the enemy the evening before.

Alerted to the main thrust of McClellan's design by the movement of Hooker's corps across Antietam Creek on September 16, Stonewall Jackson had squared off the Confederates' flank so that the Union I Corps would be making what amounted to a frontal attack, three Union divisions against three Confederate divisions. Brigadier General Alexander R. Lawton had one brigade of his division in the pasture south of the Miller cornfield, and a second brigade in line beyond it, facing the East Woods, on the farm of Samuel Mumma. Jackson posted Lawton's remaining two brigades, as well as the two-brigade division of Brigadier General John B. Hood, in reserve in the West Woods. Jackson's third division, under Brigadier General John R. Jones, was positioned a quarter mile north of the Dunker church, partly in the West Woods and partly in a meadow alongside the turnpike. Jackson's 7,700 men numbered some 900 fewer than Hooker could put into action.

The Battle of Antietam opened almost spontaneously at five in the morning as the artillerists in Jackson's and Hooker's commands began banging away at each other the moment it was light enough to see targets. The day dawned overcast and a patchy ground fog lingered in the hollows and woodlots and for a time hampered visibility. Soon the Rebel batteries under Colonel Stephen D. Lee (no relation to the commanding general) posted on the plateau near the Dunker church joined in, and were promptly answered at long range by Federal guns east of Antietam Creek. The "thunderlike cracking of the bursting shells, the whistling, rocking, shrieking of the heavy

Union and Confederate soldiers fight for control of the field at Sharpsburg. This view is from the hill behind McClellan's headquarters, which is visible in the hollow on the left. Sumner's corps is in line of battle in the middle-ground, and Franklin's corps is advancing in column to his support. The smoke in the left background is from a bursting Confederate caisson. The column of smoke in the center background is from the burning house and barn of Samuel Mumma, who gave the ground on which the Dunker Church stood. On the right is the East Wood, in which can be seen smoke from the conflict between Mansfield's XII Corps and Jackson's brigades. (Battles and Leaders of the Civil War)

missiles," one of General Meade's men wrote, soon became "one prolonged roar. . . ."

Musketry added to the din as Meade's brigade in the East Woods, under Brigadier General Truman Seymour, resumed the fight that darkness had interrupted the night before. Seymour's Pennsylvanians pushed ahead through the woods to the Smoketown road, a country lane that angled off the Hagerstown turnpike at the Dunker church, and engaged the Rebel brigade of Colonel James Walker on the Mumma farm. As a counterpoint to the spreading pall of white battle smoke, a tall column of black smoke rose over the Mumma homestead, set afire to prevent the Yankees from using it to shelter sharpshooters.

Meanwhile, Joe Hooker was putting Doubleday's and Ricketts' divisions into line of battle. Three regiments of New Yorkers and one of Pennsylvanians would lead off for Ricketts, under Brigadier General Abram Duryée, while to their right a brigade of westerners—three Wisconsin regiments and one from Indiana—led by Brigadier General John Gibbon headed Doubleday's advance. Duryée got his men moving first, and at 6:00 a.m. marched them into the Cornfield. By then most of Seymour's men had emptied their cartridge boxes and retired back through the East Woods. In the pasture south of the Cornfield, Colonel Marcellus Douglass had his brigade of Georgians lying down behind piles of fence rails and in hollows. He told his men to each take aim at his "own corn row," and when Duryée's battle line came out of the corn the Georgians stood up and delivered a surprise blast of fire that shattered the Yankees' first rank.

In what would become a characteristic scene on this bloody day, the two battle lines stood facing each other in the open, less than 250 yards apart, and fired as fast as they could load their rifles. Finally neither side could take the losses any longer and found what shelter they could and continued the firing. Colonel Walker brought most of his brigade over from the Mumma farm across the Smoketown road to a rock ledge in the pasture to join the fight, catching the Federals in a converging arc of fire, then taking heavy losses in return. Walker ordered the veteran 12th Georgia Regiment to work around the enemy's flank but only a few men responded. He went forward to urge the others on personally and found none but dead and wounded behind the ledge; the regiment began the day with 100 men and already it had lost 60 of them.

Ricketts intended that Duryée's brigade be promptly reinforced by his other two brigades, but for the men of this division September 17 would be a bad day all around. One of the supporting brigades was delayed back at its starting point when its commander was seriously wounded by artillery fire. The second brigade was thrown into confusion when the colonel in command unexpectedly lost his nerve and fled the field. Duryée's troops were left isolated at the front and under growing pressure from superior forces. Finally they gave up the fight and retreated through the corn. In its half hour of battle the brigade lost a third of its 1,100 men.

At least, in piecemeal fashion, Ricketts' remaining brigades pushed through the Cornfield to the killing ground at its southern edge. "Men now commenced to drop on all sides," a Massachusetts soldier recalled; "I remember now, as I stood loading my gun, of looking up the line and seeing a man of Co. D who I was quite intimate with throw up his hands and fall to the ground; one little struggle more and all was still." Another man wrote home, "I do not see how any of us got out alive. The shot and shell fell about us thick and fast, I can tell you. . . ." He was amazed that except for a bullet that nicked his shoe he was untouched. This was a common reaction among Antietam survivors on both sides; the air had seemed so thick with bullets and shells that they considered it miraculous they could have lived through it.

Another of Ricketts' men described the sensation of being hit. Men were falling on every side of him, he recalled, when abruptly he too was on the ground, without pain but "with a strange feeling covering my body." He looked down to find himself covered with blood, "and I supposed it was my last day on earth." What he took to be his last thoughts were of home and friends. As sensation returned he discovered he had been shot through the shoulder. He struggled to his feet and slowly made his way to the East Woods to join the halting parade of walking wounded on their way to the rear. He was one of 224 casualties in the 12th Massachusetts, which in a matter of minutes suffered the highest rate of loss, 67 percent, of any Federal regiment that day.

To meet this new Yankee advance, General Lawton had sent in a brigade of Louisianans under Brigadier General Harry T. Hays, and along with Colonel Douglass and his Georgians they pressed a counterattack right up to the edge of the Cornfield and the East Woods. Then it was the Confederates' turn to be raked by a converging arc of gunfire, and their counterattack floundered. Colonel Douglass was killed and every one of Hays' regimental commanders was shot down. Finally the two brigades fell back to their starting points in the pasture. Although the fire did

Captain James Hope's painting of Confederate Colonel Stephen D. Lee's artillery firing on Union Major General John Sedgwick's division. Hope, an Antietam veteran, painted five scenes of the battle, most of which are on display at Antietam National Battlefield. (CWTI Collection)

not slacken, the contest in the eastern half of the Cornfield and in the East Woods was stalemated.

At the same time, fighting erupted immediately to the west, where Abner Doubleday's division launched the other half of the I Corps' attack. The spearhead of this advance was John Gibbon's brigade of westerners, recently dubbed the Iron Brigade by Hooker for its fight at South Mountain. As they appeared on the field, Doubleday's forces came under a deadly artillery crossfire from Colonel Lee's batteries near the Dunker church and Jeb Stuart's guns on Nicodemus Hill.

Despite the Federals' overall 3 to 1 advantage in artillery, here as elsewhere this day the Army of Northern Virginia's skillfully managed field artillery gained the edge in firepower at the actual point of contact between the two armies. Hooker felt obliged to divert four of his batteries to protect his open right flank and duel with Stuart's gunners, and in these early morning hours his remaining five batteries were overmatched by Stephen Lee's and Stuart's batteries and Jackson's divisional artillery.

In this contest of artillery against infantry, McClellan's heavy Parrott rifles posted on the heights east of the Antietam, firing at or beyond the limit of

their effective range, could not make up the difference. But these big guns took their toll, to be sure. An air burst from one of them stunned David R. Jones so badly that he had to be replaced as head of his division by Brigadier General William E. Starke, and their counterbattery fire would cause Colonel Lee to label Antietam an "artillery hell" for his battalion. Nevertheless, on September 17 the Confederates repeatedly achieved tactical artillery superiority against the Federal infantry.

Taking its losses, the Iron Brigade pushed southward on both sides of the Hagerstown turnpike, half the line passing through farmer Miller's peach orchard and into the Cornfield, the other half into the field of clover running along the other side of the pike. Battery B, 4th U.S. Artillery—John Gibbon's command in the antebellum U.S. Army—moved up in direct support, unlimbering in the Miller barnyard. A Confederate staff officer described the sight from his vantage point in front of the West Woods: "The Federals in apparent double battle line were moving toward us at charge bayonets, common time, . . . a show at once fearful and entrancing."

The Iron Brigade's fame as one of the Army of the Potomac's best combat outfits was just beginning—Antietam was its third battle—and on this morning it tangled with one of the best-known units in Lee's army, the Stonewall Brigade, Jackson's original command now led by Colonel Andrew Grigsby. Grigsby had the Stonewall Brigade and a second brigade of Virginians under his command lying down in the clover, and as the Yankees came within range his men rose up and delivered a sudden volley that riddled the right flank of the advance. Gibbon quickly sent over strong reinforcements and the two battle lines slugged it out until finally the greater weight of the Federal force began to tell. With more than half the men casualties, Grigsby's command fell back behind the cover of rock ledges in the West Woods. Hooker pushed forward a second brigade in support, and the Federals gained an early foothold in the West Woods.

The rest of the Iron Brigade meanwhile advanced through the Cornfield to meet a surprise blast of gunfire from the pasture beyond, similar to the one that decimated Duryée's brigade earlier. "As we appeared at the edge of the corn, a long line of men in butternut and gray rose up from the ground," wrote Major Rufus R. Dawes of the 6th Wisconsin. "Simultaneously, the hostile battle lines opened a tremendous fire upon each other. Men, I can not say fell; they were knocked out of the ranks by dozens. But we jumped over the fence, and pushed on, loading, firing, and shouting as we advanced."

This engagement was taking place at the same time as the fighting along the edge of the Cornfield to the east reached its peak. "We could see them press our men," a Northern war correspondent wrote, "and hear their shrill yells of triumph. Then our columns in blue would move forward, driving them back, with loud, deep-mouthed, sturdy cheers." To a Southern newspaperman, the storm of musketry and cannon fire "sounded upon the ear like the rolling of a thousand distant drums. . . ."

General Starke met the crisis by personally leading a counterattack with his two remaining brigades— 1,150 men from Virginia, Alabama, and Louisiana— charging at the double-quick out of the West Woods and angling toward the turnpike and the Cornfield. The Yankees turned to meet this threat, and in places the battle lines were scarcely thirty yards apart. This was pointblank range; even in the blanketing battle smoke a shot could hardly miss. "Men and officers . . . are fused into a common mass, in the frantic struggle to shoot fast," Major Dawes wrote. "Every body tears cartridges, loads, passes guns, or shoots. Men are falling in their places or running back into the corn. . . . The men are loading and firing with demoniacal fury and shouting and laughing hysterically. . . ."

The counterattack halted the Federal advance, but at fearful cost. General Starke was struck by three bullets and mortally wounded. Andrew Grigsby took over, a colonel in charge of the division and its third commander in an hour. Losses among the Confederate field officers were so high that brigades were then led by captains and regiments by lieutenants. Seeing they could not hold their gains, Grigsby gave the order to fall back, and the shattered division took shelter in the West Woods.

The progress of the I Corps offensive was being communicated to headquarters by flag signal, and a little before 7:00 a.m. General McClellan was heard to remark, "All goes well. Hooker is driving them." He had established his headquarters at the house of a prominent local farmer, Philip Pry, on high ground east of Antietam Creek and behind the center of the Federal line. It was some two miles from where the fighting was taking place at the Cornfield. He and Fitz John Porter viewed the distant scene through telescopes. "General McClellan stood in a soldierly attitude intently watching the battle and smoking with utmost apparent calmness, conversing with surrounding officers and giving his orders in the most quiet undertones," his aide David Strother recalled. ". . . Every thing was as quiet and punctilious as a drawing-room ceremony."

According to McClellan's stated design for the battle, this sign of progress from the front ought to have been the signal to order Burnside to move against the enemy's other flank and for Sumner's II Corps to push forward and capitalize on Hooker's gains. However, except for sending a message to Burnside to be prepared to advance, he did nothing. Sumner had roused his troops at an early hour, issued ammunition—eighty rounds, twice the usual number—and had them ready to march by daylight. When no order came to cross the Antietam to be in position to attack, he went to headquarters to find out about it. McClellan would not see him, and the old general paced back and forth on Mr. Pry's front porch while Hooker's battle raged. It seemed that General McClellan intended to let events shape his command decisions.

Meanwhile, General Lee was anticipating events. Observing that the Federals opposite his right flank at the Rohrbach Bridge were making no threatening movements, he called on Longstreet to dispatch the brigade of Colonel George "Tige" Anderson from its posting in front of Sharpsburg to aid Jackson. The divisions of McLaws and Richard H. Anderson, the men he had ordered to start for Sharpsburg at midnight, were at hand now to serve as his reserve; he let the exhausted men rest for a time before putting them into the line. Soon afterward he ordered another command from the right, the division of Brigadier General John G. Walker, to march to Jackson's support.

In contrast to his opponent, in every instance on this day, Lee would anticipate the need for reinforcements and have them precisely where they were wanted at precisely the right moment. In every instance McClellan failed to reinforce a success or salvage a failure. And there was a similar pattern in how the two commanders were served by their subordinates. There was, for example, the contrasting performances of the two generals called on to march to the sound of the guns on September 17.

Confederate Major General A.P. Hill received Lee's order at Harpers Ferry at 6:30 a.m. He was to march to the scene of the fighting and had his men on the road within an hour, driving them unsparingly toward the battlefield. Darius Couch's division of the Union's VI Corps, which set off early that morning toward Harpers Ferry on McClellan's order, had marched perhaps five miles when a courier caught up with it in Pleasant Valley; General McClellan had changed his mind and Couch was to turn around and join the main army. He was called on to make a march that day no longer than A.P. Hill's, and if anything he had a headstart. The noise of battle reached the ears of both Couch and Hill; presumably their orders were of equal urgency. Yet Couch set a pace so undemanding that everyone could keep up

and no one straggled, and they all arrived five hours after they were needed.

Even before Colonel Starke's counterattack bought time for the embattled Confederate left flank, it was clear to Jackson that he would have to commit his last reserves to prevent a breakthrough by the I Corps. The call went out to Major General John B. Hood's division waiting in the West Woods behind the Dunker church. These were crack troops: Colonel William T. Wofford's Texas Brigade (once Hood's own command), made up of the 1st, 4th, and 5th Texas, 18th Georgia; South Carolina's Hampton Legion; and Colonel Evander Law's brigade, comprised of the 2d and 11th Mississippi, 4th Alabama, and 6th North Carolina. They were men who had displayed great striking power during the Peninsula Campaign and at Second Bull Run. At 7:00 a.m. Hood led his 2,300 soldiers out of the woods in a counterattack. "Tell General Jackson unless I get reinforcements I must be forced back," Hood announced, "but I am going on while I can!"

Hood's troops took the place of the embattled fragments of Lawton's division fighting in the meadow south of the Cornfield and made their attack on a broad front, extending from the Hagerstown turnpike on the left to the East Woods on the right. "A long and steady line of rebel gray, unbroken by the fugitives who fly before us, comes sweeping down through the woods around the church," wrote Major Dawes of the 6th Wisconsin. Hood's men raised the Rebel yell and opened fire. "It is like a scythe running through our lines," Dawes thought. ". . . It is a race for life that each man runs for the cornfield. . . . Back to the corn, and back through the corn, the headlong flight continues."

The 6th Wisconsin regiment's color-bearer went down, the fourth one hit that morning, and Dawes snatched up the flag and swung it around and around over his head, trying to rally his men. He wrote later that he gave up all hope of life, for he knew the enemy invariably focused its fire on the regimental colors. "I felt all that burning throng of thoughts and emotions that always come with the presence of Death." The I Corps was everywhere on the defensive now, and Union war correspondent George Smalley wrote, "In ten minutes the fortune of the day seemed to have changed."

The right wing of Hood's assault overpowered those of Ricketts' men who were still in the East Woods and the eastern half of the Cornfield, sending them flying for the rear. "Fear gave us wings, and strength as well, for we placed a good distance between the rebs and ourselves . . .," wrote a Yankee

The Union signal station on Elk Ridge, from where Confederate troop movements were signalled to McClellan by flag. The tower was added after the battle. (National Archives)

who had lingered in the East Woods to help a wounded comrade. The misfortunes of Ricketts' division were now complete. It had suffered almost 40 per cent casualties and an even higher toll from straggling. Ricketts admitted that of his 3,150 men which began the battle, he doubted just then if there were 300 still with the colors.

Hooker finally called on Mansfield's XII Corps for help, too late to keep up the momentum of his advance but perhaps in time to prevent his defeat. Until Mansfield's men arrived, he would have to depend on his own reserves—George Meade's two brigades—to stem Hood's counter-attack. It was not Joe Hooker's style to command from the rear, and on his big white horse he was a conspicuous figure as he pushed men and guns into the battle. The men of the I Corps, wrote correspondent Smalley, "saw their General every where in front, never away from the fire, and all the troops believed in their commander, and fought with a will." He was conspicuous to the enemy as well. When Evander Law's troops drove straight on through the Cornfield and burst out at its northern boundary, the cry went down the firing line of the 11th Mississippi, "Shoot the man on the white horse!" For the moment, however, Hooker continued to live a charmed life.

Law's men caught one of Meade's brigades in the flank as it was crossing farmer Miller's pasture north of the Cornfield and wrecked two of its regiments. But the remaining two held their ground and fought back. Federal artillery in the pasture fired double rounds of canister* trying to repel the attack, but took such heavy losses in gunners in return that soon the batteries were silenced, leaving the contest a vicious small arms fight between infantrymen.

The fighting was equally bitter to the west, along the Hagerstown turnpike. Part of the Texas Brigade was engaged in a brutal slugging match with the Iron Brigade and a brigade of New Yorkers under Brigadier General Marsena R. Patrick. Regiments charged to the front recklessly, Patrick wrote in his diary, "forgetting everything in the excitement. . . ." With the firing closing to pointblank range, the battle smoke became so thick that nothing of the opposing lines could be seen but their battle flags. A Federal officer shouted, "Shoot down that color!" at which one of his men shouted back, "Damn the color, shoot the men under it!" Four color-bearers were lost in rapid succession by the Hampton Legion in this charge.

*Light metal cans filled with lead slugs packed in saw dust. When fired from a cannon, the can, or canister, disintegrated and the lead slugs flew out in a broad pattern. A cannon firing canister worked like a large shotgun. A cannon firing double canister, or two cans at once, doubled this round's devastating power.

This seemed to be the fate of most color-bearers on both sides this day. The fourth bearer lost by Hampton's Legion was the unit's major, J.H. Dingle, who picked up the flag and cried out, "Legion, follow your colors!" and rushed to the fence bordering the turnpike and was killed instantly.

Union General John Gibbon's six-gun Battery B, in the midst of this fight, lost so many gunners that half the crews serving these weapons were soon made up of infantry volunteers. Gibbon noticed that in the heat of the action the elevating screw of one gun had run down unnoticed and its fire was sailing high above the target. Unable to make himself heard over the roar of gunfire, he hurried to the gun, ran up the screw, and the next round of canister ripped a great gap in the line of attackers.

As Hood's men pressed their assault the Battery B gunners went to double rounds of canister. To prevent a burst cannon barrel the powder charge attached to the second round was supposed to be knocked off, but one volunteer gunner could not be bothered with such niceties and continued ramming home full double charges. With every shot a massive recoil sent the gun bounding backward almost out of control, but each time it was dragged back into position to continue firing. Under this hail of rifle and cannon fire Hood's drive in the western half of the Cornfield was finally blunted.

The 1st Texas, meanwhile, charged ahead unsupported and out of control. Its Confederate commander reported "it became impossible to restrain the men, and they rushed forward, pressing the enemy close until we had advanced a considerable distance ahead of both the right and left wings of the brigade." Meade's men were waiting, rifles resting on the rails of the fence at the northern edge of the Cornfield, and when the Texans came into their sights they simply tore them apart. Eight color-bearers were shot down and the battle flag lost. Two companies were wiped out to the last man. Those few minutes cost the 1st Texas 186 of its 226 men, a loss rate of over 82 per cent.

It was 7:30 a.m. now and the opposing commands of Jackson and Hooker were spent and shattered. Each general had held back a single brigade—Jackson to guard Stuart's guns on Nicodemus Hill, Hooker to guard the batteries dueling Stuart from the Poffenberger farm. And both had thrown every other man they had into the fight. The Federals had a foothold in the West Woods and some of Hood's men occupied a part of the East Woods, but little else had changed from the positions at dawn, except that there were far fewer men to hold them.

The I Corps, fighting without the support of the

rest of the Army of the Potomac, lost 30 per cent of its numbers. More than three-quarters of its 2,600 casualties were in the divisions of Ricketts and Doubleday that had experienced the worst of the combat. The corps was, in the words of General Gibbon, "very much broken up and scattered," and the scene behind the lines was chaotic. "Hundreds were pouring back from the field, many wounded, some frightened, scores unhurt, but hurrying away to a safer region," a wounded Pennsylvanian in Meade's division recalled. Hooker's corps was finished for the day.

The picture was similar in the West Woods behind the Confederates' front. Generals and their staffs were trying desperately to reorganize broken units and find officers to command them. Batteries had fallen back to refill ammunition chests and to reorganize and consolidate after carnage had been visited on gun crews and teams of battery horses.

In the contest against the I Corps, Jackson's casualties came to 3,000 men. Lawton's division, fighting in the pasture south of the Cornfield and on the Mumma farm, lost almost half its men. Lawton himself was wounded, one of his brigade commanders was dead and another wounded, and three-quarters of the regimental commanders were hit. The regiments in the divisions of John R. Jones and Hood that fought in the West Woods and the Cornfield lost 40

and 60 per cent of their numbers, respectively, and their losses in field officers were even higher. One of the brigades in Starke's counterattack saw nine of its officers killed in the Cornfield; the 2d Mississippi lost every one of its regimental officers and nearly every company commander and ended the fighting led by a second lieutenant. Jackson had some of Stuart's cavalry rounding up stragglers, but he directed the cavalry captain not to disturb any of Hood's men found behind the lines; they had done enough fighting, even by Jackson's standards.

Chaos and Clouds of Smoke

The sight of Hood's division swarming to the attack from behind the Dunker church had finally impelled General McClellan to action, and at 7:20 a.m. orders went to General Sumner and the II Corps to cross the Antietam and march to Hooker's support. Not the entire corps, however; one of the three divisions must be held east of the creek for defensive purposes until Major General George W. Morell's division of Porter's corps came up from its camp a mile to the rear to replace it. Morell, yet another Federal officer of dull ability, required ninety minutes to make his one-mile march. By contrast Sumner

A Union charge through the Cornfield. (Battles and Leaders of the Civil War)

moved with all possible speed, but even with his best efforts he was starting from so far to the rear that it would be some time before he could reach the scene of the fighting. And McClellan still issued no orders to Burnside and the IX Corps. Except for sporadic shelling, the rest of the field remained silent.

Both sides were feeding fresh troops into the contest on the Confederate left. Major General D.H. Hill commanded the center of Lee's line, and when he saw Hood launch his counterstroke he advanced one of his own brigades, under Brigadier General Roswell S. Ripley, to the pasture south of the Cornfield in support. Hood's assault was driven home with such speed, however, that it had reached its furthermost gain and was already falling back before Ripley reached the scene. But these new troops were in time to drive back the Yankees who came through the Cornfield on the heels of Hood's retreating men. After personally posting Ripley's brigade, Hill galloped back to bring up two more brigades.

At the same time, Mansfield's XII Corps was approaching the battlefield from the north. When Mansfield went on ahead to learn where to place his men, Hooker explained that he needed help everywhere: to support the hold he had won in the West Woods, and to prevent any further breakthrough north of the Cornfield or in the East Woods. Mansfield rode back to hurry his men forward. "There is work for us to do up there," he told his lieutenants.

The XII Corps was the smallest in McClellan's army and seemingly the most unpromising for the work facing it. Fully half the 7,200 effectives were going into battle for the first time, including five regiments of new troops less than a month from their mustering-in ceremonies. Those troops that had seen action before bore an unhappy legacy of defeat at the hands of Stonewall Jackson in the Shenandoah Valley the previous spring and in the Second Bull Run campaign in August. General Mansfield was as new to combat as many of his men. He had been in the army forty years, as an engineer and on staff and routine assignments, and this was his first important field command.

His lead brigade contained three new regiments of raw troops (and their equally raw officers) with virtually no training. In their inexperience they had to be posted by the general officers. Alpheus Williams, the divisional commander, took one of them in hand and personally led it to the front. "I got mine in line pretty well by having a fence to align it on . . .," he wrote his family. The problem with so many of the new troops that day, he explained, "was that in attempting to move them forward or back or to make any maneuver they fell into inextricable confusion and fell to the rear, where they were easily rallied. The men were of an excellent stamp, ready and willing, but neither officers nor men knew anything. . . ."

General Mansfield was meanwhile personally posi-

Union Major General Joseph K.F. Mansfield posts his men minutes before receiving a fatal wound. One unit argued when he yelled that they were firing on Federal soldiers; a Confederate bullet proved the general's error. From a sketch made on the front by Alfred R. Waud. (Harper's Weekly, October 11, 1863)

J.K.F. Mansfield, a West Point graduate, was 58 years old when he died at Antietam on September 17, 1862. (CWTI Collection)

tioning other regiments in the East Woods. On one of these missions he noticed that the 10th Maine had opened a steady fire at targets among the trees. Having just heard from a I Corps officer that some of Ricketts's troops were thought still to be in the woods, he quickly rode down the line crying out that they were shooting at their own men. There were answering cries of disagreement. These Maine men had been in battle before and they said they knew Rebels when they saw them, and they saw them now.

The general took a closer look and agreed. "Yes, yes, you are right," he admitted. Just then, in grim confirmation, a Rebel bullet struck him in the chest. He was carried to the rear and placed in an ambulance and taken to a field hospital, where his wound was diagnosed as mortal. He died the next day, having commanded the XII Corps just 48 hours. He had had a premonition of his fate. The week before in Washington, D.C. he called on Secretary of the Navy Gideon Welles to bid farewell before taking the field, and as they parted he remarked, "We may never meet again."

Just before he was hit, General Mansfield had led the new 128th Pennsylvania to the front and was in the process of posting it in the East Woods and in farmer Miller's pasture north of the Cornfield. Deploying from column of march into line of battle could be done in various ways and for a well-drilled outfit there was nothing very much to it, but for these novices it was something entirely new. (Immediately after joining up in mid-August they were sent to Washington, where instead of drilling they were put to work on the city's fortifications during the Second Bull Run crisis.) Now, just as they attempted to deploy, a blast of fire killed their colonel and wounded his second-in-command, and the maneuver dissolved into total confusion. It was only with the aid of experienced sergeants and corporals from nearby regiments that they eventually formed a semblance of a battle line. The 128th's ranking officer concluded it was better to attack then continue to take casualties to no purpose where they stood, so they rushed bravely into the Cornfield. Like so many other Yankees that morning, they came out of the corn to encounter a blizzard of musketry. It was too much for them and they turned and fled back through the corn and out of the battle, having lost 118 men and accomplishing nothing whatever.

General Williams took over the XII Corps after Mansfield was hit, and he found Joe Hooker out in the open in the middle of a plowed field and received his instructions amidst what he described as "a very unpleasant shower of bullets" that kicked up spurts of dust all around them. Gibbon and Meade rode up to call for support from the XII Corps. Like Gibbon, Meade had been in the thick of the action during the Confederate counterstrokes, and a bullet hole in his cap testified to at least one close call. A buildup of Rebel strength could be seen to the south, beyond the Cornfield, and Hooker told them, "Gentlemen, you must hold on until Williams's men get up."

These threatening forces were 3,400 of D.H. Hill's men—Ripley's brigade, already on the scene, and two additional brigades, under Brigadier General Alfred H. Colquitt and Colonel D.K. McRae, advancing toward the Cornfield. They were reestablishing the Confederates' northward-facing line extending from the Hagerstown turnpike to the East Woods, where the contingent from Hood's division was still holding on. As the XII Corps took over from the I Corps the battle flared up hotly once more. The sound of it, General Williams wrote, was as if every building on New York's Broadway tumbled down simultaneously, "and amidst this, hundreds of pieces of artillery, right and left, were thundering as a sort of bass to the infernal music."

Colquitt's Georgians and Alabamians advanced into the Cornfield and became locked in a savage firefight with three regiments (the 2d Massachusetts, 3d Wisconsin, and 27th Indiana) from Brigadier General George H. Gordon's brigade that had rushed into the Miller pasture on the double-quick to fill the break in the Federal line. The pasture was on higher ground than the Cornfield, and Gordon's battle line was silhouetted and a clear target for both infantry and artillery, but it never wavered. "The whole line crowned the hill and stood out darkly against the sky, but lighted and shrouded over in flame and smoke," wrote correspondent Smalley. ". . . There was no more gallant, determined, heroic fighting in all this desperate day."

"I commenced loading and shooting with all my might," a private in the 1st North Carolina of Ripley's brigade wrote in his diary, "but my gun got choked the first round, and I picked up a gun of one of my comrades who fell by my side and continued to fire. Here I could see the second line of battle of the enemy and when their men would fall, the rest would close in and fill their places. . . . I fired as near as I could aim. . . . I do not know whether I killed any one or not."

As the fighting intensified, Colonel William L. De Rosset of the 3d North Carolina, another of Ripley's regiments, came on a new man in his command pacing back and forth behind the firing line and looking bewildered. When questioned, he said that in all the battle smoke "I have seen nothing to shoot at" and he hated to waste his ammunition. He was ordered to lie down and look for blue Yankee britches under the smoke, and soon he was firing steadily.

He was one of 100 new soldiers in the 3d North Carolina, and Colonel de Rosset testified that they did well in their first experience of combat. The Confederates used new men (in this case, conscripts raised under the draft law passed the previous spring) as replacements in veteran regiments rather than forming them into all-new regiments as the Federals did. In this way they picked up the rudiments of soldiering much more rapidly under the tutelage of experienced comrades and officers. General McClellan had made strenuous efforts to persuade the government to follow the Confederate example, but without success. Northern governors found far more political advantage and patronage in raising new regiments than in supplying replacements for their states' old regiments.

Although the Confederate system was far superior to Federal practice, it could not entirely do away with the problem of inexperienced men in combat. Colonel McRae's command, the third of Hill's brigade to go into action, also had a good many conscripts intermixed with veterans in its ranks. But in this case the entire brigade, old men as well as new, was entering the battle still badly shaken from its experience at South Mountain three days before. There it was flanked and routed and its commander killed. No sooner had this brigade entered the East Woods than a large body of Yankee troops was seen approaching off to the right. A nervous young captain in the 5th North Carolina cried out that they were about to be flanked again. There were some seventy-five conscripts in the regiment with still-vivid memories of South Mountain, and suddenly they broke and rushed to the rear, carrying the rest of the regiment and the better part of the brigade with them. It was an "unutterable stampede," Colonel McRae recalled. Many did not stop running until they were in the streets of Sharpsburg.

D.H. Hill had posted McRae's brigade in the East Woods as a guard against any Yankee flanking movement, and when it broke and ran it opened the door wide to just that possibility. As it happened, the Federals had a general on the scene who was alert to the opportunity and fully capable of exploiting it. At sixty-one, Brigadier General George Sears Greene, commanding the XII Corps' second division to reach the field, was the second oldest field commander in the Potomac army, but he was also one of its most energetic and hard-driving.

Greene pressed his lead brigade, under Colonel Hector Tyndale, into the East Woods and pivoted it to face west and take the Rebels in the Cornfield in the flank. Positioned on the outside of the pivot was the 28th Pennsylvania, a regiment going into combat for the first time and so large—nearly 800 men—that when McRae's nervous troops had seen it coming its size alone had much to do with putting them to flight. Although these Pennsylvanians were new to battle they were experienced in drill, and they wheeled precisely into line alongside the three Ohio regiments brigaded with them and unleashed a killing volley.

Their targets were Colquitt's men at the northern boundary of the Cornfield, engrossed in their fight with Gordon's Yankees in the Miller pasture. "The sight at the fence, where the enemy was standing, when we gave out first fire, was awful beyond description," the colonel of one of the Ohio regiments recalled; "dead men were literally piled upon and across each other. We had been enabled to pour a volley into an entire line, at a few rods distance. . . ." Tyndale's brigade followed up their fire with a

charge into the corn, and Colquitt's men met them head-on in a swirl of stabbing bayonets and clubbed muskets. But the weight of this flank assault, combined with the fire from Gordon's brigade on their front, was soon too much for the Southerners, and they fell back through the corn in disorder. Colquitt's brigade as a whole lost more than half its numbers. The 6th Georgia, the victim of Tyndale's flank attack, was virtually destroyed. Of its 250 men, 226 were killed, wounded, or captured—a loss ratio of over 90 per cent.

Greene sent Colonel Henry J. Stainrook's brigade in an even wider turning movement so that it emerged at the Smoketown road and the Mumma farm, and its advance forced the last of Hood's men to surrender their foothold in the East Woods. All three of D.H. Hill's brigades were in full retreat now, pressed hard by the Yankees. A two-gun section sent forward by Colonel Lee was too slow to withdraw and was captured by men of the 28th Pennsylvania. A New Yorker in Stainrook's brigade remembered that they charged ahead so recklessly that General Greene had to ride after them, calling out orders to halt until he could get infantry and a battery forward to support them. Greene's advance reached the edge of the plateau in front of the Dunker church, and Colonel Lee had to pull his batteries back beyond the woods. The 125th Pennsylvania, another of the new XII Corps regiments, was ordered to push on across the Hagerstown turnpike and take position in the West Woods, around and to the north of the church.

It was close to 9:00 a.m., and the XII Corps had turned the battle in the Union's favor. If it was called into action too late to reinforce Hooker's force, it was at least in time to rescue them. Like the I Corps, indeed, like every Federal corps that day, the XII Corps made its fight unsupported by the rest of the army. Still, it set the stage for a great victory.

In three hours of combat the Rebels had finally been driven from all of the battlefield east of the Hagerstown turnpike—the Cornfield and the East Woods, and the pasture and the Mumma farmstead to the south of them—at a cost of some 8,000 men, about equally divided between North and South. Joe Hooker would say he had never seen "a more bloody, dismal battle-field." The Cornfield had been at the center of the maelstrom, and among the trampled stalks and around its four sides the dead and severely wounded carpeted the ground.

At the northern edge of the corn could be seen an almost perfectly straight row of Evander Law's Mississippians, caught in one devastating fire during Hood's counterattack. At the southern edge were casualties intermixed from a dozen Yankee regiments, struck down in their repeated attacks. A Massachusetts man from Ricketts' division recalled the charges and countercharges there, "and so it went till the ground was fought over two or three times. The field beyond the cornfield was filled with dead men, both Yank and reb. Dan Warren counted thirty three dead rebs in the length of four fence rails."

Along the Hagerstown turnpike the bodies lay in heaps, so torn and covered with dirt by the incessant artillery fire, a man wrote, that "you were obliged to look twice before recognizing them as human beings." The post-and-rail fences along the pike were grotesquely festooned with the corpses of men killed in the act of climbing them. Men were reminded that day of the tale of the Kilkenny cats, who in the savagery of their battle devoured each other.

Sumner's Wild Advance

It became clear that D.H. Hill could not stem the XII Corps advance, so Hood sent Colonel Stephen Lee to find the commanding general and tell him the left flank would collapse unless reinforced. The colonel intercepted General Robert E. Lee on his way to the left to judge the situation personally. Already he had established a line of batteries on the high ground of Hauser's Ridge behind the West Woods to support the new, abbreviated infantry line, and ordered McLaws' division to march to Jackson's aid. Told of Hood's message, he replied, "don't be excited about it, Colonel; go tell General Hood to hold his ground, reinforcements are now rapidly approaching. . . . Tell him I am now coming to his support." Already the brigade of Tige Anderson that he had earlier called up from the right was entering the West Woods, and as the artillerist turned to leave, Lee pointed out McLaws' men advancing toward them at the double-quick.

With the 125th Pennsylvania at the Dunker church and Greene's division within supporting distance, Joe Hooker could sense victory within his reach. As he telegraphed his brother-in-law that evening, he "counted on either capturing their army or driving them into the Potomac." The men of the XII Corps were flushed with triumph. They cheered wildly as regimental officers rode back and forth in front of them, waving captured Confederate battle flags.

Then chance intervened. Riding his eye-catching white horse, Hooker came right up to the front to personally position batteries for a renewed offensive, and a Confederate sharpshooter in the West Woods put a bullet through his foot. Losing consciousness

from loss of blood, he had to leave the field. His last order was to the XII Corps' spearheads: "Tell them to carry those woods and hold them—and it is our fight!" At 9:00 a.m. General Williams reported to headquarters, "Genl Mansfield is dangerously wounded. Genl Hooker wounded severely in foot. Genl Sumner I hear is advancing. We hold the field at present. Please give us all the aid you can. It is reported that the enemy occupy the woods in our advance in strong force. . . ."

When Sumner at last arrived in the East Woods with his leading II Corps division, under Major General John Sedgwick, the guns were suddenly stilled. As the overcast burned off, the day had brightened, but men would remember the quiet, sunlit scene as strangely menacing. Sumner dressed his lines and prepared to advance. Hooker had been borne unconscious to the rear and could tell him nothing, nor could he learn or see anything of the dispersed I Corps. General Williams rode up to brief him on the XII Corps. It was widely scattered—one brigade reinforcing the I Corps foothold won earlier in the northern part of the West Woods, two brigades supporting batteries in front of the East Woods, the 125th Pennsylvania at the Dunker church with Greene's two brigades nearby. He reported that Greene was await-

Major General Edwin Sumner, the oldest Union corps commander, entered the U.S. Army in 1819. (Library of Congress)

ing ammunition resupply, and he advised Sumner to take precautions in his advance.

Sumner brushed him off. He had demonstrated the same characteristic on the Peninsula: with his mind fixed on something he was impervious to information and advice from his fellow generals. It was one reason McClellan had intended him to go into action under Hooker's control. Now he was under no one's control. Williams later complained in a letter to a friend that hundreds of lives were "foolishly sacrificed" at Antietam by generals like Sumner "who would come up with their commands and pitch in at the first point without consulation with those who knew the ground or without reconnoitering. . . ." A warning message was sent to Sumner from headquarters that "General McClellan desires you to be very careful how you advance, as he fears our right is suffering." When the courier reached the front, General Sumner was nowhere to be found.

Somehow Sumner got the idea that since the only Federal troops he could see were Greene's men several hundred yards to his left in front of the Dunker church, they must mark the army's flank—and the Rebel's flank as well. He need only march straight ahead—due west, through the West Woods—then wheel left and (in the words of the corps historian)

The ground near Dunker Church, where Confederate troops counter-attacked after driving Sedgwick away. (USAMHI)

"sweep down the Confederate line, driving it before him through Sharpsburg, and heaping it up in disorder before Burnside, who, crossing the lower bridge, will complete the victory."

Had he taken ordinary precautions for his flanks (or had McClellan put him on the field an hour or even a half an hour earlier, when the enemy was weak and disorganized), he might have escaped the worst consequences of this misjudgment. Instead, he elected to march in deployed brigades, advancing on a front some 500 yards wide, the three brigades in parallel lines only 30 yards apart. "Not a regiment was in column," wrote Francis Palfrey, who was wounded and captured in this advance, "—there was absolutely no preparation for facing to the right or left in case either of their exposed flanks should be attacked."

When Hood's counterattack was repulsed, Jackson's force holding the Confederate left was reduced to perhaps 1,400 infantry—his single uncommitted brigade, under Brigadier General Jubal A. Early, and several hundred men that Andrew Grigsby had managed to rally. This precariously thin line was not tested, however. By the time Sumner reached the field, Tige Anderson's brigade from the right and three brigades under Lafayette McLaws from the reserve gave Jackson 3,000 fresh men to counter the new offensive. With 5,400 men in Sedgwick's division, and the 125th Pennsylvania at the Dunker church, the Federals had an edge in manpower, but the Rebels more than offset this by having the advantages of position, of artillery, and of surprise.

It was shortly after 9:00 a.m. when Sumner ordered the advance. He would lead it personally, as if he was heading up a charge of the old 1st Dragoons in the Indian wars. In his impatience he did not wait for his second division, commanded by Brigadier General William H. French, to catch up. (His third division, under Major General Israel B. Richardson, was only just then being released by General McClellan to cross the Antietam.) Ironically, Edwin Sumner was one of the few Union generals on September 17 who recognized the importance of time, but in this instance it led him toward ruin. When French arrived in the East Woods Sumner was already gone. Whether French misunderstood his orders, or had none, is not clear; at any rate, he did not follow. General Sumner's array of misfortune was now complete: Sedgwick's division would enter a deadly ambush alone and unsupported.

When Jackson's line contracted, Jeb Stuart had pulled his batteries back from Nicodemus Hill to Hauser's Ridge. When the Yankees began their new advance he lobbed shells over the West Woods into their ranks with deadly effect. The gunners could

A cannonball bursts into the cellar of the Kretzer house in Sharpsburg, where terrified women and children sought safety during the violent fighting. Sketched by F. H. Schell. (Frank Leslie's Illustrated Newspaper, October 25, 1862)

hardly miss, wrote Palfrey; any shell that overshot the first line "was likely to find its billet in the second or third." Taking losses, Sedgwick's men pushed through the Cornfield, crossed the Hagerstown turnpike and the clover field beyond, and entered the West Woods. Riding at the point of the advance with Brigadier General Willis A. Gorman's brigade, Sumner noticed that the 1st Minnesota was marching with cased colors. "In God's name, what are you fighting for?" he roared. "Unfurl those colors!" Gorman's line emerged at a lane on the far edge of the woods and got into a sharp fight with some of Grigsby's men posted among the outbuildings on the Alfred Poffenberger farm. The second and third brigades, under Brigadier Generals N.J.T. Dana and Oliver O. Howard, halted close behind them in the woods. Suddenly there was an outburst of firing some 250 yards off to their left and rear, near the Dunker church.

Colonel Jacob Higgins, commanding the 125th Pennsylvania, had grown more and more uneasy at his exposed position near the church. The ground there was broken and difficult and the trees and rock

outcroppings limited visibility, but he began to suspect that the woods to the south and west were full of Rebels. Abruptly his suspicions were confirmed. A barrage of gunfire opened on his troops and rapidly spread until it was striking them from front and flank. The raw troops did the best they could, but the fire was overwhelming, and presently they broke and ran. Two more minutes, Colonel Higgins reported, and "I would have lost my whole command."

Just then two strayed regiments from Sedgwick's division turned up at the church, in time to catch the next Confederate volleys. They were veteran troops and stood the fire longer, but finally they too had to fall back. A Georgian in Tige Anderson's brigade recalled that "where the line stood the ground was covered in blue, and I believe I could have walked on them without putting my feet on the ground." The fugitives fled the woods and headed across the turnpike toward the East Woods, with South Carolinians of Brigadier General Joseph B. Kershaw's brigade on their heels. A Federal battery loaded canister to meet this charge, but could not get a clear field of fire when the Pennsylvania novices persisted in running in front of the guns. "At last our cannoneers became so impatient to fire that it was impossible to restrain them any longer, and the battery opened," one artillerist wrote. "Some of our men, I have no doubt, were killed but it was better to sacrifice a few of their lives than to allow the rebels to capture our battery. . . ." Kershaw broke off the pursuit.

Jackson now directed the full force of his concentration on the exposed left flank of Sedgwick's division in the West Woods. Jubal Early's Virginians and two of McLaws' brigades, under Brigadier Generals William Barksdale and Paul J. Semmes, spearheaded the attack. In their formations deployed to the front the Federals were helpless against this devastating fire, and almost equally helpless to react to it; the three lines facing west were so close together that it was all but impossible to pivot the regiments to form a new front facing south.

The result was chaos. One Northern colonel said his regiment lost sixty men before they could return a single shot. As soon as he realized what was happening, Sumner spurred his horse toward the rear formations to try to get them out of the closing trap. The troops saw him riding toward them, shouting and waving his hat, but could not hear him in all the noise and assumed he was calling on them for a charge, and with a cheer they fixed bayonets. Finally he was close enough to be heard as he cried out, "Back boys, for God's sake, move back! You are in a bad fix!"

The regiments forming the left of each brigade line took the worst of the hammer blows. The 42d New York of Dana's brigade was wrecked and scattered by three successive volleys that cut down half its men. Next in line to it was the 59th New York, troops seeing battle for the first time that day, and when they tried to wheel to meet the enemy they overlapped the 15th Massachusetts in Gorman's brigade in front of them. In the smoky confusion they panicked and opened fire and shot down scores of the Massachusetts men. Finally Sumner rode into the middle of the tangle and bellowed for the New Yorkers to cease firing; they never forgot how he "cussed them out by the right flank." Caught between the fire of friend and foe, the 15th Massachusetts suffered 318 casualties in those few minutes, the highest count in the regiment in the Potomac army on September 17. The 72d Pennsylvania, the left flank regiment in Howard's brigade, lost 237 men, the third highest toll.

"In less time than it takes to tell it," Francis Palfrey wrote, "the ground was strewn with the bodies of the dead and wounded, while the unwounded were moving off rapidly to the north." One of those left behind with a wound in the neck, thought at first to be fatal, was the future notable justice of the Supreme Court, Captain Oliver Wendell Holmes, Jr. of the 20th Massachusetts. His brigade commander, General Dana, was wounded but able to continue the fight. John Sedgwick, the division commander, was hit three times and carried from the field.

Howard's command, known as the Philadelphia Brigade, had caught the heaviest fire at the beginning of the attack and was the first to collapse. The same fate soon enough overtook Gorman's and Dana's brigades. The right and left of the Rebel battle line curled forward until its fire was striking the Yankees from three directions. To the west Stuart advanced his batteries apace, pouring shell and round shot into the Federal ranks. The only escape was to the north, past the Miller and Nicodemus farms. Regiments or companies would try to make a stand at a fence line or behind a rock outcropping, only to be outflanked or overrun by the tide of fugitives. "Again and again, and at every command of the officers we formed, but the fire was so hot," a man in the 19th Massachusetts wrote his family. Carried along in the retreat were the two brigades from the I and XII Corps that earlier had won a foothold in the West Woods.

Major General John Sedgwick. Wounded three times at Antietam, he had to be carried from the field. But he was back to active duty within three months. (National Archives)

After half a mile or so the fight finally ended at a makeshift line of artillery and I Corps troops, rallied after their early morning's fight, and in the face of this the Confederates broke off the pursuit and retired to the West Woods. Sedgwick's division, together with the 125th Pennsylvania, had suffered 2,355 casualties in Jackson's attack, by far the largest share of them in the opening minutes of the fighting. Jackson's losses came to less then a thousand men. Old Sumner's conspicuous bravery in the heat of the action was much admired by his men—one of them wrote that he and his company would have been taken "if Gen Sumner himself had not road in through a terrific fire of the enemy and brought us off"—yet his blundering tactics had turned the course of the battle once again in the Confederates' favor. "Re-inforcements are badly wanted," Sumner notified McClellan by flag signal. "Our troops are giving away." Among the reinforcements he sought were the troops of French's division of his own II Corps. "If you know where they are, send them immediately," he asked plaintively.

While Sedgwick's division was in the midst of its trials, Sumner had called on Alpheus Williams of the XII Corps to send him any uncommitted troops he could, and Williams ordered two regiments to the West Woods. When they reached the scene, however, they found only a well-placed Rebel battle line that promptly riddled them with a deadly fire. Once again General Lee timed his reinforcements perfectly; this was a brigade from John Walker's division that he had ordered up from the right flank earlier, and it sent Williams' men back to their starting places.

The second of Walker's brigades fared less well when it attempted to drive George Greene's command from its position east of the Dunker church. Greene's troops were resupplied with ammunition now and had already beaten off one attack, by Kershaw's South Carolinians, and they met this second attack with a fire so withering that Walker's men (in the words of an Ohio officer) "fell like grass before the mower." With a cheer the Yankees rushed after their retreating foes and seized a lodgement in the West Woods at the Dunker church. They were in small force—perhaps 700 men in all—and Greene dispatched an urgent call for reinforcements. But for the second time the Federals had won a hold on this critical piece of ground.

One of McClellan's staff, dispatched to the front for an appraisal, sent back a brief, pointed report: "Things look blue." It was shortly after 10:00 a.m., and after more than four hours of the most savage fighting either army had ever experienced McClellan's design for the battle appeared no closer to success (except for Greene's sortie) than when Hooker opened the fighting at sunrise. The I Corps was incapable of further offensive action, and its commander wounded. The XII Corps had made important gains, but it was also much diminished, and its commander mortally wounded. The single division of the II Corps that had joined the attack on the Confederate left was wrecked, and its commander wounded.

Of the 75,000 troops General McClellan could have put on the firing line that morning—had he ordered all his forces to the battlefield as promptly as possible—just 21,200, considerably less than a third, had been committed to what he termed his "main attack." Futhermore, he put these troops into action "in driblets" (in Sumner's phrase), with neither timely support nor reinforcement. The Confederates had faced this series of attacks with two-thirds as many men—Stonewall Jackson's wing of the army, D.H. Hill's brigades, and the reinforcements called up by General Lee—yet they fought the Federal offensive to a standstill.

To this point, McClellan had half the initiative, however imperfectly it was managed. With Sedgwick's repulse, however, he lost control of events. The Battle of Antietam would now follow its own bloody logic to a conclusion beyond his ability to manage. He became totally preoccupied with guarding against defeat instead of seeking victory.

"The Consuming Blast" at Bloody Lane

Despite McClellan's later claim that he sent Ambrose Burnside's orders at an early hour, it was in fact not until 9:10 that morning that he directed him to advance with the IX Corps. The wording of the dispatch made it clear why he had delayed. "General Franklin's command is within one mile and a half of here," it read. "General McClellan desires you to open your attack. . . ." Only when he could be assured that the VI Corps was arriving from Pleasant Valley to replenish the tactical reserve would he commit additional troops to the battle.

When William French and his division reached the East Woods at 9:15 a.m., he found no sign of Sedgwick's division that he had been following. If one of Sumner's staff officers was left behind with instructions he did not find him, and once Sedgwick's troops crossed the ridge on which the Hagerstown turnpike ran and entered the West Woods beyond, they were out of French's line of sight. The noise of battle was plain, however, and rather than waiting for some word from Sumner or sending back to army headquarters for orders—or waiting for Richardson's divi-

The 7th Maine, with fixed bayonets, marches over Confederate dead in the Sunken Road. The Federals faced fire from two sides. Painting by Captain James Hope. (CWTI Collection)

sion to join him—French determined to go to the front without delay. The only Federals then in sight were Greene's men off to his left, in front of the Dunker church, and he decided to position his division on Greene's left. At 9:30 a.m., as Sedgwick was being routed in the West Woods, French set off in a direction that would take him into action three-quarters of a mile to the south. Unbidden by General McClellan and contrary to his plan, the focus of the battle was shifting away from the Confederate left flank.

Both Lee and Longstreet were with D.H. Hill, the Rebel commander in this sector, watching French's advance. The Yankees came on, Hill wrote, "with all the precision of a parade day." Hill's position, dictated by the nature of the ground, was in the form of a large salient at the center of the Confederate line. Six hundred yards south of the Dunker church a farm lane ran eastward from the Hagerstown turnpike for something over a quarter of a mile, turned southeasterly for another quarter-mile, and then angled southward to meet the Boonsboro turnpike halfway between Sharpsburg and Antietam Creek. Over the years heavily loaded farm wagons on their way to a gristmill on the creek had worn the lane down until for much of its length it was several feet below the level of the field on either side. It was in effect a long, naturally formed trench, and would be marked on the military maps as the Sunken Road. Over the next few hours it would earn another name: Bloody Lane.

To defend this position Hill had his two uncommitted brigades, Alabamians under Brigadier General Robert E. Rodes and North Carolinians under Brigadier General George B. Anderson, plus fragments

from Colquitt's and McRae's brigades collected after their earlier rout in the Cornfield and the East Woods, and a small brigade from McLaws' division. (Hill's fifth brigade, under Roswell Ripley, was behind the West Woods and out of the fight.) These 2,600 men were outnumbered better than two to one by French's Federals, but the Sunken Road was an extremely strong position, and Hill's men added to its strength by throwing up a breastwork of fence rails. General Lee sent back orders for his last reserves, Richard Anderson's division, to move up to Hill's support.

French's division was a patchwork affair, only recently assembled for this campaign. Of the ten regiments, four consisted of raw troops with virtually no training, and three others had served previously only on garrison duty and were also seeing combat for the first time. Under the circumstances the fortunes of war were bound to be hard enough on these men, but to make matters worse they were led by another of the Federal generals who (like Sumner) went into battle on September 17 with no clear idea of what they were facing or how best to meet it. French would be as surprised as his men by the reception he met.

The first wave of Federal attackers, the three regiments of former garrison troops under Brigadier General Max Weber, encountered artillery fire during the advance but little musketry. Defenders and attackers could not yet see each other. Running along in front of the Sunken Road and fifty to eighty yards from it was a low ridge, and as the Yankees approached the crest they fixed bayonets and on Weber's order charged forward at a run.

"I would not give the command to fire until I could

see the belt of the cartridge boxes of the enemy, and to aim at these," the 30th North Carolina's colonel recalled. "They obeyed my orders, give a fine volley, which brought down the enemy as grain falls before the reaper." It was like the earlier slaughter at the Cornfield and the Hagerstown turnpike: an aimed shot could hardly miss at this range. Colonel John B. Gordon of the 6th Alabama compared his regiment's first volley to a bolt of lightning. "The effect was appalling," he wrote. "The entire front line, with a few exceptions, went down in the consuming blast." The charge was stopped cold, and in those few moments Weber lost 450 men, a quarter of his brigade. The only return fire was delivered by men who subsequently lay down behind the cover of the ridgeline.

Next to be thrown into the fight were Colonel Dwight Morris' three regiments of new troops—14th Connecticut, 108th New York, 130th Pennsylvania—and their reception was equally bloody. In a letter written the next day, Captain Samuel Fiske of the 14th Connecticut recorded what it was like to go into combat for the first time. It was, he wrote, "a scene of indescribable confusion. Troops didn't know what they were expected to do, and sometimes, in the excitement, fired at their own men." The victims of the Connecticut recruits were some of the troops of Weber's first wave, and the fire put them to rout. "After a few minutes," Fiske wrote, "the troops . . . before us broke, and came running back upon us, crying out, some of them, 'Skedaddle, skedaddle!' Some of our men tried to stop them; and a few, it must be confessed, joined in their flight. But in the main, for green troops, I think we behaved well; the men firing with precision and deliberation, though some shut their eyes, and fired up into the air."

The rest of Morris' new troops crowded up to the ridgeline to try to continue the fight and were shot to pieces. In their new, unfaded blue uniforms and with their faces blacked by powder and battle smoke, they made dark silhouettes against the skyline, and Rodes' and Anderson's men screamed at them, "Go back there, you black devils!" The Confederates suffered their only serious casualties when some of them left their well-sheltered positions in impromptu counterattacks. Soon Morris' men could take no more of it and fell back behind the ridge. French's third brigade took up the fight.

Three of Brigadier General Nathan Kimball's regiments were the only veteran units in the division. Bringing the brigade up to strength was the 132d Pennsylvania, another of the army's new regiments. "The nervous strain was plainly visible upon all of us," a man in the 132d recalled. "All moved doggedly forward in obedience to orders, in absolute silence so far as talking was concerned. The compressed lip and set teeth showed that nerve and resolution had been summoned. . . . A few temporarily fell out, unable to endure the nervous strain, which was simply awful. . . ." The tension was broken unexpectedly as the regiment crossed the farm of William Roulette and a shot from a Rebel fieldpiece bowled over Mr. Roulette's beehives. Swarms of bees sent the rookies scrambling in all directions, and it was some time before they could be herded back into line. General Kimball encouraged his troops with a little speech before sending them into battle. "Boys, we are going in now to lick the rebels," he told them, "and we will stay with them, all day if necessary."

It was soon obvious, however, that veteran troops could make no more headway against the formidable Sunken Road position than the inexperienced troops who preceded them. "We had seen a great deal of service before now," a sergeant in the 8th Ohio observed; "but our fighting had been mostly of the desultory, skirmishing sort. What we see now looks to us like systematic killing." As Kimball's brigade fell back to regroup, like the two brigades before it, the sergeant heard Kimball say, "God save my poor boys!" With this repulse French's division was finished as an offensive weapon. Its losses on September 17 would total 1,760, second only to Sedgwick's division, by far the largest share of them coming in the first half hour of its assault on the Sunken Road.

Continuing the Federal pattern of piecemeal attacks, Israel Richardson's division arrived on the scene after the last of French's men fell back in defeat. Richardson's 4,000 II Corps veterans might well have been used to exploit the foothold George Greene had won at the Dunker church, but Greene's sortie seems to have had little impression on headquarters. McClellan still made no effort to direct operations or shape the action toward his original design, and consequently Richardson moved southward to join French's battered force in front of the Sunken Road.

At the same time, there was a brief flurry of gunfire from the south, in the direction of the Rohrbach Bridge. McClellan's courier had reached Burnside's headquarters shortly before 10:00 a.m. with the order to open the attack on Lee's right, and Jacob Cox immediately set about putting the IX Corps into action.

The plan here was to test the Rebel defenses at the bridge with a straight-ahead charge by Colonel George Crook's brigade of the Kanawha Division, which had recently joined the Potomac army after campaigning in western Virginia. The 11th Connecticut would form a regiment-sized skirmish line along the creek bank to open the way for Crook's storming party. At the same time, the division of Brigadier

General Isaac P. Rodman, reinforced by the second Kanawha brigade, would set off downstream to cross the Antietam two-thirds of a mile below the bridge at a ford McClellan's engineers had picked out the day before, so as to take the bridge defenders in the flank. The remaining two IX Corps divisions would exploit the opening. It seemed a sound enough basic plan, yet nearly everything went wrong with it.

There was no doubting that the bridge would be exceedingly difficult to seize. The Rohrbach Bridge road came down from Sharpsburg through a ravine to reach the creek upstream, ran along the bank before turning sharply to cross the bridge, and then ran southward again close by the water on the Federals' side of the creek for a quarter of a mile before angling off to Pleasant Valley. On both banks were steep hills, those on the Confederate side slanting right down to the water's edge. The bridge itself was a three-arch stone structure 125 feet long and 12 feet wide. Despite the fact that there were 12,500 men in the IX Corps, only a small fraction of that number could try to cross this narrow bottleneck at any one time. McClellan had inspected the site on September 16 and termed its capture a "difficult task." He promised Burnside that once his corps was over the creek he would be supported by troops from the reserve who would cross upstream at the Middle Bridge.

Defending the Rohrbach Bridge were 400 men of the 2d and 20th Georgia under Colonel Henry L. Benning, whose nickname "Old Rock" suggested the stubbornness of any defense he would make. His men were well dug in and commanded every approach to the bridge at a range of no more than 100 yards. Five batteries backed them up on high ground to the rear. The Georgians formed their line on a hillside in an old quarry and behind a stone wall, improving these positions with piles of fence rails and logs, and it was obvious that a great deal of firepower would be needed to dislodge them. It was now four hours since Hooker had opened the battle, and any possible profit to be made from a diversion on this front had long since disappeared. Nothing had prevented Lee from ordering all the troops he dared spare from this sector to reinforce his other flank. That left it to Burnside to get the IX Corps promptly across the Antietam to open yet another front that Lee would be forced to defend.

The high command of the IX Corps was afflicted by a seeming mental paralysis on September 17, beginning at the top with General Burnside. In his sullen determination to obey instructions from headquarters to the letter and nothing more, he made no preparations for his role in the battle. Not a single reconnaissance was carried out in this sector by the corps. Rodman's flanking column had not been advanced to its fording side to be ready to cross the moment the signal was received. In the confusing command situation General Cox took no more initiatives than Burnside. It was McClellan's practice (as it was Lee's) to leave the tactical details of an operation to his generals; in the case of Ambrose Burnside, that proved to be a fundamental mistake.

Only the skirmishers of the 11th Connecticut actually carried out their part in the attack plan, and they

Federal troops cross "Burnside Bridge." Major General Burnside is on horseback, at center. Painting by Captain James Hope. (CWTI Collection)

discovered soon enough that the closer they approached the Rohrbach Bridge the more helplessly vulnerable they became. One company attempted to wade the creek and was picked off almost to the last man, including the company commander. The regiment's colonel was struck by four bullets and mortally wounded. After a third of the Connecticut boys were hit the rest retreated. Meanwhile, Colonel Crook's storming party somehow became lost in the woods. Eventually it appeared 350 yards upstream from the bridge, where it spent the next few hours firing at Rebel skirmishers across the creek.

General Rodman's 3,200-man flanking force experienced equally embarrassing difficulties. It was belatedly discovered that the ford where it was supposed to cross was unusable for artillery and even infantry, with high banks and a 160-foot bluff blocking the approach. When the Federals first arrived in front of Sharpsburg local citizens told them of Snavely's Ford, a good crossing downstream from the bridge, but no one in the IX Corps had made any effort to locate it. This was normally a matter for the cavalry, but with McClellan holding Pleasonton's troopers in his reserve they had not been available, and the headquarters engineers sent in their place muddled the reconnaissance. Now a party was sent out to find any place to cross. Snavely's Ford was finally located, but it was a hard two-mile march from Rodman's starting point, and a quarter of the corps was going to be some time getting to the scene of action.

While Burnside and Cox waited for some evidence of progress from Rodman, they could think of nothing better to do than order the bridge to be stormed a second time. Brigadier General James Nagle's brigade was picked for this attempt. To prevent anyone getting lost, the approach would be along the creek bank on the road leading to the bridge, with the 2d Maryland in the lead. Every artillery piece that would bear was brought into action. As the charge began, the divisional commander, Brigadier General Samuel D. Sturgis, was heard blistering one of his colonels. "God damn you to hell, sir, don't you understand the English language?" he shouted. "I ordered you to advance in line with the 2d Maryland, and what in hell are you doing flanking around in this corn?"

With bayonets fixed, at double-quick time, the Marylanders charged down the road toward the bridge 250 yards away. There was not a shred of cover against the murderous flanking fire from across the creek, and in perhaps a minute and a half they lost 45 per cent of their numbers. In this torrent of musketry and artillery fire there was not a chance they could reach the bridge, and finally they could take no

more and broke for cover. At about 11:00 a.m. an observer's report was forwarded to headquarters: "He says he cannot see that Burnside has done a thing. He sent two Regts to cross the bridge & were driven back like sheep by enemy's artillery."

As the grim results of the fighting against the enemy's left and center reached headquarters, McClellan had grown increasingly impatient with Burnside's seeming inactivity. "What is Burnside about? Why do we not hear from him?" staff officer David Strother heard him say, and messengers were hurried off to speed the XI Corps' movements. Burnside was irritated in his turn. "McClellan appears to think I am not trying my best to carry this bridge," he snapped at one of the couriers; "you are the third or fourth one who has been to me this morning with similar orders."

The sounds of Burnside's feeble efforts died away and the Sunken Road once more became the central focus of action. As Richardson's division joined the fight, the Confederates under Richard H. Anderson came up in support of D.H. Hill. Anderson's division was the last of Lee's reserves on the field; with the exception of A.P. Hill's division on the march from Harpers Ferry, the entire Army of Northern Virginia was now committed. Batteries, too, were shifted to the defense of this sector, and once again the Confederate artillery achieved an edge in firepower at the point where the infantry forces clashed.

The first of Richardson's units to arrive was the celebrated Irish Brigade, going into battle under its emerald banners. Brigadier General Thomas F. Meagher had recruited his three Irish regiments—63d, 69th, and 88th New York—in New York City, and he led them through the hottest fighting on the Peninsula. (During the campaign they were reinforced by the 29th Massachusetts, which reduced the brigade's Irish content to 75 per cent.) Meagher put his men in on the left of what remained of French's division. Heavily fortified with drink, he ordered a bayonet charge.

Resting their rifles on the fence-rail breastworks, Hill's men shot the attack to shreds. Those in the rear of the Rebel line passed loaded guns to the first rank to double the rate of fire. More than half the Irish Brigade was shot down in these few minutes; Meagher himself was spared when the whiskey proved too much for him and he fell off his horse and had to be carried from the field. The gallantry of the charge led General Richardson to exclaim to the 88th New York's colonel, "Bravo, 88th—I shall never forget you!"

Like French's troops before them, the Irish Brigade survivors fell back behind the crest of the ridge and lay down to maintain a fire against the Sunken Road's defenders. With hardly a pause, Richardson put in Brigadier General John C. Caldwell's brigade on Meagher's left. "Fighting Dick" Richardson had earned a reputation for reckless bravery during the Mexican War, and he often told the men of his division that he would never take them into any action where he was not willing to go himself. He came up on foot right behind the firing line, one of his men recalled, waving his sword, his face "as black as a thunder cloud" as he cursed the field officers who had stayed in the rear when they sent their men into the fight.

Fresh troops appeared on the Confederate side as well, as more of Dick Anderson's men came onto the field. It was close to noon by now, and as seen from the high ground east of the Antietam the panorama of battle was a spectacular sight. "On the great field," wrote newspaperman Albert Richardson, "were riderless horses and scattering men, clouds of dirt from solid shot and exploding shells, long dark lines of infantry and white puffs from the batteries—with the sun shining brightly on all this scene of tumult. . . ." Correspondent George Smalley was similarly moved: "Four miles of battle, its glory all visible, its horrors all hidden, the fate of the Republic hanging on the hour—could any one be insensible of its grandeur?"

Dick Anderson's 3,400 fresh troops appeared to insure solid support for D.H. Hill's men holding the Confederate center, but paradoxically they produced exactly the opposite effect. The ground behind Hill's line, the farm of Henry Piper, sloped upward toward the Hagerstown turnpike and was in plain view and well within range of the Federal infantry stymied at the Sunken Road, and when Anderson's reinforcements appeared they drew a heavy fire. The most serious loss was General Anderson himself, down with a bad wound almost the moment he reached the field. His division came under the command of Brigadier General Roger A. Pryor, whose background was more political than military and who found high command beyond his grasp. The reinforcements milled around in Mr. Piper's cornfield and orchard without direction, and those who did try to crowd into the Sunken Road caused only confusion. Abruptly and without warning the entire Confederate center fell apart.

On the Confederate right there was a growing sense of confusion that began when the brigade commander there, George B. Anderson, had his foot shattered by a bullet, a wound that would prove fatal. Casualties mounted among the reinforcements pushing into the crowded lane. Colonel Carnot Posey took his newly arrived brigade right through the defenders in a counterattack that was repulsed with heavy loss. These Mississippians, a man recalled, "flowed over and out of the road and many of them were killed in this overflow. The 16th Mississippi disappeared as if it had gone into the earth." As they fell back into the Sunken Road, Colonel Posey tried to extricate them from the confused mass of troops there and the movement was soon out of control. Word spread down the lane that the entire position was being abandoned.

Suddenly men by the hundreds began to clamber out of the road and run for the rear. "We had either to run or surrender," a man in the 9th Alabama recalled. "We ran *rapidly* back through a large orchard." The Yankees redoubled their fire at this rush of targets. "The minnie balls, shot & shell rained upon us from every direction . . .," a North Carolinian wrote. The tide of fugitives carried many of the reinforcements from Dick Anderson's division back with them.

A similar mix-up in orders caused the Confederate left to collapse at almost the same moment. The one exposed segment of the Sunken Road position was the shallow angle where the line turned from an easterly to a southeasterly direction. Not only was the lane here close to ground level, affording little protection for the defenders, but as Meagher's and Caldwell's men extended the Federal battle line southward the angle came under an increasingly deadly enfilading fire. Hardest hit was the 6th Alabama of Robert Rodes' brigade, and after the 6th's colonel, John B. Gordon, went down with his fifth wound of the day, the lieutenant colonel replacing him went to Rodes to explain the situation and get his orders. Rodes told him to withdraw the regiment's right wing from the exposed angle to a point in the road where it had better cover.

The young officer unaccountably misunderstood this direction, and when he returned to the battle line he ordered the 6th Alabama to about face and forward march. Hearing this clear implication of retreat, the commander of the next regiment in line asked if it was meant for the whole brigade. He was assured it was. All five of Rodes' regiments promptly scrambled out of the Sunken Road and ran for the rear. Just then Rodes was assisting a wounded staff officer from the field, and he returned too late to correct the error. As a consequence of the Army of Northern Virginia's single significant command failure of the day, the entire center of Lee's line was shattered.

The long-suffering men of the II Corps pushed forward with yells of triumph. The 2d and 14th North Carolina tried to make a last stand in the lane, but were hit from two directions and broken. A blue tide of Federals rushed across the Sunken Road

into the Piper cornfield beyond. "In this road there lay so many dead rebels that they formed a line which one might have walked upon as far as I could see," Lieutenant Thomas Livermore of the 5th New Hampshire wrote. Fighting Dick Richardson drove troops forward relentlessly, collaring units of French's division as well as his own to keep the pursuit moving. "I shall never cease to admire that magnificent fighting general who advanced with his front line," Lieutenant Livermore recalled.

The breakthrough was clearly visible from Army of the Potomac headquarters at the Pry house. A Boston newspaperman described the scene: "Ah! what a crash! A white cloud, gleams of lightning, a yell, a hurrah, and then up in the corn-field a great commotion, men firing into each other's faces, the Confederate line breaking, the ground strewn with prostrate forms. The Confederate line in Bloody Lane has been annihilated, the center pierced." Colonel Strother wrote that he was standing with General McClellan during the climax of the Sunken Road fight, "and when it was over he exclaimed: 'By George, this is a magnificent field, and if we win this fight it will cover all our errors and misfortunes forever!'"

Praying for Nightfall

Confederate officers worked desperately to dam the break in the line and to reform broken units to meet Richardson's continuing assault. To gain time

they sent in counterattacks that were little more than forlorn hopes. "Though the Confederates had but fragments here and there," General Longstreet wrote, "the enemy were kept busy and watchful lest they should come upon another surprise move."

During the hottest of the Sunken Road fighting, when George B. Anderson's brigade was being hard pressed, Longstreet had sought to relieve the pressure with an attack on the opposite Federal flank, held by French's division. The only uncommitted troops he could find were two regiments from John Walker's division, the 3d Arkansas and the 27th North Carolina, and a small brigade from McLaw's division. He put Colonel John R. Cooke of the 27th North Carolina in command. It was intended that the left wing in the Sunken Road, Robert Rodes' Alabamans, join the counter-stroke, but by the time the advance was made, Rodes' line had collapsed. That left Cooke to make the assault with fewer than a thousand men.

The little force made a wide swing to the north of the Sunken Road and struck the II Corps flank in Samuel Mumma's cornfield. Although he caught the Yankees by surprise, Cooke had the misfortune to miss entirely all of French's rookie units and hit instead the 8th Ohio and 14th Indiana, two of the only three veteran regiments in the division. They got into a slugging match in the corn, with the battle line barely 200 yards apart. "It was the hottest time I ever saw," a North Carolinian wrote his family, "and I am very thankful that I came out unhurt for I hardly thought I could escape where so many were falling."

son," a man in the 9th Alabama remembered, "walking up and down our lines and speaking words of encouragement. . . . Genl. Hill in a clear loud voice gave the order—*Attention—Charge!*"

The men of the 5th New Hampshire crouched among the heaped corpses in the Sunken Road to take the charge. The attackers came at them through the Piper cornfield shrilling the Rebel yell. This battle cry was sometimes known to unnerve even veteran Yankee troops, but the 5th New Hampshire's Colonel Edward E. Cross had a novel way of countering it. He shouted to his men, "Put on the war paint!" and they smeared their faces with black powder from torn cartridges. "Give 'em the war whoop!" Cross yelled, and high-pitched Indian war whoops rang out in competition with Rebel yells. Lieutenant Livermore was not sure how this affected the enemy, but he thought that at least it "let him know we were unterrified."

The counterattack was pressed so hard, Livermore wrote, that a Southern color-bearer reached to within fifteen yards of their position. In virtual unison a dozen men shouted, "Shoot the man with the flag!" and there was an answering volley of shots "and he went down in a twinkling and the flag was not raised in sight again." The 81st Pennsylvania came up in support and finally the flank attack was repulsed. Soon afterward D.H. Hill picked up a rifle and personally led 200 men in a second charge. "We met,

The Federals pushed in reinforcements and finally Cooke had to fall back to his starting point behind the Hagerstown turnpike. More than half his men were casualties.

Almost unnoticed during this new explosion of musketry was the collapse of the hard-won Union foothold at the Dunker church. For two hours George Greene had clung to this salient deep within the enemy lines; now, shortly after noon, he was driven out in a matter of minutes. When he began his counterattack, Cooke had brushed up against one flank of the Federal position near the church at the same time that, entirely by coincidence, another regiment from Walker's division, the 49th North Carolina, smashed into the opposite flank. In this double envelopment, the 49th drove into two regiments of new troops that had been advanced to support Greene and sent them flying, carrying the rest of Greene's men with them. With that, Federal troops had seen the West Woods for the last time on September 17.

On the Piper farm behind the Sunken Road, D.H. Hill was also seeking to buy time with counterattacks. He and his officers rallied a mixed lot of troops and directed them against the II Corps' southern flank. "At this point Genl. D.H. Hill was with us in per-

The harsh realities of war: Famous Civil War photographer Alexander Gardner's view of the bodies of Confederate artillerymen at the Dunker Church. (CWTI Collection)

however, with a warm reception," Hill wrote, "and the little command was broken and dispersed."

Each of these doomed charges gained time for more Confederate guns to come up to form a second line behind the shattered front. Captain M.B. Miller posted his battery of the Washington Artillery of New Orleans in the middle of Mr. Piper's apple orchard and blasted the advancing Yankees with canister. When the crews began to take casualties in return, Longstreet put his staff to manning the guns while he directed their fire. As the range shortened, Miller went to double charges of canister, and the guns bounded a foot in the air with each discharge.

After casualties and straggling hardly 2,000 infantrymen remained to hold the Confederate center, and they were almost entirely without organization. Longstreet later wrote, "We were already badly whipped and were only holding our ground by sheer force of desperation." But now there were twenty guns supporting them. The Parrot rifles across the Antietam took aim at this artillery line but could not silence it; once again, the range was too great for truly effective counterbattery fire. These big guns scored hits, certainly. As a South Carolina battery swung into position, a shell struck one of its caissons and it disappeared in a stupendous·explosion seen and heard from one end of the battlefield to the other. Yet the battery was quickly in action and fired seventy rounds of canister with murderous effect.

In the face of such fire Richardson's advance lost momentum and finally came to a halt. The men were fought out and short of ammunition, and Richardson pulled them back across the Sunken Road to the shelter of the ridgeline. He did so with no thought that the II Corps was through fighting. As soon as his troops were reorganized and ammunition resupplied—as soon as headquarters sent him reinforcements and rifled field batteries to suppress the enemy guns—he intended to resume the offensive and split the Rebel army in two.

At the same time, on the Confederate right flank, the IX Corps also gained the upper hand. While he continued to wait for some sign of progress from the flanking column—Rodman's command was only now reaching Snavely's Ford—General Cox had organized a third assault on the Rohrbach Bridge. Two more regiments from Samuel Sturgis' division, the 51st New York and the 51st Pennsylvania, were chosen for this attempt. Cox returned to the original idea of sending the storming party straight down the hillside facing the bridge, only this time he provided considerably more fire support from infantry and artillery. As the battle against the Confederate center reached its climax, the two regiments set off toward the bridge at a run.

They were hardly halfway down the slope when Hard Rock Benning's Georgians met them with a savage fire, and the Federal company commanders saw that the column would never make it across the bridge in this one rush. In the meadow at the foot of the hill they turned the men off the right and left, the Pennsylvanians taking cover behind a stone wall along the river bank above the bridge and the New Yorkers finding somewhat less effective cover along a split-rail fence bordering the road downstream. "We were then ordered to halt and commence firing," wrote the 51st New York's Lieutenant George Whitman, the poet's brother, "and the way we showered the lead across that creek was noboddys business."

Under the unceasing barrage the fire of the Georgians began to weaken. They had been holding this spot for three hours and their ammunition was running out. The colonel of the New York regiment, Robert B. Potter, saw Rebels leaving the line a few at a time and running for the rear, and he ordered a charge. As his men sprinted for the bridge approach, the Pennsylvanians on the right joined them, and with the regimental flags side by side they stormed across the span. A thunderous cheer came from their comrades on the hills behind them. It was 1:00 p.m. and the Rohrbach Bridge was finally, and literally, the Burnside Bridge.

It was at 1:00 p.m., too, that Israel Richardson went down with a mortal wound from a Confederate artillery shell, and General McClellan was confronted with a critical decision. From his vantage point at army headquarters he had witnessed the struggle for the Sunken Road from start to finish, and seen the II Corps triumphantly break the Rebel line. Richardson had called for artillery and infantry to support a further advance, and there were ample numbers of both guns and men at hand. A few hundred yards north of the Sunken Road was a line of seven batteries, several equipped with the rifled pieces needed for counterbattery fire. The divisions of Major Generals William F. Smith and Henry W. Slocum, of Franklin's VI Corps, had arrived from Pleasant Valley and were on the field. Fitz John Porter's V Corps had not been engaged in the morning's fighting. Longstreet wrote that "ten thousand fresh troops could have come in and taken Lee's army and everything it had." McClellan had 20,500 fresh troops.

He revealed his decision when he personally instructed Richardson's replacement, Brigadier General Winfield Scott Hancock. Presently Hancock galloped onto the battlefield at the head of his staff and rode the length of the Federal line facing the Sunken Road. "Now, men, stay there until you are ordered away," he cried out; "this place must be held at all hazards!"

General McClellan's state of mind at this decisive moment may be judged from the dispatch he drafted for General-in-Chief Halleck in Washington and sent at 1:25 p.m. "We are in the midst of the most terrible battle of the war, perhaps of history—thus far it looks well but I have great odds against me," he wrote. ". . . I have thrown the mass of the Army on their left flank. Burnside is now attacking their right & I hold my small reserve consisted of Porter (5th Corps) ready to attack the center as soon as the flank movements are developed. It will be either a great defeat or a most glorious victory. I think & hope that God will give us the latter."

Before he sent the message he crossed out the final two sentences and substituted the wish "that God will give us a glorious victory." It was, however, the fear of "a great defeat" at the hands of the Rebel host that haunted him. Following the rout of Sedgwick's division in the West Woods, his every action that day would be directed at saving the Army of the Potomac. He did not resume the offensive against the Confederate center. He would not initiate a new offensive anywhere on the field. No report of success, or the prospect of success, would persuade him to commit a single man for reinforcement. The situation at midday on September 17, Francis Palfrey wrote, was a "remarkable case of a battle won without the victor's knowing it."

From the left came Burnside's report that he had succeeded in crossing the Antietam and was confident he could hold his bridgehead. McClellan reacted angrily. If Lee was not kept occupied defending a front south of Sharpsburg, he had every expectation that his opponent would throw his uncommitted thousands into a counterstroke against the Federals' right flank in the East Woods. To meet that threat he had posted Franklin's two VI Corps divisions as they arrived to guard the right, supporting them with a

After the battle: A barn near Antietam Creek becomes a makeshift Union hospital. (Battles and Leaders of the Civil War)

majority of the army's field guns. He sent Colonel Thomas M. Key of his staff to Burnside with positive orders to continue his advance. (He said nothing of his earlier promise to send him supporting forces across the Middle Bridge from Porter's corps.) If Colonel Key was not satisfied that the instructions would be carried out, he was to deliver an order relieving Burnside of command.

Burnside promised to go forward at the earliest moment, but presently a new set of problems was discovered. General Sturgis, whose division had expended the most effort storming the bridge, had his men across the creek before it was noticed that they had also expended all their ammunition. Bringing up the trains would require some little time, so it was decided to replace Sturgis' division at the front with that of Brigadier General Orlando B. Willcox. That proved to take some little time as well, for it had not occurred to anyone to deploy Willcox earlier, and he was three-quarters of a mile to the rear. When his men finally reached the bridge they lined up patiently to await their turn to cross. Wading Antietam Creek in waist-deep or chest-deep water under fire had been an understandably daunting prospect; now the concern was apparently that Willcox's troops might get wet. Then Rodman's flanking column had to be brought into position after its long detour, and all in all two hours passed before everything was ready. It was 3:00 p.m. when the IV Corps was ordered forward.

In those two hours after McClellan refused to resume the assault on the Confederate center, what one man termed "savage continual thunder" on that front had died down to a scattering of rifle fire and random shelling. North of Sharpsburg, within an area of fields and woodlots perhaps a mile square, some 18,500 men were dead, wounded, or missing, approximately one of every three who fought there that morning. A number of Antietam veterans would recall thinking the battle would only end with mutual extermination. Those who had survived prayed it would soon be over. A Yankee who had fought in the East Woods remembered hoping "we might not be called upon again, and lo the luck of the 10th Me. was with us and we were undisturbed." A North Carolinian manning the thin line holding Lee's center wrote, "the sun seemed almost to go backwards, and it appeared as if night would never come."

Shortly after the last of his two VI Corps divisions reached the field, Franklin and his lieutenants Smith and Slocum worked out a plan to attack the Confederate left in the West Woods. When they took the plan to General Sumner, in command on this part of the field, he vetoed it as too dangerous. In his characteristic fashion he jumped to a conclusion based on intuition rather than fact; if Franklin should be repulsed, he said, there would be no fighting men left to meet an enemy counterstroke. By all accounts, old Sumner had been totally demoralized by Sedgwick's defeat. All the Federal troops on that flank "have suffered severely," he told one of McClellan's aides. "Hooker's troops are scattered badly and demoralized—but sir I have rallied these troops in the woods and behind the fences and got them in line—Sir, tell the General I will *try* and hold my position—tell him sir, I *will* hold it, I *will* hold it sir."

Although Franklin could not budge Sumner from his conviction, he did send a staff officer to headquarters to make his case directly to McClellan. His message was the sole note of optimism McClellan had received from that quarter since early morning, and apparently it energized him. At 2:00 p.m. or soon afterward he rode to the front to discuss the matter firsthand with his generals.

At Sumner's headquarters McClellan listened to that general's views and to Franklin's, but it is not clear if he also sought information on the actual condition of the I and XII Corps directly from Meade (who had taken over for the wounded Hooker) and Williams. In any event, it was Sumner's view that prevailed. "General Sumner expressed the most decided opinion against another attempt during that day," McClellan wrote.

Franklin had 10,500 fresh troops for an offensive, and if McClellan inquired he would have found there were perhaps 10,000 more men from the I and XII Corps fit at least to support them. (Under the leadership of strong-willed officers, a surprising number of even the most battle-weary troops could be pressed into action again. No division on the field had seen more violent fighting that day than John B. Hood's, yet Hood had managed to rally 800 men—two-thirds of those who survived the morning's battle—and had them posted in the West Woods.) It is clear enough that McClellan had little trust in Edwin Sumner's judgment, and he was ready enough to replace another general, Ambrose Burnside, for a lack of aggressiveness. Yet he could not bring himself to overrule the demoralized Sumner, or to put another general, such as Franklin, in his place. The pull of his inbred caution was too great. As Franklin remembered it, McClellan told him, "as the day had gone so well on the other parts of the line it would be unsafe to risk anything on the right."

General Lee was meanwhile looking for some way to seize the initiative that his opponent had surrendered. About noon, while the fight for the Sunken Road was in the balance, he called on Stonewall Jackson to devise a counterstroke to take pressure off D.H. Hill. Like Longstreet, Jackson could find only a few uncommitted troops, but he cobbled together a mixed collection of one infantry regiment, a few batteries and parts of batteries, and seven regiments of cavalry, put them under Jeb Stuart's command, and instructed Stuart to swing around to the north and take the Federals in the flank and rear. As Stuart gathered his forces, Jackson told the troops in the West Woods to be prepared to advance the moment Stuart's guns were heard behind the enemy.

The lull in fighting was broken at 3:00 p.m. when the IX Corps at last moved forward. There were some 8,500 troops in the three attacking divisions, with Sturgis' division in reserve. The defending force under Brigadier General David R. Jones came to about 2,800 men. Jones was guarding not only Sharpsburg and the ground south of it, but also the army's line of possible retreat to Boteler's Ford on the Potomac. Thanks to the fumbling leadership at headquarters and in the IX Corps this attack was beginning four or five hours later than need be, but even so four hours of daylight remained in which to drive the Army of Northern Virginia into final defeat.

The plan worked out by Burnside and Cox was to attack in two parallel thrusts on a broad front three-quarters of a mile across. On the right Willcox's division, backed by a brigade of the Kanawha Division, would advance directly toward Sharpsburg along the axis of the Rohrbach Bridge road. On the left Rodman's division, supported by the other Kanawha brigade, would follow a course taking it south of the town, then swing to the right to cut the Boteler's Ford road and turn the Confederate flank. The ground here was clearly visible from headquarters, Colonel Strother wrote, "and the movements of the dark blue columns, with arms and banners glittering in the sun, following the double line of skirmishers, dashing forward at a trot, loading and firing alternately as they moved, was one of the most brilliant and exciting exhibitions of the day."

The terrain in front of Willcox was hilly and broken, marked by an alternating pattern of meadows and orchards and stubbled fields, and with the Rebel defenders making a stand at every fence line and farm building the advance was slow and difficult. Rather than one great battle it was a series of small, bitter struggles for possession of a stone wall and an apple orchard and a farmer's house and mill. The Confederates had batteries posted on high ground in front of the town, and once again their shells and canister took a heavy toll on the Yankee infantry.

A young private in the 17th Michigan wrote his father that "it was rather strange music to hear the balls scream within an inch of my head. I had a bullet strike me on the top of the head just as I was going to fire and a piece of shell struck my foot—a ball hit my finger and another hit my thumb. I concluded they ment me." He decided that war was not quite what he had expected. "I have . . . seen pictures of battles—they would all be in line, all standing in a nice level field fighting, a number of ladies taking care of the wounded, &c &c but it isent so. . . ."

When Willcox first advanced he had help on the right from two regiments of V Corps regulars who had crossed the Middle Bridge about noon in support of several artillery batteries. This appeared to be the reinforcements that McClellan had promised when he first ordered the IX Corps into action. Cavalryman Pleasonton also crossed the Middle Bridge, and he detected what he termed "the embarrassing condition of the enemy" defending Sharpsburg and sent back a request for more of Porter's corps to exploit the opening.

Instead, the regulars were recalled to their station guarding the guns at the Middle Bridge and told to stay there. Word came from headquarters that General McClellan "has no infantry to spare" for this sector. "Decisive victory which was then within grasp was lost to us by this inaction & apathy . . .," Pleasonton remarked in his official report. (McClellan deleted the comment before he submitted Pleasonton's report to the War Department.) Like every other Federal command that made an attack that day—Hooker's I Corps, Mansfield's XII Corps, the three divisions of the II Corps under Sedgwick, French, and Richardson—the IX Corps would make its fight unsupported by the rest of the army.

As Willcox's troops fought their way toward Sharpsburg, Rodman's two brigades on their left, under Colonels Harrison S. Fairchild and Edward Harland, were confronting an equally daunting fire. The ground here was open and rolling, rising gently but steadily to a low ridge extending southward from the town on which ran the Harpers Ferry road, and at the crest of this ridgeline General Jones had posted a dozen guns with a clear field of fire over the fields in front of them. "The practice of the rebel artillerymen was something wonderful in its accuracy," a New Yorker wrote. "They dropped shot and shell right into our line repeatedly. They kept the air fairly filled with missiles of almost every variety. . . ."

It fell to Fairchild's brigade of New Yorkers to make a charge against this line of guns a half mile away. On the command they jumped up and ran forward through a fire so heavy that unconsciously they ducked their heads as if they were going out in a hailstorm. Shell and canister knocked down men as if in windrows. Eight dead were counted from the explosion of a single shell. There was a hollow in the meadow half way to the ridgeline, and the officers halted the charge in this shelter to align ranks for the final rush. The colonel of the 9th New York went along his line exclaiming, "Bully, Ninth! Bully, Ninth! Boys, I'm proud of you! Every one of you!" So intense was the excitement and strain of the moment that Private David Thompson was reminded of Goethe's description of battle in the Napoleonic Wars, when "the whole landscape for an instant turned slightly red."

They were up and running again, coming on, one of the Confederate gunners recalled, "like Pharaoh's locusts." As the range closed the batteries limbered up and went to the rear, and the infantry brigades of Brigadier General James L. Kemper and Thomas F. Drayton moved up in their places. Kemper's Virginians and Drayton's Georgians and South Carolinians lined up behind a post-and-rail fence and a stone wall to take the charge. They had the advantage of cover, the Yankees the advantage of manpower, about 700 to 590.

The opposing lines were too close for the Confederate artillery to fire without fear of hitting their own men, and the guns fell silent. The ground just in front of the Rebel position sloped upward more steeply and the two sides could not see each other. As the Rebels waited, resting their rifles on the fence rails and the wall, they could hear the shouted commands of the Union officers. As Private Alexander Hunter of the 17th Virginia remembered it, "The first thing we saw appear was the gilt eagle that surmounted the pole, then the top of the flag, next the flutter of the stars and stripes itself, slowly mounting, up it rose, then their hats come in sight, still rising the faces emerged, next a range of curious eyes appeared, then such a hurrah as only the Yankee troops could give, broke the stillness, and they surged against us."

The two lines were fifty yards apart when they opened fire, and at this pointblank range—a rarity on most Civil War fields but a grim commonplace at Antietam—men went down by the score. After several volleys Fairchild's company officers led the way in a final charge. Yankees and Rebels came together in a brief flurry of hand-to-hand combat, and then the outmanned Confederates broke and ran for the rear. The New Yorkers, one of Kemper's men wrote, "began to give regular *methodical* cheers, as if they had gained a game of base ball."

The collapse of this line put the entire Confederate right flank in immediate danger of final collapse. Retreating troops and batteries crowded into Sharpsburg's narrow streets, pursued by Union shellfire that smashed through houses and splintered storefronts. The Federal infantry crowded closer, with their skirmishers dodging among the houses on the outskirts of town. Lee was on the scene, ordering up every artillery piece still serviceable to throw against the attackers and for a time going in among the broken ranks to help his officers rally them. He then rode to a commanding knoll outside of town for a better view of the situation.

Off to the south he could make out a column of troops. He called on a passing artillery officer for his telescope. Both of Lee's hands were bandaged from a fall some days earlier and he could not use the glass, but he told the officer to focus on the distant column. "What troops are those?" he asked.

After a moment came the answer: "They are flying the Virginia and Confederate flags." As if he had expected no other answer, Lee remarked calmly, "It is A.P. Hill from Harpers Ferry." Something over two days after taking his stand at Sharpsburg, his army was finally united. Hill was coming on the battlefield at precisely the right place—and at the last possible moment.

"This Is the Battle of the War"

A.P. Hill left Harpers Ferry that morning with 3,300 men, but straggling on the hard march and the delayed arrival of his trailing brigades cut the number he actually put into action to about 2,000. Yet their impact was multiplied by the elements of position and surprise.

That Hill reached the battlefield undetected was the direct consequence of General McClellan's mishandling of his cavalry. It was one of the most basic rules of war—"the practice of the centuries," as one Union officer phrased it—to post cavalry on an army's flanks to guard against sudden and unexpected attacks, and the officer remarked that "one of the surprising features" of Antietam was McClellan's failure to do so. Even this lapse might have been of less consequence had General Couch marched his VI Corps division from Pleasant Valley to Burnside's front with anything like the energy A.P. Hill displayed. Rather than having to fight Couch's veterans, however, Hill encountered the wide open and poorly manned left flank of the IX Corps.

On this flank were three regiments of Harland's 8th and 16th Connecticut and 4th Rhode Island. The Rhode Islanders and the 8th Connecticut had seen some light action on the North Carolina coast earlier in the year, but the 16th Connecticut was another of the raw Federal regiments utterly unprepared for the grim lessons of combat. To make matters worse, a mix-up in orders put the 8th several hundred yards ahead of the other two regiments in the advance.

Just then the divisional commander, Isaac Rod-

man, sighted Hill's column angling toward them from the south. He galloped forward to warn Fairchild's brigade of the new threat, but a Rebel bullet hit him in the chest and wounded him fatally. He was the ninth Union general struck that day, and the third whose wound was mortal. Colonel Harland had meanwhile ridden back to warn the two trailing regiments, had his horse shot out from under him, and had to make his way toward the endangered flank on foot.

The 8th Connecticut pushed on alone in a bold dash at a Rebel battery near the Harpers Ferry road and succeeded in capturing it, only to be hit front and flank by a vicious counterattack that killed or wounded half the regiment and drove the rest out of the fight. The victorious Southerners reclaimed their battery.

Half a mile to the rear, the 4th Rhode Island and 16th Connecticut were entering a large cornfield on the farm of John Otto. Mr. Otto's field was full of deep hollows and mounded hillocks and was altogether a bad place to make a fight. Just as the Connecticut rookies entered one of these hollows they were hit by surprise volleys from two directions by the lead brigade from Hill's division, South Carolinians under Brigadier General Maxcy Gregg. The order was just given to advance, the 16th's Lieutenant B.G. Blakeslee wrote in his diary, "when a terrible volley was fired into us from behind a stone wall about five rods in front of us. . . . In a moment we were riddled with shot."

The attack threw the rookies into a panic. They tried to return the fire, but had only loaded their rifles for the first time the day before and in the

Bayonet charge of Hawkins' Zouaves, part of the Federal effort that pushed the Confederate right wing back into Sharpsburg. (Frank Leslie's Illustrated Newspaper, *October 11, 1862*)

Hill had three of his brigades in the contest now, and they ran head-on into the brigade of Ohioans from the Kanawha Division assigned to support Rodman. In a renewed struggle for the Otto cornfield the Ohioans, like the Rhode Islanders before them, had trouble distinguishing friend from foe. Some of Hill's men had supplemented their ragged uniforms from the Union quartermaster stores captured at Harpers Ferry, and by the time the Yankees figured out what was happening they were outflanked and had to fall back. Riding forward to spur on his North Carolina troops, Brigadier General L. O'Bryan Branch was shot through the head and killed instantly. He was the ninth Confederate general to fall on September 17 and the third killed or mortally wounded, matching the Federals in those grim statistics.

Lee had supplemented the divisional batteries of A.P. Hill and David Jones with guns scavenged in ones and twos from battle-scarred batteries involved in the earlier fighting north of Sharpsburg, and as Hill's counterstroke picked up momentum it was supported by 43 fieldpieces collected from no fewer than 15 batteries. Against their fire the Federal artillery west of the creek was badly outgunned and forced to withdraw. General Cox was now working desperately

excitement many forgot the complicated procedures. A IX Corps surgeon remarked that day on the surprising number of men, even veterans, who in the heat of combat "load and forget to cap their pieces and get half a dozen rounds into their muskets thinking they have fired them off." The regiment's organization collapsed in a moment. "Many necessary orders were given which were not understood," Lieutenant Blakeslee noted. "Neither the line-officers nor the men had any knowledge of regimental movements." The rookies were picked off by the score as they milled about helplessly in the corn.

From their high ground the South Carolinians poured an equally destructive fire into the 4th Rhode Island. The New Englanders fought back as best they could, but in the eddys of battle smoke and the tall corn it was difficult to identify targets. The Rhode Islanders' colonel thought they were shooting at a national flag and ordered a cease fire until it could be identified. The colors turned out to be those of the 1st South Carolina, a discovery that cost the 4th's color-bearer his life. In the meantime Gregg worked his men around to the Yankees' flank and their line began to unravel. Just then the Connecticut men broke in complete rout, carrying the Rhode Islanders with them. It was nearly 4:30 p.m. now, and the entire left flank of the IX Corps was swept away.

A.P. Hill's successful counterattack left the Federal forces that had reached as far as the outskirts of Sharpsburg in sudden isolation. With no support from the V Corps on the right both their flanks were wide open, and Cox ordered them to pull back. They went back cursing, furious at having to give up such hard-won gains.

Major General Ambrose P. Hill, whose successful attack after a forced march from Harpers Ferry saved Lee from disaster at Antietam on September 17. (National Archives)

to assemble a last-ditch line to hold the Burnside Bridge crossing. Among the reserves he called up was the 35th Massachusetts, yet another raw Federal regiment fresh from home; it lost 214 men, the second highest regimental toll in the IX Corps that day.

From his headquarters at the Pry house General McClellan was witness to this alarming change of fortune on Burnside's front, and at the same time there came an explosion of cannon fire from the extreme right. It seemed to herald the enemy counterattack he had been expecting in that sector since morning. The fire did in fact signal Lee's attempt to capture the initiative, if in no such strength as McClellan feared, and it ended before it was well begun.

General Meade had assembled the I Corps artillery in a solid rank on the Joseph Poffenberger farm facing west to overlook the mile of ground to the Potomac, and when Jeb Stuart attempted to break this line with his own batteries they were pounded into silence in fifteen minutes. It was the one major Union artillery victory of the day. Recognizing that there was no way to get his force, especially the cavalry, through

The battlefield at the close of day. Neither army seemed willing to resume the struggle the next day. (CWTI Collection)

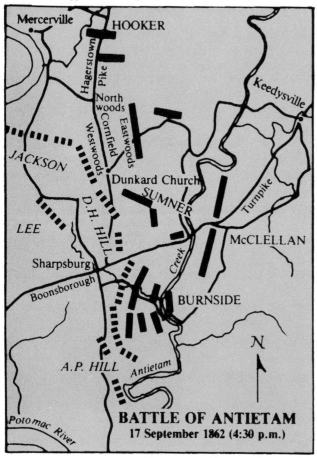

BATTLE OF ANTIETAM
17 September 1862 (4:30 p.m.)

the narrow corridor in the face of such a fire, Stuart cancelled the movement. Nevertheless, its very threat was one more thing to weigh on General McClellan's mind.

Correspondent Smalley was recording events at headquarters as the afternoon waned. "McClellan's glass for the last half-hour has seldom been turned away from the left," he wrote. "He sees clearly enough that Burnside is pressed—needs no messenger to tell him that. His face grows darker with anxious thought." Smalley saw the general scan the V Corps troops held in reserve in front of him and then cast a "half-questioning look" at Fitz John Porter at his side. "They are Porter's troops below, are fresh and only impatient to share in this fight," Smalley wrote. "But Porter slowly shakes his head, and one may believe that the same thought is passing through the minds of both generals. 'They are the only reserves of the army; they cannot be spared.'"

Smalley read the two generals' minds with accuracy. At very near this time, 4:30 p.m., headquarters sent a message to Pleasonton at the Middle Bridge. "Gen. Porter has sent off as much of his infantry as he can spare," it read. ". . . The infantry he has is the *only* infantry the General in Chief has now to rely on in reserve."

McClellan soon made the decision official. He and Porter set out for the left flank and had gone as far as the Boonsboro turnpike when a courier from Burnside met them. He reported that the IX Corps must have more men and guns to hold its position. According to Smalley's account, McClellan glanced at the darkening sky and replied, "Tell General Burnside this is the battle of the war. He must hold his ground till dark at any cost. I will send him Miller's battery. I can do nothing more. I have no infantry." As the courier started to ride off, McClellan called out, "Tell him if he *cannot* hold his ground, then the bridge, to the last man!—always the bridge! If the bridge is lost, all is lost!"

On that note of melodrama for all practical purposes the Battle of Antietam came to an end. The IX Corps would finally hold the Burnside Bridge on its own; the Confederates on this part of the field were simply too few to drive them into the Antietam, although in the day's fighting they inflicted 2,350 casualties on the Federals at a cost to themselves of barely a thousand.

The stalemate continued on the northern part of the field as well. The sun, glowing blood-red in the smoky twilight, went down and the light faded and the battlefield quieted. "Gradually the thunder dies away," wrote newspaperman Charles Coffin. "The flashes are fewer. The musketry ceases and silence comes on, broken only be an occasional volley, and single shots, like the last drops of a shower." The bloodiest single day in all American history was finally over.

Just how bloody the day had been was not immediately realized. So many men were missing from the ranks that night that it was assumed straggling must have been unusually heavy and that most would eventually turn up. A company officer in the Federal I Corps wandered through the bivouac with a huge slab of salt pork on his sword, asking anyone he met what he should do with it; it was the company's meat ration, he said, and he could not find a single man of the company to share it with. Hundreds of lanterns were seen flickering in the fields and woodlots as medical orderlies searched out the injured. Men returned to the places where they had fought in hopes of finding missing comrades. "Half of Lee's army was hunting the other half," Jackson's aide Henry Kyd Douglas recalled. The last stops for the searchers were the field hospitals, nightmarish places where blood-smeared surgeons labored in a stream of wounded that seemed never-ending.

It would be some time before casualty counts could be made. The Confederate records are incomplete and an exact count would never be known. By the best estimate, however, casualties in the Army of Northern Virginia on September 17 came to 1,546 dead, 7,752 wounded, and 1,018 missing, for a total of 10,318. General Lee would say shortly after the battle that he had put no more than 35,000 men into action, a figure probably including primarily infantry and artillery. The most careful investigator of Antietam's numbers, Ezra A. Carman, rated Lee's effective strength of all arms that day at just over 38,000. Very few of that number did not see at least some fighting. According to Douglas, "there were no unfought soldiers, no spectators, no reserves in the Army of Northern Virginia that memorable day."

The count on the Union side came to 2,108 dead, 9,540 wounded, and 753 missing, a total of 12,401. Ninety-six per cent of that toll came in four army corps—I, II, IX, XII. Porter's V Corps suffered hardly 100 casualties, all in skirmishing by the few regulars sent across the Middle Bridge. Franklin's two VI Corps divisions that reached the field lost 439 men, but three-quarters of these were attributable to the drunken adventuring of Colonel William Irwin, a brigade commander who launched two irrational and unauthorized attacks that achieved nothing but additions to the casualty rolls. Couch's division did not appear on the field at all. Of McClellan's 75,000 effectives, fully a third did not fire a shot that day.

The casualties of the two sides, inflicted in those fourteen hours of daylight, totalled 22,719. The Civil War would have many terrible days, but none more terrible than this.

The figures have an even darker dimension to them. It is a certainty that of the 1,771 marked down as missing, a great many were in fact dead, buried in unrecorded graves. Civilians returning to their farms after the fighting buried uncounted numbers of corpses they found in their cellars and outbuildings or under haystacks and in thickets, where the mortally wounded men had crawled to die. A hired man recalled burying 24 soldiers on the Jacob Nicodemus farm, 15 of them in an unmarked mass grave he dug at the corner of one of the fields. Other men listed as wounded would die days or weeks later. For example, in the Army of the Potomac files is a tabulation of Confederate wounded captured at Antietam, with the notation, "160 died in hospital." It is possible that the actual count of the dead was many hundreds greater than the 3,654 listed.

That evening Lee's lieutenants gathered at headquarters to make their reports. They gave little cause for optimism, but Lee heard them out and then issued orders for rounding up stragglers and getting rations cooked and distributed and rearranging some of the front-line position. Nothing was said of retreat. If General McClellan elected to resume the battle the next day, the Army of Northern Virginia would be waiting for him.

From the tone of McClellan's dispatches sent early on September 18, it seemed that the fighting would indeed be resumed. At 8:00 a.m. he telegraphed General Halleck in Washington, "The battle will probably be renewed today." His private view was no different. "The contest will probably be renewed today," he telegraphed his wife at the same hour. There was, however, a vital if unstated qualification to this. The Battle of Antietam would only pick up again if General Lee began it. If the matter was left to General McClellan, there would be no fighting that day.

And so it happened. There was a truce to bury the dead and collect the wounded and the day passed peacefully, and that night the Army of Northern Virginia withdrew unchallenged across the Potomac and into the Shenandoah Valley. Porter's V Corps made an attempt at pursuit across the river the next day and captured four artillery pieces, but then A.P. Hill counterattacked and drove the Federals into the river and back to the Maryland shore. In the engagement still another of the raw Federal regiments, the 118th Pennsylvania, was badly routed and lost 269 men, a third of its numbers. With that the Maryland campaign was over.

Of all the Civil War battles General Lee fought it was said that he took the most pride in the contest at Sharpsburg. At no other time did he face longer odds or greater risks, yet at the end of the day his lines were unbroken and he had inflicted one-fifth more casualties than he suffered. In that narrow sense he could claim a tactical victory, and in defiantly facing down his opponent on September 18 he could perhaps claim a moral victory as well.

Colonel William Allan, who served on Jackson's staff in the battle, wrote in his history of the Army of Northern Virginia that whatever might be said of Lee's decision to stand and fight at Sharpsburg, "the conduct of that battle itself by Lee and his principal subordinates seems absolutely above criticism." Even had he known every detail of the enemy's strength and intentions, Allan concluded, "it is difficult to see how he could have more wisely disposed or more effectually used the means he had at hand."

General McClellan's contemporaries, by contrast, were highly critical of virtually every aspect of his conduct of the battle. Francis Palfrey, an officer in the II Corps and Antietam's first historian, found nothing to praise but his decision to fight voluntarily instead of being forced to it. He cataloged the vagueness of McClellan's planning and the indecisiveness of his leadership, and complained especially that "He made absolutely no use of the magnificent enthusiasm which the army then felt for him." General Peter S. Michie, McClellan's first biographer, wrote, "It does not seem possible to find any other battle ever fought in the conduct of which more errors were committed that are clearly attributable to the commander of the Army of the Potomac. . . ." Ezra A. Carman, colonel of the 13th New Jersey and author of the definitive tactical study of the battle, was in full agreement. At Antietam, Carman wrote, "more errors were committed by the Union commander than in any other battle of the war."

McClellan's refusal to fight on September 18 drew particular censure, yet (as Palfrey put it) "It is hardly worth while to state his reasons. . . . The fault was in the man." General McClellan would take a pride in Antietam equal to Lee's. "Those in whose judgment I rely tell me that I fought the battle splendidly and that it was a masterpiece of art," he wrote his wife, and in that delusion, like his delusion of the enemy's numbers, he took comfort.

Paradoxically, he and Lee viewed the battle in the same light. As McClellan saw it, his great achievement on September 17 was to stave off defeat against great odds and thus preserve his country by preserving its principal army. He had no intention, on September 18, of running that risk a second time. That Antietam was a unique opportunity to gain a truly decisive victory—a victory his army repeatedly very nearly won in spite of him—was something he would not, and perhaps could not, acknowledge.

If Antietam was not as decisive battle as it might have been, it proved to be a decisive event. Lee's gamble for a major victory on Northern soil had failed. That was sufficient cause for President Lincoln to feel his position was at last strong enough to announce his policy of emancipation. Emancipation, in turn, made it impossible for any European nation to intervene in America's war: no power dared recognize the Confederacy now that it was clear the South stood for slavery and the North for freedom.

Antietam thus changed the war's course, linking the abolition of slavery with the preservation of the Union as Northern war aims. That was a turning point of incalculable importance and a fitting enough consequence of what one soldier described as "a great enormous battle, a great tumbling together of all heaven and earth. . . ."

President Lincoln meets with McClellan near Sharpsburg on October 3, 1862. One month later, Lincoln would order McClellan to hand over his command to Burnside. (CWTI Collection)

Emancipation at Home and Abroad

Waiting tensely for word from the battlefield, Lincoln received a telegram from McClellan on September 19: "Maryland is entirely freed from the presence of the enemy, who has been driven across the Potomac. No fears need now be entertained for the safety of Pennsylvania." This was both reassuring and disappointing. "Destroy the rebel army, if possible," Lincoln had wired McClellan a few days earlier. This goal had been in the realm of possibility, but McClellan let it slip away. In his diary, Secretary of the Navy Gideon Welles wrote on September 19: "Nothing from the army, except that, instead of following up the victory, attacking and capturing the Rebels, . . . they are rapidly escaping across the river. . . . Oh dear!"

Lincoln was not happy with the failure to win a more decisive victory at Antietam. But he called the cabinet together on September 22 to put the final touches on the Emancipation Proclamation. He had made a covenant with God, Lincoln told the cabinet, that if the army drove the rebels from Maryland he would issue the Proclamation. "I think the time has come," he continued. "I wish it were a better time. I wish that we were in a better condition. The action of the army against the rebels has not been quite what I should have best liked."

The Pry house, which served as "Little Mac" McClellan's headquarters during the Battle of Antietam. (CWTI Collection)

"President Lincoln, writing the Proclamation of Freedom." Lincoln took advantage of Confederate withdrawal from the North after Antietam to unveil the policy. *(Library of Congress)*

Nevertheless, Antietam was a victory. The Proclamation declared that on January 1, 1863, slaves in all states still in rebellion "shall be then, thenceforward, and forever free." Of course this edict would have no effect unless Union forces conquered the South and won the war. But Lincoln hoped that it would help win the war by attracting more slaves to Union lines and correspondingly weakening the Confederacy. And it proclaimed a new and powerful war aim. After January 1, the Union army would become an army of liberation. The North would fight to create a new Union, not to restore an old one.

Emancipation would also strengthen northern foreign policy, which had already received an important boost when the news of Antietam reached Europe. The battle had "done a good deal to restore our drooping credit here," wrote an American diplomat in London. Prime Minister Viscount Palmerston told the British cabinet in October that American matters had changed considerably from a month earlier, "when the Confederates seemed to be carrying all before them. . . . I am very much come back to our original view that we must continue merely to be lookers-on till the war shall have taken a more decided turn." When news of the Emancipation Proclamation reached England, it further crushed Confederate hopes for recognition. Given the antislavery sentiments of most Britons, the government could not appear to support the side fighting for slavery against the side fighting to end it. "The Emancipation Proclamation," wrote young Henry Adams from London, where he worked for his father, the American minister to Britain, "has done more for us here than all our former victories and all our diplomacy."

But proclamations do not win wars; armies do. Lincoln urged McClellan to seize the initiative, cross the Potomac, and attack Lee's army in Virginia before it could recover from its setback. Lincoln even traveled up to McClellan's headquarters to try to prod the general into action. But McClellan found one excuse after another for delay, until Lincoln finally gave up on him and removed him from command on November 7. Meanwhile, attention shifted to the western theater, where Confederate offensives also came to grief in October, helping to ensure that Lincoln's party would retain control of Congress in the November elections.

—James M. McPherson

THE
WESTERN THEATER
AFTER SHILOH

Confederate Offensives in the West by James M. McPherson
Victory at Corinth by Albert Castel
Perryville by Stanley F. Horn
The Battle of Stones River by James Lee McDonough

Confederate Offensives
in the West

by James M. McPherson

The batteries and encampments along the riverfront at Cairo, with the Illinois Central Railroad Depot.
On parade are the soldiers of Colonel Morgan's regiment. (CWTI Collection)

For two months after the bloodbath at Shiloh, matters went from bad to worse for Confederates in the western theater. On April 8, one day after southern soldiers began their weary retreat from the Shiloh battlefield, 7,000 rebel troops at Island No. 10 on the Mississippi surrendered to a small Union army commanded by John Pope. Island No. 10 was so named because it was the tenth island in the big river south of its confluence with the Ohio river at Cairo, Illinois. Situated near the Kentucky-Tennessee border, where the Mississippi made a large S curve, the island was fortified by Confederate artillery that could blow out of the water any Union boat that tried to pass it. But in the midst of spectacular nighttime thunderstorms in early April, two Union ironclad gunboats ran past the batteries relatively unscathed. Pope crossed his troops below the island and invested its Confederate garrison from the rear. Outnumbered and surrounded by 20,000 Yankee soldiers and seven gunboats, the garrison surrendered on April 8. It

Gunners keep up a constant firing at Island Number Ten, which fell into Union hands on April 8, 1862. (CWTI Collection)

was an almost bloodless victory, and it earned Pope a reputation and a summons to a command in Virginia, where he lost his reputation at Second Manassas.

Meanwhile, the Union navy won its most spectacular victory of the war by capturing New Orleans, the South's largest city and principal port. The Confederacy had stripped southern Louisiana of troops to fight at Shiloh, leaving behind only 3,000 half-trained militia, a few steamboats converted to gunboats, two

The Louisiana State flag—known at the time as the "Lone Star flag" because of its single yellow five-pointed star—is lowered on the City Hall following the Union's occupation of New Orleans. (Battles and Leaders of the Civil War)

uncompleted ironclads, and two forts on the Mississippi seventy-five miles below New Orleans. This was a mistake, for the Yankees were coming in force, commanded by a remarkable non-Yankee, David Glasgow Farragut. Born in Tennessee, Farragut had gone into the navy at the age of nine and had fought in both the War of 1812 and the Mexican War. Sixty years old when the Civil War broke out, he refused to follow southern friends into rebellion. "Mind what I tell you," he said to them; "you fellows will catch the devil before you get through with this business." They would catch much of it from Farragut himself. In February 1862 he took command of a Union fleet of eight steam sloops of war and fourteen gunboats carrying a combined total of more than 200 guns. Accompanying this fleet were nineteen mortar boats to bombard the Confederate forts, and 15,000 soldiers whose infantry firepower turned out to be unnecessary in this campaign. After a week of blitzing the forts with mortars without much effect, Farragut

decided to run most of his fleet upriver past them. In a crashing battle before dawn on April 24, thirteen of the ships got through. They destroyed the puny Confederate fleet, then steamed on and forced the surrender of New Orleans with eleven-inch naval guns trained on its streets. Behind them the forts capitulated to Union soldiers.

Southern Louisiana was now under Union control. Farragut took his ships up the Mississippi, dropping off Union troops to occupy Baton Rouge and Natchez, and continuing to Vicksburg. There he met the Union river fleet that had fought its way south from Island No. 10, destroying eight Confederate river gunboats and capturing Memphis on June 6. Nor did this exhaust the Confederate tale of woe in the western theater. After a cautious campaign lasting a month, a Union army of 110,000 men under General Henry W. Halleck—with Ulysses S. Grant as second in command—had captured the crucial rail junction at Corinth in northern Mississippi on May 30. The defending Confederate force of 70,000 escaped, but during the previous four months more than 50,000 square miles of Confederate territory, including two state capitals (Nashville and Baton Rouge) plus New Orleans and prime agricultural and industrial regions, had fallen to Union conquerors.

But having hit bottom in the West, Confederates began to bounce back there about the same time that Jackson and Lee launched their counteroffensives in the East. The Confederate bastion at Vicksburg, situated on a high bluff overlooking the Mississippi and bristling with heavy guns, proved too tough a nut for the Union navy to crack in 1862. Illness among Union soldiers and sailors unacclimated to a deep-

Union gunboats played an important role in Federal advances in the western theater during 1862. Here: Gunboats in action during the Battle of Memphis on June 6. (CWTI Collection)

South summer took a debilitating toll at Vicksburg. His fleet in danger of being trapped by low water, Farragut dropped downriver in July and northern forces gave up their first attempt to take Vicksburg. Southern units also fortified Port Hudson in Louisiana; for the time being the Confederacy controlled the 200 river miles between Vicksburg and Port Hudson.

When General Halleck was called to Washington in July to become general in chief of all Union armies,

he left Grant in command of 65,000 Union troops in west Tennessee and northern Mississippi, and Don Carlos Buell in command of another 50,000 in central Tennessee and northern Alabama. Grant's job was to administer his region and prepare for a new campaign against Vicksburg. Buell's task was a campaign to capture the important railroad center of Chattanooga.

Both Union commanders faced not only formidable Confederate armies in their front, but equally

Railroads were critical, but extremely vulnerable to attack. Here: Bridge No. 2 over Sullivan's Branch in the Nashville & North Western Railroad in Tennessee. (National Archives)

Generals Nathan Bedford Forrest and John Hunt Morgan, whose cavalry brigades created much trouble for Union forces in the western theater, cutting vital supply lines by destroying bridges and tearing up rails. (Both: CWTI Collection)

dangerous enemies in their rear. The very dimensions of Union success in the West had become a source of weakness. Having conquered so much Confederate territory, northern troops had to occupy, defend, and administer it. These troops had to be supplied by rail because a severe drought reduced rivers below navigable depth in the summer of 1862. Railroads made possible the unprecedented mobility of Civil War armies, but they were extremely vulnerable to attacks by enemy cavalry and guerrillas. A bridge burned or a mile of track torn up could interrupt traffic for days; several bridges destroyed could cut off supplies for weeks. "Railroads are the weakest things in war," wrote General William T. Sherman, Grant's principal subordinate in west Tennessee. Although "our armies pass across and through the land, the war closes in behind and leaves the same enemy behind. A single man with a match can destroy or cut off communications." It was the fate of any "railroad running through a country where every home is a nest of secret, bitter enemies" to suffer "bridges and watertanks burned, trains fired into, track torn up, and engines run off and badly damaged."

Confederates in the West developed cavalry and guerrilla raids into a high art. Generals Nathan Bedford Forrest of Tennessee and John Hunt Morgan of Kentucky commanded hell-for-leather cavalry brigades that roamed with impunity in the Union rear, wrecking bridges and tearing up rails. These horse soldiers could live off the land because most citizens in the areas where they operated supported the Confederacy. Grant and Buell were compelled to disperse their forces in small units to defend the railroads and supply depots. Isolated from each other in unfriendly territory, these units were themselves vulnerable to hit-and-run attacks by rebel guerrillas or by Forrest's and Morgan's troopers. By the end of August, Buell's advance on Chattanooga had ground to a halt and Grant had been virtually immobilized in west Tennessee by such raids. This taught Union commanders, especially Grant and Sherman, two important lessons that they would put into practice in future campaigns: the only way to counter enemy cavalry was to develop a comparable cavalry force of your own; and the best way to operate deep in enemy territory was to cut loose from your supplies and live off the enemy's land.

But this did not happen until 1863. In the late summer of 1862, Forrest's and Morgan's raids enabled the armies confronting Grant and Buell to seize the initiative. General Braxton Bragg had taken command of the principal Confederate force in the West, the Army of Tennessee. Leaving behind 32,000 men in Mississippi under Generals Sterling Price and Earl Van Dorn, Bragg shifted the remaining 35,000 to Chattanooga, from where he planned to drive through Tennessee and into Kentucky to regain control of both states for the Confederacy. Bragg would be supported by a 20,000-man army under Edmund Kirby Smith that would strike northward from Knoxville. Bragg also ordered Van Dorn to attack Grant in northern Mississippi and drive up through west Tennessee. If all went well, wrote an enthusiastic Bragg, "I trust we may all unite in Ohio." As matters turned out, these operations by several Confederate armies in the West coincided with Lee's invasion of Maryland. These movements represented the Confederacy's largest combined offensive of the entire war. But it was a bid for victory that came to an abrupt halt at Corinth, Mississippi, and Perryville, Kentucky, not long after Lee had been forced to retreat back into Virginia.

Victory at Corinth
by Albert Castel

Spring 1862 was a time of disaster for the Confederates in the West. Their armies were driven from Kentucky, shoved out of middle and west Tennessee, and dislodged from the Mississippi River all the way down to Vicksburg. Albert Sidney Johnston's desperate attempt to turn the tide failed bloodily at Shiloh and the Yankee legions pushed on into northern Mississippi. But then they stopped to digest their conquests, dispersing into a number of smaller armies spread between Memphis and the approaches to Chattanooga. This gave the battered Southern forces time in which to recover and rebuild. Now, in mid-summer, under the over-all command of General Braxton Bragg, they sought once more to regain what they had lost.

Using railroads and steamboats, Bragg began transferring the bulk of his army to Chattanooga, from where he planned to launch an offensive through Tennessee into Kentucky. Behind, at Tupelo, Mississippi, he left 15,000 troops under Major General Sterling Price. He instructed Price to prevent Major General U.S. Grant, who commanded Union forces between Memphis and Corinth, Mississippi, from aiding Major General Don Carlos Buell's Federal army at Nashville. Also he authorized Major General Earl Van Dorn, commanding at Vicksburg, to join Price should it prove necessary or desirable.

The last of Bragg's army left for Chattanooga on July 29. Price at once began preparing to move against Corinth, where a large Union force under Major General William S. Rosecrans was stationed. Rosecrans constituted Grant's left wing and thus would be the most likely to reinforce Buell. However, since Grant overall had an estimated 40,000 to 50,000 men available and could rapidly shift reinforcements to Corinth by rail, Price believed that he could not successfully attack Rosecrans unless supported by Van Dorn. Hence during August he repeatedly urged Van Dorn to join him. In addition Bragg, who mistakenly believed that Grant already was sending large numbers of troops to Buell and hence was vulnerable, telegraphed Van Dorn to unite his army with Price's and invade west Tennessee.

But Van Dorn, preoccupied with what proved to be a futile effort to capture Baton Rouge, balked. Not until August 24 did he agree to join Price for an "aggressive

The 63d Ohio meets the attack of the 2d Tex[as], the Union fortifications in the background i[n ...]

e bloody Battle of Corinth. The artist has improved upon
rz & Allison lithograph.

General Braxton Bragg.

Major General Earl Van Dorn.

campaign'' into west Tennessee. Meanwhile Price, spurred by insistent demands by Bragg to attack the Federals, advanced to Iuka, Mississippi, hoping to surprise Rosecrans, who had moved southeast from Corinth to that town. Instead, on September 18-19 Price himself was nearly destroyed in a trap set by Grant, who personally led a column to Iuka on learning of the Confederate advance. Only hard fighting, Union blunders, and sheer luck enabled Price to escape with his army intact. He then fell back to Ripley, Mississippi, where on September 28 he and Van Dorn finally linked up.

Van Dorn as senior in rank assumed command of the joint forces. These consisted of Price's two divisions under Brigadier Generals Dabney H. Maury and Louis Hébert, and Major General Mansfield Lovell's division, which Van Dorn had brought from Vicksburg. Supporting them were the cavalry brigades of Brigadier General Frank C. Armstrong and Colonel William H. Jackson, and a sizable artillery train. In all the Confederates numbered about 22,000 men, most of them veterans from Missouri, Arkansas, Texas, Mississippi, and Alabama.

Now that he was in the field, Van Dorn was eager for battle. A handsome, dashing, Mississippi-born West Pointer, he was an avowed glory-seeker who kept a bust of Napoleon on his desk. In addition he was anxious,

one might say desperate, to restore his military reputation, which had been badly damaged in March when he had been defeated at the Battle of Pea Ridge in Arkansas and further tarnished by the recent Baton Rouge fiasco. Hence he proposed attacking Corinth at once. Price, who had served under Van Dorn in Arkansas and considered him rash and arrogant, concurred in this objective but advised waiting until their army could be bolstered by the 12,000 to 15,000 exchanged prisoners (Confederates captured at Fort Donelson in February) who presently were being rearmed and reorganized at Jackson, Mississippi.

This would take too long, Van Dorn countered. They must strike immediately if Corinth were to be taken at all. Admittedly the risks were great: The town was strongly fortified, Rosecrans was known to have over 20,000 men, and Grant could send him help quickly, as demonstrated at Iuka. But the fruits of success would also be great: The Confederates would gain control of the two strategic railroads (Mobile & Ohio, Memphis & Charleston) which bisected Corinth and open the way for a thrust through west Tennessee and on to the Ohio River, which Van Dorn planned to make as soon as he could bring up the exchanged prisoners. Price, although he still had misgivings, admitted that the importance of Corinth ''warranted more than the usual hazards of battle.''

On September 29 the Confederates set out from Ripley. They headed due north, a move which, as Van Dorn designed it to do, rendered Grant uncertain as to their intentions. A three-day march brought them to Pocahontas, Tennessee. From there they swerved east across the Hatchie River at Davis' Bridge and on to Chewalla, Tennessee. Here, ten miles northeast of Corinth and astride the Memphis & Charleston Railroad, they bivouacked on the night of October 2.

Van Dorn hoped that this indirect approach to Corinth would confuse Rosecrans and prevent him from concentrating his full strength inside the town's fortifications. In fact Rosecrans, whose cavalry kept him posted on the Confederate movements, did conclude that his old West Point classmate "Buck" Van Dorn was merely feinting an attack on Corinth and that his real purpose was to cut the Mobile & Ohio Railroad north of the town. Nevertheless he called in all of his outlying units, thereby assembling a total of 23,000 troops, a majority of whom were battle-experienced midwesterners. Also he sent Colonel John M. Oliver's brigade towards Chewalla to feel out the Confederates.

At dawn on October 3 Van Dorn's army resumed its march on Corinth. As it did so, three distinct earthquake tremors shook the ground and made the trees sway. Was this an omen, and if so, what kind—good or bad? Soon the Confederate advance guard encountered Oliver's brigade. The Federals fell back, skirmishing but offering no serious resistance. About three miles from Corinth, Van Dorn ordered Lovell to form for battle on the right side of the Chewalla Road and Price, commanding Maury and Hébert, to do the same on the left. All three divisions then moved towards Corinth's outer defenses, a chain of fortifications constructed by the Confederates in April when they occupied the town following their defeat at Shiloh. These works, which were protected by a belt of fallen timber 400 yards wide, were manned by approximately one-half of Rosecrans' troops. He had stationed them there on discovering that Van Dorn indeed intended to attack Corinth. The remainder of his army he kept in reserve behind a line of forts immediately surrounding the town in order to guard against a possible assault from some other direction.

When the Confederates reached the fallen timber in front of the outer defenses they paused briefly, then rushed forward, jumping over and dodging around the obstructions. Then, on reaching the fortifications, they climbed up the steep dirt embankment in small groups. Field officers even tried to ride their horses up the parapet, but most of them slid back ingloriously and had to dismount and continue on foot. The Federals, astonished by this wild onrush and too few to cover adequately such a long front, retreated in considerable disorder and with sizable losses.

Major General Don Carlos Buell.

Shouting triumphantly, the Confederates pursued the Federals for half a mile before halting to regroup and rest. It was now midafternoon, the temperature was in the nineties, canteens were empty, and many of them had fallen from sunstroke and sheer fatigue. After about an hour they again advanced. However this time the Federals held a much shorter front and put up a far stronger resistance. As a result the Confederates had to

Major General Mansfield Lovell.

the afternoon Rosecrans had attempted to deliver what he was sure would be a crushing attack on the Confederate left flank with Brigadier General Charles S. Hamilton's division, but because of a combination of obscurely worded orders on his part and of (perhaps deliberate) obtuseness on Hamilton's part he had been unable to do so. It had been most frustrating.

Van Dorn also felt frustrated. But he remained confident of ultimate and complete victory. Misled by the size of the Federal force which had opposed him during the day, he believed that Rosecrans had no more than 15,000 troops on hand. Hence, during the night he issued orders for renewing the battle in the morning. Three artillery batteries posted on a ridge west of Corinth were to open fire on the town at 4 a.m. Then, at daybreak, Hébert would attack the Union right and try to outflank it. As soon as he was "heavily engaged" Lovell was "to move rapidly to the assault" against the enemy left, which he was to roll up by forcing his way "inward across the low grounds southwest of town." At the same time Maury would strike Rosecrans' center. Thus the Federals would be assaulted simultaneously all along their line and their flanks turned. Once driven from their works, Armstrong's and Jackson's calvary, posted to the south and east of Corinth, were to intercept them. If all went well, Rosecrans would be destroyed.

Shortly after four the Confederate batteries opened up. However they did little damage and far more power-

fight hard for every yard they gained, and although they inflicted heavy casualties, their own losses were not light. Not until twilight did the defenders withdraw behind Corinth's inner line of fortifications.

Scores of Price's troops, who had borne the brunt of the fighting, sank down exhausted from heat and thirst. Van Dorn asked Price's opinion about continuing the attack. Price answered that his men could take Corinth provided Lovell's division, which had lagged behind, supported them. However, since this was doubtful, he believed that it would be best to postpone the final assault until morning. Van Dorn concurred and ordered the battle suspended. His soldiers fell back to a line of timber about a half-mile from Corinth.

Afterward some Confederates argued that by failing to press ahead with the attack when, so they believed, the Yankees were defeated, Van Dorn threw away a golden opportunity—indeed his only real chance—of capturing Corinth. And Van Dorn himself later asserted that if he had had only one more hour of daylight he would have carried all before him. But, as already noted, Rosecrans had half his army in reserve and almost certainly could have repulsed the weary Confederates. Moreover, if Van Dorn desired an extra hour of daylight, so did his Union counterpart. All through

Two views of wartime Corinth. Above: A carte-de-visite showing the Tishomingo Hotel. Below: Another carte-de-visite, with cotton bales in the foreground and Corinth House in the background.

ful Union artillery soon silenced them. Worse, Hébert's division failed to advance at the appointed time. Perturbed, Van Dorn sent in succession three staff officers to inquire why—but none of them could locate Hébert! Finally, at 7 o'clock, Hébert appeared at Van Dorn's headquarters and announced that he was sick. Price, who was present, immediately ordered Brigadier General Martin Green to take command of Hébert's division. But Green, one of his officers later testified, was "hopelessly bewildered, as well as ignorant of what ought to be done." Consequently another hour passed before the division was ready to attack.

Meanwhile Maury's division became engaged with enemy sharpshooters. This skirmishing quickly developed into a full-fledged fire fight which the Union cannons joined, pounding the Confederate positions. Without waiting for Hébert's division to attack first, Maury's troops began moving forward. As they did so, Green finally advanced. By 9:30 Price's entire corps was in action. Only Lovell remained out of contact with the enemy. His division, after slowly advancing a short distance, halted well beyond musket range of the Union works. Brigadier General John S. Bowen, whose brigade had been designated to spearhead the assault, sent three separate couriers to Lovell urgently requesting his presence at the front. But Lovell did not come forward nor did he issue an attack order.

Thus Price's troops were left to fight the battle alone. Marching shoulder to shoulder in dense columns,

The defense of Battery Robinett by the 43d, 63d, and 39th Ohio. From a wartime sketch.

they advanced steadily toward Corinth. To a spectator in the town it seemed as if a "prodigious mass, with gleaming bayonets, suddenly loomed out, dark and threatening" beneath the harsh Mississippi sun. When about 300 yards from the Federal line they halted briefly to dress ranks, then with a wild cheer swept forward on the run. A terrific fire from rifles and artillery hit them but they charged on, "their faces averted like men striving to protect themselves against a driving storm of hail."

"We advanced," wrote a Missouri Confederate to his father a week later, "through open hilly ground on which there was not a single bush to screen a person from the terrible storm of shot and shell from their heavy siege guns, which were in full view for over a mile, and looked like if hell had been let loose. Shells bursting all around you; round shot plowing the ground everywhere; grape and cannister [sic] sweeping down the hill almost by the bushel; it is a miracle how anyone escaped."

At practically the same instant the right wing of Hébert's division and the left portion of Maury's struck the Union center, which was held by Brigadier General Thomas A. Davies' division. Davies' men, who had suffered heavily in the previous day's fighting, broke and fled. Exultant Southern infantry promptly poured through the gap and penetrated into the very streets of Corinth, reaching the railroad junction, seizing Rosecrans' reserve artillery, and almost capturing Rosecrans himself.

Victory, gallantly won, seemed to be in Confederate hands. But now the lack of coordination in the attack produced its fatal effect. The Union divisions on either side of Davies (Hamilton's and Brigadier General David S. Stanley's) turned about and raked the Rebels with crossfire. Also they detached units to bolster Davies, who rallied his division and brought up reserves. Beset on front and flank, the storming column reeled backward. Then, as a member of Van Dorn's staff later reported, it melted "like snow in thaw" under the deluge of Federal fire. The remnants either ran back across the fields over which they had advanced, suffering heavy losses as they did so, or else by the hundreds threw up their hands in surrender.

drove toward Battery Robinett, a log and dirt redoubt containing four cannon and situated atop a small hill west of Corinth and north of the Memphis & Charleston tracks. Rifle bullets and canister shredded their ranks but they stepped over the fallen and kept going. About 100 yards from the redoubt they encountered a row of logs and sharpened stakes. At this point they broke into a run and the straight lines gave way to a seething mass of yelling men. Urging them on, Rogers grabbed the regimental flag from the third man to die bearing it. His horse was shot from under him but he scrambled to his feet, still carrying the flag, and climbed up the parapet, followed by scores of his soldiers. The defenders fled, abandoning their cannon, and Rogers lifted the flag in triumph—only to tumble backward from a pistol bullet fired by a drummer boy.

As he did so, three Ohio regiments and a Missouri Union regiment which had been stationed behind Battery Robinett for just this purpose, counterattacked. Soon Moore's troops were pinned down by a withering fire. Frantically waving handkerchiefs on sticks or bayonets, they cried, "For God's sake, stop!" Those who did not surrender or manage somehow to escape were shot or bayoneted. The Federals found Rogers, his clothes rumpled and dust-covered, lying beneath the rampart. Pinned inside his coat was a note telling whom to notify in case he was killed.

Price's two divisions had fought magnificently and both had been cut to pieces. Out of the approximately

Battles and Leaders of the Civil War

Colonel William P. Rogers was killed leading his Texans in the forlorn-hope assault on Battery Robinett. From a photograph.

Only the 1st Missouri Brigade, fighting desperately, managed to hold the redoubt it had captured. But then it had to retreat when its ammunition gave out. Ordered by Maury to retake it, Brigadier General William L. Cabell wept as he led his Arkansas troops forward. Screaming fiercely, they reached the parapet, then broke, leaving behind one-third of their number dead, wounded, or captive.

But the Confederates were not finished—at least not yet. West of the Mobile & Ohio tracks Brigadier General John C. Moore's brigade of Maury's division rallied for a second assault. Leading it, astride his horse, was Colonel William P. Rogers of the 2d Texas Sharpshooters. Marching in perfect formation, his men

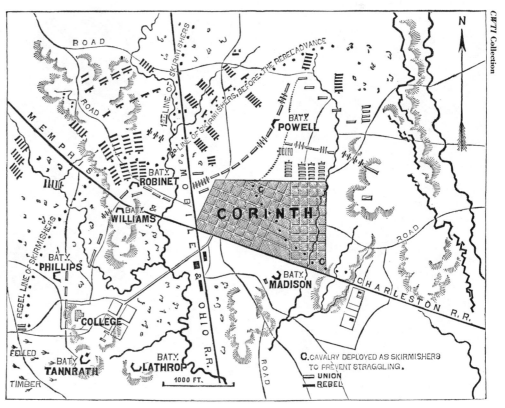

Map of Corinth, showing troop alignments in the battle.

4,000 troops Maury took into battle, over one-half were dead, wounded, and captured. As for Hebert's division, it lost 1,500 out of 7,000. In contrast Lovell's division, according to the Union commander opposite it, engaged only in some "heavy skirmishing" and its casualties were trifling.

At noon the Confederates began falling back on the Chewalla Road, leaving behind hundreds of wounded. Some of the harder-hit units were completely demoralized, hundreds of stragglers wandered about with glazed eyes, and only Lovell's division was capable of serious battle. Had the Federals counterattacked, probably Van Dorn's army would have been utterly smashed. But Rosecrans and his troops were physically and emotionally drained. Not until the next day did they start to pursue the retreating Rebels.

By then Van Dorn, who had halted for the night at Chewalla, was well on his way to Davis' Bridge on the Hatchie. However, just as his advance guard crossed the bridge, it was driven back by a column of 5,000 Federal infantry which Grant had sent to reinforce Rosecrans.

For a while it appeared that the Confederates were trapped. However Armstrong's cavalry found another place to cross the Hatchie farther south at Crum's Mill, where there was a dam that could be used as a makeshift bridge. Late that night the rear of Van Dorn's army safely reached the west bank of the river. The following day, October 6, the weary and dejected Confederates trudged through the rain to Ripley, where they rested overnight before resuming their retreat, which ultimately ended at Holly Springs. Grant, believing that it would be impossible to subsist a large force in this sparsely settled region, halted the Union pursuit at Ripley.

So ended Van Dorn's Corinth campaign. All he had to show for it were 5,000 killed, wounded, and missing soldiers, compared to half that number of Federal casualties. Moreover, instead of his liberating west Tennessee and sweeping on to the Ohio, the way was now open for Grant to launch his first attempt to capture Vicksburg. At the same time the Corinth debacle was one of the reasons why Bragg, who had penetrated deep

Below: Group of Confederate dead. Colonel Rogers lies at the left supporting the body of Colonel Ross.

into Kentucky, decided to retreat back into Tennessee. Thus the great Confederate counteroffensive in the West failed on both fronts. Soon the Union armies were again pushing southward.

Van Dorn should not have tried to take Corinth in the first place. The odds against success, as events demonstrated, simply were too great. He could have better served the Confederate cause by constantly threatening Grant's defense cordon and disrupting Union communication and supply lines. At the very least he should have followed Price's advice to wait until he was reinforced by the exchanged prisoners before attacking Corinth. It is unlikely the resultant delay would have made any substantial difference in Federal preparations and the additional manpower would have given him a much better chance of victory. But, as has been noted, he was eager to redeem his previous defeats at Pea Ridge and Baton Rouge. For that reason the bloody repulse at Corinth almost drove him mad with disappointment. After the retreat to Chewalla he actually proposed marching his shattered army to the south of Corinth and from there making another assault on the town! It took the combined protests of Price, Maury, and several other generals to dissuade him from this folly. "Van Dorn," said Maury to him, "you are the only man I ever saw who loves danger for its own sake. When any daring enterprise is before you, you cannot adequately estimate the obstacles in your way."

As for the Battle of Corinth itself, Confederate defeat resulted from the following:

(1) Rosecrans' prudence in concentrating all of his forces at Corinth by October 3 and in employing only one-half of them during the first day's fighting. This practically assured ultimate Union victory.

(2) Van Dorn's rashness in attempting to storm Corinth on the second day. Later he explained, and to a degree tried to excuse, the failure of this attack by claiming that during the night of October 3 Rosecrans received heavy reinforcements by rail. In support of this contention, he cited the fact that trains were heard moving into and out of Corinth. However, Rosecrans was merely redeploying his troops. More to the point, at the time it was occurring Van Dorn declared that the movement of the trains indicated that Rosecrans was evacuating the town. When, in the morning, he could see that this was not at all the case, he should have postponed the assault until he determined definitely the enemy strength. But he refused to consider the possibility that his strategy of striking Corinth before Rosecrans assembled his entire force had not worked. Desperate for victory, he deluded himself into believing that he had a four-to-three numerical superiority over Rosecrans and that he could take Corinth in one great, overwhelming rush.

(3) The "illness" of Hébert (testimony from a number of Confederates in a position to know makes it unlikely that he was actually sick) and Lovell's failure to carry out orders. These ruined whatever slight chance the Confederates had of taking Corinth. Probably both Hébert and Lovell concluded that an assault on the Union fortifications was foredoomed and so decided to have no share in it. Like Longstreet at Gettysburg they were correct in their evaluation of the tactical situation, and also like him they were guilty of not fulfilling their duty to their commander. Significantly, soon after Corinth both were relieved of their commands and neither ever again headed troops in the field.

(4) The superiority, which prevailed almost always during the Civil War, of defense over offense, especially when the former had the extra advantage of fortifications as the Federals did at Corinth. Through sheer nerve Price's men at Corinth did what Pickett's men did at Gettysburg and Hood's men at Franklin: Charged, reached, and even broke through a strongly held enemy position. But in achieving this they were so depleted both in numbers and physical strength that they could neither exploit their success nor stand against the counterattacks of fresh enemy troops. After the fighting ceased at Corinth a wounded Confederate prisoner from Arkansas said to Rosecrans, "General . . . we gave you the best we had in the ranch." That best was very good indeed—but it simply was not good enough.

Major General William Starke Rosecrans, victor at Corinth.

Perryville
by Stanley F. Horn

THE BLOODY battle fought at Perryville, Kentucky on October 8, 1862, was the climax, or rather the anti-climax, of General Braxton Bragg's movement of his army in a bold sweep from Tupelo, Mississippi, to the bluegrass region of Kentucky in a brilliantly conceived campaign that marked the high tide of Confederate military activity in the western theater.

The battle was unique in several ways. Both sides claimed it as a victory. Both Federal and Confederate leaders were vigorously censured for alleged mismanagement of their troops before, during, and after the battle. As the action developed it became plain that neither of the opposing commanders had more than a vague idea of the strength or whereabouts of his adversary. And, adding a modicum of confusion to the normal fog of battle, there was the mystery of the acoustical phenomenon that prevented nearby potential reinforcements from hearing the sound of musketry and cannon fire only a short distance away.

Following the Battle of Shiloh in April 1862,

Maj. Gen. Don Carlos Buell

General Bragg (who had succeeded General P. G. T. Beauregard) had spent most of the summer months in vigorously training the battered Confederate army and transforming it into a well-drilled, well-disciplined force of 35,000 men. Meanwhile Major General Henry W. Halleck, then the top Federal commander in the West, was breaking up the splendid forces that under Major Generals Ulysses S. Grant, Don Carlos Buell, and John Pope had advanced from Shiloh and occupied Corinth, Mississippi. In this dispersal of Federal troops, Buell with 25,000 men was ordered to move eastward along the Memphis & Charleston Railroad in the direction of Chattanooga, repairing the railroad as he went, with the apparent objective of eventually occupying East Tennessee.

MAJOR GENERAL Edmund Kirby Smith, who with 20,000 men was in command of the Confederate forces in East Tennessee, became increasingly uneasy as Buell drew closer and closer to Chattanooga. Bragg, however, was keeping an eye on Buell. On July 21 he started his whole force to Chattanooga, where he hoped to unite with Kirby Smith's army and, as he said, "strike an effective blow through Middle Tennessee, gaining the enemy's rear, cutting off his supplies and dividing his forces so as to encounter him in detail."

Bragg preceded his troops to Chattanooga, where he

and Smith worked out what Bragg described as "measures for mutual support and effective co-operation." Though he ranked Smith, Bragg seemed reluctant to display too much authority in Smith's official territory. Consequently there were two autonomous commands, under two independent commanders, operating in the ensuing campaign. In this awkward state of affairs, it is perhaps no great marvel that a fatal sort of uncertainty and muddling developed.

THE CAMPAIGN started off smoothly enough. Kirby Smith, reinforced by Pat Cleburne's two brigades from Hardee's corps, on August 14 moved out briskly from Knoxville into Kentucky, bypassing the Federal force at Cumberland Gap and striking straight for the heart of the bluegrass region. On August 30 a Federal force under Major General William Nelson attempted to check the Confederate advance at Richmond, Kentucky, but in a hard-fought battle Nelson's force was practically annihilated. Most of his men were either killed, wounded, or captured, and all his artillery, wagon trains, supplies, and most of his small arms captured. Following this smashing victory, Kirby Smith swept on to Lexington where he remained in virtual control of central Kentucky, while his cavalry raided northward to the immediate environs of Louisville and even to Covington, across the river from Cincinnati. He triumphantly occupied Frankfort, the capital of Kentucky, with 1,500 cavalry, causing the officials of the state government to flee to Louisville, to which the state archives and funds had already been transferred.

Maj. Gen. A. McD. McCook

While all this was going on, Bragg, with his army organized into two corps or wings under Major Generals Leonidas Polk and William J. Hardee, had been moving northward from Chattanooga through Tennessee. Buell, uncertain of his enemy's intentions, cautiously moved on Bragg's left flank, keeping his force between the Confederates and Nashville. After learning of Nelson's disaster at Richmond, Buell marched his whole army on to Nashville and prepared to defend it from the attack he thought was coming.

PRIOR to this Bragg himself seemed none too certain of his own plans—whether to invest Nashville or to conduct a full-scale invasion of Kentucky. At this juncture, however, he concluded to push on into Kentucky where, he later said, he hoped to join Kirby Smith and gain such a decisive victory over the Federal forces as would encourage the pro-Southern Kentuckians to enlist under the Confederate banner and give him greater manpower for further conquest.

But Bragg's plans never quite jelled. Buell, thoroughly alarmed, now set out for Louisville with most of his army, leaving Brigadier General James S. Negley with 6,000 men to defend Nashville. Bragg, by a quick thrust, captured Munfordville, Kentucky, and its garrison of 4,000 men, and was thus in a strong position between Buell and Louisville. So far his campaign had been well planned and well executed; but, now that he had the enemy army in a disadvantageous position, he strangely shrank from combat. Instead of precipitating a battle, after marching his army 600 miles for that avowed purpose, Bragg sud-

Maj. Gen. B. F. Cheatham, C.S.A.

denly decided to move aside to Bardstown without further contesting Buell's advance. Eagerly accepting the unexpected opportunity, Buell pressed on to Louisville, where he arrived on September 25 in time to avert an incipient panic growing out of the threatening presence of Bragg's army at nearby Bardstown. Buell quickly absorbed the troops available at Louisville, mostly recruits, whipped his army into shape, and on October 1 moved out to offer battle to Bragg at Bardstown.

BUELL'S army was organized into three corps, under Major Generals A. McD. McCook, T. L. Crittenden, and C. C. Gilbert. As they advanced, Brigadier General Joshua W. Sill's division, along with Brigadier General Ebenezer Dumont's, moved on the left in the direction of Frankfort. The remainder of Buell's force marched directly on Bragg's position at Bardstown. McCook advanced through Taylorsville, Gilbert through Shepherdsville, and Crittenden through Mount Washington—roads from all three of these places converging on Bardstown.

Bragg, however, was not at Bardstown. He had other things on his mind. On the 28th he had gone to Lexington, where he arrived on October 1. The

Gen. Braxton Bragg, C.S.A.

On the skirmish line (BL)

next day he ordered Kirby Smith to concentrate his army at Frankfort, where he planned to stage elaborate ceremonies inaugurating Richard Hawes as Provisional Governor of Kentucky as one of the Confederate States of America. Kirby Smith says he begged Bragg to give up the idea of the inauguration, in spite of whatever political importance it might have, and concentrate the two armies at once so that they could fall on Buell while he was marching in divided columns. Bragg was unmoved by this plea, however, and proceeded with the inauguration plans. But the affair was broken up by the approach of Buell's advance column under General Sill. Hawes, interrupted in the midst of his inauguration address by the sound of Federal shells bursting in the city, hurried back to the army, along with Bragg and the other generals who were taking part in the ceremonies. Thus Kentucky's experience as a political unit of the Confederate States was spirited but brief.

WHILE BRAGG was at Frankfort on his ill-advised political errand, he had left the army at Bardstown under Polk's command. Polk was instructed that, if attacked in force, he should fall back toward Bryantsville, where Bragg had piled up the stores captured in Kentucky and where he was maintaining his temporary base.

Buell, in later outlining his strategy, stated that he planned to mislead Bragg by making a feint on his left, and in this he was eminently successful. Bragg, apparently completely in the dark as to Buell's whereabouts, had written to Polk on September 30, instructing him to move towards Louisville, occupying Taylorsville, Shepherdsville, and Elizabethtown. Before Polk could carry out these orders, however, his

cavalry brought him word that Buell was moving out from Louisville. Polk reported this to Bragg, commenting pointedly: "It seems to me we are too much scattered."

Bragg now gave Polk revised instructions, based on the mistaken assumption that the main Federal objective was Frankfort. Under the spell of this delusion, he ordered Polk to move on Frankfort by way of Bloomfield, striking Buell's flank and rear while Kirby Smith attacked in front. Bragg's strategy was based on an erroneous theory; but Polk, fortunately for the safety of the army, deviated from his commander's orders. Feeling himself pressed so closely on his own front that it was impossible to do anything but fall back slowly before the superior force facing him (which was in line with his original instructions), he called his wing and division commanders into a council of war. They were unanimous in supporting Polk's judgment, and he accordingly notified Bragg respectfully that compliance with his latest orders was "not only eminently inexpedient but impracticable."

BRAGG SENT another message to Polk, telling him that the movement on Frankfort was evidently a feint, directing Polk to "act accordingly." Revealing his complete befuddlement, he instructed Polk to "place one flank at Taylorsville"—blissfully unaware that Taylorsville was already within Buell's lines. Next morning (the 9th) Polk received orders to concentrate "in front of Harrodsburg." Bragg informed Polk that he intended to give battle to Buell "just as soon as we can concentrate," going on to declare: "We can and must defeat them."

Bragg, however, seemed to be still under the impression that Buell's main effort was directed at Frankfort; and, instead of concentrating, he further weakened Polk by ordering him to send Brigadier General Jones M. Withers' division from his corps to Kirby Smith's support. Then, on October 7, realizing that the opposing armies were now approaching climactic contact, he issued a "Confidential Circular" to his generals, outlining plans for an engagement which he evidently thought would take place somewhere between Frankfort and Harrodsburg, probably at Versailles. This order gave detailed instructions for the disposition of the troops:

> Cheatham's division will move forward tonight to Withers' position, and both divisions of the right wing [that is, Withers' and Cheatham's] will move tomorrow to Lawrenceburg, thence to Versailles, and to follow General E. Kirby Smith's command.
> General E. Kirby Smith's command will move tomorrow to Versailles, throwing a division toward Frankfort. Allston's cavalry, now at Salvisa, will cover Cheatham's movement, reporting to Major General Cheatham.
> Major General Hardee, commanding left wing, Army of the Mississippi, will follow these movements as circumstances allow, notifying these headquarters of his move. Colonel Wade's infantry will join the guard at the depot at Bryantsville, reporting to the commanding officer there, and his cavalry will report to Colonel Wheeler, commanding cavalry of Hardee's wing.

NEATLY worked out on paper, it sounded simple; everybody was told exactly what he was expected to do. But battles have a disconcerting way of not following the commanding generals' blueprints. While Bragg was so carefully formulating his plans for an engagement near Versailles, the Fates (aided by General Buell) were making other arrangements. Bragg was quite right in thinking a battle imminent, but he misjudged its location by twenty miles.

Fort at Munfordville, Ky., captured by Bragg on Sept. 17, 1862. (BL)

Hardee with his corps had reached the village of Perryville, ten miles from Harrodsburg, by the evening of October 7, closely followed by Gilbert's corps of the Federal army, which was now in the center of Buell's advance. Throughout the day Gilbert's progress had been stubbornly and skillfully contested by Colonel Joseph Wheeler's cavalry, acting as Hardee's rear guard. By the time Gilbert arrived in the vicinity of Perryville, he found Hardee strongly positioned there on a ridge beyond Chaplin River [Gilbert calls this Chaplin's Fork of Salt River]. Advance troops were beyond Doctor's Fork [also called Doctor's Creek].

This section of Kentucky had been suffering a severe drought for several weeks, and most of the springs and creeks were dry, greatly to the discomfort of the marching troops. In the bed of Doctor's Fork, a tributary of Chaplin River, however, there were still some precious pools of palatable water, sorely needed by Gilbert's men and horses, so he struck vigorously to seize these water pools. A furious fight went on until dark, before the Federals were able to dislodge Wheeler's troopers from the ridge commanding Doctor's Fork. Before daybreak on the 8th Gilbert gained a position covering the pools in Doctor's Fork, and these were his only water supply for the next two days.

Although Hardee did not realize that Buell was now concentrating his whole army in front of Perryville, he did sense that the force facing him was more than he could take care of with his single corps. He appealed to Bragg for reinforcements. Bragg responded, late in the afternoon of the 7th, by directing

Perryville, Ky., looking southeast from the Mackville Pike.
(BL)

Polk to divide his corps and move with Cheatham to Hardee's relief, while Withers' division continued to Versailles. Bragg instructed Polk to "give the enemy battle immediately" at Perryville, concluding airily: "rout him, and then move to our support at Versailles"—still under the delusion that the climactic action would be there.

BRAGG'S misguided dissipation of the Confederate forces was so manifestly unwise and haphazard that Hardee, a seasoned and expert tactician, was deeply disturbed—so disturbed that on the night of the 7th he resorted to the unusual procedure of sending a friendly and informal but polite protest to his superior officer:

"Permit me, from the friendly relations so long existing between us, to write you plainly. Do not scatter your forces. There is one rule in our profession which should never be forgotten; it is to throw the masses of your troops on the fractions of the enemy. The movement last proposed will divide your army and each may be defeated, whereas by keeping them united success is certain. If it be your policy to strike the enemy at Versailles, take your whole force with you and make the blow effective; if, on the contrary, you should decide to strike the army in front of me, first let that be done with a force which will make success certain. Strike with your whole strength first to the right then to the left. I could not sleep quietly tonight without giving expression to these views." And he added a pregnant postscript: "If you wish my opinion, it is that in view of the position of your depots you ought to strike this force first."

There is nothing in the record to indicate that Bragg had any inclination to heed his subordinate's admonitory lesson in elementary tactics. Even if he had, he did not get the opportunity. While his men were marching hither and yon in scattered detachments—some under Hardee, some under Polk, some under Withers, some under Kirby Smith—a battle was about to be forced on him where he least expected it. As Basil Duke caustically says: "He kept more than two-thirds of the force under his command idly maneuvering in a quarter where nothing could possibly be accomplished, and permitted less than twenty thousand men to become engaged upon a field where more than forty-five thousand could have been hurled upon them."

BRAGG WAS not alone in his uncertainty and indecision. Seldom in warfare have the commanders of opposing armies been so completely confused as to each other's location and plans. Buell, informed that Bragg's main force was at Perryville, was endeavoring to concentrate the full Federal strength there. On the other hand, Bragg up to the last minute was convinced that Sill's and Dumont's divisions marching through Shelbyville toward Frankfort was Buell's main army moving to strike him there, and he was intent on massing in that area to meet the supposed threat. Hence he left fewer than 20,000 men at Perryville to fight 58,000, while he moved 36,000 to meet Sill's 12,000.

That night the main body of Buell's army was closing in on Perryville. Gilbert's corps in the center was already in position along the Springfield Pike, only a few miles west of town; McCook was coming up on the left, and Crittenden on the right. Major General George H. Thomas, second in command of the entire army, accompanied Crittenden and was temporarily in personal command of that corps. Gil-

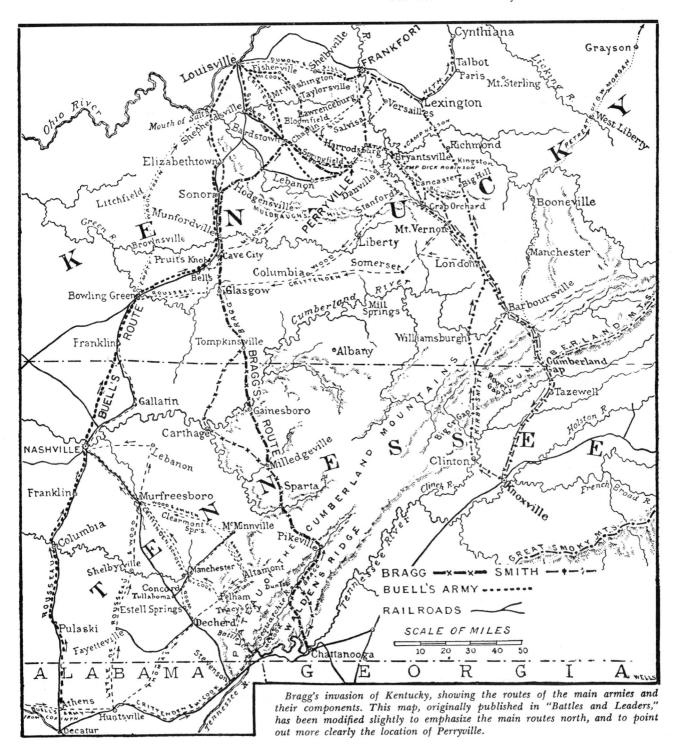

Bragg's invasion of Kentucky, showing the routes of the main armies and their components. This map, originally published in "Battles and Leaders," has been modified slightly to emphasize the main routes north, and to point out more clearly the location of Perryville.

bert, in the center, was farther advanced by several miles than McCook and Crittenden; at 3 a.m. on the 8th they were ordered to move up into line with Gilbert, and to report to Buell as soon as they were in position. Buell expected this alignment to be accomplished by 7 a.m., and he planned to order an attack immediately thereafter. But, here again, the execution fell short of the planning.

POLK, now in command of the Confederate forces at Perryville by reason of his seniority, had taken a strong position on a ridge along the east side of Chaplin River, north of the town, with his three divisions arrayed from right to left under S. B. Buckner, Patton Anderson, and B. F. Cheatham. The Confederate left, resting on the town, did not extend beyond the Federal center, and was dangerously exposed to a flank movement if the Federal right should operate with any enterprise.

"For him there would be no surrender." Detail from a drawing by Sidney H. Riesenberg. The Battle of Perryville—the highlight of Bragg's invasion of Kentucky—was fierce, and casualties were high. The Union lost 845 killed, 2,851 wounded, and 515 captured or missing. The Confederates lost 510 killed, 2,635 wounded, and 251 missing. (*CWTI* Collection)

Across Chaplin River from Polk's position was another range of hills, and beyond these hills was Doctor's Fork, flowing roughly parallel to Chaplin River and into that stream two miles below town. It was on the high ground on both sides of Doctor's Fork that the ensuing battle was fought.

Unfortunately for Buell, his arrangements did not work out as smoothly as he had planned and expected. Neither Crittenden nor McCook reached the field at the appointed time. Crittenden had been delayed during the night while he made a detour looking for a camping ground supplied with water, and he did not get into his assigned position until about 11 o'clock the next morning. Even then, he was so faultily aligned and so harassed by Wheeler's cavalry that only a small portion of his force got into action. McCook's corps was also tardy, arriving about noon; upon their arrival they were placed on Gilbert's left in a line formed along the crest of the hills to the west of Doctor's Fork. McCook's right, when he got into position, was separated from Gilbert's left by a ravine through which the creek ran, the interval between the two corps being nearly half a mile.

COLONEL DANIEL McCOOK'S brigade of Sheridan's division had advanced early on the morning of the 8th to insure the retention of the vital water supply in Doctor's Fork. The Confederates made a half-hearted and futile attempt to recover possession of the creek bed, but showed no signs of attempting a general advance. Most of the morning passed in desultory skirmishing along the center and a listless exchange of artillery fire—a noisy but ineffective gunnery exercise called "shelling the woods."

Polk, kept informed of the enemy's movements by the alert and energetic Wheeler, was becoming increasingly aware that a large force was building up in his front. Despite his recognition of this development, however, he seemed indecisive. His orders from Bragg were explicitly to "give battle immediately," and Wheeler thought that an attack would be launched at daylight. But Polk did not order an advance. Instead, at dawn he called a council of his general officers, where it was decided, Polk said in his official report, "to adopt the defensive-offensive; to await the movements of the enemy and to be guided by events as they were developed." Polk wrote afterward: "I did not regard the letter of instructions as a peremptory order to attack at all hazards, but that . . . I should carry the instructions into execution as judiciously and promptly as a willing mind and sound discretion would allow."

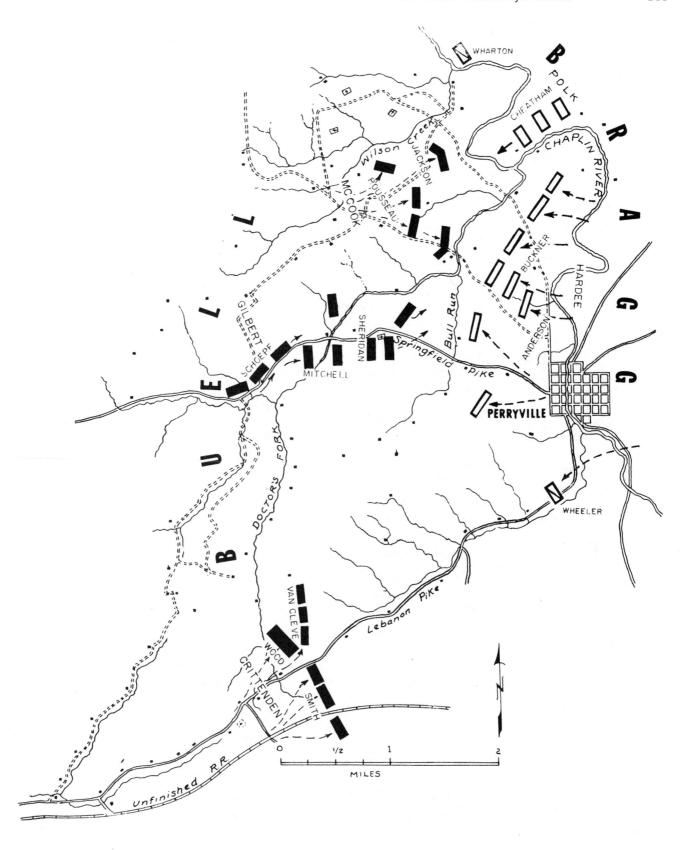

The Battle of Perryville, showing the situation from 10:30 a.m. to 1 p.m., October 8, 1862. The events shown did not occur simultaneously; Crittenden's corps was late, not arriving in position until 11 a.m., and exerted little effect until late in the day. Except for an early-morning advance by part of Sheridan's division, McCook's corps did not arrive until noon. The main force of the Confederate attack, shown developing at 1 p.m., fell on McCook. This and the succeeding map have been adapted from detailed maps prepared by Edwin C. Bearss. The rectangles represent brigades, but only the divisions are indicated by name.

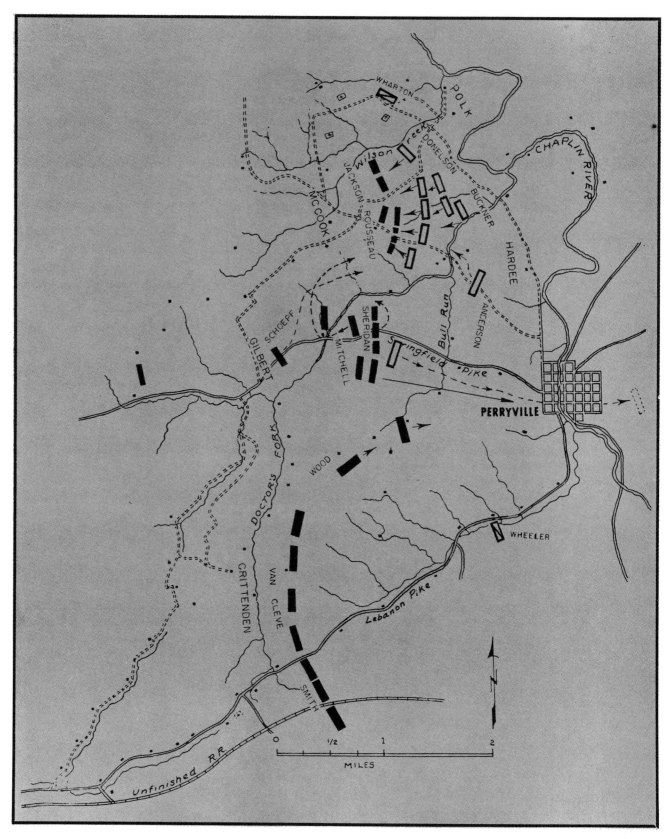

This shows the course of the Confederate attack subsequent to 3:30 p.m. McCook's divisions were crushed and driven back in confusion. Mitchell's division of Gilbert's corps has driven back Powell's brigade, but other than this, that corps has contributed little. Mr. Bearss points out that by the close of the day the Confederate attack on the north flank had enjoyed considerable success, "but were not doing so well on the Springfield and Lebanon Pikes (the latter is the road on which Crittenden's troops were deployed initially)." At dark, though not shown hereon, Wood's division of Crittenden's corps had reached a line north of where Wheeler is shown on this map.

MEANWHILE Bragg finally concluded that perhaps there might be more of a Federal force at Perryville than he had suspected. He waited at Harrodsburg, expecting to hear the sounds of battle early in the morning of the 8th; but Polk's only activity, as Bragg anxiously waited, was to send Wheeler out skirmishing briskly on his left flank, while Liddell's brigade was thrown forward in the center to check Sheridan's aggressive advance brigade. The sound of the skirmish firing and the desultory artillery fire, because of peculiar acoustic conditions, was not heard by Bragg; so at length, hearing nothing, he made up his mind to go to Perryville in person.

Bragg arrived on the scene about 10 a.m., to find that Polk had been reconnoitering the high ground between Chaplin River and Doctor's Fork Creek and was just about to advance to occupy it, which movement Bragg approved. Polk had observed some signs of activity on the Federal left, and to strengthen his position against possible pressure from that side he switched Cheatham from his left to his right. Here Cheatham's brigades were massed under cover of the hills overlooking the confluence of the two streams. The new Confederate right now overlapped the Federal left, and was extended farther by Colonel John A. Wharton's cavalry brigade.

ABOUT one o'clock in the afternoon the whole Confederate force moved forward in a general attack, the first shock of the assault falling on McCook's corps on the Federal left. Bragg had the good fortune to launch this thrust at the most inopportune time for the Federals. McCook, after placing his corps in position a few hours earlier, had gone to the rear. In his absence an over-zealous division commander,

Perryville battlefield from photo made in 1885. Looking northeast from the center of Rousseau's line. (BL)

Brigadier General L. H. Rousseau, lured by the desperately needed water in the creek bed, decided on his own responsibility to move forward and take it. He was just forming two of his brigades (Lytle's and Harris') for this purpose when the Confederate attacking force broke out from their cover. McCook's whole corps was quickly thrown into confusion. Rousseau's deploying brigades, surprised, had difficulty in re-forming for defense. Another of McCook's divisions, composed largely of raw recruits, dissolved quickly and fled. By the time McCook himself had been notified and had returned to the front, he found his corps nearly demoralized.

This corps, however, had a hard core of staunch, seasoned troops who stood their ground and fought ferociously. In later years, veterans said that some of the most desperate hand-to-hand fighting of the whole war took place on this front. But, despite this courageous resistance, the Federals were driven back steadily, though slowly, for three-quarters of a mile or more. The Confederate infantry fire and bayonet charges were effectively supported by the skillful marksmanship of their artillerists, who blasted the Federals out of successive places of refuge behind stone walls and fences as they retired.

McCOOK appealed to Sheridan of Gilbert's corps for assistance, but Sheridan had his own hands full and was unable to help. Most of Hardee's army had closed in on McCook's exposed flanks, taking advantage of the gap between him and Gilbert. But Patton Anderson with two brigades had moved directly on Sheridan's division, posted west of Perryville across the Springfield Pike, and occupied him so vigorously that he was completely deceived as to the force in front of him and did not venture to assume the offensive, as he might well have done. Late

Battle of Perryville—engagement of Starkweather's brigade on the Union right. (BL)

in the afternoon Brigadier General Robert B. Mitchell of Gilbert's corps moved up with two of his three brigades and outflanked Powell's brigade, driving him back on the town. But by this time the battle was over.

A previously mentioned peculiar feature of the Battle of Perryville was that, because of a head wind or sharp temperature gradient, or both, the sonic rays constituting the battle sounds were bent or refracted upward into the higher atmosphere, never descending to earth. Therefore the gunfire was not heard at any great distance from the scene of the action. Bragg at Harrodsburg had heard nothing of the morning firing, and Buell at his headquarters a few miles back from his front lines did not hear the furious musketry fire and sharp cannonading throughout the early afternoon.

It was not until four o'clock in the afternoon that the receding tide of battle came close enough for Buell to hear the steady roar of the guns that notified him of the serious nature of the engagement in front of him. "That is something more than 'shelling the woods'," he exclaimed to General Gilbert, who was then at his headquarters. "It sounds like a fight." And he hastily sent Gilbert to find out what was going on. Gilbert soon met one of McCook's staff officers

bearing a belated report of his desperate plight and an appeal for aid. This was the first time Buell realized that his army was fighting a full-scale battle in his immediate front. As soon as he received the bad news from McCook's messenger, Buell sent a brigade from Mitchell's division under Colonel Michael Gooding to the rescue, but it too was driven back by the now irresistible Confederate thrust, and Gooding himself was captured.

AT THE CLOSE of the day it seemed clear to the Confederates that they had won a complete victory. The right section of the battlefield was in their possession; McCook's Federals had been driven back over three-quarters of a mile or more, broken and disorganized. Two Union brigadier generals, James S. Jackson and William R. Terrill, had been killed and a large number of officers had been wounded. The Confederates had lost no general officers, but General Polk himself had a very narrow escape from capture or death late in the evening, when he stumbled into personal contact with a body of enemy troops on the Federal left. Befriended by his dark blouse and the increasing obscurity of late evening, he later related, he decided that his only hope was to "brazen it out" by identifying himself as a Federal officer—a form of deceit which the bishop-general probably considered pardonable in the dire circumstances.

The battle, though of relatively short duration,

was exceptionally fierce, with stunning casualties. The Federal loss was 845 killed, 2851 wounded, 515 captured or missing. The Confederates lost 510 killed, 2635 wounded, 251 missing. General Buell said the battle would "stand conspicuous for its severity in the history of the rebellion." General Bragg wrote in his official report that "for the time engaged, it was the severest and most desperately contested engagement within my knowledge."

DURING THE following night Bragg seemed to be overwhelmed with a resurgence of caution, not to say timidity. Apparently now realizing that he was confronted by Buell's main force, he ordered a prompt movement to nearby Harrodsburg to consolidate with Kirby Smith. The Confederates formed a battle line shortly before reaching Harrodsburg, to confront Buell if he advanced; but, beyond sending out a cautious skirmish line to the outskirts of Perryville, Buell showed no inclination to renew hostilities.

Bragg by October 10 had joined with Kirby Smith and was able to draw up at Harrodsburg a battle front made up of his greatest available force. Buell, after being joined by Sill, moved on toward Harrodsburg, and that night the two armies faced each other in battle array on the outskirts of the town. In both armies there was certainty that the next day would bring on a decisive battle. But again Bragg recoiled from the idea of combat, unable to bring himself to assume the offensive; then, after much deliberation, he fell back, beginning the movement during the night. Next morning Buell moved warily, evidently expecting some tactical ruse. Bragg did make a stand after crossing Dick's River, where his position was so strong that Buell did not dare attack. On October 13 Bragg began his active and definite withdrawal from the state, his flanks and rear protected by Wheeler's cavalry. Buell kept up the semblance of a pursuit until they reached London, where he abandoned the chase. Bragg then moved on into East Tennessee unmolested.

REPERCUSSIONS, on both sides, followed swiftly. Bragg, for the ostensible purpose of reporting personally to President Davis, hastened to Richmond as soon as his army was safely back in Tennessee and, in explaining his misadventure in Kentucky, fastened the blame on Polk. Davis was not willing to condemn his old friend, Polk, without hearing his side, so Polk was summoned to Richmond. There he told Davis flatly that the Kentucky campaign had failed because of Bragg's incapacity. He generously gave Bragg all proper credit for skill as an organizer and disciplinarian, but voiced the candid opinion that Bragg was "wanting in the higher elements of generalship" and should be removed from command of the

army. Polk's defense evidently was effective, as he was soon afterward promoted to the rank of lieutenant general (as were Hardee and Kirby Smith); but Polk emphasized his opinion of Bragg by asking to be relieved of further service under him.

Buell's conduct of his side of the Kentucky campaign had been highly unsatisfactory to the Federal authorities, and the last gun at Perryville had hardly been fired before he was being bombarded with questions and censure from Washington.

Buell, following Bragg's retreat, felt that his obvious strategic move was to get back to Nashville as quickly as possible and consolidate his forces there in defense of that important base. But President Lincoln at that time was still trying personally to direct the movements of the Federal armies. Therefore he instructed Halleck to inform Buell of the President's opinion "that your army must enter East Tennessee this fall, and that it ought to move there while the roads are passable." Buell courteously explained why he thought a movement into East Tennessee was not practicable at that time, telling why he deemed it imperative to concentrate at Nashville at once. Lincoln and Halleck did not discuss the matter with him further; the next communication Buell received from Washington was an order on October 30 to turn his command over to Major General William S. Rosecrans.

It was thought for a while that a similar fate would overtake Bragg, but Jefferson Davis was reluctant to believe that his friend was as incompetent as pictured by his critics. Davis did, however, adopt the halfway measure of appointing General Joseph E. Johnston department commander, with supervision of the commands of Bragg and Kirby Smith (now transferred to the Trans-Mississippi) and also over Lieutenant General Pemberton in Mississippi—a move which was unsatisfactory to all those involved and ineffective in bringing about any improvement in operating conditions.

So the ill-fated Kentucky campaign was brought to an unhappy close. Bragg's men had marched a thousand miles, fought a bloody battle in which they drove their enemy back with heavy losses, and were now being marched back to Murfreesboro, not far from where they had started two months before. The campaign had extended over more territory than any other of the war, but the results were just exactly nothing—except that the tarnish on Bragg's prestige was now a little more pronounced.

The Battle of Stones River
by James Lee McDonough

Winter Quarters: On picket duty. (Harper's Pictorial History of the Great Rebellion)

December 30, 1862. The American Civil War was more than halfway through its second year. The Union's Army of the Cumberland, some 44,000 strong, stood drawn up about thirty miles southeast of Nashville, Tennessee. Positioned along the banks of the west fork of Stones River, near the little town of Murfreesboro, it faced the Confederacy's Army of Tennessee, a force numbering almost 38,000.

Just as soldiers of both armies prepared to get some needed sleep, one of the strange events of the war took place. In the stillness of the winter night, the military bands, Union and Confederate, began to play their favorite selections, and the music-making became something of a contest. "Yankee Doodle" was answered by "Dixie," and the Confederate tune "The Bonnie Blue Flag" brought a resounding version of

"Hail Columbia." Ultimately, a Federal band struck up the familiar and cherished "Home Sweet Home." "Immediately a Confederate band caught up the strain," wrote a member of the 19th Tennessee Infantry, "then one after another until all the bands of each army were playing 'Home Sweet Home.' And after our bands had ceased playing, we could hear the sweet refrain as it died away on the cool frosty air on the Federal side." It was a strange and melancholy prelude to one of the bloodiest battles of the war.

Thomas L. Livermore, noted authority on losses during the conflict, computed total casualties for both sides at Stones River at 24,645. No other Tennessee battle's casualties quite equalled that figure.

Much preceded the winter carnage at Stones River. In late summer 1862, Confederate fortunes seemed to be at high tide. Rebels advanced in both East and West, in the one great counter-offensive of the war, invading Maryland and Kentucky.

It was a startling turnabout. Shortly before, in spring 1862, the Confederacy had been on the defensive everywhere. Tennessee had been pierced by Union armies, New Orleans captured, the South Atlantic coastline overrun, and a Federal army had advanced up Virginia's Peninsula to within a few miles of the Confederate capital, Richmond.

Then, just as many Northerners thought the end of the war was at hand, the Southerners held firm at Richmond. Attacking and forcing the Federals to retreat on two fronts, by September General Robert E. Lee's army crossed the Potomac River, carrying the war north into Maryland. At the same time, Rebels were on the move in the war's western theater, marching northward from middle Tennessee into Kentucky, compelling a retreat of Union forces at Nashville.

It was all for nothing. Lee's hope of a major victory on Northern soil came to a sanguinary end at Sharpsburg, Maryland, September 17, with more than 10,000 of his soldiers dead or wounded along the banks of Antietam Creek. Within two days Confederates were recrossing the Potomac.

In the west, too, fate seemed aligned against the Rebels. Following a frustrating retreat from Kentucky, General Braxton Bragg's Confederate Army of Tennessee took up a position near Murfreesboro, blocking the main road and rail route to Chattanooga.

Bragg was a 45-year-old West Point graduate who had gained fame in the Mexican War as an artillery captain and who enjoyed a close relationship with Confederate President Jefferson Davis. A quarrelsome, pessimistic, and stubborn martinet, Bragg was possibly the most controversial high-ranking general in the Confederate army. Possessing a lowering brow and a haggard, no-nonsense look, he was, as historian Grady McWhiney has observed, too ambitious to be

satisfied with himself or others and represented "an unusual combination of potentially dangerous eccentricities and high ability." For better or worse, Bragg would command the Confederacy's main western army longer than any other general.

Perhaps many of the Confederates gathering at Murfreesboro were like Captain Napoleon Monroe Bearden, Company E, 8th Tennessee Infantry, who possessed a burning ambition to drive the Yankees from Tennessee. Perryville, his first major battle, ended in disappointment. Now he hoped for another chance to carry the war to the Federals and drive them from the Volunteer State. Almost a year had passed since he wrote, "We have tried a government given us by our ancestors, and found it of no value . . . Now to erect one that will stand the test of time we must make great sacrifices—true and noble spirits must perish on the battlefields." Within a short time Bearden would lead his men to battle on behalf of the government he envisioned, and he would see and experience, first hand, the price in "true and noble spirits" the attempt to establish that government would cost.

Braxton Bragg, however, apparently had no intention of fighting again soon. Bragg hoped to occupy middle Tennessee in force and, if possible, hold the land between the Cumberland and Tennessee rivers through the winter. And, since most of his soldiers supposed the army would remain at Murfreesboro throughout the winter, they began building various types of huts and houses to protect themselves from the cold winds sure to come.

In the Union camp at Nashville, the Army of the Cumberland, having returned from Kentucky, had a new commander who was expected to attack. The administration of President Abraham Lincoln placed the mantle of leadership on Major General William Starke "Old Rosy" Rosecrans, a 43-year-old man with an impulsive, excitable personality. He had beaten Robert E. Lee in western Virginia during the early days of the conflict. Later at Corinth, Mississippi, his troops made a determined stand, turning back a Rebel attempt to reclaim that important railroad junction. His star seemed to be rising.

Nearly six feet tall, the general was compact, with little wasted flesh. He was a dedicated Catholic who seemed to enjoy religious discussions as much as military ones. Speaking rapidly while tearing and chewing on a cigar, from which he seemed inseparable, Old Rosy inspired hope and confidence throughout the army. Many thought he was just the man to lead them in significant action against the Rebel forces gathered around Murfreesboro under the irritable and austere-looking Bragg.

Union dress parade in Nashville on March 4, 1862, shortly after Federals seized the city. Shown: the 51st Regiment Ohio Volunteers, the first to enter the city. (Library of Congress)

Colonel John A. Martin, 8th Kansas Infantry, wrote: "On the whole, the army rejoiced to learn that Rosecrans had been assigned to command. To those who served under him in Mississippi, his presence was particularly gratifying, and the enthusiasm with which they hailed his coming was unbounded. . . . The glory of his recent victories gave a fresher and greater charm to his name."

It was not long, however, before President Abraham Lincoln, Union Secretary of War Edwin M. Stanton, Chief of Staff Major General Henry W. Halleck, and others in Washington, D.C. decided Rosecrans was wasting time in launching an offensive. Again and again telegraphic messages from Washington urged him to move out against the enemy. But several problems concerned Lincoln's general in Nashville. Because of the abnormally dry weather, the Cumberland River, looping around Nashville on the east, north, and west, was too shallow to serve as a dependable supply line. The Louisville & Nashville Railroad needed repair in places and some of its guard garrisons strengthened. Also, Rosecrans hoped to lull Bragg into a false sense of security—to have him believe that the Yankees intended to go into winter quarters.

A few days before Christmas the situation began turning in Rosecrans' favor. The general was pleased to see the Cumberland River rising. With a five weeks' store of rations then accumulated at Nashville,

the Cumberland rose enough to provide the means of rapidly and safely augmenting this supply, even if the railroad were broken again by Confederate cavalry.

Furthermore, there was news. Word that Confederate Brigadier General Carter L. Stevenson's 7,500-man division departed Murfreesboro for Mississippi soon leaked through the Federal lines to Nashville; equally good, Brigadier General John H. Morgan's Confederate cavalry had been dispatched into Kentucky and Confederate Brigadier General Nathan B. Forrest's cavalry into west Tennessee. The Rebel raiders might work much havoc on these forays, but they would not be within range to assist Bragg.

Rosecrans' own army was in excellent condition. This, he determined, was the time to strike. At a conference with his subordinate commanders, the animated general reportedly sprang to his feet, slammed his mug of toddy down on the table and spoke with intense feeling: "We move tomorrow, Gentlemen! Press them hard! Drive them out of their nests! Make them fight or run! *Fight them! Fight them!* Fight, I say!"

Brigade commander Colonel James P. Fyffe of Ohio would have offered a hearty "amen" to the effervescent Rosecrans had he been within hearing. Filled with a love of country and a sense of duty, Fyffe had gone to war for the Union, filled with an adventurous desire to participate in, as he expressed it to his wife Willa on December 11, 1862, "the grandest events that have shaken the world since Peter the Hermit preached the Great Crusade for the Rescue of the Holy Land." Fyffe would soon get his wish.

Meanwhile, among the Confederates at Murfreesboro, social life had been above average in recent December days. Families from nearby counties took advantage of the opportunity to visit the men, and almost every day saw scattered groups of relatives converging on the army from all directions. Perhaps the most notable occasion was the visit of Confederate President Jefferson Davis, who dined with the general officers at Bragg's headquarters and reviewed Lieutenant General William J. Hardee's and Lieutenant General Leonidas Polk's corps, pronouncing the latter "the best appointed troops he had seen—well appointed and well clad." Also, perhaps fatefully, Davis made the strategic decision, over Bragg's protest, to send Stevenson's division to Mississippi.

Another highlight of the Christmas social season was the whirlwind courtship and marriage of the vivacious, 17-year-old Mattie Ready and 36-year-old general of cavalry John Morgan. It was a military wedding in the most complete sense of the word. The

Mr. and Mrs. John Hunt Morgan, the hits of the Christmas social season. Their wedding was performed by Episcopal bishop Lieutenant General Leonidas Polk. (Library of Congress)

ceremony was performed by General Polk (the Episcopal bishop of Louisiana before the war), wearing his vestments over his gray military uniform. The bride's home was the scene of the nuptials, and General Bragg and most of the high-ranking Rebel officers in the area were in attendance. Within a few days Morgan was off raiding again (perhaps to allay fears on the part of some that the marriage would harm his command proficiency).

As Christmas drew still nearer, social life for the troops in Bragg's army approached a climax. The orchards of middle Tennessee yielded their fruits in abundance; these fruits were soon converted into their liquid form, and some of the Confederates began their celebrating early and did not sober up until much later. And certainly many of the Yankees in Tennessee's capital city were doing their best to keep up with the Rebels in the Christmas celebration. Another battle was shaping up; perhaps it would be more costly than any yet experienced. Living only for the present, believing their joy was likely to be of short duration, some of the soldiers, Yank and Reb, simply could not get enough alcoholic beverage. The story was told of a new recruit who was sent by his veteran comrades to invest a dollar in food and drink. When the young Rebel returned to camp with ten cents' worth of bread and ninety cents' worth of whiskey, he was severely reprimanded by those who thought it was ridiculous to have spent so much on bread.

Christmas day at Murfreesboro was observed by horse racing, card playing, and other merrymaking traditional to Christmas celebrations in the South. "The morning after Christmas Day," lamented one of Brigadier General Joseph "Fighting Joe" Wheeler's cavalry captains, "I felt feeble; but, being anxious to be with my men, reported for duty."

The Federal army at Nashville, of course, had less chance for contact with family and friends than did the Confederates at Murfreesboro. Perhaps for that reason, that Christmas the writings of Union soldiers seemed solemn and dreary. John Chilcote, a member of the 90th Ohio Infantry, wrote, "This is Christmas, and what a contrast between *our* Christmas and those who are at home in good, comfortable houses, with plenty to eat and good beds to sleep in, and good nurses when sick . . . The measles, mumps, chicken pox, smallpox and about everything else has broken loose and taken hold of the boys. . . ."

In Murfreesboro, invitations were out for a big ball to be held the day after Christmas. But the day after Christmas General Rosecrans started out from Nashville, and soon all festivities in the Confederate camp were forgotten or postponed indefinitely. The two armies would fight for control of middle Tennessee's railroads and rich farms. More significant, this would be the first big battle in the Union campaign to split the southeastern Confederacy, driving along the line of the railroad from Nashville through Chattanooga to Atlanta, the campaign that would finally end with Major General William T. Sherman's "March to the Sea" and capture of Savannah in December 1864.

Marching Through Middle Tennessee

The Federal army, as it moved out toward Murfreesboro on December 26, was divided into three organizations, led by Major Generals Alexander McDowell McCook, Thomas Leonidas Crittenden, and George Henry Thomas. All were re-

spected. But of the three, McCook, who had served on the frontier fighting Indians and as a tactical instructor at West Point, was somewhat arrogant. He irritated many people. "General McCook prides himself on being General McCook," drily observed one Union soldier at Nashville.

Crittenden was a son of the distinguished Kentucky senator, John C. Crittenden, who had tried so hard to work out a compromise between North and South in the tense weeks before the Southerners' bombardment of Fort Sumter ignited the war in April 1861. His older brother, George B. Crittenden, was a general in the Confederate army. With a thin, staring face and hair hanging to his coat collar, Thomas Crittenden's appearance, some thought, was rather wild looking.

The best commander in Rosecrans' army was George H. Thomas, an 1840 West Point graduate, with experience in the Second Seminole War, the

This general map shows the routes of Rosecrans' three wings from Nashville to the vicinity of Murfreesboro. The march, which started on December 26, was retarded by Wheeler's cavalry, so Rosecrans did not arrive northwest of Murfreesboro until December 29. On the 30th, both sides made moves preparatory to attacking on the 31st. (CWTI Collection)

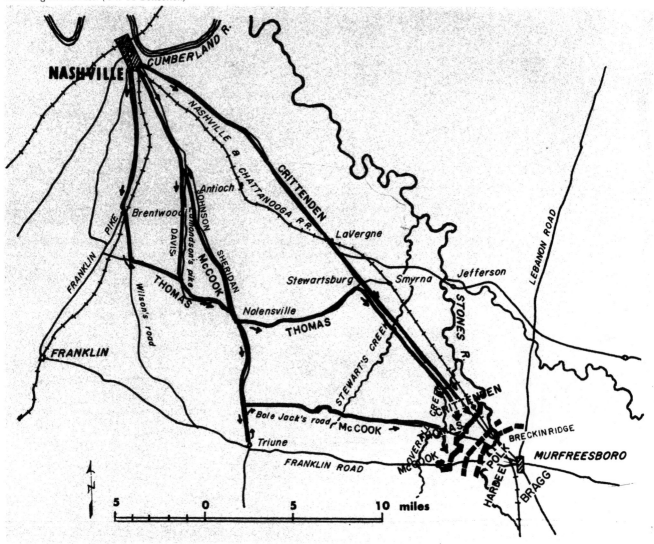

"Dragging Artillery Over the Mountains." Rosecrans' army marched nearly thirty miles, moving men, animals, artillery, and equipment through drenching rain and over muddy roads to the Murfreesboro battlefield. (Harper's Pictorial History of the Great Rebellion)

Mexican War, and as an artillery and cavalry instructor at West Point. An army man all his adult life, the general's later exploits would earn him such sobriquets as "the Rock of Chickamauga" and "the Sledge of Nashville."

Thomas' command was to constitute the center of the Union army, with Crittenden and McCook on the left and right wings, respectively. Uncertain about where the Confederates would decide to make a stand, Rosecrans speculated that Stewart's Creek, a stream several miles west of Murfreesboro with steep banks offering natural defensive advantages, could be the site. Wherever the confrontation came, the Federal commander decided to march his columns along different roads, but in position to support one another if necessary.

Crittenden's troops, on the left, moved southeast, out the Nashville-Murfreesboro Turnpike through La Vergne, about 14,500 strong. McCook's force of approximately 16,000, the largest of the three, was farther to the west, marching in a more southerly direction through Nolensville and Triune. Thomas' 13,500 men started out the Franklin Road, tramping almost due south until they reached Brentwood, then swung eastward across McCook's rear, ultimately to come into place as the center of the Union army.

An Illinois soldier said the march "began in a drenching rain." It created, he thought, "the worst mud I ever walked in." Indeed, the weather was miserable. "A cold rain fell the greater part of the night," an Indiana soldier reported, "and, as we were not permitted to have fires, we were very uncomfortable."

As the Union army pressed its advance, heavy skirmishing and sometimes small-scale fighting terrorized unfortunate civilians who found themselves in the path of destruction. Confederate Colonel Arthur Middleton Manigault, some two-and-one-half miles west of Murfreesboro on the Nashville Pike, recalled watching an unfortunate farmer's heavily loaded wagon, "his household goods piled to an immense height, far beyond what one would suppose to be the capacity of the vehicle, women and children occupying every available position, apparently at great risk to their necks." Horses, cows, sheep, hogs, and pigs formed an attendant drove, said the South Carolina officer, "in charge of the lads or Negroes belonging to the family, the proprietor himself assisting in some way or superintending everything, leaving behind his once happy home, possibly even then a heap of ashes, and seeking shelter and protection in the rear of our lines."

General Bragg, waiting to receive the Federals along the banks of the west fork of Stones River, had his army divided into two corps, one led by Lieutenant General William J. "Old Reliable" Hardee and the other by Bishop Leonidas Polk, recently promoted, as was Hardee, to lieutenant general. Hardee was already famous as the pre-war author of *Rifle and Light Infantry Tactics*, commonly referred to simply as "Hardee's *Tactics*," a manual of arms by which many of his and his enemies' soldiers drilled. Polk, a West Point graduate, had been a missionary bishop to the Southwest, the Episcopal bishop of Louisiana, and founder of the University of the South, before casting his lot with the Confederacy.

It was the railroad from Nashville to Chattanooga that gave the community of Murfreesboro military importance. The railroad passed through the heart of the little town that Polk and Hardee were charged with defending. But Bragg's decision to hold a position on the western edge of Murfreesboro, along the banks of Stones River, was questionable. The normally rich Stones River valley had already been depleted of much food and cattle by Nashville's Yankee garrison. The Federals' advance required a supply line, whether by pike or rail, of only thirty miles from their Nashville base. The Confederate army's rail link with its supply base at Chattanooga was 100 miles long, and there was no direct pike for wagon transportation.

Worse, Murfreesboro could be easily flanked. The only approach readily blocked was the Nashville & Chattanooga Railroad. The Lebanon Pike, which led due north from Murfreesboro, was a very good possible route for a Federal flanking attack. And still another road led into the town northeast of the pike

to Lebanon. Concerned for this northern flank, Bragg stationed Major General John C. Breckinridge's five-brigade division, the largest in the army, on the east bank of Stones River. Breckinridge's task was to guard the Lebanon Pike, as well as occupy Wayne's Hill (the name is of later vintage), a strategic elevation that could command much of the ground on the river's west bank.

Murfreesboro was also vulnerable from the west and south, by the pike from Nashville through Triune. From Triune an army could march upon Murfreesboro by the road from Franklin, or swing farther to the southeast and then approach along the road from the hamlet of Salem.

Just as Rosecrans was unsure of Bragg's plans, so Bragg was in a quandary as he attempted to fathom

Murfreesboro courthouse, 1863. During the Civil War the town's name was spelled "Murfreesborough." It was named for Colonel Hardy Murfree, an American Revolution soldier who once owned some village land. Stones River was named for Uriah Stone, who almost 100 years earlier had followed the stream inland from its confluence with the Cumberland. (Library of Congress)

Rosecrans' intentions. Bragg, in the first place, had not expected the Union army to advance. His intelligence reports, from questionable sources, were confusing and misleading. When the Federals began moving out of Nashville the day after Christmas, Bragg groped for information, not sure their march was anything but a demonstration in force. While a cold drizzle soaked the ground in the dawn hours of December 27, Bragg, still uncertain of Rosecrans' plans, realized his army was in a perilous position and began drawing it together.

For almost three days, Bragg did not know where Rosecrans' army was, or from which direction the Federals would approach. When at last he succeeded in concentrating his army, Bragg's position west of Murfreesboro left much to be desired. Outcroppings of limestone ledges, heavy woods interspersed with open farmlands, and cotton fields lined with rail fences characterized the landscape. Not only was much of the ground rough and uneven, and the country on every side, in General Hardee's words, "entirely open, and accessible to the enemy," but worst of all, potentially, was that Stones River split Bragg's line in two. Because of a bend in the river northwest of Murfreesboro, the Nashville Pike ran parallel to the river at the Nashville & Chattanooga Railroad for some distance before crossing the river into town. In order to block the Nashville Pike, Bragg had to place parts of his army on each side of the river, awkward positions made worse by the rising waters.

Fortunately for the Confederates, General Rosecrans' cautious advance was disturbed by Rebel cavalry. Forrest and Morgan were gone, but some 4,000 troopers under the leadership of 26-year-old Brigadier General "Fighting Joe" Wheeler, recently appointed commander of all the cavalry in the Army of Tennessee, made a two-day ride around Rosecrans' whole army. They captured approximately 1,000 Federals, burned parts or all of four wagon trains, and seized weapons and remounts for themselves. Wheeler's trail of devastation obviously could not have helped Rosecrans' confidence as he sought his enemy.

Often it has been said that both Rosecrans and Bragg, in their blind groping, decided upon the same strategy: an enveloping flanking movement against the enemy's right. While both commanders did focus on their foe's right wing, actually Bragg employed an oblique order attack from south to north (a maneuver that would steadily mass strength against one wing of the enemy's battle line until it buckled, while using smaller forces on other sectors to fasten the enemy's attention and prevent the transfer of troops to the threatened wing). Rosecrans' strategy *was* to envelop the Confederate north flank—Crittenden's corps crossing Stones River, slashing in on Bragg's right flank, driving it out of the action, opening the road into Murfreesboro, and taking the Rebel left in reverse.

As outlined to his subordinate commanders on the evening of December 30, Rosecrans' plan was for McCook to "hold all the force on his front." Thomas and Brigadier General John M. Palmer were to "open with skirmishing, and engage the enemy's center and left as far as the river," while the principal assault in force was to be made by Crittenden, east of the river: "Crittenden to cross [Brigadier General Horatio P.] Van Cleve's division at the lower ford, covered and supported by the sappers and miners, and to advance on [Confederate Major General John C.] Breckinridge; [Brigadier General Thomas J.] Wood's division to follow by brigades, crossing at the upper ford and

Confederate commanders at Stones River, from left: John C. Breckinridge, a former U.S. vice president (CWTI Collection); William J. Hardee, nicknamed "Old Reliable" (Library of Congress); Leonidas Polk, former Episcopal bishop of Louisiana (Library of Congress); Braxton Bragg, who aroused animosity in both officers and common soldiers (CWTI Collection).

moving on Van Cleve's right, to carry everything before them into Murfreesboro."

Rosecrans later explained that, "This would have given us two divisions against one, and as soon as Breckinridge had been dislodged from his position, the batteries of Wood's division, taking position on the heights east of Stones River, in advance, would see the enemy's works in reverse, would dislodge them, and enable Palmer's division to press them back, and drive them westward across the river or through the woods, while Thomas, sustaining the movement on the center, would advance on the right of Palmer, crushing their right; Crittenden's corps, advancing, would take Murfreesboro, and then, moving westward on the Franklin road, get in their flank and rear and drive them into the country . . . with the prospect of cutting off their retreat and probably destroying their army."

Meanwhile, Bragg planned to leave Major General John C. Breckinridge's division on his right, to hold the high ground on the east bank of Stones River, while the rest of Hardee's corps massed on the left of his line, west of the river, and smashed into the Yankees' right wing. He outlined his plan of attack in his "After Action" report: "General Hardee was ordered to assail the enemy at daylight on Wednesday, the 31st, the attack to be taken up by Lieutenant General Polk's command in succession to the right flank, the move to be made by a constant wheel to the right, on Polk's right flank, as a pivot; the object being to force the enemy back on Stones River, and, if practicable, by the aid of cavalry, cut him off from his base of operations and supplies by the Nashville pike."

Bragg's plan was probably too ambitious. An oblique order attack is most often used to turn a defender's line away from an objective located behind his rear, but at Stones River the maneuver was questionable. The Nashville Pike and the railroad ran at a diagonal away from the direction of attack, necessitating a three-mile advance across broken, wooded terrain before reaching Bragg's stated objective. The general discovered an oblique order attack is difficult to coordinate. Subordinates need visibility to properly conduct the wheeling motions associated with the movement. Considering distance and terrain, the maneuver was asking too much of his troops and commanders.

As both generals planned their attacks (each choosing to begin his assault early on the morning of December 31), Rosecrans decided he would deceive Bragg, making the Confederate commander think the Federal right was longer and stronger than was actually the case. To insure that Bragg would not strengthen the northern end of his line, Rosecrans ordered campfires built hundreds of yards beyond McCook's right, creating a phantom battle line in the black December night. The strategy worked, but the result was not what Rosecrans had intended. Bragg believed the Federal lines did extend far into the distance, and so simply ordered his attacking columns to sweep more widely to the west. Consequently, when they struck, Bragg gained the ascendancy by moving first. The Rebels came in at a more advantageous angle, extending far beyond McCook's flank.

December 30 was a dreary day. "Rain had fallen almost constantly," reported A.M. Crary of the 75th Illinois Infantry, "and the soldiers were saturated with water. Toward night the wind swept coldly from the north, and . . . no [forward] bivouac fires were allowed . . . " A soldier in the 90th Ohio Infantry said that some of the men, "having lost their blankets and knapsacks, suffered terribly from the cold."

While several officers sat perched on fences, warming themselves at their own nearby fires, Colonel Julius P. Garesché, the assistant adjutant general (chief of staff) to Rosecrans, kept apart from the rest. His cold hands partially covered by a greatcoat, this 21-year-veteran of the Regular army (a man who had refused a commission as a major general following the fall of Fort Sumter, saying he would earn his stars on the battlefield) was reading Thomas a Kempis' *Imitation of Christ*. This battle was to be his baptism of fire.

As the fight drew near, Garesché remembered an impelling and macabre circumstance: an old woman in Washington predicted, years before, he would be killed in his first battle. And, a little more than a year earlier, his own brother, a Catholic priest, was reported to have prophesied the same. Garesché showed no evidence of fear, but he did not expect to survive the next day's engagement.

Over on the Confederate lines, another man had a strong premonition of death. Frank Crosthwait, Company E, "Smyrna Grays," 20th Tennessee Infantry, had a brother Shelton, who was killed at the engagement of Fishing Creek in southern Kentucky in January that year, and another brother, Bromfield, who died at the Battle of Corinth, in October. As the Battle of Stones River approached, Frank Crosthwait expected to die.

A Federal soldier later recalled that Brigadier General Joshua W. Sill, commanding the 1st Brigade, 3rd Division of McCook's corps, came in from the cold to see his aide, who had been severely wounded during the day's skirmishing. The Yankee's attention was fixed upon the general. "Just before leaving," he said, General Sill "stood for a while leaning on his sword, wrapt in deep thought, and I imagined a shade of sadness on his fine face. The next morning, when he was killed almost instantly at the opening of the battle, I wondered whether some sad presentment of his fate was not passing through his mind as he stood the evening before, gazing silently upon his wounded aide."

Assaulting the Left

Dawn, Wednesday, December 31, was cold, wet, and miserable. Rosecrans' orders called for the opening attack by Van Cleve's division to be launched at 7:00 a.m., and some of the Union camps were stirring, although others continued to sleep. On the Federal right, McCook's sleepy-eyed Yankees gazed upon the dismal, winter landscape of dark cedar thickets and forlorn cotton and corn fields. Some of the soldiers were preparing breakfast, officers generally expecting the battle would begin an hour later and three miles away at the other end of the line.

Rosecrans believed his planned attack against the Confederate right would relieve any potential danger to McCook's troops. Despite the confidence of the Union commander, a few of McCook's soldiers had been very uneasy about the signs of Rebel activity just beyond their lines. Long before daylight, about 4:00 that chilling winter morning, Brigadier General Philip H. "Little Phil" Sheridan assembled his division under arms, cannoneers at their pieces. He had been strongly encouraged in making such preparations by Joshua Sill, commanding Sheridan's 1st Brigade, camped on the division's right.

Although General Sill would not survive the battle to make a report, J.H. Woodard was with Sill at his headquarters sometime before midnight. Woodard later wrote that as he looked east and south from Sill's headquarters, large bodies of enemy troops could be detected in the distance passing across the Union front toward the right of the Federal army. Sill said the movement had been going on since dark and probably indicated the Rebels were massing in force for a strike against the Union flank. His apprehension growing steadily, Sill mounted up and rode to Sheridan's headquarters, where he found "Little Phil" awake and also concerned. The two soon went to consult McCook, but their commander did not seem impressed by their fears of a Rebel attack. Sheridan and Sill took action anyway.

Unfortunately for this Union army, McCook's other division leaders, Brigadier Generals Jefferson C. Davis and Richard W. Johnson, did not take the same precautions. And this was not because they had failed to receive any warning. Shortly before daylight, McCook seemed to have second thoughts and sent a message to both men, saying he was apprehensive that an attack would be made upon his lines at daybreak. He instructed that their men be under arms and on the alert. But all Johnson and Davis did was relay the order to their brigade commanders. They did nothing to insure that the order was obeyed, although Brigadier General Edward N. Kirk, a brigade commander in Johnson's division, who, like Sill, would be mortally wounded during the first few minutes of the Confederate attack, did get his men up and under arms with a picket line covering their front and flank.

Then, in the gloomy half-light, shortly after 6:00, the Confederate infantry streamed out of the clumps of black cedars, charging toward the Federals' extreme right, near the juncture of Grisham Lane with the Franklin Road. The full force of their assault fell on the brigades of Kirk and Brigadier General August Willich, both of Johnson's division.

Though Kirk's men were up and under arms, just before the attack some of the artillery horses were unhitched and taken to water. It was at this instant that the yelling Rebels came stampeding into them. The resulting confusion was compounded when General Kirk was mortally wounded.

Willich was not with his brigade, having gone to see Johnson. His men were cooking and eating breakfast, their arms stacked. Willich, returning, rode right into a group of Confederates and was captured before giving an order—except to the Rebels whom he mistakenly supposed were his own troops. Instantly, somebody shot his horse and one of the Confederates to whom Willich had been giving orders curtly informed the general that Confederate officers wore a different colored uniform from the one he had on. Dismay and panic swept Willich's brigade, made worse by the terrorized men of Kirk's brigade who, racing pell mell for the rear, ran directly through the ranks of Willich's command, trampling some of his men into the ground.

Certainly not all the Yankees ran. Many of the surprised Federals fought gallantly. But, overmatched and confused, they were forced to give ground. And perhaps there were a few who neither fought nor ran. According to J.A. Templeton, Company I, 10th Texas Cavalry (dismounted), writing some years later: "I noticed one of their dead some two hundred yards to their rear who had been killed still holding firmly to his pot of coffee."

Nine months earlier the Confederates had shocked a Union army early on a beautiful Sunday morning at Shiloh Church, Tennessee. There also, Hardee's corps spearheaded the charge that initially overwhelmed the startled Federals. As at Stones

River, the onslaught at the Battle of Shiloh had come from the south, at the same time of morning, and resulted in panic, sending Yankees fleeing from the front lines. "The truth was," acknowledged a Federal medical attendant, "we were surprised and 'Shiloh' was the word we exchanged when we had time to reflect."

A key to Confederate success was the role of Major General John P. McCown. With three brigades of infantry in the Confederates' advance division, he was to drive in and hit the Federal flank near the junction of Gresham's Lane, running north from the Franklin Road. McCown *should* have swung his division gradually to the right as he moved forward, smashing the Union flank and driving along the length of the enemy line, while subsequent Rebel attacks were launched from left to right. Yankee defenders would have faced threats on their rear and flank from McCown's units, as well as simultaneous assaults in their front. Instead, McCown continued northwest, veering away from his proper line of advance, while Confederate Major General Patrick R. Cleburne's division was turning to the north.

Within a few moments enemy skirmishers were firing all along Cleburne's front, and the general realized McCown's division had disappeared. Cleburne, an Irish immigrant, a veteran of Her Majesty's 41st Regiment of Foot, was not a West Point graduate like McCown. But he quickly demonstrated he was more than a former Royal Army corporal. Recognizing the gap being left in McCown's wake, Cleburne put skirmishers forward immediately and moved up his division to continue the attack and maintain momentum. Cleburne's division swept onward for several hundred yards across ground obstructed by numerous fences and thickets and raked by musketry. Then it hit a solid line of Federals, some waiting in a large cedar brake and others positioned in an open field.

Meanwhile, the front brigades on the left side of Polk's corps were driving in on the right of Cleburne and McCown, as Confederate Brigadier General John A. Wharton's cavalry swung around the Federal right, slashing at their right and rear.

Johnson's Federal division was routed and the Confederates fell upon Jefferson C. Davis' division with great impact. Davis' troops only delayed the Confederates long enough for Sheridan to prepare his division to receive the first shock of attack, before they joined Johnson's men in rapid retreat.

The Confederates, in double line of battle, drove the Union soldiers, with great slaughter on both sides. For nearly two miles, through the cedar brakes toward the Nashville Pike, the Federals ran until they managed to establish a new line, manned by infantry and artillery, along the intervening Wilkinson Pike.

But in driving the Yanks, the Rebel advance gradually lost coordination and momentum. Intermingling of units was a problem. For example, Brigadier General St. John R. Liddell, leading the brigade on the left of Cleburne's division, became separated from Cleburne by following the movement of McCown's command. And some of the men in gray were fatigued and their ammunition exhausted. Time was lost in replenishing supplies and in reorganizing.

On the right of Cleburne's division, the Rebel attack was experiencing more problems and confusion. There, on the eve of battle, Leonidas Polk rearranged his corps command structure so that his two division leaders, Major Generals Jones M. Withers and Benjamin F. Cheatham, were each directing part of the other's division. This probably contributed to the confusion that characterized the Confederate assault.

It was Withers' men who first struck Sheridan's command, the left division of McCook's corps, and suffered the first Confederate repulse. Sheridan's Yankees received the Rebel attack on terrain that was largely cultivated, offering little cover. But they threw back three successive attacks by Cheatham and Withers.

Cheatham's attack was not coordinated. Colonel J.Q. Loomis, directing the far left brigade on Cheatham's front, was late moving forward. About 7:00 a.m. Loomis' troops charged across a cornfield and open woods and ran head-on into Joshua Sill's brigade of Sheridan's division. Making the situation worse for the Rebels was the failure of the brigade on Loomis' right, that of Colonel Arthur M. Manigault, to advance until about 8:00 a.m. Cheatham then had to commit both supporting brigades, led by Colonel A.J. Vaughan and Brigadier General George Maney, in the first hour of the fight.

Maney's brigade soon suffered casualties under shelling from a Federal battery. Maney, however, believed the shells were coming from a Confederate battery, and refused to fire on the gunners. Finally, in desperation, Captain Thomas H. Malone, Maney's adjutant general, certain the shelling came from the enemy, went to the front and ordered a Confederate battery to fire on the Federals. This was done with good effect, and division commander Cheatham appeared and ordered a charge.

But Maney, still believing the canoneers were Confederates, at first refused to charge. Captain Malone later described this incident: "I found General Cheatham vehemently urging him to attack the line that had supported the battery, asking, why, in the name of sense, he made such delay and did not comply with his orders. General Cheatham was manifestly somewhat excited by drink, and General Maney called my

Confederate major generals, from left: Patrick R. Cleburne (CWTI Collection) and Benjamin Franklin Cheatham (Alabama Department of Archives & History).

attention to that fact and gave it as a reason for still hesitating to obey the order. But General Cheatham vehemently insisted. . . ." At last Maney's men charged and drove the Federals away.

Cheatham was a native Nashvillian, descended on the maternal side from James Robertson, founder of the city. A powerfully built, fierce fighter, his physical strength and cursing became legendary. So, too—if the allegations of some are accepted—did his drinking. Apparently, at least upon this occasion, Cheatham identified the enemy more clearly when drunk than did Maney when sober.

As Manigault's brigade moved forward to join in the fight, a conspicuous act of heroism led to one of the rare events on any battlefield of the Civil War— promotion on the field for distinguished gallantry. Company A of the 10th South Carolina Infantry was deployed as skirmishers when a squadron of Yankee cavalry swept in from the flank, capturing the company's commander, Lieutenant C. Carrol White, and several of his soldiers. Although a prisoner, Lieutenant White called out to the rest of his men in a loud voice, "Company A! Rally on the right!" The men rallied but were reluctant to fire, fearing that they

would kill their captured comrades. White then shouted, "Don't mind us. Commence firing!" White and his fellow prisoners dropped to the ground, his order was quickly obeyed, and the deadly fire from several score Enfield rifled-muskets flew into the enemy ranks, emptying many saddles. Rising up instantly, White and the others grappled with their captors, who soon found that they had become the prisoners. Lieutenant Francis S. Parker, aide to General Bragg, happened to be on that part of the field and observed White's unusual example of both presence of mind and courage. Parker reported the incident to Bragg, and the general immediately ordered Lieutenant White promoted to captain.

Manigault's brigade, making three charges in this sector of the battle, sustained a heavy loss in officers and men. In Vaughan's brigade, the horses of every officer of the field and staff, except one, and the horses of all the officers of the field and staff of every regiment, except two, were killed. One-third of the entire force of Vaughan's brigade was lost in this effort.

The Rebels were paying an awful price, but at last mustered sufficient manpower. Cleburne's division pressed in to support Wither's left, as Confederate brigades of Colonel J.G. Coltart (replacing Colonel Loomis, who was disabled by a large limb sheared from a tree), Vaughan, Maney, and Manigault, hammered relentlessly at the Yankee stronghold. Units led by Brigadier Generals J. Patton Anderson and Alexander P. Stewart assaulted Sheridan's left, posted south of the Wilkinson Pike, and pounded Brigadier General James S. Negley's division of Thomas' corps north of the pike.

Sheridan was at last compelled to withdraw. He tried establishing a new line stretching from the Gresham house and bending back to the north, where Colonel George W. Roberts' brigade would anchor the position just south of the Wilkinson Pike. But the strength of the Confederate attack was too great. Roberts' brigade, for example, threw back three infantry attacks only to ultimately retreat again. Colonel Roberts died in the carnage.

Another of Sheridan's brigades, led by Colonel Frederick Shaefer, was out of ammunition. Sheridan's right flank was unsupported. The rest of McCook's corps had already been driven farther north. Once more Sheridan's division fell back, finding a new line of defense in the cedars north of the Wilkinson Pike.

By 10:00, McCook's 16,000 men, the largest corps in Rosecrans' army, was forced from its line of battle and sent reeling back through the cedars. Only Sheridan's division had been able to conduct a fighting retreat and continue in action. Davis' and Johnson's divisions were driven for three miles to the Nashville Pike. There, remnants regrouped between the railroad and the pike. Two-thirds of the Federal right was wrecked, the center fallen back.

Sheridan's brigade made one more stand, completing a decisive fighting retreat, saving the Federal army at Stones River. It was a brave withdrawal, possibly unsurpassed during the Civil War. By their actions, these soldiers occupied large numbers of the attacking force and allowed commanders of panicked Union units time to organize new defense lines far behind their original positions.

Sheridan's Federals were in a position described by one of its defenders as "a confused mass of rock, lying in slabs, and boulders interspersed with holes, fissures, and caverns which would have made progress over it extremely difficult even if there had been no timber." But there was timber, a brake of cedars whose trunks "ran straight up into the air so near together that the sunlight was obscured." Sheridan then occupied better defensive ground than he had been driven from earlier. Also, he had significant support from other Union divisions. Negley's division linked up at a right angle with Sheridan's left and extended northeast toward the Nashville Pike. Major General Lovell S. Rousseau's division advanced into

the cedar brakes, coming up on Sheridan's right and rear. Rosecrans ordered Van Cleve's division to take position on the right of Rousseau, while Colonel Charles G. Harker's brigade was sent still farther to the right of Van Cleve. On the other end of the Federal line, Brigadier General John M. Palmer's division took position to the left of Negley's soldiers, extending itself northeastward across the Nashville Pike toward the river, there linking up with Colonel George D. Wagner's brigade of Wood's division, completing the left of the Union line and anchoring it on the river.

The key divisions were Sheridan's, with Rousseau's and Van Cleve's to his right and Negley's on his left. The Yankee situation depended greatly upon whether there would be time for the rest of Thomas' corps, reinforcements from Crittenden's corps, and stragglers to re-form so that the Union line could be bent back—"refused," in the language of Civil War dispatches—along the southern side of the Nashville Pike.

Rousseau's and Van Cleve's troops engaged Cleburne's Rebel division and McCown's re-formed command in a furious fight. Then a gap in the Yankee line gave the Confederates an opportunity. The grayclads charged into the opening between Colonel James P. Fyffe's brigade of Van Cleve's division and Harker's brigade. Outflanked on his right, Fyffe fell back, as the Rebels applied pressure all along Van Cleve's front, forcing the rest of his division to retreat. Apparently it was also the right flank of Rousseau's division that first collapsed in the face of Confederate pressure. As troops from Rousseau's and Van Cleve's divisions retreated toward the Nashville Pike, the right flank of Sheridan's division was once more in peril.

It was about 11:00 a.m., possibly later, when Sheridan's division withdrew from the cedars. It had lost more than one-third of its fighting force, with three brigade commanders killed (Sill, Schaeffer, Roberts). It was also out of ammunition. Sheridan's withdrawal forced the withdrawal of Negley, whose division soon came under a heavy fire, with the enemy coming around his right flank. And in retiring, Negley had to drive some Rebels from his path of retreat while holding back an enemy column pressing his rear. After a severe fight, Negley at last reported with his two brigades—less some guns left behind—to General Thomas, who then had his corps together.

By noon the Federals had been driven back to what turned out to be their final defensive position. The Federal line was doubled back like a half-opened jackknife, until its right wing was at right angles to

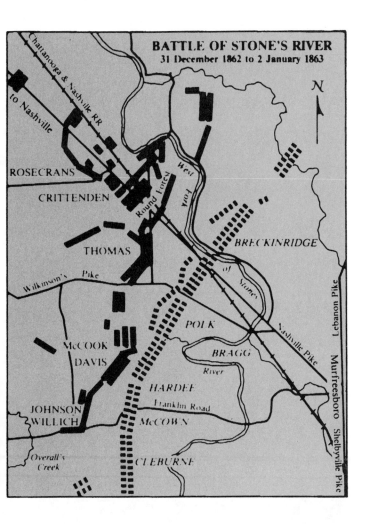

BATTLE OF STONE'S RIVER
31 December 1862 to 2 January 1863

the Union line, the Confederates very possibly could have destroyed McCook's entire corps and won the battle. It was not to be. The Confederate assault, though devastating, was not fatal.

Meanwhile, Rosecrans had used the time Sheridan and the others bought him to good advantage—even though the struggle had been raging for an hour before the Federal commander realized the crisis he faced. Near the left, or northern, flank of the Union position, Rosecrans had first thought the distant noise of musketry on the army's right wing indicated McCook was carrying out his instructions. The general was confident McCook held the Rebels' attention with a spirited demonstration on the right, while Crittenden's Federals moved into attack position. One of Crittenden's divisions was already crossing Stones River, and the other two were prepared to follow.

"Tell General McCook to contest every inch of ground," Rosecrans told a courier. The man had reported that McCook's corps was being assaulted and needed reinforcements. McCook neglected to report the rout of Kirk's and Willich's brigades and the withdrawal of Davis' division, misleading Rosecrans about the actual situation on his right. "If he holds them," said Rosecrans, "we will swing into Murfreesboro with our left and cut them off." He assured his staff, "It's working right."

When news of General Sill's death came, Rosecrans looked grim but said, "We can not help it. Brave men must be killed."

But the rising din of battle on the army's southern flank, coming continually nearer, was obviously more than the sound of a holding action.* Aware at last that the Confederates were engaged in an all-out attack against the right flank, Rosecrans ordered Crittenden to have Brigadier General Horatio P. Van Cleve's division, which had not yet advanced against Breckinridge's troops, to recross the river. Two brigades of Brigadier General Thomas J. Wood's division, already heading for the ford, were instructed to reinforce the army's collapsing right at once. Wood's other brigade and Brigadier General John Palmer's division were to hold their ground between Stones River and Thomas' corps.

As Wood headed his horse in the direction of the fighting, he yelled back to Rosecrans, "We'll all meet at the hatter's, as one coon said to another when the dogs were after them!" Considering the dire situation, Rosecrans likely found little humor in Wood's joke.

the original line of battle. It still, however, protected the Nashville Pike and the railroad.

Bragg's plan to cut off the Federals from their Nashville base went unrealized. Although it had surprised, mauled, and driven much of the right of the Union line for nearly three miles, the Rebel assault gradually lost momentum. Several factors contributed to this. Key personnel had been lost. (For example, when Brigadier General James E. Rains, directing the advance of his troops against an enemy battery, fell, shot through the heart, his brigade recoiled in confusion.) Improperly executed wheeling tactics resulted in inefficient use of manpower. Organizational and leadership problems also contributed to a weakening of the attack. And in order to plug the gaps in the line, the Rebels committed their reserves to the attacking force. Bragg had made no provision for reinforcements to rejuvenate the original Confederate thrust. A part of Breckinridge's division, the largest in this Southern army, might have been used for the purpose. But in those vital morning hours it was idle on the opposite side of the river. By continuing to press their advantage, pounding the weakest part of

---

*The tumultuous, ear-splitting noises were diminished by distance and an atmospheric peculiarity, "Acoustic Shadow." This may help explain how the battle raged for more than an hour before Rosecrans realized not only that his plan had gone awry but that the army was facing imminent disaster.

"At The Hatter's"

In the bedlam behind the Nashville Pike, an observer saw Colonel Julius P. Garesché dismount and enter a small grove of trees. Then, after opening his prayer book and reading for a few moments, he remounted and joined Rosecrans.

The commanding general had taken personal responsibility for forming a new defensive line. It would be at a right angle to the old line, cutting across the path of both Federals trying to escape and Rebel pursuers. Detached companies, regiments, and pieces of artillery, streaming through the cedars to the south of the Nashville Pike, were halted and placed in patchwork alignment facing the enemy. Shouting encouragement to spur the flagging spirits of his men, Rosecrans rode along the lines and across the open fields. In full view of Confederates drawing ever closer, he became a prime target. Following close to the commanding general were his chief-of-staff and two orderlies.

Colonel Garesché thought Rosecrans was recklessly exposing himself to death and pleaded with him to be more careful. "Never mind me," Rosecrans is reported to have replied to his friend who was also a

William S. Rosecrans worked well with common soldiers and subordinate officers but not with superiors. (National Archives)

Colonel Julius Garesché. More than being Rosecrans' chief of staff, Garesché was his personal friend. (National Archives)

Catholic. "Make the sign of the cross and go in." The only way to be safe, he said, was to destroy the enemy. "This battle must be won," he kept repeating.

In spurring from one part of the field to another, near the Nashville & Chattanooga Railroad, Rosecrans narrowly escaped being hit by a cannonball. The same ball tore through a cedar and decapitated his friend Garesché. According to a witness of the gory scene, as the colonel's horse plunged forward his headless body rode on for almost twenty paces then slid off. Rosecrans' coat was spattered by blood, causing many who saw him afterward to assume he was wounded. "Oh, no," he would say, "that is the blood of poor Garesché."

The new position of the Union line, as established late in the morning, created a short salient at the center. In this salient, on a slight elevation on both sides of the railroad track just east and north of the Nashville Pike, was a thick clump of trees covering about four acres. In and around this forest Rosecrans assembled several brigades and backed them up with artillery on high ground in rear of the infantry position. "After Action" reports referred to the general area of this stronghold as the Round Forest, the name by which local citizens knew it. Before the day was over, however, it became known to the soldiers who fought there by a new name, "Hell's Half Acre."

The infantry posted in the Round Forest were soldiers from Colonel William B. Hazen's and Brigadier General Charles Cruft's brigades, supported by Colonel William Grose's brigade, all from Palmer's division, and Brigadier General Milo S. Hascall's and Colonel George D. Wagner's brigades of Wood's division.

Twice in the late morning, while fighting still raged in front of Sheridan, Rousseau, Van Cleve, and Neg-

The decapitation of Garesché, drawn by eyewitness and news artist Henry Lovie. Garesché was killed by a cannonball that almost hit Rosecrans. (The New York Public Library)

ley, the Rebels attacked up the axis of the Nashville Pike and railroad, trying to drive the Yankees out of the clump of cedars. The first Confederate assault on the Round Forest was made by Brigadier General James R. Chalmers' men of the Mississippi Brigade, troops who had been waiting forty-eight cold hours without fires in shallow trenches. Possibly they felt some sense of relief from their misery, despite the obvious risk of mutilation or death, when they were at last permitted to enter the action. And no unit, on either side, could have shown more courage that day. Serving at Pensacola, Florida, in the early months of the war, it had been dubbed the "Mississippi High Pressure Brigade" by garrison commander Braxton Bragg. On this morning, less than two years later, brigade troops, men of the 44th Mississippi, ran into battle armed only with sticks. Other brigade troops, men of the 9th Mississippi, charged on with rifles rendered wet and useless by the previous evening's rain.

Rising and charging across cotton fields, aiming themselves at one of the strongest points of the Union line, they gave the eerie Rebel Yell and rushed toward the Cowan House—a farm residence fronting the Federals' position. There they felt the full crush of enemy artillery fire. Still they advanced, some plucking cotton and stuffing it in their ears to diminish the hellish noise. Then, concealed in the cedars and posted in the field south of the pike, the Union infantry opened fire. General Chalmers was struck in the head and carried from the field. Some regiments lost a half-dozen color-bearers. The Confederate lines wavered, became disorganized and fell back, leaving a third of their numbers dead or wounded in the open fields.

Then came Brigadier General Daniel S. Donelson's brigade of Tennesseans from Cheatham's division. It was near noon when these men surged across the same ground where Chalmers' troops had been turned back.

The Cowan House, with its yard and garden fences, split Donelson's line into separate forces, with Colonel John H. Savage's 16th Tennessee and three companies of Colonel John Chester's 51st Tennessee going to the right, the rest of the brigade to the left. Leading one of the companies of the 16th Tennessee was Captain D.C. Spurlock, who had been visiting his mother and father in a hotel on the town square only a few hours before the battle. He did not advance far (one account said less than fifteen yards) when he was shot and killed, thus joining in death his brother, who had been slain only a few weeks before at Perryville. In fact, every officer in Spurlock's company was killed. A private, Wright Hackett, led the men on toward the enemy. The Yankee fire was at its concentrated worst.

Colonel W.L. Moore was out in front, leading the 8th Tennessee. As Colonel John Anderson watched, he saw Moore's horse fall and assumed that the colonel had been killed. The 8th's color-bearer, J.M. Rice, was shot down, but crawled forward on his knees, still holding the colors up, until a second bullet killed him.

The Rebels were plunging into the Federal-filled woods when Colonel Moore overtook his regiment. Unharmed, freeing himself after being pinned under his dying horse, he dashed after his regiment. Sword in hand, he was once more boldly urging his men onward when he went down, shot through the heart.

Sweeping into the woods, the Confederates fell upon the Yankees' first line. It gave way before the vicious attack. A second Union line also failed to stem the Tennesseans. But the men in gray gained only temporary success. A strong Union counter-attack soon drove them away. Then everything was just as it had been before the assault, except for the dead and the wounded.

The 8th Tennessee Infantry went into the battle with 425 men; 306 became casualties, most of them in this costly charge. In one of its companies, out of twelve officers and sixty-two men engaged, only one corporal and twenty enlisted men escaped unhurt. And what happened to the 8th Tennessee also hap-

Above: Men of the 9th Mississippi in camp at Pensacola, Florida, in 1861. These troops suffered severe casualties at Stones River on December 31, 1862. (State Photographic Archives, Strozier Library, Florida State University)

pened, roughly, to the rest of Donelson's brigade. The 16th Tennessee lost 207 of its 396 men who went into the fight. It appeared that if the Yankee salient was to be broken, the Confederate high command had to bring up reinforcements.

The Rebels prepared for what they hoped would be the final attack, a strong assault on this sharp salient at the center of the Federal line protecting the railroad and the Nashville Pike. General Bragg decided to use Breckinridge's five-brigade division, the largest in the army, still stationed on the east bank of Stones River. To Breckinridge, a son of Kentucky, had fallen the task (when Bragg had earlier feared that part of the Federal army was approaching from the north) of guarding the Lebanon Pike as well as occupying Wayne's Hill, a strategic elevation commanding much of the ground on the river's west bank. Thus his division had sat idle as the struggle raged indecisively across the river.

Though Bragg finally decided to employ Breckinridge, a combination of bad intelligence, poor leadership, vacillation, and bad judgment combined to offset the potentially decisive strength of the Kentuckian's division. Early in the day Breckinridge received renewed word that there could be Yankees coming from the north on the Lebanon road. This

Below: Colonel Beatty's Ohio men meet Cleburne's troops late on the morning of the first day of battle. By noon, the Union right and center were pushed back toward the Nashville Turnpike, though the left stood firm. (Library of Congress)

Fresh brigades of Breckinridge's division assault Union defenders of the Round Forest early on the afternoon of December 31. Terrific artillery fire drove the Confederates back. Both sides suffered shocking loses during the day's fighting. (Library of Congress)

was soon followed by a report that one of Crittenden's Union divisions had crossed the river in his front. Although these Federals rapidly recrossed without a fight, it was a long time before Breckinridge discovered that fact. Bragg also received information that Yankees were crossing the river, and he ordered Breckinridge to attack them before they advanced.

Breckinridge moved forward, engaging Federal skirmishers who remained on his side of the river. But he still did not realize most of the enemy had left his front. He halted the advance when he could move no farther without losing a precarious hold on the Lebanon Pike. At that point he received new instructions from Bragg, ordering him to pull back on the defensive and send help to Polk's corps. Bragg called, according to his own account, for two brigades. Breckinridge said the request was flexible, asking for one, or two if another could be spared.

The brigades of Brigadier Generals Daniel W. Adams and John K. Jackson were at once ordered to cross the river and march to the support of General Polk. Then Bragg changed his mind again. Convinced by the latest reports, including one from Breckinridge, that a Yankee force still threatened on the west side of Stones River, Bragg canceled the brigades' marching orders. Instead, he next, to the vexation of many, contemplated strengthening Breckinridge with two brigades from Polk.

Meanwhile, Breckinridge took care to learn the truth about reports of Federals on the east bank,

discovering no enemy either on his front nor the Lebanon road. This he reported to Bragg. New reports reaching Bragg from his own scouts provided support for this conclusion. Bragg then ordered Breckinridge to send four of his brigades across the river at once, leaving only Brigadier General Roger W. Hanson's brigade to hold Wayne's Hill, an eminence considered strategic in defense of the Confederate right and rear. Polk was at last to be reinforced. The time was near 1:00 p.m. In confusion and vacillation approximately three hours of time had been lost—and possibly the battle.

The Kentuckian gave word for Adams and Jackson, who had already started, to continue their march, while he followed with the brigades of Brigadier General William Preston and Colonel Joseph B. Palmer. By this time Bragg's attention was fixed upon the Round Forest. When the first brigades from Breckinridge arrived, Bragg soon sent them into the fiercest of the fight. Even if the assault against Hell's Half Acre failed, Bragg thought it would compel Rosecrans to withdraw enough reinforcements from the Union right to allow Hardee to reach the Nashville Pike.

After the failure of Chalmers' and Donelson's assaults, it should have been evident to Bragg that piecemeal attacks, one brigade after another, could not succeed against the Yankee salient, especially when the Federals had been given significant time (an hour or more) in which to strengthen their position and bring up ammunition. Nevertheless, when Adams and Jackson arrived from across the river, between 1:30 and 2:00, Bragg sent their units forward, one after another, across ground thickly strewn with the dead and wounded of the brigades that had gone before. They fared no better.

When Breckinridge arrived at the fight and found his first two brigades already crippled, he determined to lead, in person, the two fresh ones into the inferno called the Round Forest. On the right flank of Preston's brigade, as men formed for the charge, was the 20th Tennessee Infantry. A member of the regiment, James L. Cooper, later recorded his impressions in the diary he kept.

"Excited as I was, I looked around and thought, 'What an awfully sublime scene.' Wounded men were coming in a stream, dead were lying all around, and on every living face was seen the impress of an excitement which has no equal here on earth. . . . But the finest sight of all was our brigade ranged in order of battle, awaiting the command 'forward.' We were formed across a . . . hill on perfectly open ground, so that every regiment could be seen. . . . About the time we started forward the firing had almost ceased, and a most unearthly silence prevailed. We moved forward slowly at first . . . When we had advanced two hundred yards, the sharpshooters commenced popping away, killing and wounding numbers of our men. Our walk then quickened into a run, and the whole line dashed forward with a shout."

Frank Crosthwait of the 20th Tennessee's Company E, with his strong premonition of death, reportedly told a close companion just before the charge, "I would willingly give a limb to be safely through this fight. I shall not come out of it. When it is over, do not think I was taken unawares, for I feel the nearness of death as I have never felt it before." His friend said he replied: "Frank, I would not go into this charge feeling as you do. Keep out of this fight. You will never be criticised, for we all know your courage; and you are too useful a soldier to be spared." Frank's response, as the friend recalled, was: "I would rather die a soldier than to live a coward."

Within a few minutes Frank Crosthwait was dead. Later he was found lying with his face turned upward and his handkerchief, with which he had tried to stop the flow of blood from a severed artery, clasped in his left hand.

Shell and shot plowed through the Rebel ranks. Volley after volley of rifle fire crashed from the Federal line, tearing into the Confederates, felling them by scores. James L. Cooper was advancing in the front rank. He said his rear rank man, George Jones, was shot in the throat, killed instantly, the missile having severed a large artery. The strange

thing to Cooper was the memory of an earlier fight, where he had been advancing in the rear rank when his front rank man, Tom Brown, had also been shot in the throat.

As the sun sank low behind the cedars, the gray-clad wave of attackers rolled on. Their courage and abandon won the admiration of the Round Forest defenders. One Federal who witnessed the assault said, "the gallantry of this advance is indescribable. . . . The Confederates had no sooner moved into the open field from the cover of the river bank than they were received by a blast from the artillery . . . Huge gaps were torn in the Confederate line at every discharge. . . ."

Breckinridge's attack came nearer to success than those before. The Union defenders gave ground. But they were far from crushed, and the strength of this final, sacrificial Rebel assault waned. Breckinridge's advance stopped in the cedars. At length the short winter twilight deepened to darkness, putting an end to the day's fighting. Hardee and Breckinridge, riding along the line, concluded their troops were too weak to make another assault. They ordered the men to go into bivouac for the night.

There had been a good opportunity for Breckinridge's brigades to deliver a decisive blow. Had the four attacked together, and at once, the Round Forest would probably have fallen to them, the center of the Union line shattered, and Rosecrans been forced to either abandon the field or risk overwhelming defeat. Another good chance to win the battle had slipped from the Confederates' grasp. This was a tragic example of the piecemeal attacks that time and again foolishly destroyed huge numbers of soldiers in this war.

Both armies had suffered shocking losses but the Confederates, having driven the Federals from their positions on the right for a distance of some three miles, believed the day was theirs. Bragg triumphantly telegraphed Richmond. "God has granted us a happy New Year." Saying he had won a great victory, Bragg announced Rosecrans had been "driven from every position except his extreme left," and claimed "the enemy is falling back."

Counsel and a Plan for Disaster

The Federals were not falling back, although Rosecrans seriously considered retreat. That evening, in his headquarters by the side of the Nashville Pike, he counseled with his corps commanders about the proper course of action. McCook, whose command had just been shattered, advised a retreat to Nashville. So did Brigadier General David S. Stanley,

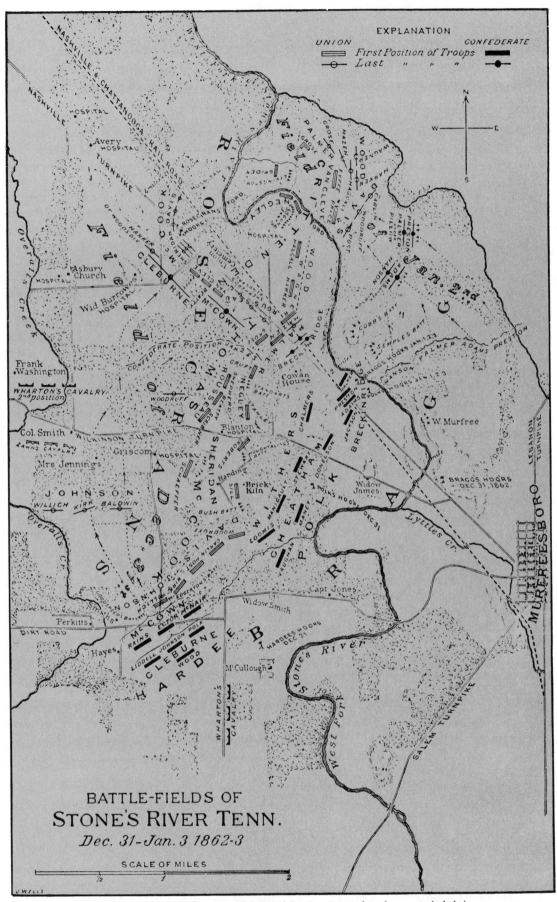

BATTLE-FIELDS OF
STONE'S RIVER TENN.
Dec. 31–Jan. 3 1862-3

SCALE OF MILES

This map shows all three days of the engagement. The Round Forest mentioned in the text included the right of Harker's first position and all of Hazen's position, field of December 31st. (Historical Times Illustrated Encyclopedia of the Civil War) commanding the cavalry. Crittenden, and possibly Thomas, assured Rosecrans they would support him in whatever decision he made.

Did Thomas play the dramatic, decisive role with which several writers have credited him? It is a moot point. Dozing through most of the conference, according to a popular story, Thomas was suddenly aroused by the mention of the word "retreat." Stoically, he muttered, "This army does not retreat, and I know no better place to die than right here." Credit has likewise been given by some to Sheridan who, picking up on Thomas' remark, is said to have sprung to Thomas' side, speaking forcefully to the same effect and requesting for his battered division the honor of leading an attack on the next day.

All these stories, while perhaps inspiring, do not alter the fact that the decision to remain and fight was Rosecrans' alone. In his report, the general explained his final decision: "After careful examination and free consultation with corps commanders, followed by a personal examination of the ground in the rear as far as Overall's Creek; it was determined to await the enemy's attack in that position; to send for the provision train, and order up fresh supplies of ammunition; on the arrival of which, should the enemy not attack, offensive operations should be resumed."

It should be noted, in regard to Rosecrans' "personal examination of the ground," that there is another version of what transpired during the night. Some contend Rosecrans, inquiring of surgeon Eben Swift if he had sufficient transportation to move the wounded, fully intended to retreat. Then, after riding out at midnight for an inspection of his lines and seeing firebrands moving in the night close to the Nashville Pike, the general concluded he was surrounded and to withdraw was impossible. Actually, Federal cavalrymen, suffering from the cold, had disobeyed orders against kindling fires, but Rosecrans assumed they were Confederates and were forming line of battle by torchlight. Only then, goes the story, did he send word to his subordinates that the army must "prepare to fight or die."

Braxton Bragg, meanwhile, convinced he achieved a great success, was certain the Federals would withdraw during the night toward Nashville. He had no evidence though on which to base such an expectation, except perhaps that, in Rosecrans' situation, Bragg would have retreated. So confident was Bragg, he appears to have made little effort even to examine his own lines or the condition of the troops he expected to lead in triumphant pursuit the next day.

While the generals made decisions, the wind blew strongly. Rain often beat hard against the fields and glades. Both sides, exhausted and badly mauled, with the number of dead and wounded in each army about the same, seemed relieved. The night, miserable though it was, finally brought an end to the fighting. In the cedar thickets and among the limestone boulders tormented men spent agonizing hours. All night long wounded soldiers, Confederate and Federal, called out for help, for a fire, for a stretcher, for water—or for death.

Uncomfortable in a cold that became still colder toward morning, amid wreckage and corpses, a Federal soldier remembered "for a long time sleep fled my eyes; the past day seemed more like a month, when measured by events and especially by the contrast between my feelings and anticipation in the morning, and our actual condition at night. This was New Year's Eve, such a one as I had never before seen."

A Confederate soldier from the 2d Tennessee Infantry remembered how men brought in all the wounded within reach, laid them in rows upon the ground, both friend and foe placed together, and then made fires between each row, in an attempt to prevent them from freezing to death.

Another Confederate of the 14th Texas Cavalry (dismounted) wrote, "the dead and wounded were thick all around us . . . Among the wounded was a Yank quite young and intelligent, shot . . . through the breast . . . We divided water and rations with him, and next morning our young Yank, with assistance to rise, could sit up for awhile."

On the Union side of the field a similar scene occurred. Henry Freeman crouched in a crevice between two rocks with a smouldering fire at one end, hardly visible a few feet away. Only a short distance from him, Freeman said, "were two severely wounded Confederates, for whom nothing could be done more than to supply water from my canteen to allay their thirst. One of them seemed very grateful. Both were dead when the morning of the new year, 1863, at length dawned . . . Some kindly hand covered their faces with their hats and spread blankets over the . . . remains. . . ."

A few of the dead were given special attention. Colonel William B. Hazen searched along the railroad tracks for the body of his friend, Julius Garesché. Locating it, Hazen removed the West Point ring from his comrade's finger, picked up the copy of *The Imitation of Christ* Garesché always carried, and sent a detail to remove the body to a less exposed place. Later in the night, on high ground at the rear of the Union left, Hazen watched a burial squad dig Garesché's grave.

Among the Confederate dead was Lieutenant R. Fred James, a young lawyer from Murfreesboro, whose colonel had sent him forward to tell some Rebel gunners that they were firing on their own troops. The colonel was mistaken. The battery proved to be a Yankee unit. James was shot down by its infantry support—falling very near his mother's farm.

A lady who went into Murfreesboro in search of her son wrote, "On entering town what a sight met my eyes! Prisoners entering every street, ambulances bringing in the wounded, where the doctors were amputating arms and legs. I found my own safe, and, on being informed that another battle was expected to begin, I set off on my way home, and passed through our cavalry all drawn up in line."

At dawn New Year's Day, Confederate skirmishers went forward all along the line, but nothing beyond a prodding action was intended. Soon it was determined that the Federals, instead of retreating, were in a strong defensive position in the new line they had established during the night and early morning. Rosecrans had modified and blunted the sharp angle in his line, withdrawing from the salient in the Round Forest. Polk's troops quickly moved up into this position. Ironically, this bastion, before which so many Rebels had courageously, uselessly sacrificed their lives, was freely relinquished to them. Rosecrans realized his position could be made stronger by not holding "Hell's Half Acre."

The day probably was not what either army expected. Neither Bragg nor Rosecrans planned an attack or a withdrawal. Before the battle, both prepared to assault the enemy's right. This morning both waited to see what the other would do. All day, the Federals reorganized and consolidated their positions. Part of Crittenden's command crossed the river again, where it formed a line of battle facing Wayne's Hill. Breckinridge, with the brigades he had brought across the river as reinforcements the previous afternoon, returned to his original posting, rejoining General Hanson's brigade east of the river. Once again, however, Breckinridge's scouts failed him, and he did not know how much strength the Federals had in his front.

Confederate cavalry under Wheeler hacked away at the Union rear, attacking wagon trains going to and from Nashville. An attack was made on the stockade at La Vergne after the capture of one of the Federal trains. This onslaught was beaten away but one of the Yankee officers later wrote, "the pressure of the enemy's cavalry in heavy force on the communications of the army . . . produced the wildest confusion from Stewart's Creek to the vicinity of Nashville. This excitement in the rear was in striking contrast with the comparative quietness reigning over the field, where each army was awaiting the action of the other."

In his official report Bragg said, "The whole day . . . passed without an important movement on either side, and was consumed by us in gleaning the battlefield, burying the dead and replenishing ammunition."

Bragg was wrong. A significant tactical movement did take place January 1, 1863, on the east bank of Stones River. While Bragg did not think about occupying the hill east of the river, overlooking McFadden's Ford, a Union division crossed the stream and claimed that strategic ground. About 3:00 a.m., Federal Colonel Samuel Beatty, who had succeeded to the command of Van Cleve's division when that officer's wound worsened, was ordered by Crittenden to move the division across the river and occupy the hill overlooking the ford.

By daybreak, Colonel Samuel W. Price's lead brigade was fording the river, a strong skirmish line from the 51st Ohio pushing out in front. Only a few hundred yards beyond the river the skirmishers flushed a Rebel outpost from Pegram's cavalry, drove it back after a short clash, and moved on to gain the high ground lying about a half-mile away from the river. The Federals were then on the scene of what would be the last major fight at Stones River.

Price massed his brigade in double line of battle, perpendicular to the river. These Yankees, sheltered by woods, looked southeast over a large field, perhaps a quarter-mile across, broken only by cornstalks from the previous year's crop and a few small buildings on their right. Price's right flank was anchored on Stones River. Colonel James P. Fyffe's brigade marched up next, filed into position northeast of Price and forward into the cornfield. Fyffe also deployed in double line of battle, with a gap of at least a regimental front between him and Price, his left or eastern flank resting "in air" on a country lane.

Beatty's third brigade, under Colonel Benjamin C. Grider, was placed astride the river; two of its regiments sat in a hollow slightly east of the stream, ready to support Price and Fyffe if necessary; the other two remained on the west bank. Meanwhile, the Confederates began sending out combat patrols from their position on Wayne's Hill, harassing Federals from about mid-morning throughout the rest of the day. Beatty became increasingly concerned about his left flank, fearing the Rebels might be attempting to divert his attention while massing troops to strike his position on its eastern extremity. Beatty's worried communiqués to Crittenden persuaded the general to send another brigade across Stones River; Colonel William Grose's command, from John M. Palmer's division, forded the stream. Near dark, however, Beatty judged that the enemy intended nothing more than harassment. Grose's brigade returned to the west bank of the river for the night.

Friday, January 2, was a cold, gloomy day. From

daybreak until near noon there was very little activity east of the river. Then General Breckinridge decided to make an estimate of the strength of the Yankee force holding the hill that commanded McFadden's Ford. Soon the familiar sounds of rifled musketry brought the front alive once more, and deep-throated artillery sounds added to the din, as Confederates tramped into the cornfield where they were greeted by the fire of Federal skirmishers. The skirmishing became severe and the Yankees first gave ground but then counterattacked and drove the Rebels back across the field. Some of the buildings in the field were set afire.

Breckinridge, in company with his son Cabel, Theodore O'Hara, and Major James Wilson, rode toward the river, coming upon Polk, Hardee, and Colonel William D. Pickett. Together they rode along the river to make a reconnaissance. Soon Hardee and Polk were summoned back to their own lines by staff officers. Breckinridge, attempting to gain a better vantage point, ordered enemy skirmishers driven in so that he could see what was behind them. This done, the general soon gained a site from where he could examine the Union bridgehead and see a sizable enemy force occupying the crest of a gentle slope partially covered with timber. These Federals were in a line almost at a right angle to the front of his own division. The intervening ground lay open for about 500 yards back from the river.

Breckinridge was trying to determine the size of the Yankee force when a staff officer from Bragg interrupted, saying the army's commander wanted to see him at once. The Kentuckian reluctantly broke off his reconnaissance and rode to Bragg's headquarters.

While this restless sparring unfolded on the east bank of the river, a noisy artillery duel raged on the west bank. Colonel Charles G. Harker, a brigade commander, said the action was "the most fearful artillery engagement" he had experienced. Brigadier General Milo S. Hascall called the Confederate bombardment "the most terrific fire of shot and shell that we sustained during the entire engagement."

The Confederates had twenty-two pieces of artillery north of the Cowan House, firing shot and shell, striking up the railroad and Nashville Pike. The Yankees quickly fought back but some of their guns were in an exposed position; others, of the 8th Indiana Battery, lacked sufficient range. Worst of all, the 6th Ohio Artillery, which had been contesting the Confederates blow for blow, suddenly found itself fired upon from the rear by the Chicago Board of Trade Battery, whose gunners apparently had mistaken the Ohio artillerists for Rebels.

Although the Confederates more than held their

own in this fierce duel, it was of no consequence. Casualty figures were relatively low. And even if the Rebel artillery dominated this action on the west bank, the coming afternoon fight would belong to the Union cannoneers.

Shortly after noon, events moved toward a conclusion. Breckinridge rode up to Bragg's headquarters along the Nashville Pike, west of the wrecked bridge that had spanned Stones River. He learned that the general expected him to attack with his division and take the high ground occupied by the Federals on his front. Bragg was particularly impressed by the discovery that Beatty's division occupied the ridge in Breckinridge's front "from which Lieutenant General Polk's line was commanded and enfiladed." Bragg deemed it "an evident necessity" that the Yankee force be dislodged or Polk be withdrawn from the advanced position he held.

Bragg decided to attack. And since Breckinridge's division, he claimed, suffered little in the battle of December 31, it was being given the assignment. But there is no evidence the commanding general of the Confederate army was familiar with either the terrain involved or the troop positions. Apparently, he had not consulted Hardee, Breckinridge's immediate superior, nor Polk, whose soldiers were allegedly threatened by the Yankee guns. (Polk shortly volunteered the opinion that the attack was not necessary for his protection.) Nor had Bragg summoned Breckinridge for the purpose of soliciting the Kentuckian's opinion, but merely to tell that officer what to do.

Breckinridge, when advised of Bragg's plan, was emphatic in voicing his objections to it. The movement was sure to be disastrous, he protested. The Federals holding the high ground west of the river completely commanded the ridge and would rake it with their guns, even if he did succeed in taking it from the Federal infantry.

Bragg was not moved. Reportedly, he said: "Sir, my information is different. I have given the order to attack the enemy in your front and expect it to be obeyed." Breckinridge was to proceed with the attack, "drive the enemy back, crown the hill, intrench his artillery, and hold the position."

The assault was to be launched at 4:00 p.m. To distract the Yankees from the real objective, a heavy fire was to be opened from Polk's front at the same time. This was done.

Dismayed by his orders, the dejected Breckinridge returned to his command and began preparations for the attack. None of his brigade commanders approved of Bragg's order. General Hanson, doomed to die in the assault, wanted to kill Bragg. Breckinridge's son Cabel later said Hanson denounced the attack order as "murderous" and was so infuriated he wanted to go to headquarters at once and shoot Bragg. General Breckinridge and Brigadier General William Preston talked him out of it. Breckinridge, however, told Preston the division would do its duty, but if he was killed, he wanted Preston "to do justice to my memory, and tell the people that I believed the attack to be very unwise, and tried to prevent it."

Meanwhile, Crittenden rode along the Nashville Pike on the west side of Stones River, accompanied by his chief of artillery, Major John Mendenhall. They observed Breckinridge's movements as he formed his division for the assault.

Excited, Crittenden ordered Mendenhall to assemble all available artillery. And within a short time after the Rebel attack began, the artillery chief had massed fifty-seven guns, completely commanding the ground on the east side of the river. Twelve of these guns were located almost a mile southwest of McFadden's Ford. Before the Confederate onslaught began, there were twenty-four guns (six batteries) emplaced on the commanding ground west of the river. After the attack started, Mendenhall moved up another fifteen guns (three batteries) from the reserve to that ridge. And when the six-gun 3d Wisconsin Battery was forced to retire across the river, it too took position on the high ground west of Stones River. So, in all, Mendenhall succeeded in massing forty-five guns on the commanding ground west of McFadden's Ford, complemented by the twelve that were positioned to the southwest. It was a murderous array of artillery.

Massing the Guns

Promptly at 4:00 Breckinridge moved forward with approximately 5,000 men. They were preceded by heavy, concentrated Rebel artillery fire. The Confederate brigades participating in this assault on the east bank of Stones River were not as numerous as those in the famous charge that broke the Union line on the last day of the 1863 Battle of Chickamauga, or the ill-fated Rebel assault that would take place twenty miles to the west at Franklin, Tennessee, in November 1864. But when Brigadier General John C. Breckinridge's colorful Confederates moved out in impressive alignment across an open field west of Murfreesboro, steadily tramping toward the Union line, they participated in a pageant unsurpassed by any of the war's more massive assaults.

Tense Yankees on the high ground above McFadden's Ford, their weapons ready, watched silently as the Rebels marched toward them. This time there would be no surprise. This time the Federals were peering down their gun sights as the Confederates came on.

The afternoon of January 2, 1863, was marked by heavy artillery action. Union gunners fired with deadly effect and forced the Confederates to fall back. (Campfires and Battlefields)

But front-line Union forces, with Colonel Price's and Colonel Fyffe's brigades lying in double line of battle, were less than 2,000 strong. Even counting Colonel Benjamin Grider's reserve brigade and Colonel William Grose's brigade from Palmer's division, the Yankees did not have 4,000 soldiers east of Stones River. The Confederates, enjoying more than a 2-to-1 advantage over the Union front line infantry, had another 2,000 cavalry at hand. Some Federals in the front line, seeing the Rebels move up the rise, doubtless knew they were significantly outnumbered.

The first Yankee volley, fired when the Rebels were within 100 yards, did not come close to arresting the Confederate charge. And there was no time to reload. The grayclads were upon them, mounting their works from end to end. The fighting was desperate, hand-to-hand, and short. Men shot their opponents at point-blank range, clubbed them with rifle butts and pistol handles, or stuck them with bayonets. Overwhelmed and demoralized, Price's brigade fled to the rear while Confederates reloaded, poured a deadly fire of musketry into their routed ranks, and screamed in triumph.

If Grider's reserve brigade could have been brought into action earlier, Price's command might have held its ground. But Grider's unit, thinking the Rebels would not attack until the next day, had stacked their weapons and relaxed. The Confederate onslaught did take this one brigade by surprise. Grabbing their rifled-muskets and hastily forming into line of battle, Grider's regiments marched to the fight at the order of their division commander, Colonel Beatty. Apparently undaunted by the desperate situation, they moved eagerly toward the battle only to be met by Price's regiments, racing headlong for the rear, running directly through their ranks.

Meanwhile, a little farther to the east, the Rebel assault reached high tide, and calamity struck Fyffe's Union brigade. When the Confederates launched their attack, Colonel Fyffe was back near the ford, talking with Colonel Beatty and General Rosecrans. Their discussion ended abruptly. A courier galloped up with news that the enemy was about to advance; Fyffe mounted and rode to his headquarters. He arrived in time to see the advancing lines of Hanson's and Brigadier General Gideon Pillow's brigades collide with Price's Yankees. Only one of Fyffe's regiments, the 44th Indiana anchoring his right flank, was close enough to give fire support to Price's line as heavy masses of Rebel infantry bore down upon it.

Fyffe told his regimental commanders to wheel their units to the right, for he intended to take the graycoats on their exposed right flank. Unfortunately, he had not reckoned with the second oncoming Southern battle line; composed of two brigades, it moved to the attack. Suddenly Fyffe realized Price's whole unit had collapsed, his own right flank was unsupported, and worse, the Rebels were closer to McFadden's Ford than he was. Fearing his brigade would be cut off, Fyffe ordered a retreat. It soon turned into a shambles. Fyffe himself was thrown from his horse and disabled. At least one of the regiments, Fyffe's own 59th Ohio, panicked and ran right through the Federals' 23d Kentucky, trampling some of its men lying behind a rail fence. In no more than thirty minutes from the start of Breckinridge's assault, three Yankee brigades were routed.

The Federals probably had enough manpower east of Stones River, if used effectively, to hold their front line. But Grider's reserve brigade never got into action until Price's front line infantry was routed. In Fyffe's front line brigade, only one regiment supplied effective flanking fire on the attacking Rebel columns driving Price. Then, when Price was overwhelmed, Fyffe's soldiers found themselves outflanked and while trying to retreat, panicked and went to pieces. Finally, William Grose's brigade, expected to anchor the Union left, was, like Grider's reserve, never in the fight until both front-line brigades had gone to the rear.

The weight of the Rebel assault, four brigades strong, went in against Price's lone brigade and two

Indiana regiments, the 79th from Grider's command and the 44th from Fyffe's brigade. The Rebel force was concentrated while the Union strength was dispersed, enabling the Confederates to dispose of the Yankee infantry in piecemeal fashion.

A glorious victory was at hand, or so it must have seemed to the jubilant Southerners. The Federal line retreated before them. Some Confederates, infantry from the 6th and 2d Kentucky and Randall Gibson's Louisiana brigade, even charged across the river in pursuit of the fleeing Yankees.

But what seemed the forerunner of victory was a prelude to disaster. As retreating Federals were pushed back toward the river, they drew the hotly pursuing Rebels down the forward slope—within range of the forty-five cannon massed on the hill west of Stones River. Union artillerists had the chance they had been waiting for, to shoot at the foe without harming their comrades. Unleashing a fierce blast, darkening the sky with smoke, striking across the river into Confederate ranks, the Federal guns dealt destruction up and down the lines. The soggy river bottom over which the Yankees had been driven became a death trap, as Federal gunners blazed away with deadly effect. For the Confederates, there was nothing reasonable to do except fall back.

When Bragg heard Breckinridge's troops were beginning to withdraw, he ordered Brigadier General J. Patton Anderson's brigade to cross the river and provide reinforcement. The battle, of course, was all over when Anderson arrived, too late for his infantry to help. Besides, the Federals had mounted a strong counterattack.

With heavy reinforcements at hand and little daylight remaining, the Yankees acted quickly, although it was apparently an impatient brigade commander who sensed that the time was right and triggered the attack. Generals Thomas Crittenden, James Negley, John Palmer, and Rosecrans looked on from the ridge that bristled with Union artillery. Colonel John F. Miller of Negley's division, without waiting for orders from his general, moved out against the Rebels. Then Colonel Timothy R. Stanley's brigade joined him, ordered forward by Rosecrans and Negley.

Cheering wildly, they surged after the retiring Confederates. The Federals realized the momentum of battle had changed. Other units joined in; thousands of Federals splashed across the stream to the east bank. Grider's and Price's shattered commands, anx-

Overleaf: Federal troops charge across Stones River on January 2. From a sketch by Henry Lovie for Frank Leslie's Illustrated Newspaper. The next day, Bragg ordered a Confederate withdrawal to the Tullahoma area, 36 miles south. The bloody Battle of Stones River was over. (CWTI Collection)

ious to redeem themselves, quickly responded. Units from Fyffe's brigade and from other commands all pursued the Rebels, forcing Southern artillery back from the ridge above the ford, compelling them to take up their original line along Wayne's Hill. Nothing had been changed by the short, bloody fight. The Yankees regained everything they had held before the assault.

Fyffe of Ohio, whose front line brigade was driven back in panic by Breckinridge's attack, was a veteran volunteer soldier and a man of many talents. An army lieutenant in the Mexican War, a veteran of the 1846 Battle of Monterrey, he later studied law and, in 1851, went to California to seek gold. A fine amateur writer, he kept an interesting journal of his California gold field adventures and his return trip to the East Coast by sea. And years later he wrote letters to his wife and mother during Civil War campaigning.

The letters he wrote following the Stones River battle help modern readers visualize the human drama of the January 2d fight. And they contrast sharply with letters he wrote before and long after the battle. His light-hearted, chit-chat approach, the continual fond and romantic references in letters to his wife, are replaced by a grave, brief, and matter-of-fact tone as he contemplates the crisis he had just survived.

"In the last day of fighting," Fyffe wrote to his mother, "the great charge made by Breckinridge's force just missed my brigade, where it stood in a single line, without any reserves whatever, and fell about two hundred yards to the right, where Colonel Beatty's troops . . . were posted, sweeping them backward like fall leaves before a wintry wind; one after the other the lines were swept away. If it had fallen on me, in place of where it did, I do not see how a single man could have escaped of my brigade . . . I hope Ma, you won't fret about the war. Somehow or other I have got to believe that it may all come out right, that the Great Being who rules over all things [will conclude it] for the best."

And to his wife, Fyffe wrote: "Lieutenant Dancer, 11th Kentucky, on my staff, was wounded in the last day's fight, and my horse, frightened by a shell, became frantic and threw me off, dragging me by the foot, . . . bruising my face and back and disabling me . . . right in the midst of a terrific charge." In a postscript, he added, "Adjt. Charles King goes to Nashville today to send Gus Pems' body home. Henry Liggett is also going to take his brother's remains . . . Tom Macabeer got back from Nashville yesterday. I had a hard time while he was gone—no wagon—no tent—no blankets—no cooking utensils—nothing to cook if we had; I tell you—we have had a 'Bad time. . . .'"

Colonel Fyffe, in spite of his troubles, was actually fortunate. William McKay, a Tennessean in the ranks of the Rebel army, was badly wounded in the thigh during Breckinridge's assault. He experienced a seemingly unending nightmare of pain and anguish. "I remained helpless and partially unconscious until our command retreated," he wrote. "I saw the Yankees coming and attempted to get up but could not. Our men moved up a battery of three guns and planted them just over where I lay. The fire from the guns was nearly hot enough to burn my face, and the Yankee bullets rattled on the gun carriages like hail."

Finally the Confederates, with most of their battery horses killed, left their guns. Suddenly, as McKay lay between the lines, fragments and concussion from a bursting Rebel shell broke his left arm and badly bruised his body. For hours he remained in the field, chilled by drizzling rain mixed with sleet, as Federal soldiers marched by and over him. "I lay where I fell until about midnight and received *brutal* treatment from some of the Yankees," McKay later recounted. "The commanders of companies would say as they passed me, 'look out men; here is a wounded man' and some of them would step over me carefully while others would give me a kick, called me a damned Rebel, and I was covered with black spots from the bruises."

At last, two Federals, searching the battlefield for a friend, took pity, secured an ambulance, and had McKay taken to a Federal hospital. The horror was far from ended. Overworked attendants, thinking he was too near dead to waste their time, laid him out on the ground. "I lay all day Saturday in the rain without any attention being paid me," he wrote. "I would ask for water they would say 'you don't need water. We will take you to the graveyard after a while.' . . ."

In the bloody charge of Breckinridge's division it must have seemed for a while as if nobody would escape unscathed. Confederate Colonel J.B. Palmer received three wounds: a shot passing through his right shoulder, another through the calf of his right leg, and a shell fragment striking one of his knees. Confederate Lieutenant L.D. Young of Kentucky wrote, "The great jaws of the trap on the bluff from the opposite side of the river were sprung, and bursting shells that completely drowned the voice of man were plunging and tearing through our columns, ploughing up the earth at our feet in front and behind everywhere. . . . While lying on the ground momentarily a very shocking and disastrous occurrence took place in Company E, . . . A shell exploded right in the middle of the company, almost literally tearing it to pieces. When I recovered from the shock, the sight I witnessed was appalling. Some eighteen or twenty men hurled in every direction."

During the initial advance, Breckinridge watched

From a lithographer's fertile imagination, "Battle of Murfreesboro—Capture of a Confederate Flag." Of the 88 Confederate regiments present at Stones River, 23 suffered over 40 percent casualties. (Tennessee State Library and Archives)

his troops move forward and cried out: "Look at old Hanson!" A short time later, Colonel W.D. Pickett saw a group of men gathered around the body of a fallen comrade, and upon closer examination found Breckinridge kneeling beside the wounded soldier, attempting to stop the flow of blood. The wounded man was General Hanson, who had been so adamantly opposed to the attack. He died a short time afterward.

Another Confederate who experienced the awful reversal sustained by the attackers said that when the order was given to retreat, "some rushed back precipitately, while others walked away with deliberation, and some even slowly and doggedly, as though they scorned the danger or had become indifferent to life. But they paid toll at every step back over that ground which they had just passed with the shout of victors. In addition to the execution done by the main body of the Federals, who had now become pursuers, they were terribly galled by Grose, who, in

the main, had held his ground, and was pouring a destructive enfilade fire into the shattered column."

The January 2d fighting was over. And it was tragic—tragic because the Confederate brigade commanders and their division commander had known it would not succeed. Having overwhelmed enemy infantry, the Rebels still confronted the Yankee artillery, which Breckinridge previously thought would doom the attack to failure. And it did.

Knowing he had been correct, but at the cost of a shattered division, must have provided Breckinridge little satisfaction. In about an hour, over 1,500 Confederate soldiers fell before the awesome power of the Federal cannon. "I never, at anytime, saw him more visibly moved," recalled a Rebel officer as he spoke of Breckinridge's conduct after the awful assault. "He was raging like a wounded lion, as he passed the different commands from right to left, but," the officer continued, "tears broke from his eyes when he beheld the little remnant of his old brigade—his personal friends and fellow countrymen; and a sorrowful exclamation escaped his lips, to find, as he said, his 'poor Orphan Brigade torn to pieces.'"

Although it took Bragg some time to admit it, this crushing blow meant that the Rebel commander's "victory" of December 31 was reversed. The general, however, never admitted the truth, except perhaps by, ultimately, retreating. But for all practical purposes the Battle of Stones River was over when the last Confederate soldier of Breckinridge's command dragged himself out of the range of the Yankee guns.

Of the eighty-eight Confederate regiments present at Murfreesboro, twenty-three suffered over 40 per cent casualties. Of the infantry regimental commanders, 40 per cent were killed or wounded. In several regiments every field officer was lost. Eight of the twenty Confederate brigades fighting at Stones River sustained more than 35 per cent casualties; 25 per cent of the infantry brigade commanders were killed or wounded.

Doubtless many of the unusually high number of Confederates listed as missing in action at Murfreesboro, 2,500, were dead or dying. Many of the wounded eventually succumbed to their injuries. Captain Peter Bramlett, 2d Kentucky Infantry, was treated by Federal surgeon Dr. F.G. Hickman. The doctor dressed Bramlett's chest and leg wounds. The captain asked if his wounds were fatal; Hickman said his chances were not good. Captain Bramlett was then carried to a shed nearby and laid on some unbaled cotton. "I gave him some water and brandy," wrote the surgeon. "The night was very cold; I got an order for a pair of blankets and placed them over him and told him that I would see him in the morning, but I failed, as he was sent to Nashville very early . . . Ten days later I saw his death announced in a Nashville paper."

A Mrs. Payne, a frequent visitor at the hospital, related "that she cared for several Confederate soldiers, one of whom was Captain Bramlett, who had died at her house. She said that when he was about to die she concluded to remove the coarse blankets and replace them with neater ones; that he caught her hand and said: 'No, do not remove those blankets, for they saved my life at Stones River. They were placed over me that cold night by the hand of an enemy, but a brother. You may come across him sometime; and if you should, tell him I died under the blankets he placed over me that night.'"

Years later, James W. Robert of Nashville, who said he was ten years old at the time of the Battle of Stones River and living in the Murfreesboro suburbs, recorded that a wounded lieutenant named Kelly from a Mississippi regiment, was brought to his father's home. One of Kelly's thigh bones was shattered. The attending surgeon said his leg would have to be am-

putated to save his life. But the lieutenant refused to submit to the operation. "He lingered two or three months," wrote Robert, "and died, and was buried at the old city cemetery. Four other Confederates were fatally wounded, and were carried to a neighbor's residence, where they all died within two weeks. . . ."

The night following Breckinridge's charge, Captain Spencer Talley of the 28th Tennessee reported to the Confederate hospital set up in the courthouse on Murfreesboro's town square and waited for the overworked doctors to examine the wound he received that afternoon. The body of his colonel, P.D. Cunningham, was brought from the battlefield and placed nearby. "When his body was brought to the Hospital my heart was full of sorrow," wrote Talley, "and regardless of my wound I secured a vessel of water and washed his blood stained face, and hands . . . I removed the stains from his coat as best I could with the cold water and a rag, combed his unkempt hair and whiskers and laid his body with many others in the Court House at Murfreesboro." Talley could not help but stare at Cunningham's torn and blood-saturated coat; it was the same one the colonel had lent him a few nights before to wear to a grand ball.

In the deluge of confusion, anguish, sorrow, pain, bitterness, and cold weather that swept over the battlefield area, a wounded Union soldier, W.H. Steele, was loaded into an army wagon and taken into Murfreesboro. Laid down on the upper floor of a brick house, he reportedly remained there three days with only a canteen of water and an ear of corn for nourishment. After the Confederates pulled out of Murfreesboro, Steele was found by his brother, who had left a hospital in Nashville to look for him. The story was told that when Steele's pants were removed, "they were so stiffened by his blood that they, being placed on the floor in an upright position, remained so as readily as two pieces of stovepipe would have done."

John Gorgas, lucky to still be alive, was more fortunate than Steele. On the picket line of the 34th Illinois at the battle's beginning, Gorgas was pulling back to the main body of troops when he was shot in the hip. Still running in spite of the wound, he was hit twice more, in the left side of the neck and in the shoulder, and fell to the ground. Fortunately, however, he was taken by the Confederates to the house of a planter who for the next several months gave him the best of care while he recovered.

Another lucky though wounded Yankee, Arnold Harrington, was captured, then fell into the hands of friends from Texas. These acquaintances from his old Texas adventures gave him all the care possible under the circumstances.

Some Confederates made the supreme sacrifice.

There was Captain Monroe Bearden. His father first heard of his son the captain being wounded some two days after the event. Sending word to his wife of what had happened, the elder Bearden started at once from Fayetteville, Tennessee, for the scene of battle. As he recorded in his diary, after a search he found his son, "wounded in every conceivable manner" and lying in Soule Female College, an institution being used as a hospital. That night, Monroe's mother and sister also arrived at Murfreesboro in a wagon, accompanied by two neighbors who wished to do what they could to help the family. The two men who accompanied them were eventually arrested by the Federals and sent north to prison. Initially it appeared Monroe was improving, but soon his plight became much more serious, and his father's diary records that Monroe died on January 22, 1863.

According to Bearden family legend, as reported by historian Robert Womack of Murfreesboro, Federals would not permit the parents to take the body from Murfreesboro. It was only after the remains were hidden under a cargo of clocks that his body was smuggled past sentries. Womack also noted that if this is true, the elder Bearden did not record it in his diary. He did record that on March 12, 1863, Captain Bearden's body was deposited "in a vault prepared for its reception in my garden, a large crowd of our friends and neighbors being present."

Who Is To Blame?

The letters, diaries, and regimental histories tell more than personal tales of horror and distress. They tell the story of the terrible, and important struggle at Stones River. It was a battle of great significance, as bloody as Shiloh—yet there were not as many men engaged at Stones River as at Shiloh. It was a fight for control of middle Tennessee's railroads and rich farms —and it secured the area for the Union. It was the first big battle in the Union campaign to seize the Chattanooga-Atlanta corridor—the campaign that finally ended with Union Major General William T. Sherman's "March to the Sea" and his capture of Savannah, Georgia, in December 1864. It was a Union victory that helped offset disasters suffered elsewhere—at Fredericksburg, Virginia, early in December 1862 and Chickasaw Bayou, Mississippi, later that month. And at a time when the possibility of European intervention on behalf of the Confederacy still seemed quite real, victory at Stones River gave the United States ambassador to Great Britain, Charles Francis Adams, more evidence that the Union could win the war—evidence he used well to discourage intervention.

Neither then, or later, was Stones River recognized for what it was. Relative to the number of men engaged, it was the bloodiest battle fought in Tennessee, and perhaps one thing more. Historian William C. Davis has written: "The guns of Stones River ceased firing on January 2, but the sound of them reverberated louder and longer than any other battle of the troubled western theater." As he eloquently put it, the intra-army feuds begun at the Battle of Stones River did lasting, irreparable internal damage to the Confederate army's high command in the West. They caused a hemorrhage from which the army would never fully recover.

Braxton Bragg at first intended to stay on the field and resume the battle on January 3d. But others had very different thoughts. The idea that the Confederate army should retreat after the repulse of Breckinridge on January 2d originated with the Kentuckian's subordinate commanders. Alone with their decimated divisions, Generals Cheatham and Withers remained west of Stones River as rain and sleet fell after dark and the river started to rise. Fearful of being isolated, shaken by Breckinridge's debacle, and lacking confidence in Bragg, Cheatham and Withers that night drafted a letter to Bragg urging that "this army should be promptly put in retreat." They said some of their men were demoralized and they feared "great disaster from the condition of things now existing" unless the army withdrew. The letter went from Cheatham and Withers through Polk, who endorsed his division commanders' judgment, remarking he greatly feared "the consequences of another engagement at this place." Then he added, "we could now perhaps get off with some safety and with some credit," provided "the affair is well managed."

When this document reached Bragg about 2:00 a.m., January 3, he read only a portion before replying briefly to Polk: "We shall hold our own at every hazard." Then he went back to bed. Polk, disturbed by Bragg's message, took up the subject with Hardee, who said he considered Bragg's decision "unwise in a high degree." But when the two consulted with Bragg the next morning they discovered the general had changed his mind.

During the night McCook's captured papers had been brought to his headquarters and, reading through them, the Confederate commander became convinced that Rosecrans had a much larger force than previously estimated. Rosecrans, he said, had 70,000 men and was receiving reinforcements. After consideration, Bragg thought they had better retreat, even though it meant abandoning hundreds of wounded men in Murfreesboro. Polk and Hardee readily agreed and the former led the withdrawal, with Cheatham's division moving out toward

Shelbyville in the early morning hours of January 4. Breckinridge's division covered the retreat as the army slowly traveled about thirty miles southeast to the vicinity of Tullahoma.

In estimating the Federal reinforcements received during the night of January 2, Bragg was probably misled into magnifying the number of Yankees added to Rosecrans' forces. Actually, only one brigade and one regiment joined the Federal force that night. The reports of Bragg's scouts might have exaggerated the number of these fresh units but deceptive actions taken by Rosecrans probably were most responsible for misleading Bragg. The Federal commander mentioned this in his report of the battle, while one of his officers described Rosecrans' scheme in more detail: "In order to deceive General Bragg, he organized a large number of men endowed with stentorian voices, who were to represent the commanding officers of companies, regiments, and brigades composing a division. As soon as these men were properly positioned, a loud voice could be heard calling out:

'Fourteenth Division, halt!' Immediately afterward other voices could be heard commanding brigades and regiments to halt, followed by a number of company commands. A few minutes intervened, and again these loud voices could be heard in the stillness of the night, giving the necessary orders by which the imaginary regiments were to take their respective camping grounds, and companies to stack arms and break ranks."

Soon after, Rosecrans ordered the men to build campfires in front of the phantom reinforcements.

The public's estimate of Rosecrans rose in the aftermath of Stones River, his first big-scale battle. President Abraham Lincoln telegraphed him on January 5, "God bless you and all with you."

Meanwhile, Bragg's image fell to a new low. Criticism had been heavy following his loss at Perryville but denouncements were even more severe when the truth was learned about Murfreesboro. Bragg's dispatches on the night of December 31 had encouraged people to anticipate a great victory. But, as at Shiloh and Perryville, at Stones River Confederate forces at first seemed successful, only to retreat in the end.

Bitter sentiments were focused upon Bragg. Newspaper editorials were aggressive and highly critical. Perhaps his greatest tormentor was the Chattanooga *Daily Rebel*, which stated the army disliked Bragg, had no confidence in him, and that the retreat from Murfreesboro was made against the advice of his generals with whom he had no rapport anyway.

The newspaper was incorrect about the retreat, of course. But its story so angered Bragg that he asked all corps and division commanders to verify in writing that they had advised a retreat. Then he went so far as to ask if it were true that he no longer enjoyed their confidence, promising to resign if his men and officers no longer believed in him. That he would make such a statement to men, none of whom liked him and some of whom despised him, simply reveals how much Bragg was out of touch with reality.

The generals supported him in the matter of the retreat though some, such as Hardee and Breckinridge, pointed out that they had not been consulted until the decision had been made. But in response to Bragg's other statement, all replied that he had lost the confidence of the army. Hardee phrased the matter straightforwardly: "Frankness compels me to say that the General officers whose judgment you have invoked are unanimous in their opinion that a change in the command of the army is necessary. In

Union troops march into Murfreesboro following the Battle of Stones River. This victory earned Rosecrans the praise of President Abraham Lincoln, who telegraphed him on January 5, "God bless you and all with you." Eyewitness sketch by Union veteran Horace Rowdon. (West Point Museum Collections)

this opinion I concur." Hardee and Polk had both asked President Davis to place General Joseph Johnston, a hero of the Virginia theater, in command. And Cheatham was said to have remarked, soon after the battle, that he would never serve under Bragg again.

The relationship between Cheatham and Bragg soon became worse. Reports that Cheatham was drunk on the first day of the battle for Murfreesboro caused Bragg to order Polk to censure that general in writing. Polk did this but in his After Action Report he also commended Cheatham for his leadership of his command at Stones River.

Bragg was angry and in his report of the battle blamed Cleburne's heavy December 31 casualties on Cheatham. He contended that the Tennessean had failed to attack promptly. Cheatham considered re-

signing from the army but his friends persuaded him to stay on.

Bragg also blamed McCown for delaying the morning attack on the first day of the battle. McCown was vocal in criticizing Bragg. Finally, Bragg ordered him arrested and a court-martial found McCown guilty of defying army regulations but not of delay on December 31. McCown was suspended from command for six months.

Bragg's longest, most bitter struggle was with John Breckinridge. The newspaper attacks on Bragg increased and at least one of the most critical came from a member of Breckinridge's staff (although done without the major general's knowledge). Bragg became convinced Breckinridge was the chief culprit, that he had turned the rest of the generals against him. By mid-February Bragg resolved to rid himself of the man he considered his chief enemy.

Bragg charged that Breckinridge was late in coming to reinforce Polk on the first day of the battle and had failed to align his troops properly or to use his cavalry effectively on the last day. He implied such failures could have cost a Rebel victory. It was contended that Breckinridge did not like Bragg personally, was angry with him over the military execution of one of his Kentucky troops a few days earlier, and was even more angry at being ordered to make the January 2d attack. Bragg believed that, consequently, Breckinridge did not give the assault his best effort, failed to coordinate the assault with supporting arms or keep his units under control, and allowed his troops to rush beyond the objective.

To support his criticisms of Breckinridge, Bragg kept busy obtaining statements from artillery Captain Felix Robertson (a corruptible man whom he coaxed into sending in a second report containing criticisms of Breckinridge), staff member George Brent, and Brigadier General Gideon Pillow (who hid behind a tree rather than accompany his brigade in the January 2d charge). Also, Bragg made a commentary on the strengths and losses of his various divisions in the Murfreesboro battle, singling out Breckinridge's for detailed analysis, using unqualified statistics to deliberately diminish the percentage of loss in the command, thus implying it had not fought well. Bragg managed to ignore the fact that two of Breckinridge's brigades suffered the most losses in the army.

The Kentuckian was almost as busy as Bragg, requesting to see Bragg's report of the battle (which the general refused to allow, having already, contrary to established army procedure, sent his own critical report to Richmond even before he received Breckinridge's report. This put his version of the battle on record first), marshalling statements from his staff members to refute Bragg's charges, and calling for a court of inquiry. Feelings were so intense that some of Breckinridge's subordinates, convinced Bragg had selected the Kentuckian as a scapegoat for his own failures, urged him to resign from the army and challenge Bragg to a duel.

This clash seemed to promise interminable difficulties. Then Breckinridge was transferred to Mississippi. Tempers cooled temporarily. But bitter feelings between the two men never subsided. The next autumn, during the critical Siege of Chattanooga, the feuding resumed.

Following the loss at Stones River, Confederate President Jefferson Davis reassessed the generalship of the Army of Tennessee, a command reeking with dissension. Davis ordered the vaunted Joe Johnston to replace Bragg. But Johnson, the Eastern hero, the replacement favored by Polk and Hardee, seemed keenly concerned that he would be criticized for having sought, perhaps even intrigued to gain, Bragg's position. And he appeared to show some sympathy for the crusty general, whose wife was then fighting a serious illness.

Johnston, once head of the Confederate army in Virginia, had suffered a serious wound in fighting around Richmond in spring 1862. It was troubling him again and providing a graceful way out of a vexing professional and ethical conundrum. Johnston reported to his president that he was physically unfit

for field duty; Bragg's presence with the Army of Tennessee was therefore required. He was to remain in command.

So a bloody battle, fought beside a little-known river and an obscure town, ended in a controversy that left the major Confederate army in the West nearly unfit to fight. Buoyed by this dissension among their enemies, as much as by their ability to battle some very famous Confederates to a standstill at Stones River, Union soldiers confidently pressed their opponents in summer 1863. Then in September came another clash with Bragg. That battle, fought along Chickamauga Creek in north Georgia, demonstrated that the Army of Tennessee could still be a lethal weapon.

The fight at Chickamauga would be a disaster for Rosecrans and his army. But in early 1863 that calamity was still many months away. For the time being, the major general commanding the Federals' Army of the Cumberland could bask in the gratitude of his countrymen and his president. In a letter written to Rosecrans on August 31, 1863, Abraham Lincoln reiterated the Union's appreciation for what the general had done. It was a sentiment that may have comforted a soldier who would know trouble in the years ahead. "I can never forget," the president wrote, "whilst I remember anything, that about the end of last year and beginning of this, you gave us a hard-earned victory, which, had there been a defeat instead, the nation could scarcely have lived over."

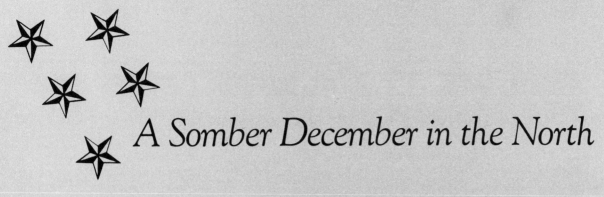

A Somber December in the North

The nation "could scarcely have lived over" a defeat at Stones River because such a defeat, had it occurred, would have come on top of two other dispiriting setbacks in December 1862. One of them was a bloody and humiliating repulse of Grant's and Sherman's first campaign against Vicksburg (described in Volume III). The second was the bloody and humiliating repulse of Burnside's attack at Fredericksburg, Virginia.

A reluctant Ambrose E. Burnside had taken command of the Army of the Potomac on November 7, after Lincoln dismissed McClellan because of his chronic caution and hesitancy. Nearly all modern historians agree with Lincoln that McClellan was incapable of a successful offensive because he had "the slows," as Lincoln graphically put it. But "Little Mac" was enormously popular with the soldiers. They gave him an emotional farewell when he left the army. Some threatened to resign or desert. A few

The Confederate repulse of Union troops at Vicksburg and Fredericksburg helped create a morale crisis in the army and on the homefront. Wrote one disgruntled Northern soldier: "I am sick and tired of disaster and the fools that bring disaster upon us." (CWTI Collection)

officers muttered darkly about marching on Washington, overturning the government, and installing McClellan as dictator. Nothing came of this, in part because
McClellan gracefully yielded command to Burnside and urged the army to follow
their new leader as cheerfully and obediently as they had followed him. Nevertheless,
morale in the Army of the Potomac plunged to a new low. Even the courageous
Captain Oliver Wendell Holmes, Jr., a future Supreme Court Justice who was recovering from a severe wound received during the Battle of Antietam, yielded to the
prevailing pessimism in December 1862. "The army is tired with its hard and terrible
experience," wrote Holmes. "I've pretty much made up my mind that the South have
achieved their independence."

This mood scarcely boded well for the success of Burnside's planned offensive. For
the new commander was about to ask his army to carry out one of the most desperate
assaults of the war.

—James M. McPherson

THE
BATTLE
OF
FREDERICKSBURG

by Edward J. Stackpole

FREDERICKSBURG, Virginia was shrouded by a
dense fog that reduced visibility almost to zero in
the wintry, pre-dawn darkness of Thursday, December 11, 1862. Pickets of Brigadier General William
Barksdale's Mississippi brigade, Confederate Army of
Northern Virginia, shivered in the raw morning air
as they stood guard along the banks of the Rappahannock River at the eastern edge of town. General
Robert E. Lee's watchdogs had for some time been
waiting for Major General Ambrose E. Burnside,
newly appointed commander of the Union Army of
the Potomac, to commence the long-awaited crossing
of his vast body of troops.

Early that morning the nocturnal quiet was suddenly broken by the sharp bark of two Confederate
cannon posted on the range of hills immediately west
of Fredericksburg. With this signal from Read's battery, Major General Lafayette McLaws, responsible
for the immediate security of the town, alerted the
sleeping Confederates of Longstreet's corps to the fact
that the Union army was at long last on the move.

THE PROSPECT of action that would end the
suspense of waiting day after day must have quickened the pulses of the men in ranks. The opposing
armies had been fully assembled in the Fredericksburg
area, facing one another across the Rappahannock,
for ten days, during which the Federal commander
deliberated in a welter of uncertainty as to when,
where, and how to initiate his offensive.

This period of watchful waiting was lightened by
an occasional snowball fight on the Confederate side
of the river, with at least one evening of conviviality
when several bored Union bands, near their end of
the partly demolished railroad bridge, decided to
break the monotony. Tuning up their instruments,
the combined bands broke into "Hail Columbia" and
"The Star Spangled Banner" without eliciting any
reaction from the Confederates. Finally they struck
up "Dixie." That broke the ice, figuratively speaking,
and caused much cheering and laughter on both sides
of the river. But the friendly concert proved a costly
bit of fun for the Federals because it aroused the
suspicions of McLaws, who promptly put his men to
work digging additional rifle pits from which his
sharpshooters would later be able to pour a lethal
fire against Burnside's bridge-building engineers.

Burnside's Initial Actions

AFTER the Battle of Antietam, fought on September 17, 1862, the two armies faced each other warily
across the Potomac. Why were they now, nearly three

months later, still confronting each other on opposite
sides of a river, but seventy-five miles farther south?

Though Major General George B. McClellan had
dallied in place almost two months after the advantage he had gained at Antietam, he finally moved
ponderously southward; early in November his army
of 120,000 men occupied the positions shown on Map
1. This placed "Little Mac" between the widely separated wings of Lee's 90,000-man army, so that by
striking each successively he might have defeated Lee
in detail. But he couldn't do it. He was too slow.

Four regiments were sent over in boats to secure a lodgement in Fredericksburg and drive Barksdale's men far enough away from the river to permit the pontoon bridges to be completed. ("Harpers")

Lee, knowing this, was unworried. Lincoln had the same opinion of the snail-like McClellan. His patience exhausted, the President relieved McClellan and placed Burnside in command of the Army of the Potomac.

Burnside, after assuming command on November 7, proposed an entirely different strategy for the coming campaign. It was to feint toward Culpeper Court House, then move the entire army rapidly to Falmouth, where he would cross the Rappahannock on pontoon bridges that Secretary of War Stanton would ship from Washington, following which his army would advance on Richmond. It was the same old "on to Richmond" obsession that had blinded previous Union generals to the basic fact that, as Lincoln repeatedly pointed out, the principal objective of the army was to engage and defeat the enemy in battle rather than strive to capture the Confederate Capital.

ONE OF BURNSIDE'S first acts upon taking command was to reduce the number of generals reporting directly to him. He did this by grouping the several infantry corps into wings that he called "grand divisions," each having two corps of three divisions plus artillery and a cavalry brigade. Major General Edwin V. Sumner commanded the Right Grand Division, Major General Joseph Hooker the Center Grand Division, and Major General William B. Franklin the Left Grand Division.

Overruling General-in-Chief Henry Halleck's preference for McClellan's plan of campaign, the Presi-

dent approved Burnside's proposal on November 14, even though his own judgment coincided with Halleck's. No doubt Lincoln concluded that Burnside showed promise of positive action, in contrast to McClellan's inactivity. Halleck's telegram to Burnside, quoting the perceptive Lincoln, stated: "The President thinks the plan will succeed if you move rapidly; otherwise not."

Initially Burnside displayed the celerity Lincoln desired. Within hours after receiving the President's message he started Sumner's grand division towards Falmouth, followed the next day by the rest of the army. Sumner covered the forty miles in less than three days, arriving at Falmouth on the 17th. On the 20th the entire army was assembled in the new area. The pontoons had not arrived, but Sumner on the 17th could have waded the river at one or more of the upstream fords had Burnside so ordered. Burnside won the race with Lee for Fredericksburg only to throw away this prime advantage by his obstinacy

Map 1. THE CONCENTRATION AT FREDERICKSBURG. The routes of the several corps of both armies are shown from the beginning of Burnside's march on November 14 until both armies were facing each other across the Rappahannock at Fredericksburg. This map shows clearly that with an abler commander than McClellan or Burnside the Federals were in position prior to this march to strike either Longstreet at Culpeper or Jackson at Winchester before the other could intervene.

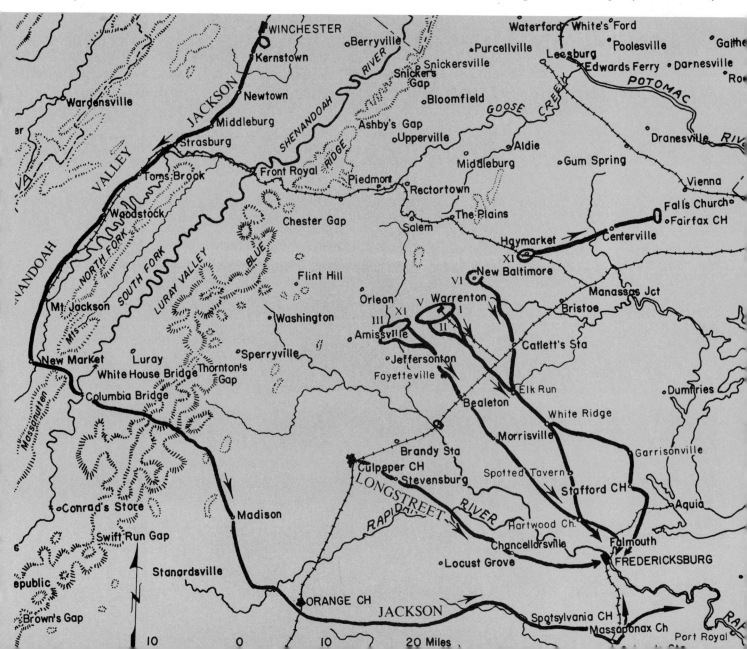

McClellan turning over command of the Army of the Potomac to Burnside. From an A. R. Waud drawing in "Harpers."

in waiting for the bridging material. Two days later, with Longstreet in possession of Fredericksburg, the rains descended, the river rose rapidly, and by then it was too late.

Lee's Reaction

WORD of the Federal change of command reached General Lee while he was considering how he would react to the several possibilities open to McClellan's invading army. Burnside's march on Fredericksburg rather than southwest toward Culpeper Court House came as a surprise, so that Sumner's wing was already at Falmouth before Lee could be certain that Fredericksburg was indeed the major Union objective. Only then had Longstreet been ordered to move in haste, from Culpeper, and at the same time Jackson's corps was directed to leave the Shenandoah Valley for Orange Court House, where he would halt, still thirty-five miles from Fredericksburg, until Lee could re-evaluate his own strategy in the light of Burnside's next move. On November 26, almost a week after the Union army had reached Falmouth, Lee wrote Jackson to bring his divisions to Fredericksburg. They arrived December 1, having marched approximately 150 miles in twelve days.

Rather than make a stand at Fredericksburg, Lee would have preferred to fight thirty miles farther south, along the line of the North Anna River, which he believed offered a more favorable opportunity to turn the defensive into a counteroffensive. But Jefferson Davis, concerned as ever about the safety of the Capital, thought differently, and Lee did not press the point.

Uncertainty as to where Burnside would cross, if he should finally make that decision, prompted Lee to dispose his forces to meet any contingency. It seemed probable, because of the topography and the presence of Federal gunboats at Port Royal, that the main effort would be an attempt to turn Lee's right flank in the area below Fredericksburg. In order to provide against the most likely Federal actions, Lee disposed Longstreet's corps along the high ground west of the town, from the Rappahannock to Hamilton's Crossing, to serve as the Confederate fixed defense. To the south, Jackson's divisions were spread over a wide area, in positions of maneuverable readiness; at Guiney's Station on the Richmond, Fredericksburg & Potomac Railroad; at Yerby's, three miles to the right rear of Longstreet's right flank; at Skinker's Neck; and opposite Port Royal. Stuart's cavalry brigades were posted in observation on either flank of the 20-mile-long Confederate line.

Snow ball fight between Confederate units prior to the Battle of Fredericksburg. These were organized affairs, involving large units and conducted with all the seriousness and attention to tactical detail of a real battle. This drawing, from "Battles & Leaders," is by A. C. Redwood, a Confederate veteran.

Burnside's Preliminary Orders

ON December 9 Burnside issued a warning order to his three Grand Divisions to prepare to cross the river on Thursday morning, December 11, in accordance with the following plan: The troops would cross at three points simultaneously as soon as the engineers finished laying the pontoon bridges, two of which were to be at the northern and one at the southern extremities of Fredericksburg; two more just below the mouth of Deep Run, about one mile below the town. Three of the five bridges would have approaches prepared for artillery, designated batteries of which were to follow the infantry into the combat zones. (Later a bridge was added at Deep Run.)

The attack was to be two-pronged, with Sumner's Right Grand Division slated to take Fredericksburg and then attack the Confederates on their ridge position beyond the town. Meanwhile Franklin's Left Grand Division would occupy the plain south of Fredericksburg, then maneuver the Confederates off their high ground near Hamilton's Crossing. Hooker's Center Grand Division would be held in reserve,

prepared to intervene wherever the attack needed bolstering.

BURNSIDE summoned his generals and their staffs to a conference on December 10, at which he discussed additional details as to their actions once they had crossed the river. Instead of issuing clear, concise, and definite written orders, Burnside is reported to have given the commanders long, rambling, and vague instructions of a general nature. If he had a well-rounded plan in mind, it was not revealed to these officers, and there is considerable doubt as to whether he was clear in his own mind as to how the attack would be pressed after the crossing had been accomplished. Burnside certainly deserves criticism for this; and his subordinates were at fault, too, in not asking enough questions to resolve their doubts and problems.

During this conference Burnside did learn, however, that his officers lacked confidence in his plan. The most outspoken critic was Brevet Brigadier General Rush C. Hawkins, a brigade commander in Getty's division of the IX Corps, Burnside's former command. In reply to a casual inquiry as to what Hawkins thought of the plan he had just outlined, Hawkins replied, "If you make the attack as contemplated, it will be the greatest slaughter of the war;

there isn't infantry enough in our whole army to carry those heights if they are well defended." Colonel J. H. Taylor of Sumner's staff added, "The carrying out of your plan will be murder, not warfare." Even that seasoned campaigner, Major General Darius N. Couch, while more restrained in his judgment, nevertheless reported that "there were not two opinions among the subordinate officers as to the rashness of the undertaking."

Though Burnside showed no inclination to change his plan, these outspoken comments must have jarred him and further weakened what little self-confidence he still possessed.

The Crossing

THE actual throwing of the bridges by the Federal engineers was scheduled to start at daylight December 11, but the noise made in moving the bulky equipment into position reached the ears of Confederate

Pontoon train en route from Aquia to Falmouth. ("Harpers")

pickets in Fredericksburg while it was still dark. General McLaws, convinced that the long-awaited crossing was about to commence, at about 5 a.m. had ordered two guns to fire a prearranged warning signal.

Through the early morning haze Confederate sharpshooters watched for the pontoniers to appear. Then the crackle of Rebel musketry rang out, toppling the leading Federal engineers into the water and spurring the rest back into the protection of the fog. Again and again the undaunted bridge builders attempted to advance their equipment, but each time they were driven back. Covering fire from Federal infantry along the bank was ineffective against the Confederates, protected as they were in pits and behind walls and buildings.

THE TENSE DRAMA continued halfway through the morning, both sides withholding artillery fire for fear of striking their own men. The muzzles of Brigadier General Henry J. Hunt's guns on Stafford Heights could not be depressed sufficiently to blast out Barks-

Engineers attempting to lay a pontoon bridge under the cover of a heavy artillery bombardment. ("Harpers")

dale's riflemen, while Lee's artillerymen could not see the river line, their view being blocked by the houses and further obscured by the fog. Finally, however, the Federal guns bombarded Fredericksburg for two and a half hours, firing sixty shells a minute for a total of 9,000 rounds. Fires sprang up all over town, but as soon as the firing ceased the undamaged Confederates popped up from their cellars and rifle pits and resumed their deadly work.

The Federals finally realized that they could not lay the bridges during daylight under such accurate fire. General Hunt proposed that volunteers ferry over a strong enough force to drive away the sharpshooters, establish a small bridgehead, and form a screen to protect the engineers. Four regiments—from Michigan, Massachusetts, and New York—accepted the call. The leading elements jumped into pontoons and paddled rapidly across. In a short time they had established their bridgehead, losing only one man killed and several wounded.

ALTHOUGH bitter street fighting continued through the remaining hours of daylight, Federal infantry poured across the completed bridges in a steady stream, fanned out to widen the bridgehead, and finally forced Barksdale to withdraw his 1,600 men from the town.

While all this was taking place at the upper bridges

opposite Fredericksburg, two others at Deep Run, for the use of Franklin's Grand Division, were completed by 11 a.m., with but little opposition from the Confederates. Had Burnside been more alert and allowed discretion to his subordinates, Franklin could have passed a couple of divisions over quickly, then swung north and driven out by the flank the sharpshooters who for long hours had blocked the laying of bridges in Sumner's sector. But Franklin delayed crossing until 4 p.m., five hours after the completion of the lower bridges. Even then, after several brigades were across, countermanding orders were received, with the explanation that the construction of the three upper bridges had been delayed. So back across the river marched Franklin's advance elements, leaving a single brigade on the southwest shore to cover the crossing of the main body of that Grand Division the next day. That night another bridge was laid at Franklin's crossing.

Burnside's Battle Orders

AS the Union divisions moved into position behind their artillery on Stafford Heights and opposite Deep Run, and the engineers struggled vainly to complete the bridges, Burnside issued his first written battle orders. These had been belatedly completed early that morning of December 11, about the same time the engineers were pushing the first pontoons into the water. That Burnside was merely feeling his way toward battle is evident in his fragmentary messages, which were surprisingly imprecise and incomplete. The essence of the order to Sumner was:

Your first corps, after crossing, should be protected by the town and the banks of the river as much as possible until the second corps is well closed up and in the act of crossing; after which you will move the first corps directly to the front, with a view to taking the heights that command the Plank road and the Telegraph road, supporting it by your other corps as soon as you can get it over the river. General Hooker will immediately follow in your support, and will see that your right flank is not troubled.

General Franklin crosses below, as you are aware, thus protecting your left. The extent of your movement to the front beyond the heights will be indicated during the engagement.

Franklin received this gem:

General Sumner will, after crossing the river, move immediately to the front, with a view to taking the heights which command the Plank and Telegraph roads. I have ordered General Hooker to hold himself in readiness, as soon as he has crossed the river, to support either General Sumner's column or your own. After your command has crossed, you will move down the old Richmond road, in the direction of the railroad, being governed by circumstances as to the extent of your movements. An aide will be sent to you during your movements.

TO HOOKER, commanding the army reserve, Burnside passed along the instructions already addressed to the two other wing commanders, while directing him to hold himself in readiness to support either column; then added: "Should we be so fortunate as to dislodge the enemy, you will hold your command in readiness to pursue by the two roads." The order incidentally neglected to specify what roads were meant; and the phrase "snould we be so fortunate" is not indicative of confidence.

These were no more than movement orders, indi-

Barksdale's Mississippians opposing the laying of the pontoon bridges at Fredericksburg. (BL)

Advance skirmishers of Sumner's Right Grand Division driving Barksdale's men from Fredericksburg. Looting seems to have commenced. Alfred R. Waud in "Harpers."

cating that Burnside intended to put his army in close contact with the Confederates on their side of the river without immediately committing them to battle. The orders were silent on how either Sumner's or Franklin's divisions were to react if the enemy should become active while Burnside prepared and issued further instructions. Those to Franklin in particular, considering the fluidity of his assignment, afforded the more striking example of how *not* to start an offensive. It was Burnside's intention that this largest of his grand divisions, with a strength of more than 46,000 men comprising six divisions, would make the main effort that he counted on to dislodge

Maj. Gen. Ambrose E. Burnside (LC)

Map 2. THE VALLEY OF THE RAPPAHANNOCK, SHOWING LEE'S DISPOSITIONS ON DECEMBER 10.
Jackson's corps is on the right, the divisions being indicated by numerals, as follows: 1. D. H. Hill; 2. Early; 3. Taliaferro; 4. A. P. Hill. Longstreet's corps was occupying the ridge west and southwest of Fredericksburg, from the river on the left to Hamilton's Crossing on the right. His divisions are indicated as: 5. Hood; 6. Pickett; 7. McLaws; 8. Ransom; 9. R. H. Anderson. Stuart's cavalry is located as shown, the brigades being: 10. W. H. F. Lee; 11. Fitzhugh Lee; 12. Hampton; 13. Rosser. The Federal army was in camps north and southeast of Falmouth, generally back about a mile and a half from the river.

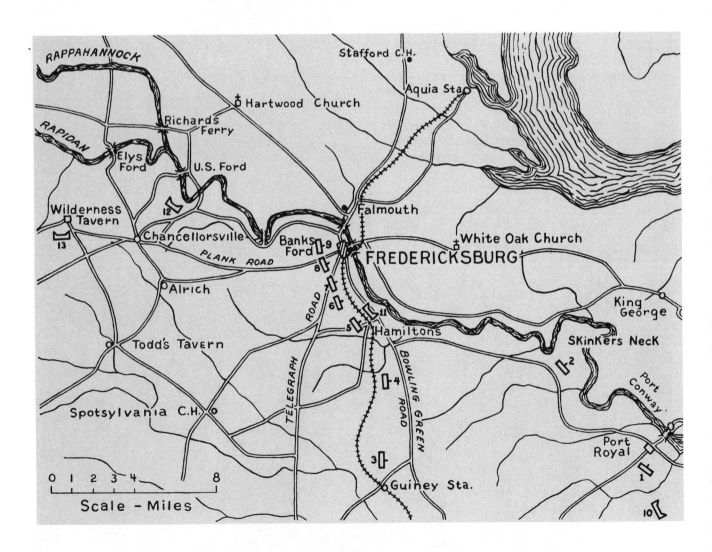

Burnside and His Lieutenants

IN SELECTING Major General Ambrose E. Burnside to succeed McClellan, President Lincoln could scarcely have done worse. Burnside's first performance at the Battle of Bull Run in July 1861, pointed accurately to what might be expected of him. In command of a Rhode Island regiment, he had asked permission to withdraw "to replenish ammunition" after a few minutes of combat. He withdrew nearly a *mile,* and did not again approach the front. He was not a coward personally, but he could not bear to expose his men to danger, and he proved this repeatedly, as at Antietam, in the Wilderness, and later. He simply was not a fighting man; he was too tender-hearted, and he knew it. Although Fredericksburg appears to be an exception, it was not. The bloodshed there temporarily deranged Burnside.

The Administration, desperately seeking a commander who would give them victories, was attracted to this 38-year-old West Pointer who, as an independent commander in a campaign in North Carolina, had boldly attacked and captured Roanoke Island, taking seventy-nine Confederate guns and 3,600 prisoners in the process. Burnside then looked like a winner to Lincoln, and with his warm, engaging smile and ease in making friends, appeared to the President to be a logical choice.

On two previous occasions Gen. Burnside had been offered command of the Army of the Potomac. Both times he had refused, modestly insisting that he did not consider himself qualified for the post, a self-evaluation which the Fredericksburg Campaign would justify. His performance as a corps commander under McClellan seemed to confirm his own judgment at South Mountain and Antietam, where he proved to be not only inadequate, but downright incompetent, as his friend and superior, General McClellan, could have told Lincoln. In that campaign Burnside's mental reflexes, never very fast, seemed to observers to become even more sluggish in the heat of combat. Such a defect, when coupled with inexperience and a lack of self-confidence, is bad enough in an officer of lesser rank. In an army commander it can be nothing short of tragic.

AN IMPETUOUS old man, by Civil War or any other standards, Major General Edwin V. Sumner was in 1862 a 66-year-old former cavalryman whose commissioned service in the Regular Army dated back almost to the War of 1812. He had fought with distinction on the Indian frontier and in the Mexican War, and had been a solid, although far from brilliant, corps commander under McClellan. He was prone to lead his troops personally into battle, for which they admired him; but this was a custom which even in the 1860's was not considered appropriate for higher commanders, and which may have been why Burnside, during the Battle of Fredericksburg, gave him strict orders not to cross the river with his troops.

Sumner's personal courage was matched by a fighting heart, and it's a pity Burnside would not allow him to cross his grand division by fording the river immediately upon reaching Falmouth. Although Sumner seems to have had as serious misgivings concerning Burnside's ability as the other senior officers in the Army of the Potomac, he supported the latter loyally and did not become a party to the efforts of several who worked to undermine Burnside. Sumner was poorly repaid for this loyalty. After the battle Burnside persuaded Lincoln to relieve Sumner, who died soon thereafter.

MAJOR GENERAL JOSEPH HOOKER, 48 years old, was, like Burnside and McClellan, a West Point graduate who had resigned from the Army after the Mexican War, and re-entered as a Volunteer officer in 1861. An illuminating example of his unbounded egotism is his telling Lincoln that he would make a better general than any who served at First Bull Run. Lincoln took him at his own evaluation and made him a general. Hooker had done fairly well up to now. He was a fine-looking man, military in appearance, and with considerable personal magnetism. But he was conniving, continually carping at his superiors, and trying, by political influence, to supersede the army commander. Lincoln saw through him, but liked him nevertheless.

Ambitious, insubordinate, and disloyal to any superior whom he regarded as standing in the way of his own aggrandizement or personal advancement, Hooked had the effrontery at Fredericksburg to write directly to Secretary of War Stanton inquiring whether rations could be made available to his command at Port Royal within three days, in connection with an independent maneuver which he had proposed to Burnside, but which the latter disapproved. Since Burnside was not entirely lacking in perception, his action in designating Hooker's Grand Division as the army reserve may have implied that he was unwilling to allow "Fighting Joe" to get out from under his immediate eye.

WILLIAM B. FRANKLIN, a native of York, Pennsylvania, graduated from West Point in 1843 as No. 1 cadet in the same class as U. S. Grant, who was No. 21. His military career had followed a normal pattern for the times, including the Mexican War, but his principal activity between 1847 and 1861 centered in Washington, where he was in charge of the construction of the Capitol dome and similar governmental assignments. To judge Franklin as a division and corps commander is somewhat difficult, because under McClellan's army command, Franklin's corps seems to have been sidelined on the fringe of combat more often than not. On the record before Fredericksburg he stands revealed as only an average field commander, and in his last opportunity to prove himself, as one of Burnside's three grand division commanders, the picture was so distorted by Burnside's own inept leadership that the reader must judge for himself whether Franklin was not perhaps more sinned against than sinner.

Edwin V. Sumner (BL)

Joseph Hooker (NA)

Rush C. Hawkins

William B. Franklin (BL)

Lee's army from its position. Therefore he was derelict in not giving Franklin a more specific directive for the attack. At the very least he should have indicated his objective in clear, unmistakable language, then left it to the wing commander to execute the mission in his own way.

The halting efforts of the Federal army, with its commanding general attempting to direct its every action by remote control and with virtually no coordination between wings, accomplished just about what might have been expected. Instead of briskly effecting the passage of the river in the early hours of December 11, and advancing at once to the attack in accordance with clearly defined orders that would allow reasonable discretion to the wing and corps commanders, forty-eight hours went by before either Sumner or Franklin received word to put into effect the confusing, fragmented messages that came down from army headquarters.

Contrast in Leadership

THE striking contrast between the generalship of Lee and Burnside can be noted in virtually every facet of the army commander's sphere of activity—strategy, overall tactical direction, logistical planning, the ability to make decisions, the issuance of clear operational directives, the fixing of objectives, and in the maintenance of troop morale. In the important task of making troop dispositions for battle, about the only positive measure that Burnside ordered was the siting of artillery along the dominant position on Stafford Heights, actually the work of General Henry Hunt, easily the best artillerist in either army. On that high ground across the river, the army's Chief of Artillery placed 147 of his 312 guns, covering the five crossing points.

The real problem would arise later when the Federal forces would undertake to storm the strongly defended Confederate line on the high ground west of Fredericksburg. To reach those heights after passing through the town, Hunt's guns would have to displace forward, a dubious undertaking. Some of the longer-range artillery on Stafford Heights, such as the rifled 3-inch guns and Parrotts, especially the 20-pounders, had effective ranges of from 2,000 to 3,000 yards and could deliver counterbattery fire against Longstreet's artillery on the ridge opposite Fredericksburg, but much of the Confederate line below the town was beyond effective range. Only around Hamilton's Crossing, on the right of Jackson's position, could Hunt expect to do any real damage to the enemy artillery, and then only at extreme range and against uncertain targets concealed in the ridge's heavy woods. The solution would have to be to cross the divisional artillery with the infantry and, hopefully, to employ the field pieces to the best advan-

tage, as accompanying guns with their respective infantry units or for use in counterbattery fire on targets of opportunity.

IN employing his numerous cavalry, Burnside followed the precedent established by earlier Union army commanders who never learned how properly to use the mounted brigades. As a result they, and Burnside, dissipated the cavalry strength instead of assembling a strong mounted force on the critical left flank to seize the key terrain along the river east of Hamilton's Crossing, from which Franklin could have more effectively launched his enveloping attack. Except for several half-hearted attempts at battle reconnaissance, which accomplished nothing, Pleasonton's cavalry would sit out the Battle of Fredericksburg.

Lee's plans and dispositions, after Burnside's rapid surprise march to Falmouth, which suggested that the new Federal commander might be a more aggressive opponent than McClellan, were based on the presumption that his opponent would probably undertake a turning movement on the south flank from the direction of Port Royal, where he would have room to maneuver. Consequently Lee decided on a flexible defense, so disposing his forces as to encourage Burnside to expend his strength in attacking the Confederate defense heights, after which Lee would

Joseph B. Kershaw, C.S.A.

Thomas R. R. Cobb, C.S.A.

John Pelham, C.S.A.

Maxcy Gregg, C.S.A.

Thomas J. Jackson, C.S.A.   *Robert E. Lee, C.S.A.*

Southern Key Division Commanders

MAJOR GENERAL Lafayette McLaws of Longstreet's corps and Major General Ambrose P. Hill of Jackson's corps commanded the two divisions of the Confederate army which played the major roles in Lee's left and right wings respectively, although Early's division ran them a close second in number of casualties.

McLaws, a classmate of Longstreet at West Point, served with distinction under that officer throughout the first three years of the war, but later aroused his superior's displeasure, in the 1864 Knoxville Campaign, and was relieved from command. At Fredericksburg he was still in Longstreet's good graces, was first on the field, and was assigned the responsibility of occupying Fredericksburg and holding the river line at that point against an attempt by the Federals to cross the river; as the situation developed, it was McLaws who was charged with the defense of Marye's Heights, from which the repeated Federal attacks were repulsed. That he was a sound tactician and hard fighter was amply proven on that and other occasions.

A. P. HILL, commander of the crack Confederate "Light Division," was considered by Lee to be the best division commander in his army. A fiery combat leader, Hill was in the habit of leading his troops while wearing a bright red shirt, and would not hesitate to lay his sword over the back of an officer who might appear to the general to be lagging in the battle. He and Stonewall Jackson had their differences, but both were hardy fighters and strict disciplinarians, and both placed their strong sense of duty ahead of personal feuds. Hill was a tower of strength to Jackson in major battles, notably at Cedar Mountain, Second Manassas, and Sharpsburg. Something must have occurred in Hill's make-up to slow him down when he was promoted to command of a corps after Jackson's death, because thereafter he seems to have lost his touch. At Fredericksburg, however, it was his division to which Jackson gave the post of honor at the sensitive spot in his sector, protecting the railroad as the most likely target of a Federal attack.

And it was Hill who met Meade's penetration attack on the afternoon of December 13, contained it, and then with the help of other brigades drove him back to his own lines. Hill's division suffered over 2,000 casualties, twice that of any other division in Lee's army.

Lafayette McLaws, C.S.A.   *A. P. Hill, C.S.A.*

launch a counterattack to drive him back across the river.

Lee anticipated that there would be two key defense positions in the forthcoming battle. The best remembered would be the stone wall along the sunken road at the foot of Marye's Heights. The other, Hamilton's Crossing, was a tactically significant crossroad that marked the southern terminal of the seven-mile-long range of hills that formed the backbone of Lee's defense. Both landmarks became the center of attention for Federals and Confederates alike. Most of the fighting and killing would occur in their vicinity.

ON THE RIDGE west of Fredericksburg, Longstreet's guns were zeroed in on the likely river crossing points, and his infantry guarding the heights had familiarized themselves with the fields of fire across the open fields and roads the Federals would be forced to use to reach the Confederate positions. In 1862 the armies in Virginia had not commenced to dig the extensive fieldworks that became the vogue in late 1863 and especially in 1864.

At Hamilton's Crossing the Mine Road from the west joined a new military road, recently built by the Confederates behind the ridge, and another road from the south that crossed the main line of the Richmond-Fredericksburg railroad at that point to join the Richmond Pike, a much-travelled highway paralleling the Rappahannock about midway between the ridge and the river. Massaponax Creek, a wide and marsh-fringed stream that is marked as a river on modern maps, about 800 yards south of Hamilton's, anchored the right flank of the Confederate line, and it was this maneuverable area upon which General Lee concentrated his attention as the more sensitive, vulnerable sector.

IN EQUALLY striking contrast to the sedentary Burnside, Lee spent much preparatory time in the saddle visiting corps and division commanders, examining the siting of his 275 guns and correcting faulty battery positions, making certain that the guns would be able to deliver enfilade fire across their front, and scrutinizing closely the features of the terrain. Having initially established his command post at Hamilton's Crossing, on the arrival of Jackson's corps Lee moved his headquarters to the highest elevation in Longstreet's sector, an ideal observation post that overlooked both the town and the open terrain to the south. This hill, on Telegraph Road, which marked the approximate center of his defense line, thus became the point from which Lee directed the defense, and which thereafter became known as Lee's Hill.

From this point the Confederate commander frequently trained his binoculars on Stafford Heights,

336

where the Federal artillery had emplaced nearly half its guns, and on which was to be seen Ferry Farm, the boyhood home of George Washington. There was also Chatham (the Lacy house), which Lee had frequently visited in his youth, but more importantly where he had courted his future bride, Mary Custis. At the time of the battle, the Lacy house was serving Federal General Sumner as his field headquarters.

FROM his observation post on the hill Lee watched the Federal artillery shell Fredericksburg on the morning of December 11, but the efforts of the enemy engineers to lay their pontoon bridges could not be seen from that point. Seemingly unconcerned by the unfolding events of the day, even after he had received reports that the bridges had been successfully completed and Federal troops were crossing on both upper and lower bridges, Lee made no move to recall Stonewall Jackson's four divisions, two of which would have to march ten to fifteen miles. Lee evidently interpreted the troop crossing at Deep Run as a feint to cover a larger movement from the Skinker's Neck-Port Royal area. In any event, he would wait for Burnside fully to expose his hand before summoning Jackson.

Only after darkness had fallen on December 11 did Lee decide to send for two of the divisions of the Second Corps, which had been at Yerby's and at Guiney's Station. These two units, A. P. Hill's division and Taliaferro's, upon arrival were ordered to extend Longstreet's line to the right, relieving Hood's

Confederate troops awaiting action at the railroad curve near Hamilton's Crossing. (BL)

division of the First Corps, which had been stretched thinly to the south pending the arrival of Jackson's corps.

ON THE MORNING of December 12, with a heavy fog again concealing the terrain, Lee again deferred the calling up of Jackson's more distant divisions. Sporadic firing from the guns on Stafford Heights were the only sounds to disturb the morning calm. When the fog lifted about noon, Lee rode off to the right with Jackson in an effort to discover what "those people over there" might be up to. A member of Stuart's staff, the huge Prussian volunteer Major Heros von Borcke, joined the two generals and reported that the Federals were massing in front of the Confederate right, that he had seen them himself and would be happy to take the generals to a place where they could observe the large enemy concentration. This was vital intelligence, so off the three horsemen rode, toward Deep Run. Dismounting at von Borcke's suggestion, as they approached the place where he had spotted the enemy, the distinguished trio crept along a covered ditch to within rifle range of the Federal troops, where they halted to peer through their field glasses. As far as the eye could see, Lee and Jackson observed regiment after regiment of Blue infantry moving down from the Federal side of the river and crossing two of the bridges, while over the third, in tight column, came artillery and wagon trains.

That was all Lee needed to know. It was now clear that Burnside's pivot would execute a holding attack to keep Longstreet occupied at Fredericksburg, while the major attack, as expected, would be

directed at the more vulnerable Confederate right flank, although not in the wide sweeping movement that Lee had feared. Burnside's now-revealed plan was, in Lee's judgment, vastly more advantageous to the defenders than a turning movement from the vicinity of Port Royal, which might well have forced the Confederate leader to disengage in the face of a superior force and fall back the thirty miles to his originally planned line on the North Anna River.

Urgent orders were immediately dispatched to Jackson's two absent divisions, D. H. Hill's at Port Royal and Jubal Early's at Skinker's Neck, to march at once. When they arrived, during the night of December 12, Jackson assigned them to positions on the ridge, so that by daylight, December 13, the Confederate defense line was fully manned all the way

The Battlefield Terrain

SITUATED at the head of navigation of the strategically important Rappahannock River, fifty miles from Washington and an equal distance from Richmond, Fredericksburg was a vital consideration in the war councils of both capitals. It was destined to change hands seven times in four years, and was fiercely fought over in two major battles.

As is true of most campaigns, geographical and strategic considerations, coupled with the area topography and the character of the terrain, heavily influenced Lee's plans for the defense. Burnside, however, who had envisaged Fredericksburg merely as a stopping off point en route to Richmond, does not appear to have fully evaluated these important factors.

Despite superiority in manpower and artillery, and the availability of several of the recently approved gas-filled balloons for observation, Burnside was confronted with a difficult problem in hazarding a river crossing directly in the face of a determined foe occupying a strong defensive position. Among other disadvantages, he had almost at the outset lost the element of surprise, and would have to fight on ground selected and strengthened by the Confederates, and in an area of limited maneuverability for his own large army. As he thought the situation over and considered the possibilities, it is little wonder that the bemused Federal commander, inexperienced as he was in commanding an army, hesitated long in making up his mind.

THE TERRAIN to which Burnside finally committed his troops presented greater tactical hazards for the attacker than he knew, since there is no evidence of any Federal battlefield reconnaissance beyond what could be seen at a distance from balloons and from Stafford Heights. If Burnside had thought to direct a careful reconnaissance in force when Sumner's Grand Division reached Falmouth on November 17, or consulted officers who had occupied the area earlier in 1862, he could have learned at least some of the following facts:

In front of Longstreet's sector was the upper end of a broken plain which, between the Confederate position on high ground and the river, widened out from about 600 yards opposite Falmouth to two miles in the Deep Run area, and then narrowed to a mile at the lower end.

The range of heights below Fredericksburg was broken by ravines and small streams, two of which—Hazel Run and Deep Run—offered obstacles in the path of a deployed, advancing body of troops—especially when exposed to enemy rifle or artillery fire. In December 1862 both streams flowed through ravines that in some places were thirty feet deep and hidden by woods and dense undergrowth. Hazel Run in particular was an important tactical feature that would strongly influence the outcome of the Federal attack against Marye's

from the Rappahannock northwest of Fredericksburg to Hamilton's Crossing. Stuart's two cavalry brigades and horse artillery covered the mile-wide open space on the army's right flank between Hamilton's and the river. Lee was covering so wide a front that no units were available as a general reserve, but each corps had local reserves.

WHEN HIS divisions were all posted, Lee's keen tactical sense and appreciation of the military uses of terrain became apparent. Longstreet's corps of approximately 40,000 men occupied a frontage of five miles, while Jackson's 39,000 were positioned in depth within the space of only two miles. Faced with no danger from a Federal turning movement, Longstreet could defend against a frontal assault with less density per man-yard of front, but Jackson's

Hill. Twenty feet in width at the point where it is crossed by the Telegraph Road, it was more of a psychological and physical deterrent in the dead of winter than would have been the case in warmer weather, when the effects of a thorough soaking could be accepted by the soldiers with greater equanimity.

THE HILL slopes of the Confederate positions were covered with woods that afforded the occupying troops exceptional advantages of concealed observation. The two hills at the north end, Taylor's and Marye's, are together known as Marye's Heights, which at its lower extremity is cut by Hazel Run. Marye's Hill rises steeply and abruptly from the flat ground below, a mental as well as physical hazard for the boldest attacker. The most prominent features of the extensive ridge are known as Stansbury's Hill, Cemetery Hill, Telegraph (Lee's) Hill, and Prospect Hill. All rise forty to fifty feet above the lower level.

The town of Fredericksburg at the time of the battle extended from the river bank to the west perhaps a quarter of a mile in the direction of Marye's Heights. The generally open terrain between the western limits of the town and the Confederate position on the heights would appear to offer room for maneuver, were it not for the water-full canal that bisected the area and the wide, neighboring drainage ditch that carried off its waste water.

IN 1862 there was a dam several miles above Fredericksburg, where the canal originated. The canal is still very much in evidence today. The diversion of water through the canal, together with the rapids below the dam and a fine collection of big rocks in the river bed, combined to discourage troop crossings, other than by bridges, of either the river or the canal, which latter would turn out to be a serious handicap to the assaults by the Union divisions against Marye's Heights.

Three main roads and several minor ones led from the streets of Fredericksburg across the battlefield-to-be. The Plank Road, of later Chancellorsville fame, crossed the drainage ditch over a wooden bridge in front of Marye's Heights and, ascending the ridge, ran on to Chancellorsville and Orange Court House. The Telegraph Road crossed Hazel Run and, passing around the base of Marye's Hill, headed southward. At the foot of Marye's Hill it became a sunken road, with a 4-foot high stone wall on the side facing Fredericksburg, which continued for over 500 yards and was destined to prove the major stumbling block to Federal penetration of Marye's Heights.

The old Richmond stage road and the main railroad to the Confederate capital ran south between the river and the foothills to the west. The bridges by which these two crossed Deep Run had been either destroyed or damaged, as had those by which the Plank and Telegraph Roads crossed the ditch obstacle in front of Marye's Heights.

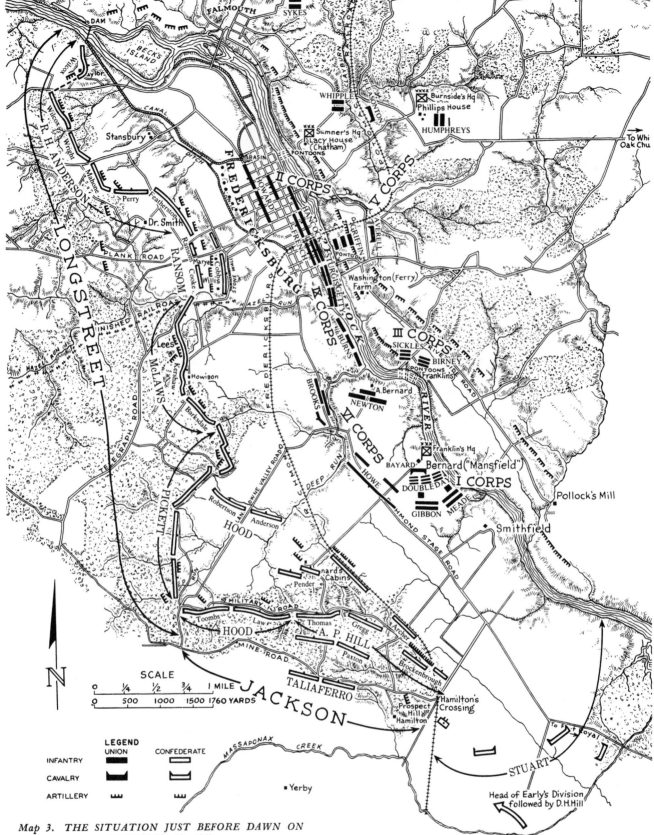

Map 3. THE SITUATION JUST BEFORE DAWN ON DECEMBER 13, 1862.

Federal divisions selected to make the attack have crossed the river and are bivouacked in the positions shown. The Confederates, having watched or heard them cross, are aware that an attack is pending, but are uncertain as to where the main effort, if any, will be made. But by now Lee is satisfied that there will be no wide turning movement to the south, in the Port Royal area, and he is moving Jackson's two flank divisions up to the vicinity of Hamilton's Crossing, where they will arrive about daybreak. The positions of Hunt's reserve artillery east of the river are indicated though the *names of the batteries are not shown. Similarly the Confederate battery positions are shown by symbols which do not necessarily indicate the number of guns in each emplacement. It will be noted that a sixth pontoon bridge is now in place, making three at Franklin's crossing site. This bridge was built late on the 11th. There were few displacements of artillery during the battle, except for the release of some of the organic batteries accompanying the attacking Federal divisions. Therefore, for simplicity, artillery positions will not be generally repeated on succeeding maps.*

BELLE PLAIN, one of two Federal bases on Potomac, whence supplies received by water were transshipped by rail or wagon to Falmouth. (LC)

assignment was one that called for flexibility and a readiness to shift troops on short notice to counter possible penetrations or flank action. The new military road that the Confederates had constructed transversely along the rear of their position had been ordered by Lee with that very possibility in mind.

The positions of the major components of the opposing armies at daylight, December 13, was as shown on Map 3, except that Early's and D. H. Hill's divisions (shown approaching on the right) had arrived and moved into their assigned slots; Early in the third line abreast of Taliaferro and in rear of A. P. Hill's two front lines; D. H. Hill south of the Mine Road west of Hamilton's Crossing. The latter division served as corps reserve, in a position of readiness which might become the front line if the Federals should succeed in penetrating or enveloping Jackson's line.

More of Burnside's Incompetence

DURING the late afternoon of December 12, General Franklin, informed that Burnside was coming over for a conference, had summoned his corps commanders, John F. Reynolds and William F. Smith,

to join him at his field headquarters, the Bernard house, formerly a large plantation known as Mansfield. While awaiting Burnside's arrival, the three generals compared notes and decided unanimously that the only sensible attack plan for their wing would be to form up in two assault columns on either side of the Richmond Road and to turn Lee's right flank, no matter what the cost. When Burnside arrived and the plan was submitted to him, all three generals received the distinct impression that he had given his tacit approval, which would be transmitted in the form of written orders as soon as he returned to his headquarters. So they stayed up half the night, working out specific action details for their divisions and waiting for the expected orders. Finally the three tired generals turned in for a few hours' rest, still uncertain as to what battle orders they should transmit to their divisions.

At 7:45 a.m. December 13, the delayed orders arrived, but Franklin and his two chief lieutenants were startled to discover that their own plans were useless. Instead of approving Franklin's attack plan, the new dispatch repeated Burnside's original directive about keeping the Left Grand Division "in position for a rapid movement down the old Richmond road," adding only the instructions "to send out at once a division at least to pass below Smithfield to seize, if possible, the height near Captain Hamilton's, on this side of the Massaponax, taking care to keep it well supported and its line of retreat open."

IT IS DIFFICULT to avoid the conclusion that Burnside had only a vague conception of the size and complexity of his task, but as army commander he could hardly admit to his subordinates that he didn't quite know what he was doing. Obsessed with the idea that his plan of action would force Lee to relinquish his hold on the high ground and commence a retreat to the south, Burnside had also ordered Hooker to send two divisions to await orders at the bridges used by Franklin's wing, prepared to support the latter in the main effort. These divisions, with Bayard's attached cavalry, brought Franklin's strength to about 54,000, which in Burnside's view was ample to do the job.

But there were two major flaws in the plan: in ordering a single division to penetrate Lee's line, Burnside was committing his major striking force piecemeal, the besetting sin of Union commanders. And the very tone of the order was one which could hardly be construed as aggressive, inspiring, or even positive in its implications. Troop commanders should not tell their men to seize a position *if possible,* or to *keep their line of retreat open.* It is little wonder that the Army of the Potomac was becoming disheartened in the face of repeated evidence of incompetence at army headquarters, in a situation in which its chances of being extricated would depend chiefly on sheer guts.

ONCE the die was cast so that no choice remained to Franklin, orders were issued and the Left Grand Division stirred. For the directed attack with a view to piercing Lee's line, Franklin designated the corps

of General John Reynolds, who in turn selected his smallest division, only 4,500 men under the command of Major General George G. Meade, a capable leader whose Pennsylvanians constituted one of the best outfits in the army. John Gibbon's division was assigned to support Meade's attack, while Reynolds' remaining division under Abner Doubleday, as corps reserve, was told to deploy as left flank protection between the Richmond Road and the river, at a refused angle facing south. All the other divisions of Franklin's wing would merely stand to arms in readiness.

The deployment of Franklin's massive force began while the plain between the river and the Confederate position was still covered by the dense morning fog, which again served the Federals well in concealing their movements from the Confederates on the hill. The latter could hear a variety of noises in front of them, even the occasional sharp bark of commands all along the front, but they could see nothing through the curtain of fog.

The Action Near Hamilton's Crossing

ABOUT 10 o'clock the brilliant rays of the sun rapidly dispelled the mists, disclosing an exciting panorama to the grayclad audience on the heights. The bright sun was reflected from thousands of flashing bayonets; officers dashed up and down on galloping horses as adjutants were observed moving to the front of their regiments and reading battle orders; a strange anachronism to the modern day veteran, but a blood-tingling extravaganza that would never be forgotten by the men of Jackson's corps who occupied the front row seats.

At 8:30 a.m., forty-five minutes after receiving Burnside's order, Meade's division moved out in a

THE pontoon bridges at Franklin's Crossing. The hills occupied by Stonewall Jackson's command are seen in the distance. (LC)

southeasterly direction, crossing the fields in column of brigades, followed by Gibbon's division on Meade's right rear. After paralleling the river for about 600 yards, Meade turned right, heading directly for the Richmond Road which here as at other points was sunken, with six-foot banks on either side. When the heads of the columns reached the fence-bordered road, they came under direct fire from several of Jackson's guns (Walker's battery) as well as enfilading fire from two guns of Stuart's horse artillery, under the command of young Major John Pelham, stationed at the point where the Mine Road crosses the Richmond Pike. Continuing the advance in spite of this fire, Meade finally was forced to pause while still 600 yards from his first objective, the railroad skirting the base of the high ground on which Jackson's men were posted. Pelham's two guns, served audaciously by that young officer, were manipulated so rapidly and effectively, in the face of the potentially overwhelming Federal force on his immediate front, that Meade's advance was held up for two hours. Only when a large number of divisional artillery batteries that had crossed with Franklin's wing poured such a heavy fire on Pelham that one of his guns was disabled and the destruction of the other became an eventual certainty, would he withdraw, but even then it required a peremptory order from Stuart, to force him to pull his two guns out of action. Meade then resumed his advance, assisted by Federal counter-battery fire that partially neutralized the effect of Walker's guns from Jackson's ridge.

JACKSON'S infantry remained carefully concealed in their woods on the ridge, and his artillery withheld its fire during the morning, even after the fog had lifted, rather than waste shells in attempting to reach for Franklin's assembled masses at the extreme range of the Confederate guns. When Meade resumed the advance, however, shortly before 1 p.m. and after the removal of Pelham's annoying guns, the gunners on Jackson's right opened vigorously, hoping to slow the Federal attack and weaken the Blue lines before they could reach the railroad and cover of the protecting woods. Four batteries with Reynolds' corps immediately trained their guns and returned the fire of the Confederate guns, at the effective range of 1,000 yards. For almost an hour the artillery slugging match continued, until the Federal guns were silenced to avoid dropping their shells among Meade's men as they neared the enemy position.

About a mile below Deep Run could be seen a point of woods that jutted into the open plain, an easily noted reference point that Corps Commander Reynolds had pointed out to Meade as his initial objective. Fortuitously, as it happened, this particular section of woods afforded a more gradual ascent for

On the Picket Line
Federal Advance Against Jackson's Corps

THE MIST still clung to the river and the lowlands as the army began to cross the stream. Our brigade was among the first to cross, and upon reaching the opposite bank, halted for further orders. As the mist rolled away and the sun made its appearance, it was a magnificent sight to watch the troops, many of them in new uniforms, marching from all directions toward and across the bridge and then double-quick up the opposite bank.

In crossing a pontoon bridge men are cautioned not to keep in step. A pontoon bridge is not a very substantial structure, therefore any regularity of step would tend to sway it from its moorings.

We then marched along the bank of the river in an easterly direction about half a mile and halted; whereupon the colonel was asked by General Gibbon if he could deploy his whole regiment as skirmishers at once, and being promptly answered that he could, he was directed to do so. The ground in front of us was a flat, unobstructed plain of considerable extent, where every man of the regiment could be seen as he deployed. On our right was a Vermont regiment and on our left a Pennsylvania regiment, also deployed as skirmishers. These three regiments constituted the skirmish line of the Left Grand Division, and it advanced firing at will and slowly driving back the Rebel skirmishers toward their main body. After dark we arrived at the Bowling Green Road which, being a sunken road, afforded us protection from the enemy's fire. Here we remained all night as a picket guard for the I Corps. The regiment was divided into three reliefs, each of which was sent out in turn some distance beyond the road and within talking distance of the Rebel pickets.

DURING the night the enemy set fire to some buildings near by, illuminating a considerable extent of country, while hundreds of men of both armies swarmed to the fences to watch and enjoy the sight.

All night long we could plainly hear the sound of axes in the enemy's camp, which we subsequently learned were being used in the preparation of obstructions against our advance in the morning.

While we were deployed as skirmishers a captain of one of the companies observed a man, who up to this time, had always failed to be present on any important occasion, endeavoring to escape to the rear. The captain called out in a loud voice, "C———, get into your place, and if you see a Reb, SHOOT HIM!" A few minutes later the man disappeared and was not seen again until the "surgeon's call" was established in camp, some days later.

An incident happened shortly after our skirmish line returned to the Bowling Green Road that afforded us a great deal of amusement. The boys had just started fires for coffee when a young officer, whose new uniform suggested recent appointment, approached with arbitrary voice ordered fires to be put out, at which the colonel exhibited an asperity of temper that surprised us, who had never seen him except with a perfectly calm demeanor. Our experience on the picket line had taught us how to build fires without attracting attention of the enemy, and we were not pleased that a fledgling should interfere with our plans for hot coffee. The colonel's remarks were quite sufficient for our guidance, so we had our fires and our hot coffee, while the officer went off about his business.

ANOTHER incident occurred to add to the occasion. Our pickets, as already stated, were so near to those of the enemy that conversation was easily carried on. One of the Rebel pickets was invited to come over and make a call, though the invitation might have appeared to him like the spider to the fly. After some hesitation and the promise that he would be allowed to return he dropped his musket and came into our lines and was escorted to one of the fires, probably to his great delight, inasmuch as coffee and hardtack was cordially offered him, being not so abundant in the South as to allow a distribution of it as an army ration. "If thine enemy hunger, feed him; overcome him with good." Fill him with lead, good lead, was what we tried to do most of the time. After that he enjoyed our hospitality as long as he dared and then returned.

On the following day while we were halted at the Bernard house, who should be brought in as a prisoner but this same man, who was greeted with shouts of welcome and friendly shaking of the hand. Some years later, a member of the regiment, while travelling in Ohio, became acquainted with a man tarrying at the same hotel. After supper the two sat down to talk, and very soon the conversation drifted to the war, when it was discovered that each had served in the war, though on opposite sides. The Southerner, learning that his new-found friend was a member of the 13th, remarked that it was rather a singular coincidence, for "I was entertained by that regiment once at Fredericksburg and a right smart lot of fellows they

were." And then he told what had happened. As our comrade was present at that battle, and a member of the company that did the entertaining, he was perfectly familiar with the facts, whereupon mutual expressions of pleasure followed and an adjournment for "cold tea."

—13th Massachusetts History

Map 4. *THE ATTACK OF REYNOLDS' CORPS. ACTIONS ON THE SOUTH FLANK UP TO ABOUT 1:30 P.M.*

As described in the text, Meade's initial rush penetrated A. P. Hill's center, turned the flanks of and partially broke up Lane's, Archer's, and Gregg's brigades, and gained the new military road. Gibbon advanced only to the railroad. His men, seeing that no one on their right was advancing, and not being told that they were not to be supported by a general advance, were wavering and drifting to the rear. A. P. Hill has requested help from Early, and it is on the way, as the sketch shows.

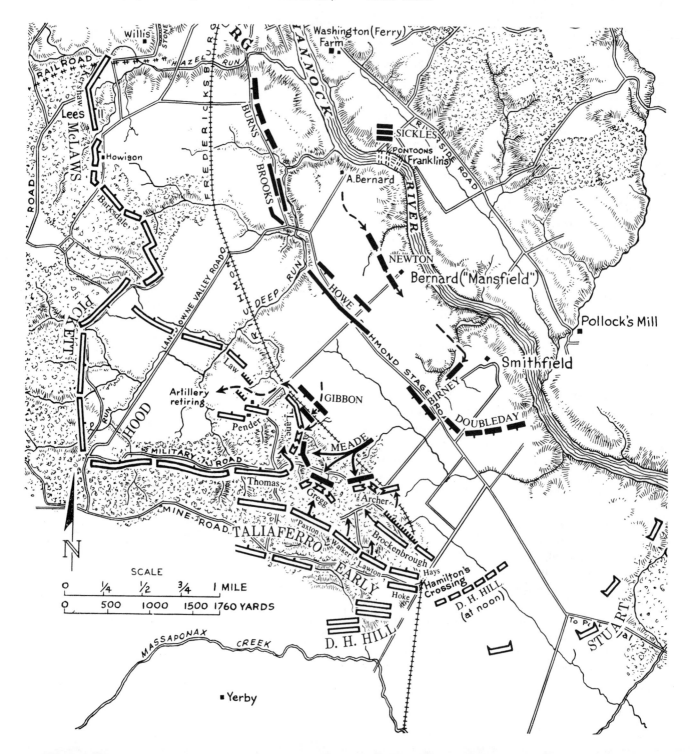

Meade's men charging across the railroad a mile northwest of Hamilton's Crossing. (BL)

the attackers than other parts of Jackson's line. The bulk of the Confederate artillery here appeared to be massed in the vicinity of Hamilton's Crossing, in view of which Reynolds' plan called for Meade's division to turn left, after gaining the crest, in the hope of immobilizing and perhaps destroying these guns.

WITH Gibbon's division advancing on Meade's right rear, the latter's leading assault echelons rushed the hill, broke into the Confederate line, took several hundred prisoners, and then paused for breath as they reached the military road that ran along the rear of the Confederate line. It looked like the breakthrough that Burnside had hoped for, and so it might have been if more adequate preparations had been made and communicated to those charged with the performance. The fault was primarily Burnside's, but Franklin must bear a share, in spite of the restrictive character of the army directive. For, once committed to the fight, it was inexcusable that supporting divisions were not rushed forward to exploit Meade's initial success.

Gibbon's division advanced only as far as the railroad, discovered that no other troops were on their right, and began to waver. By this time the able Confederate general, A. P. Hill, reacting to the break in his line, sent for help to expel the invaders. Early's division and other brigades were dispatched by Jackson to plug the gap. Moving at a run, the Confederate brigades counterattacked just when Meade's formations were somewhat disorganized after their successful dash through the woods and up the slope. By midafternoon Meade's division, suffering heavy casu-

alties and unsupported by Franklin's idle divisions, was driven back in confusion, the men making their way to their own lines, singly and in groups. Reynolds, Meade, and other officers tried unavailingly to halt the retreat, and there is no telling how many of the Pennsylvanians would have got back alive had it not been for a rescue party in the shape of Birney's division of the III Corps, which had crossed the river on Franklin's summons and was thrown into action at the critical moment. As the men of Meade's and Gibbon's divisions streamed to the rear across the plain, Birney struck the right flank of the pursuing Confederates, drove them back in turn, and inflicted a loss of more than 500 killed and wounded.

IN SPITE of Franklin's objections to Burnside's plan for his heavily reinforced left wing, once he became locked with the defending Confederates and had committed Reynolds' corps and later a division of the III Corps, there was little excuse for his failure to engage at least some of his unemployed divisions to support and exploit Meade's penetration of Jackson's line. Even Doubleday's division of Reynolds' corps was allowed to remain in place, east of the Richmond Road, as an immobilized flank guard facing Stuart's Confederate horsemen.

Franklin's lack of initiative was especially noteworthy in the case of Smith's VI Corps of 25,000 men, the largest in the Union army, which was deployed along the Richmond Road with its right on either side of Deep Run, two divisions in the line and one in support. About all this corps did during the entire afternoon was to engage its organic artillery in lively duels with Confederate guns on the ridge, while the main body of its infantry sat out the battle, with one exception. That was a spirited bayonet attack by

Continued on page 350

With the Skirmishers of Gibbon's Division

ABOUT 9 o'clock in the forenoon we were again deployed as skirmishers, and ordered to advance over the fence into the damp clayey soil of the ploughed ground beyond, the enemy firing and slowly retreating.

Our batteries were speedily brought into position and began shelling the woods, while the enemy's guns in turn, opened upon us. We were between two fires, and the greatest caution was necessary to prevent a needless loss of life. Very soon we were ordered to lie down as close as possible to the earth in the soft clay, rolling over on our backs to load our guns. We were now engaged in the very important service of preventing the enemy from picking off the men of Hall's 2d Maine Bat-

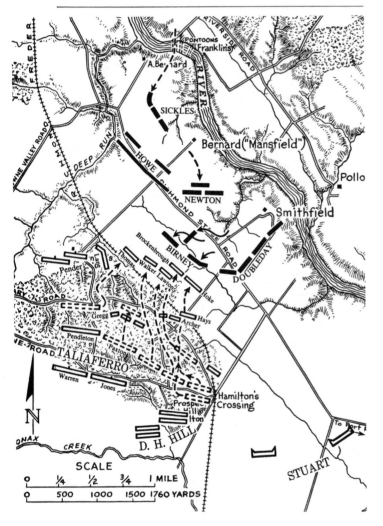

Map 5. THE CONFEDERATE COUNTERATTACK. SITUATION ABOUT 2:30 P.M.

Early's prompt and vigorous counterattack struck Meade at a time when his brigades had become attenuated and had lost cohesion in the woods. The Federals were driven down the hill, out into the open, and back half way to the road. Gibbon's division became involved in the rout. The Confederates were stopped by several batteries of light artillery posted on the rise from which Meade had launched his assault, and by Birney's division, just arrived. Newton has arrived in support and Sickles, also sent for, is approaching. Doubleday is held in check by the threat of Stuart's cavalry. Meade's and Gibbon's broken units are streaming back through Birney's lines, to be re-formed on the ground where they had bivouacked the previous night.

tery, then shelling the enemy from a position slightly elevated from ours in our rear. In order that this battery might do effective work it was ordered to point its guns so as to clear us by one foot. This was a terrible position to be in. An earnest protest was sent back to Captain Hall, asking him to elevate his pieces, or every man of us would be killed. Suddenly a shell or solid shot from his battery struck the cartridge box of one of the boys while he lay on his stomach. Some of our number crawled out to where he lay and dragged him in. He lived about six days, having been injured in the hip. It was bad enough to be killed or wounded by the enemy, but to be killed by our own guns excited a great deal of righteous indignation.

ABOUT ONE O'CLOCK a general advance was ordered. Those on the left moved first and then came our brigade. As skirmishers we advanced in front of our division until the firing became so rapid that we were not only of no advantage, but interfered with the firing of our troops, so we were ordered to lie close to the ground while our troops passed over us. Toward night we were withdrawn to the Bernard house, which had been turned into a hospital, and replenished our empty boxes with ammunition.

Our losses were three men killed, one officer and twelve men wounded, making a total of sixteen.

As we were withdrawn from the skirmish line to the rear our appearance excited a good deal of mirth among the old soldiers, who knew too well what rolling round in the mud meant, for we were literally covered with the clayey soil that stuck to our clothing like glue. We had had a pretty hard time of it, as after each time we fired, we turned over on our backs to reload our guns. Hours of this work told on our appearance as well as our tempers, so when some of the men of a new regiment asked us why we didn't stand up like men and fight, instead of lying down, we felt very much like continuing the fight in our own lines.

TO BE THROWN out as skirmishers in front of a line of battle seems more dangerous than when touching elbows with your comrades in close order, but as a matter of fact it is not generally attended with so great a loss. It is a duty requiring, when well done, nerve and coolness on the part of both officers and men. You are at liberty to protect yourself by any means that may be afforded, such as inequalities of the ground, a bush, a tree, a stump, or anything else that you may run across as you advance. The fire which you receive is usually from the enemy's skirmishers, and is less effective than when directed toward an unbroken line.

You are supposed to load, fire, and advance with as near perfect coolness and order as you can command because on that depends the amount of execution you are able to perform. It is no place for skulkers, as every man is in plain sight, where his every movement is watched with the closest scrutiny. As soon as the skirmish line of the enemy is driven back, the main line advances, and very soon the battle begins in earnest; whereupon the skirmishers form in close order and advance with the rest of the line, except in cases like the one just related, when it was necessary to replenish the boxes of ammunition.

We had acquired a good deal of proficiency by constant drilling for many months in this particular branch of tactics, long before we were called upon to put our knowledge into practice. We growled a good deal at the colonel in the early days of our service for his persistence but we had already realized how valuable a lesson he had taught us. There were occasions that will be later seen, when this kind of service was very dangerous, but as a whole, our losses on the skirmish line were lighter than some other regiments, and we think it is not unfair to attribute the fact to the thorough instruction we had had. It was the old story—the oftener a man does a thing, the better he can do it.

History of 13th Massachusetts

A Portfolio of Fredericksburg Photos

LOWER LEFT—Ruined buildings in Fredericksburg after the bombardment. (LC)

TOP LEFT—Fredericksburg as seen from Stafford Heights. One source states that Brady took this picture while under enemy fire, whereas the plate was made by T. H. O'Sullivan, date unknown but likely not during firing. (LC)

ABOVE—Observation basket attached to one of Prof. Lowe's observation balloons, flown from Stafford Heights during the Battle of Fredericksburg. This photo, however, was made during the Peninsular Campaign earlier in 1862. (LC)

LOWER RIGHT—The ground over which Sumner's divisions charged against the stone wall. The photo, probably made in May 1864, shows in the left background a brick house that Couch says was 150 yards from the wall, and was used as a rallying point. Marye's Hill is on the skyline in the center. (LC)

ABOVE—The stone wall, as seen from the Confederate side. Veterans of the 1944 fighting in Normandy will find this scene reminiscent. After a battle, a position is marked by broken bodies, pieces of clothing, personal possessions, and abandoned weapons. This photo was made after the successful Union attack in the Chancellorsville Campaign, since no Northern photographer saw it in December. Kershaw, whose troops (and Cobb's) occupied this portion of the line, said, in part: "Our chief loss was from the fire of sharpshooters, who occupied buildings on my left flank during the early part of the engagement and were only silenced by the continuous fire of one company of the 2d Regiment."

BELOW—The Lacy house (Chatham), used by Sumner as his headquarters. (NA)

ABOVE—During the battle Burnside used the Phillips mansion as his headquarters, though he spent a considerable time with Sumner at the Lacy house, which was nearer the river. In February the Phillips house caught fire, and despite efforts of the soldiers to save it, it was largely destroyed. This photograph was made while the ruins still smouldered. (NA)

Battery M, 1st Connecticut Heavy Artillery, consisting of three 4½-inch rifles. These guns fired to cover the river crossing and also the main attack. The Schenkl projectiles were not very effective, according to the battalion commander, because the plungers on the projectiles failed to take the grooves of the rifling, thereby endangering the front-line troops. (LC)

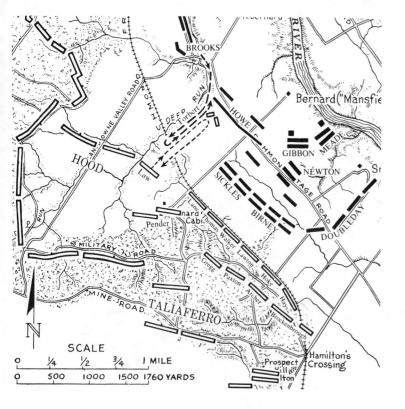

Map 6. ACTIONS ON THE SOUTH FLANK FROM ABOUT 3 P.M. TO DARK.

Virtually the only action of Howe's and Brooks's divisions is that shown on this map. Torbert's brigade made a short run up Deep Creek, captured 15 prisoners, then was chased back by Law's brigade of Hood's division and severely punished. This map also shows the general disposition of all units on the south flank at the end of the day's fighting.

Continued from page 343

Colonel Alfred Torbert's brigade of Brooks's division, which about midafternoon tried to drive the Confederates from a railroad cut on their immediate front at the Lansdowne Valley road, about 600 yards in advance of Brooks's position. Torbert succeeded in driving back a regiment of Pender's brigade (A. P. Hill's division), but was in turn attacked and forced to withdraw by Law's brigade of Hood's division. Other than that single foray, no further effort was made by Smith's corps either to back up Torbert or to test the Confederate defense for weak spots.

The Federal attack had lacked both power and depth, and although Reynolds managed to hold the railroad line for several hours, it soon became apparent that this particular effort had failed. By late afternoon the troops were withdrawn and reformed in the shelter of the Richmond Road, from which the attack had been launched in the morning. Instead of a major, well-supported turning movement against Lee's right flank, the engagement had turned out to be a relatively ineffectual one in which only part of each of the opposing forces was involved. That it was sanguinary, however, is reflected in the casualties: 4,861 on the Federal side, approximately 3,400 on the Confederate.

Sumner Attacks Marye's Heights

WHILE Franklin's reinforced grand division was being deployed on the open plain below Fredericksburg and Meade's assault division was marching up the hill and down again, affairs on the north flank were brought to a head. It will be recalled that Burnside's explanation of his plan of action was for Franklin to maneuver Lee's right into an untenable position and then, at an appropriate time, he would give Sumner to the north the go-ahead signal to push two divisions "in the direction of the Plank and Telegraph Roads, for the purpose of seizing the heights in rear of the town."

The Federal army commander evidently reached the conclusion, after several hours had passed and Franklin had made only slow progress, that an early success on that front would not be achieved. For at 11 a.m., three hours after Sumner received his orders, Corps Commander Couch received a dispatch, over a recently installed field telegraph circuit from the Lacy house, to put the troops in motion. Couch designated French's division for the advance via the Telegraph Road, with Hancock's to follow, while Howard's division was formed up in a position of readiness, to move towards the Plank Road if and when released by Couch.

AT NOON French's leading brigades moved out from the center of town, as described by Couch (the corps commander):

". . . by two parallel streets, the one on the right, which was Hanover Street, running into the Telegraph road, and both leading direct to Marye's Hill, the stronghold of the enemy. On the outskirts of the town the troops encountered

a ditch, or canal, so deep as to be almost impassable except at the street bridges, and, one of the latter being partly torn up, the troops had to cross single file on the stringers. Once across the canal, the attacking forces deployed under the bank bordering the plain over which they were to charge. This plain was obstructed here and there by houses and fences, notably at a fork of the Telegraph road, in the narrow angle of which was a cluster of houses and gardens; and also on the parallel road just south of it, where stood a large brick house. This cluster of houses and the brick house were less than 150 yards from the stone wall, which covered also as much more of the plain to the left of the brick house. A little in advance of the brick house a slight rise in the ground afforded protection to men lying down, against the musketry behind the stone wall but not against the converging fire of the artillery on the heights."

Thus the Federals were under fire, either from musketry or artillery or both, from the moment they debouched from the edge of town—and to a certain extent they took casualties from artillery even while in the streets. They lost many men while still in column before they could double-time over the two bridges on the canal to the slight cover on its far side; and their losses increased from musketry fire as they advanced in line beyond this swale.

Longstreet had assigned the divisions of R. H. Anderson, Robert Ransom, and McLaws to the defense of the range of hills extending from the Rappahannock on the north almost to Deep Run on the south, with McLaws on the right and Ransom supporting him in the area between the Plank and Telegraph Roads. It was on McLaws' front, where the stone wall at the foot of Marye's Heights afforded the Confederates their most effective defensive positions, that the major fighting would occur.

Lieutenant Colonel E. P. Alexander, commanding a battalion of Longstreet's artillery, had confidently declared that the fields between the western edge of the town and the high ground where the Confederates awaited attack were so thoroughly targeted by the artillery on the ridge and the muskets of the infantry at its foot that "not even a chicken could live to cross." It was a grim but prophetically accurate appraisal, one that Burnside might have made for himself with a modicum of imagination and appreciation of terrain, in addition to taking the precaution of conducting a few reconnaissances.

The Sunken Road Makes History

GENERAL Cobb's Georgia brigade and the 24th North Carolina Volunteers of Cooke's brigade manned the sunken road with its protective four-foot stone wall, both of which were invisible to the attackers, who had no idea what a formidable obstacle stood in their way. When this road was built, the dirt had been thrown to the far side, thus concealing the existence of the wall from those approaching it from the town. These units, in preparing their reception for the Federals, formed two successive lines in their narrow, protected causeway so that a continuous band of musket fire could be laid down on the attackers, one line loading while the other fired.

The congestion in the streets of Fredericksburg, and the confusion caused by the intermingling of

Troops crossing on Sumner's lower bridge, just downstream from the ruined railroad bridge. ("Harpers")

Drawing by Henry Lovie shows the approach of Sumner's troops to the stone wall. Confederate lines on Marye's Heights are well defined in the background of the drawing.

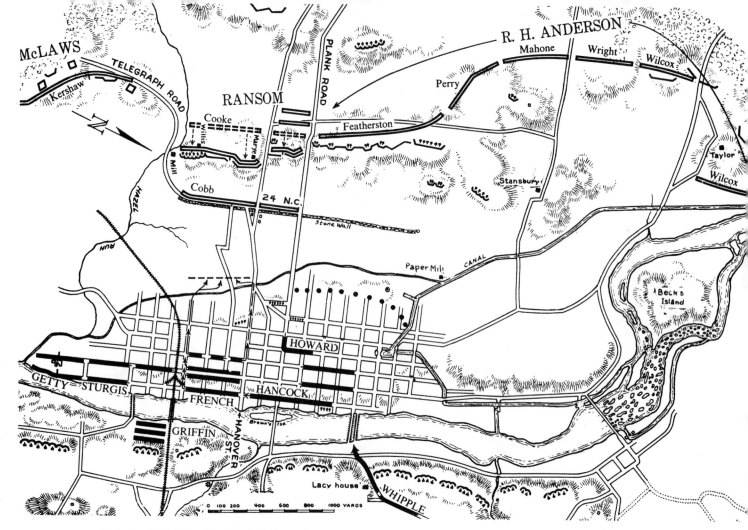

*Map 7. ACTIONS ON THE NORTH FLANK,
ABOUT 11 A.M. TO NOON.*

Federals: French's division formed up about midmorning in the streets where his brigades had spent the night. Three regiments detailed as skirmishers moved at 11 a.m. toward the front, marching in two columns—the right via Hanover Street and the left on a street parallel to the railroad. They trotted from the western exits of the town, across the bridges over the sluice, turned left and right, respectively, faced into line and advanced. They were met by heavy artillery fire from Marye's and Willis' Hills, but continued to dash forward. The skirmishers were followed by the brigades in the order 1st, 3d, and 2d, at intervals of about 150 yards. Then came Hancock's division in the same formation. Meanwhile Howard had formed his brigades on the right of Plank Road, having been told that he would attack on the right of French and Hancock. But these orders were countermanded and his men were held in column in the streets, ready to advance. Sturgis' division also formed up in the streets, preparing to move out in column along the railroad. Whipple's division moved down from its bivouac north of the Lacy house, crossed over the upper bridge, and commenced taking over picket duty in the northwest portion of the city from Howard. Getty's men remained crouched at the lower end of the town near the river.

Confederates: Longstreet's defense was largely entrusted to McLaws, supported by Ransom. Cobb's brigade was behind the stone wall at the foot of the heights, with the 24th North Carolina Volunteers of Ransom's division occupying that portion of the front between Plank Road and the extension of Hanover Street. The remainder of Ransom's division was held back of the artillery on the heights; but when the Federals appeared, Cooke's brigade was rushed forward to the crest, from where they reinforced the small-arms fire of the troops behind the wall. At least initially, the greatest damage to the advancing Federals was caused by the Confederate artillery firing from Marye's and Willis' Hills.

large masses of infantry and artillery, proved a serious handicap to the attackers. Nineteen divisional batteries of artillery had crossed with the foot soldiers, ten of them assigned to Couch's corps, but only seven of the nineteen found the opportunity to fire their pieces, either before or during the actual assaults.

The converging gun fire of the Washington artillery descended on the advancing Federals as soon as they emerged from the shelter of the buildings in the town. It was so destructive that it undoubtedly accelerated the rate of the Federals' advance as they dashed across the narrow bridge of the drainage ditch to the comparative security, however fleeting, of the depression in the ground beyond the ditch. But the effect of the gunfire, though devastating, was less than that of the blinding sheets of musket fire that assailed them as soon as they came within range of the grimly waiting Confederates behind their stone wall.

THE ADVANCE of French's division from the western exits of the town was accompanied by only two guns, manned by heroic cannoneers, who did their best, even though it was of little real help to the charging infantry. The only effective artillery support came mainly from a few of Hunt's long-range guns across the river, but even that was of limited assistance because of the necessity for ceasing fire when the Blue infantry entered the fire-swept zone in front of the wall.

For some strange reason it did not occur to any of the Federal generals that there were other parts of the Confederate defense line that might have been approached with better chance of success, at least after observing how the leading attack waves were being mowed down before reaching the stone wall. Instead, brigade after brigade was rushed headlong into disaster in monotonously bloody succession, all directed at the same limited objective and over ground covered with a rapidly increasing number of dead and wounded. It was as though the stone wall possessed some sort of awful, magnetic attraction that with difficult ground on the flanks, funneled its victims into a valley of death from which there could be no escape.

IN THE FACE of the withering hail of bullets from Cobb's infantry in the sunken road, the guides of the leading brigade of French's division succeeded in planting their guidons within 100 yards of the wall. Encouraged by the sight, the men of the brigade grimly continued to advance, ignoring heavy casualties, until they were only sixty yards from the Confederate muzzles. At that point flesh and blood and courage could take no more, and the lines melted

A. C. Redwood sketch of the Washington Artillery firing on the Union troops charging Marye's Heights. Note the excellent observation and open field of fire enjoyed by these batteries. (BL)

away. The brigades that followed, those that remained of French's division, then Hancock's, rushed successively across the killing ground, each one cresting a bit closer to the wall, until Hancock's final charge, which was stopped only forty yards from the wall. By that time McLaws had rushed additional regiments from Ransom's division into the sunken road so that the Confederates were using four relays of infantry, with a resulting speed-up in the rate of fire, delivered point-blank in the faces of the charging Federals.

Two Union divisions in the space of a single hour had been decimated in the fruitless sacrifice, and the plain over which they advanced was covered with the dead and wounded, adding up to 3,200 casualties alone in the divisions led by French and Hancock.

AS GENERAL COUCH watched the slaughter from the cupola of the Fredericksburg Court House, it finally dawned on him that there might be a better way to execute Burnside's order. Howard's division was the only one that remained under his control, so Couch ordered Howard, who had lost an arm at the Battle of Fair Oaks, to take his division off to the right in order, if possible, to flank the stone wall by piercing the Confederate line beyond its protection. Without taking time to send out a reconnaissance patrol to determine a feasible route of ap-

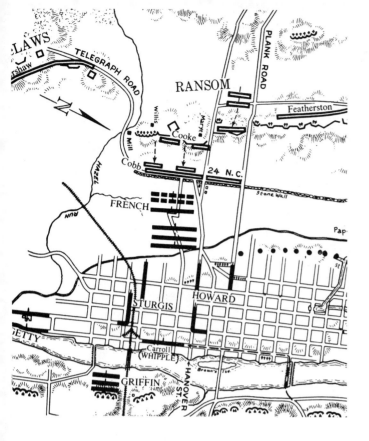

Map 8. THE SITUATION ON THE NORTH FLANK FROM ABOUT NOON TO 1 P.M.

Federals: This sketch shows the charge of French's and Hancock's divisions against Marye's Heights. The picture may be likened to successive waves of a surf dashing against a shore, breaking up, receding, leaving a thin line on the sand to mark their farthest reach. Each Federal brigade suffered heavily from artillery fire as it came in sight at the edge of the town, then encountered long, tearing sheets of musketry volleys as the men neared the stone wall. The leading guides planted their guidons within 100 yards or so of the stone wall, but the lines for the most part melted away. Couch says that the plain seemed to be alive with men, some lying down, others running about, while a steady stream of wounded was returning to the town. Whipple, who crossed the river about noon, has used one brigade to take over picket duty on the right from Howard. His 2d Brigade (Carroll) has moved down to the left behind Sturgis. Howard, having received orders to support Hancock, is moving two brigades to the left toward Hanover Street.

Confederates: Two of Cooke's regiments ran down the slope into the sunken road with Cobb's men. Ransom has brought the remainder of his own brigade to the crest just south of Plank Road. Cooke is wounded. Cobb suffers a cut artery in the leg and bleeds to death quickly despite surgical aid. Mc-Laws orders Kershaw to bring up his entire brigade and to assume overall command in place of Cobb.

Federals: The remnants of French's and Hancock's divisions are scattered in front of the stone wall. Survivors who have drifted to the rear are being rallied in the small ravine along the ditch. Sturgis is following Hancock, Ferrero's brigade in the lead. Nagle's brigade starts to deploy on the left, then sidles to the right oblique and follows Ferrero. Howard, deployed on the right with two brigades, is advancing; his third brigade is held in reserve on the right of the Plank Road. Griffin's division, coming in as part of the Fifth Corps reinforcing the Ninth Corps, has crossed the bridge and is moving forward on the left; Carroll's brigade of Whipple's division, ordered to support Sturgis, has joined Griffin instead and is moving forward with him. Sykes has moved down to the upper bridge. Humphreys is still in bivouac.

Confederates: Kershaw has moved two of his regiments to the top of Marye's Heights thence down into the sunken road to reinforce Cobb's regiments. Three additional regiments are following to the top of the hill. Ransom has brought his regiments forward to the crest and one of them is in the sunken road reinforcing the 24th North Carolina.

The attack on Marye's Heights as seen from the Confederate side.

proach, Howard started his regiments across the lone bridge used by his predecessors, with instructions to change direction after crossing. The hapless soldiers of his division, however, in angling off to the right, ran into marshy ground which caused them to veer to the left, so that they soon found themselves headed for the selfsame stone wall and in as deep trouble as those who had gone before. Result: 900 additional casualties.

Unwilling to admit failure, or mentally incapable of modifying his suicidal tactics, Burnside from his remote headquarters across the river kept sending orders to continue the attack. Perhaps he thought the Confederates would run out of ammunition, or lose heart, if he kept hammering at them. He still had two uncommitted corps, Willcox's IX and Butterfield's V. (Whipple's division of Stoneman's III Corps had already been attached to Couch and was standing by awaiting orders.)

IN THE COURSE of the afternoon all seven of these divisions, having been directed to support Couch either by attachment or as collaborators, were poured into the cauldron, wholly or in part, some directly against Marye's Heights, others a short distance to the south of it. All to no avail, as the casualties mounted and the troops began to wonder whether their absent commander was in full possession of his senses.

Burnside Loses His Head

EVERYTHING had gone badly for Burnside, who chose to remain throughout the battle on Stafford Heights across the river, where he could neither see nor get the feel of the fighting. All he could think of, seemingly, was that his original plan would succeed and therefore required no modification in spite of the disheartening reports that flowed in to his headquarters from all parts of the field. His unwillingness to allow the least discretion, or departure from his orders, to his grand division commanders, was equalled by a lack of that flexibility of mind that is so necessary in adjusting to battle conditions as they develop, including a willingness to modify preconceived tactics and unhesitatingly discard plans that prove unworkable. But these changes of pace cannot be made irrationally, or without adequate communication with subordinate commanders. For example, when Franklin's battle was slow in developing, Burnside decided to throw Sumner's divisions into repeated canalized attacks against the unyielding Marye's Heights, without even coordinating the change of plans with Franklin.

As the divisions on the north flank successively bloodied themselves against Longstreet's hard anvil, and the dead and wounded piled up in the narrow zone before the stone wall, Burnside in desperation ordered Franklin to charge the enemy with his whole force in an effort to take the pressure off the right

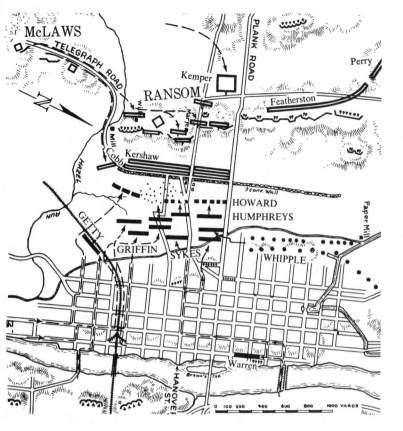

Map 10. *SITUATION ON THE NORTH FLANK FROM ABOUT 2:30 P.M. TO DARK.*

Federals: Howard's two leading brigades have reached a line near the stone wall. His third brigade has been moved to the left of the Plank Road in the shelter of a ravine. Humphreys crossed the river shortly after 2:30 p.m. and formed a battle line in the ravine, to the right and left of Hanover Street. At dusk he advanced in a bayonet charge, which was repulsed. Meanwhile Griffin, with Carroll's brigade attached, has advanced astride the railroad for a short distance then driven straight for the stone wall. His brigades attacked successively but were repulsed. Sykes moved to the upper bridge at 2 p.m., crossed at 4 p.m., moved out Hanover and George Streets, and formed line with two brigades in the ravine. At 5 p.m. Getty advanced on the left in a column of brigades. His leading brigade almost reached the stone wall before being thrown back. The supporting brigade remained behind the railroad embankment. By dark the foremost elements of the Federals in this sector were pinned to the ground in front of the stone wall. Another irregular line was in the ravine.

wing. Franklin disregarded the order, stating afterward that it came too late; but by then, it may be, he and his generals had made up their minds that *any* order from army headquarters could not be trusted or considered intelligent.

CONCURRENTLY with this order to Franklin, Hooker was directed to renew the attack against the stone wall with the two uncommitted divisions of his reserve wing. While these divisions were crossing the river, Hooker did what Burnside himself should have done, rode to the front to see the situation for himself and to confer with Couch and the division commanders whose men had already attempted what everyone but Burnside had now concluded to be impossible.

Hooker's opinion was that further suicidal sacrifices should be ruled out. He then rode back to the eastern bank to dissuade Burnside, who refused to entertain the recommendation that the order be revoked. By the time Hooker had crossed the river for the second time it was late afternoon, foreshadowing

Confederates: Kershaw's three remaining regiments are placed in position near Marye's house. A battalion is moved forward to the gap in the unfinished railroad embankment on the right of Willis' Hill in order to stop any Federal advance up Hazel Run. At 4:30 p.m. the Washington Artillery Battalion, being out of ammunition, is replaced by Alexander's battalion. Ransom, fearful that his left flank would not be supported by Featherston, asked for reinforcements. Kemper's brigade of Pickett's division was sent to him at 4:30, and two of its regiments were placed in the sunken road to relieve the 24th North Carolina. Other readjustments of units were made after dark. The Confederates had repulsed the Union attack so easily and with so little loss to themselves that Lee could hardly believe there would be no renewal of the attack the next day.

HOT WORK FOR HAZARD'S BATTERY.

an early December twilight that would shortly reduce visibility to the point where Hooker might safely defer ordering a further assault on the premise that it could not be effectively completed before dark.

WHILE Hooker was visiting the army commander, one of his divisions, Humphreys', had already crossed to the town and was in formation, prepared to take up the assault, when Hancock advised Couch that his men had just noticed some Confederates apparently leaving their position. Although this movement was only the relief of one artillery battalion by another, the Federal generals interpreted it as the start of a general withdrawal, and Couch promptly told Humphreys it was a good time for him to attack. Humphreys immediately ordered his men to fix bayonets without taking time to load their muskets, and

Hazard's Battery B, 1st Rhode Island, going into position. About 3:30 p.m. he placed his six guns on a low crest only 500 yards from the Confederates. Hazard fired rapidly on the Confederates on Marye's Heights until Humphreys asked him to stop so that the infantry could advance through. Hazard's losses were heavy. Though most of the horses were down, the men preserved the old artillery tradition by dragging away the guns by hand. Gen. Howard, who watched the action, said, "Captain Hazard's conduct was equal to anything I ever saw on the field of battle." (BL)

A. R. Waud sketch of the attack by Hooker's Center Grand Division. This was an on-the-spot drawing, and therefore represents quite accurately the appearance of the scene. This shows clearly that the tactics of 1862 were concerned more with keeping a parade-ground alignment of troops than in taking advantage of folds of the ground or using dispersed formations to minimize losses. ("Harpers")

led them toward the stone wall. Whether the cold steel gave them courage, or they covered the ground more rapidly because they didn't have to stop to load their pieces, they did manage to approach closer to the Confederate line than any of the previous attackers. But they, too, failed to reach the wall, and their wave likewise crested and receded, leaving 1,000 additional dead, wounded, or missing.

The Federal casualties in front of the stone wall had now mounted to 6,300, following the sixth and last (Humphreys') contribution to the senseless slaughter. This marked the end of the day's fighting, with twilight already covering the battlefield as Hooker ordered his troops to fall back from their advanced position with the sardonic comment in his battle report: "Finding that I had already lost as many men as my orders required me to lose, I suspended the attack."

As soon as the semi-darkness made it safe for a man to stand erect without attracting Confederate fire, Sykes's heretofore unused division moved out to within a stone's throw of the Confederate position, to serve as a shield against enemy interference with the painful Federal task of pulling back from close contact and removing as many wounded as possible during the hours of darkness. Some undirected, sporadic firing from nervous Confederates occurred during the night, but no forward movement was undertaken by either side, which was understandable after more than five hours of active combat in so small a sector, where no more than 6,000 Confederates and twenty guns had withstood the driving attack of seven Federal divisions whose battle strength exceeded 40,000 men.

Kershaw's troops defending the stone wall at the foot of Marye's Heights. This drawing was made by Confederate veteran A.C. Redwood. (BL)

THE PAPERS of Jedediah Hotchkiss in the Library of Congress consist of a diary and letters to his wife and brother Nelson. The following excerpts, from a typescript which Hotchkiss himself made in 1897, concern the Battle of Fredericksburg.—Editor

DECEMBER 7, 1862. The Yankees had gunboats at Port Royal, 15 miles below Fredericksburg, but were unable to get any higher. They had to get across the river before they could throw shells at this side, and then we could pick off their men with sharpshooters. So we peppered them well and drove them out.

The Yanks are thick on one side of the river and we on the other. The opposing pickets have a talk now and then. One of the Yankees asked one of our sentries if Jackson had resigned. Our man said, "Yes." "Why?" asked the Yank. "Because your General Banks," replied our man, "Jackson's reliable Quartermaster General, has failed to supply us lately with stores."

FRIDAY, DEC. 12th. After breakfast General Jackson started for Fredericksburg, sending for Brown and myself to come along.

Hood's division was moving into position to the left of Deep Run and A. P. Hill's division was moving into the woods in which Hood had been and where Hill afterwards fought. Gen. Hill had his Hd Qrs. on a high wooded hill, near John Yerby's. Our line of battle was formed parallel to the Mine Road east of and about ¼ mile from it, the right resting on the R.R. near Hamilton's Crossing.

The day was spent getting the troops into position. Gen. Jackson rode down to the river from Hamilton's Crossing, taking me with him, and examined the country to and near the river bank. We then rode back to our camp, the general whistling as we went along. We found our wagons near A. P. Hill's Hd Qrs. and encamped just in his rear. Our Hd. Qrs. are about 2 miles from Hamilton's Crossing near John Ewing's. The morning was cold but as the day advanced it moderated. The smoke and fog were very dense and concealed the army movements on both sides.

SATURDAY, DEC. 13th. We were up at an early hour and off to the battle field by daylight. The morning was cool but the sun rose red and fiery and soon drove away the fog. The tents were struck and the wagons loaded and sent to the rear. All our troops were early in position; A. P. Hill in front, Early on the right, and Taliaferro on the left as supports, and D. H. Hill along Mine Road in reserve. At about 10 a.m. the enemy advanced and the battle opened with artillery. The Federal infantry advanced at 1:30 p. m. and an incessant firing was kept up at intervals during the rest of the day until about 2:15, when it slackened some. It was renewed at intervals during the rest of the day. Most of the fighting was on the right of Jackson's line and on the left of Longstreet's. The enemy was repulsed with great loss; our losses were also great. The cannonading was very heavy.

About sundown we opened a very heavy artillery fire on the enemy. Gen Jackson had ordered an advance if the enemy wavered much; but, although the enemy was driven back, a delay occurred, as the orders had not been received in time by all the division commanders, consequently some confusion ensued and the advance was not made. Gen. Jackson had intended to push the enemy to the river. We took a good many prisoners. We drove the enemy back ¾ of a mile, their repulse being complete.

Our position was a very fine one, our men sheltered by woods, but we had many killed and wounded by the shells of the enemy from long range guns. One battalion of our artillery had 119 horses killed and disabled and 98 men. The line of battle was four miles long, and the enemy had three lines of troops reaching about that distance and then masses of troops besides.

TUESDAY, DEC. 16. The enemy recrossed the river last night, took up their pontoons, and made good their escape. Towards noon it was reported that the enemy was crossing at Port Royal. As the Second Corps was in position nearest in that direction, it was ordered to march to meet the reported movement. We started from Hamilton's Crossing at about 1 p.m., Early's division in advance followed by Taliaferro's, A. P. Hill's; and D. H. Hill's in rear, going by Grace Church. The advance got to near Moss Neck, where a messenger from Gen. Stuart, who had preceded us, gave information that there was no enemy at Port Royal; so a halt was called just where the head of our column was, in a narrow road hedged by dense and well-nigh impenetrable pine thickets. The troops had been ordered to go into bivouac.

The general, who was in front, tried to get back to the rear unobserved by his men. He gave his horse to a courier and attempted to go back through the woods and "flank" his line. But he could not succeed, and had to come back and remount his horse and ride back along the line of march. The soldiers at once "caught on" to the situation and cheered him vociferously as we galloped in a single file through the opening they made for us along the middle of the road. The men were in fine spirits and kept cheering for the entire staff and escort that followed the general. They added: "Close up! You will get lost and never find him."

After getting through the thicket-enclosed road we turned to the right and rode down through open woods to a sheltered hollow and went into bivouac where the fallen leaves were abundant. Someone started a fire at the base of a large, hollow tulip poplar, the ascending sparks of which afforded a subject for conversation between the general and the staff. We tried to induce the general to go into a house, as the air was sharp and raw, and we had nothing to eat. But he refused, and we soon laid down in a circle around the roaring fire with our feet toward it. About 10 p.m. the tree burned off and fell with a crash, but fortunately did not hit anyone. By that time we were all well chilled and when we renewed our request to go to a house he yielded and Pendleton and I rode forward in search of Corbin's place, and having found it easily secured an invitation to come to "Moss Neck," the palatial home of Corbin, and Hd. Qrs. were established there late in the night. The troops bivouacked near where they were halted.

War's Desolation

Things have changed much since we came here. One large forest covered the crest of the chain of hills running from one to two miles from the river, and stretched back for nearly a mile. In the edge of the woods, peeping out towards the river, were the baronial mansions of the F.F.V's of the "Northern Neck." But now we have our camps along these hilltops, and the trees have disappeared [used for firewood and corduroying the newly built military roads], and houses that never looked at each other in the near-century they have been standing, stare at each other impudently, having barely the trees that surround them left to tell of the lordly race from whose destruction they are spared. So it is here; but across the river they too are gone, and whatever new generation shall live in that land, they cannot say that they sit under the trees their fathers planted.

We pay nearly one hundred thousand dollars for damages to the farms on which we have encamped, and from that you may form some idea of the "abomination of desolation" an army produces.

After the Battle of Fredericksburg collections were taken up in Lee's army to relieve suffering of the civilian population of the town, who were without food and whose homes had been severely damaged by artillery fire and looting. One Georgia regiment raised $500, and Gen. T. J. Jackson personally gave $100; his headquarters gave $800, and A. P. Hill's division donated $10,000.

On the left is a modern view of the Marye house, taken by Ralph Happel and reproduced by courtesy of the National Park Service. The building is now a part of Mary Washington College. On the right is a photograph of the Marye house taken during the Civil War.

After the Battle

THE night of December 13, after the battle, was bitterly cold for Sykes's men, forced to snatch what fitful sleep they might on the cold, damp ground less than 100 yards from the stone wall. But it was much worse for those wounded who were not evacuated, many of whom during the night died from their wounds and exposure. Blueclad corpses by the hundreds, stiffened by death and the chill of the night air, were rolled into positions where they served as parapets for the living.

At daylight the usual morning fog allowed the front-line men of both armies to move about, restoring circulation and smoking with impunity, until the sun broke through to expose a macabre sight. Where hundreds of blueclad dead had dotted the field could be seen only naked white bodies. Many thinly clad Confederates, having decided that these Federals had no further use for clothes, thought the living might as well replenish their own wardrobes.

As the fog rolled away, Sykes's men were startled to discover how close to the lethal stone wall they had spent the night, but they were even more surprised to see their enemy casually moving about only a few yards away, cooking breakfast, cleaning muskets, and performing other peaceful camp chores. The Confederates saw them at the same time, grabbed their guns, and opened fire, as Sykes's exposed lines hit the dirt, almost as one man. Their position was unenviable, to put it mildly; they had not been ordered and were not expected to attack, and they couldn't retreat from what little protection was offered by their shallow swale without inviting certain death from the sharpshooting Confederates. So they stayed where they lay, all through the doubly long hours of December 14, until the welcome relief of the second night of their ordeal ended their misery by enabling them to fall back to the shelter of the buildings in Fredericksburg.

IN THE MINDS of the Union generals the feeling was universal that another attack would be attempted on Sunday, December 14, although Burnside had not yet divulged his intentions. Either that or Lee's army would counterattack to drive them out, since one or the other would naturally be expected to take the initiative. One officer, however, had positive views and the fortitude to express them in opposition. At nine o'clock on the evening of the battle, in a conference with several generals including Butterfield, Meade, and Humphreys, the outspoken Rush Hawkins again inveighed so vehemently against another attack that he persuaded the others and was promptly designated as their spokesman in an attempt to bring Burnside around to the same view.

So they all repaired to the Phillips house, where

they found Sumner, Hooker, and Franklin, who in turn listened to Hawkins' estimate of the situation and were convinced. Burnside at the time was not at headquarters, but at 1 a.m. he entered the room with the abrupt announcement, as Hawkins related the incident: "Well, it's all arranged; we attack at early dawn, the IX Corps in the center, which I shall lead in person." Seeing Hawkins, he added, as though on the spur of the moment: "Hawkins, your brigade shall lead, with the 9th New York on the right of the line, and we'll make up for the bad work of today [yesterday]."

The dead silence that met this statement seemed to astonish Burnside, but after questioning the others and finding none to approve, he said, lamely, that since he was alone in his opinion, the attack would not be made. The following day he called another council to consider whether to stage a general retreat or simply withdraw from the plain while retaining possession of Fredericksburg. The consensus was that there should be no retreat and no further attacks for the time being. The army would hold the ground it presently occupied and at once initiate defensive measures.

Then ensued, for the second time in a month, an uneasy period of watchful waiting between the two armies, as each rested on its arms expecting the other to renew the battle. Sooner or later, something was bound to happen, but neither Lee nor Burnside seemed anxious to shift from their defensive postures.

SUNDAY the 14th passed with only an occasional exchange between opposing skirmishers. So did Monday, and still neither army showed any intention to move. Lee was puzzled, believing that Burnside would certainly now attempt the turning movement that he had expected in the first place, to counter which Lee reshuffled the position of his divisions for greater flexibility.

On the afternoon of the 15th Burnside sent a flag of truce with the suggestion that time out be taken to allow his men to bury the dead that cluttered the ground in front of Marye's Heights. Lee consented and the gruesome work was accomplished without the Confederates being able to determine whether Burnside's action foreshadowed a resumption of the battle or a Federal withdrawal.

That night the rains descended and the winds blew. Next morning wondering Confederate scouts who reconnoitered the Federal lines discovered that the entire Union army had quietly recrossed the river under cover of darkness. The storms had drowned the noise of the retreat from the Confederates. It was conducted so efficiently, quietly, and rapidly, and the bridges were taken up with such alacrity, that the Federals were able to regain some measure of

self-respect after their defeat. On the other hand, considerable chagrin was felt by Lee and his generals, in spite of their satisfaction at having so easily and cheaply repulsed Burnside's hosts, that their enemy had been allowed to escape without punishment.

An Appraisal of the Battle

THE Battle of Fredericksburg served to illustrate, to an unusual degree, the controlling influence of competent top generalship on the one hand; and conversely, how little superiority in manpower and weaponry contributes to battle success for the army that is burdened by ineffectual leadership.

The scales were heavily weighted in favor of the Confederates, despite their lesser strength, simply because Ambrose E. Burnside, inexperienced as an army commander and lacking the vital ingredient of self-confidence as well as that of his subordinate commanders, was pitted against the best general in either army, by any criterion, the experienced Robert E. Lee.

Granted that Lee was fortunate in having lieutenants such as Jackson, Longstreet, and Stuart, nevertheless it was he who bore the responsibility, planned the strategy, coordinated the tactics, evaluated the characters and limitations of the opposing generals, and assigned to his corps commanders the missions that they consistently executed so superbly.

During the heavy fighting of December 13, in the restricted area on both flanks, the ease with which Burnside was defeated is revealed in the fact that only four of Lee's nine infantry divisions, a small percentage of his 275 pieces of field artillery, and none of Stuart's three brigades of horse cavalry, had become actively engaged.

LEE MADE proper use of his numerous cavalry after contact, assigning to Stuart the job of protecting Jackson's right flank and at the same time denying maneuver space to Franklin's Grand Division between Hamilton's and the river. Burnside, however, merely attached elements of his cavalry to his three grand divisions and gave them no further thought. Nor did Sumner or Franklin employ them any more effectively. More imaginative wing commanders would have been alert to seek useful missions, such as harassing Longstreet's rear on the north flank, or sending Bayard's strong cavalry force to keep Stuart occupied on the south flank, thus releasing Doubleday's division to strengthen Reynolds' attempted penetration of Jackson's line.

Lee and Longstreet were justified in their belief that the latter's position was virtually impregnable, an opinion shared by most of the Union generals except Burnside. It must therefore have amazed the battle-experienced Confederate leaders to find their opponent desperately beating his head on so narrow a front against their unyielding stone wall, while the largest part of his army stood passively by on the open plain, after failing on the first attempt to split Jackson's line wide open.

At no time during the fighting on December 13 or subsequently, until the Federals had recrossed the river, did it occur to Lee that Burnside would so readily acknowledge defeat, after his initial repulse, particularly after a Federal soldier had been captured with a message disclosing that Burnside had ordered a renewal of the attack for the following day.

THE ONLY principle of war that Burnside succeeded in putting into effect was when he made an unexpectedly fast march from Warrenton, and finally, although in reverse, when he withdrew his entire army from close contact without Lee's knowledge. In between, the entries on the Burnside ledger were all on the liability side, an accounting which Lincoln correctly analyzed by removing him from command a few weeks after the battle.

In reviewing Burnside's strategy, it is difficult to understand his reasons for deciding to march his entire army directly from the Warrenton area to Falmouth, preparatory to crossing the river on pontoons, rather than employing the more expeditious and infinitely simpler method of crossing the Rappahannock and Rapidan at one or more of the upper fords (as Hooker was to do in April 1863), and then moving overland, with a minimum of obstacles, to the occupation of Fredericksburg as the initial objective. In either case, if he had proceeded without pausing, he would have been unlikely to encounter effective

---

Franklin's divisions recrossing the Rappahannock during the withdrawal. ("Harpers")

opposition from the Confederates, nor should he have had serious difficulty in establishing his base of supply at Aquia Landing and concurrently occupying Fredericksburg and the high ground to the west before the rains could cause a rapid rise of the Rappahannock River.

ON THE Confederate side, Lee followed his usual strategy, refusing to be hurried until all the cards were on the table and he could appraise Burnside's probable intentions. The Confederate commander's ability to concentrate his forces at a time and place of his own choosing, without apparent concern for what might appear to be his own temporary disadvantage, had been demonstrated repeatedly, most recently at Second Manassas and Antietam. Seemingly unconcerned that some day a thoroughly capable opponent might take advantage of the situation (so far such a Union general had failed to make his appearance), Lee correctly assumed that Burnside would not attack until the additional facilities required at his supply base at Aquia could be built. Consequently he felt no need to hasten the concentration of his army at the critical point. As it turned out, Jackson's corps reached Fredericksburg ten days before Burnside finally made ready to cross the river.

WHERE BURNSIDE would decide to effect his river crossing became the subject of a major guessing game by both sides, because the narrow, winding course of the river offered numerous opportunities above, at, and below Fredericksburg. Lee knew perfectly well that he could only hinder, not prevent, the crossing in the face of Burnside's heavy concentration of artillery on Stafford Heights, but he was equally sure that he could make it hot for Burnside once he got across.

In trying to make up his own mind, Burnside's vacillation was painful to behold. The longer he hesitated, the more confused he became and, if his lack of mental clarity can be judged by his subsequent decisions and orders, he never did develop an intelligible plan for the conduct of the battle. A single incident, characteristic of the shallowness of his tactical perception, illustrates how blind Burnside was to realities. While riding along Stafford Heights with the commander of the VI Corps, he told General Smith "in the strictest confidence," as Smith later put it, that "he knew where Lee's forces were and expected to surprise them and occupy the hills before Lee could bring anything to bear against him."

His basic plan for the army attack was equally naive and unrealistic. He imagined that by sending one division to frontally attack Longstreet opposite Fredericksburg, and another in the same manner against Jackson, these two widely separated divisions could succeed without massive support in piercing the Confederate line at two points, with the effect of forcing Lee's army to evacuate the ridge and hasten off to Richmond. At once thereafter, according to the visionary Burnside, Franklin and Hooker would be all ready to promptly pursue, intercept, or whatever.

BURNSIDE'S amazing blindness to the military facts of life was similarly displayed in the area of communication with his subordinate commanders. When the battle commenced, about all they understood was that when Burnside should give the word, the two divisions earmarked for the penetration attack were to head for the enemy lines. Nothing more than that!

At a later Congressional committee meeting, before which both Burnside and Franklin testified, Burnside stated that he had learned about the new military road the Confederates had constructed, that he wanted possession of it as a means of separating Lee's two wings, and that his instructions to Franklin anticipated that the latter would capture the road as a prelude to an aggressive assault by Sumner against Longstreet's position. One searches in vain for anything in either Sumner's or Franklin's orders that conveyed any such meaning.

FRANKLIN in turn testified that he interpreted the order which he received at 7:45 a.m. December 13, as calling for what he described as "an armed observation to ascertain where the enemy was." He also stated: "I put in all the troops that I thought it proper and prudent to put in. I fought the whole strength of my command, as far as I could, and at the same time keep my connection with the river open."

Franklin may have interpreted the order too literally, but was certainly less than accurate in the statement above quoted. Smith's corps of three divisions was not used, and Franklin had been negligent in not promptly calling into service two of the three divisions of the III Corps (Hooker's wing), which were waiting at the river for the express purpose of being employed as needed. When he did belatedly bring Birney into the action the results suggested how much more he could have done had he not been almost as mentally inflexible as Burnside himself. Instead of "fighting the whole strength of his command," as he stated, he had actually put only three divisions, one-third of his available strength, into the attack.

Franklin may have been obtuse, uncooperative, and unaggressive, and Hooker could have shown a more constructive attitude, but the fact remains that the primary responsibility for the fiasco rested on Burnside for poor planning and even worse execution. With more speed, normal coordination, an evidence of aggressiveness from the top and a confident, experienced army commander, a night crossing followed by a well-organized dawn attack in strength to outflank Lee's right, would at the very least have made Fredericksburg a less one-sided battle.

LEE'S CONDUCT of the defense was well up to his usual standards, the victory at Fredericksburg adding one more to his string for the year 1862. Nevertheless Lee made one major miscalculation with respect to Burnside. He overestimated his opponent's ability as an army commander to such an extent that it caught the usually perceptive Lee unprepared to turn the Federal defeat into what might have become a debacle. Understandably Lee gave Burnside credit for a normal degree of military know-how, even though this was his first campaign as army commander, and the natural corollary to that assumption would be that the December 13 attack was only the preliminary to a second-day assault on a broad scale, employing the troops who were not engaged in the first phase. When Burnside made no further attempt for two days, and then quietly recrossed the river without being discovered, Lee forfeited the opportunity to stage a counterattack that could conceivably have seriously hurt the Army of the Potomac and created interesting strategic possibilities that might have made Fredericksburg a really profitable victory for the South.

The campaign as a whole had proved to be a major exercise in mutual frustration, causing casualties of some 18,000, only one-third of whom were Confederates, and solving nothing. Both armies were right back where they had been on December 10. Lee's superiority had again been demonstrated, against inferior opposition it is true, and Burnside was marked for removal. But the incomplete victory gave Lee little satisfaction, considering his not inconsiderable losses, the destruction of homes and buildings in Fredericksburg, and the escape of the Federal army.

An Irishman's View of Battle

By
Thomas Francis Galwey

From the diary of Thomas Francis Galwey, 8th Ohio Infantry (Published by Stackpole Co., under the title The Valiant Hours. *Presented here by permission of the copyright owner, Colonel Geoffrey Galwey, USA-Retired.)*

DECEMBER 11. Dusk is coming on. The city has taken fire at several points. From our position on the bluffs north of the plateau we can see, by the light of the conflagration, the skirmishers fighting in the streets, dodging about from house to house. As night comes on, the sight is indeed awe inspiring. The whole heavens are lit up by the burning city. On the heights beyond the city, for a mile or more, flashes of white light show through the smoke, as the enemy's artillery seeks to demolish our bridges, which by this time are all laid.

At daylight we march down to the river bank and cross the river. Just after passing the bridge we halt near tobacco warehouses. The men pillage them at once. We are marched up to the principal street of the city, which runs parallel to the river, and here we stack arms. Later in the day we are assigned quarters, each company taking one house. Excepting the colored people, the inhabitants have all fled. And they seem to have fled in great haste, because we find ladies' apparel tumbled on bedroom floors, as if it had been changed very suddenly.

Pillage

IT is a strange sight, a city given up to pillage. Not for more than an hour after we had stacked arms and broken ranks, did I notice any attempt to get the men, who had been wandering about, back to their commands. That certainly did not prevent pillage, for each company could very well sack the house where it was quartered. And they did it very effectually.

The Bank of Virginia was plundered in the afternoon, and its safe blown open. I heard one of the men who put the powder into the safe complain that he had found nothing but worthless paper. No telling how valuable these papers were to the owners. One man in our house packed up a sewing machine which he found in the house, and in some way or other he got it to the river to send to his home. I heard of pianos being taken across the river to send north.

THE FURNITURE in the house that we occupy is old-fashioned but rich. Everything bespoke the former comfort of its owners. At night we brought all the bed ticks down stairs and laid them on the floors. We did this because the enemy was shelling the city, and the slates, shingles, windowpanes, and chimney bricks were flying in all directions.

A few survivors of the charge. These are New York Irish soldiers of Meagher's (pronounced Mahaar) brigade, and they are not as clerically minded as the appearance of the gentleman at the center would indicate. Meagher lost 545 men out of 1,315 in the desperate assault against Marye's Height.

After a while, as night came on, the cannonade slackened. All night, however, there was a rattle of musketry on the outskirts of the city and a rumble of artillery moving in various directions to take position for tomorrow's work. Nearly all the men were drunk, but at last nearly everyone fell asleep. I know that I slept soundly until daylight, when a fragment of shell came crashing through the window above me and struck the mantel on the opposite side of the room, knocking down some of the candles, which it seems some one before going to sleep had had enough sense to extinguish.

AT DAYLIGHT on Saturday the 13th everything was stirring. The plundering had continued all night. Many of the men are already drunk again. A heavy fog covers the city and entirely envelops the valley between it and Marye's Heights, where the enemy's works are. Yesterday we could plainly see the Rebels moving about on the heights; this morning they are entirely obscured by the fog. Towards noon the fog began to lift, and Franklin's men, away to the left, began the attack. All is in motion now. The 1st Delaware, the 4th Ohio, and our own 8th Ohio, are detached to open the attack of our division (French's) in skirmishing order. Our regiment moves out Hanover Street toward the western outskirts of the city. The other regiments take the adjacent streets, it being the intention to deploy and to connect our lines when we shall have cleared the houses and have reached the open ground beyond. Just as we reach the edge of the city and before we have time to deploy, we are met by a fire from the enemy's skirmishers (Barksdale's brigade, we learn from a wounded Confederate) who are at the foot of the hill which descends from the city into the open valley.

Attack Against the Stone Wall

General Couch orders the advance. With a cheer we deployed and went forward at a run. Our color bearer as usual was conspicuous for his bravery. Several times he outran his comrades so far as to incur the danger of being captured with our precious colors. We halted for a few minutes behind a light rise of ground to reform and to give the short-winded men time to come up. Then with a lusty cheer we bounded forward again, not halting until we had taken the house at the fork of the road. Here the fighting became desperate. We distributed ourselves among the houses in the vicinity, firing from behind fences, out of windows, and from every possible cover.

AT THE angle of the road, forming a "flat-iron," was a small brick grocery store. The blunt end of the house, which was presented to us, was wide enough for a door which we found barred on our approach. A few blows from the butt of a musket opened it and we carried our bleeding comrades in, laying them first on the counters and then, as their number increased, on the floor—where, in fact, there was more room. Strangest of all, here we found a woman who, either by accident or a foolhardy desire to save her property, had, after barring the door, descended into the cellar.

This house was right in the vortex of the whirlpool of destruction. Bullets whistled through it in every direction. Shells [shattered] every glass window. The wounded began to beg for water, and their comrades, after looking everywhere in vain for a well, dragged the poor woman out of her cellar. Opening the back door which looked out on the enemy's terrible batteries on the heights, they forced her out into the pelting shower of missiles to show them the well. Poor woman! She must have gone mad with fear, if she finally escaped with her life.

FIGHTING continues unabated. The air is alive with fireworks. Along the crest of the hill just outside the city, our batteries are extended, firing over our heads at the heights in front of us. From the latter belch flashes of enemy artillery fire. At the foot of the heights are several stone walls, and between them as well as on top of the heights, are lines of rifle pits. All are teeming with Gray Backs. Line after line of our men advance in magnificent order out from the city towards us. But none of them pass the position which we took at our first dash and which we have continued to hold until now, in spite of the concentrated fire of the enemy's batteries and the destructive fusillade of his infantry. There is one exception, the Irish Brigade, which comes out from the city in glorious style, their green sunbursts waving, as they waved on many a bloody battlefield before, in the thick of the fight where the grim and thankless butchery of war is done. Every man has a sprig of green in his cap, and a half-laughing, half-murderous look in his eye. They pass just to our left, poor glorious fellows, shaking goodbye to us with their hats! They reach a point within a stone's throw of the stone wall. No farther. They try to go beyond but are slaughtered. Nothing could advance farther and live. They lie down doggedly, determined to hold the ground they have already taken. There, away out in the fields to the front and left of us, we see them for an hour or so, lying in line close to that terrible wall.

But we have plenty to occupy our attention on our own front. It seems that Franklin, on the left, has retired. Rumors of that sort have spread along our line; how, I know not. At any rate the enemy's fire, if it is furious before, becomes tremendous now. Our artillery does little firing. No battery seems to be able to hold a position with us in the valley, and the artillery on the northern banks of the river open only occasionally, being afraid of destroying us.

THE BALLOON is up, near General Burnside's headquarters on the other side of the river. We can see it very plainly now and then, when the smoke blows away. Several times the enemy have thrown shells at it, and once it was wrapped in smoke but escaped damage.

Destruction of Fredericksburg caused by the bombardment. The amount and types of loot collected by the Federal troops is also quite evident in this drawing by Henry Lovie.

Column after column issues from the streets of the city, and after deploying into line, advance across the open valley under the murderous fire, to lose their share of men in the vain attempt to carry those impregnable heights.

With the most of our men I spend the greatest part of the day at the brick grocery store, saving our ammunition and only firing when the smoke allows us an unmistakable target. Others of our company are around the blacksmith shop across the road.

AT ONE TIME a horse with his saddle swinging under his belly came dashing past us from the enemy's line where, I suppose, he left his disabled rider.

Two new regiments had been attached to our brigade just before we went into battle. A part of one of them remained near us during a good part of the time, and although they did not actually run, yet they were very nervous all the time. At one time a group of these Jersey men were beginning to grow used to the affair, when a couple of shells one after the other exploded almost in their midst. Captain Butterfield of our regiment, noticing their terror, assured them that the Johnnies could not successively put three shells in the same place. When his words were beginning to reestablish their confidence, another shell exploded with a tremendous crash right among them. The poor Jersey boys took to their heels and were soon lost to sight in a depression in the ground, away to our rear. So much for misplaced confidence.

We Withdraw

LATE in the afternoon our regiment, being out of ammunition, and Hooker's Grand Division coming up to take over, we were withdrawn. After halting for about a half hour near the canal, we moved back up the low hill into the city. As dusk came on, a streak of fire came from every gun, cannon, and bursting shell, so that the whole valley, and the face and crest of Marye's Heights were full of lurid flames. Above us the dark sky was interlaced in every direction with the streaks of light from the burning fuses of coursing shells. The roar of artillery, the awful crash ("rattle" is too weak a word for it) of musketry volley, and the cheers and yells of the two armies, made an excellent representation of Hell.

Though it was December, the weather had been warm all day. As we reached the top of the hill or low ridge where the city comes to an abrupt edge, we halted for a short time. Hooker's men were just going into the fight, flush with ammunition and cheering just as courageously as if a thousand of good men had not spent themselves on the same ground. The sight was one never to be forgotten.

A Federal battery was trying to go into position just where we had halted a few minutes ago, during our return. They wheeled to the left from the road, and, in spite of what appeared to be the concentrated fire of most of the enemy's batteries on the heights, as we moved again back to the river they still were bravely holding their own.

IT HAS BEEN a fearful day! We are brought back to the banks of the river, where we light fires and boil coffee. As night comes on, the city presents a strange and terrible sight. A section of artillery stands at every cross street to meet any sudden emergency which may arise. The fighting has ceased with the dark, but an incessant picking fire is kept up by the enemy on Hooker's men, who occupy our old position. Every building in town is a hospital. Churches, school-houses, barns, and all the larger sort of residences are taken for this purpose. Their floors are splattered with blood. Surgeons are operating everywhere; ambulances are coming and going; and above all there is the rumble of the ammunition wagons coming up with their new supplies, of batteries returning from the front, and of others taking new positions for the morning.

Sleep comes for some of us; but not for the men who are hugging the ground in the front. During the day they watched *our* desperate advances. During the night we dream of their vigilance over our sleep or, perhaps, of some more peaceful and homelike scene.

WE WAKE in the morning, moving not to the "lascivious pleasing of the lute," but to the now familiar sound of cannon, loud and deep, and of musketry, sharp and rattling. But as the morning passes away it seems clear that our army is too much shattered to attempt another assault.

The enemy is only too glad that he has passed almost unscathed through so desperate a battle, and will not attack us in our present position. Behind us is the river, crossed by two double pontoons at the city, and by one double pontoon farther down at Franklin's position. Should we be attacked now, we would have to make a desperate fight, as the bridges would be altogether inadequate to an orderly retreat. All day long, trains of ambulances with their sad loads cross the bridges to the other side.

MONDAY still finds us on the bank of the river, while the rest of the army is in very much the same position as yesterday. It is evident, however, that we are booked for retreat. Heavy artillery is being placed in position across the river, and all surplus stuff is going back over. After dark we move up into one of the streets running parallel with the river, and here we stack arms. Wagon trains continue to pass us until about eleven, when the order is quietly given us to move. A few minutes brings us to the end of the pontoon bridge. Here a provost guard is stationed to prevent any of the private property of the citizens being taken away. Most of the men have "gobbled" something. Whatever was of value was taken away from the troops and added to what was already an immense pile. I had found a piece of embroidery, a very fine one, too, and a bedspread, which I carried unmolested over the bridge only to throw it away (the bedspread) in disgust when it had gotten between my legs several times and under my feet in marching.

The bridges were covered with straw to prevent the noise of our crossing reaching the enemy's ears. But something better than the straw came to our rescue. About midnight a terrific rain storm came up. For days the weather had been uncommonly warm for that time of year, and now the thunder almost rivalled the cannonade we had heard for two days.

Under cover of the storm, the army continued crossing all night. By daylight all except the pickets were north of the river; they too were soon got over without much trouble.

ON TUESDAY the 16th we returned to our old quarters; but in our absence the camp followers—dog-robbers and pot whollopers, as they are called—had pillaged comfortable huts, leaving nothing but mere shells.

SEVERAL DAYS were sufficient to restore our winter quarters to the state in which we had left them when we had sallied out a few days before to storm those terrible entrenchments across the river. We returned to the old routine of picket duty and police work. Gambling and carousing were resumed with much equanimity, although many of the gamblers and sots had met their death or been crippled a few days before.

A few days after the battle a flag of truce came from the enemy, with a regiment and a detail to assist us in burying the dead. One man from each company in the army was taken for this. Jim Gallagher went from ours. When the details returned at night from their day of grave digging, they were full of stories how they had passed the day in company with the Confederate details engaged in the same work. They all, Confederate and Federal, parted on good terms and bade one another a sincere goodbye.

After a few days everything resumed its course, as if no great battle had taken place. Picket lines were again formed along the river banks and on other grounds, as they had been before.

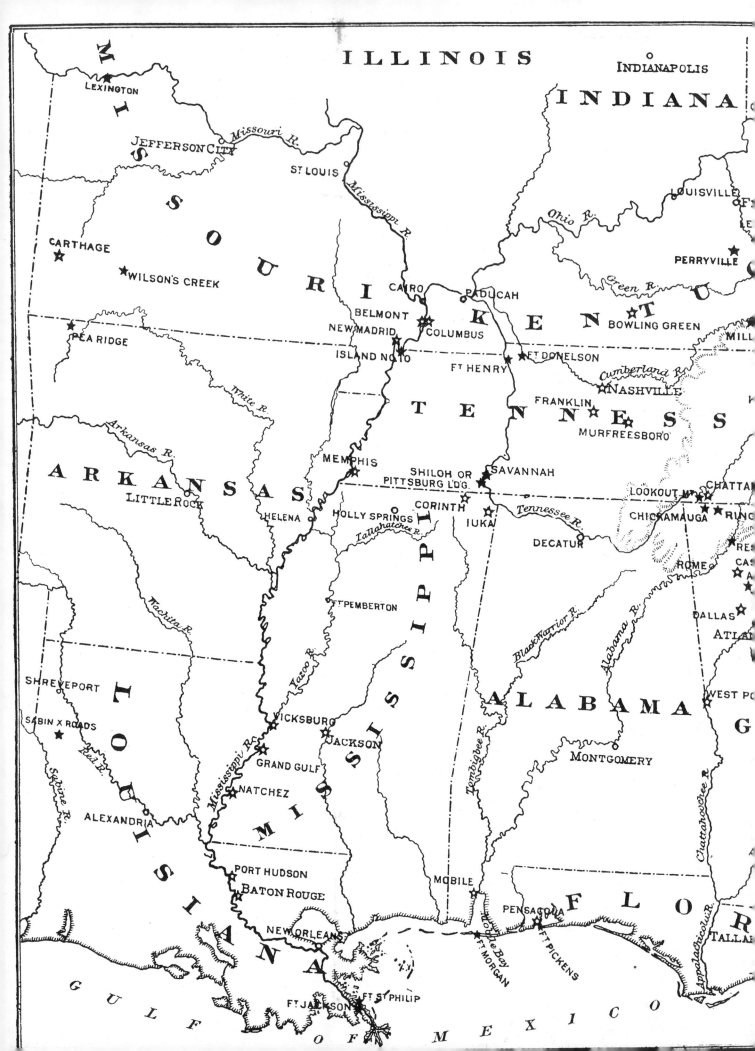